Dreams of Adventure,

Deeds of Empire

DREAMS OF ADVENTURE, DEEDS OF EMPIRE

MARTIN GREEN

ROUTLEDGE & KEGAN PAUL
London and Henley

First published in Great Britain in 1980
by Routledge & Kegan Paul Ltd
39 Store Street, London WC1E 7DD and
Broadway House, Newtown Road,
Henley-on-Thames, Oxon RG9 1EN
Printed in Great Britain by
Redwood Burn Ltd
Trowbridge & Esher
Copyright © 1979 by Martin Green

ISBN 0 7100 0509 1

FOR

Linda Bamber, Patsy Vigderman, Rich Moran,
and other friends I first met
as graduate students at Tufts

Contents

Contents

Prefatory Notes

(1) Perhaps some readers, standing on the steps of a fairly massive structure, may be encouraged by being given a floor plan. The first two chapters of this book are preparatory, Chapter I in matters of history, Chapter II in matters of literature. They define the concepts of the argument to follow, and describe usefully similar cases. Adventure, it is argued, is the energizing myth of empire; and empire is to be found everywhere in the modern world, disguised as development or improvement. The third and fourth chapters discuss two authors, perhaps the most important in the history of the adventure novel in English. Each one's work is characterized, and also the relation between the two in matters of form—the transformation undergone by Defoe's motifs when taken over by Scott. The third pair of chapters moves the discussion out away from England, to first America and then Russia. We see how the American and the Russian adventure novels, which derive from *those* cultural matrices, are like and unlike the English version. Chapter VII returns the reader to nineteenth-century England, but to the popular and the children's literature of the time, to study cultural images related to adventure. The next three chapters discuss individual authors again. One is English, one American, and one Polish, so they follow an already established pattern. (A master pattern is of course chronological; each writer is simply related to those before and after him in the nearly three hundred years from Defoe's birth to Kipling's death.) And Chapter XI presents contemporary cultural images.

(2) This book is about a big subject; not only the adventure novels of nearly three hundred years, but the imperialist history of that time (in more than one country) and moreover the relation between the two. But I have addressed my argument, as always, to the general reader. (I keep hoping he exists, or can be conjured into existence by the sound of a voice.) That means that my argument is

simplified; I have cut out many cases, qualifications, and general considerations, in order to make a readable book. But if the general reader does exist, I know he won't open his mouth—won't make any response to my argument. It is the specialists who will be scrutinizing and judging me. So I have relegated a lot of the material I cut to the back of the book, as notes. These are sizable paragraphs, in some cases miniature essays. The Defoe, Scott, and Kipling chapters, in particular, have each a kind of appendix on other books by that author— those three being the peaks in the mountain chain of adventure. In the main text I discuss only one or two books by each of them, so it behooved me to show that I knew some others.

(3)   This is the second of three volumes of a series to be called *The Lust for Power*. In the first I talk about Gandhi and Tolstoy. In this one I try to apply their teachings to literature and history. I try to find something to do, within my own field of activity, which will not betray the idea, the insight into the human situation, they entrusted to us. So this is a study of imperialism, shaped to satisfy the criteria of scholarly objectivity and free speculation, but also shaped to suit a practical purpose, to fit a social situation which I see as a moral and spiritual crisis. Its immediate reference is to England, but the argument applies to all the Western countries.

When I went to school, a striking feature of maps was still the large areas colored red; geography and history were taught in implicit relation to England's imperial career. The world was ours, so it seemed. In reality, it wasn't, any longer; but the walls of the schoolroom screened out a lot of news. Correspondingly, in ways that were only half-conscious, I learned that a margin of privilege surrounded England, a reserve on which I personally could draw at any moment I chose to leave the island. For instance, other nations needed to learn English, and would pay me for what I had got free. That map and that margin are no longer there, and the Empire manifests itself now in somewhat reverse manner. Instead of being a frontier, a free space outside England, waiting for use, it has moved inside, in the form of immigrants, who are instead an impediment on our freedom of movement. Within the island we feel cramped, limited, our margins shrunk; and abroad we wear only the tattered insignia of our former privileges. (The English accent begins to have a tawdry sound, like tattered lace, now that American is standard.)

We have lost our power; that's what it feels like to us; but in fact, we have still far more than other people. For us, as for all the nations of the West, the big question of the day involves not recouping but renouncing. Will we find a way to give up what we have taken, over the last three hundred years; to give back to the others what we took from them? We took a lion's share, and developed a lion's nature, and unless we can renounce both, we shall ruin ourselves and the world. For instance the per capita rate at which the United States consumes energy is two hundred and fifty times the per capita rate of Nigeria, and England's rate is half America's; the absolute figure for the U.S. is twice the combined total for Africa, the rest of the Americas, and Asia apart from Japan; and the United States and the USSR together account for 60 percent of the $3 billion a year that the world wastes on weapons. Can we renounce our nature as predators? As a speculative question, that is nugatory. As a practical problem, and for students of the humanities, it involves a paradox. For the way to do it is to move into and through that nature, toward and beyond our imperialist fathers, understanding what they did and what they thought they were doing, their dreams of adventure and deeds of empire. The more obvious strategy, to turn one's back on the problem and push away from imperialism, has been tried—as we shall see. Now is the time for a new effort. At least in England, where the nerve of conquest has so suddenly gone slack, it might be possible to influence action through reflection. But only if we imagine the power we once had generously, imagine not only how we lost it but how we won it, without resentment.

The London of today is radically different from the one I grew up in—and much more different from my father's London. I was taught that Trafalgar Square was the Hub of the Empire, and I saw it as such —even if it was the revolving neon ads which really made me think of a wheel. Now I see an imperial city in decay, a Rome peacefully barbarized, unprotestingly ravished and barely aware of her fall. It is a city organized to service foreigners richer than ourselves, a tourists' city, culturally a colonial city. Prominent buildings are sign-posted in Arabic; prominent companies are run by Americans; and our houses are too big for their occupants—modern lives clutter and clatter loosely inside buildings that fitted their forebears snugly. And so it is across the country; the cities are full of ghettos, and are troubled by clashes of race instead of class; imperialism has come home to roost, the anthropoemia has reversed itself. We are often told that the English are glad to be relieved of their size, and the responsibilities and privileges that went with it; and undeniably they have been liberated from manifold tensions, social, sexual, political; they feel free, supple, simple, light. But when they think about large issues, they feel diminished.

Such a situation calls for a radical change in culture, if we are to escape resentment, deep down. It calls indeed for many changes, but the one I am thinking of is in our high culture, our system of value-bearing ideas, and art objects as things to study. There too we need to start again, to go in new directions. In literature, for instance, it would be well to concentrate on new books, which we can come to freshly, and to study them in new ways. And it seems to me that these should be the adventure novels I have been discussing. These are the books that explain how England came to acquire an empire, and so how our immigrant population comes to be English. More exactly, these books ask for a critical commentary which leads into that explanation. In themselves, they are romances, so have some character of personal fantasy, some of social myth; they explain how empire building felt to the men who set out to explore and exploit and acquire, and to their friends and relations at home. But there are other sources—and the classrooms of England now supply them—to tell us how it felt to the native populations they adventured among.

The teaching situation now seems to me very like that which prevailed at the end of the last century and the beginning of this, especially in adult education, when people studying literature found in the great eighteenth- and nineteenth-century novels moral discriminations and literary achievements that invited explanation in terms of the class system and the Industrial Revolution. Those novels told the story of the sisters and their courtship. But critics and scholars who were concerned about the political and social condition of the country found a way to give them a commentary which led naturally into political truths, without ceasing to be literary criticism. Those were the great days of the Workers Educational Association classes, where the classics of English literature were set before the working-class reader, and both books and readers were tested and extended, each by the challenge of the other. To those teachers and critics, I think, the working-class readers felt like the true People of England, disinherited of the treasures of their own culture, defrauded by an upper class—sometimes called Bloomsbury—which trivialized those treasures as it appropriated them. Nowadays, I think the innocent and disinherited readers are not working class but immigrant. *They* are the People of England; theirs are the hands we see reaching up in the public libraries for the big volumes so strange to them, so familiar to us.

It was the Great Tradition novels which could be explained in terms of class conflict and industrialization. It is the adventure novels which could be explained in terms of empire; and which could, in the explanation, bring together native population and immigrants, if they were properly studied. That would not mean studied with an overbearing condemnation of the spirit of adventure—the books were written to be enjoyed, and that pleasantness is one of their strengths in the educational situation—but the readers should identify with the adventurer with a complementary sense of how he looked to his adversaries and subordinates—how Crusoe looked to Friday. It would not be easy, but it should be possible, to create the sort of stasis of interest within which all the people in the English classroom, however various their heritages and their politics, could come to understand each other and themselves better. And if that understanding cuts sharp enough, deep enough, out of it might grow a new mood, ready for seriousness, ready even for renunciation.

Dreams of Adventure,

Deeds of Empire

I

Modern Empire, Caste, and Adventure

MY argument will be that the adventure tales that formed the light reading of Englishmen for two hundred years and more after *Robinson Crusoe* were, in fact, the energizing myth of English imperialism. They were, collectively, the story England told itself as it went to sleep at night; and, in the form of its dreams, they charged England's will with the energy to go out into the world and explore, conquer, and rule.

I shall describe some of the best known of those tales, in terms of both their forms and their themes, and trace the tradition of their development which connects them to each other across the decades. I shall discuss their authors, defining their place in literary history, and the relation of each to the "serious" writing of his times. (What I mean by serious will emerge; the books I discuss are to be taken seriously, and according to literary criteria of seriousness, but the criteria are unconventional.) And I shall put the tales into the appropriate imaginative contexts, from the history of imperialism; especially important being the historical heroes of empire, who were both like and unlike the heroes of adventure fiction.

By empire I mean primarily a country possessing colonies; but

3

the word is also appropriate to some other political systems, in which one group is dominant over others whom it regards as alien and inferior. And in such systems—which are to be found in all large states—the arts, science, and ideas, become charged with the same energies as the politics, and can be called in some sense imperial. This is true even of that serious literature which, implicitly if not explicitly, resisted the cult of empire, and is all the truer of the adventure tale.

To go back to the primary meaning, empire is surely the most exciting kind of politics, and in morally noble as well as merely appetitive senses of the word exciting. As J. A. Froude said in *Oceana* (p. 355), "A man who is a citizen of an imperial power expands to the scope and fullness of the larger organism. . . . His thoughts are wider, his interests less selfish, his ambition ampler and nobler. . . ." Thus empires are analogous to large spiritual institutions, like churches or religious orders. Froude continues, "Individual Jesuits are no more than other mortals. The Jesuits as a society are not mortal at all and rule the Catholic world." But except from an ecclesiastical point of view, even the Roman Catholic Church is only an analogy. The great type, the archetype, is empire, and the great example of this excitement, at least in English history, is to be associated with the Imperialism of the end of the nineteenth century—of which Froude's *Oceana* was one of the trumpetings, and Kipling's stories the great fictional expression.

This excitement is often said to begin with Disraeli's speech of 1872, in which he asked England, "Will you be a great country, an Imperial country, a country where your sons, when they rise, rise to permanent positions, and obtain not merely the esteem of their countrymen but the respect of the world?" But Disraeli was merely introducing into the language of official politics what had been gathering force for centuries, as an idea and even more as a feeling. From 1688 on England had been expanding, and the pride of Englishness had been swelling, particularly with reference to the country's overseas possessions. This had been noted even by non-Englishmen, like Emerson. "In the island they never let out all the length of the reins, there is no Berserkir rage, no abandonment or ecstasy of will or intellect . . . [But they have been] pouring out now for two hundred years from the British islands

4

. . . carrying the Saxon seed . . . to the conquest of the globe."*

This profound excitement (felt not just by Englishmen or Americans about England, but by other Europeans about their empires, in their degree) has been a major motive force in world history for the last four hundred years. It has found innumerable forms of expression, in politics, in economics, in literature, in philosophy, in science and technology; forms of expression that were also the food of further pride and the tools of further conquest. Indeed, if we take empire to refer generally to Europe's power over the rest of the world, we will find it difficult to name any form of European life above the folk level that was not influenced to some degree.

Even the expressions of passionate dissent and organized resistance to that excitement partook of it. Only the work of Tolstoy and Gandhi, and the pacifist-anarchist traditions of thought and action which they subsumed, seem to me really opposite in tendency, and really powerful. But Tolstoy and Gandhi belong to another book. In this one I want to study the way this excitement showed itself and reinforced itself in one literary genre, the adventure tale; and the way that genre related to serious literature, and to the larger culture.

What date shall we take as a starting point? Some of the things we group together under the title of "the British Empire" were to be found in the England of Elizabeth I; most notably, the feeling of excitement just discussed, and the expression of that feeling in literature; Shakespeare can reasonably be called a literary spokesman for that imperialism. Nevertheless, historians tell us that there are reasons for dating the British empire's rise at the end of the seventeenth century, in fact at the Union of England with Scotland, in 1707; which is to say, at the very historical moment when the adventure tale began to be written, since *Robinson Crusoe* appeared in 1719. Defoe was one of the English government's agents in negotiating that union. And Defoe, rather than Shakespeare, is my candidate for the prototype of literary imperialism.[1]

In his history of the word "empire," Richard Koebner points out that Henry VIII officially claimed to wear "an imperial crown," but that in uses of that kind "imperial" was, as it were, a qualitative adjective. It referred to the king's "imperium," his abstract power,

---

*English Traits, Boston, 1856.

not to the concrete territory he possessed. And territorially it was felt improper to use the term for anything less than the whole British Isles. England had conquered Wales in the Middle Ages, and Ireland in Elizabethan and Cromwellian times; but it could not call itself imperial until it ruled Scotland also. James I, being king of England and of Scotland, spoke of his imperial monarchy, but even this use was felt to be rhetorical rather than literal, because the two kingdoms were separate, even though James was king of both. There had to be an administrative union of the two before Englishmen, or Britons, could speak of Britannia, and His Britannic Majesty. Cromwell much desired that Union, William III worked for it, it was achieved under Anne—and one of her ministers' main agents in Edinburgh was Daniel Defoe.

Most of us don't nowadays think that the United Kingdom was or is an empire; though Scots and Welsh nationalists do, and the rise of their nationalism is the mark of an epoch ending. What we nowadays think of as the empire seemed then rather a string of trading stations and plantations; but they too of course caused a growing excitement of possession in Englishmen, an excitement which had one of its climaxes at roughly the same time, about 1700. John Bowle, in *The Imperial Achievement,* says that the empire's period of reconnaissance and early settlement lasted from 1500 to 1650, ending with the Navigation Acts of Cromwell's government in 1650–1651 and in 1657. By these acts, Cromwell's government won for English shipping the monopoly of the Atlantic trade, and ordered other countries' ships to bring to English ports only the produce of their home countries. England also seized Jamaica, and launched the Western Design against Spain in the Caribbean. The age of empire proper began. And Koebner says that it was around 1688 that England acquired, one by one, the attributes of a model kingdom, according to the ideas of the modern world system; its liberties, its navy, its power in Europe, and finally, its Union.

And in those years the other countries in that system, like France, acknowledged the same criteria for a model kingdom, and so admired and envied England. Over the next fifty years, many famous symbols of imperialism (or mercantile patriotism) were gradually introduced into English culture. (And earlier symbols, like Parliament itself, took on their modern meaning.) In 1717, the mint introduced the golden guinea into the coinage. (Both "gold" and "guinea" are terms charged with imperialist meaning, as we shall see.) In 1736 came Thomson's ode to "Liberty," and in 1740 his masque "Alfred," which culminated in the song "Rule Britannia." (A giant figure of Britannia stood on the roof of the East India Company building in the City.) In 1745 "God Save the King" was popularized. And there was Young's ode, "The Merchant," Lillo's play, *The London Merchant*, and Glover's epic, *London: The Progress of Commerce.*

From 1688 on, therefore, English culture spoke in a triumphal mood, with which we are all familiar, which persisted throughout the eighteenth and nineteenth centuries, and into this one, and which was clearly related to a complacency about England's possessing an empire. And no one has ever doubted that Defoe (born in 1660) was a very representative spokesman for that mood, so to connect him with imperialism will occasion no surprise. But I want to claim, beyond the general connection, that *Robinson Crusoe* is the myth of that imperialism in specific ways, which throw light in both directions, both on empire and on the novels. That novel's silence about the actual empire of Defoe's day, for instance, illustrates certain complexities within the English idea of possessing an empire.[2]

First of all, it must be established that their empire did not always call itself empire. In fact, even in the late nineteenth century, the overt imperialism of Disraeli and Froude had to struggle for some time against the moral and political habit of ignoring the colonies, a deliberate habit of serious England. And in the historical case I will be first considering, England in the early eighteenth century, imperialism usually called itself patriotism or protestantism or freedom of trade, and used the term empire for its enemies, whether Spain or Louis XIV; just as, later, England saw Napoleon, the Tsar, and the Kaiser, as emperors greedy to swallow their peaceful little community of traders. What we now see to have been the English Empire—what was occasionally admitted to be that then, but humorously, or sentimentally, or poetically—was more seriously thought to be England's part in the modern world system.

That is the phrase that a modern historian, Immanuel Wallerstein, has found for the phenomenon, and since he sees it not too differently from the way seventeenth- and eighteenth-century Englishmen felt it, we must not dismiss their self-image too quickly. Let us recapitulate Wallerstein's theory, which he has worked out with reference to the fifteenth and sixteenth centuries, 1450–1650, when the system first developed.

The Modern World System

Charles V, coming to the joint throne of Spain and the Holy Roman Empire in 1519, ruled a territory comparable in extent with that of his contemporaries, Suleiman the Magnificent and Ivan the Terrible. And *his* territory consisted of the heartland of all Europe, plus the vague enormousness of the New World. Thus it seemed that a world age of empires was beginning, and Vienna and Madrid were charged with the excitement of conscious imperialism. But in 1556 Charles abdicated from his joint throne, and the Habsburg possessions split into two halves, never to be reunited. The idea of empire was discredited.

There followed eighty years of fighting in the Netherlands, which rebelled against Spanish rule. This led to the ruin of the great Habsburg port, Antwerp, the flight of Flemish capitalists and artisans to England, and the rise to commercial predominance of Amsterdam and London. But it was not a new age of city states that was beginning, any more than of empires. The Italian cities fell into a long decay, displaced by the republic of Holland and the kingdom of England, and the economic system directed from that joint center.

Thus the modern world system began, as the unacknowledged structure by means of which these territorial states of northwest Europe wielded power over the rest of Europe increasingly after 1550, and over the rest of the world after 1650; an unacknowledged empire, which was not politically unified, as the old, self-acknowledged empires were, nor administered by a tax-gathering bureaucracy. This system worked by the means of indirect domination politically, of capitalism economically, of protestantism religiously, of rationalism philosophically; and its military and industrial powers were energized by a new science and technology.

The core countries of the system at its beginning—up to and including Defoe's time, let us say—were Holland and England. They exerted power over a semiperiphery to the system, the countries of southern Europe, and a periphery, eastern Europe. One effect of this system was that England and Holland grew stable and unified politically, and economically they freed their artisans and yeomen from feudal bondage, in proportion as in the other countries the political structure grew feeble or brittle, and the workers entered bondage. The former happened in eighteenth-century Spain and Italy, the latter on the huge agricultural domains of Poland, Hungary, and Russia. We shall see the effects of this on the worlds of literature and thought when we come to Tolstoy and Conrad.

Socially, the core countries were dominated by merchants rather than nobles. The degree of this dominance corresponded to the centrality of that country within the system. Thus in England the merchants married with and merged with the nobility, and so became politically stronger than their equivalents in, say, France. The city of London and the new class, "the gentry," became dominant in the seventeenth century. England became a mercantile state, and a mercantile world power. In the 1690s, the state made itself the source of financial credit, instead of private houses, and the administration was generally modernized. This it did in imitation of Holland, and Holland, even more a merchant oligarchy, was England's great model. She was also the great rival, in trade and colonization. Thus the core states intertwined with each other, in political and military mimicry, competing against each other for the profits to be derived from exploiting the periphery and trading with the arena surrounding the system. As the system waxed strong, its perimeter moved out, and more and more of the arena became periphery. And unconsciously or indifferently the core countries weakened the state machinery and cultural life they encountered out there, reducing these states to dependencies if not to colonies.

Colonies, in one form or another, were essential to the system. As it came into existence, Wallerstein says, it needed three things in order to survive: politically strong core states, new labor controls (to facilitate a new diversification of work), and geographical expansion. At its very beginning, the European system had covered the Mediterranean (commercially organized by the Italian cities) plus the Flanders-Hanse network. The conquest of the New World by Spain meant an increase in territory from three to seven million square kilometers. The ratio of land to labor within the system increased enormously, prices rose, and wages fell. Where labor was so strongly organized that wages were maintained anyway, as in north Italy, commerce declined.

The outer arena—notably China, India, Turkey—supplied the system with precious goods, luxury items, exotica. The periphery supplied the lower-ranking, less-rewarded staples. And the labor systems diversified correspondingly. Mines and the sugar industry employed slaves; the large agricultural domains (in East Europe and in South America) employed serfs. Meanwhile in the core states, farming was done by yeomen and skilled work by artisans, new industries were born, ever new skills had to be learned, work became specialized and differentiated. At the semiperiphery the farming work was done by coerced sharecroppers; while at the periphery, for instance in Russia even in the sixteenth century, serfdom was introduced.

The political and moral ideology of this development are easy to trace right up to our own times, in the connotations of phrases like "East of Suez," "South American politics," or "Balkanization." They mean that once you're far from the core countries geographically, anything goes, morally and politically. To take a random example, in *The Political Economy of the War*, F. W. Hirst says, "It would be naive to imagine that the standards of business ethics in the Balkans and in South America in the '70s and '80s were the standards of Whitehall or the Bank of England. Bribery was not accidental or occasional, but essential and systematic in every field of commerce." And we shall come across many such manifestations of the centrifugal cultural field set up by the modern system.

The system developed an ideology in which freedom and morality were the main values; freedom and morality in religion meaning protestantism; in commerce meaning capitalist enterprise; in politics meaning a gentry republic or constitutional monarchy. This ideology was anti-imperialist; the system worked by means unlike those of the old military, centralized, tax-gathering empires, their towering structures crowned by some divinized emperor who blazed forth glory. The new empire was, or felt like, a community of freely competing equals, and called itself a nonempire to draw attention to that difference. Its means and values flourished in the core states, and their gospel was taken to the periphery and beyond, in all confidence that they could take root there, by an act of will. When they did not take root, that was attributed to a failure of will.

Defoe's writings, fictional and nonfictional, are animated by that ideology. It supplies their moral structure, and supplants the imperialism that is not named. I mean that Defoe seems morally unwilling to outright glory in England's power and wealth, its empire, so puts his stress on England's core qualities, its moral *solidity.* [3] (This is an example of what made foreigners call Englishmen hypocritical.) The great value of Wallerstein's theory is to help us to understand why and how Defoe (and the other writers who were in the spirit of the modern system) had to make such substitutions, had to be covert in their fables of imperialism. We must not expect to find in the adventure novels outright celebrations of empire; we must not expect to find outright imperial topics tackled; and we must expect to detect political meanings by interpretation.

We must also expect to find only hints of the more sordid aspects of the trading expeditions that *are* represented in adventure tales, and the more appalling aspects of the technology that the traders employed. It will be necessary to keep in mind some of the basic history of industry and war.

In the sixteenth century, the industrial history of the different countries of Europe diverged. (This is according to John U. Nef in *War and Human Progress,* whose account coincides with Wallerstein's.) In Spain and the Holy Roman Empire, there was less industrial enterprise and more agriculture than there had been before, but less output on the whole; there was even a fall in population. Spain was much less populous in 1660 than it had been in 1550, while Joachimsthal, the mining capital of the empire, had a population of only eight hundred in the 1630s, in place of 200,000 in the 1530s. (The wars were the immediate cause.) In the same period, in France, Italy, and Switzerland, there was a slight increase in heavy industry, and a large increase in the luxury and art trades; France, in particular, developed technical and administrative aptitudes in those trades, modeled on Renaissance Italy. But in England, Holland, and Sweden, the Protestant powers of the northwest, there was a great growth of heavy industry.[4] Between 1564 and 1634 the shipments of coal from the Tyne to the south of England increased by a factor of fourteen, and the use of iron in the country as a whole increased by a factor of between five and six between 1540 and 1620. In Sweden, iron and copper metallurgy developed under the guidance of the great Calvinist capitalist, Louis de Geer, whose headquarters were in Amsterdam; which shows the manifold interconnections of the Protestant states. De Geer had great influence over Gustavus Adolphus, king of Sweden and military hero of Protestant Europe (one of Defoe's heroes, for instance). He who produced iron, or rather he who controlled its production, dominated the scene. Iron is the emblematic metal of the system, and symbolic play upon it runs through the literature of these two hundred years.[5]

Lewis Mumford points out, in *Technics and Civilization,* that mining and metals in general has always been specially linked to capitalism (which is to say, to the modern system) and to militarism.[6] It is linked to the first because mine work broke away from the labor controls of the guild system very early in the history of capitalism; and because mining produced the silver on which the Fuggers' fortune was based, and the Fuggers financed Spanish imperialism. It is linked to militarism because the mines produced the metals used in weapons and armor, and used the gunpowder also used in petards and guns.

Mining was also a great source of industrial mechanization because of its connection with smelting, refining, smithing, and casting. Half the skills needed to mechanize other processes of production and distribution derive from it. And in its social and ecological effects it has always been destructive, opportunistic, and exploitive. In most cultures, the mine is associated with Hell, and in its moral and political character as well as its physical. It employed slave labor even in Europe until the late Middle Ages, and in Scotland serfs worked in mines long after their equivalents in agriculture had been freed. The work was done in darkness and danger, and required power tools and high temperatures, and it created around the mines the inorganic environment of slag heaps. For all these reasons, it was deeply shameful to the modern system, and to its humanism; so was hidden or exiled to a geographical periphery as much as possible.

But it was also vital to the modern system. For instance, in matters of war, metal gradually displaced wood and stone. Besides guns themselves, bayonets began to be attached to guns about 1660 and, like many military innovations, seemed particularly devilish at the time. Voltaire called them the demon of war. The Swedes used them only against the Russians, and the Austrians only against the Turks; that is, against enemies on the periphery or outside the system, and so not fully human.

And the importance of metal was matched by that of gunpowder, which was culturally of a very similar character. About 1660, Robert

Boyle observed that gunpowder had quite altered "the conduct of martial affairs, by sea and land." The invention of the gun had been attributed by folk legend (and also by scholars like Polydore Vergil, in 1499) to a sinister monk called Schwartz; and it was generally considered to be the devil's work. This was partly because of the origin of gunpowder, and more particularly of saltpeter, an essential ingredient.[7] One way to obtain this ingredient was from excrement —even human excrement—and men were commissioned to collect this for royal authorities. Partly for reasons of safety, it was prepared in small installations, and in lonely parts of the country, for fear an enemy might capture the deadly powder. Several aspects of the trade, therefore, made it abhorrent; another instance is its association with forced labor. Coal mines, salt works, and alum works, which also used excrement, were among the first factories. Sulphur, that other ingredient of gunpowder, was also associated with the devil and excrement and danger. When Cortes invaded Mexico, one of his men was lowered four hundred feet into a volcano to scrape sulphur off the walls, to make gunpowder. And Cortes' guns were of crucial importance in his conquest of Mexico. So the metals, mines, and explosions we meet all the time in adventure settings have political resonances we must not miss.

Guns and explosives have had a world character of being especially European and modern system products. China first developed gunpowder, but used it for fireworks and not for artillery. It was not China but England, therefore, that exported one thousand barrels of powder to India in 1629. European gunners sold their services outside the modern system. In India, for instance, the Moghuls employed European gunners until 1707, and the Muslims, who replaced them after that, were considered much inferior. Gunnery was a white man's art. For different reasons, but with a similar effect, in the English armies the sepoys or Africans were not given access to the artillery or to the Gatlings.

But probably even more important than the modern system's introduction of new weapons was its imposition of drill and organization. That is what made the European soldiers superior to, for instance, the Indian armies they fought. And Michael Howard in *War in European History* tells us of the nadir of brutality and near-anarchy which the Thirty Years' War reached at the end of the feudal period, when the old empires were dying. Warfare escaped rational control and became purposeless violence, except in the United Provinces, where the modern system was established. There armies were regularly supplied and paid, and fighting made political and social sense. The Dutch made their soldiers work, at digging and drilling. And later the Swedes introduced the further rationality of uniforms and mechanical maneuvers. (This is another example of the connections between the Protestant countries.) Prince Maurice of the United Provinces taught Delagardie, who later became military tutor to Gustavus Adolphus. It was the latter, Howard says, who provided the rest of the world with the modern blueprint for getting an army under the control of a single will. He showed how "the violent element which permeated European society could be canalized and put to the purposive, legitimized uses of the developing state machine . . ." (p. 60). It was the Bourbon kings of Catholic France who applied that blueprint; by 1680 the French forces were 300,000 strong; the wonder of Europe. And the Hohenzollerns imitated the Bourbons, and the Romanovs the Hohenzollerns.

Thus the Dutch model was gradually followed all over Europe in what Howard calls "The Wars of the Professionals," in the eighteenth century. Long before 1800 all the core countries had the state machinery to pay, feed, arm, and clothe a full-time force on foot, in war and peace. This was the militarism of the modern system, though developed furthest by the Bourbons and the Hohenzollerns. Those dynasties and their regimes were not as *typical* of the modern system as English merchants—at least if one is contrasting that system with the feudal—but they were not wholly atypical. That system still had its military castes, though they were "officially" subordinate to the merchants. England's style in war was superficially different, because she relied mainly on her navy. She was in some sense a nonmilitary nation. But Cromwell's Roundheads and the Ironsides will remind us that England too had an army, and of the modern kind.

Thus the English empire (and the modern system of which it was a part) grew by a great variety of means, some of which, like mining and militarism, were obscured by the system's ideology. We need to remind ourselves therefore of those hidden means; but our principal concern will be with that ideology, and the special character of its energizing myth, adventure. The modern system's kind of adventure —exemplified in the fiction of Defoe—differs from other kinds because of the merchant caste's dominant position.

Caste

Caste is a concept I shall use often, and throughout the book, to explain the imaginative characteristics of the modern system and its literature. By caste, I mean the social character men derive from their profession or vocation, or from their parents' vocation, for these traits are often acquired in childhood. These traits, friends and enemies alike agree, are independent of the caste members' individualities. They manifest themselves primarily but not exclusively in matters connected with that profession. But play habits can be as important as work habits; thus the military caste habitually, in all countries, hunts; an activity that clearly relates to their profession, and prepares them for war even in times of peace, but which also characterizes them in other ways, social, political, economic, not directly connected with war. (Think how important hunting is in the country squire's life described by Tolstoy.) Thus a caste is not formally organized as such, and its members do not necessarily constitute an active group. It is often a tendency rather than an action which the term points to. On the other hand, to speak of "caste" is appropriate only if that tendency and those traits amount to an important characterization of an important number of people.

It seems to be true also that—within the modern system—the term applies best to the members of one profession; the one that has no cultural function proper in the system. I mean the military caste, whose members, judged by that system's work ethic, function only degradedly in times of peace, as fighters and consumers, unproductive, essentially idle, overprivileged. Times of war are very abnormal, according to modernist ideology, so normally speaking the military caste have status rather than function—that is why they are defined as a caste. (Of course they were seen very differently while they were the dominant caste, in the feudal system that organized society in premodern times.) By analogy with them, moreover, it seems possible to talk of a merchant caste, as being the dominant one culturally, in seventeenth- and eighteenth-century England. And there was also a group we can call a Brahmin caste, mostly scholars and clergymen, the society's "writers," who had in their keeping its conscience and to some degree its imagination.[8]

15

Caste is an awkward term. It is an acceptable category according to a feudal ideology, but in a modern system—which was anti-feudal in origin and feeling—its terms are always prejudicial. We are not supposed to be caste members ourselves or caste conscious about others. Caste thinking is the prototype of class- and race-thinking—something dangerous and disgraceful, although we all do it. It ties status to vocation. We are supposed—especially in America, the most modern of modern system countries—to take everyone on his merits, and accord him the status appropriate to them.

The prejudicial status of the concept caste is however deceptive. Like class (and race) caste lives a powerful subterranean life, which is independent of economic or social-scientific fact. Caste exists, as an inhibition and an inspiration, wherever people think it does; and they *like* to think it does; it is one of the games people play. Society therefore always has lively ideas in circulation of what constitutes a typical house or a typical child, or a typical marriage, for each caste. The range of human possibility is divided up between them, and to some extent each caste has its own set of typical stories, its own myth. But the whole society enjoys all these stories, barely acknowledging their caste connections. One difference between those sets, which bears on the history of the novel, is that erotic idealism attaches itself more easily to the military than to the merchant or the Brahmin castes; the young officer is a more romantic figure than the young shopkeeper or the young curate; and this feeling is felt by the society at large. Crusoe is not a romantic figure, but Waverley is, because Scott wrote for the military caste, Defoe for the mercantile.

Then certain kinds and degrees of political participation have seemed appropriate to certain castes also. For instance, in *The Complete English Tradesman,* Defoe tells us of an upholsterer who became so concerned for the liberties of his country that he fell into debt, and was thrown into jail. Defoe's moral is, tradesmen should mix with tradesmen, not with gentlemen, and should stick to tradesmen's interests. That man should have shut up shop and bought himself a commission in the army, if politics was his main concern. And there is even a certain stylistic affiliation to be discerned for each caste, as Defoe indicates in the same book. "As plainness and a free unconstrained way of expression is the beauty and excellence of speech, so an easy concise way of writing is the best style for a tradesman" (p. 11).[9]

Caste, moreover, has more important effects than are officially (in a modern system) admitted, because it creates alliances and relations of trust between people in power. It is, for instance, a vital part of how establishments function. The group within which it works is often small, and the members often deny—some quite sincerely— that caste affects their relations with each other; but outsiders see its effects. Thus its signs are particularly to be looked for in symbolic figures and symbolic anecdotes, though not of the most official kind —in other words, in art.

It has also some importance in the workings of large groups, where it is habitually called "class." The difference between caste and class can perhaps be usefully discussed in relation to Defoe. Defoe was much concerned with class, and with claiming membership of the one he preferred, though he didn't speak of upper and lower. For him —as for most people in the period we are studying—the key term was "gentleman." Defoe suffered a good deal under the imputation that he was not a gentleman. This is really a caste idea, though applied within a class system.

He argued (in *The Complete English Gentleman,* for instance) that according to the true idea of a gentleman, status is not conferred by the current false criteria of a man's pedigree, or his classical learning, or his title, or his not working for a living; "gentleman" should mean (of course) the virtues and the graces. However, it is noticeable, in both Defoe's behavior and his imagination (as displayed in his novels) that, in fact, he hankered after the current false criteria, the trivial fripperies of gentility. To be De Foe, to have a coat of arms (which he achieved in 1695) and a motto (which he acquired in 1706), to challenge opponents to a duel, to be acknowledged by others as a gentleman, and (as Moll Flanders) to know how to talk genteelly, to sing, dance, and speak French, and to have a gentleman for a husband, or (as Colonel Jack) to have a genteel wife with "the fine hand of a lady."

Defoe wanted it both ways; both to disprove the criteria of the old feudal idea of a gentleman (substituting a reformed Protestant version) and at the same time to satisfy those criteria and rejoice in those gaudy privileges. Much the same could be said of later writers like Scott and Dickens, and of earlier ones like Shakespeare, and indeed of nonwriters. Success in England has always meant to join the gentleman caste. I want to suggest that this was not mere weakness of mind.

Clearly the fine hand of Colonel Jack's first wife, and the dashing demeanor of Moll Flanders' favorite husband, make no sense morally by Defoe's theory. This is not "true gentility." But then they make no sense immorally either—they bring no practical advantages. They show, I want to suggest, a disguised sense of caste at work, which looks meaningless because—using the language of class—it denies its own values as it operates. As a status system, class is overtly moral, covertly economic in its criteria. Caste, on the contrary, is hereditary —the thing a man must do is the thing he was born to. And it is amoral; or its morality is aesthetic and romantic; it values certain *styles* of being, and judges them by their graces as much as by their virtues. And as the merchants settled into power, they became sympathetic to such aesthetic views—only not bare-facedly.

Hence arose a good deal of confusion. But originally the denial of caste was a maneuver in the conflict between the feudal and the modern systems, a maneuver directed by the dominant merchants against the knights they were displacing.[10] The latter were especially associated with caste and status, and the former, as they rose to power, set up a new system of classification. According to this, nobility had nothing to do with vocation; the gentry were not the warrior class, but the privileged class; the aristomilitary caste was demilitarized.

By vocation, the nobility and the gentry had always borne arms, in both senses. But henceforth they would not carry weapons, and they would not—by birth—even have armorial bearings. They were to be recruited—the gentry directly, the nobility more indirectly— from the rich merchants. They would be those who deserved a high status in the community. This was a phenomenon Defoe was never tired of pointing to, with pride, as proving the power and dominance of the merchants in England. But that recruitment did not mean that caste had ceased to exist.

Probably caste is a universal phenomenon, and persists residually even under systems determined to eradicate it. In seventeenth-century England, at least, the concepts gentry and gentility smuggled caste feeling back into the class system. The characterizing marks of the knights did not simply disappear; after being gentry for a generation, rich merchant families tended to assume the character of the aristocracy and to slough off their old character. But this both offended against the new classification and seemed like the grossest snobbery and failure in seriousness. For it was the merchant caste that was dominant in terms of the country's serious cultural values —that was, as it were, in official alliance with the Brahmins. The military caste was held at a distance from official values. It was supposed to be at best decorative in peace time, not part of the government of the country. (Though one had only to look at France, Germany, or Russia, to see immediately and clearly what was hazy and muted in England, the functional connection between all aristocracy and the army and diplomacy and government.)

This helps account for that curious English snobbery, in life and in literature, which has so puzzled foreigners and plagued natives. Everyone wanted to be genteel—the word soon became embarrassing, but the appetite persisted—and genteel meant bearing the marks of the aristomilitary caste. But they were external marks, cut off from all social and personal function, and used for adornment, like cut flowers withering on a ball dress.

This paradox continued over centuries, as long as the modernist ideology flourished. It can be seen in the heroes of novels, or at least in the men the heroines marry—the men considered worthy to reward them; who were so often aristocrats even while the novels were teaching the superiority of the middle class. This was independent of the individual author's sympathies. There is more mere decorativeness in Scott's gentlemanly heroes and heroines than in Defoe's, despite Scott's self-proclaimed love of feudalism, chivalry, aristocracy. Scott didn't really *believe* that chivalric values could be valid again; he *believed* in modern system values, according to which the military caste had no cultural function. He had no faith in what he loved. So the use he—and his successors—made of such values was largely sentimental and snobbish. It is only when a reader meets people who did live by those values, like Richard Burton in the nineteenth century, and Isak Dinesen in the twentieth, that caste traits cease looking like genteel adornments, because one sees that they are rooted in a serious identity.

The modern novel has been largely about the conflict between castes and caste values, but in a covert and obscured way. The caste dialectic was muffled and disguised everywhere in the modern system by the dominant work ethic, which stripped the aristocrat of his vocational dignity. And in England the situation was especially confused by the greater power of its merchant caste, so anxious to dub itself gentlemanly—that is, aristocratic but not military. The English novel of adventure reflected that confusion, and imposed class terms upon it. For the purposes of this book, however, it is necessary to avoid the word class, and to sort out the caste confusion behind it.

For instance, Robinson Crusoe's character as an adventure hero, so inventive, so busy, so unerotic, and the character of his adventures, both derive from his serving—as imaginative representative—the merchant caste. Scott's heroes are different because they serve also (rather than instead) the military caste. Crusoe was prudent, Ivanhoe is chivalrous; because by 1800 England's participation in the modern system was beginning to turn into straight imperialism, and the merchant caste was almost openly allied to the military. By 1900 Kipling's heroes have very little of the merchant in them, and their chivalry is modified instead by the primitivism of saga and epic; because by then the empire felt dangerously great, and the aristomilitary caste felt in need of the crudest energies of self-assertion. Thus the caste character of the ideology, manifested in the adventure hero, changed as the empire changed.

Capitalist Adventure

The change over time in the caste character of the adventure tale could be considered not a change so much as an acknowledgment of what had been hidden—of the dependence of the merchant on the soldier. Similarly, there was a change in the character of the economy, as imagined in fiction, from the export of stout English textiles to the exchange of intoxicants and explosives (from Defoe to, let us say, Waugh and Greene). And that change also can be considered to be more properly an acknowledgment of something present from the beginning but hidden.

For instance, a major export of the modern world system was alcohol, the manufacture of which was established in the sixteenth century, consolidated in the seventeenth, and popularized in the eighteenth, according to Braudel. It soon became the practice to give it to soldiers before battle, and to "natives" with whom one traded. It was Europe's poisoned gift to America and Africa. After 1600 the Spanish state revenue in Mexico from pulque was half that from the silver mines. The Far East, with its highly developed civilizations, alcohol did not conquer. But it was an essential feature of colonization and imperialism elsewhere.

The corresponding import was spices—pepper, cinnamon, cloves, nutmeg, ginger—as dear as pepper, was a common saying in the fifteenth century, and it was in search of such cargoes that it was worth making perilous voyages. This, indeed, had been a passion of the Middle Ages; it was in full swing by the twelfth century, Braudel tells us, in *Capitalism and Material Life*. The craze passed away in the early eighteenth century, when the more characteristically modern tastes for coffee, tea, chocolate, and tobacco took its place.

Werner Sombart derived the growth of capitalism as a whole from the spread of luxury. He said that when, in the sixteenth and seventeenth centuries, men studied the growth of cities, they always attributed them to a coming-together of nobles and princes, and to the luxury trades that followed them. In the cities, the sculptors, architects, silk-weavers built around the nobles a world of fantasy—that is, a world declaring itself unlike the reality of workers' lives. He makes an important event out of the entry of the courtesan into society. "All personal luxury springs from purely sensuous pleasure. . . . In the last analysis, it is our sexual life that lies at the root of the desire to refine and multiply the means of stimulating our senses. . . . For this reason we find luxury in the ascendancy wherever wealth begins to accumulate and the sexuality of a nation is freely expressed." (p. 60) He points to the elaborate and gold-spangled costumes, feasts, galas, gifts, coaches, servants, and liveries, which marked the growth of prosperity in the seventeenth century.

This was also marked by the consumption of new commodities, like sugar and tea. Sombart gives the figures for the latter as being 100 lb. imported into England in 1668, but 26,000 cwt. in 1761, and 86,000 cwt. in 1784. Assuming that half the quantity imported was consumed in England, that means a per capita consumption of 0.01 lb. in 1700, 0.5 lb. in 1784, and 6.51 lb. in 1901. While sugar consumption in Europe as a whole is given as 4.5 million cwt. in 1800, or 0.75 lb. per head; in 1913 it was 38 lb. per head in Germany. Many scholars agree that it was these luxury trades that drove the engine of capitalism and imperialism, to begin with, and unified European culture. As Braudel says, luxury may not be a good way of supporting an economy, but it is a good way of holding a society together, because of the fascination which the haves exert over the have-nots. The mass-production and exchange of staple goods came later. Sombart points out that before the eighteenth century only colonies and armies took bulk sales of composite goods. Of course, as time went by, and methods of bulk transport improved, the modern system began to move staples too, but it was the lure of luxury that set the system going.

As we shall see, the modern system (insofar as represented by Defoe) officially disapproved of luxury. England identified luxury with frippery, and saw its own products as, on the contrary, stout and sturdy and plain. And in the adventure novel objects of use were exalted, objects of luxury degraded. Iron was exalted, gold—though ambivalently—was degraded. Crusoe values "that very useful thing called a grindstone," not the gold he finds on the ship.

But this myth (to some degree representing actual feeling and even practice) came to imaginative life only as a part of the general drive *toward* luxury—it could be called the moral luxury of the luxury trade. It was an attitude in economics parallel to the attitude in politics that opposed empire, and to the attitude in adventure fiction that opposed romance. (In fiction, the posture of Robinson Crusoe was antithetical to that of Amadis de Gaul.) In all three cases, that posture, though meaningful and of course sincere, must not be allowed to obscure the underlying truth. British textiles were a form of luxury, just as the modern system was a form of empire, and the adventure tale was a form of romance. In fact they were *the* forms, for the nearly three hundred years from the birth of Defoe, in 1660, to the death of Kipling in 1936.

The paradox here is related to the old paradox of worldly Puritanism, which Max Weber explained, and which in a sense everyone had always understood. The Puritans and Protestants who dedicated their lives to religious values learned a disciplined energy which led them to greater worldly power than anyone else. They became more worldly than anyone else—modern-worldly. They knew this. Defoe at least was perfectly aware of the importance of his own class and sect as agents of modernization—as was Burke from an opposite vantage point—and the Dissenters themselves in the eighteenth century acknowledged their relation to the bourgeoisie they led. What I called the excitement of empire was in modern times quite largely the self-congratulation of that worldly Puritanism.

But Puritans could never associate themselves overtly with empire. It was only the military caste that could exult in outright imperialism. So we must learn to recognize caste alliances that lie hidden beneath apparent hostilities, or beneath terms that have become too familiar to us. Underneath the term Puritanism lies a powerful alliance between the merchant caste and the Brahmins. The writers of modern England devised an ideology and a myth which served the purposes of her merchants. That myth is to be our primary object of study here.

Let us begin with an attempt to define adventure, first in general, and then in the modernist meaning appropriate to Defoe and his successors. I am thinking, as will be obvious, primarily of adventures in books, but the definition has its applications to real life too. In general, adventure seems to mean a series of events, partly but not wholly accidental, in settings remote from the domestic and probably from the civilized (at least in the psychological sense of remote), which constitute a challenge to the central character. In meeting this challenge, he/she performs a series of exploits which make him/her a hero, eminent in virtues such as courage, fortitude, cunning, strength, leadership, and persistence.[11] That seems to cover most kinds of literary adventure, down to girl detectives battling opium fiends in San Francisco's Chinatown. (Of course, it doesn't cover, for instance, commercial or financial adventure, which are quite important to consider in connection to Defoe; associated meanings like that will have to be specially introduced whenever relevant.)[12]

In the modernist adventure, that kind especially representative of the modern system and its imagination, the adventurer defeats the challenges he meets by means of the tools and techniques of the modern world system. By tools I mean guns or compasses, and scientific knowledge, such as of when an eclipse is due, and so on. By techniques I mean things like keeping a diary and keeping accounts and the Puritan examination of conscience and the conviction of righteousness; but also any rationalized and systematized and demystified habits of thought (Twain's *Connecticut Yankee* provides some good examples).

This definition, however, needs to be qualified by other ideas, equally important and partly contradictory. In later adventure writers, in fact from Scott on, the adventurer himself is not simply identified with such tools and techniques. (Because, as I have pointed out, Scott's heroes are part-chivalric, and not all-mercantile.) In Scott, the character of the modern world, and its contrast and conflict with another ancient or exotic world, is often emphasized by other, sometimes subtler, means. Waverley, for instance, has no tools; he *observes* the ancient and exotic world of the Highlands with the eyes of modern (Hanoverian) England. Sometimes, notably in Cooper, the adventurer contains within himself the conflict between modernist tools and those of that other world—Natty Bumppo embodies the Indian world too; he is both white and Indian. So the definition of modernist adventure is not absolutely simple to apply; but it will enable us to distinguish the adventures we are concerned with from *Amadis de Gaul* and the romantic adventures of chivalry. Amadis makes no use of modern tools or techniques, and does not represent the modern world in any way. (It will also help us to distinguish between the romances and the adventures amongst our own books: using romance for the Scott and Scott-type books, adventure for Defoe and his affiliates.)

But between the individual hero, like Robinson Crusoe, and the British Empire, there stretches an incommensurability. To fill in that blank space, it is necessary to describe some real-life adventurers of empire, and to relate them to the heroes of fiction. (In many ways, this book will be a history of the WASP hero.*)

What has been said so far is true of the adventurer of fiction (and those real-life figures who resembled him) while there are various differences between him and the adventurer of history; using that phrase for the military conquerors on whom historians spend a lot of their time. (In action, as I have indicated, the modern system has been quite largely military, though in ideology it has been mercantile and anti-militarist.) I am not talking about a difference between reality and imagination, but between two embodiments of imagination. Studying that difference will, I think, bring out a hidden structure, a cultural character, to the "literary" form of imagination.

Let me describe three of the great historical adventurers of empire. None of the three has a close connection with any of the fictional

---

*The White Anglo-Saxon Protestant concept is a facet of the modern system ideology, and I shall use the acronym often.

heroes I shall be concerned with. That distance between the two groups is a part of my point. But they and their stories powerfully excited and stimulated the West's imagination of itself and its opponents, and of human possibilities generally. Embodying individual and small-group struggle, but also large-scale achievement and power, they created our idea of the hero quite as effectively as our fictional heroes did. Indeed the narratives of the historians have been more important than those of fiction in shaping the image of the culture heroes of empire. We must contrast them with the adventure heroes, to see what the novelists don't mention.[13]

The three are Cortes, Clive, and Napoleon. I shall have much more to say about Cortes than about Clive, and very little about Napoleon. That distribution of attention derives from my particular focus on English fiction. If I were dealing with French literature, or for that matter most other European literatures, I should say a great deal about Napoleon—for instance, about how much he meant to Tolstoy alone. But except for Byron, English writers treated Napoleon simply as a moral scandal, up to the very end of the nineteenth century. Conrad was clearly fascinated by that figure, Kipling and Conan Doyle, too, but the 1914 war put an end to that nascent development of fictional interest.

Cortes had no more direct influence on English literature than Napoleon, but his connection with the Spanish romances so interestingly parallels and contrasts the connection between the English voyagers and the English adventure tale that it is instructive to consider him at some length. As before, the literary question is inseparable from the political and the economic. The English adventure tale differs from the Spanish romance in the same way as the English empire differed from the Spanish. The fiction that Defoe made out of the English facts, is, like those facts themselves, in the purest spirit of the modern system; it is a story of individual enterprise, Protestant piety, hard work, and self-help. While what we meet in the story of Cortes and the conquest of Mexico is the spirit of chivalry's archaizing romance and glory, and conscious flamboyant imperialism. (Cortes addressed his Emperor as Caesar in his despatches, and played the Roman general himself. Indeed, his Emperor dreamed of chivalric deeds himself, and in 1536 challenged his political enemy, François I of France, to single combat.) Spain, and the phase of the world system it dominated, was never modernist in spirit, which was one reason it soon lost power. The supplanting of Seville by Amsterdam and London, in the realm of finance, exactly paralleled the supplanting of *Amadis de Gaul* by *Robinson Crusoe* in the realm of fiction.

In Defoe (and Richardson and others) our literature made an alliance with the mercantile caste. That is why we have a large difference to note between Cortes, the Spanish hero, and Crusoe, the English hero, representing military and commercial castes respectively. And the mercantile hero continued to be dominant in English adventure tales right through to the days of John Buchan. But of course since England *had* a military caste, Defoe's triumph was only partial and passing; concurrently the military caste made its claims felt, in the form of a demand for romance, from Scott's time on; and if military heroes are rarely to be found in novels, there are often adventures which turn the merchant into a temporary soldier. While in Kipling's time, at the end of our period, the hidden heroism of the soldier was revealed, and he triumphed over the merchants and their allies among the children of light.

That is another reason why it is important to examine the historical heroes of adventure. Their stories, even if written by historians and not novelists, powerfully expressed the imagination of the military caste, and therewith the claims of that caste also to represent or lead the imagination of the whole society. Those stories can be felt as a pressure on the writer, when reading, say, Scott; though most serious writers resisted that pressure, which they thought morally unserious. Those stories are full of the value of warfare, and empire, and aristocracy.

For instance, our three adventurers belonged to old and honorable but impoverished families. And they used the rewards of their success to reestablish their families as noble. Through them and men like them, the riches of the empire and frontier strengthened the aristocracy. Hannah Arendt has shown that this link is what made imperialism attractive to the ruling classes of most European countries, even when the governments were opposed to it.

Thus John Strachey tells us, in *The End of Empire,* that the first Sir Henry Strachey, who was Clive's secretary, was helped by him to redeem his family estate in Somerset. That is where the plunder of Bengal was spent, rebuilding the fortunes of the English gentry. And Warren Hastings grew up in Daylesford, a village whose manor had belonged to his family for hundreds of years, but had been lost to them. At the age of seven he took a vow to redeem those acres, and achieved his vow by means of the wealth he took from India. Cortes became a great nobleman of Spain with his American wealth, and Napoleon, of course, set his brothers and sisters upon half the thrones of Europe. This is an imaginatively potent idea, but not one to be approved by modernist ideology.

In England, modernist ideology (compounded of half-truths, like other ideologies) developed an energizing myth of adventure, with heroes who represented mercantile capitalism. But England lived by other myths also, notably militarist ones, though they were told by historians rather than novelists. So in responding to the adventure tales and their heroes, we have to glance at the historical heroes also, that shadowy company behind and between the men the novelists paint.

Cortes, Clive, and Napoleon

Since I am concerned with what these heroes meant to those who heard about them, I shall consider Cortes and Clive via a famous historian's account of each—in Cortes's case, W. H. Prescott's *Conquest of Mexico* (1843); and shall refer to a more modern account —J. M. White's *Cortes and the Fall of the Aztec Empire* (1971)— to allow for the biases of the first.

The way Prescott saw Cortes was directly borrowed from his Spanish sources. In his diary he spoke of the Spanish chronicles of the Conquest as being sprinkled with the gold dust of imagination; but his use of that gold dust himself testifies to his own similar excitement by the story—though of course to some degree he distanced and ironized Cortes's achievement and his adventure. The latter is not presented as a model in the way that Crusoe's is. Prescott's hero-worship is "romantic"—that is, aesthetic, not quite serious.[14]

The essence of the Cortes story is that he landed in Mexico on Good Friday, 1519, met the Aztec emperor Montezuma on November 8 of that year, and by 1521 the whole Aztec empire had capitulated to him; he could have become its king, merely for the asking. He arrived with only eleven ships, five hundred soldiers, sixteen horses, ten bronze guns, four falconets, and thirteen muskets. Some of those men he had to send away, as dissidents, so only four hundred reached Mexico City. But he acquired 200,000 allies along the way, mostly Tlascalans, who constructed thirteen ships, to Spanish design, and transported them in parts to Mexico Lake, assembled them there, and made him master of the water, so that he could defeat Aztec forces enormously greater than his own. He took over the kingdom.[15]

The story of the other great conquistador, Pizarro, is in its disproportions even more extraordinary; he left Panama for Peru with only one ship, a hundred and eighty men, and thirty-seven horses. The chief Inca, Atahualpa, had thirty thousand men in his army; but Pizarro brought three or four thousand to a meeting with him, seized him, had him strangled, and took over the kingdom.

These stories have a profound effect, stimulating pride in those who can identify with the winning side, fear in those who can't—of an intensity which only myth can express; and Europe's self-image in the eighteenth and nineteenth centuries derived from many such acts of mythic self-identification. No doubt her men of conscience always or often repudiated such identification; but the consequent split between conscience and imagination has not been entirely to the culture's advantage. The pride was there, whatever the guilt. One crude manifestation of that pride is the nationalist slogan: Shakespeare's Henry V said that one Englishman was worth three Frenchmen; but Columbus said, with a magnification suitable to the greater cultural gap, that a thousand Indians would not stand before three Spaniards.[16] Crude as such formulas are, and the emotions behind them, they are better indications of the sources of world-system psychology than more sophisticated ideas.

Prescott treated the Cortes story as romance, explicitly; and in fact it reminds us of romance—adventure in fiction—I mean the stories of Scott and Rider Haggard, not those of Defoe. It is suited to the military-caste imagination, not the mercantile. At the beginning of his book, in Volume I, on page 3, Prescott says, "The subversion of a great empire by a handful of adventurers, taken with all its strange and picturesque accompaniments, has the air of romance rather than of sober history." And in Volume I, on page 7, it was "as adventurous and romantic as any legend devised by Norman or Italian bard of chivalry."

He gives Cortes a romantic character, speaking of "the amorous propensities which belong to the sunny clime where he was born," and how he was often involved in affairs of honor. (Sexual glamour is more appropriate to the aristomilitary caste than to the merchant.) When Cortes arrived in Hispaniola, he was offered land to work, but said, "But I came to get gold, not to till the soil like a peasant." In Mexico he saw himself as a Roman general, leading Roman legionaries. He told his soldiers that he would lead them to countries more vast and opulent than any yet visited by Europeans. "I hold out to you a glorious prize." But it was also for him a holy war. In all these traits he stands far from Robinson Crusoe, of course.

When Prescott's story reaches Mexico, it involves an extraordinary concatenation of the motifs of the adventure tale to come; notably the treasure, the exotic landscape, and the love of a native princess. Treasure, in the form of gold, jewels, carvings (packed in chests, often) is much stressed. Cortes wrote to the emperor that "the land teems with gold as abundantly as that whence Solomon drew the same precious metal for his temple." The precious metal spills over into Prescott's metaphors, too, so that we hear of golden reasons and golden arguments.

On page 244 of Volume I, he describes the valley of Mexico City, "the land where the fruits and the flowers chase one another in unbroken circle throughout the year; where the gales are loaded with perfumes till the senses ache at their sweetness; and the groves are filled with many-colored birds, and insects whose enamelled wings glisten like diamonds in the bright sun of the tropics." And a little later, a land "of exuberant fertility, almost impervious from thickets of aromatic shrubs and wild flowers, in the midst of which tower up trees of that magnificent growth which is found only within the tropics." This is the landscape which romance-novelists were using as late as Conrad.

And then there is the story of Malintze, or Marina, given Cortes as a slave by a Tabascan chief; apparently she was of noble birth, but sold into slavery by her mother, in order to secure to her half-brother the inheritance which should have been hers. She served Cortes as an invaluable interpreter and spy, became his mistress, and bore him a child. It was because of her persuasions that Montezuma yielded himself to the protection of the Spaniards, which event broke the back of any possible Aztec resistance. Thus Cortes seduced and mastered the whole of Mexico in the person of Malintze, at once sexually and militarily triumphant.[17]

The figure of Montezuma himself is of the greatest importance in the romance-adventure landscape, combining as it does the exotic, the imperial, and the horrifying, plus a feminine unresistant succumbing to the conquistadors. We first hear of him that he lived in barbaric and oriental pomp, and was an arrogant and sacerdotal prince. When he finally appears on the page, however, to meet Cortes, he is slim, melancholy, long-haired, timid; borne to the meeting in a royal palanquin blazing with burnished gold, he then came forward on foot, leaning on the arms of two powerful vassals. Meanwhile Cortes dismounts from his horse, throws his reins to a page and advances to meet him—all virility (Vol. I, p. 341). In the palace, "Clouds of incense rolled upwards from censers, and diffused intoxicating odours through the apartment. The Spaniards might well have fancied themselves in the voluptuous precincts of an Eastern harem, instead of treading the halls of a wild barbaric chief in the Western world" (Vol. I, p. 347). And on page 350, "In the pompous and burdensome ceremonial of the court, he saw that nice system of subordination and profound reverence for the monarch which characterize the semi-civilized empires of Asia." The conquistadors are often called men of iron, of stern visage, etc., to compare with the gold of the Aztecs. In Book V, Chapter I, Montezuma was dangerously wounded, when he addressed his people on Cortes's behalf, and they shouted at him, "Base Aztec, woman, coward, the white men have made you a woman—fit only to weave and spin," and threw stones at him. Prescott tells us that Montezuma was gentle even to effeminacy in his deportment, and constant in his affections.

Prescott's reader is implicitly called on to identify with Cortes, and to rejoice in his victories—because, for the time being, for the sixteenth century, and in this confrontation, Spain is the modern system. The Spaniards of this period were in fact habitually described by nineteenth-century WASP historians as Visigoths, and as thus full of barbaric vigor. (The Spaniards of later generations were not allowed any Gothic heritage.) Thus on page 407, "Cortes had triumphed over all his enemies. He had set his foot on the neck of princes; and the great chief of the Aztec empire was but a convenient tool in his hands for accomplishing his purposes." And at the end he is summed up, "He was a knight-errant, in the literal sense of the word. Of the band of adventurous cavaliers, whom Spain, in the 16th century, sent forth on the career of discovery and conquest, there was none more deeply filled with the spirit of romantic enterprise than Hernando Cortes."[18]

The conquest of Mexico is the other side of the coin to the cultivation of his island by Crusoe. If we consider them both as stories, Prescott's book and Defoe's are, respectively, the military caste's and the merchant caste's responses to the fact of empire. Though each is the antithesis of the other, they belong together, and each needs the other, to be fully understood. *Crusoe* is so attractive to the mercantile and Puritan mind just because it puts the best face on a complex operation of which another face is military conquest. The Cortes story is attractive to the military imagination because it puts the most romantic face upon an operation that was also sordidly economic.

Turning to England's conquest of India in the eighteenth century, the essence of the Clive legend can be given in Macaulay's words: "A handful of [our] countrymen, separated from their home by an immense ocean, subjugated, in the course of a few years, one of the greatest empires in the world."* Macaulay makes use of the Cortes legend to define Clive's achievement, and to make it demonstrably the larger of the two. Under Clive's leadership, he says, the English defeated a nation who were as highly civilized as the Spanish who had defeated Mexico. This inversion of the Cortes story, with the Spanish now in the role of the Mexicans, was a standard device of nineteenth-century history. It ingeniously intensifies the modern system pride of consciousness. Traces of it can be found in Prescott himself; it is full blown in Motley's *Rise of the Dutch Republic,* and in Kingsley's *Westward Ho!;* and it goes back as far as Defoe and Hakluyt.

In psychology as well as achievement, Clive was a military caste hero; as a child, he was a "good bad boy," as the nineteenth-century called that type, or hyperactive to use our term; he organized the idle lads of his native town to blackmail shopkeepers. As John Strachey says, Clive really was, "as we all learned at school, a boys' storybook sort of hero, if ever there was one" (*The End of Empire,* p. 23). Even when he got out to India, he was insubordinate and rude to his superiors; indeed, unhappy; he twice attempted suicide before he

---

*"Lord Clive," *Edinburgh Review,* January, 1840.

found his vocation, in war. Then, at the age of twenty-five, he led two hundred English and three hundred sepoys to the capture of Arcot, its defense for fifty days of siege, and the eventual defeat of a besieging force of 10,000. The garrison lost five or six men, the enemy four hundred. And soon after he drilled into an effective army two hundred newly landed recruits, and five hundred newly levied sepoys. His men, English and native, came to adore him.

When Surajah Dowlah locked up some English prisoners in the Black Hole of Calcutta, from which they never emerged alive, Clive led an army against him, and defeated him at the battle of Plassey, although enormously outnumbered. Macaulay tells these stories with the greatest indignation and triumph. Surajah Dowlah is made a more villainous Montezuma, feeble and luxurious; ruling of course an oriental despotism, which glitters with treasures like the Peacock Throne and the Mountain of Light. The idyllic aspect of the Cortes-Montezuma relationship was not echoed with Surajah Dowlah, but it was with Mir Jaffir, the prince Clive set on the other's throne. After things had gone wrong in India, and Clive had to defend himself in the House of Commons, he told his fellow Members, "If ever a Mussulman loved a Christian, Mir Jaffir loved me."

When a historian like Macaulay, whose prime loyalties are to mercantile values, has to comment on heroes like Clive, he, like Prescott, relies rather heavily on the amoral categories of romance and the exotic; which is yet another testimony to the way the military caste was linked with the romance genre, even in the nineteenth century.

In Macaulay's story, Hindu religion is presented as all cruelty and superstition, Hindu character as at best feminine. Macaulay's characterology is a direct reflection of the core-periphery-arena structure which Wallerstein describes. At the core one finds firmness, vigor, virility; but the farther you go from the core, the less virile you find men to be. Thus he says of the Brahmin Nuncomar, in his essay on Warren Hastings,* "What the Italian is to the Englishman, what the Hindoo is to the Italian, what the Bengalee is to other Hindoos, that was Nuncomar to other Bengalees. The physical organization of the Bengalee is feeble even to effeminacy. . . ." (p. 562). and a long passage develops the idea. While the stuff Englishmen were made of

*In *Edinburgh Review*, October, 1841.

could be seen at Plassey: "With the loss of twenty-two soldiers killed and fifty wounded, Clive had scattered an army of near 60,000 men, and subdued an empire larger and more populous than Great Britain" (*Essays*, p. 514).

Clearly the reader feels there a very powerful personification of the British empire—even though the explicit idea "empire" is attributed to the enemy. Indeed Macaulay is almost overt about his propagandist intention. He begins his essay, "We have always thought it strange that, while the history of the Spanish empire in America is familiarly known to all the nations of Europe, the great actions of our countrymen in the East should, even among ourselves, excite little interest."[19] And Macaulay's lead was followed up by, for instance, G. A. Henty, who wrote a *With Clive in India* among his nearly eighty very popular adventure tales for boys.

Looking for a cooler, in some sense postimperial version of the same story, we can take Philip Mason's *A Matter of Honour*, 1974, about the history of the Indian army. Mason's account is that by 1750, all India had discovered that the Europeans, and the English even more than the French, possessed a military secret, which enabled them to defeat much larger forces. This, Mason says, was not so much their firearms as their drill and training and organization, and the permanent and continuous policy of the English leaders. (These were, I have argued, another expression of the modern world system.) Indian armies, by contrast, were improvised for the occasion, and their commanders disappeared after a campaign. The soldiers were only paid eight months in the year, and pay was often in arrears. The organization was feudal, and many of the vassals' troops (which accounted for the enormous numbers cited) were not to be relied on; treachery was expected and accepted. The Indian social system was religious in its sources and sanctions; politically it was largely chaotic.

By contrast the English social system, as reflected in the army, was much more solid, and the links between officer and man much more vigorous. The victories in India were to be attributed to Stringer Lawrence as well as to Clive, for the former built up the organization of the army, gave the sepoys regular pay (which could be advanced before a campaign), pensions, uniforms, regular rules for promotion, court-martial, and so on. Sepoys took an impressive oath of loyalty, and their regimental colors became objects of veneration—became the emblems of their craft, comparable with the emblems every craft

33

in India venerates. This disciplined infantry was what defeated the Indian hordes, with their armored elephants and their cavalry, which was much flashier than ours. The Indian horsemen were trained to develop steely arm and hand muscles, and to pick up pistols from the ground, and to ride in gambade against the enemy, but they broke on the rock-like British infantry. The English triumph was thus a triumph of infantry over cavalry, in a sense a triumph of the merchant caste over the aristocracy; which was the pattern the English associated with all their victories. Cavalry, even within the British army, had the traditions of gentlemanly swagger, sartorial elegance, aristocratic extravagance; but the military tune every Englishman knew was "The British Grenadiers." The English were—or believed themselves to be—*yeoman* soldiers.[20]

John Strachey tells the same story in *The End of Empire*,[21] and says that Clive's victory was crucial to the history of the British empire. The decision to attack Calcutta in 1757, he says, "marked the moment in history when a daemonic will to conquer and to rule seized the British . . . and possessed them for two hundred years" (p. 31). It was also a crucial moment in the history of England. "For us in Britain," he says on page 13, "this 18th century event lives in a way that none of the other conquests of world imperialism can do. The Black Hole . . . etc. . . . are part of our national folklore. Countless British families, exalted and obscure, have served—as mine did— generation by generation in India; their children still see hanging on the walls of their homes this or that memento of the conquest." The first Sir Henry Strachey was Clive's secretary, and the historian's family has private anecdotes about him, handed down through the generations.

Thus Strachey has special reasons for responding imaginatively to the story of Clive, and he talks of ". . . the still mysterious event of the conquest of a vast empire by an only moderately successful trading company, intermittently supported by the government of a European state of the second rank, itself inhabited by less than 6 million people." Which is not to say that the historian's attitude is uncritical, either politically—his orientation is Marxist—or morally—he suggests that Clive's hysterical tears when he left India may have come from his knowledge of what he had done to Bengal. But however critical he or anyone may be, the story of Clive, like that of Cortes, is one of those great imaginative moments which changed the history of the world, and changed it for European and native alike. As Braudel says, Plassey began a new era for the world, because it marked the triumph of Europe over India. Every European afterward felt himself bigger.

But the novelists had to find indirect ways to express that feeling. Only historians, licensed by fact, were allowed to create images of imperial glory, of military conquest, and of triumphant domination. Fiction had to obey moral restraints, to celebrate mercantile virtues, and consequently to approach the facts of imperialism—individual and political—very obliquely.

The case of Napoleon can be dealt with more briefly. The poor young man who started with no advantages and raised himself by his own efforts to the heights of his profession, and then seized supreme power in France, rewrote its laws and education system and everything else, became emperor, and finally ruled Europe and dominated the world—this is a classic story of modern system qualities triumphing. Here we see the modern system and the military caste perfectly fused. Napoleon's enemies were old established systems of privilege and sentiment, feudalism, tradition, corrupt empires. He conquered Egypt—sustained the gaze of forty centuries looking down upon him —and thought of conquering India. That story energized the literature of nineteenth-century France, notably in the case of Stendahl and Balzac, for instance. It aroused young imaginations in Germany, Poland, Russia, India, all through the nineteenth century.

This had its effects in politics, of course. Alexander Herzen wrote to Turgenev in 1862, about the legacy of Napoleonic militarism in France. "Yes, if the army could be reduced to the defenders of property, the bodyguard of capital, everything would quickly reach its stable, final order. But . . . the hereditary knightly element keeps up the ferment and prevents bubbling life from settling down. . . . What is to be done with the great people who boasts of being a military people, which is all made up of Zouaves, pioupious, and Frenchmen, who are also soldiers?" Herzen saw this Napoleonic militarism as the main threat to the success of the modern system; in which "The bright image of the shopkeeper—the knight and the priest for the middle class—hovers before the eyes of the casual labourer, until his tired, horny hands drop on his sunken chest. . . ."*

*The Memoirs of Alexander Herzen, pp. 1736, 1688.

From our point of view, however, the meaning of Napoleon blends into that of the modern system. Both were aspects of the modernist imperialism. The story of Napoleon was one of the great means by which the imagination of Europe was charged with the deep and heart-pumping excitements of empire. But in England, and somewhat less in America, that story was not available to writers, except very indirectly, because British sentiment had been powerfully organized against Napoleon—depicting him as an emperor and despot, against whom Britain struggled in the name of freedom and the modern world system. Scott, the great romancer, wrote the standard British biography of Napoleon, which insulated the British imagination against him. The stimulus to the world imagination was enormous. The response, in English literature, is missing. That in itself interestingly suggests the laws and limits of literature's function within the general cultural imagination, a function which is to be a main object of this study.

These three adventurers may be taken to represent thousands of others, some only locally known, who altogether amounted to a great energizing force—an inspiration to young men particularly to achieve something similar. They are the equivalents in the Western world for the legends of Genghis Khan, Tamburlaine, Attila, and so on, among their peoples. But the Western world has been a modern world system, and not an empire. (I do not forget that this formula is profoundly false. Nevertheless it is also true. Both sides of the coin must be felt at the same time.) Therefore the high culture at its most conscientious has disapproved of adventurers of this kind, and has often averted its gaze from them, or subsumed them under other headings, *interpreted* them. The stories the most serious writers told were not adventures at all, and the less serious wrote adventures suited to the mercantile imagination.

II

Narrative, Other Forms,

and

Literature-As-A-System

I N this chapter I want to tackle "literature"; to bring that complex phenomenon, and the high culture it is part of, into relation with "empire." The most important relation imaginative writers found, as I have suggested, was adventure. To celebrate adventure was to celebrate empire, and vice versa. But not all writers could sincerely adopt a celebratory attitude to empire. In fact, the morally serious were more ready to condemn it, or purposefully to ignore it. But that equation holds good, nevertheless, and relates the form to the ideology, for writers as a whole.

Some writers (like Defoe) understood the empire to be a place where adventures took place, and men became heroes. Some (like Swift) refused to understand empire in any such favorable terms. Some (most serious novelists) refused to understand it at all as a subject for fiction. All of them took the adventure narrative to be the generic counterpart in literature to empire in politics. And by writing such narratives, the first group of writers prepared the young men of England to go out to the colonies, to rule, and their families to rejoice in their fates out there. While the others turned away from adventure, to write serious fiction—or essays and poems—which implicitly advocated a quite different career.

But before getting to full-length narratives, it is worth considering other forms, and other, more fragmentary, aspects of literature. It is worth asking what, for instance, poetry in English owed to empire; what the poets took from the voyagers and empire-builders who wrote out their exploits, or were written about.

The news of the New World stimulated the imagination of writers, like everybody else; but the effects are hard to summarize, because the evidence is contradictory. Columbus's first letter describing the New World was printed and published nine times in 1493, and by 1500 had had twenty editions. So he and America were soon notorious. And the stories of New World voyages began to appear in print soon after 1500. Francanzano Montalbodo's collection, *Paesi Novamente Retrovati,* came out in Venice in 1507, and had fifteen editions; and Ramusio's collection (these set the precedent for Hakluyt in England) followed at mid-century.

On the other hand, Charles V never mentioned America in his memoirs, and up to 1600 geographies regularly described the world as if the discovery had never taken place. In sixteenth-century France, twice as many books were published about the Muslim threat as about the American promise. The facts were undeniable, and exciting; but they were hard to assimilate, at the serious levels of the imagination; and so in a sense they *were* denied. Only after 1650 did Europe's mental horizons expand in rebellion against antiquity's authority.*

We can take an example of this that relates to Columbus himself. His first account of the Caribs he met was friendly, vivid, and moderate; he noted with appreciation their handsome bodies and good faces, their neat and clean houses, their ingenious nets and hooks, etc. He was in this first letter the most realistic ethnographer since Herodotus;† but his later accounts were quite fantastic. As the habits of European culture reasserted themselves in his mind, he ceased to see the non-Europeans clearly. His first account was less medieval-

*J. H. Elliott, *The Old World and the New, 1492–1650.*
†Margaret T. Hodgson, *Early Anthropology in the 16th and 17th Centuries.*

fantastic than Walter Raleigh's was to be, of the same people, a century later; even though Raleigh was an intellectual. And this pattern was to prove typical; the European mind, even at its most adventurous and ambitious, did not absorb the new facts easily, and often retreated before them, into fantasy.

Notably the men of letters, the men of the arts in general, were not seriously curious about the news. Dürer noted having seen works of art sent from the New World, but neglected to record or speculate about what he saw. Rabelais used the New World news for purely playful, satiric, or fabulous purposes. In some ways, the high-culture imagination of Europe remained medieval in the sixteenth and seventeenth centuries. In medieval times, curiosity, *turpa curiositas,* was not given high status as an intellectual motive; new information, at least of a geographical kind, was not intellectually important. After the discoveries, that status changed, but gradually and slowly. The high culture and the serious mind of Europe lagged far behind the work of her sailors and adventurers. Among even Augustan men of letters, it was only Defoe—who was only marginally a man of letters—who participated fully in the new interests.

Defoe was a geographer, and geographical exploration is the most empirical form of inquiry, the most destructive of a priori reasoning. Like medicine and war, navigation and cartography were comparatively free from classical precedent. But for men of letters that precedent was not a merely inert pressure; it actively denied the new ideas—deriving energy from the denial; and humanist culture has gone on doing that these two hundred and fifty years. Humanism is essentially conservative, in both good and bad senses.

Education gradually accepted the knowledge, especially the education of the Dissenters. For instance, Defoe (like Locke) particularly recommended geography for a gentleman's education, and in history put a stress on the modern. He wanted boys to know the stories of Cortes and Pizarro. And in Germany we find J. H. Campe's *Discovery of America, for the Use of Children and Young Persons,* translated into English in 1759. (Campe also wrote *Robinson der Jüngere,* a hugely successful adaptation of Defoe's book.) In these ways education gradually made use of the new knowledge, in the course of the eighteenth century. But that knowledge did not replace the classics, especially in the education of the ruling class. And literature was even slower to respond to it.

Of course the excitement of new wealth (of windfall, to use W. J. Webb's phrase) can be felt in such early and important works as *Doctor Faustus* (1588) in lines like,

> I'll have them fly to India for gold
> Ransack the ocean for Orient pearl.

And again in *Paradise Lost,* a century later:

> High on a throne of royal state, which far
> Outshone the wealth of Ormus and of Ind,
> Or where the gorgeous East with richest hand
> Showers on her kings barbaric pearl and gold,
> Satan exalted sat. . . .

But such uses imply deep uneasiness as well as excitement.

The Milton passage is thought to derive from Sir Thomas Roe's description of Jahangir, the Mogul emperor to whom he was sent as ambassador. Its being used to evoke Satanic rather than Divine state is typical of the imaginative geography the modern system developed. The same flavor of excess, of the forbidden, is after all implicit in the Marlowe passage. The new lands were sometimes described as Paradise, sometimes as Inferno; and judgments as to whether they were Heaven or Hell sometimes varied within a single account. They seemed to combine characteristics of both. But the diabolic element (often personified in "savages") counted for more in the reflections of morally realistic writers. There was a resistance in the moral mind, a reluctance in the literary imagination, facing those lands.[1]

Empire was also discredited by the opposite element, the childlike innocence of the natives—or more exactly by the cruelty and deceit of the European traders who took advantage of that innocence. The cruelty of the Spaniards to their Indian subjects was a constant theme of Protestant moralists everywhere. And it was linked to their wealth. If America and India were seen as treasure houses of gold, gold had always had sinister connotations, for moralists.

Columbus himself began the stories that so appealed to the European mind, of Indians childishly trading gold, *pure* gold, *solid* gold, for trifles like beads, mirrors, knives, and so on. Peter Martyr's *De Novo Orbe* (1500–01) exaggerated Columbus's account; he spoke of golden trees and fishooks, golden cannon, and kitchenware. Hakluyt described natives dancing with eagles of gold hanging on their breasts, and pearls in their ears. The implicit message to the reader was plunder. England saw America as a fountain of gold and gems, says R. R. Cawley, in *The Voyagers and Elizabethan Drama*. Also as an earthly paradise; Raleigh said the Indies lived in a perpetual spring, and in Mexico the wheat grew high as trees. But that paradise was purely material, and associated with moral failure. Thus in 1658 Davenant had natives appear on the London stage carrying baskets full of ingots of gold and wedges of silver; but the title of his play was *The Cruelty of the Spaniards in Peru*.

Of course, many Elizabethan writers wrote enthusiastically about the new lands, and the English colonies on them. J. H. Parry says that propaganda was a vital part of English and Dutch imperialism (as distinct from Spanish) because those two countries needed capital investment by city merchants. The enterprise depended on persuading the latter to put their money down—men like Sir Thomas Smythe, who contributed to the Muscovy Company, the East India Company, and the Virginia Company, in turn. The English crown paid for much less of the total costs of empire than the Spanish crown; hence English propaganda was mercantile in character; and hence it was England that had a Hakluyt and later a Defoe.

It was from the persuasive propaganda of the Hakluyts that the creative writers took off; Spenser, Bacon, Drayton—whose ode "To the Virginian Voyage" draws directly on the Hakluyts; and later Middleton, Fulke Greville, in his 1633 *Life of Sidney*, and finally Defoe. But by definition, propaganda is repugnant to the literary conscience. Literature-as-a-system relegates such writing to exile, far from its value center.

Of course, the subject of the relegated writing may flourish in literary exile. As a cultural image, it may root itself in every imagination, even if rejected by literature—and may return to haunt writers at a later date. Thus one of the most famous imperial projects of Elizabethan times was to colonize Guinea/Guiana; a project to be associated with Raleigh, both as colonizer and as propagandist. (And Defoe, a great admirer of Raleigh, took the scheme up later.) The scheme was given literary praise by Marston, and by Chapman in his "De Guiana Carmen Epicum," which begins, "Riches and Conquest and Renown I sing." Its tone can be gathered from lines like these:

> Guiana, whose rich feet are mines of gold,
> Whose forehead knocks against the roof of stars,

> Stands on her tip-toes at fair England looking
> Kissing her hand, bowing her mighty breast.

This shows us literature in subservient alliance with imperialism.

But we can take Raleigh's scheme to be typical, not only because of its imaginative glitter at the time—Guinea was the land of the El Dorado legend—but also because of the many forms in which it returned to haunt the literary imagination. Though Raleigh's project failed completely, the Pilgrim Fathers considered Guinea a possible site for their colony, as late as 1619; another Guinea Company was founded in 1627; and Defoe promoted its colonization a century later. While El Dorado recurred as a motif of the most serious literary meaning, as late as Conrad's *Nostromo,* and Naipaul's *Loss of El Dorado.* (By the twentieth century, a Pole and a Trinidad Hindu, both writing in English, were involved in the myths of West European imperialism.)

So clearly men of letters were excited about empire, from the sixteenth century on; it contained much to simply delight their fancy. But it was not so simple to integrate that excitement with the serious moral imagination and its literary forms. That problem has been in some sense unending and insoluble. As we see in the case of space exploration today, serious literature generally is reactionary, and will not or cannot ally itself to contemporary excitements. Insofar as the problem did find a solution, it was in the adventure tale, but that was no solution for serious writers.

Other Literary Models of Empire and Adventure

The English adventure tale will be discussed in the next chapter and those that follow. But it is useful to bring to that discussion a sense of the alternatives—the like-but-unlike precedents for the incorporation of empire-excitement into large literary forms.

The first of these precedents is Virgil, and his relation to the Roman empire forms an interesting contrast (sometimes not a total contrast) to the relation of some of our authors to the British empire. The aspects of empire treated in the *Aeneid* show the moral responsibility that goes with conquest and domination, not the windfall and boom aspects dominant for the Elizabethan writers. But the two are connected, and later English writers faced the same problem as Virgil. Indeed, if we think of England's empire as the United Kingdom rather than the colonies, we shall see a similarity to Rome even in the earlier period. The establishment of the Tudor dynasty was for Shakespeare a political and moral event of the highest significance, just as the establishment of the Caesars was for Virgil.

As John Bowle puts it, the Roman empire determined the political and cultural future of Europe; while the British spread over the rest of the world; so the two demand to be put side by side. Politically speaking, however, the Roman empire was more purely a military phenomenon than the English. It was not merchant-dominated, like the modern world system. Economically speaking, the significant contrast, according to Paul Petit in *Pax Romana*, is that while Rome's commerce was highly organized, its production was run along cottage industry lines. Roman commerce had no mass production or assembly-line methods, no machines to speak of, no standardization, and only low-level technology.

On the other hand, there were great capitalists, especially in industries like pottery, tiles, and bricks; there were great financiers; and there were agricultural capitalists, working the enormous latifundia. But the important similarity for us was the predominance of the home country over the rest of the Roman empire, which must remind us of the position of England within her empire.

Petit says, on page 195, "Italy, from Sicily to the Alpine border, was the centre of political and intellectual life, the country of the master race, wholly unified in itself since all its citizens had received citizen-rights. Basking in the glory of its history and in the presence of the imperial government, it possessed over those provinces which until a few years before had been merely exploited, a superior and privileged place which guaranteed a solid prosperity in the first century of our era." The empire was of course the successor to and the inheritor from the great Roman republic. If we take the British empire's history to stretch from 1688 to 1930, then the period corresponding to that first century A.D. might be 1870–1930; in which case it would be appropriate to compare Roman authors like Virgil and Horace with English writers like Conrad and Kipling.

Petit says it was the work of Augustus, the first emperor, to repair the ravages of the civil wars (which lasted from 50 B.C., when Caesar crossed the Rubicon, to the battle of Actium in 31 B.C.), but

43

also to ensure that predominance of Italy. Between the battle of Actium and the rise to power of the Severans, in A.D. 193, the area directly administered by Rome doubled in size, her frontiers advancing in all directions away from the Mediterranean. Augustus' great enterprise was to romanize western Europe, and the profits of that enterprise drained back from the colonized countries to Rome, just as the profits of the British empire drained back to England in Kipling's time.

The concept of Empire was as new to Romans in Virgil's time as it was to Englishmen in Kipling's time. Koebner tells us that it was first in 184 B.C. that Scipio Africanus referred to the imperium of the Roman people as territory, and that usage continued to be rare. Cicero always used the word to mean the state's power to enforce the law. The territorial meaning was invoked only on monuments to successful generals. But in 38 B.C. Octavian made his position paramount, and claimed he inherited from Julius Caesar the title "imperator." In 27 B.C., the Senate granted him a proconsular imperium, and four years later that was declared permanent.

Once emperor, Augustus wanted to make his new powers seem old, to legitimize them. His "argument" was that the republican aristocracy having been ruined in the civil war, Rome's ancestral tradition should now be renewed under the guidance of the princeps (himself). He needed the support of ideas and of literature, just as British imperialism was to, and the support was lavishly given. He and his minister, Maecenas, induced Horace, Virgil, and Livy to sing the imperium romanum—in Horace's *Carmina*, in the *Aeneid*, and in the *Ab Urbe Condita*. Virgil and Maecenas are said to have taken turns reading the former's poetry aloud to Augustus. Virgil and Horace, who both lost their patrimonies in the civil war, both admired Augustus, and welcomed the peace which empire promised. They wanted to see the land resettled and the cities diminished. (This dark background of civil war was not there for the British empire Kipling and Conrad knew; it *was* there earlier—in much diminished degree —for Shakespeare and Defoe; and it inspired stresses in their work recognizably similar to Virgil's.)

As W. R. Johnson says, in *Darkness Visible*, "Virgil lived in an age when the shared metaphors which any society requires in order to exist were disintegrating. . . ." The poet was not twenty years old when war broke out between Caesar's men and Pompey's; twenty-six when Caesar was murdered, and when Cicero was trying to sum up, in *De Officiis,* what the republic had tried to be. It is not surprising that his foundation epic, the *Aeneid,* celebrates Augustus' empire as the creator of order, a boon worth any price.

Virgil was essentially an Empire poet, the spokesman for a large state, more civilized than its rivals or its own antecedents. That comes out in the ways he is praised when he is compared and contrasted with Homer. Arnold and Nietzsche preferred the Greek poet. But T. S. Eliot and C. S. Lewis (themselves citizens of a great imperial metropolis) acclaimed Virgil as *the* poet of civilization. Lewis says that Achilles was a boy, Aeneas a man; and that in the *Aeneid* European literature "grew up." And indeed Aeneas can be seen as a Stoic hero, a hero of maturity, struggling away from the primitive codes of a tribal society, toward the civilized values of *humanitas, pietas, ratio,* and *salus.* He is less single-minded than Achilles, because in Virgil's time the themes of national destiny, the birth and death of nations, and the costs of civilization, were problematical. Intellectually, Virgil is clear in his resolution of those problems; Aeneas is not to be considered an interloper in Italy; he is the instrument of fate, the agent of civilization, the agent of empire. But emotionally, Virgil's story remains ambivalent.[2]

The poem is about the problem of containing the violence of history. In Book I, line 257, Jupiter begins a speech foretelling the glory of Rome and the enchainment of Frenzy. Rome's enemies are in a sense crazy; Turnus is infected with madness by Allecto in Book VII (as is Amata, Lavinia's mother, another of Aeneas' enemies); and Dido is infected by Cupid, in the form of Aeneas' son. (Dido is the foreign queen who loves Aeneas and is deserted by him; Turnus is the native prince whose kingdom Aeneas conquers and whose bride Lavinia he marries; both figures have important parallels in our own imperial myth.)

But it is clear that Dido and Turnus are not merely crazy, and that the violence is not all on their side. Virgil gives us a strong sense that "inexcusable" violence is being employed by Rome itself, and that Aeneas' virtue, his famous *pietas,* is "inauthentic"; that is, the balance between good and evil in his conduct is palatable only when he is considered as a representative of civilization and Empire, not when he is considered as an individual. He is first called "pius Aeneas" in Book IV, line 393, immediately after Dido denounces him as a faithless lover. His piety compensates those who identify with him for his infidelity. Hunt's chapter on Dido and Turnus is headed "The Realm of Tragic Guilt," and clearly the guilt is not all theirs. Both those characters arouse a strong emotional response in the reader, which is in part sympathetic identification.

Dido is a heroine out of Greek tragedy, and Turnus is brave, handsome, passionate, patriotic. Both represent old cultural values which are going to be diminished as Roman civilization is established. In Book XI Turnus tries to awaken the ancient heroism of his people, the Latins, with the speech beginning line 415, "O si solitae quicquam virtutis adesset."

Turnus is a figure of feeling, attracting all our sympathy. He was described, when first introduced in Book VII, as the bravest of men, but the most passionate. (The comparable figures in the English foundation epics are Shakespeare's Hotspur and Scott's Fergus MacIvor.) Aeneas is a less passionate lover, and his marriage is externally arranged by fate—as it were, given to him from outside. Yet the reader is not in any doubt that Aeneas and not Turnus deserves to marry Lavinia; but the reader *is* led to question the concept of "deserves." Just so Carthage is depicted as luxurious and epicurean, and Dido is associated, by means of literary allusions to the *Argonautica*, with Medea, the murderous witch of Lemnos. So we know it is right for Aeneas to desert her; but we are led to question the concept of "right." This is how the *Aeneid* renders empire into poetry, and it offers useful points of reference for a theory of the imperialism in English literature, despite the differences in both literary form and political structure. In Scott's *Waverley*, Flora MacIvor is a Dido figure; in Shakespeare's *Antony*, Cleopatra is; while Waverley and Octavian have the same function as Aeneas. All three writers show what is gained and what is lost when peace is established and a great civilization founded. If neither Virgil nor Shakespeare makes much of adventure, the reasons for that will become apparent, and are equally interesting from our point of view.

As I have indicated, the foundation epic of the British empire was told by Shakespeare in his history plays, and by Scott in his historical novels. Scott we shall come to in Chapter IV of this study, but Shakespeare did not write adventure tales, nor narrative in any strict sense, so I have nothing to say about him except a preliminary word here. It will perhaps be enough to quote the famous speech from Act

II, Scene I, of *Richard II,* to show Shakespeare as an imperial writer
of the ornamental or propagandist kind.

> This royal throne of kings, this scepter'd isle,
> This earth of majesty, this seat of Mars,
> This other Eden, demi-Paradise,
> This fortress built by Nature for herself
> Against infection and the hand of war,
> This happy breed of men, this little world,
> This precious stone set in a silver sea,
> Which serves it in the office of a wall
> Or as a moat defensive to a house,
> Against the envy of less happier lands . . .

What is specifically imperialist there is the precious metal and precious stone images (I would suggest that the mythological allusions
are subsumed in these) combined with the stress on defensiveness.
The language makes England into a treasure—something that needs
to be defended against both predators and barbarians. (We shall see
the same thing going on in *Robinson Crusoe,* to define our feeling
about Crusoe's kingdom, but Defoe's imaginative style is much more
modernist.)

The history plays were of course part of the Tudors' propaganda
to legitimize themselves and their idea of England; an idea which by
Elizabeth's time partook of the excitements of Empire also. Shakespeare took the task over from earlier propagandists. In *English
History in the 16th Century* Lily B. Campbell tells how Henry VII
set Polydor Vergil and Bernard Audre to writing histories that would
serve Tudor purposes. While Henry VIII set John Leland to recover
the antiquities of England, and in a report of 1546, Leland promised
"to establish the antiquity and originality of the English church, the
claims of Englishmen throughout the ages, the historical greatness of
England, shire by shire, and the true relation of England to Ancient
Rome" (*Shakespeare's Histories,* Eugene M. Waith (Ed.), p. 20).
Polydore Vergil's book (published in Latin in 1534, in English only
later), influenced Hall, whose *Union of the Two Noble and Illustrious
Families of York and Lancaster* Shakespeare used.

Hall's chronicle, which appeared in 1548, promised to prove Henry
VIII "the indubitable flower and very heir of both the sayd lineages,"
and pageants of the York-Lancaster union were presented to Elizabeth on her coronation procession. The Wars of the Roses were for

Shakespeare and the Tudors what the civil war in Rome was for Virgil and Augustus; a period of devastation from which the country was grateful to be delivered. (An equally strong feeling can be detected in Defoe against the civil war in England in the seventeenth century.) Hall's chronicle covered exactly the period of Shakespeare's two historical tetralogies. Both writers show the sin of deposing Richard II, the punishment that sin received, and its expiation in the death of Richard III and the accession of the Tudors.[3]

Critics have pointed out a connection between these plays and Shakespeare's treatments of Roman history, because both subjects bear on the same theme: empire. Traversi, in *Shakespeare: The Roman Plays*, calls *Antony and Cleopatra* the last and greatest of the English chronicle plays; and he reminds us of the *Aeneid* when he says that *Antony*'s subject is the founding of a universal empire. And Ernest Schauzer, in *The Problem Plays of Shakespeare*, says that the second tetralogy of English history plays "leads up to" *Antony* because they all deal with kingdoms, their greatness, and their costliness (the price to be paid in other values), just as Virgil does.

J. H. Walter even makes specific comparisons between *Henry IV* and the *Aeneid*. "The play gains in epic strength and dignity from Falstaff's death, even as the *Aeneid* gains from Dido's death. . . . both Dido and Falstaff are sacrifices to a larger morality they both ignore." Aeneas and Henry both neglect duty for dalliance; are recalled by divine interposition; and submit. Henry's order to kill the prisoners, at Agincourt, is an act of epic-hero's rage, just like those we see in Books X and XII of the *Aeneid*. And the justification of Aeneas, Book I, lines 504 and 505, applies to Henry also:

> rex erat . . . quo iustior alter
> nec pietate fuit, nec bello maior et armis

Thus Virgil and Shakespeare offer us major models of the literary treatment of empire. Very occasionally I shall be able to make a comparison between those models, in epic and drama, and the adventure narratives, fictional and nonfictional, which the modern world system has predominantly made use of. More generally they are valuable to my argument as a backdrop, a reminder of historical perspectives and alternatives.

One difference between these models and the adventure tale, the difference in literary dignity, is an important clue to the right critical treatment of the latter. Virgil wrote in the grandest literary genre of his time, deliberately aiming at greatness. Shakespeare took advantage of a striking flexibility in the literary system of his time, to rise to the highest levels occasionally within works which were much of the time entertainment. Both addressed the imperial theme directly. The adventure tale has been a low genre; just as—a connected fact —it has not confronted the imperial topic. That does not mean it has not dealt with that theme, or that high powers of intelligence and imagination are not at work within it. It only means that conventional critical methods will not suit the tale, and that an important topic has been neglected by literature for that reason.

The third literary model I want to sketch, that of the Spanish romances of the sixteenth century, bears much more directly on Defoe, and is more similar in literary type. Like the modernist adventure tales, the romances do not confront the imperial topic, and their literary status was never so noble as Virgil's. Like the adventure tales, they express a caste ideology (rather simple-mindedly) but a different caste, and by means of a different mode of expression.[4]

The bulk of these romances were written in Spain, at the rate of about one a year from 1508 to 1550, plus nine more up to 1588— the defeat of the Armada was a defeat for the military class they served, and a check to the imagination they expressed—so only another three appeared after that, up to 1605.[5] This is Henry Thomas's account in *Spanish and Portuguese Romances of Chivalry* (Cambridge, 1920) and he tells us what enormous influence they had, despite that simple-mindedness mentioned before. (It is not the complex works of art—that is, the spiritually rebellious—which have the most social influence. The modernist adventure tale probably was more influential than the serious novel.)

The romances were much translated, and came second in bulk of printed matter to devotional literature only. Statesmen and emperors delighted in them, abroad as well as in Spain. François I had *Amadis de Gaul* translated, and many court ceremonials under Henri II were derived from it; social historians have called it the social breviary of Henri's court, and say that international political ceremonies like the Field of the Cloth of Gold were designed by reference to it. Treasuries of thoughts, on education and courtesy, were compiled from the romances and published separately. Children were named after characters in the romances. It was widely believed that underneath and in their fantasy was to be found profoundest truth.

Amadis de Gaul, the most famous of them, was written over a period of forty years, different parts by different authors, and amounted finally to twenty-one books. It exerted great influence over, strikingly, both St. Ignatius de Loyola and St. Teresa de Avila; and perhaps even more striking testimony to its social power is the official decree against importing it into the Spanish colonies, declared in 1531, because of its excessive popularity. Its imaginative influence runs through the conquistadors' accounts of their conquests, and—there seems every reason to suppose—through their most private ways of seeing and naming their exploits. When they first saw Mexico City, Bernal Diaz says, it seemed to them like something out of *Amadis;* California was named after the Amazonian kingdom described in Book V; and so on.

John J. O'Connor, in *"Amadis de Gaul" and Its Influence on Elizabethan Literature,* analyzes it under four categories that contrast vividly with the sort of adventure tale which Defoe was to tell. It was a book of war; of which the technology was archaic, and the enemies fantastic—monsters, pagans, giants. It was a book of love; part sensual and part ideal love, but always outside marriage, between knights and princesses, and involving swoons and madness and irresistible passion. It was a book of courtesy; including whole educational treatises, based on the value of high birth and the code of honor. And it was a book of marvelous adventures; some of whose most prominent agents were magicians and Fortune. That is enough to indicate the distance between such stories and the kind we are used to. Those are four categories of the military imagination, not the mercantile.[6]

The plot is said to begin not long after the Crucifixion, but the sense of time and place have nothing to do with reality. Amadis is said to be born of a secret union between Perion, king of Gaul, and the princess Elisena. She and her maid, Darioleta, push the baby out to sea in its cradle, and it floats away up to Scotland, where Amadis is taken ashore and grows up in ignorance of his origin. Inspired by love of Oriana, daughter of King Lisuarte, he performs innumerable feats of arms, in none of which is he ever defeated. And so on.

The famous reaction against chivalric romance is of course *Don Quixote,* which appeared in 1605. Generically speaking, that book certainly was an antitype of the chivalric romance, and modernists like Twain have often claimed it as their sponsor. But irony is always a kind of tribute paid to the thing ironized, and it seems plausible to consider *Don Quixote* as the last chivalric romance rather than as the start of something new.

That is Alexander A. Parker's theory, in *Literature and the Delinquent* (Edinburgh, 1967). He says that the true antitype to romance in Spain was a new moral realism in fiction, which began with *Guzman de Alfarache*, in 1599. This was the first of a whole line of picaresque novels throughout Europe, of which the last was Smollett's *Ferdinand, Count Fathom*, 1753. One aspect of Defoe's literary activity, that represented by *Moll Flanders*, is similar to this picaresque fiction, though it seems likely that Defoe's source was that other popular form, the criminal's biography. In any case, this is not the side of Defoe's work that I shall be concerned with. The real start of new adventure narrative in England, I am convinced, was *Robinson Crusoe*.

The connection between the romances and the adventure tales is therefore not at all genetic, either in the intellectual biography or the literary genre sense, but contrastive. The romance did not give birth to the adventure. It is a social-historical contrast I am drawing attention to, between the spirit of the romance and the spirit of the adventure tale. Those "spirits" should be defined in terms of their social-cultural functions. Perhaps I can illustrate the chivalric spirit in a piece of actual history, the Paso Honroso (or exploit) of the knight Suero de Quiñones in 1434. Henry Thomas tells us that this knight and nine comrades tilted against all comers for thirty days, because he wanted to free himself from a vow he had taken to wear an iron chain around his neck every Thursday, in token of servitude to a certain lady. One man was killed and many wounded (including all but one of the ten defenders) before the exploit was stopped by the authorities. This is what the spirit of romance could inspire men to, until it was replaced by the spirit of adventure. As for the latter, the shrewd exploits of the merchant caste can be illustrated from *Robinson Crusoe*, or from William Phips's rise to wealth, as told by Cotton Mather, or from the story of any adventurous apprentice who ended up Lord Mayor of London.[7] But I shall be concerned with the form as much as the spirit of adventure.

Method of Analysis and Comparison

In order to study the adventure tale form as it develops over the two hundred years and more after *Robinson Crusoe*, I am going to use a vocabulary of critical concepts derived from the structuralists. My understanding of these concepts differs somewhat from theirs, because my interest in literature and society differs. But they are the critics (amongst those I know) who have worked in the area of theory I am concerned with, and they have developed a set of stimulating ideas which have given shape to my own. My interpretation of those ideas is in some ways radically different, but—seen from another point of view—is only an extra twist given to them to make them suit my purpose.

I am interested in narratives that are imaginatively true, and these are histories and biographies as often as fiction; so the opposite to imaginative truth is not nonfiction but imaginative falsity or deadness. Thus, though I agree with the structuralists when they say that their central problem is always "What is literariness?", I mean something different by the question. They mean, it seems, "What is imagination?" while I mean, "What is this kind of imagination?"

What they have to offer me I can suggest first by a passage from Genette's *Figures*, pages 159–160 (quoted in Robert Scholes's *Structuralism and Literature*, p. 8) when he says that structuralist theory applies most obviously "to literatures distant in time or space, infantile or popular literatures, including recent forms like melodrama and the serial novel, which criticism has always neglected . . . structuralist criticism can treat this material anthropologically, studying its large masses and recurrent functions, following the way traced by folklorists. . . ." Whereas to "living literature" hermeneutic criticism seems appropriate. But in fact, Genette goes on, the true distinction is not to be drawn between two kinds of material; we can use structuralist methods whenever the object is "other" to us. This suits my purpose perfectly, for I am concerned with particular books, the products of the highest intelligence, as much as with "large masses."

Then structuralism, says Scholes, establishes a model of the "system of literature" as the external referent for individual works. It seeks to explore the relation between them and it, and also the relation between that system and the culture of which it is a part. System in this sense means a complete, self-regulating entity that adapts to new conditions by transforming its features while retaining its structure. The idea is adapted from linguistics, where the system of a language is called a *langue;* the other of the two key terms is *parole.* (French terms are used because the theory originated with de Saussure.) *Parole* means any particular utterance, and includes poems and novels, but also slang and mere ejaculations. And yet no *parole* can be understood before you understand the *langue* in which it is spoken, while the latter is systematic and theoretical. (Of course it does not have to be learned systematically and theoretically to be used correctly, for children do not learn their native language that way. But from that correct usage a system can be induced—in fact, must be, if a language is to be taught or studied in any way other than the way native-speaking children learn it.) This is the sort of system which structuralism studies in literature, the *paroles* in this case being individual works of art, the *langue* being a genre or perhaps all literature at a given moment. (As that loose alternative suggests, literature is not so much of a system as language. But it has some systematic characteristics.) And this is what I am studying, my *paroles* being primarily adventure tales, my *langue* literature-as-a-system.

Tenn A. van Dijk, in *Some Aspects of Text Grammars,* says that we need transformational grammars of literature, to explain the deep structures that underlie particular literary texts and out of which those texts are generated. Such a grammar would be transformational in the sense that it would allow us to produce and interpret an infinite number of texts in a rule-governed way. If I understand this correctly, a transformational grammar of language gives us the rules for transforming a single affirmative statement into its negative, interrogative, past and future, compound and complex forms. Such a grammar of literature (with perhaps a genre being the equivalent of a language) would explain how a given story could be transformed into another; *Waverley* into *The Pathfinder,* let us say, or *Pamela* into *Jane Eyre.* That, at any rate, is what I shall try to do.

The structuralists say that literary study should concentrate on the motif, which is any irreducible element entering into a number of works of art. I shall define the adventure tale, and mark its development as a genre, primarily in terms of motifs; though I shall use

Lévi-Strauss's term, *mytheme,* when I think of a story as a myth instead of a tale.

But the most important formalist idea for my purposes is that of genre—genre as a mechanism of the system of literature—and here Claudio Guillen's *Literature as a System* is most useful. Guillen says that the genres are mental codes, by means of which a writer comes to terms with his writing. Taken all together, they codify the subjects available to a writer, the styles appropriate to them, and the rewards to be expected from each. There have always, he says, been styles and counterstyles, genres and countergenres; for instance, praise and vituperation, tragedy and comedy, pastoral and picaresque; together these map out the possibilities for a writer. They constitute the code of literature at a given moment.

Robert Scholes usefully extends this idea by pointing out that reading as well as writing is a generic process; we postulate a genre whenever we begin to read, and that genre implies certain expectations, against and with which the writer works. Each specimen is likely to alter slightly the laws of the genus, for this is not taxonomy —this is an artistic, not a scientific process—but they are still laws, exerting pressure on both readers and writers. This idea helps me to understand the relation of the adventure tale to other forms of fiction, notably the morally serious domestic novel. I see the state of literature at any given moment as a system of forces acting upon both writers and readers, persuading them to give "appropriate" depths and strengths of response to literary forms and their subject matters. (Perhaps the best mechanical analogy is the centrifuge, which sorts out the heavier elements from the lighter—but those elements must here be understood to be reader responses as well as the literary forms with which they are paired.)

The genre map of literature, the grid of the system, that shows which forms are dominant, and where the beginning writer may aim at greatness, changes as the larger map of culture changes. In the Renaissance, the epic poem and the tragic drama were dominant. After 1688 in England the novel was born, and gradually displaced those forms. And among the subgenres of fiction, serious literary interest came to focus on what can be called the courtship or domestic novel. The adventure novel was assigned less significance, and matched with more superficial responses. This does not mean that all the writers of adventure were nonserious, or that the thematic material was trivial. But this point I must return to. The structural anthropologists and folklorists have something to contribute to my method, too. Lévi-Strauss works with not tales but myths, and he defines a myth as a body of materials, mainly narrative, which "deal with" one aspect of a culture. The narrative often obscures the myth, in order to make that aspect of the culture palatable to its members. (As adventure obscures imperialism.) The myth is a coded message from the culture as a whole to the individual members; it can be delivered in a variety of different ways; and it remains valid as long as the culture remains homogeneous. I find this very suggestive when applied to the birth and death of the adventure tale from Defoe to Kipling.

The code of the message, says Lévi-Strauss, can be read only if we rearrange the mythemes (the motifs or units of myth) into a nonnarrative order. (This is of course what criticism does to literature, and what my interpretation will do to adventure.) Thus he breaks the Oedipus myth down into four columns of units, some of which are semantic, not syntagmatic; for instance, the fact that "Oedipus" means "swollen-foot." The culture that developed the Oedipus myth, according to his interpretation, *believed* that man is autochthonous, but *knew* that men are born of man + woman. The myth evoked that puzzle but connected it with another puzzle, involving problems of kinship and incest, which the culture had worked out. By associating the adjustments of social life with the enigmas of religious mystery, the myth made the latter familiar and acceptable.

But the value of Lévi-Strauss to me does not depend upon any particular method of interpreting, such as the column of units, much less any particular interpretation. Some of Edmund Leach's essays are much closer to my purposes and better as models. Lévi-Strauss's value above all lies in his teaching that myths, while sometimes constituting models for their societies—to perpetuate beliefs or practices—sometimes instead expose the mainsprings of their societies, in all their contradictions. A decoded myth is a theme with variations, the theme being some self-contradiction within a morality.

Edmund Leach has applied these ideas to literature, and so has brought them much closer to my own uses. In "The Legitimacy of Solomon" (1966) he shows how the Biblical story of Solomon's family origins mediates a contradiction in Jewish culture: the contradiction between the teaching of endogamy (with the idea that Palestine was a direct gift of God to the Jewish people) and the fact of exogamy (with the knowledge that Palestine was a conquered country, with a racially mixed population). This story was written at a time when religious rules were very important; because of Ezra and Nehemiah, Judah had become a religious community, represented by a high priest instead of a king. The only half-Jewish origin of Solomon, told in the story, admitted the fact of exogamy, but made sense of it in the larger context, related it to the teachings of the Divine fate of Israel.

Another study in the Leach line is even closer. This is Marguerite S. Robinson's "The House of the Mighty Hero or the House of Enough Paddy?." This is about Prince Dutthagamani (161–137 B.C.), the prince who restored the Sinhalese dynasty and Buddhism in Ceylon. It is again an endogamy-exogamy contradiction which lies behind the myth, and it is mediated by an equivocation about exactly how the people who tell the story, the Morapityans, are descended from the Prince. This equivocation makes the contradiction comfortable and acceptable. But the culture also contains a contradiction between priestly and kingly authority, mediated in this story by the combination of the man of peace and the man of war in Dutthagamani. That is what is announced in the title of the essay; the Morapityans have to ask, is it for his might and heroism they celebrate him, or for his skill in producing and providing? Is it not for both, even though the two legends present themselves as mutually exclusive?

At this point we can make an easy transition to the modernist adventure tale, and apply similar methods to it. For there is in Defoe's *Captain Singleton,* and in several later stories of that kind, a comparable figure, whom we can label "the bloody Quaker." This figure (in *Captain Singleton* he is called William) is both a sincere Quaker, devoted to peace, meekness, and self-denial, and at the same time a pirate, an expert in war, and ruthless against his enemies. I will explain later how Defoe, and the other writers, resolve the contradiction. But it's obvious that it arises out of a contradiction in their feelings, aspirations, and values, and in their readers' feelings—a contradiction that works in the culture itself, just as one did in the culture of the Morapityans.

And the association of the explicable with the inexplicable, which Lévi-Strauss points to in myths, is paralleled in the adventure tale by an association of the familiar with the unfamiliar, of the palatable with the unpalatable, which one can see in Kipling's "The Man Who Would be King," for instance. Much of the "theory" of human nature and history which this story implies is deeply disturbing, but it is mixed with much that is familiar and comfortable. (Of course the element of the enigmatic, which Lévi-Struass stresses in myth, is much smaller in art—at least in the serious art of the domestic novel.) The other structuralist concepts will be applied in the chapters to come, and will prove especially fruitful in explaining how a genre develops and how the system of literature relates both inwardly to the adventure tale and outwardly to the system of culture as a whole.

But it is worth describing in advance the one genre of fiction that came into existence at the same moment as the adventure tale, and with roughly the same cultural sponsorship, but which developed into a much more serious literary genre. The domestic or courtship novel, which also took an initial impetus from the hands of Defoe, gradually won a literary status for itself which the adventure novel never equalled, and indeed preempted the prestige of literary seriousness. It won itself a place in the center of the system of literature.

It did so because this form was employed to carry both key values of the ruling mercantile caste, and at the same time a protest against the crudest expansive thrusts of the modern system—including imperialism and adventure. Perhaps "protest" will seem too assertive a word for something that showed itself at first as voluntary ignorance —aversion of interest. But there is spiritual energy in fiction like Richardson's, and the curve of that energy, at least by extrapolation, carries the reader away from the triumphant capitalism and militarism of eighteenth-century England; while in the nineteenth century there was of course demonstrable protest, against industrialism, in the domestic novel. The serious writers, reacting against what they hated in their civilization, could indirectly attack it in the courtship novel, while more clearly asserting the caste values they shared with their audience. They created a literature of largely silent resistance. The adventure novel, on the other hand, did not protest. This is the source of the distinction, serious vs. nonserious: though of course individual writers had to give a literary validity to the distinction, by the imaginative effort they put into the domestic novel.

It is also worth sketching briefly the history of this genre because it is a paradigm of the development of a genre, of both the changes and the continuity in its motifs. Because these books are so well-known, and because great writers have written so often in this tradition, it is easy to demonstrate the development in their case; and then we can use that demonstration in considering the adventure tale. We find there a very different development, all stops and starts, with nothing consummated artistically.

Let us merely name the motifs of the domestic novel, from Defoe and Richardson to Lawrence. There is the group of marriageable girls —as in Jane Austen; the middle-class family life—as in George Eliot; the wild young aristocrat—as in Richardson—who seeks one of the girls; the process of courtship, which is the main action; the young man's conversion (or not); the melodrama of seduction; the married woman who made the wrong choice (particularly frequent in Dickens and Thackeray); and repentance (particularly strong in George Eliot and Tolstoy). These can all be found in Defoe's *Religious Courtship* and *The Family Instructor*.

The Domestic Novel

The essential subject of this kind of novel is marriage, its essential action the right choice of partner for the heroine. The relations between it and the adventure novel can be described as polar, and that polarity is a major clue to the operation of literature-as-a-system in England. To keep to our previous metaphor, the courtship novel became one of the heaviest elements in the centrifuge, the adventure one of the lightest. To put it more simply, serious fiction writers in England were warned away from the adventure tale, and toward the domestic novel, even though, during this period of 1700 to 1900, the adventure material bore much more directly upon the serious history of England.

To come to Defoe's own contributions, in *Religious Courtship* he tells the story of a middle-class widower's three daughters, whose mother had been devout and had told her daughters never to marry an irreligious man nor one of a different faith. Their father is comparatively worldly, but their mother had said, "A religious life is heaven upon earth," and so each daughter has to work out her own fate between those two options. The interest of the novel derives from comparison of their fates. The youngest is courted by an aristocrat, but finds him insufficiently serious about religion, and so rejects him, braving her father's wrath. The young man goes off in high dudgeon to his country estate, but there converses with William, a poor but honest peasant, who teaches him religion, after acquiring which he is accepted. (Two motifs here were of great importance in later fiction: the *Wakefield/Werther* pastoral, and the idea that the aristomilitary caste scorn religion.) The oldest and steadiest sister, confidant of the others' problems, declares she won't marry at all, because the times are so wicked (though at the end she gets a suitably unexciting partner). But the middle one, being morally lazy, accepts a man who turns out to be a crypto-Catholic and keeps a disguised altar in his closet, and causes her a great deal of grief in the long run.[8] And at the end of the book, the father too is converted to seriousness by his daughters' sufferings.

This story is told at considerable length, with dialogue and imagined scenes and settings, though more sketchily than a real novel such as Richardson was to write. But the plot is of the type that was to be of great use to Richardson and subsequent novelists, notably Jane Austen. *Sense and Sensibility, Pride and Prejudice, Mansfield Park, Persuasion,* are all strikingly similar to this story.

Conjugal Lewdness (1727) also contains several anecdotes about wicked aristocrats marrying sober citizens, and about tyrannical fathers interfering with their children's choice of partners. Max Novak, in his introduction to the 1967 edition, says that Defoe here was the first to depict conjugal quarrels in realistic fiction, complete with feminine irony, masculine defeat, and the sexual implications of apparently remote differences of opinion.

But I would like to spend more time on *The Family Instructor,* where the stories are developed at more length.[9] In the Preface, Defoe says that some have called this a religious play, and he had at first intended to treat the material in a dramatic poem, which is perhaps some indication of the seriousness with which he had imagined it. In Part I, "Relating to Fathers and Children," a father and mother, suddenly aroused to religious consciousness, decide to reform their family. Though their children are not immodest or dishonest, the elder daughter, for instance, loves to play cards all night, to go to the playhouse, to wear patches, to read romances, and to sing idle songs: ". . . they were bred up with gaiety and gallantry, as being of good fortune and fashion; but nothing of religion. . . ." (p. 71).

The parents' reform begins with a family rule that the children shall not go to the park after church, and this provokes a big quarrel, the elder daughter and the elder son being bitterly resistant. A younger brother and sister are amenable, having seen the advantages of religion in other houses they have visited. But the older ones, in an ingeniously conceived scene, walk out into the garden back of the house while a family meeting is held, giving the impression they have gone to the park, without risking such outright disobedience in reality, in order to test their parents' reactions. Later they both leave home.

Part 2, "Relating to Masters and Servants," tells quite a different story, of good and bad apprentices. On the whole this story fell into the hands of moralists rather than novelists in later years, so I shall not occupy myself with it.[10] Part 3, "Relating to Husbands and Wives," takes up again the story of the family. The elder daughter, who had been in love with Sir Anthony, an aristocrat and a rake, marries a serious-minded citizen with old-fashioned Protestant principles. He will take her to the playhouse door, but will not go in himself; in fact he institutes family prayers, to her disgust, and teaches the children religion. They quarrel; she repents her malice against him; falls into a fever, and repents her evil ways as she recovers. The elder brother, on the other hand, having joined the army and lost an arm in the wars, comes back to England unrepentant, and so dies rejected by his family.

And Vol. II, Part 1, "Family Breaches," tells the story of two bad wives, married to two pious citizens who are friends. The first wife objects to her husband conducting family worship, on the grounds that he is unworthy—it is clear that she is morally jealous of him. She becomes pathologically angry, falls sick, goes mad, and when she recovers doesn't fully remember what has happened—is diminished. The second wife is born an aristocrat (her brother is called Sir Richard) and so is used to luxury, and to riot and gaming. She mocks her husband when he asks that grace be said at her brother's table. Sir Richard is much struck by her husband's integrity, however, and when she returns to her brother's house in dudgeon, he quarrels with her and is even himself converted to moral seriousness by the spectacle of her dissipation. He takes her back by force to her husband, and there she falls sick and eventually repents.

The motifs of these stories echo through the rest of eighteenth- , nineteenth- , and even twentieth-century serious fiction; in the Brontës' novels, in Dickens, in Thackeray, in George Eliot, in Hardy; they are to be found, somewhat transvalued, in D. H. Lawrence. (Indeed, crudely as they are written, there is evidence elsewhere in Defoe—notably in *Roxana*—that he had a novelistic imagination of no mean order, and could, given other circumstances, have won himself a place in the history of serious fiction.) This is the story of caste psychology and intercaste conflict, of manners taken seriously and marriage taken solemnly, with which we are all familiar because it has been central to our literary culture.

Of course the story develops and changes. One cause is that a talented artist will not simply repeat his predecessor. The sexual assault upon Pamela, by which Richardson demonstrates her virtue, is refined away to practically nothing in *Mansfield Park*. While Richardson's Mr. B. undergoes an enormous development to become Mr. Rochester in Charlotte Brontë's novel. But Pamela, Fanny Price, and Jane Eyre are the same figure, have the same function, to use Propp's term. In the second half of the nineteenth century, a different kind of change occurred in the heroine, which involved a more complex development in the story. In the hands of George Eliot and her successors, the girl becomes more substantial. Physically and morally, Dorothea Brooke and Maggie Tulliver are larger than the girls they stand beside—while their predecessors were smaller than their equivalent contrasts. Hardy and James were more equivocal about physical size, but at least some of their girls can seem large, figures to be admired rather than pitied. The girl's counterplayer, an aristocrat to begin with, is often given foreign blood instead by George Eliot, a proletarian origin by D. H. Lawrence, and East-European or American-radical credentials by Doris Lessing. It is, I think, obvious, what external forces caused these substitutions and displacements. The more striking fact is surely the continuity.

Why was this story taken up by major writers while the adventure tale was not? Of course, there was resistance to this story too, at first, as we see in Fielding's mockery of Richardson. But that resistance did not last long; Fielding's last novel, *Amelia,* is Richardsonian, or one might say, thinking of these books, Defoesque. It seems clear that the difference derives from the close alliance that was forged in the early eighteenth century between literature and the religious-moral-sexual interests of Puritanism. Though Pope and Swift might keep those interests at arm's length, Steele and Addison embraced them in their writing for *The Tatler* and *The Spectator*, which include many short stories comparable with those Defoe told.

Puritanism was a major—many historians would say the major—element in the ideology of the modern world system. Its energies can be found at work everywhere, in religion, in morality, in commerce, in science.[11] Of course it was not unopposed, but its relations with its opponents within the modern system ideology seem to be a good example of the Hegelian triad, in which Puritanism was the thesis. (Puritanism was the merchant caste's form of Christianity, so the dialectic just named was also the dialectic of the castes.) Thus in the case of literature it seems clear that Defoe and Richardson and the novel they invented represent a thesis, to which Fielding, among others, opposed an antithesis; but the novels of the end of the eighteenth century, even Fielding's own *Amelia*, bore the marks of the thesis. By then Puritanism was in alliance with other social forces which it had fought before—that is the crucial point.

The Puritan army (at least in its lower ranks) had been radical, but the economic sinews of Cromwell's Commonwealth, the London merchants, were conservative. Though Presbyterian, they were lukewarm about even the Scots' Presbyterian Church, and grew tired also of supporting Cromwell's adventurous militarism. They made an alliance with the conservative forces in England, on which the subsequent settlement was based, and to this settlement the Brahmins (scholars, writers, clergymen) gradually subscribed.

These merchants even brought the Stuart Charles II back to the throne. A pamphlet of 1680* claimed that Presbyterians were not radicals, did not oppose either king or state, but were rather the natural heirs of the Elizabethan Puritans, men who wanted a *moral* revolution. That was what the Restoration Puritans engineered after 1688, by means of their Societies for the Reformation of Manners (led by Queen Mary and Archbishop Tillotson), and their Dissenting Academies, of which there were forty-seven by 1702. These were essentially merchant caste reforms, in education and morality, and as vital to the modern world system as the new habits of work imposed on the factory hands.

*H. G. Plum, *Restoration Puritanism*, 1943.

Literature cooperated, in the persons of Addison and Steele, and all that their famous journals, *The Tatler* and *The Spectator*, stood for. These immensely successful innovations in taste brought literature and culture into alliance with the merchant caste. Defoe felt that *The Tatler* continued the work he had begun with his *Review*. Together, they saved literature from the control of schoolmen, rakes, and aristocrats. On the stage the New Comedy, for which Steele's *The Conscious Lovers* set the model, did the same. And Defoe and Richardson created the novel. Pope and Swift, on the other hand, felt a loyalty to older and fiercer modes of literary intelligence; and the reason is that they would not identify themselves with the merchant caste, or with the new gentleness, the glorious and bloodless moral revolution, which was in its service.

This moral revolution redirected spiritual intensity toward home life, marriage, and sex; away from older objects of devotion, like the liturgical life of the church, and the cults of the aristomilitary caste. When the spirit of religion came out of the monastery, to adapt a famous phrase, it settled in the home as well as in the marketplace, making its altar the bedroom and the bed. Indeed, as far as the serious novelists were concerned, it was the home and *not* the market that was important; the treaty of mutual support between the merchant caste and the serious writers referred exclusively to the private life of the former, and did not cover the public life of commerce in England, much less in the empire. (By the same token, that treaty referred exclusively to the moral concerns of the serious writers, and did not cover their theological or specifically religious interests.)[12]

The colonial enterprise did not attract the participation of Brahmin seriousness, so it did not undergo the imaginative transformation that serious writers gave to family life in the courtship and domestic novel.[13] Serious writers facing the colonial theme felt an inhibition or a prohibition, from which they turned away, to the courtship theme. This is what the novelists above all took up (one sees that theme treated crudely in *The Family Instructor*) and the greatest example is Richardson; that is why there is that extraordinary concentration on sex in *Pamela* and *Clarissa* which has misled so many commentators. Of course it was a Puritan kind of sex that Richardson could celebrate. It was passive and feminine sex which was idealized in such novels, while the chivalric romance had idealized the active and masculine kind. Passive sex and spirituality were most seriously and inextricably wedded, or identified, by that author and those readers.

Thus even the theological and spiritual heritage of Puritanism did not entirely lose connection with the serious novel. We can find a structure of feelings closely related to Richardson's in the hymns of Isaac Watts, perhaps the major representative of Puritan piety in eighteenth-century England.[14]

> We are a garden walled around
> Chosen and made peculiar ground
> A little spot enclosed by grace
> Out of the world's wide wilderness.

And

> Watched by the world's indignant eye
> Who load us with reproach and shame
> As servants of the Lord most high
> As zealous for His glorious name,
> We ought in all His paths to move,
> With holy fear and humble love.

Clarissa persecuted by Lovelace, even Pamela persecuted by Mr. B., was, I think, the heroine of feelings like these. Persecution is a main mode of action and fantasy in Richardson.[15] You don't find anything comparable in the adventure novel.

Out of the negative and shadow figures of the Puritan drama, moreover, out of Milton's Satan and Richardson's Lovelace, comes the Byronic hero, and the Nietzschean superman. Such figures, when transvalued, are spiritual adventurers. They appear even in domestic novels, where all the action is transferred indoors, and almost all inside personal relations, and are moral imperialists. Lovelace says, "I have three passions that sway me by turns; all imperial ones. Love, revenge, ambition, or a desire of conquest." He often sees himself as "an imperial personage." While Clarissa takes modesty as her motto, and desires to slip through life unnoticed.[16] She is anti-imperialist. (These are puns, of course, but it is history that is making them.)

This disapproval of the military, aristocratic, and adventurous hero was a very powerful impulse within English seriousness, which persisted a long time, even though it always evoked some contradictions (voluntary contradictions in Fielding, Swift, Scott, as well as the involuntary ones in Milton and Richardson). For instance, Harriet

Byron in *Clarissa* attacked the aristocratic concept of honor from the mercantile-bourgeois point of view of duty. "Murderous, vile word, Honour! . . . the very opposite to duty, goodness, piety, religion." But we find Thomas Arnold in the nineteenth century saying something very similar.* "I confess that if I were called upon to name what spirit of evil predominantly deserved the name of anti-Christ, I should name the spirit of chivalry—the more detestable for the very guise of the 'Archangel ruined,' which has made it so seductive to the most generous spirits—but to me so hateful, because it is in direct opposition to the impartial justice of the Gospel, and its comprehensive feeling of equal brotherhood, and because it so fostered a sense of honour rather than a sense of duty."[17] Presumably Arnold meant to condemn Scott's novels and adventure novels, in general, for spreading the spirit of chivalry. In fact, the most serious voice in Scott comes down for duty against honor; and Defoe's adventure tales are not in the least chivalric. But serious moralists like Arnold (and Dr. Johnson) were sometimes impressed by the domestic novel as a spokesman for seriousness; never by the adventure tale.

Thus of the two genres which Defoe helped to found, only one was embraced by morality and by literature. Of course, one must take into account Defoe's weaknesses as a writer: his failure to achieve interiority, personality, with language and with literary form; his lack of artistic and intellectual scruple, which meant a lack of intensity of meaning. But in the case of the courtship novel there was a Richardson to take up where Defoe left off, and to create that intensity; in the case of the adventure novel there was not, even though *Robinson Crusoe* was much more of a success than *Religious Courtship*, by every measure of success. The adventure novel never became serious enough literarily for moralists like Arnold and Johnson to read.

We tend to think of that unseriousness as the *cause* why moralists (and the most gifted writers) neglected it. But it was *effect* just as much—writers were never told how to combine the adventure subject with political seriousness. Clearly English literature had organized itself into a system, of which the central seriousness was hostile to the material of adventure and therewith of empire and frontier. The writer who took up that material knew that he was providing entertainment.

*Quoted in John Lord, *Duty, Honor, Empire*, p. 83.

III

Defoe

Defoe and his England

IN a work of this size and purpose, there is no room for any but the most schematic biography of the authors. But Defoe acted out his temperament and represented his caste in a dozen different political and economic roles.[1] He was a representative man of his times. So it helps to remember his social activity while reading his adventures. Therefore I am going to pick out those "themes" of his life story which relate most importantly to *Robinson Crusoe* and *Captain Singleton;* and to my general subject, the modern world's imagination. I would say that Defoe embodied that imagination.

First, then, he was born into a Dissenting family, and knew, at least by family tradition, some religious persecution. It always remained one of his major interests to speak for and to Dissenters; and he could, on occasion—for instance, in his *Memoirs of the Church of Scotland* —talk the old Puritan language about "persecuted saints" and the "worldly men," the "men of blood," who oppressed them. But more characteristically, his stress fell on reconciliation, in religion as in politics. He had a modern kind of tolerance, and wanted to reconcile the Dissenters to the rest of England, and vice versa—put a modern stress on moderation. Thus in "An Appeal to Honour and Justice" (1715) he says, "I was from my first entering into knowledge of public matters, and have ever been to this day, a sincere lover of the constitution of my country; zealous for liberty, and the Protestant interest; but a constant follower of moderate principles, a vigorous opposer of hot measures in all parties. . . ." (p. 232). Both parties, he says, have succumbed to hot opinions. But he has been loyal to the country and the king.

This stress on England-as-a-whole, as an escape from factionalism, is also very characteristic of Defoe. The bitter memories he cherished were of civil war rather than of class or sect persecution. The happy future he foresaw was of prosperity and respectability, with the Dissenters fully members of the middle class.[2] This is modern system Puritanism, as distinct from earlier kinds.

Equally significant, and a second trait to stress in Defoe, is his loyalty to the king. Royalty rose above faction and above all ideologies except that which it embodied, the ideology of the nation-state itself. And for Defoe there was one king above all kings, William III, the Dutch prince invited to ascend the throne in 1688. Defoe was twenty-eight at the time of the Glorious Bloodless Revolution. He joined William's forces as they approached London, and cut something of a figure in the City of London's processions of welcome. He defended William in his poem "The True-Born Englishman," gave William a lot of advice, in pamphlets, saw him face-to-face, and claims to have been a valued consultant. And indeed his loyalty to William's memory after the king's death was unequivocal and warm in a way almost unique among Defoe's political passions. He always celebrated the anniversary of William's landing in England.

What William meant to Defoe was probably what he meant to most people; which was expressed in the official toast to the king's memory: "To the glorious, pious, and immortal memory of the Great Deliverer . . . who rescued us from Popery, Prelacy, Brass Money, and Wooden Shoes." Financial probity and material progress there go hand in hand with religious liberty, all supreme values of the merchant caste.

And it is not irrelevant to remember also that William III was a Dutch prince. In him the two leading core states came together; you might say that Amsterdam yielded precedence to London finally in 1688.[3] Certainly the contrast between the Protestant Dutchman and the Catholic Stuarts, who were half-attached to France and even to Spain, was a contrast full of meaning to those who believed in what we are calling the modern world system.

Then, born a Dissenter, Defoe began adult life as a tradesman. His family had been Flemish artisans, who had fled the persecution of Philip II; a group whose migration helped establish the English wool trade—a crucial element in English wealth of Defoe's time. He was also an economic journalist, indeed a major propagandist for exponential growth and all the changes that brings. But Defoe himself was not a successful merchant. From his early thirties on, he was never clear of debt, and he went bankrupt in 1692, for £17,000. He was one of nineteen marine insurers ruined in the French wars. (Insurance was one of the key new professions, a keystone in the great structure of finance capitalism.) He paid off all but £5,000 of his debt in ten years, but lost a lot again in 1703. At that time he was in jail for a political offense, and while there his Tilbury brick and tile works failed. Between 1688 and 1694 he was defendant in eight lawsuits, all accusing him of sharp practice. Thus he had profound, as well as varied, experience of modern capitalism.

(It is, I think, no accident that three of the writers I am treating at length, Defoe, Scott, and Twain, all went bankrupt; and failed on the scale of firms, not merely of private individuals. They did so because they *were* firms, commercial enterprises, as Jane Austen, George Eliot, D. H. Lawrence were not. They participated in the capitalist activity, and the other three did not.)

Defoe was also a journalist, most notably in *The Review,* which he edited, and largely wrote, from 1704 to 1713. As such he was engaged in political propaganda, and semipolitical intrigue, and was one of the Grub Streeters whom Pope put into the *Dunciad.* As Pat Rogers shows in *Grub Street,* Defoe was very representative of the group which Pope repudiated, the group from whom he dissociated himself and literature, as being sordid and semicriminal. (Between 1720 and 1726 Defoe was *Applebee's Journal*'s reporter, interviewing criminals in Newgate prison.) Literature at its most dignified maintained a distance between itself and the modern system; but Defoe did not belong to literature.

As a journalist, he can be associated with Twain and Kipling; and the work of all three is more made up of newspaper fact and newspaper interest than the work of, again, Austen, Eliot, and Lawrence. Indeed, it is no accident that the first three, and this time we can add Scott also, were very interested in hoaxes. In Defoe's case, the most famous is the pamphlet, *The Shortest Way with Dissenters,* which earned him a spell in pillory and jail. In Scott's case, I am thinking of his long denial of being the author of the *Waverley* novels; in Twain's and Kipling's, stories like "The Man Who Corrupted Hadleyburg" and "The Village That Voted the Earth Was Flat" show their fascination with fraud and hoax.

Then Defoe was a government agent, a secret agent, sent to Edinburgh to facilitate the Union of England with Scotland, which was forced through—against a lot of Scottish opposition—in 1707. The Scottish parliament was abolished, and the Scots were given forty-seven seats in the English House of Commons and sixteen in the English House of Lords. Defoe discharged his duties by writing pamphlets and poems, but also by masquerading as a merchant—dropping hints, picking up information—his glee at being in disguise is obvious in his letters to Harley, the minister who employed him. "I am perfectly unsuspected," one letter begins, and closes, "I am all to everyone that I may gain some." This glee he took in disguise seems peculiarly characteristic of the heroes of the modern world system, especially the literary heroes (it is prominent in *Kim,* for instance) and is related to the taste for hoaxes. Defoe delighted in the idea of secret policy, and made a minor cult of Cardinal Richelieu.

But it is just as important that this work was done for the union with Scotland, the foundation of the British empire. Defoe believed in that Union not merely as extending English power but as improving Scottish life—introducing the benefits of progress, of the modern world system, where they were not known before. (Of course, those two values, Empire and Progress, were natural twins to his mind.) The Scots, and particularly the Highlanders, were for Defoe men on the very periphery of the system, psychologically and sociologically—and to bring them inside the Union was to benefit them. This was true for many others beside Defoe, and remained so throughout the two centuries we are studying. It will be interesting for us to watch the different figures that Scotland cuts in relation to England's modernist idea, in subsequent adventure novelists, like Scott and Kipling.

One last point; Defoe was a rationalist. Not in the most philosophic sense: he was very interested in supernatural and providential phenomena, and quite ready to accept explanations in such terms. But in the more literary sense of a distaste for myths and fables, he was a rationalist. His "The Storm" is, like *Journal of the Plague Year,* a nonfiction novel which professes to give us all the facts about a natural phenomenon. In the Preface, he says that ancient history is mostly lost to us by the empty flourishes and romance of ancient historians, and the lives of great men, who could have been of use to us, are "drowned in fable." For instance, the true story of Daedalus, a man who cleverly made his way out of an Egyptian maze by using a clue of thread, "is grown into the fable of making himself a pair of wings, and flying through the air." A drought in Samaria gets turned into a tale of Phaeton. And so we have the silly romances of Arthur, St. George, Guy of Warwick, Bevis of Southampton, all "legends of fabulous history which have swallowed up the actions of our ancient predecessors." These are the native equivalents of *Amadis,* the fiction of the feudal system in England.

And in *The New Family Instructor,* Defoe derives the words "romance" and "romantic" etymologically from "Roman Catholic"; saying that they were first applied to the saints' legends and supposed miracles of that religion. That derivation indicates pretty clearly the revulsion felt by the merchant caste for romance, and their own affiliation to adventure instead.

A Dissenter and a rationalist, therefore, a journalist and a secret agent, a merchant and a patriot, Defoe embodied many of the dominant forces of the modern system in England, and was admirably equipped to devise the literary form of its energizing myth.[4]

Defoe's Fiction

Defoe wrote many kinds of fiction, was a first practitioner of many subgenres, as *Moll Flanders, Memoirs of a Cavalier, Journal of the Plague Year, Roxana,* and *Colonel Jack* will remind us. Indeed, one aspect of his importance to my argument here is that he was so generally gifted and inventive as a writer of fiction. That he in effect invented the novel for England and therefore for the world, is part of that sense of him I want to invoke, in order to give importance to *Robinson Crusoe,* or to that significance of *Robinson Crusoe* which I am going to describe. But I trust the reader to supply that himself, for there has been a good deal of interest in those books in literary circles recently; and what I would say is not so very different. The only ones I shall talk about are his tales of adventure. It is generally accepted that all Defoe's adventure fiction derives from (one might say, crystallizes out of) the flood of travel writing of his own youth and Elizabethan times. William Hallam Bonner tells us, in *Captain William Dampier,* that the Term Catalogues of 1668–1709 show voyages to have been the most popular genre of literature published then, and that this was a new popularity. Voyages were popular in Elizabethan times also, but there had been a falling off after 1626 for two generations. But Defoe's personal library included forty-nine voyages, and he styled himself a master of geography—he wrote the text for the very large and expensive *Atlas Maritimus et Commercialis.* And when an interest in pirates developed, after Exquemelin's book* appeared in 1684, Defoe produced the first English book on the subject.

Among particular titles that constituted precedents for Defoe's work, one could cite Dampier's *New Voyage Round the World.* Dampier was a roughly parallel figure to Crusoe and Singleton, almost certainly something of a model for them, and in fact sailed on the expedition which brought home Alexander Selkirk, the major model for Crusoe. Dampier also brought home a Friday figure, a "painted prince," from the Spice Islands, who was put on exhibition in England, but died soon after of smallpox. Dampier's book came out in 1697, and had three editions in nine months. He personally had a great success—dined with Pepys and Evelyn, and appeared before the Council for Trade to describe the Isthmus of Darien.

The major such title, however, is Hakluyt's *Voyages—The Principal Navigations, Voyages, Traffiques, and Discoveries of the English Nation,* in three volumes, 1598–1600.[5] The volumes include letters, ruttiers, navigation training manuals, battle reports, logs, diaries, official reports, and projected and imaginary voyages as well as real ones. When merchant adventurers formed companies, they consulted Hakluyt. He and his uncle founded geography in England, and prepared England for empire, by—in the *Voyages*—praising England, hailing its great captains, rallying support to the navy, recommending colonization, describing new lands, revealing Spain's weaknesses. Irwin R. Blacker, editor of the 1965 edition of the *Voyages,* says they are "the very papers of Empire," and "the epic of the

---

*A. O. Exquemelin, *The Bucaniers of America,* London, 1684–1685.

English people as they told it themselves." Defoe's novels retold that epic, but in fiction and a new kind of fiction—formally appropriate to the modernist material involved.

One of the fiercest episodes in the *Voyages*, fierce in its imperialist exultation, is Raleigh's account of Grenville's last fight on the *Revenge* and of the defeat of the Armada. Raleigh was one of Defoe's heroes; in 1719, the year of *Robinson Crusoe*, he also brought out a *Voyages of Raleigh*. But there was a difference between the styles of imperialism of the two men, the difference between the modernist and the Elizabethan. Raleigh's *History of the World* spread the dream of English empire far and wide, infecting amongst others Cromwell. But his idea of Guiana was all made of gold. Hidden in the interior was supposed to be a race of Incas of fabulous wealth; with a capital city, Manoa, full of gold, and a king, El Dorado, who was smeared with turpentine and then daubed with gold dust for his coronation. Manoa was sought by European adventurers, including Raleigh himself, for 240 years.

That sort of material—or more exactly, the reflection in the general English mind of that sort of material—is what Defoe started with when he began to write adventure tales. But he made something different out of it. I want to summarize briefly two other works of his of that kind before I come to *Robinson Crusoe* and *Captain Singleton*. The first is *A New Voyage Round the World*, in 1725, in which the anonymous captain-narrator describes a career in trading, exploring, privateering, from which he returned rich. The adventures he meets are largely typical of the genre. At the Cape of Good Hope the captain cleverly put down a mutiny. At Madagascar he enlisted hundreds of pirates, who were fed up with their leaderlessness and self-dividedness. In Borneo he traded with trinkets, and in New Guinea got gold from innocent savages; these were vegetarians, who had had no contact with the world, and so had no rapine or violence in their manners or their agriculture; whose faces were "singularly honest and sincere."[6]

The most interesting episodes occur at the end of the book, in South America. As he traded along the west coast, the captain kept inquiring about the Andes and how to cross them. He captured a Spaniard who owned a villa near Baldivia, and won his trust and affection—won him away from his national loyalties. The Spaniard became a sort of Montezuma to the captain's Cortes. He told the captain how few Spaniards there were in Peru, and how they did not deserve to own that country. There were only 7,000 Spanish families there, and they neither worked nor explored. "Seignior," says he, "we have so much pride that we have no avarice, and we do not covet enough to make us work for it" (p. 361). (Pride was the quality characterizing the Spanish, according to modern system characterology.) The English would make a valuable property out of Peru; there were several mountains as rich as Potosi that had never been worked.

The Spaniard invited the captain to his villa, and treated all the Englishmen like kings—also leaving his sons on board the English ship as hostages—and gave them much gold and silver plate. (Gift-giving is an important motif in Defoe.) He led them up into the mountains, where the volcanoes light up the valleys by night, and they saw a river of fire, etc. (p. 396). (This is one of the great landscapes of adventure fiction; it recurs notably in Rider Haggard and Conan Doyle.) Half the streams and pools had gold in them, ready to be picked up. But the captain led his men, and Defoe leads us, on past that, down the mountain's other side, onto a great plain. This is what Defoe wants us to reach out toward. The Spaniards, we are told, don't care about this land (which is what we now call Argentina).[7] The land is like Salisbury Plain, and they see vast herds of black cattle, wild, and think of what the land would be like "if it had but half the art and industry of a European nation to assist the natural fertility of the soil." The gold, as always in Defoe, is a semisinister value; it breeds a fever among the men, who break discipline more than once. But the land, empty land, asking to be worked, is the beatific vision of modernist adventure, recurring in Rider Haggard and Conan Doyle at the end of the nineteenth century. This marks the difference between Defoe's imperialism and Raleigh's.

Indeed, that England should occupy that particular piece of land was a message Defoe returned to several times during his life. In *History of the Principal Discoveries,* for instance, he recommends a colony 120 miles south of the Rio de la Plata. Defoe was an enthusiast for colonies generally. He wanted England to occupy Canada, Max Novak tells us, and to claim California, on the basis of Drake's explorations. In 1711 he was considering emigration himself. *Moll Flanders* and *Colonel Jack* are, amongst other things, propaganda for emigration to Virginia and Maryland. Indeed, all Defoe's adventure and picaresque fiction can be regarded as propaganda for emigration. An Act of 1717, just before he began his career as a fictionist, made it possible to deport much larger numbers of criminals than before, and Defoe consistently depicts the experience as regenerative. The land and the gold are, then, two adventure motifs in the *New Voyage*.

The other adventure tale is even more interesting: *The Four Year Voyage of Captain George Roberts* (1726). The book is anonymous but usually attributed to Defoe; as in several other cases, it is quite possible that he acted only as its editor or even its scribe, but that makes little difference to its interest for us. Defoe is not important for the idiosyncrasies of his style, or even the integrity of his individuality, but for the way he represents by participation, the way he merges into the whole activity he describes.

The tone of this book is very severe, factual, sober, and the narrative implicitly develops the captain (the narrator) as WASP hero, that is, as modern world system hero. He is contrasted, implicitly, with other men (for instance with his first commander, Captain Scott), all of whom turn out to lack crucial WASP qualities, to be either incompetent or untrustworthy.

There is a long episode with some pirates who capture his ship. The quartermaster general of the pirate company, though normally of remarkable intelligence and generosity, takes a dislike to Roberts; jealous (one gathers) of his greater piety, firmness, virtue. Roberts refuses to join the company, and the other pirates are willing to let him go free, but the quartermaster becomes vindictive, persuading Roberts' mate to desert him, denuding his ship of all provisions, and all sails but old ones, and leaving him with only "a boy" and "a small boy." It is a remarkable study in the jealousy and malignity that can feed on virtue itself in the close quarters of ship life; a precursor of Melville's and Conrad's studies of that kind; for this motif will often recur in later adventures.

After the pirates disappear, there is much Crusoe-like detail about Roberts making do with inadequate materials. Then he falls sick, and cannot look after himself properly. The boy goes ashore at St. Nicholas, in the Cape Verde Islands, and does not return. Then seven young blacks come aboard, and the other interesting episode of the book begins. They profess to help Roberts, but in fact get drunk, do everything wrong, and leave; except that three have hidden aboard. These three are very affectionate and helpful—in intention—but entirely undisciplined. They refuse to man the pumps at Roberts' command, and, giving up all hope, lie on deck like dead men. Then one of them claims to know the coast and its ports—to be able to guide the ship to anchorage, but in fact cannot do so.

This man jumps overboard, and swims ashore, abandoning the captain, who cannot swim, and soon after the other two do likewise. However, they and their friends on the island come back to the ship, and get the captain ashore, on a narrow beach at the foot of unclimbable rocks. There he is stuck for a whole month, still sick and helpless, and they look after him. Domingo puts Roberts' head on his lap so that he may sleep. Manuel gets killed by a falling rock while tending him. Roberts reflects on their virtues; humility, hospitality, reverence for age; "how vastly they exceed us . . . who pretend to so much learning and knowledge." The book ends with a long factual description of the Cape Verde Islands, calculated to be of use to merchants and sailors, including maps. But it is the mythic aspect that concerns us—though it is important to note how closely that relates to the factual aspect. Mythically it gives us the fullest and most complex picture of "natives" and—more implicitly—of the WASP captain confronting them, two of the most important motifs of the modernist adventure.

Robinson Crusoe

And so now we come to Defoe's best-known work. I must, in order to economize time and space, pass very lightly over those features of my interpretation which I expect to be assented to easily, however important they are to my argument. I expect a consensus (not of course a total one) on the following points: the imaginative importance of tools and techniques in the story—the exploration and dramatization of work—as in the famous passage about the complex operations necessary to bake a loaf of bread;[8] the imaginative predominance of reason and prudence—so vivid that the passages of emotional melodrama (for instance, Crusoe's reactions on first arriving) fade from the view, or never grip the mind, of most readers;[9] the literary achievement of formal realism, to use Ian Watt's term —in Defoe's case, a how-to-do-it realism, as when Crusoe does not notice the rope dangling from the wreck until the second time he swims by it; the striking lack of interest in erotic feelings—Crusoe's marriage barely mentioned, and only the portrait of Friday having a strong (though innocent) erotic coloring; the role of religion, as a powerful engine for the virtues which make Crusoe the hero, but as a perfunctory mechanism from other points of view. All of those features of the book are important, in making it correspond to the modernist imagination, but I count on their being obvious.

Nor shall I spend much time arguing, what I can expect no consensual agreement to, that the spiritual autobiography aspect of the book is unimportant. There is no question that Defoe made use of that form, that framework, for his story. But it seems to me that he used it up in doing so—that it would never occur to another writer to use that framework again, for that purpose, because everything that is vivid and exciting in the book is independent of that framework. He got where he wanted to by means of that crutch, but in arriving he let it go. This brusque declaration cannot hope to convince those scholars who have invested their energies in the opposite idea. But I hope to carry with me the rest.

Among the ideas I do want to put some stress on is that of value. What Crusoe does on his island is primarily to create value. He brings together the ship and the island, two things which before were of no use to anyone, and he creates—and we participate in the creation—something that is very valuable. That is the central pathos of the story, I would suggest, and it makes *Robinson Crusoe* a central myth of the modern system. The ship is a wreck; it is no longer any use; the island is a desert; it has never been of any use. But Crusoe, swimming out to the wreck, and paddling back with loads of planks, ropes, nails, carpenters' tools, sews the two together and creates something new out of the two of them; creates a property.

It is always in jocular terms that Defoe names the island as property: "my castle," "my bower," "my country estate," "my subjects," and at the end the elaborate masquerade of playing royal governor to fool the mutineers. ("My property," taken to an extreme, becomes "my kingdom"—this is the mercantile feeling about kingship.) But there can be no doubt that Crusoe *feels* it as property, that the feeling is an excited one, which runs deep, and that the reader, unless alienated from the book, shares that feeling.

We are made to share it by means of a number of other, simpler feelings—or perhaps they are parts of this larger one. There is the feeling of glee, first of all. I quote from pages 57 through 58 of the Penguin edition. "Neither was this all; but my goods being all English manufactures, such as cloath, stuffs, bays, and things particularly valuable and desirable in the country, I found means to sell them to a very great advantage; so that I might say I had more than four times the value of my first cargo, and was now infinitely beyond my poor neighbour. . . ." I'd suggest that that note, that innocent gloating over possessions and achievements, runs through the book, and makes the experience of reading it very different from what we call serious fiction. The lust for possession is something "literature" is very nervous of.

Related to glee is luck. I quote from page 74. "But that which comforted me more still, was that at last of all, after I had made five or six such voyages as these, and thought I had nothing more to expect from the ship that was worth my medling with; I say, after all this, I found a great hogshead of bread, and three large runlets of rum or spirits, and a box of sugar, and a barrel of fine flower. . . ." That which one does *not* deserve, has *not* planned for, can be taken by the virtuous and prudent man as even sweeter profit, as confirmation that grace is with him. It is first cousin to another feeling I want to call greed, though it is not a matter of appetite but of possession, and is excited by the counting over of what one has, the arranging of them neatly, or the dividing of them up into convenient packages —as when "I finished this work in about a fortnight, and I think my powder, which in all was about 240 lb. weight, was divided in not less than a hundred parcels. . . ." (p. 79).

Closely connected to glee, luck, and greed are the more anxious emotions of possession, like the need for security; and no literary reader of *Robinson Crusoe* needs reminding how much effort and emotion the hero puts into his defenses, his stockades and his muskets and his cellars, his caves and his camouflage and his movable ladders. But those readers, being of literary interests, and so deeply suspicious of and hostile to the modern world system, will find that those features jump to the eye. I am concerned to argue that Defoe in fact gives us a very complete and all-round exploration of the emotions of possession—the *relationship* of possession, which is also a relationship of creativity. The creation of value, the joy of possession, the anxiety of security, they are all there, and their interdependence. The

Defoe

modern system feels itself quite specially the creator of value, and
Defoe's book answers to that feeling.

So much for the book's themes. I have not said anything radically
different from what Ian Watt said, I believe; how could I, since to
anyone not blinded by literary "science" it has always been obvious
what *Robinson Crusoe* is about.[10] (Of course, as one's general vocabulary shifts, one wants to phrase the idea a little differently.) But I
have promised a structuralist criticism here, and so it is the motifs
I must say most about, though I want, in nonstructuralist fashion, to
give them an imaginative context from imperial history.

The first group I want to draw attention to includes trifles, objects
of use, and gold. In Guinea, Crusoe finds how easy it is to purchase
"for trifles, such as beads, toys, knives, scissars, hatchets, bits of glass,
and the like, not only gold dust, Guinea grains, elephants' teeth, etc.,
but Negroes, for the service of the Brasils, in great numbers" (p. 59).
This became an idea of great potency in the core states, so it recurs
often in their adventure tales; that the bright, brittle, valueless trifles
or toys they made in large quantities could be exchanged for gold. It
is an image that relates to that of their own solidity, for the trifles
are eminently fragile and impermanent (not stout or sturdy). Gold
is the opposite, a refulgent source of power, like the sun. In *The
Review*, III (4), page 13, Defoe says in so many words that gold and
silver have an intrinsic value and appropriateness to be money, as
opposed to "insignificant and unvaluable trifles, as beads, shells,
feathers, and stones."[11] Gold is heavy and shining, the opposite of
the brittle trifles, so soon rusted. But the weight suggests guilt, the
gleam is of blood, the whole thing means passion and fever. In the
polarity of gold and trifles nothing is wholly good or reliable. What
stands independent of that fatal polarity is the tool, the object of use
—the holy emblem of the modern system.

Crusoe values "that most useful thing called a grindstone. . . ."
This is perfectly sincere, and he takes deep satisfaction from tools and
devices, so that a phrase like "a snug contrivance" contains a great
deal of feeling. But of course the gold, though from a higher point
of view to be despised, is in fact always worth acquiring, as Crusoe
shows in the famous passage where he moralizes over the uselessness
of gold in his shipwrecked situation, but nevertheless appropriates it.

This group of motifs will recur in many other adventure tales, but
it is perhaps worth putting it into a historical context here. The idea

78

of trifles is a widespread myth of imperial power, which covers un-truth as well as truth. For instance, the Chinese got gold dust, spices, etc., in return for trifles (coins, combs, lacquer-boxes) in Indo-China. On the other hand, they paid lavishly in real values for the trifles they relished like swallows' nests. And just so, as Braudel points out, England paid lavishly for turtles to make turtle soup, and Holland paid lavishly for tulip bulbs, and both paid highly for porcelain. In such cases, the imperialist power handed out gold, and got trifles in return.

Trade between the modern system and other empires never did conform to the "official" model. In the East it was England that paid gold; the Indians and Chinese did not want our goods as much as we wanted theirs; and that trade, and the East India Company itself, was disapproved by Defoe, for instance, because it took bullion out of England. One thing we did sell to Turkey and India was gunpowder; in 1606, 500 barrels went from England to Turkey, in 1629, 1000 barrels to India. And in North America fur trappers, Indian and white, were often paid in guns and powder, which was the key transaction between the state government and the Cossacks in Russia also. But this was all subsumed, or obscured, under the image of the shrewd man, who himself cared only for objects of use, selling trifles and getting gold.

Of course there was a feverish imagination of, and appetite for, gold. John Smith in his *Generall Historie* (1624) says that among the English colonists in America, "there was no talk, no hope, no worke, but dig gold, wash gold, refined gold, load gold." And back in England the gold they found (and silver and jewels) were much displayed. It is calculated that 20 percent of what came back was used in decoration; gold and silver lace and embroidery, cloth of gold, silver plate and toilet sets, rings, watches, chains, etc. The voyages made a big difference to such styles.[12] Raleigh and Charles I wore earrings, Queen Elizabeth was famous for the quantity of jewels she always wore. Not to mention the new perfumes, and tobacco, and slaves. The slave trade was called England's silver mine—her consolation prize for not getting Potosi. Thus most *objets de luxe* can be considered forms of, or allusions to, gold.

The next group of motifs includes guns, natives, slavery, and canni-balism. Guns and powder are of the first importance to Crusoe always, and Defoe dramatizes their arrival on the island very effectively. "I believe it was the first gun that had been fired there since the creation of the world; I had no sooner fired, but from all the parts of the wood there arose an innumerable number of fowls of many sorts, making a confused screaming, and crying every one according to his usual note. . . ." (p. 72). That is surely a very eloquent evocation of the theme of guns; all the more eloquent for its aesthetic and intellectual innocence, its lack of development, of larger design. Defoe's art is in a sense no-art, almost totally transparent. The gun itself pokes through the page at us.[13]

And guns are related to natives as directly—and fatefully—as gold is related to trifles. Guns were the supreme tool, the supreme example of the modern technology, on which the modern system was built. It was at the sight and sound of guns that natives fell on their faces and worshiped—as Friday does in the novel. Any unnatural conjunction of the two motifs, as when a native himself fired a gun—as Friday does—gave the reader an almost sacrilegious thrill. These two, and slavery and cannibalism, define the most aggressive aspect of the modern system.

The idea of slavery is charged with very strong feeling, because it is imposed on Crusoe by his Moorish captors, and is the very worst of fates; freedom being a specifically modern system idea. And yet Crusoe sells his faithful Xury as a slave, when he has the chance; and he determines to enslave a savage—"to get a savage into my possession"—before Friday arrives. To be a slave is a fate worse than death; to have a slave—from a race outside the system, of course—is almost better than ordinary life. Like gold and guns, it raises the pitch of life thrillingly. In the relationship with Friday, as has often been observed, Crusoe achieves a warmth and ease of feeling he has not displayed before, and will not display toward his wife, at least in the narrative.

And the slavery is justified above all by the natives' cannibalism. ". . . all my apprehensions were bury'd in the thoughts of such a pitch of inhuman, hellish brutality, and the horror of the degeneracy of human nature; which, though I had heard of often, yet I never had so near a view of before. . . ." (p. 172). And when seen as threatening white men, cannibalism resolves all Crusoe's doubts and hesitations about killing the natives.

Cannibalism is heavily stressed in adventure tales. It is the archetype of everything monstrous and appalling in primitive cultures.

The books' feeling against it seems to be connected with the horror and fascination of abandoning oneself into the hands of men of another color and culture. In India, one of the luxuries of native servants was they would shave a man while he was still asleep—as well as dress and undress him, etc. That image, turned sinister, is for instance taken up by Melville in "Benito Cereno." No doubt there are fantasies of homosexual rape at work beneath the surface also. But it is cannibalism (in *Omoo,* for instance) which is named as the ultimate horror.

I hope it is not irrelevant to introduce here the thought of Lévi-Strauss, who remarks on how vividly cannibalism reversed and antithesized the process whereby the European nations filled their colonies—a process he calls anthropoemic; they vomited forth by exile or imprisonment those people who caused them trouble. Cawley tells us that that idea of social spitting or spewing forth was habitually used in Elizabethan times in describing the settlement process. Colonies would rid England of her idle and her incendiaries. Thus Rome too had used its colonies, to get rid of its beggars, its idle, and its mutinous. The same was true of Spain; and Cortes himself was a natural rebel, as was Clive; the great conquerors themselves did not fit happily into their native societies, and were in some sense forced to go abroad. Australia was the most famous example of a prison colony, with convicts sent there from the late eighteenth century on. But all England's American colonies save those of New England were penal settlements. So, though I claim no historical connection between anthropoemia and cannibalism (or the horror at cannibalism), I think that an imaginative connection must hold them together in our mind.

The most important motif is the most obvious one, that Crusoe is a man absolutely alone, and on a desert island. This appeals to our imaginations in many ways, some of them, especially the magical-subconscious, not directly relevant to imperialism or the modern world system. But in Defoe's novel these other appeals are subordinated to the island's function as a perfect setting for adventures in reason and work and the creation of value. That becomes clear if you compare Defoe's story with the true story he began with, the story of Alexander Selkirk, a much gloomier and more violent man than Crusoe, psychologically. Defoe minimized that material; though it seems it would have found a ready response from his audience. Max

Novak says that seventeenth- and eighteenth-century discussions of man's beginnings often worked with the image of an individual alone, and often assumed that a man in Crusoe's position would go in constant fear, and would probably go mad. Pufendorf, whom Defoe read, describes such a one creeping into a cave, covering himself up with leaves, and trembling at the approach of fellow creatures. When Crusoe does such things, they are subsumed into a larger image whose main emotional scheme is quite different—the triumphant emotion of modernist adventure. "Island" as Defoe uses it means the perfect setting for that adventure.

And finally we must remind ourselves that *Robinson Crusoe* is basically a romance, though one radically transformed to become appropriate to the modern world system. If we take Frye's definition of romance, in *Anatomy of Criticism*, we see that many traditional elements he mentions, like the necessary mutilation, and the redemption of a "loathly" lady, are not to be found in this book; nor, except by very far-reaching displacement, can we speak of buried treasure or even a quest. And where it is possible to recognize the presence of traditional romance in Defoe's mind, it is dysfunctional.

Sometimes an incident will occur which belongs to an older kind of romance—for instance, when one of the men Friday rescues turns out to be his long-lost father, an incident which belongs in Greek or chivalric, but not in modernist, romance. That sort of coincidence does not pay enough tribute to realism, which Defoe introduced into romance as a constant pressure, in adapting it to the modern world system. However, the three main stages of a romance, according to Frye's scheme: a journey, a crucial struggle (in this case Crusoe's struggle with the inertial forces of nature), and an exaltation of the hero; these are recognizably the three main stages of *Robinson Crusoe*. So are the reader's intense feelings of identification with the hero; Frye says romance offers the reader the ideal heroes and villains of the current ruling class. And most romance-like of all is the very strongly shaped curve of feeling, which is quite crucially carried, I think, by a young man hero. Crusoe's father begs him not to "act the young man," but he does, and the reader is of course delighted that he does, without needing to feel that the father is wrong. It is, I think, misleading to talk of Crusoe's *sin* of disobedience; that is what he says, but it is not what the reader can feel. Crusoe is being a young man.

Formally speaking, this is a romance device, but here again I find a historical perspective useful. Empire, frontier, exploration, have been peculiarly associated with that "young man"; the key content of that phrase being not so much youth as bachelorhood. The 186 young men who rode north into Mashonaland with Cecil Rhodes to found the city of Salisbury in 1890; the young men advertised for in St. Louis in 1822, to go up into the Rockies for two or three years (Mike Fink was one); the Cossacks who moved out from the settlements into the free land of the Russian frontier—these are the men (not all of them so young in the literal sense) for whom Crusoe stands.

One of the most vivid expressions of this young man idea is to be found in *Roughing It,* where Twain describes the California he first knew as "an assemblage of 200,000 *young* men—not simpering, dainty, kid-gloved weaklings, but stalwart, muscular, dauntless young braves, brimful of push and energy, and royally endowed with every attribute that goes to make up a peerless and magnificent manhood—the very pick and choice of the world's glorious ones. No women, no children, no grey and stooping veterans—none but erect, bright-eyed, quick-moving, strong-handed young giants . . ." (p. 132). It is worth remembering that Twain was known as "Youth" to his wife, and made a good deal out of embodying young manhood even in his old age. "It was that population which gave to California a name for getting up astounding enterprises and rushing them through with a magnificent dash and daring. . . . It was a wild, free, disorderly, grotesque society: *Men*—only swarming hosts of stalwart *men*—nothing juvenile, nothing feminine visible anywhere" (p. 133). America was a young man's country—was that country for all Europe—and in America young men went west.

Subsequent history brought out these meanings to the phrase "young man," but the concept was a potent one for Defoe to use because these meanings were always potential within it. *Robinson Crusoe* is a central mythic expression of the modern system, of its call to young men to go out to expand that empire; and the more you know about the latter, the richer the meanings you find in the former.

Defoe

Captain Singleton

This is the story of an orphan who goes to sea, takes part in a mutiny, leads his fellow mutineers across Africa, makes a fortune and loses it. In the second half (the book is divided in two with mathematical exactitude), Captain Singleton becomes a pirate and makes another fortune, undergoes conversion, and returns to England in disguise, to enjoy a peaceful prosperity and do good works. In the second half of the book, also, the captain finds a comrade, but Defoe's stress does not fall on that comradeship so much as on the isolation of the man in command.

The story of adventure, as Defoe tells it, is always built around an isolated individual, who leads subordinates against alien opponents. He emphasizes the figure of the solitary captain. But seen in a larger generic conspectus, that story seems to be a linked alternate to a story of brothers, or comrades, or brothers-in-arms, who are loyal to or in love with each other. Thus in Greek epic the *Odyssey,* an isolate's story, structurally like *Captain Singleton,* is linked to the *Iliad,* a story of brothers-in-arms. (Hindu epic, as I pointed out in a note to Chapter II, is about literal brothers, bonded also by being all in love with the same woman.)

To link the two structurally seems paradoxical, since they are so different, but history presents them so linked; it is clear that the imaginative character and cultural purpose of both versions is the same. Moreover, we have a comparable case in the story of marriages, the story of the sisters; for famous examples of that story are *Pamela* and *Clarissa,* both about very isolated figures; and yet clearly linked to the sisters' stories told by (among others) Jane Austen. And the link is not that of fragments to a whole. *Clarissa* is no more a fragment of, shall we say, *Persuasion,* than *Captain Singleton* is a fragment of *Westward Ho!* or *The Three Musketeers.* The connection is quite different; they are alternative fictional forms, alternative versions of a mythic form.

They are linked alternates, the story of the isolate and the story of the band, and they bear the same mythic message. Therefore we can call Defoe's adventures, on certain occasions, examples of the story of the brothers—which is generically distinct from and quite unlinked to the story of the sisters. The former of course has a longer history, going back to epic, while the latter seems to arise only where there is a highly developed leisure culture, and not always there. Presumably its development in eighteenth-century England had something to do with the status of women then; just as the character of capitalism then had presumably something to do with the early development of the isolate alternative in both the sisters' and the brothers' stories. We begin with dramatically solitary figures, Robinson Crusoe and Pamela; it is not until we reach the works of Scott and Austen, both minds in which the Puritan thesis had been matched and mellowed by something opposite, that we get the stories of the groups. This is the historical development of fiction, as a genre of the modern imagination.

Many of the same motifs appear in *Captain Singleton* as in *Robinson Crusoe*, because it also is a modernist adventure. Thus I shall say very little about its treatment of Eros, gold, guns, natives, etc. But there is an important difference in this being not the story of an individual alone on an island, but of a group on the move across the world; in the first half of the book, on land across Africa, in the second half on a ship across the oceans.[14] In some sense it is *not* the story of a group, since the story takes no interest in group psychology, and scarcely any in individual psychology. It is the story of a captain, and, in the second half, of his comrade also. Nevertheless, it *is* a group story, in a *formal* sense, as the contrast with *Robinson Crusoe* brings out; many of its features are tied to the idea, however unrealized that may be artistically, that this is about a group of men on the move. And quite as many later romances have followed *Singleton* (using the group pattern) as have followed *Crusoe*. The immensely popular *Westward Ho!* is a Victorian example.

Another important innovation is Captain Singleton's career as pirate. Defoe wrote several narratives of pirates; in fact he is the inventor, so far as England goes, of that pirate genre that went on to become one of the most popular the modern world has told itself (equalled only by the much more recent cowboy story). But the reader must note, in *Singleton,* the curious equivocation that most of the time the narrator sounds like a merchant. In Defoe's time the lines separating merchant, privateer, and pirate were often blurred, and in certain times and places could be crossed without invoking the ordinary moral sanctions. Defoe makes use of that in *A New Voyage Around the World.* But in *Captain Singleton* the blur is of a different kind. Except when he *says,* at the beginning of each half of the book, what a wicked fellow, he, Singleton, is, the narrator writes in the same reasoning, prudent, constructive voice as Crusoe used—and of course Moll Flanders, and all Defoe—because that modern system voice was the one Defoe thought in. The cause of this is no doubt Defoe's habitual haste and carelessness; he didn't imagine things intensely, or perfect them esemplastically. But the effect is to create an effective artistic equivalent for the blur in the adventure-reader's mind, the blending of the desire to preserve the law in general with the desire to break it oneself. (The artistry is effective only for adventure-readers —not for those trained in the school of "serious" fiction.)

A third motif is explosion. This is closely related to that of guns and gunpowder, but is sufficiently distinct. When Singleton's group of sailors is baffled in a fight with some Indians, who retreat into a cave, they blow the latter up. The captain has said it was time to give up the struggle, even though "it would vex any Body to be so baulked by a few naked ignorant Fellows." But William, the captain's Quaker comrade, is determined to have some "Satisfaction" of them, though he acknowledges that there is nothing but "Curiosity" to be gratified in the attempt. He and the gunner fetch two barrels of powder out of the ship and put them in the mouth of the cave and set light to them. The force of the powder bursts out of some bushes on the other side of the hill, and they run to look.

"First, we saw that *there* was the other Mouth of the Cave, which the Powder had so torn and open'd, that the loose Earth was so fallen in again, that nothing of Shape could be discerned; but there we saw what was become of the Garrison of *Indians*—too, who had given us all this Trouble; for some of them had no Arms, some no Legs, some no Head, some lay half buried in the Rubbish of the Mine, that is to say, in the loose Earth that fell in; and, in short, there was a miserable Havock made of them all, for we had good Reason to believe, not one of them that were in the Inside could Escape, but rather were shot out of the Mouth of the Cave like a Bullet out of a Gun" (pp. 213–214).

This will immediately remind readers familiar with *Connecticut Yankee* of various scenes in that novel. But in fact, explosions, producing human debris, usually native, are a motif in much adventure fiction. Jules Verne, Conrad, Kingston, for instance, make much use of them. Defoe's distinction in the use of this subject matter—as in his use of others—is his candor. Like Crusoe's shot, this petard of William's reverberates in the reader's mind, uncontained by literature, and so unconstrained.

But the major motifs that *Captain Singleton* introduced are three figures, each of which embodies a contradiction, in the way that myths often do, according to the structural anthropologists. First of all, William, the bloody Quaker. He was a surgeon on a sloop the pirates captured, and lets them know that he wants to join them, but that they must make it seem that they are forcing him. He takes no part in actual fighting, but gives them military advice, even in the midst of battle—he tells them what to aim at and where to charge. But he is not so much murderous as mercenary. He reminds them often that their real interest is not in killing but in making money.

At the same time, William remains the representative of morality and religion in the story, and at the end effects the captain's conversion. The major means by which Defoe reconciles these two opposing sides of the character is by describing William as "merry"—alluding to his dry wit, "the cunning rogue," and so on. I need hardly say that this device does not work, for a reader trained in serious fiction. The indignation aroused by William's behavior cannot be pacified by anything to be called "humor." But Defoe was genuinely fascinated by Quakers; the theme of Quakerism turns up often in *The Review*, and in *Roxana*. It is a theme he characteristically *played* with—rather than treated seriously. Defoe or his characters *disguise* themselves as Quakers, in costume or dialect; but they also clearly regard Quakerism as the purest of moral positions. This is the source of half its fascination for them; the other source is the impulse to desecrate that purity. The paradoxical combination of Quaker and pirate expresses many feelings about this disparity, but one surely is the wish to find the former no better than the latter. And so it is not surprising that other writers have invented bloody Quakers too, notably Cooper in the Leatherstocking tales, R. M. Bird, in *Nick of the Woods*, and Melville in *Moby Dick*.

The second such figure is the Black Prince—a phrase used by Defoe himself. When the group have defeated a band of natives in Africa, "There was among the prisoners one tall, well-shap'd handsom Fellow, to whom the rest seem'd to pay great Respect, and who, as we understood afterwards, was the Son of one of their Kings" (p. 57). They cure the Prince of his wound, and he takes a vow of loyalty to them (swearing by the sun, whom his tribe worship) and it is through him that the captain manages the rest of the natives. This man represents older modes of being, those we associate with epic; his language, mostly of gestures, is much grander and more mythic than the Englishmen's. He tames a leopard, which follows him around. He commands an extravagant devotion from his followers, and in turn offers an extravagant devotion to the captain. He is handsome, splendid, a noble human being, which one would not say of the captain; but clearly he is of so much simpler an order as to be of a lower order.

This figure also appears in later adventure tales; notably as Chingachgook in *Leatherstocking Tales,* and as Dain Waris in *Lord Jim,* and other such figures in other Conrad novels. Quite often he moves in an atmosphere of tragedy; but simplified tragedy, because his principal function is to serve as an opposite pole to the white man. The other is dry, calculating, managerial, functional; and it is our shame for imposing a dry, calculating order upon other men which is discharged by building up this lay figure of nobility.[15] Besides successors there were predecessors for the Black Prince; most notably, Othello, Oroonoko, and Montezuma. All three are in different ways interesting figures, and much more fully worked out than Defoe's Black Prince; those precedents are in a sense the content to Defoe's concept, and show how much there was in his readers' minds, ready to respond to his barest phrases. (Incidentally, it is worth keeping the Black Prince motif separate from that of "my man Friday," who is essentially a slave-companion, a devoted servant, a figure of comedy rather than of tragedy. The two are similar in certain ways, but if we regard them as functions, they are worth keeping distinct.)

Finally there is the figure of the English hermit—not Defoe's phrase, but the title of one of the popular imitations of *Robinson Crusoe, The English Hermit* published in 1727, which focused on this figure. This is "a White Man indeed, but stark naked," (p. 120) whom the group find living alone—that is to say, living among Negroes. "He appeared to be a Gentleman, not an ordinary bred Fellow, Seaman, or Labouring Man; this shewed itself in his Behaviour, in the first Moment of our conversing with him, and in speight of all the Disadvantages of his miserable condition." He embraced the captain "very passionately, the Tears running down his Face," and "never was without Tears in his Eyes for several Days" (p. 121).

"As he was naked, and had no Clothes, so he was naked of Arms for his Defence, having neither Gun, Sword, Staff, or any Instrument of War about him, so not to guard himself against the Attacks of a wild Beast, of which this Country was very full" (p. 124). It is this nakedness which distinguishes him from Crusoe, and suggests a word like "hermit." I have not found any full-blown successors to this figure in the authors that interest me, but of course the strain of feeling he satisfies enters into Tarzan and Tabu Dick, and into Ike McCaslin laying aside watch and compass to enter the wilderness, and into Mailer's heroes doing the same in *Why Are We in Vietnam?*

Thus *Captain Singleton* foreshadows the adventures of the next two centuries almost as vividly as *Robinson Crusoe*. It contains fictional possibilities at least as striking as *Religious Courtship*. And yet it and its genre, even its author to some degree, were rejected by literature proper. Defoe's motifs were to be found in later adventure tales, as some of my examples indicated, but their potentialities are scarcely realized, and their development is scarcely worthy of the name. Adventure motifs are likely to seem more promising when enumerated by a critic than when met in fiction, while the reverse is true of courtship motifs. This is the result of rejection by literature-as-a-system.

Defoe, Literature, and Culture

The peripheralization of the adventure tale within the system of literature, and of Defoe's work in general, can be seen reflected in Defoe's relations with Swift. These relations can be described as a kind of polar opposition. Biographically there was an antagonism between the two men; ideologically they were on opposite sides; and in terms of literary achievement and consequent reputation, they are in the important sense irreconcilable. Swift established himself, in his own lifetime, and for futurity, at the center of literature. He and Pope and their friends were the arbiters of literary taste of their age. And by that token, Defoe was on the periphery.[16]

In *Swift and Defoe* John F. Ross says that the two men were antagonists for twenty-one years, from 1705 to 1726, and that it was Defoe who made the attacks. Swift was in the position of security and superiority, and by ignoring Defoe, his aggression could be merely negative. In 1705 Defoe's satiric fantasy, *The Consolidator*, attacked Swift's *Tale of a Tub*. In 1710 the two men became rivals, because both were working for Robert Harley. But Harley received Swift at his front door, and saw him occasionally at the Scriblerus Club, which met in Arbuthnot's rooms at the Palace, and at two other clubs. Defoe went to Harley's back door, and did not belong to any fashionable clubs. Literary and social values were in alliance. Though Defoe was put in the pillory and jail for "The Shortest Way With Dissenters," nothing happened to Swift for "A Modest Proposal." Defoe appeared in *The Dunciad* because everyone thought him a Dunce; he belonged completely to Grub Street, as Pat Rogers has pointed out—by his activities, by his associates, by his politics, by the kind of thing he wrote. Swift and Pope had won the battle for the leadership of literature; had made, for instance, classical models and classical learning necessary to authors, and by those standards Defoe failed. He himself said that his verse and his prose were addressed to the unlearned.[17]

In 1710 they were on different sides politically. On November 16, 1710, Swift's magazine, *The Examiner*, called "Mr. Review" a "stupid, illiterate scribbler, with a mock authoritative manner." Defoe answered from Scotland in two issues, saying that Swift was very learned, but "a cynic in behaviour, a fury in temper, unpolite in conversation, abusive and scurrilous in language, and ungovernable in passion. Is this to be learned? Then may I still be illiterate."

In the very first issue of his *Examiner*, Swift announced his position as spokesman for the landed gentry against tradesmen and stockjobbers. (Defoe often said that land, when compared with trade as a source of wealth, was like a pool as compared with a stream.) Swift hated "money-men" and opposed the institution of the National Debt. ". . . the wealth of the nation, that used to be reckoned by the value of the land, is now computed by the rise and fall of stocks, . . . such a complication of knavery and cozenage, such a mystery of iniquity, and such an unintelligible jargon of terms to involve it. . . ." Like most serious writers, Swift hated exponential growth.[18] Then in No. 22, he complained that the Whigs wanted England to become, "a common receptacle for all nations, religions, and languages, a system only proper for small populous states, but altogether unworthy and below the dignity of an imperial crown; which with us

is best upheld by a monarch in possession of his just prerogatives, a
senate of nobles and of commons, and a clergy established in its due
rights with a suitable maintenance by law. But these men come with
the spirit of shopkeepers to frame rules for the administration of
kingdoms." This is so directly the opposite of Defoe's opinions, at
several points, that it could have been aimed at him. Swift's grandfather had been a royalist under Charles I; he hated the colonization
of Ireland, and he was of course an officer of the Church of England.
In him, literature allied itself to the military caste rather than the
mercantile.

But literary considerations were also important in their antagonism. Mr. Ross maintains that Defoe was not an ironist at all but a
realist—which shows how Swift's judgment still prevails in literary
matters. But he is right to call Defoe's ordinary style a "copious,
breathless gossip," and one can see how that styleless seriousness
would irritate Swift. He called Defoe "so grave, sententious, dogmati-
cal a rogue, that there's no enduring him." Swift knew he would be
read by Berkeley, Bolingbroke, Pope, Addison, Arbuthnot, and by
their equivalents of the future. Such a consciousness, which shaped
Swift's style, is indeed a crucial element in serious writing at all times,
and Defoe—who aimed at being a serious writer early on—was gradually convinced that he must give up such ambitions. His style lacks
that shapeliness. And it was probably Swift's hostility, and a similar
hostility in others, that helped convince him.

Gulliver's Travels contains some expression of the antagonism.
Robinson Crusoe was one of the "traveller's tales" which Swift took
off from; and he satirized the material they contained. For instance,
when Gulliver offers gunpowder to the King of Brobdingnab, the
latter rejects the idea with horror. And in the very last chapter we
find this account of modernist adventure (*Works* XII 378–379):

"A crew of pirates are driven by a storm, they know not whither;
at length a boy discovers land from the topmast; they go on shore to
rob and plunder; they see a harmless people, are entertained with
kindness; they give the country a new name; they take formal possession of it for their king; they set up a rotten plank or a stone for a
memorial; they murder two or three dozen of the natives, bring away
a couple more by force for a sample, return home, and get their
pardon. Here commences a new dominion, acquired with a title by
divine right. Ships are sent with the first opposition; the natives

driven out or destroyed; their princes tortured to discover their gold; a free license given to all acts of humanity and lust; the earth reeking with the blood of its inhabitants; and this execrable crew of butchers employed in so pious an expedition is a modern colony sent to convert and civilize an idolatrous and barbarous people."

A passage like that makes it clear how Swift set himself against the spirit of the times. And making himself the center of literature-as-a-system, he made his own posture in such matters paradigmatic for other writers. Not that they must hold his opinions, but that they must display his independence of judgment, his self-dissociation from "the spirit of the times," while Defoe's strength derived from participation in that spirit. (Of course, the phrase is ambiguous; some *literary* things that could be called in the spirit of the eighteenth century were Swift's more than Defoe's; in this discussion it refers to things like colonies—the *new* forms of wealth and power and expansion.)[19] By and large, the writers did follow Swift.

For instance, amongst eighteenth-century men of letters who take a hostile attitude to the empire material one could mention Cowper, whose "Alexander Selkirk" and "The Castaway" use the Crusoe story but only in a highly moralized and unadventurous manner, and who is very severe against slavery and the East India Company. And Dr. Johnson, who in 1784 observed of Cook's *Voyages,* that no one would read them because "One set of savages is like another." Boswell tells us that Johnson was very incredulous about "particular facts."

But that does not mean that the triumph rested wholly with Swift. Literature is a system within a larger system of culture, and in the terms of that larger system *Robinson Crusoe* was an enormously successful book. Compare the pages it takes up in any large library catalog with the number of entries for any popular serious novel, like *Sons and Lovers.* By 1895 there had been 196 English editions, 110 translations, 115 revisions, 277 imitations. Defoe did not need to establish adventure as a genre. His book was a genre in itself. I must say more about that in a minute, but for the moment let me note the keenest irony against Swift. Despite his satirical intentions, *Gulliver's Travels* was read as yet another traveler's tale. It became a children's classic, but a classic of adventure. It was Defoe who triumphed, and Swift was carried along in his wake. One hears for instance that Daniel Boone was reading *Gulliver* one day when he was interrupted by an Indian attack, and to commemorate the occasion he named a nearby creek by a name out of the book. Now Boone was not a literary man; one can be pretty sure that he was reading *Gulliver* for its Defoe content, not for the ironic slant Swift gave to that content. And thus Swift's book came to play a part in the history of the frontier and empire and adventure—despite the effort of mind and will the author had directed against them.

To return to the career of *Crusoe*, one may say that it was an international genre also. There were forty-nine French translations, beginning with one in 1720, and twenty-one German. Of the German imitations, J. H. Campe's *Robinson Der Jüngere* (Hamburg, 1799) (in which Robinson started off with no utensils at all) itself had 117 editions by 1895, and was translated into twenty languages. Another very famous adaptation was *The Swiss Family Robinson* by Johann Wyss. This substituted a family for the isolated individual. It was published in 1814, written probably twenty years before; translated into English in the year of publication, it became nearly as popular and as often adapted as Defoe's story. These are obvious examples of a story being modified in the course of compulsive retelling. (Such modifications are less radical than the transformations we shall come to in Scott.)

And among testimonies to *Robinson Crusoe*'s influence, we might select Rousseau's use of it in his ideal education, in *Emile* (1762). *Crusoe* is to be the whole of Emile's library for a long time—"the text of which all our discussions of natural science will be a gloss. I would like him to be infatuated by it. I want him to identify himself with Robinson." Thus at the end of the eighteenth century *Robinson Crusoe* came to life again in France, and Germany, and all Europe; it remained alive all through the nineteenth century. All the political economists, including Marx, made use of the story. Missionaries took it with them, along with the Bible, to pagan empires and primitive tribes. It was a part of their gospel. The colporteur, George Borrow, writing in 1851, tells how he himself was first induced to learn to read (having long resisted his teachers) by hearing the story, and how he absorbed himself in it. ". . . it was a book which has exerted over the minds of Englishmen an influence certainly greater than any other of modern times, which has been in most people's hands . . . a book, moreover, to which, from the hardy deeds which it narrates, and the spirit of strange and romantic enterprise which it tends to awaken,

England owes many of her astonishing discoveries both by sea and land, and no inconsiderable part of her naval glory. Hail to thee, spirit of De Foe! What does not my own poor self owe to thee?" (*Lavengno*, p. 24). But still Defoe was not a figure in literature proper.

Of course, literature's rejection of Defoe in the eighteenth century was to some extent a passing phenomenon, not a permanent literary institution. There were, as I have said, contradictions within the system of literature which ultimately produced a revolution, which we call the Romantic Movement. This was from one point of view a revolution in the status of authors and genres, and it brought about a change of rank for Defoe and for Swift. For instance, Coleridge explicitly contrasted the two men, in 1818, to Defoe's advantage. "Defoe makes one respond to the experience, not to his comment on it, as Swift does." He said the character of Crusoe is a representative of humanity in general, and his story always interests, never agitates. Coleridge compared Defoe to Hogarth and Shakespeare, as being peculiarly English, and this is the note struck by other Romantic critics—Lamb, Hazlitt, Scott, and Carlyle. Defoe was a great Englishman, a great Protestant, patriot, and democrat. It was the nineteenth-century biographies (Wilson's in 1830, Lee's in 1869) that established his reputation, rather than critical appreciations. He became accepted as a sort of proto-Cobbett.

All this, obviously, was more effective as a cultural rehabilitation than as a literary one. Thus Scott praised Defoe's plain language and his realism in the handling of coincidence and supernatural events; he did not praise anything that could be called Defoe's imagination. As long as the reaction against the Augustans was strong, Defoe had an assured place as a reproach to them. But he was no precursor or pre-Romantic. If the Romantic system of literature was anti-ironical in tendency, it was Carlyle who was the great exemplar of that tendency, and he was closer to Swift than to Defoe. Carlyle spoke for the heart and for the people, against eighteenth-century wits, dandies, and ironists. But his weapon against them was a greater irony. Defoe could be no ally to Carlyle. While Wordsworth's and Coleridge's weapons against the eighteenth century were taste and theory, they spoke for plain and simple meanings, strong and deep feelings, but under the aegis of literature at its most sophisticated. Neither of them was any Defoe.

Thus by these writers Defoe was used rather than imitated—used

against the Augustans or as a source of new material, as the voyagers were used, by Coleridge in "The Ancient Mariner," for example. The Romantics did not mean to be like Defoe themselves, as men of letters, any more than they meant to be like the Dampier or Hakluyt they also used. Once the defensive movement against the Augustans was over, I think it is true to say, Defoe again found himself on the periphery of literature, and a serious writer would not think of ap-
•prenticing himself to Defoe or of writing an adventure tale.

Defoe's meaning and message were carried to later generations not by the novelists or poets but by moralists like Benjamin Franklin and Samuel Smiles. (And by the Encyclopaedists in France.) Franklin's link with Defoe is explicit in more than one dimension. He says in his autobiography that he learned a lot from Defoe, both stylistically and intellectually; mentioning Defoe's "Essay Upon Projects" in particular. Biographically, we know that Samuel Keimer, who printed Defoe's writings in London in 1715, went to America six years later, employed Franklin in his printing house, and brought out more Defoe there in 1723. And the *Autobiography* contains adventures like Crusoe's in spirit, though confined in scope.

Smiles' anecdotes are very often of full-blown adventure, and his famous *Self-Help* (1859) has a final chapter entitled "Character: The True Gentleman," which is very close to Defoe's *Complete English Gentleman*. Defoe's definition of the gentleman is essentially in terms of maturity, seriousness, and responsibility; and so he claims the title for tradesmen and dissenters, and denies it to most squires, whom he depicts as red-faced, hard-drinking boobies. Smiles describes the distinction as being between "gentlemen" and "genteel men" or "gents."[20]

But I shall return to Smiles, in Chapter VII. Franklin is worth dwelling on for a moment here, because he was of great importance in the eighteenth and indeed the nineteenth century, as a propagator of modern system values in other lands. He was in his lifetime made a member of thirteen academies, from London to St. Petersburg, and there were many books for children with Franklin for hero; for instance, in England, Thomas Percival's *A Father's Instructions,* London, 1775.* In France, Franklin was of course a cult by the time of his death; in a book on Franklin and Germany he is described as

---

*Michael Kraus, *Atlantic Civilization*, Ithaca, 1949.

the living presence of the new age there; and in *Benjamin Franklin and Italy*, Antonio Pace puts special emphasis on his nineteenth-century reputation as a moralist. "Franklin's posthumous success as a moralist is, unlike his predictable reputation as a scientist and a statesman, quite extraordinary and a fact of considerable importance for the cultural historian. . . ."

That career as a moralist indicates the spread of modern system values—of the Defoe gospel. *Poor Richard* became very popular in Italy around 1830, and remained much read until after the achievement of national unity. "The fortune of Franklin's moral writings and his personal popularity prove in fact to be a sensitive indicator for gauging the formation of Italian bourgeois self-consciousness. . . ." Max Weber and Werner Sombart have both shown Franklin to be a touchstone of the European middle-class temper. "Moreover, the connection between Franklin's vogue as a moralist and the nationalistic movement is of great interest. . . . Franklin's rise from obscurity and poverty to prestige, power, and independence seemed prophetic of the course Italy had to take in order to achieve regeneration and her national destiny" (Pace, *Benjamin Franklin and Italy*, p. 234).

It was in the nineteenth century, we may say, that Franklin's and Defoe's message really reached the semi-periphery. Smiles' *Self-Help* was also very popular in nineteenth-century Italy. While Sarmiento, the great liberal hero of nineteenth-century Argentinian nationalism, as a young man devoted himself to Franklin, reciting the famous Turgot epigram, "Eripuit caelo fulmen, sceptrumque tyrannis," as his motto. Meanwhile, in the core countries a powerful reaction was developing, of which one expression was D. H. Lawrence's attack on Franklin in *Studies in Classic American Literature.* By the 1920s the keenest minds in England felt they'd had their fill of Franklin's virtues, not to mention Smiles' and Defoe's. (H. G. Wells, in many ways a twentieth-century equivalent of Defoe, could not maintain his literary reputation after 1918.) Those writers had never been allowed into the circle of literature, and now they were to be driven out of high culture altogether. That is why it is necessary, fifty years later, to remind ourselves of how living those ideas were for two centuries and more, whether conveyed in essays or in adventure tales.

IV

Scott

ALMOST a century stretches between *Robinson Crusoe* and *Waverley*. During that time the myth of adventure, with its message of empire, was spread by a variety of means. By the revisions and adaptations of *Robinson Crusoe* itself—very frequent in the second half of the century; by the biographies of adventurer heroes and the descriptions of exotic lands; by the teaching of history and geography. But it was not spread, to any significant degree, by fiction, and scarcely at all by the fiction of serious and ambitious authors.

All through that century, however, the power and pride of England were swelling, and the power and pride of the modern system generally. The rulers of England and the empire wanted fictional images to stimulate and educate their sense of self. When Scott finally devised such images, their grateful response was immediate and tumultuous. But the same cultural inhibitions that had so long restrained men of letters from creating such icons, now disguised and distorted the images they produced. Scott's stories did not express contemporary exploration and conquest as simply as Defoe's did. They seemed to bear no likeness to Defoe's.

And later writers followed Scott. That is why, if we accept the idea that Defoe was the founder of modernist adventure, and so the progenitor of a line of writers that runs down to Kipling and Conrad, we are likely to be puzzled by the occurrence in the work of these later writers of traditionally romantic features of just the kind that

Defoe exorcised from his stories. In many of them, perhaps particularly in Conrad, one finds that the atmosphere is far from factual, prosaic, or utilitarian; the landscape, charged with grandeur, is oppressively present; the hero, and even more the heroine—her very existence denied by Defoe—are figures out of opera; and so on.

All of this is so because of Scott's work—because of what Scott made of the Defoe heritage. Without really abandoning the modernist scheme of imaginative fiction, Scott introduced into it new materials—deriving from romantic history—which were superficially, and perhaps profoundly, too, antagonistic to the form. The measure of the resultant complexity is that he was often read as an antithesis to Defoe; for instance, he was so read, it seems, in the South of the United States, and certainly by Twain when he made his celebrated charge that Scott was to blame for the American Civil War. I don't think that antithesis was complete, as I shall explain, but certainly Scott represented the aristomilitary caste, and introduced into the adventure tale literary materials bearing the ideology of that caste.

Scott's reader was invited to imagine himself a knight in armor, engaging in tournaments for points of honor, and commanding the devotion of savage retainers; or else an Elizabethan courtier, or a Highland chieftain; or something else equally remote from the banks and counting houses and trading companies most readers saw as contemporary reality—as the source of the wealth around them. To some extent, then, Scott sold day dreams, dealt in illusion. But he also served a reality which their common sense ignored, being a mercantile common sense. For England was in his day depending more and more on its soldiers and sailors and rulers of colonies and makers of treaties, and so on. The imperial wealth and power was not the work of solitary Crusoes and freebooting Singletons. It was a ruling class, an aristomilitary caste, that wielded the power and took the responsibility; and that caste had been denied a voice and an image in the serious literature of the culture. Scott supplied a stream of rather fanciful images, rather obliquely related to reality, to the sons and daughters of that caste, and to those of the rest of the nation who admired them. Romantic, fanciful, merely historical as those images now seem, they clearly gave a satisfactory form, and a fuller life, to the aspirations of a large audience.

As I have said, Romanticism was a revolt of the genres within the system of literature. To a considerable extent, as its name indicates, it was a revolt of romance in a general sense; that is to say, of everything not realistic—legend, superstition, the saga, the epic, the exotic, and all the motifs of the marvelous to be found in Greek or Spanish romances. But in a more particular sense, this material was linked to the military caste, in Scott's world as in earlier times.

The great Romantic poets incorporated that new material into their verse, in various ways acceptable to the system of literature; they evolved the categories of sense and sensibility appropriate to it; and —except in certain cases—cut its connections to the military caste.

It was not so easily accommodated into fiction, and at first was restricted to subgenres, the Gothic and the historical novel. Of these, the first only gradually and partially became respectable, but the second leaped into enormous popularity with a very large audience. For Scott's contemporaries, he was a great writer because he incorporated a great deal of romance material into fiction, and did not fall into moral or intellectual nonsense—that is, he contained that material by means of suitable categories of sense and sensibility. After his death, critics declared those categories literarily inauthentic. The system of literature rejected or at least degraded him. From my own point of view, concerned with the caste character of literary materials, it was a great achievement that he incorporated romance into modernist adventure.

Scott, I may as well say here, knew Defoe's work well. He edited what was then thought to be a complete edition—the first. In *Rob Roy* he used Defoe's *The Highland Rogue*, though without realizing its authorship. He also used the *Tour* in that book. And in *Old Mortality* he used an episode from *Memoirs of the Church of Scotland*. Almost certainly there are other such particular borrowings, but the interesting point is the general connection, the tradition of thought. For instance, Defoe had plenty to say about Scotland and its relation to the modern system, which is not really unlike Scott's theory.

When Defoe writes about Scotland he stresses its antiquity, and the contrast between that and English modernity. In "Caledonia" he writes,

> The antiquity which other nations boast
> Would here turn modern, and in age be lost . . .
> Here mighty ancestors preserve their style,
> From long prescription, ancient as the isle.

And in *The True-Born Englishman* he says that the Scots aristocracy is older than the English. His interest in this idea (like Scott's interest, later) focuses on the ethos it betokens—is a cultural-anthropological interest. Thus in the Review III (12) he says that in Scotland people wear a national habit, and so put on the same suit until it wears out. In England, people wear a suit only until it ceases to be fashionable. And that interest inspires his fascination with the Highlanders. In a letter to Harley he says,

Indeed, they are formidable fellows, and I only wish her Majesty had 25,000 of them in Spain, a nation equally proud and barbarous like themselves. They are all gentlemen . . . [as opposed, we might add, to citizens] . . . will take affront from no man, and insolent to the last degree. But certainly the absurdity is ridiculous, to see a man in his mountain habit, with a broadsword, target, pistol or perhaps two at his girdle, a dagger and staff, walking down the street as upright and haughty as if he were a lord—and withal driving a cow. Bless us—are these the gentlemen! said I—" (*Letters*, pp. 146–147).

His tone there is as urbane and citified as Steele, but his interest went deep; as you can see when you consider how much that portrait resembles Robinson Crusoe crossing his island. Defoe was fascinated, as were all the great adventure writers in this series, by the contrast between the modern world citizen and those who embody another mode of being; and the fascination included admiration and emulation, as well as less positive emotions. In *Review* V (10), page 3, he wrote that Highlanders are "The best body of raw men in the world; they are all provided with arms, and understand them; they are entirely under subordination to their superiors, and may be perhaps the most formidable little body of men in their rude circumstances in these parts of the world." His criterion there is military—these are England's Cossacks—but there is also some sense that they are more *men* than others.

The Novels

We shall find the equivalent in the *Waverley* novels, but let us note first that the whole series is dedicated, in the edition of 1829, to the King's Most Gracious Majesty; and different as were the two kings and the two authors, Scott's feeling for George IV *is* parallel to

Defoe's for William III. In both cases, the king represented the order and dignity which the writer needed to find at the apex of the social system.

Scott says that he hoped to do for Scotland what Maria Edgeworth had done for Ireland. She had accomplished "more than all the laws towards completing the Union" (of England with Ireland), and Scott had worked on that other union, of England with Scotland. This is the political character of his work. So we, from our point of view, may say that he tried to complete what Defoe began. Francis Jeffrey, the *Edinburgh Review* critic, said he did complete the Union.[1]

Let us note also the date of the individual novel, *Waverley*. It is significant that it came out in 1814, for the Waverly series as a whole arises naturally out of England's long struggle against Napoleon. To English eyes, as Alexander Welsh puts it,* Napoleon was an embodiment of will, ambition, passion, while England herself seemed an embodiment of reason, prudence, realism—humbler but stronger qualities, merchant-caste qualities, opposing the aristomilitary. Scott himself was an unequivocal patriot, whose opposition to Napoleon and admiration for Wellington was quite as strong as Defoe's feeling against Louis XIV and for Marlborough.[2] And his fiction was (as Defoe's was not) a literary equivalent of the national resistance.

In the General Preface, Scott tells us of the formation of his mind. As a boy he told his friends tales of knights-errant, and at fifteen, when he was ill a long time, he filled his head with "the romances of chivalry." But also with histories, memoirs, and voyages. That is the double heritage of adventure fiction, both military and mercantile myths. Scott began his literary career by writing ballads, and his first project in prose narrative was a *Castle of Otranto* fantastic romance. But then he saw the advantage of Scottish history as a subject; "the ancient traditions and high spirit of a people, who, living in a civilized age and country, retained . . . manners belonging to an early period of society" (p. 8). This historical change was his subject, and the need to accept both terms and their interrelation was his point, as Jeffrey and Coleridge, for instance, saw immediately. Jeffrey said that the novels' interest was that "in our own country and almost in our own age," we discover "manners and customs we had been accustomed to consider as belonging to remote antiquity or extravagant ro-

*In his *The Hero of the Waverley Novels*, New Haven, 1963.

mance."* And Coleridge defined the main theme as the transition from an age of heroism to one of prudence.

To connect this with Defoe, let us say that both authors treat the theme of a conflict between the modern world system's life-style and its alternatives. In *Tristes Tropiques*, Lévi-Strauss speaks of "that crucial moment in modern thought when, thanks to the great voyages of discovery, a human community [Europe] which had believed itself to be complete and in its final form suddenly learned, as if through the effect of a counterrevelation, that it was not alone, that it was part of a greater whole, and that, in order to achieve self-knowledge, it must first of all contemplate its unrecognizable image in this mirror. . . ." (p. 367). That moment of thought is not something which took place, once and for all, in the sixteenth century; Lévi-Strauss describes it to explain his own experience in the 1930s in approaching the Tupi-Kawahib. And it is what Defoe was writing about in the eighteenth century, and Scott in the nineteenth, though both presented the idea in fragmentary and oblique form. Defoe does not contemplate the unrecognizable image of man—he conjures up an unrecognizable environment; Scott places the unrecognizable image in the past. But both writers evoke the passionate interest—mingled glee and anxiety—which the modern citizen takes in his unique situation.

But what one might call the axis of sensibility has rotated through perhaps 90°, from geography to history; whereas Defoe's motto might have been " 'Tis a Thousand Miles Hence," Scott's was " 'Tis Sixty Years Since." And therewith the place of nature (the alien conditions with which Crusoe had to struggle) has been taken by culture: the mode of life of the Highlanders. And so naturally the interest in technology has been replaced by an interest in ethnography. The form has also developed toward an interest in larger historical units; larger units of time, and larger institutions; the armies are larger and the battles last longer. Instead of Singleton's band of pirates, we have the 1745 rebellion, a doomed rising, larger in every way.

Of course, there are other differences, which don't fit into so simple a scheme. For instance, the central position, narratively speaking, is no longer occupied by a man of action, but by an observer-participant. The effect of this is discussed by Alexander Welsh, in his

*Quoted on p. viii of James C. Corson's Preface to the Everyman's edition of *Waverley*, 1969.

Hero of the Waverley Novels. The dominant virtue of the novels is prudence, he says (in this the continuity from Defoe is obvious) but Scott's heroes are all passive (while Crusoe is a model of active prudence). Scott's heroes are not even calculatingly prudent, and they allow social authority to win their rights for them—even their sexual rights. They deserve the girl they love by being good, and they inherit the property they end up with. They do not make money by trade or in any other way, or make love; though a hero may often seem to, or seem about to, kill an enemy or seduce a woman, this always turns out to be mere seeming. The novels' scenes of violence and disorder are soon over, and have the character of being a disturbance of reality, while the Byronic villains, dark figures of passion that at first glance look more lively than the heroes, are in fact more merely literary. It is significant that they belong often to some geographically as well as morally remote origin—Fergus to the mountains, Saladin to the desert, Staunton to the West Indies. Reality is characterized by a middleground in every category, including character. Scott's values, despite his love of aristocratic stylishness, were more passive and compromising than Defoe's—perhaps because his position was a compromise between the chivalric and the mercantile.

In the Introductory to *Waverley,* Scott compares the spirit of the past with that of the present contrastively, but rather ambiguously. "The wrath of our ancestors, for instance, was coloured gules; it broke forth in acts of open and sanguinary violence against the objects of his fury. Our malignant feelings, which must seek gratification through more indirect channels . . . may be rather said to be tinctured sable. But . . . the proud peer, who now can only ruin his neighbour according to law, by protracted suits, is the genuine descendant of the baron, who wrapped the castle of his competitor in flames, and knocked him on the head as he attempted to escape from the conflagration" (p. 65). A passage like that suggests the complicated scheme of feelings and values which Scott offers. The contrast between gules and sable is to the advantage of the past; but the Cockney cynicism of "knocked him on the head" alerts us to a realistic assessment of that "open and sanguinary violence." Scott's judgment of things feudal is often not much different from Twain's. Indeed, he often made exactly the same point as Twain, that in medieval times rooms were too cold, and behavior too hot. Although Twain saw Scott as the romantic, and therefore as antithetical in spirit to Cervantes the ironist, in fact Cervantes was favorite reading of Scott's. Scott was a skillful homogenizer of moral feelings, as Welsh puts it. He minimized antitheses.

Scott's purpose was more conciliatory, in literary terms too, than Defoe's. He genuinely liked both the modern world adventures and the old world romances, and tried to satisfy both the military and the mercantile castes. This is the source of his weakness, as we shall see, his lack of authenticity; or perhaps that derived from his attempts to conciliate his public's various tastes, rather than express his own. There is a fatal gentility to the *Waverley* enterprise; one aspect to it is a game with chivalric trappings for readers who make their money in trade—a literary equivalent for the social pursuit of titles and coats of arms. Like the snobbery of genre in the eighteenth century (the greater prestige of epic poetry), and the shame of trade among families like the Bingleys of *Pride and Prejudice,* the *Waverley* enterprise also derives from a distaste for the public face of the modern world system, and amounts to a kind of concealment. But this compromising and conciliatory purpose is also a sign of Scott's strength. He is much more knowledgeable and much more ambitious than Defoe in literary matters. He clearly had some sense of literature as a system, and set out to manipulate it, and succeeded, temporarily.

Waverley

We can perhaps divide the story of *Waverley* into two main parts. In the first, the observer-participant is moved from his place of origin in Hanoverian England (a commercialized and rationalized England, where he can find romance only in a debased and literary form) up north to Scotland. There an older form of social organization survives, most intensely and purely in the Highlands, supporting a life which gives a central importance to the passion, gallantry, and death, which elsewhere seem banished to a moral periphery. On the borders of the Highlands, Waverley enters a village described to us in terms of its poverty, its discomfort, its comic picturesqueness (described, that is, from a modernist perspective); and this impressionism rests on a detailed analysis of the crops, the agricultural methods, the drainage, the ownership, etc., from the same point of view. Then Waverley enters Baron Bradwardine's manor house, which is seen as both grotesque and picturesque, and is dominated by carvings of bears, the family emblem, here rendered in so many sizes and materials as to carry some totemic and tribal suggestion. And the first person Waverley meets is a Shakespearian fool. All this, I am suggesting, is the equivalent, in historical, cultural, ethnological terms, of Crusoe's discovery that he is alone on a desert island, and must defend himself against its wild animals, its storms, its unknown fruits, etc. The representative of our modern life meets a challenge that we the readers are usually exempt from.

But this is only a halfway stage on Waverley's journey into the Highlands. Rose Bradwardine describes to Waverley an incident—seen by her at the age of ten—in which real Highlanders were involved.

Three of the Highlanders were killed, and they brought them wrapped in their plaids, and laid them on the stone floor of the hall; and next morning, their wives and daughters came, clapping their hands, and crying the coronach, and shrieking, and carried away the dead bodies, with the pipes playing before them. I could not sleep for six weeks without starting, and thinking I heard those terrible cries, and saw the bodies lying on the steps, all stiff and swathed up in their bloody tartans (p. 148).

Waverley's reaction to this anecdote is the essence of Scott's meaning.

"Waverley could not help starting at a story which bore so much resemblance to one of his own daydreams. Here was a girl scarce seventeen, the gentlest of her sex, both in temper and appearance, who had witnessed with her own eyes such a scene as he had used to conjure up in his imagination, as only occurring in ancient times, and spoke of it coolly, as one very likely to recur. He felt at once the impulse of curiosity, and that slight sense of danger which only serves to heighten its interest." He feels himself in "the land of military and romantic adventures," and determines to have a share of them himself. (Scott had a clear if intermittent sense of the interplay of chivalric and mercantile caste sensibilities in his stories.)

When Highlanders appear on the page, the first one is described as a figure of epic poetry, in terms of his costume and arms; the dirk and pistol, the broadsword, target, and fowling piece. And from his mouth we hear epic speech.

"Fergus MacIvor Vich Ian Vohr," said the ambassador, in good English,

greets you well, baron of Bradwardine and Tully-Veolan, and is sorry there has been a thick cloud interposed between you and him, which has kept you from seeing and considering the friendship and alliances that have been between your houses and forbears of old; and he prays you that the cloud may pass away and that things may be as they have been heretofore between the clan Ivor and the house of Bradwardine, when there was an egg between them for a flint, and a knife for a sword (p. 151).

This is the equivalent in language (and in a work of literature of course language has a very special potency) of romantic styles of behavior and relationship, and of patriarchal modes of authority, land tenure, land cultivation, etc. This is life in the grand style—attractive, impressive, challenging, threatening. Waverley is led by Evan Dhu on a visit to Fergus MacIvor, and on his way he hears of the latter's retinue.

There is his *hanchman,* or right hand man; then his *bard,* or poet; then his *bladier,* or orator, to make harangues to the great folks whom he visits; then his *gilly-more,* or armour-bearer, to carry his sword, his target, and his gun; then his *gilly-casfluich,* who carries him on his back through the sikes and brooks, then his *gilly-comstrian,* to lead his horse by the bridle in steep and difficult paths; then his *gilly-trushharnish,* to carry his knapsack; and the piper and the piper's man, and it may be a dozen young lads beside, that have no business, but are just boys of the belt, to follow the laird, and do his honour's bidding (p. 153).

As they talk, they see the mountains rising around them, and the eagles flying, and in general the landscape suits itself to a grander moral and social scenery, grander in various ways. Waverley feels conscious of an imputation (p. 155) "which Evan seemed to entertain of the effeminacy of the Lowlanders, and particularly of the English." For it is manhood that is under test, here in the Highlands as it was on Crusoe's island. And at Glennaquoich Waverley meets Fergus and Flora MacIvor, the principal embodiments of this virility and splendor.

In the second part of the story, the spectacle of Highland life, that has been unrolled before Waverley like a painted panorama, is replaced by the 1745 Rebellion, in which the MacIvors involve him. Essentially his role in this second part is as passive, or at most as tentative, as his role was in Part I, but geographically he moves a great deal, and socially he moves up and down the ranks of Scottish society, reaching the circle of the Young Pretender himself. But at the battle of Prestonpans he meets Colonel Talbot, a forceful spokesman for English reason at its best, and under Talbot's guidance realizes the weaknesses and dangers, practical and moral, of the romance world he has entered. This education coincides with, and rationalizes, the defeat of the Rebellion, and the retreat of Waverley to private life in England again.

But Waverley has gained much from the experience. At the end of the story he has become a man, and has won a highly desirable though entirely domestic bride. (There is less conventional rounding-off in Defoe's story, but—by the same token—the sense of reward and relief at the end is stronger; Crusoe's triumphs as mock-governor of the island, like Charles Edward's triumphs as Pretender, have to end; but Crusoe's financial investments, so lavishly detailed, and his difficult journey home, are less conventional than Waverley's rewards.) And clearly the curve of Waverley's experience is to be echoed in the sympathizing reader, who has tempered his own loyalty to modern reality by indulging a yearning for the opposite, in a measured and controlled experiment that leaves him all the more firmly what he was before.

If we examine *Waverley* structurally, we find that the rotation of the romance axis already described has made confusion of most of the old motifs. We must be struck by the profusion of new ones, like the historical figures and local details (costume, houses, food, etc.), the epic speech, the romantic landscape, and the heroines. These last are a feeble invention, who bring with them an operatic sensibility badly at odds with modernist adventure.[3] Flora MacIvor's "effects" (in both senses, theatrical properties *and* splendid tableaux; her harp and her diamonds, but also her political passion and her tragic fate) turn every place and event she enters into papier-mâché. Rose, the inheriting blonde, is less recalcitrant but no more rewarding. But from Scott's time on, romance was burdened down with a stock of such lay figures, Cooper's narrative pace being particularly hobbled.

Fergus's function is like that of the Black Prince, but it would be stretching that term too far to apply it to him. "Black" is not inappropriate, but it will not apply in Defoe's sense—the sense of belonging to another race and culture; Fergus is black in the moral sense. He is a prince, but because the hero has become passive in *Waverley* his opposite number has to become active, and this makes another development to the figure as Scott used him. He is much more of a threat, to the hero and to the story, than Defoe's Black Prince was.

Perhaps Scott's most successful invention in the way of romance motifs is the large scene; like the ball at Holyrood, the army on the march, or the battle. This is something Defoe did not attempt in his modernist adventures, though in *Memoirs of a Cavalier* he came closer. Scott had of course read *Memoirs of a Cavalier*, and one might say that his whole achievement was to blend together material from several of Defoe's kinds of books. But that is not true in any sense derogatory to Scott's originality, for in large scenes of this kind his extraordinary feeling for (and knowledge of) how institutions work, both the formally and the informally organized, finds truly vivid literary expression.[4]

Scott's Career and Reputation

We know much more about Scott than about Defoe, but it isn't feasible in his case either to develop biographical detail here, except in the matter of his literary career, which is peculiarly representative of the adventure novelist's.

Scott began his literary career with narrative poems, and immediately showed that he knew how to make literature pay—how to make it popular. In 1809 he published *The Lay of the Last Minstrel*, the first best-selling poem. A significant predecessor was Defoe's *The True-Born Englishman*, but Defoe's sales and even more his earnings could not compete, because of the underdeveloped state of publishing then. Scott's poem had sold 44,000 copies before the Collected Edition of his works appeared in 1829. Then came *The Lady of the Lake*, which sold 25,000 copies in eight months, and made the western Highlands a tourist attraction forthwith. Houses and inns there were filled that season, and posthouse duty in Scotland rose from the date of its publication. In 1813 came *Rokeby* and *Triermain*. The first sold 10,000 copies, which would have been a great success for anyone else, but he regarded it as a failure. In fact, Byron had begun to write similar poems, and since he could charge their Romantic heroes with autobiographical excitement, he outshone Scott. Scott said to his publisher, "Since one line has failed, we must stick to something else." So in 1814 he produced *Waverley*.

On his deathbed, he is supposed to have said (according to Samuel Smiles, *Character*, p. 187), "It *is* a comfort to me to think that I have tried to unsettle no man's faith, to corrupt no man's principles, and that I have written nothing which on my deathbed I should wish blotted out." The phrasing of that is implausibly mealy-mouthed, but one can imagine that he said something to that effect. Scott did mean to reinforce the constructive energies of his people; that is just what makes him, and the other adventure-tellers, so unlike serious writers. That remark is after all not so far from another entry in his Journal for June 16, 1826, "I am sensible that if there be anything good about my poetry, or prose either, it is a hurried frankness of composition which pleases soldiers, sailors, and young people of bold and active disposition." As opposed, obviously, to people of literary taste. (In our day, Donald Davie has said it is science students, not literature students, who read Scott.) In fact, in 1831 a cruise in a warship, on the Mediterranean, was arranged for Scott, because he was such a favorite author of the navy's; a favor extended later to Kipling, but not to George Eliot or Henry James.

The system of literature gradually moved Scott to its periphery in the course of the nineteenth century. At the beginning, the novelty, the profusion, the pleasure given, the very popularity of *The Waverley Novels,* overbore all criticism. That popularity was quite unprecedented. Ten to thirty journals reviewed each one as it came out, and copies were eagerly awaited from the packet from Leith. Weeklies had advance copies rushed down by coach. *Waverley* sold six printings in one year, *Old Mortality* (1816) sold 4,000 copies in six months, *Rob Roy* (1816) 10,000 in two weeks, *The Fortunes of Nigel* (1822) 7,000 by 10:30 of the first day it was for sale. They earned him £10 to 15,000 a year. So England found in Scott the stories it wanted to hear, and not only England.

French translations came out within the year of publication in English, and the rest of Europe was not far behind. *Ivanhoe,* for instance, was translated into French, Spanish, and German by 1832, Portuguese by 1838, Italian by 1840, Greek by 1847, Polish by 1865. Cheap editions in England began in the 1860s, while in 1871 Scott's biography sold 180,000 copies.

Soon after 1870 he began to be relegated to children, and versions of his work adapted to their taste appeared. This is a sure mark of relegation to the periphery of literature, though that very shift may be a move to something like the center of culture; for the books that shape ourselves as a nation or as a class are surely the books we read as children.[5] What we read as adults, at least what we read seriously, cannot have that effect, just because serious critical attention disinfects the reading process. (I am thinking of that infection which Tolstoy said was the great power of art.) Ideally, of course, critical reading is a process which ensures that we get infected or excited only by those ideas and images which deserve to excite us. Practically, however, critical reading is often more aggressive than that. The reader's mind acts upon the text, and in doing so crushes its seeds of meaning.

The best reviewers understood what Scott was doing from the beginning. Jeffrey reviewed *Waverley* enthusiastically in the *Edinburgh Review* in 1814, and spoke of how it showed "feudal chivalry in the mountains, and vulgar fanaticism in the plains; and startled the more polished parts of the land with the wild but brilliant picture of the devoted valour, incorruptible fidelity, patriarchal brotherhood, and savage habits of the Celtic Clans. . . . [elsewhere] so long superseded by more peaceable habits, and milder manners. . . . When the glens of the central Highlands . . . were opened up to the gaze of the English, it seemed as if they were carried back to the days of the Heptarchy."*

Generally speaking, Scott was seen as being morally affirmative and effective, at least by conservatives. He inspired the nation; particularly its military men, as we have seen, but not exclusively them. Newman in 1839 said Scott's novels prepared men for conversion to Catholicism, and gave them nobler ideas, and, set beside Pope and 18th century literature, "look almost as oracles of truth confronting the ministers of error and sin." On the other hand, Hazlitt was always largely hostile, in the name of political radicalism; and Carlyle delivered the crucial Victorian verdict, which in the long run relegated Scott to the periphery. Reviewing Lockhart's biography of Scott in 1838, for the *London and Westminster Review,* he said the latter had no faith in anything but power. Nor did he disbelieve. He "quietly

Scott: The Critical Heritage, John O. Hayden, (Ed.), p. 80.

acquiesced, and made himself at home in a world of conventionalities."* He was at ease, not in Zion, but in Babel. A man of letters, Carlyle implies, is not supposed to be at ease with the world around him. He is supposed to be a hero of resistance.

Twain's criticism of Scott, in *Life on the Mississippi* (1883), is in a sense irrelevant to our argument, but deserves a short comment, just because we are concerned with both Twain and Scott. Twain says Scott set the world in love with dreams and phantoms; "with decayed and swinish forms of religion; . . . with the sillinesses and emptinesses, sham grandeurs, sham gauds, and sham chivalries of a brainless and worthless long-vanished society" (p. 375). This is partly a political attack. In the same chapter, Twain praises Napoleon and the French Revolution for their permanent services to liberty, humanity, and progress; and Scott was Napoleon's major literary antagonist in England. But it is partly literary criticism, and that part is purely modernist. Twain is attacking Scott (and the same is true of his attack on Cooper) for not being enough like Defoe.

His attack is not quite relevant to our argument because Twain is not thinking of the Scott represented by *Waverley*, but of the author of *Ivanhoe* and other such novels; and even more of what the plantation aristocrats of the South made of *Ivanhoe*, with their mock-tournaments, etc. But (of course) I must acknowledge that the Scott of whom I speak also wrote *Ivanhoe*, and several other books, in which his nostalgia for the past is not effectively balanced or shaped by his moral realism and by that interest in cultural anthropology which was its intellectual expression. The Waverley novels were not all like *Waverley;* but the best ones are, and the form I described is potentially present within the whole enterprise.

If Carlyle delivered the verdict against Scott, and relegated him to the periphery of the Victorian literary system, it was Coleridge who played a part closer to Swift's part against Defoe. Coleridge was the genius who seemed to his literary contemporaries to sit at the very centre of the system, and to incarnate its best qualities of judgment and discrimination. The antagonism between him and Scott, and his refusal to "accept" the other man, is of crucial importance. Coleridge understood the Waverley novels. He said Scott's stories could never be obsolete, because their subject is† "the contrast between the two

---

*Scott, Hayden, p. 347.
†Quoted in David D. Devlin, *Author of Waverley*, Lewisburg, Pa., 1971, p. 53.

great moving principles of social humanity; religious adherence to the past and the ancient, the desire and the admiration of permanence, on one hand; and the passion for increase of knowledge . . . on the other."

But he thought the novels not serious enough in their treatment of that subject. In a letter of 1821, he described Scott as popular reading that aimed "to amuse without requiring any effort of thought and without exciting any deep emotion. The age seems *sore* from excess of stimulation." And when he heard of Scott's financial failure, in 1826, he wrote, "When I think of the wretched trash that the lust for gain induced him to publish for the last three or four years . . . even my feelings assist in hardening me. . . . I should indeed be sorry if any ultimate success had attended the attempt to unite the Poet and the Worldling."

Scott took a tone of philistine heartiness about Coleridge. He referred in his *Journal* in 1828 to meeting him—that extraordinary man—"Zounds, I was never so bethumped with words," and told Mrs. Davy in 1831 that most of Coleridge's prose was nonsense. But in effect he accepted his own banishment from the central position Coleridge and Wordsworth held in literature. In an entry for 1827, he says Wordsworth is unwise and unjust to himself in choosing subjects which the popular mind cannot sympathize in. "He fails to receive the universal suffrage he deserves because too subtle in subject, too blunt in expression." He compared himself rather with Tom Moore. "We are both good-humoured fellows who rather seek to enjoy what is going forward than to maintain our dignity as Lions. . . ." (*Journal*, p. 6).[6]

Scotland and India

Most of Scott's fiction made only indirect mention of the colonies as such. At the end of *The Heart of Midlothian*, Effie's son kills his (illegitimate) father and goes to America to escape justice. There he conspires against his master, and finally renounces white culture altogether, joining an Indian tribe. His parents' sin works itself out in his loss of white identity. This is one of the rare occasions when the colonies appear in Scott's fiction. The function assigned to them is eloquently "anthropoemic," but rudimentary. (Other Victorian novelists also made this use of them.)

Another tantalizing reference comes in Appendix III to the General Preface to *The Waverley Novels,* in which Scott describes a subject for an adventure novel, with which his brother Thomas toyed, and which derived from an incident in their youth. The Scott brothers and their friends engaged in boyhood battles against the poor children of their neighborhood, and "one very active and spirited lad . . . a youthful Goth," who led their armies, got wounded rather severely. Scott and his brothers tried to bribe him to silence, but he refused either to "sell his blood" or to inform on them. "Such was the hero whom Mr. Thomas Scott proposed to carry off to Canada, and involve in adventures with the natives and colonists of that country" (*Waverley,* p. 50). Scott shows himself much struck with the boy's "nobleness of sentiment," and calls him an Achilles and an Ajax, so the anthropoemic elements of the story are enriched by antithesis. He says nothing about the boy's lowly origins, but of course that is another element of interest. It is indeed a very promising subject for an adventure story of a kind closer to Defoe's than anything Scott did in fact write. For of course the striking fact this calls our attention to is that Scott's adventure tales do not involve either empire or frontier. So that even that limited respectability which he won for adventure did not extend to the crucially important contemporary subject matter.

But in the Prefatory to *The Surgeon's Daughter,* he says he has been advised to write a story about India. "India, where gold is won by steel; where a brave man cannot pitch his desire of fame and wealth so high but that he may realize it, if he have fortune to his friend." He has been advised to take a story from Robert Orme's 1763 three-volume *History of the Military Transactions of the British Nation in Indostan 1745–1761.* This is the story of Clive, and Scott sees its adventure potential. He agrees that the subject is wonderful. All the English soldiers "are distinguished among the natives like the Spaniards among the Mexicans. What do I say? They are like Homer's demi-gods among the warring mortals. Men like Clive and Cailliaud [a 19th century French traveler in Africa] influenced great events like Jove himself. . . . Then the various religious costumes, habits, and manners of the people of Hindostan—the patient Hindoo, the warlike Rajahpoot, the haughty Moslemah, the savage and vindictive Malay. Glorious and unbounded subject! The only objection is, that I have never been there, and know nothing at all about them" (p. xiv).

But that is not a sufficient explanation, since he had never been in the rebellion of 1745, for instance. And it seems clear that Scott did "know something about them," in fact, did think of going to India. He spoke of it in 1810, when there was some chance that his friend, Lord Melville, might go out as governor general. Scott's wife's brother had made a fortune there. Indeed, his family, like other Scots, had many connections with the colonies. His brother Thomas went out to Canada, his brother James to the West Indies. Scott was very aware of the world destiny of the British—that, ultimately, was his subject. But the connection between Scotland and India was particularly close.

The East India Company was of course a large part of the British empire, and a very striking fact from our point of view; that an empire —a subcontinent much larger than England itself, in every sense of large—should be ruled by a commercial company, is a striking example of how the modern world system worked—how it blended empire with nonempire. The Company was, among other things, a huge source of wealth to England. It paid £400,000 a year to the Treasury, as well as making very large loans on occasion. It is usually now considered that this was the wealth which financed the Industrial Revolution in England.[7] One example of the profits involved is the case of the E. I. C. ship *Berrington*, which in 1784 carried to India a cargo of lead, copper, steel, wool cloths, naval stores, worth £27,000, and brought back cotton goods, yarn, indigo, silk, and saltpeter, worth £120,000. And the effect in terms of imperialist psychology was also huge.

Like other parts of the empire, India was a living promise of lordship or royalty to Englishmen. In *Adventures of a Younger Son* (1831), his purported autobiography, Trelawney says, "If the English conspired against our liberty . . . India, with her thousand kings, was open to us . . . In India Europeans lorded it over the conquered natives with a high hand. Every outrage may be committed almost with impunity, and their ready flexibility of temperament has acquired a servile subordination. . . ." (p. 46). One example of what he is talking about is given us by James Morris in *Pax Britannica*. Sir David Ochterlony, East India Company Resident at Delhi in the eighteenth century, used to travel with thirteen wives, each on her own elephant.

This was just one of the facts that made nineteenth-century liberals and radicals deeply suspicious of and hostile to the empire. It attracted the wrong kind of Englishmen from their point of view, and brought out the wrong tendencies in them. And this feeling was closely related to caste loyalty. Cobden and Goldwin Smith described the colonies as being linked to the army, the navy, the established church, and the aristocracy. "Merely accessories to our aristocratic government," Cobbett called them in 1836; and in 1838 Bronterre O'Brien said, "Our aristocracy and merchants possess colonies all over the world, but the people of England—the real, veritable people of England—do not possess a sod of ground in their own country, much less colonies in any other."* It was the military caste who governed the colonies; the public schools were training boys' characters, and the new boys' literature was training their imaginations, in the ways of the military caste. Nineteenth-century imperialists like Froude saw the colonies as a way for England to return to farming and landowning, and to get away from trade and commerce.

Morally, too, the effects of this imperial wealth were manifold, and most of them the cause for disapproval by the serious mind of England, perhaps especially the serious literary mind. Cowper's *Expostulation*, line 82, says

> Hast thou, though suckled at fair freedom's breast,
> Exported slavery to the conquered East . . .
> With Asiatic vices stored thy mind
> But left their virtues and thine own behind?

Burke's attack on the East India Company as birds of prey and birds of passage is well-known. And in 1770 Chatham said to Parliament, "For some years past there has been an influx of wealth into this country, which has been attended with many fatal consequences, because it has not been the natural produce of labour and industry. The riches of Asia have been poured in on us, and brought with them not only Asiatic luxury but, I fear, Asiatic principles of government. Without connections, without any natural interest in the soil, the

*R. Hyam and G. Martin, *Reappraisals in British Imperial History*, London, 1975, p. 9.

importers of foreign gold have forced their way into Parliament by such a torrent of corruption as no private hereditary fortune could resist."*

The special importance of India for Scotsmen can be given in Scott's own words, when he described the India Board as "this corn chest for Scotland, where we poor gentry must send our youngest sons, as we send our black cattle to the south." Young Scotsmen, above all young gentry, could retrieve their family's fortunes there. The connection was made largely via his friend Henry Dundas, Lord Melville, who was Pitt's political manager of Scotland, and who dispensed a large patronage in the East India Company after 1784. Englishmen commonly said that no one but a Scot could get a job in any Indian province where the chief was a Scot, and Boswell in 1762 spoke of knowing a Scot who saw London only as a place to join the Company. Men spoke of the Indian-and-Scottish interest in politics, and James MacIntosh said you could see "a little stream of Indian gold" in Scotland "spreading cultivation and fertility and plenty along its narrow valley."

For thirty years another channel of Company patronage to Scotsmen was Charles Grant. Though also a friend of Dundas, Grant was very unlike Scott in his views, for he was a fervent Evangelical, a powerful member of the Clapham sect, and an agent of the Victorianization of the Company, the substitution of missionary moralism, which Scott would have hated, for the old Enlightenment tolerance. Nevertheless, it is worth saying something about Grant here, because both his family and history and his own career bear importantly on the operation of the modern world system, in Scotland and in India.

He was born in 1746, and his father, called Alexander Grant the Swordsman, was a very colorful figure in the 1745 rebellion. Charles was named after the prince, and was baptized just before his defeat at Culloden, having to clasp the hilts of two swords held crossed over him. He grew up to be the very opposite of Jacobite romanticism—to be an embodiment of Evangelical seriousness. After Culloden, Alexander, like many other Jacobites and Highlanders, went out to the West Indies. He died soon after getting there, but another Alexander Grant became Charles's protector and patron. This Alex-

*R. A. Huttenback, The *British Imperial Achievement*, p. 7.

ander had also fought at Culloden, but then emigrated to India, and fought under Clive at Plassey and won prize money there amounting to £11,000. Charles went to London to work for him in 1763, and then to India. (It is interesting to note, as an example of Scots-Indian nepotism, that Charles had two brothers and two cousins in India with him, besides his wife's sister.) He became Secretary of a Board of Trade in 1774 and made a lot of money, and was converted by the Danish missionaries out there.

This was the time of such conversions, the time of missions abroad and the Evangelical movement at home. There was a general reaction against the eighteenth-century rationalism and skepticism. From our point of view this shows the modern system recharging itself with primitive energies which had begun to drain away from at least the conscious mind and will of the system—primitive both in the sense of crude and in the sense of original. The conviction of righteousness, individual and collective righteousness, strong in Defoe and Raleigh, much eroded in Hume and Gibbon (and their readers in, for instance, the East India Company), was renewed in Macaulay and Grant.[8]

The latter's case is especially interesting for us, because of his close biographical connection with the forty-five, and all the colorful Jacobitism which his father represented and which Scott celebrated. Charles Grant, after his conversion, turned away from that colorfulness (predominantly aristomilitary colors) toward the black and white of Puritanism. This was the movement of the whole serious mind of England then, and it meant that the adventure novel as Scott wrote it was swimming against the tide, morally speaking, and would not become a major literary genre.

Between 1780 and 1790 Dundas imposed government control on the Company. Grant came back to Scotland in 1790, and became M.P. for Inverness in 1799, keeping the seat for fifteen years. In 1794 he became a director of the Company, which he is said to have dominated after 1804 because he did so much of the work. He attacked Sir William Jones and the other Orientalists, who had studied and celebrated Indian culture. Grant saw that culture as being in a state of decadence and India as needing redemption by means of an infusion of English culture; for instance, he wanted to have missionaries sent out there and to have support be given them by the Company. He spread a nondialectical, single-valued view of history and progress. But the point for the moment is that in this typically Victorian form the patronage connection between Scotland and India continued.

So when we read Scott celebrating the ancestral virtues of Scotsmen—virtues no longer rife in modern England—we should think of India as being implicitly referred to. Those virtues habitually found an important political function and a large economic reward, in the administration of India. And also that ancient character-structure, and the social structure behind it, explained India and Indians to his readers. Scott was in a sense writing about the nineteenth-century empire under the guise of writing about feudal Scotland. That is another reason why his readers were so engrossed by him, until the system of literature persuaded them he was not serious.

Emigration and Empire

But this sketch of a historical context for Scott must be expanded still further. That connection between Scotland and India is only part of a larger pattern connecting the British Isles with the colonies, and that in turn is part of the modern world system migration. In "The Migration of Human Populations," (*Scientific American*, September 1974) the demographer Kingsley Davis tells us that in the sixteenth and seventeenth centuries the world was dominated by a single migratory network, built around the advanced states, and it was thanks to this network that they were able to achieve their Industrial Revolution. The first territories to be exploited were tropical and uninhabited (that is, no "civilized" people lived there); lands like the Caribbean islands, where the Europeans grew spices, sugar, rice, coffee, etc., by means of slave labor. Between 1451 and 1870, 11 million slaves were exported from Africa and 9.6 million reached their destinations. When the slave trade was stopped, indentured labor, from India, China, and Java took its place. Some 16.8 million left India, 4.4 million for good.

The second sort of lands to be exploited were temperate and uninhabited; and these attracted the European migrants. They were moving in considerable numbers from 1720 on, but it was after steamships began to operate in 1827 that those numbers expanded; by 1830, it is estimated, 52 million had changed their land of residence. In 1897 145,000 emigrants left Britain alone, 50,000 for the colonies. Associated with migration is a remarkable increase in population. C. F. Carrington says that in the course of the ten generations following the days of Raleigh and Drake, the population of Britain increased (counting those living in the colonies and the U.S.) from 7 to 140 million, a rate unexampled among other races. Davis says that between 1840 and 1930 Europe's population rose from 194 million to 463 million, a rate of growth twice the world's average, and Europeans abroad increased at a rate even faster. Between 1750 and 1930 the European-occupied areas of the rest of the world increased their population by a factor of 14, while the world rate was 2.5. In 1750 these areas held 3 percent of the world's people, while in 1930, 16 percent. Caucasians increased by a factor of 5.4, Asians by a factor of 2.3.[9]

One importance of this to us is to remind us of the literature that necessarily accompanied this vast shift of population. Two categories that jump to mind are first the literature of promotion, from the poems of Marston and Chapman to the twentieth-century pamphlets of the Canada office in London; and second the flow of correspondence by means of which emigrants kept in touch with family and friends at home. This literature kept the idea, in some sense the experience, of the empire in the minds of the home population, however the serious writers of the time might slight it. From this point of view we can discern two different meanings of the word literature, and can say both that there was no significant literature of empire in nineteenth-century England, and that there was a very rich and significant one. Scott's leatherbound volumes, with their indirect mythic message, joined forces with millions of pamphlets and letters and miniatures and mementos of those abroad. The swarming of WASP's over the rest of the globe was being recorded and celebrated.

Another literature of that kind, to do with missions, developed in Scott's time. Although the Roman Catholic church had sent missionaries to foreign parts from the beginning of the age of exploration, Protestant missions, much more important from our point of view, did not begin effectively until the 1790s. In 1792 William Carey founded a London Missionary Society (Baptist); in 1795 a group of mostly Presbyterians founded their London Missionary Society; in 1799 Evangelicals founded the Church Missionary Society, who began to publish the *Christian Observer* in 1802, and so on. The

Scott

Moravians (the first Protestant missionaries generally) had gone to Bengal in 1777, the first English missionaries followed them the next year, but it was not until 1813 that the numbers became considerable. But more considerable, on the whole, was the homeland role played by missionaries in pious Victorian society. Probably the greatest hero of the whole nineteenth century for that half of England was the missionary Livingstone. And we must imagine all the church- and chapel-goers hearing sermons and reading church-magazine reports about missionaries in foreign parts, regularly. On the whole, that segment of Victorian culture remained distinct from the literary segment, but there were figures who crossed the line, like George Borrow. He also showed the connection between missions, empire, and adventure, when he said it was a "crown of glory to carry the blessings of civilization and religion to barbarous, yet at the same time beautiful and romantic lands."

This aspect of modern system ideology also can be associated with Scotland.

Livingstone of course was a Scot, as was his missionary father-in-law, Moffat, and many other missionaries. The African Lakes Company that ruled Nyasaland did so on the behalf of both the Free Church and some Glasgow merchants. And the missionary enterprise blended with others in which the Scots were prominent. Scots explorers, like James Bruce and Mungo Park, were famous for their journeys. And Scots soldiers, like Charles Napier and Colin Campbell, were famous in India. The Hudson's Bay Company was largely Scottish, in fact largely Orcadian, and whole villages considered themselves "Company folk." And the Canadian Pacific Railway was carried through by Scottish financiers and engineers.

It is clear that Scotland had, as England's subordinate partner, a special destiny in the modern world system.[10] John Galt the novelist founded a Canada Company in 1824 to organize emigration there (70-acre land grants were being made in Canada in the 1820s) and there was a British-American Land Co., appealing to Highlanders, in 1834. During the nineteenth century a high proportion of Scots emigrants were skilled workers; engineers, shipbuilders, iron smelters. A typical Scots emigrant city was Pittsburgh, and its great success story was Andrew Carnegie.

It is no wonder that when R. L. Stevenson went out to America by emigrant ship in 1879, he described emigration as "this great epic of self-help. The epic is composed of individual heroisms. . . . For in emigration the young men enter direct and by the ship-load on their heritage of work; empty continents swarm, as at the bo'sun's whistle, with industrous hands, and whole new empires are domesticated to the service of man" (*From Scotland to Silverado*, p. 10). His tone is ironic, for he sees on his ship that most emigrants are in fact already defeated men. But on board the emigrant train to California he is caught up by the old excitement, at the building of the railroad. Think, he tells us, "how at each stage of the construction, roaring, impromptu cities, full of gold and lust and death, sprang up and then died away again, and are now but wayside stations in the desert; how in those uncouth places pig-tailed Chinese pirates worked side by side with border ruffians. . . . If it be romance, if it be contrast, if it be heroism that we require, what was Troy Town to this?" (p. 129).

Stevenson saw the subject. But then Scott had done that much. And neither one could in fact marry that subject to the serious writer's modes of sense and sensibility. The trick could be turned in children's literature; vivid narratives of that kind were produced; they were written by Stevenson, as by Ballantyne before him—both Scots writers. If anyone could have written the serious novel of adventure, it probably would have been a Scotsman, because of the mode of Scots participation in the Empire—the disengagement (compared with England) despite the deep involvement. But it seems that the polarity holding literature always in some opposition to that genre and subject-matter was too strong.

Historians and Historical Novelists

Despite his "official" demotion from literature, Scott exerted an enormous influence on writers, partly just because of his sales. (The same was true of Defoe before him, and it is one reason why students of literature need to study both of them.) But Scott (and Defoe) also exerted influence in the larger realm of high culture—were, odd as it sounds, intellectuals. They were Whig ideologues. This influence constitutes another imaginative context for the adventure tale, explaining its potency by naming its allies. In Defoe's case, the influence was felt in the field of economics. In Scott's case, this influence centered in the realm of history, where the deeds of kings, generals, and armies always bulk larger than they do in literature. He was himself a historian. His *Life of Napoleon*, which appeared in nine volumes in 1827, earned him £18,000, and is said to have shown Carlyle and Macaulay how profitable a work of history could be made. But his greater influence on history-writing was exerted through his novels. Via Scott, the adventure ethos entered history, in the work of the nineteenth-century Whig historians of England and America, carrying in solution also nationalism and historical romanticism. Even Macaulay, in some ways a Utilitarian, wrote patriotic ballads (about the Armada) which would have shocked Hume. It was the infusion of adventure that made the difference between eighteenth- and nineteenth-century historiography, and it was Scott who made the infusion.

In many ways Scott himself was an eighteenth-century Whig historian, as he was an eighteenth-century sensibility in general. His Toryism, and his Romanticism, though they seemed to his contemporaries so unlike the attitudes of his predecessors, are rather superficial changes from the point of view of anyone considering the progress of the modern world system. He only introduced a dialectic, which complicated but also enriched the Whig historians' system of ideas.

In *The History of Historical Writing*, J. W. Thompson calls the period, 1715–1789, the Age of Reason. (We might call it the Age of the Encyclopaedists, and imply Defoe also.) In those years, historians' ideas were derived from Descartes, and their metaphors were derived from mechanics. They promoted peace and prosperity, fought superstition and splendid tyranny. Their ethos was neither adventurous nor zealous; especially in France, historians tended to oppose both the army and the church, and to mock both kings and empires. Voltaire is an example. Scott reacted against much of that. His sense of history was unlike Voltaire's. On the other hand, another of the representative French historians of that time was the more conservative Montesquieu, whose political model was constitutional monarchy in the English style, and whose enemy was military despotism in the style of Louis XIV. And that was Scott's position as much as Defoe's. Scott's Toryism (his aristomilitary sympathy) was not of a kind to divide him from Montesquieu, or from the English Whigs.

History, in the Age of Reason, seemed to be on England's side. Thompson says that eighteenth-century writers throughout Europe used history as an arsenal with which to bombard the ancien régime with irony, in the name of freedom. In England, with all its faults, historians felt that they had freedom; or at least that the worst cases of unfreedom were abroad. The greatest ironist of them all, Gibbon, served the same cause. He first intended to write the history of liberty in Switzerland, then one of the holy places of Protestantism and freedom. And freedom represented all the values of progress; the Scots historian, Robertson, said his *History of Charles V* would mark the steps by which Europe advanced from barbarism to refinement. These historians spoke as clearly for modernism—as Defoe himself.

The difference between their attitudes and Scott's is that his loyalties were more divided, even in *Waverley*, where he made the issue to the conflict clearer than usual. The comparative narrowness and simplicity of the eighteenth-century historians' view is clear in this remark of Robertson about Loyola. "The wild adventures and visionary schemes in which his enthusiasm engaged him equal anything recorded in the legends of the Roman saints; but are unworthy of notice in history." Robertson also deplored the reading of conquerors' exploits while "the useful arts and the branches of commerce sink into oblivion." One glimpses there an aridity and narrowness of mercantile rationalism which Scott and the Romantics reacted against.

But he was not really skeptical of the values of progress and modernism. He merely held those values dialectically. Avrom Fleishman, in *The English Historical Novel*, has shown that Scott was consciously a sociologist, in the Scots school of speculative history, which had its roots in 18th century Whiggery, but refined upon it. His Whig friend Adam Ferguson, in his essay on the *History of Modern Society*, warned against the effects of wealth and liberty (in polished and commercial nations) because they dissolve the bonds of patriotism, loyalty, blood brotherhood, etc. That is exactly Scott's message. And Dugald Stewart, another such friend, made a sharp distinction between natural and historical aristocracy, which, as Fleishman says, is a very important distinction for Scott, as a way to refurbish aristocracy for the modern world. Scott ". . . throughout his poetry and fiction may be said to have worked towards a refinement of the aristocrat ideal [towards creating] . . . a paidea for modern life" (p. 52). He carefully analyzed the idea of a gentleman. (In this work, of course, Scott was next in line from Defoe and next before Smiles.)

Thus Scott's adventures, though less directly than Defoe's, translated the Whig interpretation of history into fiction.

In his famous essay, *The Whig Interpretation of History* (1951), Herbert Butterfield defines this interpretation as "The tendency in many historians to write on the side of Protestants and Whigs, to praise revolutions provided they have been successful, to emphasize certain principles of progress in the past, and to produce a story which is the ratification if not the glorification of the present. . . ." (Preface, p. v). Clearly this is a specification, in terms of historiography, of the general line of thought and sensibility we are studying. On page 4, Butterfield says that "the great patriarchs of history-writing" divided people between those who furthered history and those who impeded it, and introduced value judgments at every turn, so that history might be their judge and their defender. Butterfield's irony is of course another sign that by 1951 people were feeling that this long historical movement was over, and that other intellectual attitudes must be devised. But in the period we are concerned with, that could not or did not happen. The modern enterprise dragged the modern mind after it.

In the nineteenth century, Thompson says, we should consider Thiers and Guizot Whig historians, while in England the supreme example is Macaulay; no other history has ever approached Macaulay's *History of England* in popularity. Three thousand copies were sold within ten days of publication, 13,000 in four months; and in America, Harper sold 40,000 in a cheap edition, more than anything else but the Bible.

The specifically Victorian note is perhaps struck by Macaulay's confident declaration on page 516, "No *state* has achieved anything by a breach of public faith, and the British government in India has gained everything by having always kept its promises." Scott would have found that a bit much to swallow. But in "The State of England in 1685," Macaulay puts the stress where Scott put it—and even more exactly where Defoe put it—on the excitements of progress. North of the Trent, England in 1685 was in a state of barbarism. Middlesex was to Northumberland as Massachusetts is to America west of the Mississippi, where settlers impose the law of the gun and the knife. A quarter of England has been turned from a wilderness into a garden in little more than a century. There has been an immense increase in wealth of every kind, and of refinement, arts, skills, learning and specifically comfort. Macaulay was, as Herzen says somewhere, the Scott of his generation, and the poet of the middle class.

The nationalist and racist historians of later in the century, Froude, Freeman, Green, etc., who more clearly owed a lot to Scott, were nevertheless Whig in Butterfield's sense. They wrote histories that were also adventures. Froude produced *A History of England from the Fall of Wolsey to the Defeat of the Spanish Armada*—a foundation epic—between 1856 and 1870; and *English Seamen in the 16th Century*—a book of heroes—in 1895. Freeman made heroes of Harold and Godwin, using the idea of the Norman yoke which Scott had employed in *Ivanhoe*. And J. R. Green described his *Short History* as a chronicle of the English people, showing their development from primitive democracy.[11]

But all this, though relevant to the larger subject of the modern world's imaginative transactions with its empire, is rather remote from Scott. Let me conclude this chapter by describing his influence on subsequent novelists, especially on historical novelists. Their number was enormous; at times in the nineteenth century, half a year's new fiction was historical. Of course not all had serious meanings, and among the serious books, not all held by Scott's ideas. But it is clear that for some years Scott was at the center of fiction as a production system, and his kind of novel promised rich rewards even to serious writers. A high point seems to be the early 1860s, as far as quality goes, when we have Flaubert's *Salâmmbo* in 1862, and George Eliot's *Romola* in 1863, and Charles Reade's *The Cloister and the Hearth* in 1861. Even in the '80s we have *John Inglesant* (1881), and *Marius the Epicurean* (1885) and the works of George Moore; but by then the influence of Scott was quite adulterated by mixture with other ideas. The big producers of historical fiction in England were of course lesser writers, such as G. P. R. James, who wrote about sixty novels, beginning with *The Life of Edward, the Black Prince* in 1822. Harrison Ainsworth (1805–1882) was closer to Dumas in style. Lytton and Kingsley, for that matter Dickens and Thackeray, wrote historical novels. R. D. Blackmore introduced a somewhat new style in 1869, with *Lorna Doone;* and Stevenson another, with *Treasure Island, Kidnapped,* and *The Master of Ballantrae.*

More important, in terms of the quality of minds shaped by Scott's influence, and as testimony to his place in the system of literature, was his imitation abroad. In the other modern system countries, writers had every incentive to become proto-Scotts, in the field of their own national history. Among the early works in France, we can list de Vigny's *Cinq-Mars* (1826), Balzac's *Les Chouans* (1829), Dumas's *Henri III et sa Cour* (1827), Mérimée's *Chronique du Règne de Charles IX,* and Hugo's *Nôtre Dame de Paris,* as early specimens from drama and fiction, not to mention the historical painters who clearly owed a lot to him. The great nineteenth-century passion of nationalism was largely shaped by such works of art. It is obvious that Scott had found a formula, which would for the time being produce a notable work every time a talented writer worked on it. (The same was true, in a less spectacular degree, of Defoe's *Tour,* and other of Defoe's nonfiction work; but in his fiction he did not fully develop his formulas.) Then in Italy we must mention Manzoni; in Germany Ebers, Hausrath, and Freytag; in Poland Mickiewicz and Sienkewicz; in Russia Tolstoy and Merezhkowski. And why did this formula work so well? Why was there this avid interest in the past for writers to tap? Because of the nationalist passion, especially in countries still struggling for independence. Because the change from the past, once rightly named, was the energizing myth of the modern system. The Scott novel could be adapted to any European public, because indirectly it celebrated the triumph of the whole white race.

Meanwhile in America, as we shall see, Cooper twisted the formula in some ways back towards Defoe, so that the material of contemporary and frontier adventure could be included. That was the privilege of the American, which other writers could only envy. And Cooper's extraordinary success in other countries, despite the manifest ineptitudes of his performance, seems to be a proof that such material had a very privileged status in the imagination of readers everywhere.

Scott and Defoe

But before turning to Cooper, I should like to sum up the development of the adventure genre so far, the transformation of motifs and themes. What is missing from Scott is the sharply modernist interest of Defoe. His stories breathe no sense of "how to do it." When they have any sense of "how things are done," it takes the form of "how *they* did it *then*"; for instance, Fergus's banquet, or Donald Bean Lean's cave life. And there is less interest in guns, weapons, explosions; these are not *our* explosions. And consequently the adventures themselves tend to be escapades, like Baron Bradwardine hidden in his hole. Such an episode does not give the reader the Defoe-sense of a practical emergency he should prepare for imaginatively since—just by virtue of his being a civilized person—it lies in wait for him.

What is obtrusively present in Scott is the formal elaboration of "literature"; the prefaces and notes, the folklore and history, the pseudonarrators and the class conventions, the archaisms and the humor. Scott is dignifying the adventure tale by making it a high genre, with large claims on our seriousness. It is very characteristic of Scott that this attempt is clearly conscious, but also self-conscious and artful—self-deprecating. This is an artificial and synthetic genre he has invented, including a love interest, a Gothic interest, a comedy of manners, high tragedy, and above all, the materials of romance; all any reader could ask for in a single book. It might even be called a pseudogenre, since the formal elaboration does not function "organically." At its best the machinery reminds one of the form Northrop Frye calls the anatomy, which is the very opposite of adventure; anatomy devices let the air out of a fictional balloon. Scott's devices don't intensify the essential feelings of his stories so much as assure the reader that he is getting a lot for his money—like the formal devices of Victorian furniture.

Above all, Scott brought into the form of the modernist adventure motifs and feelings which represented the aristomilitary caste. Their kind of heroes, their kind of virtues, their kind of exploits, their *romance*, were fitted into the framework of prudential and realistic reflection and narrative. Merchants and men at arms were brought together—and men of letters too, to begin with.

But if in those three ways Scott is very different from Defoe, and almost his antithesis as an adventure-writer, he does continue Defoe's expression of the excitement of empire and frontier in deflected form. He (and his followers in other European countries) may be said to dodge the issue, asking not "what are we doing to other forms of life," but "how did it all start?" But they were responding to the excited awareness of Europe's world triumph, the spreading dominance of the modern system. Their response was deeply deflected, but then so was Defoe's; and it was more of a response than the serious novelists made.

And one aspect of Defoe's work Scott did carry to completion and crown: he made the adventure tale into a foundation epic of England. Here one would compare him with Shakespeare rather than with Defoe. He retold the stories of British history so that they made sense for modern readers, and sense of the energizing kind. The Hanoverians were for him what the Tudors were for Shakespeare; the Rebellions of 1715 and 1745 were his Wars of the Roses; Elizabeth was his Henry IV, Mary Stuart his Richard II, Richard the Lion Heart his Henry V, and so on.

Of course there is ambivalence in Scott's piety; particularly evident in the way his story culminates in the subordination of Scotland as a necessary feature of the triumph of England. One always has to ask about Scott, whose side is he on? And the answer is always, both. Moreover, his way of being on both sides suggests moral laziness and mental cynicism rather than anything nobler. But still there is no denying that he guided the adventure tale to a higher position and a wider scope than it had before, or since. He blended into its mercantile character that aristomilitary character which the upper class of England demanded for its myths; and he took it beyond romance to epic.

V

Cooper

IN ORDER to make the transition from Scott to Cooper, we have to overcome the intellectual prejudice that there are always immense differences between England and America, in matters of both history and literature—immense distances between Empire and Frontier. In reality, the United States were just as imperialist as the English Colonies in America. The case of Daniel Boone and the invasion of Kentucky shows how local and popular, how American, the imperialist dynamic was, even before 1776. In pouring through the Cumberland Gap, and driving the Indians out of their lands, the settlers were going against the treaties and the wishes of the government in London. The frontier—not the court—was where one saw the empire in action. And American high culture, though reluctantly, followed and reflected that action. As the U.S. gradually became the leading edge of the modern system, so did its literature develop the leading form of adventure.

Frontier and Empire

The historian whose work is most useful to us in this matter is Walter Prescott Webb. In his *The Great Frontier* he analyses the relations of modern Europe with the rest of the world as a political system relating a Metropolis to a Frontier.

The term frontier, Webb points out, has meant something different in America from what it has in Europe. In the latter it has been a line between two powers, to cross which means danger; in the former, it has been an area that invites entrance and promises opportunity and riches. But this difference in usage is deceptive. Europe, without acknowledging it, has had the same experience as America, because it has had new worlds as its frontier ever since the fifteenth century. (Clearly, when Webb says Europe, he thinks of what, following Wallerstein, I have been calling its core states; and in general Wallerstein's theory refines upon Webb's usefully.) America is the most notable case, but the Boers in South Africa, and the English in Australia, etc., also lived on a frontier. The difference is that Europe's high culture kept that experience at arm's length, did not name it or know it, did not acknowledge the frontier. By the same token, moreover, America was an unnamed empire, and its experience was unacknowledgedly imperial.

When Webb calls Europe a metropolis, he means that it was a cultural center, holding within it everything pertaining to Western civilization. But he is more concerned with the frontier experience, which was opposite in character to the metropolitan, and with the legend that centered about it. The frontier, he says, wore away European and metropolitan institutions—entail, titles, primogeniture, for instance—as on an abrasive grindstone: it set men free—made them rich—made them bold. "The frontier experience from 1500 to, say, 1900 was without doubt among the most memorable adventures mankind has had in modern times. On the rim of the Metropolis, always at its yonder edge, the beacon fires of its Great Frontier was luring men outward, stirring them to mighty deeds, achievements and sacrifices. This was indeed a heroic period, heroic for the individuals and the nations involved. People love their heroic periods, make legends about them, and vaguely hope that they will come again. . . ." (p. 280). Webb seems to me to make this nostalgia too simply chronological. "Heroic periods" can be quite contemporary, as the Frontier was. The contrast is with something different, not past, and the nostalgia it evokes is for something culturally out of style, not for something literally nonexistent. But economically, in any case, it was clearly an overwhelming force, acting on the Western world as a whole.

Webb argues that the frontier was, for Europe, above all other

things, a windfall of natural resources: precious metals, furs, amber-
gris, slaves, pasturage; things that brought immediate profit or things
into which little work had to be put. And the windfall created a
boom, and the boom modified economic and political structures. He
says that most of the institutions Western man has developed since
1500 are boom-born; which means that "the modern age was an
abnormal age . . . with exceptional institutions. . . ."

This way of naming the excitements of Empire makes us realize
that they are to be found on the frontier as much as in the metropolis.
The modern empire has not meant so much a scepter and an orb as
a rifle and an axe, and Natty Bumppo embodied those excitements
better than George III. This should remind us of the extraordinary
response, all across Europe, to *Robinson Crusoe*. That was a response
to the new kind of empire. And observers at the right distance saw
the identity of that empire with frontier. Alexander Herzen habitually coupled the images of Crusoe and Natty, to name a single
concept, the free spirit, the man creating his own life, modifying the
conditions of nature, and rejecting the conditions of civilization. And
the social-political consequences of releasing this free spirit in the
citizens of the core states were empire.

After 1500, Western man's condition improved, Webb says, not
in a moderate way, but extraordinarily. But around 1830 the land-
population ratio, for Europe and its frontier together (that is, for the
modern system) reached the same level it had been at in 1500 for
Europe alone; that is, about twenty-seven persons per square mile.
The rate of expansion began to slow down, although it took a long
time for the full effects of the arrest to show themselves.

Historians have criticized Webb's theory quite severely, on the
grounds that he does not know in sufficient detail what the complicated economic relations of Metropolis and Frontier actually were.
And I myself would say that in literature, Europe's sense of its
frontier was significantly different from America's, and so the American word can be used for the colonies only metaphorically in literary
studies. Nevertheless, that metaphorical use of the word seems to me
brilliantly illuminating, for one striking difference between literature
(and high culture generally) in England, and literature in America,
is that the latter made much more of the frontier experience and the
boom. There were many justifying reasons for that difference. But it
may be possible to say, as a generalization, that England's indiffer-

ence to, or undisturbedness by, what was happening on its frontier, amounted to a falsity, and falsified the values her high culture was enunciating.

The great virtue of Webb's theory is to suggest an analogy between American experience and British, and so a propriety in holding up British literature against the model of American—and against American real life. If we look at Robinson Crusoe as being a first cousin to Daniel Boone, we shall be struck by new features of the way Defoe presents him. And we shall better understand Natty Bumppo, too, for American studies also will benefit from breaking down the false isolation in which they have so long worked. *Robinson Crusoe* is, as John Seelye has pointed out, the true archetype of much American as well as English fiction.

Cooper's Books

In Cooper we find an exaggerated version of Scott's posture (his blending of the aristocratic style with the mercantile) set in a cultural situation which makes that posture seem eccentric to begin with. The American situation was much more hostile than the English to anything aristocratic. For that reason, Cooper in his forest tales chose an aggressively unaristocratic and unmilitary hero; but tried to make him answer to the aspirations, satisfy the sensibility, *represent*, his own aristomilitary caste. It was an absurd project, and the debris of literary disaster is everywhere in those tales; and yet the ruins are impressive.

Cooper's father was a self-made man, or rather a self-made aristocrat, as we shall see. And Cooper himself was a military man, in the American navy; imaginatively though not literally a captain. Those were the two determining experiences of his imaginative life; partly because they were not approved as determining experiences by official American culture. Thus he had a special vocation to speak, as novelist, for the aristomilitary caste. He had to defy the overreaching claims of the mercantile mind, but at the same time to conciliate American culture—to make his own caste the favorite son of the American imagination.

Within Cooper's writings, the Leatherstocking Tales are what most concern us, and within them, Leatherstocking himself. They, and above all he, mark the next great stage in the growth of the WASP adventure tale and adventure hero. Taking them in the order of their publication, we have *The Pioneers* (1823), *The Last of the Mohicans* (1826), *The Prairie* (1827), and *The Pathfinder* (1840) and *The Deerslayer* (1841). Taking them in the order of Natty Bumppo's biography, the first is last and the last is first; and we also find a change in the mode of his depiction, from realism to romance. As indeed their respective titles indicate, the first published book is more "about" the beginnings of American society, while the last, though describing a much earlier historical period, feels less distant in time —because it relates to those beginnings only symbolically. A change from realism to romance sounds like a change from Defoe to Scott. But in fact Cooper showed very little sense of, or awareness of, Defoean realism, even in *The Pioneers*. That unDefoean quality is, I think one may say, Cooper's greatest weakness as a writer of modernist romance—his feeble interest in fact and process, and his flimsy caterings to our interest in them. He was very heavily influenced by Scott; from beginning to end, one needs nothing more than Scott's varying styles to explain all the variations amongst Cooper's fictional forms. The difference between *The Pioneers* and *The Deerslayer* is rather that between *Waverley* and *Ivanhoe* than that between *Waverley* and *Crusoe*.

In his Preface to the Leatherstocking Tales, Cooper says that his hero is a man "with little of civilization but its highest principles as exhibited in the uneducated; and all of savagery not incompatible with those great rules of conduct." The complicated phrasing obscures the meaning, and is perhaps related to the paradox in the idea itself—to the elements of self-contradiction in Cooper's enterprise. Natty is a savage, except that he has the highest principles of civilization, in simple form. As such he represents both the best of what Cooper sees around him, and the direction in which America *should* move—a direction which is only one option among many facing the country and indeed one already losing out to the others.

In both ways Cooper is pointing out the American ideal to readers who are presumed to feel themselves very remote from it—from Natty; not necessarily because they are not Americans; just being a reader of novels is enough to ensure that you are of a class to whom Natty must be a very strange figure. When he is first described,

Cooper stresses Natty's *coarse* physique, his skinny body, lank sandy hair, enormous mouth, single tooth; and his flannel underwear, his silent and ironical laugh, and his wiping his nose with his hand. All those traits are in marked contrast with those of Gilbert Stuart's portraits, for example; those pink, plump, smooth faces, every detail of physique and costume "finished" as if by a salon. That is what Cooper's readers thought they saw in each other, I would suggest. And in fact, Stuart painted just such a portrait of William Cooper, the novelist's father, who is depicted as Judge Temple in the first novel, and who is the civilized, reading American, as contrasted with Natty.

In *The Pioneers,* Natty represents natural law, and so finds himself in conflict with Judge Temple, who represents civil law; both are indignant against various kinds of waste endemic in the frontier community; but the Judge fights that with regulations which Natty feels are an infringement on personal liberty. The situation is richly symbolic, and the theme of waste, the spoliation of natural resources, is a very valuable extension of the subject matter of modernist romance. So is the conflict between law and individual liberty—both are typical of American experience, of the Frontier as opposed to the Empire; the English, in India or Africa, did not experience those problems half so acutely. But of the two, the first, waste, is felt by Cooper more deeply and originally.

Another such theme is the Indian tribes (represented by Chingachgook), in treating which Cooper employs motifs already familiar to us. In his passion and pride, and in his loyalty to Natty, Chingachgook is a Black Prince of the kind we met in Defoe and Scott. In this book, however, the Prince is degenerated into Indian John for most of the time, ruined by addiction to drink and by being uprooted. His death too is related to the conflict between his people and the whites, and is caused by the symbolic means of an explosion of gunpowder. At the end of the novel, Natty declares his intention to leave the settlement for the wilderness. The Judge's daughter, Elizabeth, goes up the mountain to take Natty a canister of powder as a farewell gift (his rifle, bullet mold, and powder keg are his constant accoutrements). Not finding Natty, she gives them to Chingachgook, who promises to hand them over but says, "This is the great enemy of my nation. Without this, when could the white man drive the Delawares? [sic] Daughter, the Great Spirit gave your fathers to know how to make guns and powder, that they might sweep the Indians from the land" (p. 418). A fire breaks out on the mountain, surrounds Chingachgook, and the powder explodes, wounding him fatally.

Such gunpowder explosions are to be found in Defoe, but the very parallels demonstrate how remote Cooper is from the spirit of Defoe; the mechanism of his explosion is so theatrical—a whole mountain set ablaze to get one spark into a canister of powder—and so implausible—if Chingachgook was being showered with sparks, surely he would put the can down? And how could it happen that the fire, having been about to consume him, retreated as soon as he was killed? Cooper's indifference to these questions (even if there are answers to them, it is fatal to arouse such questions) shows his failure to grasp something essential in modernist romance.

And indeed the central plot of *The Pioneers* is not modernist-adventurous but chivalrous-romantic. Its theme is the legitimation of the Temples' post-Revolution possession of the land, which used to belong to a family named Effingham when the colony was under British rule. The Temples are legitimized by inheritance and marriage; Elizabeth Temple marries Oliver Effingham, and the long-lost Major Effingham turns up out of hiding at the end to bless the union. The mechanism of the plot also is all romance—disguises, concealments, and mysteries; and there even seems to be a network of allusions to *As You Like It* (the "usurping" Temple is called Duke —short for Marmaduke; the inheriting Effingham is called Oliver, the old major is called a king, and there is a banishment and a forest and so on). Indeed the legitimation of an American aristocracy—by aristocratic and romantic means of legitimation—is one of Cooper's concerns in other books. He was always writing chivalric romances almost as much as modernist adventures, and he was not skillful at combining the two sets of conventions.

The Last of the Mohicans takes place at the time of the wars against the French and the Indians. Its basic story-motif is one we can identify with Cooper in general, the group-flight—something distinct from the group-quest in *Captain Singleton*. At first, Major Duncan Heyward is guiding Cora and Alice Munro to meet their father, with the help of Magua, the Mohawk scout; but Magua turns out to be a treacherous Mingo in reality, and the journey becomes a flight. This book also introduces another motif that was to be very important in frontier romance, that of the-fate-worse-than-death.

Cooper

The idea that the forest (or other such environment in another novel)
is bristling with savages lusting for a white woman, who will subject
her to the unspeakable if the white man's vigilance lapses for a
moment, is a very powerful motor for this sort of romance—and for
white race-consciousness outside literature. Obviously it is parallel to
the fear of cannibalism which Defoe made much of; this adds the
manifold energizing force of explicit sex. Cooper derives it from the
captivity narratives, so popular in America, beginning with Mrs.
Rowlandson's; the white woman, abducted and then imprisoned by
a screaming horde, becomes the ark of the covenant for white men.
But it is worth considering that serious fiction in England had also
made use of a similar motif of abduction, in Richardson and his
successors.[1] Cooper does not owe anything to Richardson directly,
but insofar as he inherited the romance pattern from Scott, he benefited from Richardson's work. Cooper brought together these two
strands of Puritan sexual melodrama, one with the prestige of polite
fiction, the other with the power of frontier racism. In this story sex
and death are closely linked; above all, miscegenatory lust is fearfully
punished. Chingachgook is accompanied by his son, Uncas, a good
Indian. Magua lusts after Cora; but Uncas modestly loves her. When
Uncas and Cora are both captured and tortured by Magua, Natty
offers himself as a sacrificial captive in exchange for her. A savage kills
Cora; Uncas kills him; Magua kills him; Natty kills him.

In *The Prairie* the-fate-worse-than-death is again prominent. Ines
is the dainty and delicate prisoner of Ishmael Bush and his sons—
a coarse-grained crew—but she is in no danger of rape from them.
It is the lust of the Indians she arouses, and with barely controllable
intensity. Even Hard-Heart the Pawnee, a good Indian, cannot take
his eyes off her. "Nothing so fair, so ideal, so every way worthy to
reward the courage and self-devotion of a warrior, had ever before
been encountered on the prairies" (p. 268). Mahtoree, a bad Indian,
tells his favorite wife to look at Ines, and then at her own reflection;
the effect is instantaneous; the wife takes off her ornaments, and
hands them, and her baby, to Ines. Ines is a heroine of civilization,
of progress; with her "intellectual and nearly infantile beauty," she
embodies a degree of sexual differentiation, and produces a pitch of
sexual-moral excitement, undreamed of by more primitive races.
Other white women are defined in terms of their coarseness compared to her, and the ultimate opposite are the withered and remorse-

less crones of the Indians, who mock and torture white captives. (The active and working women to be found in primitive societies are always a focus of horror for the novelists in this tradition.)

Another motif in this novel is the physical size of white Americans of the frontier states; size being closely related to atavism and degeneracy. The Bushes are Tennesseean, and are described as colossal, vast, gigantic, and so on. Ishmael is dull and listless, his face's lower features coarse, extended and vacant, the nobler parts low, receding, and mean. His costume is motley and gaudy, with a sash, three watches, silver buttons, silver-plated knife and rifle. His sons are indolent and inert, sullenly resistant to authority, ideas, education, and politeness. Among the Bushes even family feeling has dried up —their moral substance all transmuted into physical.[2]

This idea of the size of frontiersmen powerfully struck the American imagination; men like James Hall and Timothy Flint commented on the size of first Virginians, then Tennesseeans, then Kentuckians, as the frontier moved west and south.[3] And the idea of degeneration on the frontier was also to be found, for instance in Crèvecoeur's *Letters of an American Farmer.* But the two ideas are not usually combined, and Cooper's combination of them has a very disconcerting effect. Literarily it is a striking effect, but largely because it is out of place, as it were out of date—it would be in place in Frank Norris. It derives, presumably, from Cooper's profound dividedness. His Americanism was no stronger than his conservatism, and the spectacle of these huge new men struck him mainly with dismay. He contrasts them with Natty, the good American, but the contrast is ineffective. The difference between the two is fictionally uninteresting, and its didactic message is more dismal than Cooper intended. Natty dies in the course of this novel, and leaves no heir; he was the last, indeed, the only, one of his kind. It is the Bushes who are destined to breed, and settle the country, in their wasteful and destructive way. And one day, says Natty, "They will turn on their tracks like a fox that doubles, and then the rank smell of their footsteps will show them the madness of their waste" (p. 79). With such a vision, how can Cooper be an Americanist?

In the last two novels the religious and moral note of warning grows stronger, and conflicts even more with the adventure dynamic. Natty, who is now thirty-two years old, says on page 20 of *The Pathfinder,* "They that live in the settlements and the towns have

Cooper

confined and unjust opinions concerning the might of His hand; but we, who pass our time in His very presence, as it might be, see things differently. . . ." He thinks sadly of the men killed in the recent wars. "Generals and privates, they lay scattered throughout the land, so many proofs of what men are when led on by love of great names and the wish to be more than their fellows. . . . 'If you think I pass my days in warfare against my kind, you know neither me nor my history. . . . No, no; bloodshed and warfare are not my real gifts, but peace and mercy. . . .' " (p. 86). But he is a scout. "My real calling is to hunt for the army, on its marches and in times of peace" (p. 86). What scope does *this* give him to exercise his "real gifts"? We are bound to think of Defoe's William.

And when in Chapter 27 Natty tells of being morally tempted three times, the last and worst was when he found six Mingoes asleep and could have killed them. He overcame the temptation; but this means that he waited till they awoke, then peppered them with shot till only one limped home—Chingachgook having scalped the rest.

Yet Natty is clearly presented as a religious and moral hero in this book. When at the end Mabel Dunham appeals for peace "in the name of our holy religion," Natty endorses her plea with his forest wisdom. He's not been personally Christianized by the Moravians, but he respects them, and says, "I'm in church now; I eat in church, drink in church, sleep in church. The earth is the temple of the Lord, and I wait on him hourly, daily, without ceasing, I humbly hope" (p. 402). We are told that "His feelings appeared to possess the freshness and nature of the forest in which he passed so much of his time; and no casuist could have made clearer decisions in matters relating to right and wrong" (p. 121). And this was of course a powerful idea in American culture. Jefferson had said, in his *Notes on Virginia,* "State a case to a ploughman and a professor. The former will decide it as well, and often better than the latter, because he has not been led astray by artificial rules." That myth persisted for a long time to come. Even F. J. Turner, so much later, said, "Political wisdom is not sealed up in books and parchments. It welled up in the forests, like waters from the hillside." But Natty's claims to moral wisdom are concentrated in his manner. His actual behavior is that of a killer.

And in *The Deerslayer,* there is again talk of how Natty's sweetheart is in the forest; like his religious life, his love life is not differentiated or defined in the way that other men's are. He lives in a

138

prelapsarian innocence, in which all things merge. The price of this is his inability to choose any one creed or any one woman. In this story he is chosen by Judith Hutter, but declines. All of which amounts to a pretty total disability, in a hero of adventure. He is the victim of his author's ambivalence. Critics have often spoken of Natty's renunciations, but it is of course Cooper who has on Natty's behalf renounced all sorts of definite action for him, except self-sacrifice—in this novel, as in *The Pathfinder*, he voluntarily surrenders himself to wicked Indians. Insofar as he does act aggressively, he has to apologize immediately after, because such actions are not in accordance with his beliefs.

This book tells the story of how Natty came of age, by going on his first warpath; how he kills a man. This is greeted with joy by all his friends and acquaintances, but he himself cannot take any satisfaction in it. The novelist has to engage in a lot of aesthetic casuistry to provide him with an occasion on which he *can* kill someone; and then Natty engages in a lot of moral casuistry to justify the act. Later in *The Deerslayer* he is first given his famous rifle, and displays his prowess by shooting an eagle; but must descant immediately on why he shouldn't have done that. And it is this paradox which has such fatal aesthetic consequences; the action is intolerably slow because each action has to be elaborately prepared for and retroactively justified; and Natty, though described as silent, talks incessantly, because he has to rationalize everything he does. He's a moral hero who performs immoral acts, so his moral life has to be all in his speeches. And at the end of the book, with the rescue of the whites, comes the official slaughter, for which Natty was clearly the outrunner.

And though there is usually no profit in dwelling on an author's failings, in this case it is necessary to insist—since literary critics have often argued or implied the opposite—that these are very bad adventure tales. Moreover, Cooper's failure is interesting, because he was perfectly capable of writing a decent adventure, as his sea-novels show. In the forest stories he fails to adapt the Scott formula to the conditions of the frontier—the operatic conventions with which he handles his heroines, for instance, fundamentally conflict with any realistic sense of where they are and what they are doing. One must put some of this down to personal literary ineptitude, but it still remains puzzling, because he did so much better with other fictional problems. One is bound to suspect that the root of his difficulty lies in Natty; in the paradox of the American hero, a man who derives his moral principles from the Moravians, but achieves his manhood as a killer.

This, however, may be the place to say that Cooper's difficulties are typical of the problems of American writers in the nineteenth century; Melville's problems with, notably, *Moby Dick,* Whitman's with verse form, Twain's with the novel. All of these are genre problems, and derive from the fact that the genres (the code of the system of literature) which America inherited from England were not adapted to the imaginative material forced on her writers by her frontier experience (which irresistibly established itself as her essential experience). That maladaptation was in part cultural; the new material was associated with cultural attitudes which were hostile to gentility, and so to "literature-as-a-system." That system continued to dominate critics and publishers, and the book-buyers who put down the money for novels and poems. But it was badly at odds with the imaginative experience that pressed upon the writers, and which was in certain ways formless. That is, it existed only in minor forms —pungent dialectical anecdotes—forms outside the system, and hostile to it, in just the way the Indian tribes, and to some degree the frontiersmen, were outside the political and economic system. However, we are concerned only with Cooper's version of this problem.

Cooper inherited these conflicts, along with a strong filial pride and affection, from his father, William Cooper, the founder of Cooperstown, New York. He was one of the most energetic and successful promoters of new settlements in eighteenth-century America. He published in 1782 a do-it-yourself *Guide in the Wilderness,* and moved his own family to central New York State in 1790. William was something of a Crusoe figure, but one who had, by the time his son knew him, risen to be a gentleman, to belong to the aristocratic caste.

James Fenimore Cooper had a great admiration for his father and everything he represented. He must surely have thought of him when, in *Wyandotte,* he says, "There is a pleasure in diving into a virgin forest and commencing the labours of civilization, that has no exact parallel in any other human occupation . . . [it] approaches nearer to the feeling of creating, and is far more pregnant with anticipation and hopes, though its first effects are seldom agreeable, and are sometimes nearly hideous" (p. 42). William Cooper was, like

Judge Temple in *The Pioneers*, born a Quaker, but became an Episcopalian and a Federalist—an American aristocrat. He was the lord of his manor, a modified patroon, and died violently in 1809, at the age of fifty-five, killed by a blow from behind by an opponent at a public meeting.

William Cooper came to own tens of thousands of acres, but continued to assert himself against his opponents by means of direct physical contact, as well as by the socially privileged means of law and wealth. He would wrestle with, after arguing with, those who disagreed with him; on occasion challenging all comers, and promising to give 100 acres to anyone who could throw him. In *The Pioneers*, Judge Temple is placed in opposition to Natty the true hero; the Judge has renounced his Quakerism (as so many did during the War of Independence) and become a judge, a man of wealth, and so on. Natty is a kind of shadow self for Temple/Cooper, more really and primitively American, one who embodies all that other men have renounced. He moves off at the book's end to a purer life:—"I'm weary of living in clearings, and where the hammer is sounding in my ears from sunrise to sundown" (p. 473). But as Natty's fictional career works itself out—in response to Cooper's experience of America over nearly twenty years—it becomes clear that Natty too is living against his principles as much as Judge Temple—that to be "really American" was no escape.

By his marriage to Susan DeLancey, James Fenimore Cooper moved even further inside the American aristocracy. The DeLanceys had owned vast estates before the Revolution, and owned them by the patroon system of land tenure. Even after the Revolution they still owned a good deal of Westchester County in New York State, described by Robert Spiller as the most aristocratic bit of American soil in those days. So that Cooper became by marriage a sort of thirteenth-century English baron, to use Spiller's formula.

It is therefore not surprising that he was full of the pride of caste. And it is worth noting how conscious and clear he was about what caste meant. In *The Chainbearer*, the hero says, "I had got the notions of my caste, obtained in the silent, insinuating manner in which all our characters are formed. . . ." (p. 188). His was, of course, the aristomilitary caste. And he defines a gentleman at some length. The most general idea is that a gentleman is a man who will not stoop to meannesses, and Cooper is ready to develop that idea in distinction

from other, more "Christian" ideas of morality. The gentleman
". . . is truthful out of self-respect, and not in obedience to the will
of God; free with his money, because liberality is an essential feature
of his habits, and not in imitation of the self-sacrifice of Christ;
superior to scandal and the vices of the busybody, inasmuch they are
low and impair his pride of character . . ." (p. 172). One of Cooper's
major themes is the fate of this caste in America, a country which
dedicated itself so definitely to the modern system and the mercantile
caste.

But I must revert to structuralist criticism. Essentially, Cooper
adapted Scott's formula to a frontier condition, and to a sense of
distance that was as much geographical as historical. That phrase
suggests a return to Defoe, but there is little in Cooper's way of
handling geography that is Defoean. However, his way has its own
intermittent grandeur. Its sweep is enormous, in physical and historical geography. The Introduction to *The Prairie* begins "The geologi-
cal formation of that portion of the American Union . . ." and invokes
the largest scientific categories. Moreover, Chapter I relates the story
to come to the Louisiana Purchase, and all American history. However, there is one really striking change away from Scott toward
Defoe, in the character of the hero, away from being an observer-
participant, to being a man of action. Natty *is* much closer to Crusoe
than Waverley was. The action in question, moreover, is of Defoe's
kind, insofar as Natty does everything with his own hands and a few
essential modern-system tools, mostly the rifle and the axe, and a few
techniques in woodcraft. (On the other hand, Cooper being a philosophical novelist, Natty embodies a touch of sadness, a sense of
failure, unthinkable in Crusoe.)

There is nothing in Natty to make one think that Cooper had been
reading Defoe, but it is undeniable that Natty is much the same
figure as Crusoe. There are artist's drawings of the one that could be
used to illustrate the book about the other; the rifle, the fur cap, the
leggings, the knife. If we take Defoe's geographical axis as a horizontal line, and Scott's historical axis as a vertical, it would be possible
to represent Cooper's axis as a line bisecting the 90° angle between
the two.

Natty is another do-it-yourself hero, who earns his power over our
imaginations by commanding our participation and making us believe he in fact does solve problems we would be unable to. Cooper

being such a fictional blunderer, we often refuse Natty our participation, but when we yield, it is of this kind, and not of the kind we give to Waverley. And it is time to admit, also, that Natty commands us in some other remoter way, not when we are actually reading about him, but when we think about him at a distance from the text. After all, if Natty gave Cooper fictional difficulties he didn't meet elsewhere, he also gave Cooper his greatest fictional success. It is Natty he is famous for, and when one reads the tributes of remarkable men of letters, but when also one consults one's own experience, one can see why. Fictional characters, fictional subjects in general, can have a vitality and power which is independent of the normal criteria of realization in fictional terms. That happens—in this case at least—when a writer has linked together a number of powerful ideas which stay linked and stay powerful in our minds, despite the ineptitude of dialogue, action, characterization, etc.

Of course the power I am attributing to Natty, if unearned by fictional realization, *is* earned by Cooper's general impressiveness as a writer and thinker—and to some extent by his mere reputation. Those powerful ideas were linked together in our minds by the name of Natty partly because we were forced to read Cooper and not someone else.

Otherwise, I suspect, we would be more moved by Nathan Slaughter in R. M. Bird's *Nick of the Woods*, 1837, a much better adventure tale. Nathan is a bloody Quaker of a much fiercer kind than Natty—or than Defoe's William; and most of the themes of the frontier novel are better rendered. There is for instance a family of large Kentuckians called Bruce—of colossal stature, like Cooper's Bushes; and the proportions of their frame are "as just as they were gigantic"; with the same "lounging indifference of carriage, and something like awkwardness or uncouthness . . . but real native majesty." Bird's apter realization of the idea is evident in Mr. Bruce's commendation of his son as coming from the best stock in Kentucky for loving women or fighting Injuns; the boy took his first Shawnee scalp before he was fourteen. Cooper is too genteel to give us that sort of tone, and therefore too genteel for this sort of story. The same contrast holds true of the two representations of Western humorous boasting; by Cooper in Paul Hover (in *The Prairie*) and by Bird in Ralph Stackpole. The latter leaps, howls, boasts, cavorts, with much more power. And Bird himself enters into the spirit of farce much more completely. When Stackpole is thrown at wrestling, "his heels were suddenly seen flying in the air, his head aiming at the earth, upon which it as suddenly descended with the violence of a bombshell; and there it would doubtless have burrowed, like the aforesaid instrument of destruction, had the soil been soft enough for that purpose, or exploded into a thousand fragments. . . ." (p. 77). Bird here participates in that Western humor (which continued down to Disney) which Cooper was far too stiff to capture.

But, as I said, Cooper was to achieve his greatest fictional successes in nautical fiction. His forest adventures he never imagined with any intensity, and they are realistically implausible; while the way people talk and behave, especially the women, is generically inappropriate, because he has not imagined the genre either. He has mixed up drawing-room diction and gestures, and theater entries and exits, with the evocation of endless rolling plains and virgin woods. (In *The Prairie* Hard-Heart leaps into our view out of undergrowth that is palpably a stage trap, and exits—across the dreary and interminable plains—as if slamming a door.) But in the sea-novels, though there are lapses with the women characters, Cooper clearly knows and loves the medium of the adventure, and consequently his imagination does not stumble and flounder over plot and episode. One might take as an example of his success there, his vivid rendering of the personality of ships, their characteristic lines and movements, their human and usually feminine personalities.

One explanation of that superiority is biographical. Cooper became a midshipman as a teenager and mastered that world of experience for himself, while his experience of the forest and the frontier came to him via his father. It seems that he met only decrepit and degenerate Indians himself, and the frontier history of Cooperstown was something he knew only by anecdote. Ships he discovered for himself, and he found a ship's severely hierarchical and yet practically egalitarian social structure very congenial.

I find such an explanation quite convincing, but it leaves us facing the paradox that the sea-novels are not rated so highly—and are not in fact so interesting—as the badly flawed forest-novels. The reason for that, I believe, lies deep in the cultural history of America.

To put it briefly, after 1850 the American imagination turned decisively toward the West and the continent. But though that may explain Natty Bumppo's later reputation, it cannot explain his creation; the Leatherstocking stories had been written before that, at a time when in his essays Cooper was still declaring that America was not an agricultural but a maritime nation. Perhaps those declarations had always expressed a wish rather than an observation. As a sea-power, America could have a less threatening future greatness than as a land-power, precisely because great land-powers were empires; the British empire was sea-based, and Cooper and Americans like him implicitly exempted Britain from the infamy generally attached to "Empire." It was Austria and Russia, and France under Napoleon, that were empires in the opprobrious sense. England was essentially a trading nation, and the home of liberty, which is what America should become.

That belief, I think, explains the reluctance of Cooper's imagination to accept Natty as the agent for America's westward advance. That was the wrong direction, geographically, politically, imaginatively. ". . . the tide of emigration, which has been so long flowing westward, must have its reflux . . ." (*Notions*, p. 48). But that reluctance, that conflict of feelings and sense of doom, though it made the craftsman in Cooper so clumsy, made the artist in him rise above himself, because it generated intensity. Natty's first and last appearances in *The Prairie*, his two sunset hilltop scenes—once one knows he is in effect barring the way to the west, warning the whites back—have an intensity which nothing in the sea fiction can match.[4]

Cooper's Reputation

In the case of Cooper, some study of his reception and reputation is especially rewarding, because his readers' response was both vivid and also expressed in terms close to those of this study. For instance, W. H. Gardiner's review of the very early novel, *The Spy*, in the *North American Review* in 1822, included advice to Cooper on how to write "an American novel." The advice was very sympathetic to Cooper, in both senses; and in fact Cooper followed it. Gardiner told him to stress the sectional variety of American society (to replace the class variety of Europe, which Scott had at his disposal); and to choose subjects from the settlement period, the Indian wars and the revolutionary wars; and to celebrate the American landscape—which he should describe "with that deep moral feeling that unites the soul to beauty and breathes its own freshness and fragrance." And in fact, Cooper went on to write five novels about the revolutionary wars, and six about the Indian wars, and stressed sectional variety and landscape in exactly that way.

Gardiner was a friend of Prescott, one of the Brahmin intellectuals; and despite Cooper's prejudice against New England, he and they were on the same side culturally, being all representatives of the "responsible" class in America, the reading class. (I mean those who felt themselves responsible for America's values and cultural images.) Cooper's project was recognized, in its very earliest manifestation, as a group project in that sense, and was promoted and cooperated in by his readers.

Cooper was very successful with that class. *The Spy* went through three editions in six months, *The Pioneers* sold 3,500 copies the day after publication, and *The Pilot*'s edition of 3,000 was quickly exhausted. He was unpopular with reviewers after 1830, but this was for political reasons. (They attacked him ostensibly for introducing political ideas into his romances, but their antagonism owed more to their belonging to the opposite party to him.) Cooper took Horace Greeley and four other newspapermen to court for libel. And between 1840 and 1851, when he published sixteen novels, only four were reviewed. But this was less significant than it might seem. His sales were as high in those years as they had been in the 1820s. One guesses that this was because the people who bought his books, the responsible class, were independent of the opinions of newspapers, who directed themselves to a different audience.

We should not identify this responsible class with "advanced" literary opinions or taste. They were not responsive to, for instance, writers like Edgar Allan Poe. Poe never sold anything like as well as Cooper, and he has an interesting essay of 1843 in which he reflects on that fact. Poe says that the interest readers take in Cooper "has no reference to plot, but to theme, a Robinson-Crusoe-like detail, and the figure of the half-civilized Indian. The theme—life in the wilderness—is one of intrinsic and universal interest; appealing to the heart of man in all phases; success or popularity is, with such a subject, expected as a matter of course. So also is life at sea. . . ." (*Fenimore Cooper: the Critical Heritage*, p. 208). Here one sees the conscience of literature considering the adventure tale, and condemning it for its spiritual commonplaceness, its subservience to the dominant interests of the culture. One might say that Poe is to Cooper as Coleridge is to Scott, and Swift to Defoe, though I am not aware of a comparable intensity of antagonism. He continues, "There are two classes of fiction, the popular, read with pleasure but without admiration—in which the Author is lost or forgotten . . ." This is Cooper's; and such fiction merely feeds a well-established appetite. ". . . and then a class . . . in which, at every paragraph, arises a distinct and highly pleasurable interest, springing from our perception and appreciation of the skill employed, or the genius evinced in the composition. After perusal of one class, we think solely of the book—after reading the other, chiefly of the author. The former class leads to popularity—the latter to fame" (p. 208). He names Hawthorne, Simms, and Charles Brockden Brown in the latter class—and thinks almost certainly of himself, too. What is most striking in those remarks for us is their candor—their attribution of egotism, and thirst for fame, to his own party, the men of literature. This is the point of view we must adopt in order to study this story of the conflicts between literature and the adventure tale.

Other essays also bring out the strong alliance between Cooper and the men of action—the party of action in American culture. A review of 1827 speaks of "this naked and masculine power" and says of the author, "A sailor, and an American, he has had noble opportunities of forming an acquaintance with her [Nature], and nobly has he used them! He is not her poet, but her secretary and copyist . . . compared to him, our poets are freshwater sailors, who know nothing of the matter; he alone gives us the plain but mighty truth" (p. 121). And in 1842 William Gilmore Simms wrote that we are interested in Cooper's hero (he is talking about *The Pilot*) "by the fact that he promises nothing, yet goes to work, without a word, in a manner that promises everything. . . . He shows the capacity for work, and this constitutes the sort of manhood upon which all men rely in moments of doubt and danger . . . with ship and man we grow fascinated beyond all measure of ordinary attraction. . . ." Hawkeye he finds the same as the Pilot; a figure of self-reliance; clearly Simms sees both Cooper's heroes as heirs to or versions of Robinson Crusoe, as distinct from other fictional heroes—and distinct by being more manly. We do not love such heroes but admire them in their progress through sea and forest. "But *manhood,* true manhood, is a sight, always, of wondrous beauty and magnificence" (pp. 222–223).

It is in Cooper that we see most clearly in literature the close alliance ever potential in American culture, between manhood, adventure, and national destiny. And America was the model state of the modern world system, acting out its collective dream. Cooper, as the voice of America, was extremely popular in Europe, and translated into almost every language. Between 1820 and 1853 there were 105 German translations of individual works of his, and five collected editions; while in France, Gosselin brought out thirty volumes of the *Works of Fenimore Cooper* between 1836 and 1852. He was often set by French writers in political antithesis to Scott. Scott was seen as the celebrant of the feudal past, Cooper of the modern world system. A review of 1827 made him the emblem of everything which Europe and the Bourbons had denied. And a review signed F. A. S. in *Le Globe,* in the same year (June 19 and July 2) said, "We do not see much resemblance between the entirely new culture portrayed by the republican author, and the feudal customs which the Scotch baronet has exhumed from old chronicles" (p. 127).

Scott, the writer says, has no moral idea except the Voltairean ideal of tolerance, based on indifference and skepticism; while Cooper is full of moral energy, because he sees a moral society around him— the most reasonably constructed society in the world. It is true that America's population is divided into two colors, and that the whites hold the reds in bondage. "And yet, everywhere in America one senses a spirit of enterprise, of braving all obstacles, of pursuing one's fortune over the seas and through the wilderness." Cooper's books are a magnificent epic of the wilderness (while a French treatment of similar themes, like Chateaubriand's *Atala,* is only a work of the imagination). "On the borders of the wilderness and civilization, hosts of pioneers are rolling back the limits of the wilderness, men strongly shaped by these two influences, men who combine the vices and virtues of these two opposing orders. And in the depths of the wilderness, there is a race of men almost unknown, generous and ferocious, crafty and brave, independent and savage, despoiled of a dominion formerly their own, beaten down but never enslaved, a race for whom the light of civilization has never been anything but a devouring fire. . . ." (p. 127).

One sees there how completely the response to Cooper is part of a response to America. The critic is quite blind to what seems so vivid to us—the military caste-character of Cooper's images. But it is still a response—a marvelously intelligent one—to the books. It describes Hawkeye as embodying the first dream of Rousseau, the natural man, and Hawkeye's problems as dramatizing the conflicts between that and Rousseau's second dream, the social contract. The point couldn't be better made.

French criticism continued to be particularly illuminating during another quarter century. (Russian criticism of Cooper is also very interesting, but that will be discussed in the next chapter.) Balzac knew Cooper's work very well, and admired it; and George Sand, in 1856, named Cooper and Scott as the two great poets of the middle class. "They have no grudge against God, or society; no eccentricities, no sacred joys like Shakespeare and Byron" (p. 262). This is a point of view close to Poe's, but more generous. "The foundation of their power is this wisdom, this doggedness, this apparent simple good-heartedness which characterizes industrial society and practical education" (pp. 262–263). She recognizes them as spokesmen for the modern world system; at a moment when, in France, nearly all serious writers were already turned against it. She sees Cooper as an American hero, to whom America owes as much as to Franklin and Washington; but also as a tragic hero—because of the tragic history of American power; "This fateful situation of a power acquired at the cost of suffering, murder, and fraud, pricked his heart with a deep philosophical remorse" (p. 263). But after this decade of the 1850s, Cooper dropped down from the serious level to the popular in France.

In America, too, this happened after 1852, when Cooper died. The note struck in that year by the contributors to the Cooper memorial was most strikingly a stress on his manliness. His novels contained an elixir of the qualities needed by men of action—and other adventure writers were linked to him in that. In an essay in *North American Review,* Jan. 1852, Parkman said that Cooper and Scott were "both practical men, able and willing to grapple with the hard realities of the world. Either might have learned with ease to lead a regiment, or command a line of battle ship. His readers are not persons of sedentary and studious habits but of a more active turn, military officers and the like, whose tastes have not been trained into fastidiousness. . . ." (p. 252). Cooper deals with realities, whereas Bulwer Lytton and Hawthorne never cheat us into a belief in the reality of their conceptions. This manly realism was what the New Englanders took from him. R. H. Dana said how he and all his friends were stirred by *The Spy* when it came out, and how immediately they connected the book with the man who wrote it. Parkman said the books were his boyhood friends, and influenced his own choice of career and work. Prescott said Cooper's books were "instinct with the spirit of nationality."

Dana and Parkman are especially interesting as representatives of that "responsible class" who actually sought out adventures, and then wrote them out, in the spirit that Cooper had implicitly recommended. (This responsible class adventurism seems to have been more American than English; one might point to Borrow and Brooke as comparable English cases, but their books don't convey the same sense that these men felt their caste challenged.) In Dana's and Parkman's books, we see both the individuals and their class asserting a leadership in modern system affairs, on the strength of a capacity for adventure. Theirs was a class which American history was forcing to assume the posture of the aristomilitary caste, despite a powerful heritage of quite opposite character.

The Brahmins of New England, who had always felt themselves the enemies of English aristocrats, were now feeling themselves much more the enemy of the frontiersmen of the West of their own country; and so in need of a strenuous manliness. R. H. Dana, who was born in 1815 and entered Harvard in 1831, left the university in 1834 because his eyes were weak, and sailed all around America, to California and back, as a common sailor. In *Two Years Before the Mast* (published in 1840) he makes much reference to Cooper in the Preface, and stresses the value of such a voyage in acquiring manhood. We should also be reminded of Cooper when he describes the autocratic character of the captain's power on board ship and the discipline he exerts, but says that that is necessary and valuable.[5]

But the aristocratic qualities are combined with the mercantile adventure qualities we associate with Defoe. Adventure by 1840 combined both; or at least the New Englanders were determined that it should. Dana's voyage took him to Crusoe's island of Juan Fernandez, which he describes as "the most romantic spot on earth that my eyes had ever seen. I did then and have ever since, felt an attachment to that island, altogether peculiar. . . . [It is made sacred by] the associations which everyone has connected with in their childhood from reading *Robinson Crusoe*" (p. 47). Like Cooper he makes much of Spanish lethargy (and Indian loutishness) in California settlement society; the moral geography of the modern world system is strong. And he has his handsome sailor, Bill Jackson, "the best specimen of the thoroughbred English sailor that I ever saw" (pp. 24–25).

Parkman, who was also troubled by ill health, went out West a decade later than Dana, on the Oregon Trail; it was 1846, the year of decision in the Westward Movement and Manifest Destiny. He had been seized with a passion for the forest, like Dana's for the sea, at the age of fifteen. In *The Conspiracy of Pontiac* he says, "To him who once has tasted the reckless independence, the haughty self-reliance, the sense of irresponsible freedom which the forest life engenders, civilization henceforth seems flat and stale." His rhetoric was significantly different from Defoe's—much more romantic "The wilderness, rough, harsh, and inexorable, has charms more potent in their seductive influence than all the lures of luxury and sloth. And often he on whom it has cast its magic finds no heart to dissolve the spell, and remains a wanderer and an Ishmaelite to the hour of his death" (*The Oregon Trail*, p. 27). He responded to the American adventure, and the world of young men, though to the idea of it rather than the actuality.

Parkman's mind was very like Cooper's, though fiercer. He was as unsympathetic to the emigrants on the Oregon Trail as Cooper was to the Bushes. He saw them as "some of the vilest outcasts in the country" not in love with liberty but "shaking off restraints of law and society" (p. 7). But he tried to ally himself with their energy, for in them "seemed to be revived, with redoubled force, that fierce spirit which impelled their ancestors, scarcely more lawless than themselves, from the German forests, to inundate Europe, and overwhelm the Roman empire" (p. 88). This idea, with all its racist implications, was to be a powerful one in the latter part of the century, especially among historians. But it was the Indians that most excited Parkman's romantic feelings, just because they were doomed. He called them the conservatives of barbarism, who would not change and so must perish. "The stern, unchanging features of his mind excite our admiration from their very immutability." He went West chiefly to see an Indian war, and to study Indian character. He believed that only war saved the Indians from lethargy and abasement.

His feeling for the Indians is very like Cooper's—and probably Cooper's sympathy also owed something to a sense that they were doomed, as Parkman's certainly did. They are *his* young men, and quite unlike Twain's figures of triumphant aggression and innovation. Parkman often invokes Apollo in describing Indians, and stresses their static physical beauty. At one point he looks up to find that "superb naked figures stood silently gazing on us" (p. 155). And he is interested by the paint, the earrings, and the hair ornaments, worn by the warriors—their self-display—though he is interested just because "the proud and ambitious Dakota warrior can sometimes boast heroic virtues" (p. 155). Like Cooper, he is horrified by the withered crones, and the women who work while the men laze. He too makes a noble Indian friend, the Panther; and he invokes a moral landscape like Cooper's: "There is a spirit of energy in mountains, and they impart it to all who approach them" (p. 167).

Above all, he has a guide and bear-hunter, Henry Chatillon, who is his hero. (Melville, in a review of the book, called Chatillon the last hero, and compared him with Kit Carson. Natty Bumppo would have been more exact.) His "age was about 30; he was 6 feet high, and very powerfully and gracefully molded. The prairies had been his school; he could neither read nor write, but he had a natural refinement and delicacy of mind, such as is rare, even in women. . . ." (p. 14). In a cancelled passage, Parkman compared him with Napoleon and Nelson, but that was an excess of enthusiasm. In fact Chatillon "had not the restless energy of an Anglo-American. He was content to take things as he found them. . . ." (p. 14). This kind of passivity —not *like* Natty's, of course, but parallel in function—is partly what makes him attractive to Parkman. (The Indians had yet another kind of attractive passivity.) "He was a proof of what unaided nature will sometimes do." In these two books we see how Cooper's constituency of readers, and caste-comrades, cooperated with him in spreading the gospel of adventure; and we see another, more ruling class, character to that adventure.

Historians

In America historians seem to have been particularly representative of the culturally responsible class for whom Cooper wrote. Butterfield remarks on how many of his Whig interpreters were American. The historians gave America a new sense of nationhood in the 19th century, and they got the feel of it, in part, from Cooper.[6] In the second half of the century they, like other people, read him primarily in boyhood, and Allan Nevins, writing as late as 1954, seemed still close to the experience. In that year he introduced a selection of chapters about Natty, called *Leather-Stocking*, and recalled his boyhood in Illinois, where he lived in the world of Cooper; and of Henty and Reid, two of the principal boys' adventure writers of England, and of "Oliver Optic" and John T. Trowbridge, their American equivalents. Nevins says, "Men do not easily forget an early devotion to Scott, Dumas, Maryatt and Lytton." (He might add that even when they do forget it, that devotion continues to mold their minds.) He calls the Leatherstocking tales "the nearest approach yet made to an American epic." They deal with "our rude heroic age, our Homeric period of national life."

Of course in 1954 Nevins's remark was out of period, and something of a curiosity. But the nineteenth-century historians all felt something like that, or at least the four whom David Levin deals with in *History as Romantic Art*. These four are William Prescott (1796–1859), George Bancroft (1800–1891), John Lathrop Motley (1814–1877), and Francis Parkman (1823–1893), all Brahmin authors; and some of the relevant titles are Prescott's *Conquest of Mexico* (1843), *Ferdinand and Isabella* (1838), and *Conquest of Peru* (1847); Bancroft's *History of the United States*, which came out between 1859 and 1876; Motley's *Rise of the Dutch Republic* (1856) and *Peter the Great* (1877); and Parkman's *Conspiracy of Pontiac* (1851), *The Discovery of the Great West* (1869), and *Montcalm and Wolfe* (1884). There were close connections between the four, and between the group of them and the other Brahmins. They all disliked Hume, Locke, Voltaire, and the irony, skepticism, and materialism of the eighteenth-century Whigs, which acted as a check on the expansive energies of modernist ideology; these nineteenth-century Whigs identified themselves with those energies. They were on the side of religion—which they interpreted in the nineteenth-century fashion as "faith" or earnestness. Thus Bancroft said that George Fox towered over Descartes morally and spiritually, though intellectually their "methods" coincided.

As the titles of their books indicate, the four men's histories tell the story—celebrate the epic—of the development of the modern world system. In their hands that development becomes an adventure tale. Prescott's Spain, Motley's Holland, Parkman's England and France, and Bancroft's America, were core states, and each in turn became the leading power in that system. Cooper too tells that story, insofar as it concerns America; and the philosophical remorse of his Natty is to be found in the historians.

The true hero of history, these historians said, was The People; but in practice they focused their feelings rather upon what they called Representative Men. For instance, Isabella of Spain, William the Silent, the older Pitt, and Washington.[7] Representative men were "natural," in the sense that Natty Bumppo was. Isabella and William the Silent wore simple austere dress, and had deep-lying passion, warmth, *nature*. They were, in their historical settings, what Natty was in his. In American heroes, naturalness tended to be associated with Nature herself. Bancroft said Washington went into the wilderness as a surveyor for three years, and "Nature revealed to him her obedience to serene and silent laws . . . from her he acquired a divine and animating virtue" (Levin, *History as Romantic Art*, p. 53). And he described Daniel Boone as being, "of a strong, robust frame, in the vigorous health of early manhood, ignorant of books but versed in the forest and forest life" (p. 52).

Of the four, Parkman was the most vivid temperamentally, and can remind us of T. E. Lawrence in his physical frailty, his hardness on himself and contempt for weakness in others too, his love of heroism and his enthusiasm for masculinity.[8] He was determined to keep up the spirit of adventure, to keep the reins of progress in his own people's hands. He once said, "An uncommon vigor, joined to the hardy virtues of a *masculine* race, marked the New England type. The sinews, it is true, were hardened at the expense of blood and flesh —and this literally as well as figuratively; but the staple of character was a sturdy conscientiousness, an undespairing courage, patriotism, public spirit, sagacity, and a strong good sense" (p. 35).

This is the late nineteenth-century Whig interpretation of history, for there was a marked transition from moralism to racism in the course of the century. That went naturally with the rising power of adventure. The story of the Teutonic race became an adventure tale. Bancroft and Motley were keen on primitive epic and saga; as were Kingsley and his friends in England. Stubbs and Freeman, in England, not only traced the history of political and legal institutions, but also refurbished Anglo-Saxon art and taste; made Beowulf and Caedmon great poets. (Whereas Gibbon and Hume regarded the Anglo-Saxons as barbarians, and despised historians who glorified their own peoples.) We touch here upon what one might call the saga modification of military caste sensibility, a development I must return to. For the moment it is enough to note that Victorian manliness, a very important element in the culture's morally serious thought and feeling, owed much to this strain of adventurism. And American manliness owed more, as we shall see.[9]

The American Hero

The historians themselves are one element in the imaginative context for Cooper, as for Scott; but the most important single element is something the historians wrote about—the historical hero. The other culture-heroes of a period give the reader the crucial comparisons and contrasts for its fiction heroes. For the cases of Defoe and Scott I cited Marlborough and Wellington, and went into some detail about Cortes and Clive. In the case of Cooper, the comparable figure must be Andrew Jackson, the backwoods Napoleon, victor of the Battle of New Orleans and the Battle of the Bank.

Cooper ardently supported President Jackson's political policies against the Whigs (who were more suitable political allies for Cooper, in most ways) and ardently admired General Jackson's military victories over the British and the Indians. He liked Jackson's bluntness of word and deed, his attack on the money interests, and his strong government; he saw Jackson as embodying the moral virtue of the old rural republic, whose memory he himself cherished. Of course Cooper saw the difference, in breeding and gentlemanliness, between Jackson and the Founding Fathers, who commanded his deepest loyalty. And in *The Monikins* he satirized Jacksonianism and the political spoils system, operated by Jackson's followers. But such discrepancies only make more striking the general truth that Cooper himself was a Jacksonian.*

This is so striking because Jacksonian democracy represented what Emerson called the "savage" element in American culture, against which Cooper and his caste-comrades fought. In his essay on *Power*, Emerson wrote, "In history the great moment is when the savage is just ceasing to be a savage. . . . Everything good in nature and the world is in that moment of transition, when the swarthy juices still flow plentifully from Nature, but their astringency or acidity is got out by ethics and humanity." This was a central Romantic idea, closely related to the nostalgia for the frontier, and those Americans who chose to be sons of the Adamses and not sons of Adam were renouncing that heritage of power.[10]

The Hawkeye version of the WASP hero had been a literary attempt to resolve America's cultural dilemma in favor of the responsible class. But Hawkeye was only the most aristocratic profile of a multiform cultural image, only a mask of simple virtue dropped over one of a hydra's heads; it had only a doubtful claim to represent the cultural forces seething within that image. (In fact that dilemma is still a living one, because the responsible class has never made its case good. The irresponsible class has always seemed the more "savage.") In politics it was the presidency of Andrew Jackson that marked both the entry of "savagery" into the White House, and the defeat of the system of politicomoral ideas that corresponded to the responsible class.

Jackson was a culture hero, and his Presidency meant an alliance of the most official with the most unofficial elements in American culture, against "literature." Cooper, and the responsible class in general, had no chance against that alliance. All the eulogies of Jackson when he died said that he had embodied the spirit of his age; and his Battle of New Orleans was mythified from the moment it occurred, in 1815; it was declared to be a subject fit for Homer, Ossian, or Milton, because it showed the veterans of Europe beaten by an American militia. It showed God and Nature to be on America's side; or else it showed how American willpower and marksman-

---

*See John P. McWilliams, Jr., *Political Justice in a Republic*.

ship would always win the day.[11] This was the crucial event that turned America's aspirations west, away from Europe, J. H. Ward tells us, in *Andrew Jackson: Symbol for an Age*. The cultural nostalgia for the frontier mastered the country.

Out of the battle came the famous song, "The Hunters of Kentucky," which played an important part in subsequent Presidential elections. It was composed and sung first in 1822. The singer (a man called Ludlow) wore buckskins and moccasins, and carried a rifle over his shoulder; his appearance was greeted by an Indian war whoop from the audience, repeated at the song's climax; touches of Indian style that were directed against genteel propriety. The song itself was full of Southwestern boasting: "And if a daring foe annoys / What-e'er his strength and forces / We'll show him that Kentucky boys / Are alligator horses." This was always sung at Jackson Day dinners, thereafter. And that "Cossack" image was more successful, culturally, than Natty Bumppo.

Nature (the opposite of culture) was always invoked in the rhetoric of Jacksonianism. Bancroft introduced the subject of Jackson's presidency with the question, "What wisdom will he bring with him from the forest? What rules of duty will he evolve from the oracles of his own mind?" And he was also seen as God's chosen instrument and associated with thunder and lightning images.

The political concomitants were imperialism, as might have been predicted. The idea of manifest destiny was always historically attributed to Jackson, though it was in fact first used by John L. O'Sullivan in 1845, in reference to America's claim to Oregon. "By the right of our manifest destiny to overspread and possess the whole of the continent which Providence has given us for the development of the great experiment of liberty and self-government entrusted to us." In any case, Jackson gave political expression to that feeling. Already in 1843, indeed, he had spoken of the annexation of Texas as "extending the arm of freedom." Under his rule, America was quietistic in Europe, but aggressive in the West and toward the Indians.

Jackson was in fact the moving force behind Indian removal in the south. He was responsible for all but two of the eleven treaties of cession with the Georgia Creeks. He acquired for the United States three-fourths of Alabama and Florida, one-third of Tennessee, one-fifth of Georgia and Mississippi, and so on. Such was the political work of the real-life Natty. And this was continental imperialism, however it was named. Jackson forged the American identity, and the national state, in the struggle for westward expansion, says Michael Paul Rogin, in *Fathers and Children.* In 1820, 125,000 Indians lived east of the Mississippi; by 1840 75 percent of them had been involved in removal programs. And American politics as a whole bore the stamp of that imperialism. The years 1824–1852 are generally called the years of Jacksonian democracy, and during that period half the candidates for the Presidency were either Indian war generals or else secretaries of State involved in Indian removal.

But in Natty's case we have to contrast not only the historical hero, or his political policy, but also the frontier folk hero, a diffused cultural presence, of which four crystallizations are especially interesting—Daniel Boone, Davy Crockett, Mike Fink, and Kit Carson. These men form an indispensable context for Natty Bumppo, and bring out the purposefulness of Cooper's characterization.

To show that context we must first make clear the close connection, and then the sharp difference, between Natty and the American folk hero. The difference is that (by definition) a folk hero serves the purposes of an irresponsible class. The connection is that Cooper's idea was not a personal one; he borrowed and adapted it from— amongst other sources—the living legend of his time, Daniel Boone.[12]

In Chapter I of *The Prairie,* Cooper talks of the "swarms of that restless people which is ever found hovering on the skirts of American society," who invaded the lands of Louisiana, as soon as it was bought. The men of the new states led "long files of descendants, born and reared in the forests of Ohio and Kentucky, deeper into the land in quest of that which might be termed, without the aid of poetry, their natural and more congenial atmosphere . . ." (p. 10). One of whom was Daniel Boone. "This adventurous and venerable patriarch was now seen making his last remove . . . [leaving] . . . enjoyments which were rendered worthless in his eyes when trammelled by the forms of human institutions." We must be reminded of Boone when Ishmael Bush boasts, on p. 69, "that he had never dwelt where he might not safely fell every tree he could view from his own threshold, that the law had rarely been known to enter his clearing, and that his ears had never willingly admitted the sound of a church bell." In 1786 Jefferson had cited Boone as getting uneasy as soon as he knew there were ten people to the square mile where he lived. But if Bush is like Boone, so is Natty. (Indeed, the whole charm of *The Prairie* as a literary scheme—a charm not realized in effect—is that Bush and Natty stand for such similar ideas.) Natty had been associated with Boone since the publication of *The Last of the Mohicans*, at least; in that book Cooper borrowed significant features of Boone's Indian adventures—the rescue of the maidens, and the latter's leaving of a trail for their avengers to follow.

Boone's story was told many times in print, and in a way that testifies to innumerable tellings orally. Some of these versions of his character differ significantly from what Cooper (and other responsible-class writers) tried to make out of Boone. James Hall's *Letters from the West*, which appeared between 1822 and 1828, in Cincinnati, portrayed Boone as brave, adventurous, restless, delighting in danger and strife. (Letter 15, on "The National Character," says the Western version of that character is the most original, while Letter 16 is about Boone as a backwoodsman, the typical American.) Above all, Hall says, Boone was a hunter; devoid of selfishness and of softness; "an isolate being, professing tastes and habits of his own, and voluntarily supporting hardships, perils, and privations" (p. 407). (This can only remind us of D. H. Lawrence's famous description of the American hero—hard, isolate, stoic, and a killer.)

Hall describes seeing Kentucky men in Philadelphia in 1800, and admiring "their brawny limbs and sun-burned features . . . the rough hardy air . . . the blanket, bear-skin, and saddle bags—nay the very oil-skin on his hat, and the dirk that peeped from among his vestments. . . . He strode amongst us with the step of an Achilles, glancing with a goodnatured superciliousness." He showed, "a spirit quick to resent—he had the will to dare, and the spirit to execute; there was something in his look which bespoke a disdain of control, and an absence of constraint in all his movements" (Arthur K. Moore, *The Frontier Mind*, p. 68). This is, to use Cooper's terms, not Natty Bumppo but Hurry Harry, a nonhero; but it was Hall's version of the frontier hero who caught the general imagination.

Many figures in fiction were derived from Boone, as well as Natty, and it is interesting to note that most of them are notably old men —and each is paired with a young hunter, who is less uncouth than he, and often turns out to be genteel-in-disguise. We get something of this pattern in *The Pioneers*, where Natty is paired to some degree with Oliver Effingham, who is at first disguised as the young hunter Edwards. And in *The Prairie,* the other novel in which Natty is old, he is paired with Paul Hover, though also with Captain Middleton; in this novel, the two split between them the young man's role. The essential function of this character is to be an intermediary for the reader to the old man, and to inherit as the reader's proxy the old man's heroic qualities. Some other examples are to be found in *Westward Ho!,* a novel by Cooper's friend, Paulding; Charles W. Webber's *Old Hicks the Guide,* about the Texas Rangers; and Edward Ellis's best-selling *Seth Jones.* Of seventy-nine dime novels from 1860 to 1893 which Henry Nash Smith reports examining, forty contained old hunters.[13] They are old, presumably, because they represent the past—"America's Homeric age."

Boone was succeeded as national folk hero by Davy Crockett, who published three autobiographical volumes—two in 1834, and one in 1836, the year of his death. He was famous for killing; he says he killed forty-seven bears one month, which made 105 that year. Like Boone, and Natty, he had a much-beloved and personified rifle, Betsy. Like Boone, he was offered the chance to become a brave, by the Comanche tribe. But his story is more full of violence. He describes a truly savage fight with a cougar; and a comic scene of a man he overheard practicing eye-gouging and face-stamping, alone in the forest.

In 1835, politically disappointed—he had hoped to win the Western vote away from Jackson—Crockett set off for Texas, abandoning country, home, and family, for Texas still belonged to Mexico. He died defending the Alamo against the Mexican force sent to subdue rebellion. And the last part of his autobiography, describing his journey through the southwest toward the Alamo, is quite interesting from our point of view. It contains some vivid anecdotes that combine frontier ferocity with frontier humor in that blend which in American culture has so much force because of its implicit hostility to genteel values. Most strikingly, he describes picking up two companions, Thimblerig, a Red River boat gambler, and young Bee-Hunter, who is an erotic hero. (They also pick up later a pirate and an Indian, all on their way to the Alamo—the home of all lovers of freedom. The Bee-Hunter, he tells us, once sat down to breakfast in Texas with eleven men, all of whom were wanted for murder in their home states.) What is interesting for us is that the Bee-Hunter is so like Paul Hover in *The Prairie*. Cooper seems to have rewritten Crockett's material. It has been argued that in his last two Leatherstocking tales Cooper was reacting against the Crockett image, consciously or unconsciously; trying to rescue the Western hero from those associations of rapacity and vulgarity. (That is why there is such a heavy stress on Natty's nobility there.)

Then Mike Fink, famous as a boatman, who had in fact three separate careers as a frontier hero. In the first he was a scout/ranger/guide, like Natty, who defended Fort Pitt and spied in Indian territory. (He was always an expert rifleman, using a Kentucky rifle.)[14] In the second he was a keelboatman on the Ohio and Mississippi rivers. After the battle of Fallen Timbers, in 1793, a treaty of peace was signed with the Indians near Fort Pitt, so scouts like Fink were left with no employment. And they didn't want regular work; "they had imbibed in their intercourse with the Indians a contempt as well as disrelish for regular and steady labour."* Like the Cossacks, the frontiersmen took on the cultural traits of the tribes they fought. So they became boatmen, a trade which involved little contact with the law, and was a part of the great migration movement. In 1787, five hundred boats carried 20,000 people down the Ohio River, and the keelboats were poled even against the current by muscular boatmen. There was much singing, boasting, and taunting of rivals, as the boats passed each other; while their relations with the shore-dwellers were marked by drinking, wenching, and blackmail.

Fink's third career was as trapper and mountainman in the Rockies. This began in 1822, in St. Louis, when William H. Ashley and Major Andrew Henry advertised for one hundred young men to ascend the Missouri to its source, and to remain in the wilderness for two or three years. Several of that hundred were to become legendary, for their bear fights, human fights, or, as in the case of Fink, for being murdered. (He was killed in a brawl in 1823.) The fur trade had just then become important, and the trappers were the precursors of empire.

Fink was always described as being of Herculean proportions, perfectly symmetrical, of Indian coloring, and usually naked to the waist. He is the most physical of these heroes, and the most erotic. The language attributed to him is of the Southwestern-humor kind;

---

*Charles Cist, *History of Cincinnati*, 1845.

"I'm a Salt River roarer, and I love the wimming, and I'm chockful of fight." And his violence had a racist cast; two of his famous exploits with his rifle were first that he shot the heel off a Negro, and second that he shot the scalp lock off an Indian—both in jest. This is the sort of raucous folk image to keep in focus behind the figure of Natty, in order to appreciate Cooper's shaping hand.

Finally, Kit Carson. He was born in Kentucky in 1809, but his father believed that Daniel Boone was the greatest of Americans, and followed him to Missouri in 1813. In 1830 Kit answered an advertisement by Thomas Fitzpatrick, for men to go into the Rockies, and ultimately became the most famous of all mountain men.* Such men traveled in companies of fifty or a hundred, and often changed employers. Kit worked for the Hudson Bay Company for a time. They were also exemplars of the reckless, savage life, resistant to all laws or constraints, and inclined to Indian habits and ideas—rumored, for instance, to scalp their enemies. Timothy Flint, in *Shoshonee Valley* (1830) describes them as alternately indolent and laborious, aggressive and amorous.

When famous, Kit was offered a job with land speculators. But he met Fremont in St. Louis in 1842, and went with him to chart a route to the mouth of the Colorado River, for the U. S. Engineers; and then on a second expedition beyond the Salt Lake. He became Scout to the American army in California, and helped defeat large forces of Mexicans; he was offered a military commission during his visit to Washington.

Carson was therefore coopted by the established society, more clearly than any of the other folk heroes were. This coopting could be compared with Cooper's appropriation of the cultural image for establishment purposes. But it could also remind us of the way certain Cossacks (like Platov, or Skobelev's regiment) were employed by the Russian autocracy—exemplars of freedom employed as the agents of political discipline—disciplining those who had been freer than themselves from the modern system's laws.

For Carson later became an Indian agent. He fought the Apaches in New Mexico in 1854, and again in 1855–1856, the Apaches and the Utahs. In 1861 he was made a colonel in the Union army, and defeated a force of Texas rebels. By then he was the hero of many

*According to Noel B. Gerson, in *Kit Carson,* New York, 1964.

dime novels—the representative of America's unofficial imperialism; on one occasion he found such a novel amongst the debris of a wagon whose occupants he had been too late to save from Indian attackers. In such adventure scripts, of course, he was a brave loner; in real life, he was on the side of the big battalions. In 1863–1864 he had to fight the Navajo, and defeated them by the use of cannon; thereafter, it is said, his sleep was haunted by dreams of starving Navajo squaws and children. And he was of great assistance to General Sherman when the latter came out to arrange the treaty with the Indians in 1867.

On the political plane one may say that Carson, and the frontiersmen in general, were controlled and used by the Federal government. But on the cultural plane, it is clear that the folk hero image escaped the controls which Cooper and the responsible class tried to put on it. In literature itself Natty Bumppo has been successful, in some sense; readers have been induced to pay him quite exaggerated respect; but in the culture at large Mike Fink and Davy Crockett counted for more. Just as in literature, *Gulliver's Travels* was a masterpiece of irony, but in the culture at large it was just another adventure tale.[15]

VI

Tolstoy

I CHOSE Tolstoy as one of the authors to examine here for various reasons, one of the most important being that his books and his ideas, just because he is a Russian, throw a different light on the history of modern adventure. This is a light that comes in some sense from outside, because Russia and Russian literature lay on the periphery of the modern system, while England and America and literature-in-English lay at its center.

Russia in the nineteenth century was making a violent effort to acquire the technology of the modern system, without being infected by its ideology. That statement applies primarily to official Russia, not to the intelligentsia; but the latter too—at least Tolstoy's party, powerful within literature—opposed some Western styles of thought and feeling. Russian literature did not breathe the spirit of the modern system, or of the mercantile caste. There was no Russian Defoe. In Defoe's day, indeed, Russia had practically no printed literature. In the time of Dante and Chaucer, Russia had had no poetry, in the time of Shakespeare no drama, and before 1750 no novels. That made a difference, even in the nineteenth century.

Even more strikingly, Russian imperialism then was still under the control of the tsars, and not to be associated primarily with merchants. The merchants were a caste, devoted to traditional methods of trading, and the life-style that traditionally went with them. Not until the second half of the nineteenth century did they become

English-style merchants, entrepreneurs, and engage in capitalist expansion. Russia did have, in its advance eastward, some character of representing the modern system—spreading the benefits of civilization—but by and large it was a conscious and military imperialism; like that of sixteenth-century Spain, not that of seventeenth-century England. The nineteenth-century novel of adventure accordingly began as romance, heavily influenced by Scott (favorite reading of Tsar Nicholas I) and with a markedly aristomilitary character.

Indeed, in early nineteenth-century Russia, something like a caste system still prevailed, and the aristomilitary caste was dominant in literature. We see this in the early rise of the nobleman's genre of Sportsman's Sketches, in which Aksakov, Turgenev, and Tolstoy began their writing careers; and in the genre of childhood reminiscences, in which Aksakov, Tolstoy, and Herzen excelled, and which was also tied to the landowning caste. Later in the century, a different and somewhat opposed sensibility developed, in the work of priests' sons, like Chernyshevsky, and doctors' sons, like Dostoevsky, and the epigones of Belinsky (himself a doctor's son and priest's grandson). N. G. Pomyalovsky, whose *Seminary Sketches* appeared in 1862, was typical of a group of intellectuals of the raznochintsy—most of them priests' sons but outside the caste system themselves—whose naturalistic-satiric writing was very popular in the 1860s. *Seminary Sketches* is a childhood reminiscence, but very unlike Tolstoy's *Childhood, Boyhood, and Youth.* But these men are also unlike the English domestic novelists, and their related critics. There is for instance no implicit alliance to be detected, within such work or within the intelligentsia that read it, between the writers and the merchant caste in Russia. The intelligentsia dissociated itself from all other castes, except the peasants, and threw itself into a posture of aggressive dissatisfaction with society as a whole. Russia was a different case.

Tolstoy's position can best be understood as following from Pushkin's. In 1825 Pushkin wrote to a friend that "our writers are recruited from the highest social class. With them aristocratic pride is linked with their literary ambition. . . . Our poets do not solicit the protection of gentlemen; our poets are gentlemen themselves. [And, though the friend he was addressing, Ryleev, was a Decembrist, soon to be executed for his part in that revolt] The lack of esteem for one's ancestors is the first sign of wildness and immorality." Pushkin was proud of his six-hundred-year-old nobility. But more important, he and his friend, Prince Viazemsky, saw literature in Russia as threatened by the new nobility, appointed as noble by the tsars for services to the state—that is, to the autocracy. This threat was represented, in the '20s and '30s, by the literary journalist, Bulgarin, who, Pushkin said, treated literature as a commodity. Literature as represented by Pushkin and his friends—and by Herzen and Tolstoy later—was close to the politics of the Decembrists; who were rebels against the autocracy, but in the name of the aristocracy as much as of the lower classes (Gleason, *European and Muscovite*, p. 46).

This anachronism in the cultural style of literature (from a modern system point of view) was not accidental or atypical of Russia. Something similar was even truer in political matters. Even in its eastward expansion, Russian imperialism was not like the English kind. It was more the work of the autocracy, its armed forces, and above all its Cossacks. If that character was not reflected in the imaginative literature in any major way, it was because the conscience of literature-as-a-system was against it.

Thus in 1821 Pushkin wrote a verse tale, *The Prisoner of the Caucasus,* in which a Russian officer is loved by a girl among his Chechen captors, who helps him escape and then kills herself in despair. (Tolstoy was to write a prose tale with a similar plot and setting.) There is some fine description of the premodern life of the Chechen, and the poem was acclaimed as a triumph of Russian poetry; except that, in the epilogue, Pushkin celebrated the final victory of the Russian forces, under General Ermolov, the conquest of the Caucasus and defeat of the Chechens. (Pushkin much admired Ermolov, a military and imperialist hero, who had, he said, the head of a tiger on the shoulders of Hercules; he wanted to write his biography.) But his friend Viazemsky wrote that that epilogue stained Pushkin's verse with blood. "The blood freezes in one's veins, and one's hair stands on end, to read that Ermolov 'Destroyed and annihilated the tribes like a black plague.' " This, said Viazemsky, is an anachronism; poetry is not the ally of executioners; we should be educating the tribes, not executing them (Woolf, *Pushkin on Literature,* p. 63). This is what the conscience of literature would have said in England too, and later Russian writers were more obedient to it.

But the conscience of a literary system often unconsciously pays tribute to its connections with the political system too. By their silence Russian adventures slurred over the imperialist character of

Russia's advance east, and over the "continental" nature of Russian imperialism. In the section "Imperialism" of her *Origins of Totalitarianism,* Hannah Arendt says, "Nazism and Bolshevism owe more to Pan-Germanism and Pan-Slavism (respectively) than to any other ideology or political movement" (p. 222). And she goes on to talk about a continental kind of imperialism, in which there was no distance between colony and mother country (between frontier and metropolis, to use Webb's terms). She says that transoceanic empires sometimes suffer from a "boomerang effect," whereby the political methods and political ideas used on the frontier, usually much harsher than those approved for the home population, filter back and infect the home country. In the case of continental empires, there is no need for any such gradual effect. "Continental imperialism truly begins at home" (p. 223).[1]

There are indeed parallels between Russia's history and that of Prussia, and the Romanovs were traditionally friends and allies, even imitators, of the Hohenzollerns. (To some degree, the Russian autocracy may be seen as a sequence of German princes, dragooning a quite alien Slavic population.) But Germany as a whole did not become an empire until 1870, three hundred years after Russia. The preeminent example of continental imperialism must be Russia.

Moreover, Germany had nothing to compare with the thrust eastward, that enormous expansion of Russian power over unoccupied land—that is, occupied only by nomadic or mountain tribes who did not belong to the modern system. That expansive thrust was still continental, though it was not so consciously imperialist. Russia's conscious expansion was the territory it took from Sweden, Poland, and Turkey; the land it took from the tribes of Central Asia seemed as empty and unclaimed as Africa and the West Indies seemed to England. Historians sometimes say, comparing the expansion east with Russia's efforts to expand in other directions, that the former "happened of itself." This should remind us of the "absence of mind" in which England acquired its empire; and of America's "innocent" expropriation of the Indians.

As that reference suggests, there is much in Arendt's "continental" idea which applies particularly to the case of American culture. (While England, on the other hand, is preeminent amongst empires in which the boomerang effect was dodged and delayed.) G. A. Lensen, in *Russia's Eastward Expansion,* says in his Introduction,

"Russia's eastward expansion was part of the European tide that inundated Asia and America in the Age of Exploration," and it involved the same types—pathfinders, traders, missionaries, soldiers of fortune. They moved into Siberia in search of "the golden fleece," and during the 1630s Russia annexed territory at the rate of something like the size of France every three years.

Only America's thrust westward could compare with Russia's, and even that was smaller, in square miles occupied and in numbers of people moved. Moreover there was the difference, which made those two great powers politically antithetical, that in Russia the power of the state was concentrated in the autocracy to an extraordinary degree. Russia was the most backward state in Europe, from a modern political point of view; it had practically no liberties, even after it had begun to modernize its technology, and even after it began to produce its great literature.

Russia was the first in a sequence of modernized empires (imperial Germany and Japan were later examples) whose history is of the greatest importance in understanding the modern system. These were countries who continued to be ruled by military castes, even while they appropriated modern system skills. Their history in some sense caricatured or satirized the modern system; it mocked the hopes of countries like England that they had escaped from militarism and caste-domination, had exorcised the black magic of imperialism, had substituted the white magic of productivity, enlightened self-interest, and the pursuit of happiness.

Ever since the days of Boris Godunov, Russia had been either sending men to Europe to acquire the secrets of Western technology (sometimes these men refused to come home afterward) or recruiting European technicians to come to Russia (sometimes *these* men's passage was prevented by the kings of Sweden or Poland).[2] It was most typically military engineers the tsars wanted, and what they most definitely did not want was the liberal ideology that Europe had developed along with that technology. The economic development of Russia was not autonomous, in the Western style, but occurred under the direction of the tsars, out of phase with the "free growth of the free market," etc. It stopped and started at their behests. Thus Peter the Great had fostered the growth of a metallurgical industry, to the point where Russia's was one of the foremost in Europe. In 1800 her iron ore production was nearly equal to England's. But it was not a free-growing industry; by the end of Nicholas I's reign, in 1855, England's production had increased twelve-fold over the 1800 figure, while Russia's was much the same as before; and England was producing a thousand times as much coal as Russia.

Russia's intellectuals were bitterly conscious of belonging to an empire and not to a modern system country. Their efforts to create a great literature were bedeviled by the fear that "literature" as they understood the term—an idea derived from the literature of eighteenth- and nineteenth-century Europe—only could or only should flourish in a free country.

Thus Russian literature, in its relation to Russian culture as a whole, provides an interesting contrast to English. And amongst Russian authors, Tolstoy was a pre-eminent spokesman.

Tolstoy and Cooper and Caste

But Tolstoy is also of special interest to our argument because, of all the writers of adventure tales, he is the only one who went on to write serious fiction of the very highest level—*War and Peace* and *Anna Karenina.*

Such novels are, by definition, not our concern here. But I should say a word about *War and Peace,* which contains elements of adventure—of the story of the brothers. It is after all about Napoleon, one of the three great conquistadors I cited as inspiring the modern idea of the historical hero. When Napoleon actually appears on the page, Tolstoy gives a very disparaging account of him, and the book's tone becomes hostile to adventure. But he figures in the book also as the focus of Andrey's and Pierre's early aspirations; as the symbol of glory and achievement, and youthful genius defeating established power unaided; in a manuscript note, Tolstoy said that each of the novel's heroes was ambitious à la Napoleon. Moreover, each hero's feelings for Napoleon is a young man's worship of another young man—that is a pattern in the book, most strikingly illustrated by Nicholas Rostov's feeling for Tsar Alexander. Seeing the tsar's handsome and happy face, Nicholas "experienced a feeling of tenderness and ecstasy such as he had never before known. Every trait and every movement of the Tsar's seemed to him enchanting" (p. 264). This is a military-caste story, suffused by the love of young manhood—a love felt by young men for young men.[3] This group of motifs and themes will remind us of Scott; and the big social and battle scenes we admired in *Waverley* are developed even further in *War and Peace*.

But this novel is also about girls and whom they should marry; notably Natasha, contrasted with Sonia and Vera; and Princess Mary, contrasted with Lisa and Mlle. Bourienne. And this group of motifs and the thematic material surrounding them will remind us of George Eliot, and the English story of the sisters. *War and Peace* is a great synthesis of a novel, as has often been said. I don't know that it has been remarked that the two elements most importantly synthesized are the story of the brothers and the story of the sisters. Of course there are other elements too, but from the point of view of the history of the novel, these are the most important. And they are held together not in equality but in a subordination (Tolstoy assigns "reality" to the story of marriages and "unreality" to the story of adventures) which is also part of the history of the novel.

Tolstoy went on from that achievement in serious fiction to renounce art and denounce Empire entirely. Following his conversion, about 1880, he took up a moral position outside the system of literature as a whole, and outside the modern world system as a whole. He disapproved of the direction of development of modern history, in Russia but also outside. And looking back, we can now see the origins of that final attitude always present in his mind.

During his youth, however, Tolstoy wrote not only serious novels but also some adventures. Indeed, he never wholly ceased to work on that kind of material, as we shall see, but after his conversion he was uneasy with it. His kind of adventure was in the Russian tradition. Besides Pushkin's verse tale, and similar tales by Lermontov, there was *Ammalet Bek* by Bestuzhev-Marlinsky. He was another Decembrist, who won a pardon. He fought in the Caucasus between 1829 and 1837 (when he died there in battle) and wrote this very popular historical novel, with a Byronic hero, about the fighting there in 1810. In the Scott tradition, there were verses interspersed, and some ethnological interest shown in the life of the Chechens. Novels about the Caucasus war were a well-established genre in Russia, the genre of transposed Scott, and that was the option Tolstoy chose when he began *The Cossacks*. But if we consider Tolstoy as a whole, we are likely to see a more intimate and revealing likeness between him and Cooper than between him and Scott.

In the course of Chapter 19 of *The Cossacks*, Tolstoy makes an explicit reference to Cooper which lights up his manifold debt to adventure in English. "The memory of Fenimore Cooper's *The Pathfinder* flashed through" the hero's mind, because he finds himself involved in an adventure like those he'd read about. (In another story, Tolstoy also invokes *The Pathfinder* to mean the beauty of the forest, and the happiness of living in it.)[4] Cooper was generally popular in Russia, and with serious writers. Belinsky compared him with Shakespeare. Lermontov thought him greater than Scott, and borrowed from *The Water-Witch* for his *Taman*. Gogol's Cossacks in *Taras Bulba*, like Tolstoy's, owe much to Cooper's frontiersmen and Indians. The heyday of his reputation there was 1825–1845, Tolstoy's youth, when Cooper's novels appeared in the magazine, *Notes of the Fatherland*, and the drift of the Russian critics' enthusiasm can be caught in this quotation from an essay by Belinsky in 1839. ". . . and as for the sea and ships, here again he [Cooper] is at home: he knows the name of every rope on board ship; like the most experienced of pilots, he knows its every movement; like a skillful captain, he . . ." (Dekker and McWilliams, *James Fenimore Cooper: The Critical Heritage*, p. 189). Belinsky is impressed by the same feature of Cooper as were the American readers, his practical knowledge and skills. Annenkov, Herzen, Chernyshevsky, were all enthusiastic. Cooper was referred to in the Epilogue to *Brothers Karamazov*, and by Chekhov, and by Gorky.

Cooper's stories (despite the elements of conflict we see in them) carried the message of hope in Russia; so they did in France, and in England, to judge by D. H. Lawrence's account of his boyish enjoyment of them. They carried the modern system's energizing myth. And it seems likely that Cooper exerted a more powerful influence in Russia than anywhere else, because America was such a mirage of freedom to people living under the tsarist authority, and also because of the similarities between the two countries' geopolitical situations.

In Tolstoy's case, however, there were also personal reasons for a special affinity between him and Cooper. The latter was the youngest of five brothers; Tolstoy was the youngest of four, and the son of a father who impressed those who knew him, including his children, as remarkable. (The mother died when Lev was two.) Nikolai Ilyitch

Tolstoy was not a great achiever, as William Cooper was, but he was notably the center of his household, around whom everyone else revolved; he was not an adventure-novel hero, but he was a domestic-novel hero; he was adored by his mother, by his cousin Toinette—who did the most to bring up the children—by the servants, and by the children themselves. There were two Cooper girls, one Tolstoy girl, but in both families it seems clear that the masculine principle was dominant. Tolstoy described what he felt at the age of five, when he was moved downstairs from the nursery to join his brothers and to receive lessons—to enter the world of men, of horses, dogs, and hunting. For Cooper, too, the initiation into manhood, and aristo-cratic manhood, was of crucial importance.

For there were, also, certain sociocultural similarities between the two families. In *Fenimore Cooper: Critic of His Times,* Robert Spiller describes the Cooper house as a curious mixture of pioneering crudity and baronial grandeur, a description that would fit the early Yasnaya Polyana. (The house and estate at Aksokovo, which S. T. Aksakov describes at the beginning of his *Family Chronicle,* is in some ways even closer to Cooperstown.) The houses of the Russian nobility contained trophies of European culture, like grand pianos and marble statues, while they lacked the comforts of quite modest English houses. Spiller says on p. 28, "The tin-plate stove must have held curious conversations with the plaster busts in those pedimented doorways during those long northern nights." English travelers made very similar comments on Russian houses in the early nineteenth century.

That was the time when Sidney Smith asked the famous question, "Who reads an American novel?" in the *Edinburgh Review.* And in 1804, when Karamzin's *Letters of a Traveller* was published in English, Henry Brougham said, in the same magazine, "a book of translations from Moscow is like a horse in Venice or a tree in Scotland—its amusing badness is all that deserves attention." In some sense, everyone thought that, about both America and Russia. The *Edinburgh Review* critics were famous for sharpening to the point of insult prejudices other people softened to the mumble of shame.

The obverse side of that prejudice was the enthusiasm felt for both America and Russia as places where a new life could be begun, a new and purified European civilization. Herder, early in his career, dreamed of becoming the Luther and Solon of a new nation of the

Ukraine; Bernardin de Saint-Pierre thought a new Pennsylvania might grow up around the Aral sea. And it was in Russia and America that the radical Protestant sects persecuted in Central Europe found a place to live and grow. Moravianism, for instance, was not without its effects on both Cooper and Tolstoy, and is even reflected indirectly in their fiction. Natty Bumppo and Karataev are both figures of radical Christianity, figures of renunciation, passivity, simplicity— essentially negations of the worldly culture around them and ahead of them.

The incongruities of furnishing, etc., reflected contradictory pressures on the people who lived there, which could cause the anxious questions, "How do really modern people do this or that?" or "Is this country really civilized?" or "Do I want it to be?" Both our authors asked those questions. They were too intelligent for that self-questioning to inspire mere cultural snobbery in them. But they felt that anxiety and were angry to feel it.

They responded in part negatively to the pressure to be liberal and democratic and advanced; they asserted an aristocratic caste identity which always seemed reactionary. Here is one example of that in Cooper, from *Satanstoe,* a novel largely preoccupied with the differences between the author-representing hero and a New Englander, Jasper Newcome, who is in some ways the better educated and more earnest of the two, more the modern system hero, but who is not a gentleman. Newcome, we are told, was "ultra-levelling in his notions of social intercourse, while I had the opinions of my own colony, in which the distinction of classes are far more strongly marked than is usual in New England." The tone is of course defiant, for Cooper had to defy the pressure of all modern system ideology, to say such things. But he needed to claim a place in the modern world for his own caste. And the likeness between him and Tolstoy centers in their caste identity.

An equivalent to such caste opinions are the caste sports, like skating and riding and shooting, in which Cooper's heroes excel, and their enemies do not. And of course the same is true of Tolstoy. Hunting above all is of great importance to the aristomilitary caste. Then Cooper became a sailor, while Tolstoy became a soldier, and served in an imperialist war in the Caucasus.

In that war, Russia was putting down the resistance of mountain tribesmen, who had never before been subdued by any civilization, and who were inspired and led by their imams; it was a muridic rising, religious and populist in character, while the imperialist power they faced justified itself by its civilizing mission.

It is also worth remembering that Tolstoy was an artillery officer in those wars. Artillery, cannon, were the supreme weapon of the modern system against the rest of the world. (When he arrived in St. Petersburg, and began his career as a man of letters, he was still, officially, military inspector to a munitions factory there.) And though Tolstoy's part in the war was to some degree that of an observer, it was not entirely so. He took part in battles. Indeed, on February 17, 1853, he distinguished himself in a major attack, in which his battery silenced the enemy's guns; and that was the engagement which broke the back of Shamil's resistance. Thus he belonged to the military caste by experience—the experience of modern war —as well as by birth.

In Tolstoy's case, the most striking expression of this caste feeling in writing is this extract from a discarded chapter of *War and Peace*. "I am not a bourgeois, as Pushkin boldly said, and I boldly say that I am an aristocrat by birth, by habits and by position. I am an aristocrat because I am not only not ashamed, but positively glad to remember my ancestors—I was brought up from childhood in love and respect for the highest orders of society and in love for the refined as expressed not only in Homer, Bach, and Raphael, but also in all the small things in life. . . . I am an aristocrat because I cannot believe in the high intellect, the refined taste, or the absolute honesty of a man who picks his nose and whose soul converses with God."[*5] That last sentence is Tolstoy's fling at the Jasper Newcomes of his society. And it is no accident that both novelists' heroines are often what Cooper describes as "a spirited horsewoman." On horseback, everyone is a figure of chivalry, and we shall see in discussing Kipling how powerful that image is. In the case of Natasha Rostov, the concept has a good deal more content than it does in Cooper's usage, but as a caste index it has still the same meaning.

Tolstoy's animus against Speransky in *War and Peace* (which is probably mirrored in the more full-length portrait of Karenin in *Anna Karenina*) is another example of caste feeling. Mikhail Speransky (1772–1839) was the great bureaucrat of nineteenth-century Russia,

*Quoted in R. F. Christian, *Tolstoy's War and Peace*, pp. 102–103.

the bureaucrat as genius, and responsible for much of the modernization and Westernization of the country. According to Marc Raeff, he was "the model and teacher for an entire generation of government officials, at least in the techniques of bureaucratic work" (*Michael Speransky*, p. 350). He was a village priest's son—the typical origin for the Russian bureaucrat—and educated at a seminary.

This means more than it may seem to do at first glance, because the Russian priesthood was in effect a caste.[6] At least this was true of the "white" priests (and deacons and psalmodists, and so on) who officiated in the village churches, and who married before they took orders. Their sons almost always went to a seminary for their education, and their daughters sometimes were given a benefice as a dowry, to help them find a husband in a seminary. (The "black" churchmen were the monks and the higher ecclesiastics.) Thus, though there were of course exceptions, a priest's father was usually another priest, and so was his son. Turgenev said Belinsky was of the purest Russian blood, because he came of a priestly family—who could only intermarry with other such families. Turgenev also complained to the de Goncourts that he had been seated next to a priest at a banquet given by the Russian ambassador in Paris; in Russia, he explained, the nobles had nothing to do with the priests. And indeed, if the white priesthood was a Brahmin caste, it altogether lacked the Indian associations of purity, learning, and refinement; the parish priests of Russia were associated rather with ignorance, drunkenness, and tyranny. They had to keep records for the central authorities, and make them political reports. Even Speransky had to draw up a code of laws for Nicholas, and act as chief prosecutor of the Decembrists.

But Tolstoy's feeling was against the psychological type as much as against the cultural function: it was the feeling of the free nobleman against the office-bound clerk, of the military caste against the bureaucratic, and one can see something similar in Nabokov's treatment of Chernyshevsky in *The Gift*. Speransky became an expert popularizer and report-writer, with the traits, intellectually, of the French Encyclopaedists and the English Utilitarians, and had remarkable powers of work and self-dedication. He married an English-woman, and clearly his function in Russia was very parallel to that of the Evangelicals in contemporary England; the men like Grant, who recharged England with neo-Puritan certitude. Speransky asserted himself by means of mind and morality, not by manliness and human warmth; he manifested himself as a Brahmin, not a Kshat-triya. Socially he was always on guard, and relaxed only with inferiors with whom he felt sure of every superiority. With equals his personality was marked by a cold aloofness, which masked a hypersensitive need for admiration and consolation. This figure played an important part in Tolstoy's emotional life (as it did in Russian culture as a whole) and he discharged upon it strong caste prejudices; although in *Anna Karenina* that prejudice is counteracted by opposite feelings, and later in life he attempted to divest himself of that caste persona.

Speransky was apparently destined to be an important character in *War and Peace* from its first conception in Tolstoy's mind, and he survived the many changes that engulfed other originals. K. B. Feuer establishes this, in her study of the *War and Peace* manuscripts cited in the bibliography. She also establishes that there was a connection between Speransky and Napoleon in Tolstoy's mind—a connection Shklovsky had more intuitively pointed to, on the strength of the detail Tolstoy uses to characterize both, their plump, small, white hands. In one draft Tolstoy said that Speransky was a civic Napoleon to Prince Andrey, and in another he applied to both the same prejudicial term for seminarians, *kuteynitski*. It is clearly a nobleman's caste-dislike for them that Tolstoy is expressing; when Andrey gives vent to his disillusionment with both, in another place, Pierre says to him *"quel esprit de caste."* Such feelings were strong in Russian literary circles, even in the second half of the century. Tolstoy's friend, Strakhov, was told by a fellow conservative, Leontev, that he couldn't understand the aristocracy because "You are still just a seminarian," in a quarrel in the '70s. And both Dostoevsky and Chekhov declared they felt a handicap in matters of form and aesthetics, because they were not nobles—Chekhov said this as late as 1889.

Such caste-feeling in a novelist is important also because it bears on the sort of adventure and adventurer he imagines. Tolstoy, true to his caste, does not give us a do-it-yourself hero; he is much closer to Scott than to Defoe. His heroes are—or rather they become, for his stress is on their becoming—fiery figures of manhood, eminent in courage, and honor, and ardor—essentially, though not simply, chivalric types. His caste-loyalty persisted, against his will, all his life. In his diary entry for December 31, 1904, he wrote about his desire for a Russian victory over the Japanese, "This is patriotism. I was brought up on it and am not free from it, just as I am not free from personal egoism, from a family and even an aristocratic egoism, and from patriotism."* The literary proof of that caste-character persisting is *Hadji Murad*, the masterpiece of imperialist adventure he was working on—ashamedly—at that very time.

Earlier in his life, however, he asserted his caste-identity unashamedly and voluntarily—rooted himself in it. When he entered the University of Kazan, he began smoking, set up a horse and trap, and became a dandy. He was much impressed by his brother Sergei, who was perfectly comme il faut. Tolstoy scorned the gymnasium graduates and scholarship boys at the university, consorted only with fellow aristocrats, refused to bow first when he met someone, froze the overfamiliar. And this aspect of his personality recurred, though intermittently, over some fifteen years. In 1851 he went to Moscow with the express intent to (1) gamble, (2) marry, (3) get a post; and he wrote out for himself some Rules for Society: that he must associate only with men of higher status, dance only with important women, never express his feelings, always punish a sarcastic or insulting remark.

And this was not merely a matter of personality style; when Tolstoy became a famous writer after the Crimean War, he quarreled with his fellow contributors to *Sovremennik*, because he felt they lacked aristocratic honor, even in their intellectual life. They represented the modern system mind in literature. He doubted the quality of their convictions, found them morally flabby, and insisted on the criterion of man-to-man combat as a test of intellectual sincerity. Turgenev complained bitterly of Tolstoy's "nobleman's pride." And it is clear that Tolstoy was asserting just that by his behavior toward this group. He always wore his military uniform with them, flaunted his grooming and physical condition, and in return for their domestic hospitality entertained them at a hotel, with gypsies. He was using a caste-rooted integrity and authenticity against them, just as in our century working-class writers have used their class against their colleagues.[7]

And his close relations with his brothers are important because their mutual affection despite incompatibility of belief was the nuclear model for the caste loyalty he was asserting. In 1854—by which time Nikolai would be thirty-two—the four of them reunited at

---

*Quoted in Ernest J. Simmons, *Tolstoy*, p. 208.

Yasnaya Polyana, and talked far into the night, and then made up a bed on the floor and slept together. This speaks of an intensity of man-to-man warmth which can remind us only of Kipling. And this warmth is one of the sources of all stories of the brothers.

Tolstoy put his faith in caste-loyalty through much of his life; and, after marriage, supplemented that with a faith in family life; and both were for him alternatives to modern system values and personality styles. Both were forms of silent resistance to modern civilization— though also to the empire of Nicholas I. Thus in his hands (as indeed in Cooper's) the adventure story served antimodernist forces of the mind, too.

Tolstoy and Peter and Modernization

But one tendency in the adventure novel, one ideological implication or alliance, was in the long run repugnant to Tolstoy. This was its being finally on the side of the modern system; it might counter that tendency by an opposite sympathy with Nature and the primitive, but it could not seriously oppose it. (Tolstoy was also disturbed by the violence of adventure, but that is a separate issue.) He was nearly always uneasy about the modernization of Russia, and a natural ally of the Slavophiles rather than the Westernizers—the two great parties of the Russian intellectual debate. As time passed, his temperamental ambivalence came down more and more against the latter. It might be said that he undertook to wrestle against Peter the Great, the great modernizer of Russia, who had brought her into line with western Europe. Nicholas I, the tsar of Tolstoy's youth, saw himself as another Peter, and the spokesmen for "official nationality" made a cult of Peter. Egor Kankrin, Nicholas's minister of finance, even proposed that Russia should be renamed Petrovia and Russians Petrovians. Tolstoy, like Herzen, picked a determined quarrel with Nicholas, especially in certain late stories and essays.

All the Slavophiles, and most Russian writers, had to quarrel with the agents of their country's modernization, at one point or another. "Peter I" said Herzen, "drove civilization into us with such a wedge that Russia could not stand it, and split into two layers" (*My Past and Thoughts*, p. 1576). And Dostoevsky, announcing a new journal in

1863, said, "The reforms of Peter the Great have been too expensive for us: they have separated us from the people." It is true that Belinsky in his final phase, when he bitterly concentrated all his will and contracted all his sensibility into the demand for modernization and enlightenment, declared that Peter was his model and his religion. And in 1854 Granofsky angrily reproached Herzen with having betrayed their cause, when the latter began to write against Peter. But such incidents only show how alive an issue Peter remained to all Russian intellectuals—when he was repudiated, he was sure to be defended. As Herzen said, apropos of Granofsky's reproach, in Russia Peter's image grew more colossal every year.

Much of Russian cultural history could be written around the Bronze Horseman, the statue to Peter set up by Catherine, and a symbol of autocracy in Pushkin's poem of that name. It is the symbolic center of the modern system city Peter conjured into being—the Dutch-style naval base subsequently embellished by Elizabeth and Catherine. When Herzen first visited St. Petersburg, in 1839, he tells us he went immediately to gaze upon that statue, and to wish that the cannon that crushed the Decembrists had instead pulverized that image. Peter, his statue, and his city, were the symbols of modernism and state power to Herzen, Pushkin, Dostoevsky, and most other writers. Pushkin said Peter had made all Russia rear up like a horse when he got on her back.

Tolstoy had, moreover, a personal connection with Peter the Great, for the founder of the Tolstoy family fortunes, Lev's great-great-great-grandfather, was a personal favorite of that tsar. He went to Italy on Peter's bidding in 1697, to study naval science, as part of the modernization program. He became the first Russian ambassador to Constantinople, 1701–1710. And in 1717 he tricked Peter's recalcitrant son, Alexei, into returning to Russia from Germany, where he is thought to have been murdered to suit Peter's plans. After the death of Alexei, Peter Tolstoy was "one of the most intimate and trusted persons about the Emperor," according to Paul Birukov, the later Tolstoy's biographer.

The tragic confrontation of Peter and his son has continued to fascinate and trouble the Russian imagination. Ge, a friend of the novelist Tolstoy, painted a famous picture of the two facing each other; and D. S. Merezhkovsky wrote a famous novel, *Peter and Alexis,* in 1905, in which Peter reproached his son with listening too

much to priests and with taking no interest in military matters—
"through which we have come from darkness to light."

The part of the Petropavlovsk Fortress in which the Tsarevitch was
put to death was known afterward as the Alexis Ravelin, and it
remained an evocative name in Russian culture, because it was the
prison's death row. It was a place impossible for outsiders to visit, and
Tolstoy himself, even though the prison governor was an old friend
of his, was refused permission when he wanted to do some research
there. It was also where the famous revolutionaries of his lifetime, like
Nechaev and Kropotkin, were held. Thus there were many reasons
for Alexis, and Peter Tolstoy, and Peter the Great, to recur to the
novelist's mind.

Peter the Great was known as the Tsar Preobrazovatel, the Transforming Tsar, and what he transformed was Russia, and into a part
of the modern world system. Earlier rulers had wanted to reform
Russia, Marc Raeff tells us, "But not at the price of a loss of its
traditional spiritual and cultural identity. For Peter, on the other
hand, this identity did not have any absolute value or particular
meaning, quite the contrary perhaps" (Raeff, *Peter the Great*, p. x).
And on the next page, "Power was the most easily perceptible and
most dramatic manifestation of the new spirit of Europe. It was this
very modern and Western trait that Peter possessed to a high degree." He forced on Russia a new chronology, new script, new costume; he set up a newspaper, shaved off people's beards, reorganized
the Church, and created that metallurgy industry which was in the
eighteenth century the most advanced in Europe.

And he was a modernist in the detail of his personality, as well as
in the design of his reforms. V. O. Kliuchevsky says, "Whenever he
could, he used his hands, which were never free from calluses. When
he was young and still inexperienced he could never be shown over
a factory or a workshop without trying his hand at whatever work was
in progress. He found it impossible to remain a mere spectator,
particularly if he saw something new going on. His hands instinctively
sought for tools; he wanted to work at everything himself." He was
an epitome of the modern world system. "Even during his first
foreign tour, the German princesses who talked with him came to the
conclusion that he was a master-craftsman in fourteen different
trades" (Kliuchevsky, *Peter the Great*, p. 13). He was a royal Robinson Crusoe, but he had a populous empire to work on, not an empty

island. As B. H. Sumner says, in his *Peter the Great*, "He had, in fact, a craftsman's bent, an inventor's, an explorer's" (p. 23).

Peter evoked awe-struck loyalty from his subjects. One of his contemporaries called him, "Our Lord, Peter the Great, who has drawn us from nothingness into being," and Derzhavin said, "Was it not God, Who in his person came down to earth?" But in *Notes on Ancient and Modern Russia* (1811), Karamzin, who at first also idolized him, said that Peter had made Russians citizens of the world, but stopped them being citizens of their native land. And the revival of nationalism, after the defeat of Napoleon, strengthened this feeling. The Slavophiles glorified pre-Petrine Russia. The peasants had always resisted Peter's reforms, and had rumored that he was the Anti-Christ, because he was leading their country into the modern world system.

It cannot have been a matter of indifference to an imagination like Tolstoy's that his family's fortunes were founded by a favorite of this tsar—in a sense by Peter. He tried for a long time to write a novel about Peter and his work, but had to give it up. According to D. S. Mirsky, he failed because he became so disgusted with the person of the great emperor—"the embodiment of all he hated."

Tolstoy himself was not without modernizing and westernizing sympathies, especially early in his life. When he was young he read Rousseau with passionate enthusiasm, and imitated Benjamin Franklin by keeping a Franklin journal to record his faults and his progress in correcting them, and so on. In middle life he spent much of his energy on educational and agricultural experiments. And in his comments on the English and French soldiers he met when they were prisoners of the Russians in the Crimean war, he used modernist criteria himself. He admired their independence and skill and fully developed individuality, and contrasted the Russian soldiers with them unfavorably.

He wrote to his brother Sergei during the Crimean War (Birukoff, *Leo Tolstoy*, Vol. I, p. 176), "You should see the French and English prisoners (especially the latter); each one is better than the last, I mean morally and physically; they are a *splendid people*. The Cossacks say that even they feel pity in sabring them, and by their side, you should see any one of our riflemen; small, lousy, and shriveled up, in a way."

One of the official papers Tolstoy wrote as an officer in that war was about the fact that the Western armies had rifles, and the Russians only muskets. It was entitled "Massacre by Small-Arms." In fact, half the English and French soldiers had guns with a range of 1,200 paces, while 95 percent of the Russians' range was only 300. And they were not trained in marksmanship (Harcave, *Years of the Golden Cockerel,* p. 155). Thus Tolstoy was involved in those practical and even military affairs which involved acknowledging the superiority of the West. When he turned against Peter, he turned against part of himself.

Intellectual Russia as a whole may be said to have turned against modernization—which again meant turning against part of itself—in the course of the nineteenth century. The populist movement was in part inspired by Tolstoy, in part by Herzen and other writers. It can be seen, as James Billington has argued in *The Icon and the Axe,* as a continuation of the various forms of resistance and protest recurrent in Russia since the times of Peter himself. "The central fact of the populist era," Billington says, "which haunted the imagination of its creative artists, was that all of Russian life was being materially transformed by modernizing forces from the West" (p. 402). But this was not a new concern. The student martyrs of the populist movement in the 1870s and '80s were the heirs of the 20,000 Old Believers who had burned themselves to death two centuries before rather than accept the modernization of the Russian Church. They were the heirs of the Cossacks who had risen in defense of their liberty, and of the peasants who had declared Peter the Anti-Christ himself. And Tolstoy was one of their literary heroes.

Moreover, seeing Tolstoy as opposing Peter is also of interest to us because Defoe wrote a history of that tsar, and made him into one of his heroes of modernization. They were of course on the same side on most issues. Defoe's hero, William III, was the western king Peter most admired, and on his trip to England he visited William and was presented with an English yacht. And when Peter sent Vitus Bering exploring in 1725, the Great Northern Expedition took with it nine wagons of instruments and books, amongst which were the very recently published *Robinson Crusoe* (and *Gulliver's Travels*).

In his *Impartial History of the Life and Actions of Peter Alexandrovitz,* Defoe points out that the tsar had altered "the economy, the customs, manners and commerce of his own people. By this means, he has brought a nation, who were before the most blind and ignorant, and the greatest contemners of knowledge, and of all manner of learning, to be searchers after wisdom, studying sciences and eagerly bringing home books, instruments, and artists, from the most learned parts of the world, for their instruction. By this means, he has brought his soldiers, who were before the most scoundrel undisciplined crowds, rabbles rather than soldiers, and just good for nothing, to be regular disciplined troops, clothed, armed, and paid like other nations, and behaving on all occasions in a manner sufficient to make them formidable to those who used to despise them. By this means, he has reduced his people in general, to a legal kind of obedience to their governors; not the same kind of blind homage they used to pay to their princes, who they rather worshiped than obeyed; but, a more polite regulation, so that now the czar endeavors to convince their reason, of the real advantages which his new laws are to them, at the same time that he exacts their obedience. . . ." (p. 3). He brought them into the modern world system, taught them freedom, productivity, enterprise, enlightened self-interest.

It was not Defoe but Voltaire who wrote for Catherine the Great the official biography of Peter. Lomonosov collected the materials, and Voltaire wrote them up—and fell, like so many other philosophes, philosophically enamored of Catherine. But this was a very appropriate conjunction of personalities, which can only reinforce our sense of the greater affinity between Defoe and Peter. Voltaire and the philosophes were in many ways the more elegant heirs and belles-lettres epigones of Defoe, just as Catherine was the more elegant and belles-lettres edition of Peter; just as her Italianate St. Petersburg was the rococo efflorescence of his Dutch-style naval base.

Defoe returned to the subject of Peter quite often in other books, notably in *The Complete English Gentleman,* where we are told, "He sought wisdom, thro' the whole world; he applyed for knowledge, in every branch of science. . . ." (p. 36) and, "It was his usual saying, that every cobbler that came but from Germany or Holland knew more than he did" (p. 27). When Peter came to the throne, there was no printing press in Moscow, and the boyars didn't want the one he forced on them. "Their best surgeons knew nothing of anatomy; their best astronomers knew nothing of eclipses; they had not a skeleton in the whole empire, except what be natural in their graves; their geographers had not a globe, their seamen not a compass (by the way they had no ships) even their physicians had no books . . . even their handicrafts had no tools; there was not a Russian clock-maker or watch-maker to be found in the whole empire. . . ." (p. 67).

And though Russian intellectuals in the nineteenth century necessarily had angrier and more complicated feelings about Peter than Defoe did, still the affirmative half of their dialectic followed the lines of this argument. There were moments in Tolstoy's life when he would have assented to this account of Peter, and even when he dissented, it remained a very important idea to him.

Tolstoy's Adventures

Through much of his writing career, then, Tolstoy believed in the modern system and therefore in adventure; and even after he ceased to believe in the former, he was strongly drawn toward the latter. I will just mention, among his adventure tales, "A Prisoner in the Caucasus," "The Raid," "The Bear Hunt," and "Stories of My Dogs." Moreover, he planned a great novel about Russian history and national destiny, which would have contained elements of Cooper and even of Defoe. We find in his diary for March 3, 1877,* "In *Anna Karenina* I cherish the idea of the *family,* in *War and Peace,* in view of the war of 1812, the idea of the *people;* the central idea of my new book will be the *power of expansion* of the Russian people."

He saw this expansion in the constant migration of Russians to the new lands in the southeast, in southern Siberia, in the Belaya Reka region, in Turkestan, etc. "A great deal is heard about all this migration nowadays. We spent last summer in the Samara region, and the two of us drove to a Cossack settlement some fifteen miles from our Samara farm . . ." and met on the way a long procession of such migrants (p. 63). Just recently he'd heard of a hundred Tambov peasants going to Siberia on their own initiative; they finally found some abandoned land on the Manchurian border. "And so, although the land originally belonged to China, it became Russian soil, conquered not with blood and war, but by the agricultural strength of

*Copied into his wife's diary; see Sonia Tolstoy, *Diary of Tolstoy's Wife 1860–91.*

the Russian moujik. Occasionally the Manchurians attack them, but the Russians have built a fort and are able to protect themselves." This is in a sense a scene out of American experience which he is recording, and he is finding an inspiration for his new novel in a modern system story. On October 25, of the same year, he says this book's "main theme is the people and their strength, which reveals itself exclusively in agriculture." In Part II there will be a Russian Robinson Crusoe, who will settle on new land in the Samara Steppe. This could have been the great *serious* adventure tale. But that novel never got written; no doubt Tolstoy came to feel that "the strength of the Russian people" was a divisive theme, and that such strength was not and could not be manifested only in agriculture.

Nevertheless, even at the end of his life, Tolstoy wrote one of his finest adventure tales, *Hadji Murad;* again about the war in the Caucasus, but its sympathies directed against the Russians, or at least with the Chechens. Alexandra Tolstoy, in her *Life of My Father,* describes how Tolstoy worked on "How to Read the Gospels" and allowed himself also to write *Hadji Murad* as an indulgence. Thus in his diary for August 5, 1902, he says, "I have been writing on Hadji Murad, partly with pleasure, partly against the grain, and with shame."

Its origin is in a diary entry of 1896, about a thistle plant he saw. "There were three shoots on it: one was broken and a white, muddy flower hung from it; another was broken and splashed with mud, the stem was shattered and dirt-stained; the third shoot stuck on sideways; it was also dark with dust, but it was still alive and the centre of it was turning red. It reminded me of Hadji Murad. I'd like to write about it. It clings to life right up to the last, and it is the one thing in all the field, and somehow it has clung to it" (A. Tolstoy, *Tolstoy: A Life of My Father,* p. 371).

It is a passionate empathy with all living things that triggers this memory and this inspiration. That was a faculty which Tolstoy possessed in unusual degree. And it is connected with the values his art embodies, the worship of life. The thistle is a triumphant emblem of life surviving in spite of all difficulties—life, as distinct from beauty or goodness or anything else; and the same is true of the character Hadji Murad. And the fact that his art—and much modern art—is inseparable from life-worship, is the reason why the late Tolstoy (whose values were spiritual) was ashamed of writing the story.

In the introduction to the actual story he describes gathering flowers, and seeing the red kind called Tatar, always avoided by pickers because of its cruel thorns, and its toughness. This specimen took him five minutes to pluck, and then was too coarse for his nosegay. A little later he saw another such plant thrown away on a ploughed field, and he thought how destructive man is to other species.

" 'What a destructive creature is man, how many different creatures, how much growth he destroys to support his own life!' I thought, involuntarily striving to discover something living amid the black and lifeless fields." His attitude is very close to Lévi-Strauss's, if we make an equivalence between Tolstoy's "man" and the other's "European man" or "civilized man." When he sees the second Tatar thistle: "one of its arms lopped off, an eye put out, still it stood up, refusing to surrender to Man, the destroyer of its many brothers all around it. 'What energy!' I thought."

But all of this translates also into quite specific reference to the story he is going to tell. "Tatar" was a general name for all the savage tribes against whom the Russians made war in their expansion east. They were tough and cruel and too full of vitality to be sentimentalized, but as the empire expanded with its ploughed fields, these tribes were one by one subdued or slaughtered. One of them was the Caucasians (also called Circassians, or Chechens), against whom a Russian army was fighting in 1850, when Tolstoy joined it, and when Hadji Murad was a leading figure on the opposite side.

It is notable that Tolstoy wrote so often about this situation, rather than about, say, the Crimean War—apart from the reports he wrote at the time from Sebastopol. The Caucasian situation was explicitly imperialist—very like, in fact, the North-West frontier in India which Kipling wrote about—and that was the subject Tolstoy turned back to, time and time again. The main leader of the Caucasian resistance then was Shamil, a religious as well as military figure. In Tolstoy's story, Hadji Murad, having quarreled with Shamil, has to flee to the Russians for protection; we see him only when he arrives among the Russians; he dictates his life story, which is very bloody, at their request; he makes friends with Butler, a handsome officer in the Cossack regiment; finally he makes a suicidal attempt to return to his people, in order to save his family there, but is killed and decapitated.

Hadji Murad, the man and the story, is fierceness incarnate. The idea of a doomed rebellion, and the hero's position, vis-à-vis Shamil, roughly like Fergus's position vis-à-vis the Young Pretender, may remind us of Scott and his adaptation of the Black Prince motif. But the difference is that Tolstoy's story has no Waverley and consequently no Rose or Flora; nor, indeed, any plot, in the sense of the mild interests and satisfactions connected with Waverley himself. Tolstoy confronts us very directly with Hadji Murad, which has a much more shocking and sobering effect. But underneath and behind that sobriety is the ineluctable exhilaration of adventure. We identify with fierceness incarnate. This is a late-style adventure, closer to Kipling than to Scott. Fifty years after the event, and fifty years later in the history of the modern system, Tolstoy had to see imperialist war in more radical terms. To enjoy its excitements, one had to swallow blood, cruelty, and destruction.

The Cossacks

But Tolstoy wrote *The Cossacks,* also about that war, at the beginning of his writing career, between 1852 and 1862. This *is* another Waverley story, with an author-representing central character called Olenin, who leaves Moscow because he feels his mind and his heart going to seed in the center of a civilization, and joins the Russian army in the Caucasus as an observer-participant. While there he meets some powerful excitements and severe challenges to his manhood; from an old Cossack hunter, Eroshka, a figure of vitality, freedom, boldness; from a beautiful Cossack girl, Maryanka, with whom Olenin falls in love but does not dare marry; and from Luka, a Cossack brave whom Maryanka does marry, and who represents in many other ways all that Olenin wants to be. At the end he goes back to Moscow, defeated but enriched by the experience, like Waverley. And the background is another doomed rising (of the Chechens); though there is less bloodshed here than in *Waverley.*

The novel is significantly autobiographical. There was an Eroshka (in real life Epishka) and a Maryanka (in real life Solomonida) and a Chechen brave called Sado, who made Tolstoy his *kunak* (comrade or blood-brother). Most significant, Tolstoy felt the challenges and promises of Cossack life just as Olenin felt them. He felt the cultural nostalgia we saw in Cooper; writing to his aunt about becoming Sado's *kunak*, he told her how ancient the custom was, something "by now" honored mostly in the memory.

At the same time, *The Cossacks* is very completely and straightforwardly a translation into the terms of Russian culture of the Scott-Cooper version of modernist adventure, and somewhat closer to Cooper's rendering. Tolstoy puts, for instance, a stress on guns and hunting, and takes an interest in geography and contemporary history, which is more like Cooper's. And Eroshka, though very unlike Natty Bumppo in his psychosexual type, and the intensity of his physical presence—which is rendered in terms of a smell of blood, sweat, and gunpowder—is nevertheless a version of the old hunter. One of the diagrams of tendency in the book is a triangle of emotional vectors, in which Olenin and Luka both aspire toward Eroshka, as rival heirs to his virtue.

The triangle is the same as one in *The Prairie,* though the tendency and the conflict are blurred in Cooper. (Captain Middleton and Paul Hover aspire to be Natty's heir.) But we also think of *Waverley.* Luka is a Black Prince of the Fergus MacIvor kind, in that he is the man of action whom the observer-participant yearns to be. We switch back to a Scott-comparison here, because Luka is not separated from Olenin by race, as Chingachgook is from Natty. Moreover, Maryanka is a heroine of the Flora type (with some touches of Marina/Malintzi); she embodies the wild and barbaric virtue of her race, which Olenin could only possess by possessing her. (This was a motif Conrad was to make much use of—Nina in *Almayer's Folly,* Jewel in *Lord Jim.*)[8] There is another triangle of vectors, with Luka and Olenin both aspiring to her.

Had the novel been completed (what we have is only Part I of three projected parts) it would have reminded us even more of *Waverley.* In Part II Maryanka was decisively to choose Luka over Olenin, but the two men were to go together up into the mountains to take part in the war there. In Part III Olenin was to return alone to marry Maryanka, but the marriage was to turn out badly, and he was to be murdered, either by her or by some rival for her favors. This is a rearrangement of Scott's scheme in *Waverley;* making Flora Fergus's beloved instead of his sister; and then—a more significant change but still true to the theme—ending the story tragically and not comically. Waverley–Olenin's attempt to assimilate the wildness of the Cossacks–Highlanders is here shown to be impossible and doomed to bring about disaster.

The important new idea which Tolstoy brings to the adventure is that of Nature—his idea being a much more metaphysical and psychological one than Scott's or Cooper's. Tolstoy's is even a religious idea and so more a kind of cult. (Tolstoy's beloved brother Nikolai, the day before his death, said, "Only one thing remains—the vague hope that there is in Nature, of which in the earth one will become a part, something which will abide and will be found.")

This is what gives so much more depth to the characterization of Olenin than there was to Waverley. Olenin's motivation for leaving Moscow, what he sees as he looks at the Cossack village, his desire for Maryanka, his excitement in the fighting, all this as much as his feeling for the actual forest is a cult of nature. It is an idea very well suited to the modernist adventure story, in which the thematic crux is the exchange of values between a more primitive and a more civilized culture.

But there was something else in Tolstoy which made him avoid some of the adventure possibilities of this story; at the end of Chapter 32, Olenin is awakened by the sergeant major and told that the company is leaving on a raid into the Chechen country. This raid lasts four days, and is the most considerable military operation described —except that it isn't described. The narration jumps ahead to Olenin's return from it. The paragraph that begins with the raid ends with, "Then Olenin sat all evening long on the porch staring at Maryanka, and the whole night, without a thought in his head, he aimlessly paced the yard" (p. 145). This makes *The Cossacks* into a love-adventure, which is to say, no adventure. The writing of the story took a long time, including some complete breaks, and Tolstoy was heading towards the domestic novel by the time he finished. He had committed himself to marriage, in life and letters.

Tolstoy was always serious, always spiritually ambitious—more than Defoe and Scott, for example. He aimed at greatness always, and however skeptical he might be of the received ideas of his time, he could not resist the pressure that pushed him away from the adventure and toward the domestic novel. He did resist the pressure to write about lower- and middle-class characters, as we saw, but he yielded to the fundamental teaching of literature-as-a-system; and in *War and Peace* wrote a masterpiece of the subordination of the adventure to the other form; and in *Anna Karenina* a masterpiece of the domestic novel at its purest.

Perhaps, however, he missed one opportunity, to make a masterpiece out of *The Cossacks*. The most striking feature of Tolstoy's treatment of that story is the one indicated by the title: his presentation of Cossack life. This is striking because so appropriate, skillful, and beautiful; but it was not original, in literary terms, for it is very like Scott's treatment of the Highlanders. It was a treatment already conventional in Russian literature; the Caucasus had been for Pushkin and Lermontov already the land of nature and of heroism. Russians in general held that, as Tolstoy said of the Chechens, "These people live as nature does; they die, are born, intermingle, give birth to children, fight, drink, eat, are happy and die again, and their lives are not conditioned, except as nature herself inexorably rules the sun, the grass, the animals, the trees, and them. They have no other laws" (A. Tolstoy, *The Cossacks*, p. 123). Nor does Tolstoy stress—and this was his opportunity—those features of the Cossacks that would have distinguished them from Scott's Highlanders; their double function as both examples of freedom and agents of discipline.

Those distinguishing features he does stress, or does allow to emerge, are those which align his picture with Cooper's. For the Russian situation was strikingly like the American in certain ways. The idea of the natural or primitive that was represented for Scott by the Highlanders, for Cooper and Tolstoy was split into two figures that were at war with each other: the Cossacks versus the Chechens, the frontiersmen against the Indians. The Cossacks were fighting for the Russian state against the Chechens, though they were not part of the Russian army, and were in fact resentful and scornful of Russian individuals—seeing them as overcivilized. When Olenin joins the Russian army as observer-participant, he faces three social groups, of which the Cossacks are the middle term; they are something of a stepping stone for his imagination toward the fiercer and unimaginable primitivism of the Chechens. Perhaps they are not so much a stepping stone as an arrow pointing the way, for some Cossacks have already adopted Chechen ways, particularly the young men, and Luka and Eroshka have Chechen friends; respectable families like Maryanka's aspire to be Russian, but the young people with whom Olenin is concerned aspire to be Chechen. This is of course very like frontiersmen's feelings for the Indians (Natty's heart is with the Indians) and their *being* half-Indian, half-white. The situation is very emblematic of imperialism; Kipling's heroes too intensely admire the tribes they war against—Stalky on the North-West frontier is said to have *become* a Sikh—and are very uneasy with the Englishmen they meet in London. But not even Tolstoy took full imaginative advantage of the situation.

Of course, neither Scott nor Cooper offered him a good model. Scott's Highlanders were more like the Chechens than the Cossacks, and Cooper's frontiersmen were depicted stiffly and distortedly. While in Russian fiction, Gogol's Cossacks were almost purely picturesque. Tolstoy portrays his Cossacks close up with wonderful vividness, but fails to find the larger historical perspective they deserve, and the sterner historical seriousness that would go with that.

Thus the greatest interest Tolstoy has for us here does not derive from his artistic success with the genre of adventure. Judged from that point of view, *The Cossacks* is charming and even distinguished, but not a major achievement. Its greatest interest is of the kind it shares with *Robinson Crusoe*—the importance of the facts (including the myths) it engages our imaginations with. Tolstoy's achievement is to persuade us that there is something out there—not in *The Cossacks* but in the Cossacks—which has fixed his attention and so deserves to fix ours. The power of his treatment lies in its historical truth. This is an important imaginative context for not only his own work but all adventure fiction. And it is important in more than one way. Tolstoy's resemblance to Cooper also brings out the *international* character of modern system imperialism. This is not an American or a Russian, but a world-historical phenomenon. The Cossacks reveal to us the tendency so mutedly expressed in the frontiersmen of America and the transoceanic empires.

The American frontier too was advanced westward by the means of bands of *men;* men on their own, that is; as were the frontiers of the empires of European powers.[9] In the case of France, we find the Foreign Legion, who won Vietnam for France between 1865 and 1885; in the case of England, the Canadian Mounted Police, who rode west from Winnipeg in 1873; and the young pioneers Rhodes sent north in 1890 to occupy Mashonaland. But there were fewer of them than of the Cossacks, and they counted for less, in the running of the homeland and the character of the government. It seemed a metaphor when Marx or Herzen called the African troops of Napoleon III "Cossacks." But it was more than a metaphor, and it meant more than Marx intended. It meant not only that Napoleon III's France was getting to be like Russia, but that Russia was only like France—her Cossacks had always had their counterparts in Western Europe. Russia was in many ways—in its relation to China, the Caucasus, Tibet, the Tatars—culturally WASP. It was the agent of expansion of the modern system, in its relation to the rest of the world, although it was the patient in its relation to Western Europe.

The Cossacks

Their origin seems to go back to Muscovy's rise to power in Russia, when the national enemy were the Mongol states ruled by the successors to Genghis Khan. Mongol or Tatar parties raided Russian settlements by night, bringing baskets to carry off babies, and taking slaves to sell to the Turks. So some groups of "free" Tatars sold their services to the Russians as border guards to defend them against these raids. Then Russians who disliked settlement life moved out into the "wild" or "free" country to do the same. At first they lived out there in the summer months only, returning to the settlements in the winter. But then the authorities exerted tighter controls, and these frontiersmen had to choose —and those who chose to live like Cossacks all the time were of course the fiercer ones. The first leader of Russian Cossacks was probably Ivan Russo, who is mentioned in 1468. By 1570 there were seventy-three watchposts along the frontier manned by such men, who were granted land and hunting rights in return for their services. These were called "town Cossacks" because of their comparatively organized condition.*

They were in flight from the taxation and legalism of the settlements. From 1500 on Russian peasants had been fleeing the imposition of authority by the central government. As Muscovy established

*See Philip Longworth, *The Cossacks.*

its empire over the rest of Russia, it gave the nobles imperial rights over their peasants.

According to Wallerstein, serfdom was introduced into periphery states like Russia just as it was being ended in core states like England. The bonded peasant class was created in Western Europe between 1100 and 1300, but in Russia between 1500 and 1700. They remained bound. The last serfs were emancipated in France in 1791, but in Russia nearly all the peasants remained serfs until 1861. Feudal dues and duties increased decade by decade, and it was as late as 1581 that the decree was passed forbidding peasants to leave the village they were born in—tying them to a particular landowner. The Cossacks were those who escaped that process, from a variety of motives. They were strongly influenced by the Tatars they fought against. They used the horsetail standard of the Mongols (Genghis Khan's standard) and mated with Tatar women, whom they often abducted. For many of them, marriage was not a part of life. One of the famous settlements, the Zaporozhian Sech, was officially bachelor, and women were not supposed to enter it. They used Tatar words, like *ataman*, for their leader, *esaul* for his lieutenant, and *yassak* for tribute. They called farming a kind of slavery, and promulgated decrees against it. The plough was for them a mark of bondage. The word Cossack itself, *kasak*, is a Turkic word used since the tenth century by the Mongols to mean adventurer.

They were not, then, an ethnic group, in any strict sense; in a loose sense they were an ideological group, with an ideology of freedom. Their economic activities were to sell to the settlements the fish, fur, and hides they had caught, plus honey and wax, in return for grain and cloth, nails, and lead, powder and guns. This must remind us of the American frontiersmen; and it is typical of many similarities that when attacked on the march, the Cossacks formed their carts into a triangle (called a tabor) and fired upon the Tatars, who circled the formation on horseback, galloping and shooting arrows. (Longworth says the Cossacks were closer to our image of cowboys than were the real cowboys.) But of course their main activity was hunting and fighting; the boys were trained to gallop, to stalk, to swim horses across streams, etc.

Of all the companies of Cossacks, that of the Terek—the one Tolstoy wrote about—was generally considered the most romantic. Alexandre Dumas had written about them, in his *Adventures in the*

Tolstoy

Caucasus. They had adopted the Chechen cloaks, Chechen war cries, Chechen riding style, just as American frontiersmen adopted the Indians'. And the situation of their lives was as adventurous and romantic as any adventure-romancer would wish; bare-chested, shaven-headed Circassian braves, who one day came to the Cossack village to trade, the next day lurked in the reeds by the river to kill. The Cossacks were Old Believers—and thus religiously too they were in resistance to modern Russia—and they were defending a narrow strip of land along the Terek river, fifty miles long but only about 700 yards wide. They were fighting against mountain tribes first aroused to a holy war against Russia by Kazi Mullah in 1829, who did not capitulate until 1859.[10] Indeed, Russia had annexed Georgia in 1801, and the mountain tribes had been fighting sporadically ever since then. The conquest of the mountains had been begun by General Ermolov in 1816, but it was not easy. General Velgaminov wrote, "The mounted natives are very superior in many ways both to our regular cavalry and to the Cossacks; they can ride between dawn and sunset a hundred miles. They are born on horseback, their weapons, carefully selected, are private property, and kept in excellent condition" (W. Laqueur, *Guerilla*, p. 73).

But how did the Cossacks feel, that they should be attacking the Chechens on behalf of Russia, while their sympathies ran as much in the opposite direction? This was in fact a very typical situation for them. They had always been the advance guard of the Russian empire, Russia's frontiersmen (and also shock troops and arm of terror), but they were also rebels against the settled life of citizenship; they imposed the discipline of civilization on primitive tribes, while at the same time in flight from that discipline themselves. They played the same role as Natty and Daniel Boone, only armed to the teeth and organized into hordes of thousands.

Politically, they stood for freedom, as far as their own social organization goes. Each host, or *voisk,* governed itself by means of a general assembly, called a *krug,* and theoretically the land was communally owned. In the seventeenth century there were about ten thousand Don Cossacks, egalitarian and libertarian, unruly and marauding. And they saw themselves, and were seen by others, as free; singing and dancing were a part of their image; and even free-thinking writers were praised as "Cossacks." They were mythical heroes for the rest

194

of Russia, embodying the myth of freedom and expansion, just as the frontiersmen were for America. Pushkin's Decembrist friend, Ryleev, wrote a famous ballad, "Voynarovsky," about a Byronic Cossack hero, the heir to Mazeppa (the Cossack rebel against Peter the Great). Herzen referred to himself as a Cossack, and to his circle of friends as a Cossack brotherhood, because of their love of freedom. At the same time, he referred to the troops who put down the revolution of 1848 in France as "African Cossacks."

This is surely the most vivid example of the anthropoemia Lévi-Strauss discusses, and shows how that could serve the purposes of an imperialist power. For seen in terms of their relations with the outside world, the Cossacks were the agents of political discipline. In the 1650s the tsarist government created a military community of five regiments of Cossacks around Kharkov; other such settlements came later, and the Cossacks were pressed to conform to that pattern. (The government's control of ammunition gave them leverage over the Cossacks.) In 1654 the Zaporozhian Cossacks, who had been employed by the king of Poland as border guards, against, amongst others, the Russians, transferred their services to the tsar. This was a very important step in the development of Russian power in Europe, and brought, as its first fruits, the acquisition of the Ukraine. But even more important was the expansion of Russia toward the East, which was also the work of Cossacks.

The Cossack leader Ermak had led 540 men across the Urals in 1581, and the four hundred of them who reached Sibir there defeated a force of two thousand Tatars. This is a story like that of Cortes and Raleigh, in date and historical significance, and in frequency of retelling. (It is, incidentally, a subject Tolstoy devoted a story to.) They were sent out by a rich trading company, the Stroganovs, and they won partly because they had guns. Ermak's success advanced the Russian frontier, at one point, four thousand miles east. By 1600 a million skins were being sent back to Moscow every year. Whole areas were hunted out in twenty or thirty years. Ten percent of the state's revenue was derived from that trade, and foreigners were rigidly debarred from it. (The Cossacks acted as tribute collectors from the trappers, when they weren't the trappers themselves.) Their advance is comparable in many ways to the American advance west, but by 1630, the Russians had settlements on the Pacific coast, while the Americans had only reached the Appalachians. And the Cossacks here were the advance guard of the modern system—culturally WASP.

In the eighteenth century, however, they developed a loyalty to the tsars in particular. The government used them for military purposes, expansive or repressive. In 1792 Catherine the Great created the Kuban host, to protect and develop the North-West of the Caucasus, recently taken from Turkey. In 1867 a Seven Rivers *Voisk* was created to do the same for Central Asia. During the nineteenth century there were twelve main groups; by 1900, 7 million Cossacks were estimated to live on 230,000 square miles, and to provide the Russian army with soldiers, mostly cavalry. In peacetime they formed 45 percent of Russia's cavalry, in wartime 70 percent. Every Cossack male had to serve in the army twenty years. Napoleon called the Cossacks a disgrace to the human race, but dreamed for a time of creating a similar force in France.

Repressively they were used, for instance, against Poland, after the annexation of that country. In 1798 60,000 Poles took up arms, mostly pikes and scythes, with a few muskets; and the same happened in 1831 and 1863, when the Russian superiority was ten to one. Polish veterans of those aborted revolutions went to fight in revolutions elsewhere: Mieroslavski in Baden and Sicily; Dembinski and Bern against Austria in 1848; Mickiewicz in the Roman Republic. This was the kind of history that shaped, for instance, Conrad's feeling about Russia and about politics in general. The Cossacks played a very sinister role in that history, and—inside Russia—against Jews and students and striking workers.

On the other hand, there were Cossack revolts within Russia in the name of freedom. For instance, in the seventeenth century, the revolt led by Xmelnitski; in the eighteenth those led by Stenka Razin and Pugachev. These men were heroes of liberty to nineteenth-century revolutionaries in Russia like Bakunin and Nechaev. For that matter, Byron had made a hero out of Mazeppa, the Hetman of the Ukraine who rebelled against Peter the Great. And gradually their loyalty to the tsar wore out at the end of the nineteenth century, when they were used more and more against striking workers and protesting students. They played a major part in defeating the Revolution of 1905, but soon after they began to refuse to fire or to charge against certain kinds of rebels, and in 1917 they effectively deserted the tsar.

The Cossacks' is the great story which explains so much—not only about Russia—and which challenges and denies as well as explains; and yet it did not get taken into literature.* And behind the Cossacks themselves, a great body of Russian people, mostly peasants, moved east. Migration has, as we know, an important connection with adventure writing. And there was, in Russia, an ever-mounting drive eastward. Between 1894 and 1914, five million migrated east across the Urals, more than in the whole three hundred years preceding.

In his *Survey of Russian History* B. H. Sumner says, "Throughout Russian history one dominating theme has been the frontier; the theme of the struggle for the mastering of the natural resources of an untamed country, expanded into a continent by the ever-shifting movement of the Russian people and their conquest of and intermingling with other peoples" (p. 9). Sumner draws several parallels between Russian history and American and English imperialism. The Caucasian mountains were the equivalent of India's North-West Frontier; and Gogol's *Taras Bulba* is like Parkman's *Oregon Trail.* The agriculturalists continually advanced against forest-and-plains nomads, and the edge of the wave was the meeting with savagery—"a return to primitive conditions on a continually advancing frontier."

As in Anglo-Saxon imperial history, part of the motive power was mechanical, part political, part military. In 1886 the Trans-Caspian Railway reached to Merv, in 1888 to Samarkand, in 1898 to Herat. But there was also a Russian equivalent to the American doctrine of manifest destiny, preached by Prince Ukhtemsky. And Russia had acquired Vladivostok in 1860, and most of Central Asia between 1864 and 1878; for instance, in 1866, General Romanovsky defeated 40,000 Bokharans and took Khodjent, and in 1871 a part of Chinese Turkestan was seized. Then during the Boxer Rebellion in China in 1900, Russia acquired Manchuria, and during the Boer War, while England was otherwise occupied, Russia pushed ahead in Persia, Turkey, and Afghanistan. Here we touch on imperialism in the conventional sense.

Intellectually, Russian imperialism used the same racist and cultural apologetics as did the English and French. The explorer Przhevalsky wrote in 1887, "These poor Asiatics look to the advance of Russian power with a firm conviction that its advent is synonymous

---

*Sholokhov's novels come closest to a full-scale treatment.

with the commencement of a happier era, a life of greater security for themselves." And the philosopher Solovev wrote in 1890 that inferior races must either submit or disappear. Let us take the explorer as a final example of the historical hero, to stand beside Olenin, and Tolstoy's other heroes, to define them by contrast.

Przhevalsky

Because Tolstoy was so divided in his sympathies, the enemy as much as the celebrant of adventure, we cannot naturally associate him with the historical heroes of his time. If we look for an equivalent to Andrew Jackson and Cooper's fascination by him, the best we can do is Peter the Great, who aroused Tolstoy's hostility rather than his fascination. And though Tolstoy was as much the historian as Scott, in *War and Peace,* we cannot associate him with the writing of nationalist or racist history in nineteenth-century Russia. (There was plenty of both; the myth of the coming of the Varangians to rule the Slavs, and thus to found the Russian state, is the same Teutonic race-myth as we found in nineteenth-century America.)

We do of course associate Tolstoy, the adventure-writer, with the war in the Caucasus. But he was too young to have known Ermolov, the conquistador who captured Pushkin's imagination; while Paskevich, the general who succeeded Ermolov, was not a heroic figure. Moreover, the conquest of the Caucasus was completed in 1859, and during Tolstoy's maturity Russian imperialism was directed toward Central Asia; under the direction of the minister of war, Miliutin, who came to power in 1861 and remained there until 1881. He avoided trouble with Turkey (which was under the protection of the European powers) but was aggressive in Turkestan. He advanced the careers of General Kaufman, the dashing conqueror of that territory, and later its viceroy; and of General Skobelev, whose victory at Gek Tepe excited many people, including Dostoevsky. The last words of his *Diary of a Writer* were, "Yes, hail the victory of Gek Tepe! Hail Skobelev and his soldiers, and the eternal memory of the heroic knights who were 'withdrawn from the rolls.' We shall inscribe them on our rolls." (E. C. Thaden, *Conservative Nationalism in 19th Cen-*

tury Russia, p. 85.) There we see Dostoevsky, though not congenitally of a military temperament, succumbing to military excitement under the influence of nationalist ideas.

But we must seek a more appropriate figure to set beside Tolstoy amongst those who represent more specifically modernist forms of expansion, who represent (though equivocally) the forces of enlightenment, the explorers. The figure of Nikolai Przhevalsky (1838–1888) is an interesting one for us, partly because of a specific resemblance between him and Stanley, but more generally because he represents in Russian terms forces we are familiar with in English history. Donald Rayfield, in his *Dream of Lhasa*, describes Przhevalsky as explorer, adventurer, zoologist, and conquistador. Though he despised China and the East, he also loathed European society—"The breath of mankind is more terrible and more destructive than all the misfortunes of nature." Though, like so many nineteenth-century boys, he dreamed as a child of being another Livingstone, his adult temperament was in fact much closer to Stanley's.

His father was of a Polish Cossack family, so he inherited something of that tradition. But in 1863 he helped to crush the Polish rising against tsarist rule. He belonged to the military and ruling caste, which took its leading part in the modernization of the country; his stepbrother directed the extension of the Trans-Caspian Railway to Samarkand—a significant step in the Russification of the East.

As a boy, Przhevalsky (like Stanley or Clive) hated school, loved hunting, and read only books on travel. He joined the Russian army in 1855, but still hoped to explore "the black heart of Africa," like Livingstone. In 1862 he published his first book, *Memoirs of a Sportsman*, in the aristocratic genre which Aksakov, Turgenev, and Tolstoy had made famous. And gradually he established his status as an explorer.

His personality conformed to one of the more distorted adventurer-models, least like domestic novel heroes in general, and Tolstoy's in particular. He was an enormous eater, especially of sweets. He took no interest in women, didn't drink, and went to bed at nine. He preferred boys as companions, and imposed a playfully sadistic relationship upon them. In 1866, when he began his explorations in eastern Siberia, he took with him a young companion, who had to promise implicit obedience in advance. When the boy got homesick, he was sent home in disgrace. In 1867 Przhevalsky took another sixteen-year-old with him into the Siberian jungle, armed with twenty-five pounds of gunpowder, fifteen pounds of shot, and so on. He was passionately fond of guns, and dazzled the natives with displays of marksmanship. But he was also passionately fond of Nature and of natural science, and he returned from this trip with 130 new species of flowering plants from Lake Hanka.

Later he went still farther afield, and got to Peking in 1870. He liked the company of the Buryat Mongol Cossacks whom he employed—they were horsemen of freedom. "Like a free bird in a cage, I cannot get on with this 'civilization,' where everyone is first and foremost a slave to social life" (Rayfield, *The Dream of Lhasa*, p. 187). But for non-European civilizations he had even less sympathy. "In my opinion, only the rifles and cannons of the Europeans can do any good here," he wrote from China. "Missionary preaching, in which Europe puts its hopes, is the voice of one crying in the wilderness" (Rayfield, p. 52). On this trip he (like another Connecticut Yankee) won a reputation among the natives as invulnerable, and also as a miracle doctor, because of the cures he worked with quinine.

His great desire was to get to Lhasa, for official Russia during the last quarter of the nineteenth century hoped to create a satellite kingdom in Tibet. In 1872 he set off on an expedition there, with a Martini machine gun, two Schneiders, thirteen revolvers, and a quarter of a ton of ammunition; and a rich store of trifles, such as mirrors, magnets, kaleidoscopes, and picture postcards of actresses. He reported to the general staff that, "A thousand of our soldiers would be enough to subdue all Asia from Lake Baykal to the Himalayas. . . . Here the exploits of Cortes can still be repeated" (p. 69). He wrote a three-volume book about this expedition before setting out on the next; and that was the pattern of his life; a journey, lectures and a book, another journey. He had to give lectures and go to dinners when he was in St. Petersburg, collecting funds for his next trip, but hating to do so, and always fell sick there.

In 1876 he again set out for Tibet (which he never reached) with two new teenage companions, whom he had jovially promised would get thrashed side by side whenever that was necessary. He won their devotion; in 1928 one of them recalled how "the deep gaze of his strict, handsome blue eyes seemed to penetrate right into your soul" (p. 154). He always praised his own Spartan education, because it had hardened him, and that was what he promised his boys—that he would harden them. On this last trip he took a new £100 Lancaster Express rifle, which he called Lyan, and which he fired and polished every day of his life till his death.

Such was Russia's explorer-conquistador. He was admired by men of letters too. Chekhov wrote an obituary, and said, "One Przhevalsky or one Stanley is worth twelve polytechnics and a thousand good books. Their loyalty . . . etc. . . . makes them in the eyes of the people heroes who personify a higher moral force" (p. 203). What Tolstoy thought, we don't know, but we can be sure he would have understood and admired, during the expansive moments in his own development, and would have bitterly condemned in the other moments. Przhevalsky embodied one force in the dialectic of tendency in Russia and in Tolstoy. That conflict was in some ways fiercer in them than in England and Tolstoy's equivalents there, just because of Russia's position on the periphery of the modern system. Rebecca West, in her life of St. Augustine, draws some interesting parallels between that saint's peripheral and provincial relation to the Roman Empire, and Tolstoy's to what we call the modern system. Tolstoy, like St. Augustine, was on the periphery, and he loved and envied what he saw at the center; but he also identified himself with the opposite to all that.

After *War and Peace* and *Anna Karenina,* no one was able to drive Tolstoy out of the center of literature-as-a-system in Russia, by attacks such as those on Defoe, Scott, and Cooper. (Though there were, and are, savage claims that he *ought not* to have been a great novelist, holding such opinions as he did.) But there was a comparable contemporary criticism of the early work, *The Cossacks,* before he became so established. This was written by Eugenie Tur, a highly respected novelist and critic of the time. She described Tolstoy's novel as "a poem in which the praise is sung, not by a commonplace talent, but a very real one, of daring prowess, thirst for blood and booty, man-hunts, the heartlessness of a beast-like savage. Side by side with this beast-savage is the abased, disparaged, broken, debauched representative of civilized society. . . . The author is at great pains to prove that savages are magnificent and happy, and cultivated people are low, petty, and unhappy" (A. Tolstoy, *Tolstoy,* p. 165). This is somewhat different from the attacks on Defoe and Swift, because the critic does not deny Tolstoy's talent; but just for that reason her ideological thrust—the thrust of literature's criticism of the adventure tale—is brought out. Tolstoy is said to betray the cause of civilization; we might interpret that to mean that he betrays the Brahmin caste of writers. (In Kipling's case, the critics felt the same, but made more of purely literary deficiencies, too.)

The conscience of later Russian literature, in the form of the writers of the 1860s, like Pisarev and Dobroliyubov, made to Tolstoy similar reproaches. He accepted the challenge. He told everyone he did not want to be "a writer"; and, as we have seen, he declared his inability and unwillingness to write like a bourgeois. He wrote like and for his own caste, the military and aristocratic. (A similar defiance can be seen in modern American novelists who have been struck by the claims of adventure—Hemingway, Mailer, Faulkner.) Then he wrote two of the greatest serious novels the world has; and then he repudiated literature altogether.

And behind all his shifts of stance, which have often been condemned as uneasy egotism, competitiveness, desire to be different, lay internecine struggles of sympathy and tendency in his nature, set off by the dialectic of the modern system.

VII

Popular Literature and Children's Literature

TOLSTOY gives us the sense—proper to high culture and especially to art—that he is questioning and testing whatever he describes; both the modern system, and the adventures of its expansion. Now we must look to narratives and discussions which seem not to test but to advertise their values, which work at a lower artistic and cultural level.

Turning to popular literature will bring out the importance of the how-to-do-it strain of adventure, the Defoe/merchant-caste strain, which gets overshadowed by the chivalric romance when we restrict our attention to works of literary value (serious art being reactionary, and often allied to the aristocracy) but which was very powerful at the popular level. That strain of feeling was also more powerful in nonfiction than in even "democratic" fiction, because art at its purest recoils from predominant truisms, and perhaps especially from mercantile ones. It is in popular biographies and advice books that Defoe's adventurer lived on and inspired others, not in brilliant novels.

Books of this kind had been appearing ever since Defoe's time, though they are meagerly represented in the histories of literature. I have mentioned one or two eighteenth-century writers like Dilworth; there were the stories of the sea and sailors; and of course there was the unending sequence of reissues and adaptations of *Robinson Crusoe.* But in tħe nineteenth century, this literature changed its character somewhat, as did more serious literature, in response to changing cultural forces, and also found new forms of expression. In the first half of this chapter, then, I shall not be tracing the development of fictional motifs, or evoking the historical background that gave those motifs resonance, but categorizing the culture heroes of the time—those that were in effect variants on the adventurer theme, and reinforcements of that idea. In the second half I shall describe motifs in the children's and popular literature of the time, or that part of it that was adventurous.

My discussion in the other chapters is restricted to writers of first-class intelligence and sensibility. Even Cooper, though far from being a great novelist, was a man of great intelligence. Since we are dealing with a cultural image as it got expressed in literature, and dealing with it in a literary way, it was necessary to choose material one can respect from that point of view. But it is necessary also to remember the other expressions of that image, less respectable and substantial from that point of view, but as effective or more so as a cultural influence. (For evidence of that effectiveness I rely on sales figures; no one seems to know what happens to books once bought —what they do inside the reading audience's heads.)

First of all, the work of Samuel Smiles, who was born in 1812, and became famous in 1859 with a book called *Self-Help,* which sold 25,000 copies in its year of publication, and 250,000 by 1900. It was translated into nearly every European language, and several Indian ones, plus Japanese, Arabic, and Turkish. In Italy there was an edition which substituted examples of self-help from Italian history for those British anecdotes which Smiles had chosen—anecdotes which made up nine-tenths of his book. This book was subtitled "Illustrations of Conduct and Perseverance," and it promised in effect to explain the secret of the superior energy and success of the Anglo-Saxons, their superior adaptation to the modern system. The *Revue des Deux Mondes* review took it as that, and only feared that Frenchmen's chauvinist prejudice might deny them access to this new source of moral energy. In his *Autobiography,* Smiles said that he wrote it to illustrate PERSEVERANCE, the great word of George Stephenson, the railway engineer.

Smiles was a Scotsman, a Utilitarian, and something of a radical in early life. Not an adventurer, then, but something of a Puritan. (He was a friend of Ebenezer Elliott, the Corn Law Rhymer of Sheffield.) And what this book teaches is how to acquire, by making a cult of these examples of great men and great actions, the standard virtues of Victorian England. What those are is perhaps sufficiently indicated by the titles of his later books: *Character*, 1871, *Thrift*, 1875, and *Duty*, 1880. They contain much warning against drink, and praise of savings banks; but basically these are collections of anecdotes about great men, noble boys, and Mothers (no need for an honorific for *them*). Some of the men most often cited are Washington, Wallerstein, Wellington, and Scott—a list somewhat equivalent to Defoe's list of Protestant heroes. Cobbett is described as the typical Englishman in character, and contrasted with Herder and Fichte; he was coarse and vulgar, compared with such Continental intellectuals, but had a strong undercurrent of poetry in his nature, and the tenderest regard for the character of women; though anything but refined, he was a true Englishman—pure, temperate, self-denying, industrious, vigorous, and energetic.

In the intellectual line, the greatest man who ever lived was Newton. (This is what Defoe and the Encyclopaedists said, but it's worth recalling that Swift dismissed Newton as a mechanic; Smiles is clearly on Defoe's side—the Encyclopaedists' side—in the Swift-Defoe battle.) More controversial choices of exemplars of virtue, but characteristic of Smiles, are Savonarola and Grace Darling, the lifeboat heroine. Both of these are puritan, and in their different ways, modernist figures. On the other side, Goethe, though a great poet, is not a man to copy, because he was amoral and an aesthete. Smiles has his suspicions of art, and warns us against certain kinds of literature— the leprous book, the scrofulous book, and even the giggling book. (Petronius? Pope? Nabokov?)

Considerably more interesting are his *Lives of the Engineers*, which began with *The Life of George Stephenson*, the great railway pioneer, who lived from 1781 to 1848. Smiles complained that history had been monopolized by kings and warriors and war, and claimed attention for engineers, the heroes of peace. Some phrases from the English reviews will indicate the kind of interest this biography has. "Few romances possess so strong an interest as this life, so brave, so simple, so strenuous in its faith . . . the true history of a working man." Stephenson was a true Victorian hero, and his rise from poverty to fame and fortune was felt to be adventure in the best sense—something in competition with, though not in hostility to, literal adventure in the Crusoe sense. "We see the vast achievements and the epic story of this age of ours more than half comprised in the feats of its strongest and most successful worker . . . we may designate him a hero . . . To young men faltering, it gives lessons which should supply fresh vigour. The continuous effort, the persistent valour, the daring ingenuity, and ever-active intellect of this collier boy . . ." Crusoe's virtues are seen at work in a somewhat different setting.

Smiles's importance is that he was so typical of nineteenth-century opinion. It is easy to recognize in his idea of manliness a vulgarized version of Emerson's, and indeed of other Victorian moralists. Stephenson was a *man;* he hated foppery and frippery above all things; he didn't drink, but ran and wrestled, and above all, worked. Emerson in fact, as Smiles tells us, said it was worth crossing the Atlantic just to meet Stephenson, he had such native force of character and intellect.

Smiles connects the cult of manliness, again in no unique way, with the cult of machinery. The ideas of work and workman subsume both. "There is indeed a peculiar fascination about an engine, to the intelligent workman who watches and feeds it. It is almost sublime in its untiring industry and quiet power; capable of performing the most gigantic work, yet so docile that a child's hand may guide it" (p. 28). Such a workman often speaks of his machine "with glowing admiration." All the improvements to machinery have come from workmen, not from scientists or philosophers. "This daily contemplation of the steam engine, and the sight of its steady action, is an education of itself to the ingenious and thoughtful workman." Defoe, I want to suggest, would have assented, would almost certainly have come to some such judgment, had he lived in the nineteenth century. It is a suggestive crystallization of the technocratic idea, which was powerful all through the century, though it rarely reached high levels of expression, literarily.

It figured largely in Mark Twain's life, however (his experience with the Paige type-setting machine constitutes a sardonic comment on the last sentence quoted), and he developed it literarily in *Connecticut Yankee* and other stories. It was also quite brilliantly expressed in fiction by Kipling and Wells; and commented on by Henry Adams, in "The Virgin and the Dynamo." The cult of the engineer may be said to have replaced in the nineteenth century Defoe's eighteenth-century cult of the merchant, as the former came to seem more the hero of peace, constructiveness, and the modern system.

Smiles's later *Lives of the Engineers* are particularly interesting for us because, alongside the biographies, they include histories of particular cities from a point of view very close to Defoe's, and continue the imaginative work he did in *The Tour.* We are shown England from a modern system point of view. Thus, in the Introduction we are told that England *is* not fertile—it has been *made* fertile by its industry, its canals, and other works of its engineers and improvers (p. 74). This work is moreover quite new. Not long ago, our wool was made into cloth in Flanders, our mines dug by Germans, our windmills built by the Dutch, and so on. Our apparent luck is based on our self-help—and will last only as long as our virtue does. This is exactly the approach Defoe took in his *Tour,* and his *Essay on Projects,* and Smiles emphasizes exactly what Defoe emphasized. He tells us for instance that the roads recently built in the Highlands of Scotland have had a moral influence. Telford, the engineer in charge, called the road-building a Working Academy, which turned out eight hundred improved workmen every year, and he meant improved as citizens too. (The image, and the tone, are very close to Twain's "factory of men" in *Connecticut Yankee.*) The change this road-building has made to Scotland can be measured in the fact that back in the 1745 Rebellion, when the district of Balmoral was remote from civilization, a whole regiment of Jacobite rebels was raised there, in a district "where *now* our Queen is so beloved."

Volume I is mostly about James Brindley, who built his first canal in 1761, but it also gives an account of Manchester in 1740. Volume II is mostly about Rennie and Smeaton—the latter built his first lighthouse in 1759—but it also gives a history of docks and bridges, and of the pirates who flourished before these modernizations. Volume III is mostly about Telford and Scotland; and it is notable how many of these men were Scots. Volume IV is about Watt and Boulton—Watt's first steam engine was built in 1766, and Arkwright's spinning jenny was built three years later; but also about

Birmingham. Thus these four volumes are a history of England during its Industrial Revolution, complete with exempla and heroes, exactly what Defoe wanted, and very like what Defoe produced in that line.

In *Self-Help* Smiles also took many examples of heroism from the suppression of the Indian Mutiny, which had only just occurred; and in *Duty* he praised Sir Charles Napier, John and Henry Lawrence, and Outram, as military heroes of the Indian Service. This gives us the cue to put that kind of Victorian hero beside Smiles's engineers; such kinds of men surround and support figures like Stanley—perhaps the most famous Victorian adventurer—in a cultural pantheon. The Indian soldiers are not Cortes or Clive types, military conquerors on the grand scale. They are suitable heroes for merchants, and their allies in the modern world system. But they assimilate as much of the conquistador material as could be assimilated into a Crusoe form.

As our example of the Indian hero let us take the Lawrence brothers, and their work in the Punjab in the mid-nineteenth century. They administered this province, after England took it away from the Sikhs in 1848, and made it the showpiece of British India. It was 74,000 square miles, of which the population was only one-fifth Sikh, though they were dominant. The British built the Grand Canal of the Punjab, nearly 250 miles long; and in four years built 3,000 miles of road, and surveyed 5,000 more, that was to be the Grand Trunk Road which Kipling celebrated.

The Lawrences were a Scots-Irish military family, very poor and in most senses underprivileged. John was the sixth son and eighth child, and said that at school "I was flogged every day of my life, except one, and then I was flogged twice" (Bosworth-Smith, *Life of Lord Lawrence,* p. 15). But it must have been a ruling-caste training place, for there were other boys at the school who were to become Indian heroes—besides the Lawrence brothers themselves. There was, for instance, Lord Gough, later to be the victor of Chillianwallah and conqueror of Gujerat. It was a school like Kipling's United Services College, in effect. These poor but ruling-caste Ulstermen (like but unlike the Ulstermen prominent on the American frontier) provided much of England's imperialist strength.

Bosworth-Smith's characterization of John Lawrence in his official biography is particularly interesting. Of Herculean physique, we are told, he had the cut of the Jats he ruled, with their handsome prominent features and tall bony frames; and the Jats are said to be descended from the ancient Goths. There was no ounce of superfluous fat upon John Lawrence, and he could hold a cannonball at arm's length. His friends, we are told, called him Oliver, after Cromwell, "the greatest and most downright and God-fearing of Englishmen" (p. 100). It was of course Carlyle's *Heroes and Hero-Worship* essay on Cromwell that they and Bosworth-Smith were thinking of. And the latter's whole account draws heavily on Carlyle's value-images.[1]

Lawrence was brave and strong and rough as a giant, but tender as a woman and simple as a child. He was heroically simple; he had the rough humor, the boisterous pranks, the wild spirit of adventure we associate with the Norwegian troll. When the rugged lineaments and deep furrows of his grand countenance are described, Bosworth-Smith quotes Milton's lines describing Satan. But the Satanic associations could be misleading. Lawrence was above all things a moral hero. Smiles says, in *Self-Help,* that Delhi was taken and India saved during the Mutiny by the personal character of Sir John Lawrence. His eye glared terribly when he saw anything mean or cowardly or wrong. They called him King John on the frontier. He was made Viceroy in 1864, and came home a peer in 1869, one of the great Victorian heroes.

Comparing the Lawrence brothers, Bosworth-Smith (a schoolmaster at Harrow) categorized John as Scots in character, Henry as Irish. The latter was, it seems, the more imaginative, the gentler, the more literary. He married a rather literary woman, his second cousin Honoria, a governess who had been a great friend of his sister Letitia, who herself was an Evangelical in the circle of Wilberforce and Thornton. (This illustrates the range of ruling-class types, and the alliance between them.) John, we are told, was passionately fond of Scott, but otherwise seems to have been aesthetically philistine. Henry and Honoria were more imaginative. The brothers quarreled over the administration of the Punjab, though with great dignity and mutual respect. Henry went into semiretirement, but he emerged again to be Resident at Lucknow, where he died, a martyr, during the Mutiny.

Henry gathered around him a number of young men, who were destined to have remarkable careers in India. There were, for instance, William Hodson, famous for the corps he formed, Hodson's Foot; John Nicholson, famous for the relief of Delhi during the Mutiny; and James Abbott, who was, we are told, accepted as prophet, priest, and king, by the fierce Yusupzais of the Hozara country. This phrasing I take from Maud Diver's biography of Honoria Lawrence, and it reminds us of Kipling, but more importantly it reminds us of the enormous imaginative charge of these Indian careers, where it seemed that everyone English was a Man Who Could Be King. Another of Henry Lawrence's young men was Herbert Edwardes, who was sent to Jummu to be, as he said, a Lieutenant of Foot advising the King of the Mountains. Edwardes, who wrote remarkably well, again and again in his letters names that kind of excitement. "I found five countries oppressed by one tyrant—and I removed him. I found three chiefs in exile—and I restored them. Those countries and those chiefs rallied round me in the hour of need. When I held up my hand for soldiers, they came. When I left the province, during an imperial war, peace reigned behind me" (Maud Diver, *Honoria Lawrence,* p. 319). John Nicholson was literally worshiped by a sect, the Nikkulseynites, whom he cursed and flogged for doing so. Edwardes's obituary comment on Henry was as Carlylean as Bosworth-Smith's on John: "How much of the *man* there was in him. How unsubdued he was. How his great purposes, his fierce will, generous impulses, and strong passions raged within him, making him the fine, genuine character we knew. . . ."

One final quotation from Edwardes will make clear the moral and imaginative tone of the Victorian cult of Empire itself. In a letter of 1846, after a satirical description of some Sikhs, he continues, "These barbarous phases of society, into which an educated man descends as into a pit of lions, have, after all, a wild, almost terrible interest. There is something noble in putting the hand of civilization on the mane of a nation like the Punjab (if I may borrow Spenser's allegory) and *looking down* brute passions. What a victory! to bind a bullying people with a garland—to impose security of life, good order, and law as fine, upon a whole nation."[*] The military impulse and military pride were sanctified and subdued to other caste values.[2]

There we have a kind of Victorian hero, obviously carrying a very potent image, who might have seemed quite unrelatable to the engineer and the merchant. In fact, India was a theater of empire where the military caste provided the leading actors, and even quite displaced the merchants from public view. But administrative civilians

---

[*]*Memorial of Herbert B. Edwardes,* ed. by Lady Edwardes (his wife), p. 76.

were heroes in India; their tasks more constructive, but their powers still exhilarating. I take as an example H. M. Kisch, whose letters were published as *A Young Victorian in India* in 1957. Mr. Kisch, who was born in 1850, arrived in India in 1873, and immediately found himself in charge of "198 square miles of famine" (p. 24). He wrote home that he gave employment to 5000 people every day, and fed another 3000 a day free. He had an establishment of 300 and ruled a population of 100,000. In 1874 he recalled with pride that when he arrived he couldn't dig a tank, build a grain store, or anything else. And a little later he wrote, "Since I last wrote, I have dammed several of the rivers in my circle. . . ." (p. 45). In 1876, his subdivision was 782 square miles, and contained a population of 154,000—mostly of an aboriginal tribe, "far superior to Bengalis." (That prejudice against the Hindus, and particularly the Bengalis, was a large feature of English rule in India; an imperial power prefers to deal with a primitive or aboriginal tribe.) They treated even his music box as a god.

It was in India that the institution of Guides originated; although guides and scouts were obviously famous long before, in the American colonies; perhaps I should say, it was in India that something was instituted on the British side which was called Guides. In 1839 Henry Lawrence proposed such a corps, trained to work in forest and jungle (to discover enemy positions) where regular troops could not operate. In 1845–1846 Harry Lumsden created the Queen's Corps of Guides (he himself being only twenty-five) and Hodson was his second in command.

The institution much struck the general imagination; Kipling for instance always found such irregular troops much more exciting than the regulars. (This excitement was a fraction of that attaching to the Cossacks in Russia, for the Cossacks were irregulars.) And after the Boer War Colonel Baden-Powell, with Kipling's advice, set out to create such an institution for boys, to save England from the softness and degeneracy threatening it. Baden-Powell designed the Boy Scouts to foster specifically English-boy qualities. He wrote, "Your Englishman . . . is endowed by nature with a spirit of practical discipline. . . . Whether it has been instilled into him by his public school training, by his football and his fagging, or whether it is inbred from previous generations of stern though kindly parents, one cannot say" (Ellis, *The Social History of the Machine Gun,* p. 105). That practical discipline was what the Empire required of its administrators, and the public schools supplied. He set out to develop that English quality by means of simulated and controlled adventures. The Boy Scouts and the public schools are examples of those institutions of large cultural effectiveness which did not operate through books, and which were hardly at all expressed or reflected in serious literature.

One final hero-type in the Victorian constellation is the missionary. In *Self-Help* Smiles tells, for instance, the story of John Williams, a London Society missionary, who died a martyr on Erromanga, a South Seas island. And a book-length version of that sort of narrative is James Paton's *The Story of John G. Paton: or 30 Years Among South Seas Cannibals.* The hero was born in 1824, and after a very severe and pious Scots Presbyterian childhood, set off as a missionary for the New Hebrides in 1858. There he engaged in a thirty-year-long and more or less fruitless struggle with naked savages, who practiced horrid heathen rites, including cannibalism. And the whites he encountered were nearly all rough, swearing traders, who mocked and jostled him. It is an intensely grim life that is described, but it is offered as a call to imitation; John G. Paton is a Christian hero of Christian adventure.

But in Smiles's book there is also much about Livingstone, which gives quite a different image of missionary work; stressing how Livingstone dug canals, built houses, cultivated fields, as he labored among the Bechuanas; he taught them to work as well as to worship. It was by using this stress on the missionaries' work that a man like Smiles could best assimilate it to the work of the explorers and administrators—the work of civilization. And this was a stress by no means foreign to the missionaries themselves; they sometimes took copies of *Robinson Crusoe* with them as well as Bibles. The practice, and later theory, was that the missionary should be a trustee for Western civilization. He taught his tribe habits of work, of justice, of reason, and collected information about their language, culture, natural habitat.

Seen as such, he was first cousin to the heroes of adventure stories; and in fact R. M. Ballantyne blended both images. In his very popular boys' stories, including *Coral Island* itself, he included a strong strain of missionary feeling, quite like that of *The Story of John G. Paton.*

Beside the missionary stood the colporteur, of whom the most famous and the most literary was George Borrow. His *The Bible in*

Spain, 1842, told the adventures of an Englishman, attempting to circulate the Scriptures in Spain; but it was also full of picaresque adventures, romantic settings, and chauvinist opinions. "Yes, notwithstanding the misrule of the brutal and sensual Austrian, the doting Bourbon, and above all, the spiritual tyranny of the court of Rome, Spain can still maintain her own. . . ." And it might be Defoe himself who tells us that for two hundred years Spain was the she-butcher of malignant Rome.

Borrow learned to read on *Robinson Crusoe,* and maintained a kind of cult of it. For months, he tells us, "the wondrous volume was my only and principal source of amusement. For hours together I would sit poring over a page till I had become acquainted with the import of every line. . . ." (*Lavengro,* p. 10). Borrow was described as an Elizabethan born out of his time, and in fact illustrates that revival of primitive WASP energies in Victorian England. He traveled far and riskily with his Bibles; he went to Russia in 1823 for the London Missionary Society, and to Spain in 1835, where he told everyone that the Pope was Satan's prime minister, and that they weren't Christians, for they were ignorant of Christ and his teaching. It can give one a valuable insight into the imperialist aspect of the Victorian temperament to remember that Borrow was a pupil at grammar school together with James Brooke, who became Rajah Brooke of Sarawak.

Moreover, people in the nineteenth century continued to read the travel literature of earlier times, which made the explorer one of the great heroes of nineteenth-century culture. One reader we happen to know about is Thoreau, thanks to the researches of J. A. Christie, reported in his *Thoreau as World Traveller.* Thoreau read the collections of Hakluyt, Purchas, and Drake; but also the works of the Spaniards, like Columbus, Balboa, and Ponce de Leon; and also Frobisher, de Soto, Cartier, Hudson. But three-quarters of his travel-reading was written after 1800, and half of that was contemporary —written between 1832 and 1865. This meant books about travels in Japan, the Arctic and Antarctic, the West and South America, and, more latterly, Africa and Asia. He read, Mr. Christie calculates, about twelve such books a year.

One favorite was Alexander Henry, whose *Travels in Canada 1760–76,* Thoreau said, was "like the argument to a great poem on the primitive state of the country and its inhabitants." This—the relation to legend and myth—was Thoreau's main interest in such reading. In his *Journal* for March 16, 1852, he writes, "The volumes of the 15th, 16th, and 17th centuries, which lie so near us on the shelf, are rarely opened, are effectually forgotten and not implied by our literature and newspapers. When I looked into Purchas's *Pilgrims,* it affected me like looking into an impassable swamp, ten feet deep with sphagnum, where the monarchs of the forest, covered with mosses, and stretched out along the ground, were making haste to become peat. These old books suggested a certain fertility, an Ohio soil, as if they were making a humus for new literature to spring in." His language implies fertility even when it asserts decay. And indeed a new literature did spring up—that of Kingsley and Kipling. Whether Thoreau would have approved of that literature we cannot say; but it is clear that he was concerned for the tradition of thought we are following. (We should note a certain likeness between life at Walden and life on Crusoe's island; and a certain fondness in Thoreau for guns and hunting.) He read even the boys' books of the period; notably those of Captain Mayne Reid, whom we shall come to. He read each Reid tale, *Desert Home, Boy Hunters,* and *Forest Exiles,* as they came out in the '50s. (The last is a Swiss Family Robinson set in Peru.) He read and reread Reid's *Young Voyagers; The Boy Hunters in the North.*

Thus the engineer, the explorer, the missionary, and the Indian soldier, all in different ways continued and developed the Crusoe image of heroism. Nineteenth-century readers, at many levels of literacy, made a cult of those heroes. And at the end of the century, boys were urged to do the same, by a variety of institutional means.

If we turn now to fiction, we can begin with Captain Marryat, who wrote very popular books, first for men and then for boys, in the first half of the nineteenth century. He and Cooper together invented the genre of sea fiction at a significant level of intelligence and taste. Marryat was often said to be the best recruiting officer the British Navy had. His *Mr. Midshipman Easy* (1836) is an adventure tale of the kind we have studied, but set on shipboard. The hero's father had been mad about equality and other French Revolutionary ideas, so Jack has some hard lessons in discipline to learn when he joins a ship of the Royal Navy, but he is fundamentally good-natured—being a typical adventure hero. Thus in the course of many adventures he acquires a Black Prince, Mesty, who has tales to tell of savage despotism; a devoted friend and comrade, Gascoigne; and an exotic bride, Donna Agnes, whom he rescues from the clutches of wicked priests. Marryat used several of the motifs that Cooper used (in *The Prairie*, for instance) and which Defoe or Scott had used before him. He modified rather than transformed the energizing myth of the system.

But *Mr. Midshipman Easy* had something of Regency jauntiness, and in 1841 Marryat showed his alertness to the new Victorian mood by writing a more serious, an *Evangelical* adventure tale for children, *Masterman Ready*. This is the story of the Seagrave family who are shipwrecked on to a desert island while on their way to Australia. They learn to survive there in Robinson Crusoe fashion, their adventures rising to a climax with a battle against savages and a last-minute rescue. The differences from Defoe's book largely arise from the fact that the central figure is not an individual but a family. This change was introduced by Wyss in *Swiss Family Robinson* and Marryat consciously set out to improve on Wyss. The change brought with it not only a domestic life-style in the wilderness, but a narrative change, in the more moralistic differentiation of roles played by the different children (and the adults, but they are less important). Here William is definitively a good boy, while Tommy is naughty, and precipitates the catastrophe. By letting the water out of the drinking cask the family relies on while it is besieged by savages, he creates a critical emergency; Masterman Ready saves them by crawling out of the stockade to get water for Mrs. Seagrave and the babies, but is killed.

Ready is Marryat's crucial invention, and one that opened the way for many Victorian adaptations of the adventure tale. He is a common seaman, who has been fifty years at sea, and attaches himself to the genteel Seagrave family, and especially to William, even before the wreck; after the wreck he is their instructor in the practical arts of survival. He is a Natty Bumppo figure, except that he has a wild past to repent—which he narrates serially and edifyingly to William —and that he holds by a more Evangelical morality. His function is indicated by the name "Masterman"; he introduces the principle of social hierarchy even into the wilderness and adventure setting.

The book's Victorian prudence is indicated by its teaching about Empire and about discipline. Ready tells William, ". . . there is more work got out of men in a well-conducted man-of-war than there can in the merchant service in double the time . . . I should never have known what could be done by order and arrangement, if I had not been pressed on board a man-of-war. . . . I found that everything was done in silence" (p. 120). And William is even taught that all empires grow old and decay, that the British Empire will, too, and one day it may be the turn of black races to be great. This, then, is a highly moralized version of modernist adventure. The balance between Brahmin and merchant has shifted in favor of the former, and aristomilitary values are largely repudiated.

That story reflected the early Victorian mood, full of the vigor of English Puritanism, but at odds with the imperial situation. It was replaced in the second half of the century by something almost opposite. English readers soon passed from semi-Defoe adventure to ultra-Scott romance; to, for instance, Charles Kingsley, another extremely popular Victorian writer, and with higher intellectual claims.[3] His Elizabethan adventure tale, *Westward Ho!* was published in 1855, but reprinted very often. It was, for instance, officially distributed to English troops in the Crimean War, and after a new edition in 1857, it was reprinted three times in the '60s, twelve times in the '70s, eight times in the '80s, and altogether thirty-eight times by 1897. It was dedicated to two men, Rajah Brooke of Sarawak, and Bishop Selwyn of New Zealand, both of whom possessed "a virtue even purer and more heroic than the Elizabethan." That suggests Kingsley's key contribution to Victorianism and to the adventure tale —the idea of recapturing Elizabethan vigor (in somewhat purified form)—of assimilating the two ages to each other.

The hero is a "glorious lad," Amyas Leigh, who is much closer to the fiery hero of chivalric romance than to the prudent Crusoe-type, but who represents a new stress, derived from the sagas, on primitive and simple-minded strength. Kingsley describes him as a savage but simple-hearted giant, but also "a symbol of brave young England longing to wing its way out of its island prison, to discover and to traffic, to colonize and to civilize, until no wind can sweep the earth which does not bear the echoes of an English voice" (p. 10). The shout that greeted Amyas's victory was, we are told, "the birth-paean of North America, Australia, New Zealand, the Pacific Isles, of free commerce and free colonization over the whole earth." He is contrasted with his clever consumptive brother, Frank, and his hysterical Catholic cousin Eustace, who has been corrupted by Jesuit teachers, and whose face often writhes with envy, malice, and revenge. Amyas has been brought up by his widowed and martyred mother, and by stately Sir Richard Grenville. There is a lot of North Devon scenery and legend, and many historical characters, with elaborately Elizabethan language, verse, pageants, etc. (Kingsley's method is derived from Scott at his most "historical.") Defoe-virtues are represented only in the merchant, Mr. Salterne, a minor character and not much favored by the author. Romantic chivalry is the keynote of the author's values, and Spenser, Raleigh, and Sidney are his historical heroes.

Unlike Scott, Kingsley is very Protestant and even anti-Catholic. This, like the saga influence, derives from Carlyle, and reflects a recharging of the modern world system with moral righteousness of a more imperialist and military kind. Rose Salterne is the beauty of North Devon, and Amyas and five other glorious lads who love her form a chivalric Brotherhood of the Rose, and take an oath to all go away for three years and not court her, for fear that mutual competition may injure their mutual brotherhood. (This curious way to express their love is to be explained by the author's covert malevolence against Rose, and women, and sex.) While they are away, Rose is seduced by a Spaniard, Don Guzman, and elopes with him to Spain, and subsequently to South America, where Don Guzman is associated with the rape of Peru. Amyas sets off in pursuit of her, but she has been abandoned by Don Guzman and fallen a prey to the Inquisition, in whose hands she dies. Amyas then pursues Don Guzman, finally kills him in the battle that defeated the Armada, and—having been blinded in that battle, and so reduced to a status for which marriage is not inappropriate—marries Ayancora. She is a new and much-to-be repeated motif—adapted from Cortes's Marina; Ayancora is an Indian princess Amyas picked up in his travels, but is really an English girl abandoned in the jungle as a baby and worshiped by the savages because she is white. Marrying her, Amyas incorporates—without any real miscegenation—primitive powers. *Westward Ho!* tells the story of the ousting of Spain by England from the leadership of the modern system, one of the key episodes in the history of that system. But morally and aesthetically it is a lurid fantasy of power and revenge and hatred, on quite a different, and lower, level, from the other adventure tales.

It is worth taking a brief look at some nonfiction by Kingsley, because he was a central figure in the Victorian propaganda for empire and adventure. In *The Heroes or Greek Fairy Tales for My Children* (1868) he says that "heroes" used to mean (when nations were young) men who dared more than other men. Then it came to mean men who helped their countries. And now it means men who suffer pain and grief. (This idea is linked, paradoxically, to the atavistic worship of animal vigor in Amyas Leigh; Kingsley's moral imagination accords the primacy to pain and grief—to passivity—and as a result his historical and political imagination has no effective moral component.)

And his *The Roman and the Teuton* (1864) warns England against the fate of Rome and other empires. In the early years of Christendom, the Teutons were "Forest Children," a young and strong race, like English sailors and navvies now, while the Romans were subtle and sophisticated. (William Morris took up this story in his late romance, *The House of the Wolfings.*) The Roman palace was "a sink of corruption," where eunuchs, concubines, spies abounded. Kingsley warns his listeners, who were the undergraduates at Cambridge, where he was Professor of History, to beware of a similar corruption at home. "Forget for a few minutes that you are Englishmen, the freest and bravest nation upon earth, strong in all that gives real strength, and with a volunteer army which is now formidable by numbers and courage. . . ." (p. 32). It can happen in England, too. Unbridled indulgence of the passions produces frivolity and effeminacy, as we see in the French noblesse of the ancien régime, in the Spaniards in America, and in the Italians in their once-great cities. National life is grounded in morality, that is, on the life of the family. "The muscle of the Teuton" was always combined with moral purity, and this gave him, "as it may give you, gentlemen, a calm and steady brain, and a free and loyal heart; the energy which springs from health; the self-respect which comes from self-restraint". . . and so on (p. 38). Here we see the late Victorian version of the WASP hero, containing recognizable elements of Defoe and Scott, but also something else. That hero now embodies racist and atavistic energies.

Kingsley draws several contrasts between the Roman Empire and the British Empire in India, where the moral roles of imperial power and native population are reversed. "The Goth was very English; and the overcivilized, learned, false, profligate Roman was the very counterpart of the modern Brahmin" (p. 114). Only the English among the Goths' descendants preserved the Gothic heritage of freedom, and so they are anti-imperialist even in India. Kingsley's main hero in this book is Dietrich of Bern, who "went adventures." Dietrich, he says, has been criticized on the grounds that his civilized qualities only went skin-deep; that if you scratched him you'd find a barbarian. But this is really a high compliment, he argues. For Kingsley's message is always to cultivate the barbaric qualities in the individual and the nation; and that is one of the messages of most nineteenth-century adventure tales after him.[4]

That call sounds loud and clear in Kipling and Haggard, who form the climax to this chapter, but there are several other writers who modified or extended the range of the adventure-myth, before I come to them. For instance, there is Alexandre Dumas, one of the adventure tellers with the most international and long-lasting audiences. He will remind us of the pan-European character of modernist imperialism. Dumas was born in 1803, the son of one of Napoleon's generals, and though he lost his father at the age of three, he grew up on the tales of his father's exploits, and on the tales of adventure and bloodshed which the Napoleonic era left behind. His work is a literary equivalent to his father's career. Hippolyte Parigot said, "If Danton and Napoleon were exemplars of Gallic energy, Dumas, in *The Three Musketeers*, is the national novelist who puts it into words."*

Having read Scott, and seen Shakespeare performed in Paris, Dumas wrote *Henri III et sa Cour* (staged in 1830), and set out to do for French history what the English writers were doing for English, and the American writers for America. (In 1838 he adapted Cooper's *The Pilot* as a serial for *Le Siècle,* and it attracted five thousand new subscribers in three weeks.) In 1844 he produced *The Three Musketeers,* also as a serial; drawing his historical material, incidentally, from Courtilz, the French Defoe.[5] The confrontation at the heart of that book, between Cardinal Richelieu, compact of old-man wisdom—cold, inhuman, unhealthy—and the four healthy young men, who are a composite representation of France's young-man vitality, is an important new motif of adventure. It reconstitutes the framework of the story of the brothers. That motif was to be repeated again and again, notably by Kipling, in the *Puck of Pook's Hill* stories.

*Quoted in André Maurois, *The Titans,* p. 179.

Popular Literature and Children's Literature

Then Dumas's *Count of Monte Cristo* (1846) made triumphant use of that romantic revenge motif which was employed by later adventure writers, like Jules Verne in *Twenty Thousand Leagues Under the Sea*. And Dumas himself was another example of the writer as entrepreneur, on the largest possible scale. From the beginning he planned to put all French history into fiction; he made a fortune, built himself a great house (called Monte Cristo) like Scott and Twain; and went bankrupt, like Scott and Twain. He translated into literary terms (though terms which literature-as-a-system rejected) the encrgics of nineteenth-century France. And he distilled a version for child-readers—the new class of readers.

The Critical History of Children's Literature* says "During the years from 1840 onward, boys were exploring remote regions, sailing the high seas, escaping from cannibals or redskins in the company of heroes . . ." (p. 237). This was something radically new. The genre of children's literature had been invented, we may roughly say, by the Puritans; in verse quite explicitly by Bunyan and Watts; Bunyan's *Book for Boys and Girls,* 1686, and Watts's *Divine and Moral Songs for Children,* 1715, which was influenced by Bunyan's example; in prose, more accidentally, by Bunyan and Defoe, with *Pilgrim's Progress* and *Robinson Crusoe,* not written for children, but soon given to them to read. The only Tory who contributed was Swift, in *Gulliver's Travels,* and that was read as if Defoe had written it. Later in the eighteenth century there were big successes like *Giles Gingerbread* and *Goody Two-Shoes,* but the message and the myth remained the same. Prudence and piety were the values recommended. The new nineteenth-century development (apart from *Alice in Wonderland,* which stands by itself) was in stories which operated on almost opposite values.

The middle of the nineteenth century saw a very striking and very significant change in the culture's idea of children. Their literature was in effect captured by the aristomilitary caste. Adventure took the place of fable; and the adventure took on the characteristics of romance. Children's literature became boys' literature; it focused its attention on the Empire and the Frontier; and the virtues it taught were dash, pluck, and lion-heartedness, not obedience, duty, and piety. For instance, "Oliver Optic" in America (where children's

*See under Meigs in Bibliography.

literature had been *very* pious), wrote a Starry Flag series 1867–1869, and an Army and Navy series 1865–1894. Another dominant interest was science and invention, and that was only slightly indirect in its support of the same values. Edward Stratemeyer wrote a long series about Tom Swift, boy adventurer, full of grit and ginger, who goes up in balloons, drives an electric car, fires an electric rifle, and so on. Stratemeyer started a syndicate of writers to use his name in 1903, because he was so successful. In 1926, 98 percent of the children questioned in a survey listed a Stratemeyer title as a favorite and in the '20s and '30s the Tom Swift series sold fifteen million.

Kingsley, and for that matter Scott, were read also by children, but some authors were read only by them, and these authors too were aristomilitary by affiliation. Among English writers of boys' adventure books, one of the most notable was George Alfred Henty. He wrote nearly eighty such books, with titles like *With Clive in India*, *With Roberts to Pretoria*, and so on, stories of the achievements of the British army in colonial settings. Henty borrowed a good deal from standard histories and geographies, so his books were also educational. They rely on Anglo-Saxon racism, assigning stereotype identities to Latins, Easterners, and "natives." *By Sheer Pluck* describes Africans as being "just like children. . . . They are always laughing or quarrelling. They are good-natured, and passionate, indolent, but will work hard for a time, clever up to a point, densely stupid beyond."[6] (It is the idea implicit in Defoe's *Four Year Voyage of Captain Roberts.*)

Most of Henty's books begin with a letter addressed to "My dear lads," and teaching some homely truth. He had himself been a puny and sickly boy, who spent most of his childhood in bed, and was bullied at school. Then he took up boxing and yachting, became a man and a war correspondent; and as a writer, became a preacher of manliness. His biography by G. Manville Fenn (published in 1910) says, "There was nothing namby-pamby in Henty's writings. . . . 'No,' he said, 'I never touch on love interest.'" His study was full of pipe-smoke and native weapons, and he had a "Johnsonian" manner with the effete and impudent. When met in the Strand, he had always just returned from wide open spaces, and was sternly silent about subjects of mere chatter. Fenn says his books are "essentially manly, and he used to say that he wanted his boys to be bold, straightforward, and ready to play a young man's part, not to be milksops. He had a horror of a lad who displayed any weak emotion and shrank from shedding blood, or winced at any encounter" (p. 334). He contributed stories to boys' magazines like *Captain, Chums, Great Thoughts, Young England,* and *Union Jack.*

In *The Great War and Modern Memory* Paul Fussell says that the soldiers in that war had learned the language of patriotic duty from Henty and Rider Haggard among the novelists, and from Robert Bridges and Henry Newbolt among the poets. Newbolt was famous for "Lampaida Vitae," with the famous refrain, "Play up, play up, and play the game." He will remind us of the important part played in this manliness propaganda by the public schools. In that poem, and many others, the subject moves from a public school to a colonial battle, and the first is shown to be essentially a preparation for the second. Newbolt was the poet of Clifton College, and wrote a famous poem, "Clifton Chapel," which begins with the stanza,

> This is the Chapel: here, my son,
> Your father thought the thoughts of youth,
> And heard the words that one by one
> The touch of life has turned to truth.
> Here in a day that is not far,
> You, too, may speak with noble ghosts
> Of manhood and the vows of war
> You made before the Lord of Hosts.

(We should not take this school militarism for granted. It was something new, and Thomas Arnold would have been shocked by it.)

At the end Newbolt added a note, "Thirty-seven Old Cliftonian officers served in the campaign of 1887 on the Indian frontier, of whom twenty-two were mentioned in dispatches and six recommended for the D.S.O. Of the 300 Cliftonians who served in the war in South Africa, 30 were killed in action and 14 died of wounds or fever." Then he added a supplementary stanza.

> Clifton remember thy sons who fell
> Fighting far oversea,
> For they in a dark hour remembered well
> Their warfare learned of thee.

Fussell tells us that General Haig, Commander in Chief during the Great War, was a lifelong friend of Newbolt's, and that the latter sneered at Wilfred Owen and poets of that kind as "broken men."

Literature of this kind was spread largely by means of the boys' magazines to which Henty contributed so much. The most famous of these was G. A. Hutchinson's *Boys' Own Paper,* which brought Henty, Ballantyne, Michael Fenn, and W. H. G. Kingston to a large audience, and, as *The Literature and Art of the Empire* says, made patriots of its readers. It began in 1879, belonged to the Religious Tract Society, but was above all patriotic, though it printed foreigners like Jules Verne as well as all the famous English ones. A typical title from Volume I is Kingston's *From Powder-Monkey to Admiral;* the navy had a whole chapel to itself in the cathedral of British patriotism. There were also publishing projects like a series of biographies, edited by Sir Harry Wilson, called "The Builders of Greater Britain" and another edited by Sir William Hunter, called "The Rulers of India." (This is the background against which to see Kipling.) There was, this volume says, a literary empire, consisting of Kipling's India, Haggard's South Africa, Gilbert Parker's Canada, and inspired by the songs of Tennyson, Henley, Newbolt, and Masefield.

Comparable with Henty in popularity, and even more popular internationally, was Captain Mayne Reid, 1818–1883, for a time the most popular English author in Russia, for instance; also translated into French, German, Italian, Spanish. He was born in Ireland of Presbyterian parents, and left for America in 1839. Reid was a militant and indeed military liberal. He fought in the Mexican War, and was the first man in the U.S. force to enter Mexico City. In 1848 he published *The Rifle Rangers,* his first romance, read and admired by Dumas and Lamartine. In 1849, stirred by the news of the revolutions in Europe, he organized a legion to go to Kossuth's support in the revolt of Hungary against Austria. Then his romance *The Scalp Hunters* sold a million copies in England, and was translated into as many languages as *Pilgrim's Progress.* Another book of his published that year, *The Desert House or The English Family Robinson,* began a series.

But he also continued his political activities, and it is important to note their anti-imperialist character. He had become Kossuth's friend, and in 1852 they planned to go together to Milan to fight against the Austrians for Italian freedom. In Reid the connection between book adventure and real-life adventure was especially close. But though he was a Liberal, and Kipling a Tory, both men established rifle clubs, so that young Englishmen should get some military training; and there is no real discontinuity between them culturally, despite the political difference. Like Henty's, Reid's books care as

223

much about geography and history as about moral ideas or narrative —*The Castaways*, 1870, for instance, quotes Wallace and Livingstone for a page at a time, and has a trivial plot that seems not seriously meant. Indeed, because of the predominance of the killer albatross and the hammerhead shark over the human characters, the book produces an effect quite like those of Crane and Conrad.

A very important development in the boys' books of the second half of the century was the synthetic, framework story, like *The Three Musketeers*. One very popular example was W. H. G. Kingston's *The Three Midshipmen*. Kingston (1814–1880) wrote 150 books for children. This one begins at a school, and puts together an English, a Scots, and an Irish boy, who were to appear again and again in a whole series of books. The English boy, Jack Rogers, takes the lead; he is a squire's son, solid and pugnacious; Alick Murray is serious, clever, and cautious; while Paddy Adair is full of fun, lovable, but thoughtless. This trio is the United Kingdom in literary form, and they act out the same function—of dominating the rest of the empire.

At school the boys have to deal with a soft, fat sneak called Bully Pigeon, who embodies the least attractive aspects of Englishness and turns up later in their lives as a cowardly civilian in the Mediterranean, and then as a would-be sophisticate on their ship to China. Bully Pigeon boasts himself an atheist, but whines when he gets into trouble, and soon dies. Aboard ship, Honest Dick Needham, of the lower classes, comes to the help of the young gentlemen time and time again. In the Mediterranean, the three chase Greek pirates and smash Mehmet Ali on the Sultan of Turkey's behalf. Their adventures frequently lead to explosions, in which human limbs mingle with fragments of stone and iron. Then they go to Sierra Leone, where they chase slavers, and first meet the Portuguese villain, Dom Diogo, whom they pursue through several episodes. (England had gained great moral prestige by suppressing the slave trade in its own dominions, and Portugal great infamy by not doing so.) They meet a Black Prince and acquire a faithful Friday-style Negro, Wasser. Later they go to Singapore and Hong Kong, where they chase opium clippers. Thus they cover the whole empire, and make it, by their adventures, vivid and glorious to their readers.

Rather similar in synthetic form is R. M. Ballantyne's *Coral Island*. In this adventure three boys are wrecked on an island; Jack Martin is eighteen and a natural leader; Ralph, who tells the story, is fifteen and serious and "old-fashioned," and Peterkin Gay is thirteen or fourteen, little and quick and mischievous.[7] Like Crusoe, they land with an axe, an oar, an iron hoop, a telescope, some whipcord and a broken penknife, and have to make do. But Ballantyne puts much more stress than Defoe does on the Paradisal beauty of both land and sea, and the heroes are seen more romantically and chivalrically than Crusoe. (Ballantyne was much influenced by Scott.) Jack is lion-like; tall, strapping, broad-shouldered, handsome, good-humored; Peterkin expects him to become king of a native population. When cannibals arrive (looking more like demons than human beings) Jack goes berserk while fighting them. (The idea of an Englishman going berserk, when pushed too far, was a much-repeated device, derived from the sagas.) Later they get to Fiji, where the natives, being pagans, feed their eels with babies, and fill their temple with human bones. The story contains some Evangelical teaching, but puts more stress on the related secular virtues, for instance, cold bathing and training in observation. (This is the book which William Golding transvalued to write *Lord of the Flies,* one of the clearest cases of post-1945 reversal of sentiment.)

Another major force in fiction and ideas at the popular level in the nineteenth century was Jules Verne, and his followers. Though Verne imitated Dumas to begin with, he had more in common with Defoe than with Scott, while Dumas's affinity was the reverse. Verne's work is thought of usually as science fiction, but it is just as much adventure fiction, and his heroes are adventurers. And his case is an interesting one for us because there have been some studies of his work, in French, which are not too far removed from ours in point of view.

Jules Verne was born in 1828, and though he trained in law, always wanted to write. He met Dumas in 1849, sat in his box for the first stage performance of *Three Musketeers,* and became a sort of secretary to him. But he also made friends with Jacques Arago, a blind explorer, whose brother was an astronomer. Verne had always loved science, and also the sea and ships. In 1862 he wrote *Cinq Semaines en Ballon,* the story of a British eccentric, Dr. Ferguson, who floats across Africa in a balloon. He took this novel to a publisher, Jules Hetzel, a liberal who had been Lamartine's Chef de Cabinet in his Ministry in 1848, and thereafter for a time exiled by Napoleon III.

(This liberal connection expresses an important tendency in the books.)

Hetzel gradually saw the immense potential in Verne's work. In 1866 the latter produced *Les Aventures du Capitaine Hatteras,* about an English explorer, who races against his American rival, Altamont, to discover the North Pole; and for this book Hetzel wrote an advertising explanation of Verne's work in general: "Son but est, en effet, de résumer toutes les connaissances géographiques, géologiques, physiques, astronomiques, amassées par la science moderne, et de faire, sous la forme attrayante et pittoresque qui lui est propre, l'histoire de l'univers" (M-H. Huet, in *L'Histoire des Voyages Extraordinaires,* p. 20).

He used as models for his heroes mostly explorers like Livingstone, Stanley, Burton, De Brazza, the heroes of the nineteenth century. It is notable how many of his leading figures were Anglo-Saxon; Huet counts ninety Americans, eighty English, thirty Russians, and so on. The French tend to appear as comic savants, like Paganel, or comic servants, like Passepartout. But Verne had in fact strong anti-English prejudices; though he admired their tunnels and bridges, and their energy, sense, and progress, he hated their cruelty and love of profit.[8] But still he judged them only by their own, modern system standards.

So it is not surprising that Verne wrote several Robinsonaden: *L'Oncle Robinson, L'Ecole des Robinsons, La Seconde Patrie* (an avowed continuation of *The Swiss Family Robinson*), and *Deux Ans de Vacances.* And his work is largely an energizing myth of the modern system. It is similar to Defoe's in emotional character. His works cannot be said to be novels, someone says, because they do not deal with love. He always declared he couldn't handle that subject; on the other hand he was proud of and conscientious about the science he included. Michel Corday says (quoted by Jean Jules-Verne) that he helped young readers to escape their "stupid jail. . . . He inspired in us a desire to know about the universe, a taste for science, a dedication to masculine forms of energy."

When Chesneaux says that Verne is a Utopian Socialist, he is thinking of the Saint-Simonian brand of socialism; and in particular of the technocrats. The Saint-Simonian, Enfantin, became administrator of the French railways under the Third Empire, and other Saint-Simonians were employed in big projects like the Suez Canal and the plan for a Channel tunnel. Verne's friend Nadar, who is depicted in some of the novels, was de Lesseps's secretary. He often describes possible engineering projects, like a giant lighthouse on Cape Horn, or a canal to irrigate the Sahara. Many of his friends were polytechnicians, and he assigned that status to some of his favorite characters. "Paganel" was an avowed Saint-Simonian, and *Indes Noires* is a technocratic fantasy.

This line of imagination, which runs through much science fiction, is one we can only assume that Defoe would have found very congenial, as did H. G. Wells, the modern Defoe. Chesneaux says that Verne was, like Wells, an author of politics fiction as much as of science fiction. And though Wells had a much more literary imagination than Verne, it is fair to bracket them together. What strikes one about *The War of the Worlds* is the vivid way England is imagined —and imagined as vulnerable; Wells evokes the anxiety of riches and a panic at the rout of civilization. He presents London as an enormous magnificent city, about to be destroyed, and England as an entirely tamed country, at the mercy of fierce invaders. This is of course the vision of much imperialist fiction—a soft, rich, splendid mother country, inviting rape by the hardy savage tribes outside. It is Kipling's vision; while on the other hand the narrative structure of Wells's book is that of Defoe's *Journal of the Plague Year*.

An interesting book which connects Verne with Defoe is Emile Cammaerts's *Discoveries in England*, of 1930. Cammaerts was a Frenchman long resident in England. He says he was struck as a child by the number of Englishmen who played leading roles in Verne's stories, and finally realized that his hero, Phileas Fogg (in *Around the World in 80 Days*), was just another version of Robinson Crusoe, whom he had been in love with a long time. Crusoe was for him as a child "the ideal type of adventurer—courageous, patient, as well as wise and just in his relations with the savages"; whereas Cammaerts knew that temperamentally he couldn't emulate d'Artagnan's bravado, or the military dash of French adventure heroes in general. (He was pointing to a contrast between mercantile and military heroes as well as between English and French.) Crusoe was a settler, and carried, "in a kind of frog, instead of a sword and dagger, a little saw and a hatchet, one on one side, one on the other." This is a highly significant contrast, for Cammaerts. The English adventure novel, he says, is geographical, where the French is historical; the English dream is in a sense outside history—at least the history of militarism and domination.

Cammaerts mentions Robert Louis Stevenson's voyages as an example of the compulsion felt by every English author to live out something of an adventure himself; and Stevenson was a symbolic figure as man as well as author to many readers of adventure at the turn of the century. His family were famous consulting engineers, who had built lighthouses all around Scotland, and harbors all around the world. They were examples of Defoe's and Smiles's engineer-heroes. He had difficulty in reconciling his parents to his vocation to be a writer, but in fact he turned their engineering work to fictional images as much as Dumas turned his father's military exploits into fiction.

Stevenson finished *Treasure Island* in 1882, and it was a tremendous success, both accepting and changing the conventions of adventure. In "How This Book Came To Be," he shows how much it was a composite of earlier books in that tradition. The parrot came from *Robinson Crusoe,* the stockade from *Masterman Ready,* the chest from Washington Irving, and so on. There is much reference to Scott, whom Stevenson was very conscious of rivaling, and in fact there is much more of him than of Defoe. Stevenson's is *historical* expertise rather than practical. He said that the story began with the drawing of a map and that it was told to his stepson, with his father's collaboration. It is palpably the fantasy of men-being-boys. There is no real interest in large historical forces. What is strikingly new about it in a generic way is that a boy plays the leading part and tells the story; and that the violence is much more open and important.

The end of this sort of adventure romance was announced by another Scots writer whom it is suitable to connect with Stevenson in many ways, J. M. Barrie. The servitor imperialism of the Scots writers from Scott on has played an important part in the reinforcement of modernist values in England, as we have seen.[9] (John Buchan, another Scot, was the last of the old-style adventure writers.) Barrie was no conscious or intentional rebel against tradition. As a boy, he read Defoe, Cooper, Stevenson, and at the end of his life, when he was guardian of the boys for and about whom he wrote *Peter Pan,* he was, they tell us, always eager for them to be involved in sports and athletics, and reluctant to see them concerned with the arts. He wanted Kims and Hucks about him, not Little Lord Fauntleroys.

But his own temperament, which was expressed in *Peter Pan*, was purely whimsical and playful, and deeply averse from serious adventure or violence of any kind. *Peter Pan*, 1904, is about a Boy Who Would Not Grow Up, and though it uses all the devices of the boys' adventure story, the Indians, the hollow tree, the underground house, the lost boys, the pirates, it treats them all as conscious fantasy, and so denies their connection with the real world, a connection which is the life line of any energizing myth. But of course a work so purely playful has a thousand faces, and this one was not what most people, or Barrie himself, saw. To them *Peter Pan* seemed like a continuation of *Treasure Island*, the same themes transposed into another key. But the end of Empire was at hand, as far as England was concerned, and that feeling is transmitted, all innocently, through Barrie's work.

Treasure Island had been a very great success of the old kind; W. E. Henley called it the best boys' book since *Robinson Crusoe*, and Andrew Lang said, "Except for *Tom Sawyer* and *The Odyssey*, I never liked a romance so much." (Implicitly that comment conjures up a whole scheme of literary tradition, which would relate literature closely to imperialism, and relegate the serious domestic novel to the periphery of the system.) It prompted, amongst other things, *King Solomon's Mines*, which Rider Haggard published in 1885. This too was very popular; it sold 31,000 copies in twelve months, was praised by literary men, and read aloud in public schools. And though Haggard didn't have Stevenson's finished artistry, nor anything like Kipling's talent and taste, still some parts of his work have some literary importance.

Haggard was born in 1856, and went out to Natal with Sir Henry Bulwer, when the latter became Lieutenant Governor in 1875. When England annexed the Transvaal in 1877, it was Haggard who ran up the Union Jack there. Then he went back to England in 1881, published *Cetewayo and His White Neighbors* (which urged the Government to be aggressive in South Africa) and *King Solomon's Mines* in 1885 and *She* in 1889. *She* is a curiosity from our point of view, because the myth is implicitly erotic and in some sense feminist—the major character being an immortal incarnation of femininity; it is the sort of idea D. H. Lawrence played with, and *The Plumed Serpent* is not totally dissimilar from *She;* and yet Haggard employs many of the traditional adventure motifs, which are so tied to opposite values. (The result is to embarrass the characterization of the young man hero, whom the story keeps turning into Chéri, despite the story-teller's determination to make him stay Tom Brown.) This is the only time when one of these adventure romances is told—in part—in the service of the Mother Goddess.

King Solomon's Mines is not very interesting, though one should note the treasure motif, taken over from Stevenson, and from now on standard; and the introduction of the old-hunter narrator, Allan Quatermaine. There is no striking similarity between him and Natty Bumppo. His literal model is probably African hunters like Frederick Courtney Selous, who advised Rhodes, and planted the Union Jack in Mashonaland in 1891—"the king of the white hunters." In literary effect, the important thing about Quatermaine is a certain almost-Cockney tone, a self-deprecating and antiromantic humor which proved an effective literary crystallization of the modern man's self-awareness in the presence of primitive grandeur and savagery. It combined intimations given by both Defoe and Scott, and was developed further by Kipling and Edgar Wallace.

Haggard was deeply impressed with both the grandeur and the savagery of tribal life, and felt them to be in some sense truer than the civilized ideas of Victorian England. "Nineteen parts of our nature are savage, the twentieth civilized, but the last is spread over the rest like the blacking over a boot, or the veneer over a table; it is on the savage that we fall back in emergencies" (*Allan Quatermaine*, p. 16). The deeper philosophic note of Haggard's romances is thus quite strongly stoic and melancholy. *King Solomon's Mines* introduced, as well as an old hunter, a Black Prince, Umslopogaas (modeled, Haggard tells us, on a Swazi aide-de-camp he knew in 1860). In *Allan Quatermaine*, in which the main characters of the earlier novel return, Umslopogaas says, "Man is born to kill. He who kills not when his blood is hot is a woman and no man." And in tendency the story endorses this.

For instance, even in *King Solomon's Mines*, Sir Henry Curtis, who is usually described as an Arthurian knight in Victorian dress, in battle turns back into a Viking and a Berserker. And on page 108 of *Allan Quatermaine* we are told, "The Englishmen are adventurers to the backbone; the colonies which will in time become a great nation, will testify to the value of this spirit of adventure, which seems at first sight mere luxury." Like Kingsley, Haggard saw the value of savagery, especially for a ruling race.

Like Kipling, Haggard was deeply impressed by Rhodes, his achievements and his ideas; Haggard's fiction is in effect propaganda in Rhodes's service. *Allan Quatermaine,* published in 1887, begins in England, and the narrator's picture of the country is charged with anxiety and indeed anger. "This prim English country, with its prim hedgerows and cultivated fields . . . now for several years I have lived here in England, and have in my own stupid manner done my best to learn the ways of the children of light . . . and found civilization is only savagery silver-gilt. . . . It is on the savage that we fall back in emergencies. . . . Civilization should wipe away our tears, and yet we weep and cannot be comforted. Warfare is abhorrent to her, and yet we strike out for hearth and home, for honour and fair fame, and can glory in the blow" (p. 16).

Haggard's most impressive book is *Nada the Lily,* which came out in 1892, and was inspired by the story of Chaka the Zulu king, who ruled from 1800 to 1828, and is said to have caused the deaths of over a million people. This subject also inspired Bertram Mitford's *The King's Assegai,* which was published in 1894, and has a similar epic grandeur and ferocity. The translations of Homer taught in the public schools, and even more the Norse and Germanic sagas that aroused so much interest in the nineteenth century, provided a literary model for which these African subjects were perfect.

Haggard compares Chaka to Napoleon and Tiberius, and then dedicates his book, in Zulu style, to "Sompsen, my father," the white man who had 3000 black warriors shouting for his blood, but calmly replied that for every drop of blood they shed of his, a hundred avengers should rise from the sea; so that they gave him the Bayete and said that the spirit of Chaka dwelt in him. This is a key idea—to show natives that white heroes have as savage a splendor as they.

In his Preface Haggard says that his intention is to convey "the remarkable spirit that animated these kings and their subjects." The Zulu military organization, "perhaps the most wonderful thing the world has seen," is already a thing of the past. He says he has learned to think and speak like a Zulu, in order to tell this story. The story is told to a white man by Chaka's witch doctor, Mopo, who has known Chaka from childhood. Mopo has some of Quatermaine's antiheroic realism. Umslopogaas is Chaka's son, but is brought up as Mopo's, and consequently as Nada's brother, since Chaka always has his children killed. Umslopogaas wins a comrade, Galazi the Wolf, who has won a great club by passing the night in a cave inside Ghost Mountain, where the Stone Witch sits forever, waiting for the world to die. In the cleft between her breasts are the bones of human sacrifice. Umslopogaas also wins a great weapon, an axe, but to get it has to marry, which spoils their comradeship. "Galazi was also great among the people, but dwelt with them little, for best he loved the wild woods and the mountain's breast, and often, as of old, he swept at night across the forest and the plains, and the howling of the ghost wolves went with him" (p. 153). (Galazi was the inspiration for Mowgli, Kipling said.) When disaster finally comes, and the comrades know they must die, Umslopogaas says, "May we one day find a land where there are no women, and war only, for in that land we shall grow great. But now, at the least, we will make a good end to this fellowship and the Grey People shall fight their fill, and the old stone witch who sits aloft, waiting for the world to die, shall smile to see that fight, if she never smiled before" (p. 285). This is *not* in the spirit of Defoe or Scott; but it takes something from Kingsley, Morris, and Carlyle.

The most impressive passages are those describing battle, or meditating on it. Their stychomythic dialogues and ritual and rhythmic formulas are not original, but they have some power.

Ah, the battle!—the battle! In those days we knew how to fight, my father! All night our fires shone out across the valley; all night the songs of soldiers echoed down the hills. Then the grey dawning came, the oxen lowed to the light, the regiments arose from their bed of spears; they sprang up and shook the dew from their hair and shields—yes! they arose! The glad to die! . . . The morning breeze came up and found them, their plumes bent in the breeze; like a plain of seeding grass they bent, the plumes of soldiers ripe for the assegai. Up over the shoulder of the hill came the sun of Slaughter; it glowed red upon the red shields; red grew the place of killing; the white plumes of chiefs were dipped in the blood of heaven. They knew it; they saw the omen of death, and, ah! they laughed in the joy of the waking of battle. What was death? Was it not well to die on the spear? What was death? Was it not well to die for the king? Death was the arms of Victory. Victory should be their bride that night, and ah! her breast is fair (pp. 48–49).

The feeling that passage expresses—and there is much of it in *Nada the Lily* and Haggard's other books—is rare in English literature. That literature on the whole, and certainly in the nineteenth century, had been in the keeping of what Haggard called "the children of light"; let us say George Eliot, Matthew Arnold, John Stuart

Mill, and the novelists Tolstoy approved in *What is Art?* What Haggard introduced was a lyrical or threnodic militarism, better fitting an army-focused culture like Prussia or Russia; and in *King Solomon's Mines* there is also a new emphasis upon regiments—their organization and training, but also their pride and glory.

There was to be something of this in Kipling, too; it was the two together who demonstrated in literary terms what Hannah Arendt called the Boomerang effect. The values by which the English on their frontier lived and imagined life, though the opposite of those which they proclaimed at home, crept home in novel form. The liberal values of the modern system, productivity and enlightened self-interest, etc., are undermined. The oppositeness itself took its toll, as we see in Quatermaine's alienation from England. The two effects together produced a kind of pessimism echoed in Mopo's remark, "Nothing matters, except being born. That is a mistake, my father!" (p. 39). The story of the Zulus made a particularly strong impression on the English imagination; they seemed terrible but noble, above all "worthy adversaries." They so appear, for instance, in one of Lady Butler's most famous battle pictures, "The Defence of Rourke's Drift"; and Cetewayo, who paid a visit to England, became a figure in the popular vocabulary—in music-hall jokes, for instance.

Haggard's friend, Andrew Lang, spoke in 1901 of a new "exotic" literature, "whose writers have at least seen new worlds for themselves; have gone out of the streets of the overpopulated lands into the open air; have sailed and ridden, walked and hunted; have escaped from the smoke and fog of towns. New strength has come from fresher air into their brains and blood . . ." (Brian Street's *The Savage in Literature*, p. 11). And it is significant that Lang was an anthropologist. There was a strong racist interest in anthropology then. The Anthropological Society itself declared in 1864 that black children develop only up to the age of twelve—an idea you can find in both Henty and Kipling. To such ideas Darwin's influence added others, of man's nearness to the apes, the struggle for survival, the persistence or sudden development of monstrous specimens, and so on. This made "primitive man" seem very horrifying but very exciting. It has been proposed to call a whole group of novels that arose in the 1870s with Henty's book on the Ashanti, "the ethnographic novel." And there is also the "anthropological romance" genre which

Popular Literature and Children's Literature

Leo J. Henkin discusses in *Darwinism and the English Novel;* these are novels written between 1890 and 1940 about fossil races of men or near-men. And then there is the whole Tarzan oeuvre. These all expressed and reinforced the trepidation of the imperialist race at the height of its powers. The anxiety of possession we noted in Defoe was an individual thing; by the time of Wells and Haggard it was national.

VIII

Twain

TWAIN belongs in this sequence of writers just on the strength of his combination of great talent with enormous popularity. Because of his success alone I should have to ask what modification he introduced into adventure conventions. But he also made the idea of adventure and the frontier crucial parts of his subject-matter. He allied them to humor. His treatment of those themes was in some ways oblique and out of line with the other writers—because he was a humorist—but in one book he made a major statement out of them. And in that book he also made a wholesale attack upon the romance genre and the aristomilitary caste (in the form of a parody of Malory) and spoke himself in the voice of a self-styled modern Crusoe. Indeed, Twain habitually spoke in a version of that voice. It was natural to him, though he made full use of it only in *Connecticut Yankee*.

That voice is his great achievement—the brash triumphalism of the modern system made audible, at first self-confidently self-mocking, then savagely self-destructive. The first performance, which continues for three-quarters of the book, announces the American rebellion, the rebellion of the Defoes against the Scotts, the reself-assertion of the mercantile against the aristomilitary caste. (Scott came after Defoe, but Twain came after Scott, so he could avenge the taking over of adventure by the aristocrats.) The second, which is rather a breakdown of performance, announces the self-accusation of the whole modern system. The horror at imperialism, which men began to feel at the end of the nineteenth century, breaks down the decorum of literature, breaks through the mood of entertainment, with dramatic effect.

The *Connecticut Yankee in King Arthur's Court*

The book by Twain I want to talk most about is, therefore, *A Connecticut Yankee in King Arthur's Court*, and I want to interpret it —that is, to put it into an imaginative context that is not entirely obvious, to light up an otherwise obscured context in which the book becomes alive, interacts with the experience we bring to it in a vivid and rewarding way. So I must comment on the text in a little more detail than I have used elsewhere. But my opening remark—that Arthurian romance is *not* the book's imaginative context—will take me away from the text.

It seems likely that Arthurian romance was important to Twain. When his wife died, for instance, he quoted a part of Ector's lament for Launcelot, in Malory, to express his grief; that, and other biographical testimony, suggests a richness and intimacy of feeling on Twain's part for the Arthurian story which could—playing against his opposite feelings of impatience and antagonism—have made a wonderful subject. But in fact it was not a wonderful subject, for Twain, and the critics who have read it in the context that subject brings with it have rightly neglected the book. The more experience of Arthurian literature you bring to your reading of it, the more disappointed you will be. Twain makes only the most obvious jokes—assumes the most philistine attitudes—never evokes the spirit of romance.

Why this should have been so is not my problem; but I would guess that the difficulty was Twain's habit of simplifying and dichotomizing. We see this also in his attacks on Scott and Cooper. He attacks them, I think, because they don't go far enough in the direction of modernist realism, but he makes it appear that they are going in a totally different direction, and attacks them wholesale. This is of course an effective rhetorical device, especially for a humorist, and it works well enough for a short-term, small-scale performance. But in a full-length novel, that wholesale and unqualified scorn for the thing satirized kills the reader's interest—denies the interest the writer in fact felt. Writing a full-length novel brought Twain many problems, and one of them was that his "official attitudes" bulked too large. Twain was essentially ambivalent, and could make very few judgments without starting to feel opposite sympathies. But in a full-length book he was on his dignity, and his attitude to the subject matter (in this case, Arthurian romance) became rigid, programmatic, dismissive. After the first few pages we know that he won't ever give Malory a fair chance, that there won't be any interaction between the two modes of sensibility. A humorist—someone who habitually sees things in terms of dichotomies—is likely to be more interesting, at least in a long performance, on a subject to which he doesn't have an "official attitude," a plan or a purpose—on a subject which engages him accidentally, though completely, and very powerfully. This, I think, is to be found in *Connecticut Yankee*, but that subject is not Arthurian romance, but modern imperialism or modernization.

Before Twain finally decided to make his novel out of the King Arthur burlesque, he had thoughts of using some old material about how civilization came to the Sandwich Islands; and if we look at what he had to say on that subject, we shall get a first glimpse of the imaginative context in which to set what he did write. Twain was sent to the Islands in 1866 by the *Sacramento Union,* because of a new American interest in them, created partly by the developing sugar trade. He stayed longer than he had intended to—four months—finding a lot to say about them; he sent twenty-five letters to his paper, amounting to eighty-five thousand words; and returned to the subject in later books.

It was during this trip that he began to find his vocation, to associate with the cultural elite of America, as distinct from the miners, prospectors, newspaper-bohemians, and so on, he had known before. He became friends with the U. S. Minister to China, the honorable Anson Burlingame, who gave Twain the advice—which he says in his *Autobiography* he followed for the next forty years— "Avoid inferiors. Seek your comradeships among your superiors in intellect and character; always climb." And the effect of the association was literary as well as social; in his letters from the Sandwich Islands, Twain first began to speak for the forces of refinement and respectability (though of course he continued to speak for their opponents also).

But what concerns us primarily is the interest Twain took in the Islands' cultural contrasts—between what he called "savagery" and "civilization." For instance, he described the president of the Assembly (who was also the king's father) thus, "This man, naked as the day he was born, and war-club and spear in hand, has charged at the head of a horde of savages . . . and revelled in slaughter and carnage; has worshipped wooden images on his devout knees . . . and now look at him; an educated Christian; neatly and handsomely dressed; a high-minded, elegant gentleman . . . a grave, dignified, statesmanlike personage. . . . How the experiences of this old man's eventful life shame the cheap inventions of romance." Surely it is another version of that idea that Twain evoked in the novel he did write. And perhaps it is an even more specific clue to the origin of *Connecticut Yankee*, that the Prime Minister of the Islands then was a renegade New Hampshire man. That quotation comes from *Roughing It*, page 206; for Twain returned to the subject of the islands in that book in 1871, and again in *Following the Equator* in 1897; it was a subject that stayed on his mind.

Thus I interpret *Connecticut Yankee* to be about modernization, and find it to be variously ironic, for and against that subject. Without any interpretation, of course we would find in it some comedy of irony at the Yankee's expense, an irony through which *some* complexity of feeling is engaged. He describes himself on page 14 as "a Yankee of the Yankees—and practical; yes, and nearly barren of sentiment, I suppose—or poetry, in other words." And on page 23, "I made up my mind to two things; if it was still the 19th century and I was among lunatics and couldn't get away, I would presently boss that asylum or know the reason why; and if on the other hand, it was really the 6th century, all right, I didn't want any softer thing; I would boss the whole country inside of three months. . . ." And so on. Let me just point out the Bob Hope-tone, the flat dry uneasy overself-confidence, and the comment on that in the word "boss," which is a central word. The Yankee's title in Arthurian England is Sir Boss. On the other hand, that irony is friendly and gentle, compared with the savage ironies directed against slavery and the droit de seigneur and feudal injustice, and so on. (The end of the book is not friendly or gentle to the technology which the Yankee has introduced, but the end of the book is quite separate from the rest, as we shall see.)

The theme of modernization is explicit, and even its connections with Crusoe and Columbus are explicit. On page 47, the Yankee says, "I saw that I was just another Robinson Crusoe cast away on an uninhabited island, with no society but some more or less tame animals, and if I wanted to make life bearable I must do as he did —invent, contrive, create, reorganize things—set brain and hand to work, and keep them busy. Well, that was in my line." And this comes at the end of a paragraph in which he has deplored the lack of gas or candles, or windows, of books, paper, pen, and ink, of coffee, tea, tobacco and sugar. And on page 232, like another Samuel Smiles, he praises "the creators of this world—after God—Gutenberg, Watt, Arkwright, Whitney, Morse, Stephenson, Bell." As for Columbus, he is invoked on page 38, when, "It came into my mind, in the nick of time, how Columbus, or Cortes, or one of those people, played an eclipse as a saving trump once, on some savages, and I saw my chance." And in fact eclipses were often "played" in contemporary romances of contemporary adventure, like *King Solomon's Mines.* [1] So there are explicit parallels and connections with Defoe-adventure and mercantile romance.

But what is only implicit in the novel is the similarity between the Yankee's modernization of sixth-century England and the core countries' modernization of lands outside their system, like the Sandwich Islands. A more notable example was the continent of Africa, to which general attention was just then being attracted by the Scramble for Africa. And the crucial case there was the Congo, which was being modernized, in matters of transport and administration, by a man with whom Twain had worked as a colleague—Henry Stanley. This was a crucial case also because in reaction against the Congo and Stanley there was arising that revulsion against modernization and colonization which disturbed the whole civilized world and paralleled exactly the revulsion which disturbed the end of *Connecticut Yankee.* (Twain began writing the novel in 1886; Stanley began his last journey, during which the worst scandals erupted, in 1887, and reached his objective in April 1888; the *North American Review* held a symposium on his expedition in December 1888; Twain finished the novel, of which the end is so disillusioned, in 1889.) Parallel cases included the modernization of Germany under Bismarck; a figure and a country which Twain, like other Americans, deeply admired; and the political position of the Boss is strikingly like that of Bismarck, the power behind the throne.[2] Also the modernization of Japan, once it was opened to American influence; a case which Thorstein Veblen compared with Germany's in *Imperial Germany*.

We are bound to think of both these countries (and Russia) when we read, on page 65, "My works showed what a despot could do with the resources of a kingdom at his command. Unsuspected by this dark land, I had the civilization of the 19th century booming right under its very nose." The opposition of the Church, which finally defeats the Boss, was the great opposition which Bismarck had to face in Germany; and Twain's characterization of the Church and the peasantry would have reminded contemporary readers of the church and the peasantry of Russia. Finally, let me point out that the use of modern military technology against much more primitive equivalents was to be found in contemporary American practice against Indians; Gatling guns, dynamite bombs, wires charged with electricity dangling from balloons, all were used in attacks on Indians at the end of the century.* This is the context, I want to suggest, in which to read *Connecticut Yankee;* put into this context, the book's enthusiasm, its anecdotes, and above all its growing uneasiness, which finally explodes, all become meaningful and moving.

We can discuss the way the book works in terms of a contrast between the Yankee and King Arthur. Twain does not put a heavy or at least consistent stress on Arthur; the contrast he draws is between the Yankee and Arthurian England as a whole; but we can, for the sake of neatness, use Arthur as a way to make the points. The Yankee represents democracy, which is good, while Arthur represents feudalism, which is bad. There is a great deal of teaching of that thesis in the book, to be taken quite straight. On page 84, "You see my kind of loyalty was loyalty to one's country, not to its institutions or its office-holders. . . . To be loyal to rags, to shout for rags, to worship rags, to die for rags—that is a loyalty of unreason, it is pure animal; it belongs to the monarchy, was invented by monarchy; let monarchy keep it." And with democracy we can associate free trade, a disestablished church, an established stock exchange, and organized competition—competitiveness is one of the Yankee's prime characteristics, as we see in his argument with Dowley. Turning to Arthur's England, we might put its Bastille-type prisons in contrast with the

*S. Moskowitz, *Explorers of the Infinite*, p. 106.

stock exchange, and its general dirt, squalor and nakedness with the Yankee's clean competitiveness, and its slavery and droit de seigneur with free trade and free worship.

Then the Yankee represents technology, while Arthur represents traditionalism. The Yankee loves technology, and it plays an essential part in two of his best performances, the blowing up of Merlin's tower and the restoration of the fountain. And with that we can associate for instance his knowledge of science; his prediction of the eclipse; and his confidence that "the world was not flat, and hadn't pillars under it to support it, nor a canopy over it to turn off a universe of water that occupied all space above. . . ." (p. 133). And his West Point military academy, and his machinery imagery, and above all his technocracy.

At the end of Chapter 17, he tells a grateful serf, "I'll book you both for my colony; you'll like it there; it's a Factory where I'm going to turn groping and grubbing automata into *men.*" This is a crucial idea, politically, to make the factory the means of humanization. And after he has restored the fountain, the people fell back before him, "as if I had been some kind of a superior being—and I was, I was aware of that" (p. 160). This is that divinization of the white man which we can trace from Columbus to Kipling. With Arthur's traditionalism we can associate superstition, and romanticism in general, like Sandy's; the Church and its doctrines and mysticism in particular; and the hermits and the monks and the knights and the barons.

Then the Yankee represents vaudeville, while Arthur represents legend. Both the Yankee's use of language, and shaping of anecdotes, but also the things he does, like the blowing up of the tower, are vaudeville, calculated to strike an audience with surprise, to deflate their pomposity, and to make them laugh. And we can associate that with his Cockney sensibility—the feeling of the quicker, cleverer, more knowing, townie, facing the slower-witted countryman or pompous aristocrat or tradition-bound native. And his elaborate and ingenious lying; and his journalism, in which he delights. ". . . when outside there rang clear as a clarion a note that enchanted my soul and tumbled 13 worthless centuries about my ears: 'Camelot *Weekly Hosannah and Literary Volcano*—latest eruption—only 2¢—all about the big miracle in the Valley of Holiness!' One greater than kings had arrived—the newsboy" (p. 186). While to the legends and legendariness associated with Arthur we can add the jousts, the cere-

241

monies, the tournaments, the colorfulness, the figure of Merlin, and the quotations and pseudoquotations from Malory.

Finally, the Yankee represents brains, while Arthur represents brawn, or, to put it more kindly, physical splendor. When the Yankee challenges the chivalry of England, 25,000 knights, he says, "Therefore, you have no chance—none whatsoever. Reflect: we are well-equipped, well-fortified, we number 54. 54 what? Men? No, *minds* —the capablest in the world; a force against which mere animal might may no more hope to prevail than may the idle waves of the sea hope to prevail against the granite barriers of England" (p. 311). This is a challenging assertion—exactly the faith that modern prophets, like Susan Sontag and Norman Mailer, have blamed the modern dilemma on. And with those brains we might associate the Yankee's faith in argument, and in reason, and his delight in finding that as a slave he fetches a much higher price than Arthur. While with the latter's physical strength goes his natural royalty, and the splendor of Lancelot and the others, but also their childishness and stupidity.

It is easy to see how this novel fits into the genre we have been studying. It is a recrudescence and further radicalization of the Defoe model of mercantile adventure. David Beard, who illustrated the *Yankee*, wrote to Twain on November 12, 1889, that he wanted to see a copy in every American home, "because I consider the story a great missionary work to bring Americans back to the safe honest and manly position, intended for them to occupy, by their ancestors when they signed the Declaration of Independence." Beard's illustrations delighted Twain, and they stressed the book's antiaristocratic and antichivalric feelings, by introducing caricatures of English notables. Merlin was drawn from Tennyson, for instance. The mention of Independence, which is exactly right, will remind us of Franklin, and so indirectly of Defoe again.

Directly Twain does not mention Defoe much, and there seems to be no evidence of "influence," but there is plenty of evidence of similarity of mind. For instance, Twain played with statistics in the way that Defoe did—though Twain's play is more typically humorous. (I am thinking of pieces like "The Dangers of Lying in Bed.") And the love of figures is only a crystallization of the general love of fact, the preference for the empirical and the pragmatic over the imaginative and speculative and high culture generally. Both *Life on the Mississippi* and *Following the Equator* are books in the genre of Defoe's *Tour;* each gives a progress report on civilization.

Often when Twain says Cervantes, moreover, I think we have the right to think of Defoe, because what he means is that force which displaced chivalry from our imagination. Thus in *Life on the Mississippi* he says that *Don Quixote* swept away the world's liking for medieval chivalry—though *Ivanhoe* had such effect in the South that *Don Quixote* was a wasted effort there. "As far as our South is concerned, the good work done by Cervantes is pretty nearly a dead letter, so effectually has Scott's pernicious work undermined it" (p. 378). That good work was in fact done for the Anglo-Saxon mind by Defoe.

The Yankee is a latter-day Crusoe; he has the same practical ingenuity, the same love of material possessions and the same creation of value, and perhaps the most striking, the same glee. For three-quarters of the book the dominant tone is gleeful, though that dominance is more and more disturbed, and finally overthrown, by its opposite, guilt and horror. King Arthur, though not personally attached to, or subordinate to, the Yankee, like a Black Prince, is a development of the Black Prince motif; he represents his people, commands them magically or religiously, and through him the Yankee commands them. And Clarence is a development of the Friday figure. But we must be more struck by the differences—by the way these categories have become more formal than substantial as a way of linking this book with *Robinson Crusoe.* The reason is just that this is a fundamentally different *kind* of book; just because it is a humorous book, and as such contains no real adventures.

There are adventures, but they are unreal; because permeated by and subsumed in an alien spirit, the spirit of humor. That does not mean that adventure and humor are not allied here—it means that they *are.* One of Twain's interests for us is that he shows just how those two went together in nineteenth-century culture (low culture). Twain sums up and embodies the long tradition of American humor, which found its most pungent form in the Southwest humorists. (There were elements of something similar in English humorists, and elements of that humor in English writers from Defoe on, but in Twain's time the English sense of humor—let us cite Dickens and Thackeray as examples—was more gentlemanly. After Twain made his impact, however, English laughter became more democratic, in Kipling and Wells.) The central figure who unites adventure and

humor is the shrewd and calculating trader who triumphs over various
grander, grosser, or more traditional opponents. Thus Twain exem-
plifies an alliance between adventure and something else that resembles the alliance between adventure and history-writing in Scott.
Such alliances are the crucial joints and gears in the workings of a
culture.

There being no real adventures does not make the book so different
as it might seem, for us, for we are concerned with the larger cultural
meanings of those adventures in *Crusoe*, and the same meanings are
treated in the *Yankee*. I said that the change from Defoe to Scott
was like a 90° rotation of the axis of the first book, from geography
to history. This change is like another 90° rotation, but in another
plane, from adventure to humor. The point of each anecdote is
different; or shall I say that the shape is different because in Twain
it has much more point. The "reality" is different; the element of
hypothesis is much stronger and livelier in Twain. And so on. But the
writer's, and the reader's, adventure of spirit is the same in both
authors—except that in Twain that adventure comes to a horrible
end.

Some of the power of that ending, and of the book as a whole, is
prophetic. When we read of, for instance, the setting up of the
military academy, we can think that within the decade of the novel's
publication, after the Spanish-American War, Harvard began its
School of Business Administration (in the belief that an imperialist
nation needed a trained foreign service) and the University of Chicago created a Department of Military Science and Tactics. When
we read of the factories to turn groping and grubbing automata into
men, we can think of the Congo, and the scandal that broke after
Roger Casement's investigations. And when we read of the rings of
barbed wire on which the knights hang dead, what can we think of
but the Somme in 1916?

Tom Sawyer, Huckleberry Finn, etc.

Although *The Yankee* is not an adventure novel, Twain was interested in that genre, and in fact most of his fiction carries the word
adventure in their titles; but they belong to the genre of children's-

adventure, and to the subgenre of children's-adventure-for-adults. That makes a considerable difference; the adventures of Tom Sawyer and Huck Finn are mock adventures, and their point is most often a humorous point, so that those books are halfway between *Crusoe* and *The Yankee.* That is why I shall not make a great deal of them here.

In *Life on the Mississippi,* Twain talks about Murel's Gang— desperadoes who hid out on an island in that river, a nineteenth-century equivalent to Rob Roy. But Twain could not tell their story, as Defoe and Scott told their equivalents'. Such stories made him too nervous to tell them full-scale. He wrote always about the world of adventure, but he could not take the adventurer's point of view—or he took it only to renounce it with a self-deprecating joke. His treatment of such material is represented by "The Private History of a Campaign that Failed," which is a vivid example of humor as an escape from painful truth. Twain is not as purely playful as Barrie about adventure, but he is of the same moment in the history of adventure. He is much more playful than Stevenson. His eye is on the adult reading over the child's shoulder, in collusion with that second reader. He is ambivalent, as always; and to some degree he undermines the adventure and the whole genre.

It is worth remembering that William Dean Howells had to convince Twain to promote *Tom Sawyer* as a book for boys. This was Howells's invention; not adventure but a new genre, whose real reference was to safe domesticity always. It was Howells who had heralded Thomas Bailey Aldrich's *Story of a Bad Boy* in 1870 as a landmark. He said that it was written with "so great desire to show what a boy's life is, and so little purpose of teaching what it should be" that it established a new pattern of fiction.* And Howells himself wrote books of that sort; boy's-life stories, rather than adventure stories. Their purpose was realism rather than excitement, though realism of a sentimental-nostalgic kind. They weren't part of an energizing myth.

Neither were Twain's, because he thought of the adventures as jokes for grown-ups. According to F. L. Mott, in *Golden Multitudes,* page 157, Twain wrote to Howells about *Tom Sawyer,* "It is not a boy's book at all. It will only be read by adults. It was only written

*Richard Darling, *The Rise of Children's Book Reviewing, 1865–1881.*

for adults." On the other hand, *Tom Sawyer* contains most of the motifs of adventure: the cave, the treasure, the captain, his comrade, and his band, a Friday figure, and a wicked Indian. There is even some development of those motifs, of a kind significant for later, more serious adventure. In *Huckleberry Finn*, Huck's relationship with Jim is clearly a development of the Crusoe-Friday relationship, and led on to Kim-and-the-Lama. The Crusoe-type practical ingenuity is now devoted to trick, fraud, and hoax purposes, as in Huck's disappearance from his father's house, or the release of Jim from imprisonment. And the King and the Dauphin carry some sardonic allusion to Scott-type romance.

What is importantly new—and antienergizing—is the sense of the sordid and horrible, which broods at the edge of the narrative, and is crystallized in the figure of Pap, his appearance at Huck's window, and his final appearance as a corpse. That whole sense of the sordidness of the frontier is something that doesn't appear in British adventures; and it is of course appropriate that it should be an American who brought it into relation with the rest, since the Americans always knew their Frontier more realistically than the English knew their Empire. Even the part of the book that is beautiful, Twain's lyrical evocation of the river, and all nature, and of drifting with the current, depends on that sense of the sordid and horrible. The innocent stressless beauty is evoked in revulsion from the incidents of frontier life. One is bound to remember that at eight Samuel Clemens found a stabbed body on the floor of his father's office one night, and at nine he witnessed a murder, of which the perpetrator was acquitted. Huck wants to get away from everything rather than into adventure. He does take pleasure in some of the new places and people he meets, and above all in being released from the containments of the settlement, but his is a very passive kind of adventuring.

Twain's nearest approach to adventure as we are defining it is to be found in *Life on the Mississippi*, in the description of his own training as a river pilot. He is as ambivalent as ever about most things he describes, but the skill he learns, the pride in that skill, and the sense of Mr. Bixby as a master craftsman, these are solidly in the line of Anglo-Saxon modernist adventure. The pilot is contrasted with both the captain and the mate as being a man of *skill;* and of the three it was a pilot Sam Clemens wanted to be. That central element in his imagination is finally Crusoe-like.

Biography and Reputation

There were of course other elements in his personality, and they were combined very unstably. The most important thing about Twain as a person, from our point of view, is that he was born the child of the Frontier culture, but grew up to become the favorite writer of the new financier-capitalist culture. He experienced the growth of America in himself—a growth so violent it was like a change of nature.

His childhood was passed in a small settlement, he traveled up and down the river as a youth, and in 1861 went to Carson City, Nevada, and there became a prospector, a silver-miner, and hoax-journalist. *Roughing It* gives a vivid impression of the effect this environment had on him. Henry Nash Smith picks out, as especially revealing, that book's story of a dog ineffectually chasing a coyote, which Twain makes into a fable of the superiority of Frontier values over those of conventional culture; the tenderfoot dog (with a higher self-esteem than he can validate in the West) will always be defeated by the veteran coyote (who looks disreputable but commands the situation). And the imaginative touch which brings the story alive—just because it announces Twain's bedazzlement by Frontier values—is that the coyote seems released from Nature's laws by its extraordinary speed, subtlety, and cunning. He is a Frontier hero, like the Yankee, a hero of invention and practical cunning. So it was straightforwardly, despite the burlesque, the excitement of the Frontier (of Empire) that dazzled Twain.

Frederick Jackson Turner makes some comments on the Frontier mind, which both explain that excitement and can connect Twain again with Defoe and Crusoe. "That coarseness and strength combined with acuteness and inquisitiveness; that practical, inventive turn of mind, quick to find expedients; that masterful grasp of material things, lacking in the artistic but powerful to effect great ends; that dominant individualism, working for good and for evil, and withal that buoyancy and exuberance that comes with freedom . . ."* That is the legend the Frontier created for Anglo-Saxons generally—and a real enough legend, and school of character.[3]

*"The Significance of the American Frontier," in *The Frontier in American History*, p. 37.

The effect of that training in Twain's case was not in any psychological sense democratic. One of the strongest impressions the reader gets from *Roughing It* is of a land peopled by great men, who subject lesser mortals to humiliation all the time. These were boatmen and pilots, in Twain's early years, and then stage coach drivers and division agents; all of them men who need not reply when spoken to, men of brutal social power, that was sometimes physical and even fatal in its manifestations. One of the division agents was the murderer Slade, "A man who awfully avenged all injuries, affronts, insults, or slights, of whatever kind—on the spot if he could . . . a man whose face would light up with a terrible joy when he surprised a foe and had him at a disadvantage" (p. 62). Slade had killed twenty-six men, and the moment when Twain breakfasted with him is in many ways the emotional climax of the book.[4]

It was partly a derivative of this education that Twain hankered —half-humorously—after princely status. Meeting some Austrian royalty in 1898 made him confide to his diary his regret at not being a prince himself. "It is not a new regret but a very old one. I have never been properly and humbly satisfied with my condition. I am a democrat only on principle, not by instinct—nobody is *that*." But since his culture was capitalist (mercantile) Twain could only play with the idea of aristocracy, as Crusoe played at being Governor. In his later years he was playfully called "the King"; and his millionaire friend, Rogers, was "the Rajah"; both men "held court."

Another derivative of his cultural formation was Twain's self-deprecating and self-destructive attitude to literature. It is worth noting both that his *Innocents Abroad* trip was an act of promotion for a shipping company, and also that 100,000 copies of the book were sold, over two years, door to door, by subscription publishing. "Anything but subscription publication," he said, "is printing for private circulation." But everyone knew that that was the mode of publication of vulgar books, not of literature. Both facts remind us of how intimately Twain associated himself with capitalism in its rawer and more thrusting experiments. He spent a great deal of money and time and energy on get-rich-quick schemes; most notably, and tragically, on the Paige Typesetting Machine. He associated his machine with his novel, *The Connecticut Yankee*, as enterprises (he formed the company the week before he began the novel, and he hoped to have done with both together).

He also promoted a patent food, Plasmon, was director of an Accident Insurance Company, and invented a number of things himself—for instance, Mark Twain's Self-Pasting Scrapbook, and an Adjustable Strap for Garments. And he spent his profits largely, in the manner of other self-made men; for instance, spending $125,000 on his house in Hartford. And making his friends among other great success-figures of capitalism, like William Huddleston Rogers, of Standard Oil. He said of Rogers, "He's a pirate all right, but he owns up to it, and enjoys being a pirate. That's the reason I like him (Kaplan, *Mark Twain and His World,* p. 157). But it was Rogers who saved Twain after his bankruptcy, and Twain could never have saved Rogers; there is a bitter note to what he said to Rogers, "You and I are a team; you are the usefullest man I know, and I am the most ornamental." Rogers, and his secretary, were much involved in Twain's affairs; she had power of attorney, and access to his safety deposit box. Twain was in the power of the millionaires.

In *Mark Twain: God's Fool,* H. Hill says that family, investments, and his literary career were the three strands of Twain's life. Financial schemes were always on his mind, and he was forever suing and suspecting treachery, especially at the end of his life. "Both suspicion and an almost blinding lust for fortune were a part of his nature; he speculated, suffered, and sued as instinctively as he wrote" (p. 80). All this makes him one of the major figures in our literary history, in a sense quite unlike the use of that phrase by literary critics, but a very important sense.

He identified himself with, and participated in, all the fevers of American capitalism in the Gilded Age. He took advantage of none of the opportunities of withdrawal and detachment which "literature," amongst other things, offers to its representatives. It seems a natural consequence that Twain suffered a deep cynicism and depression. "It could probably be shown by facts and figures that there is no distinctively native American criminal class except Congress" (Kaplan, *Mark Twain,* p. 98). And he felt very deeply the corruption that was coming over the country; at times he blamed it on the '48 Gold Rush, which had "introduced the change and begot the lust for money which is the rule of life today, and the hardness and cynicism which is the spirit of today." When the diamond rush began in South Africa, he sent an old Nevada friend called Riley to gather materials there for a book, for he saw that rush as likely to "sweep the world like a besom of destruction." (However others might blind themselves, Twain saw the likeness between the frontier and the empire.)

More than the other writers we have been studying, therefore, Twain knew that he could not claim to represent literature, or to write for the "discriminating reader." The "discriminating reader," in America even more than in other countries, stood in indignant opposition to other forces of the culture, and Twain had allied himself to them. He always declared an antipathy to Jane Austen—when he read her, he felt "like a bar-keeper entering the Kingdom of Heaven"—and to George Eliot and to Henry James. And another famous expression of his feelings about literature was the hoax lecture he gave in Boston on December 17, 1898, at a dinner to honor Emerson, Holmes, and Whittier. These men represented literature; but Twain told a story about three tramps using their names, and the trouble they caused in a cabin in the Rockies; which gave him a chance to use the sacred names disrespectfully, and vent his resentments in humorous form; only unfortunately those resentments seemed too evident to the audience, who did not laugh. Another famous expression of this was his letter to Andrew Lang in 1890, in which Twain declared that he didn't write for the brain or mind of his society but for the belly and the members.

But it was probably Matthew Arnold who principally represented to Twain the judging and rejecting faculty of literature. And in this confrontation between literature and the adventure writer, we know more about the latter's feelings than we did in the other cases of Defoe, Scott, etc.

Arnold began to criticize America in a way that bore on Twain in particular in the late 1880s. In 1887, he reviewed General Grant's *Memoirs* (published by Twain himself) and complained of their lack of style, and of American boasting and lack of distinction. In 1888 he wrote "Civilization in the United States," in which he said that the country lacked the discipline of awe and respect, and had not solved its human problem. "The glorification of the average man, who is quite a religion with statesmen and publicists there, is against it. The addiction to 'the funny man,' who is a national misfortune there, is against it. Above all, the newspapers are against it" (Kaplan, *Mr. Clemens and Mark Twain,* p. 299).

Twain was bound to apply these criticisms to himself. He was a newspaper humorist, who had come to England as early as 1872, giving funny-man lectures on the Sandwich Islands and the Silver Frontier. (It was in the frontier humorist, one may say, that England first met frontier life, and as we would expect, literature was against it.) Indeed, he was already familiar with the charges. Literary Americans like the popular moralist, Josiah G. Holland, often complained of their humorists' lack of respect. And Twain himself wrote to Mrs. Fairbanks from England in 1873, "God knows, I wish we had some of England's reverence for the old and great." Such criticism often took the form of a cultural threat, moreover, reminding him of his dependence on mere popularity. A literary history of 1888 (published in New York) said that Twain and his ilk "must make hay while the sun shines. Twenty years hence, unless they chance to enshrine their wit in some higher literary achievement, their unknown successors will be the privileged comedians of the republic" (Kaplan, *Mark Twain*, p. 299).

Naturally, Twain had his defenses against such attacks. In May 1886, he wrote in his diary, "My books are water; those of the great geniuses are wine. Everybody drinks water." And he had a position; he didn't care about, didn't believe in, poetry and fiction; he liked history, biography, travel, science—"books with the root of the human matter in them." And he had his allies, powerful voices on the Victorian scene, like Smiles and Macaulay, spokesmen for the modern system. Sydney J. Krause says, "If there was any one writer Twain would rather have been other than himself, I believe it would have been Macaulay. He read and re-read him" (*Mark Twain as Critic*, p. 229). He particularly loved the Macaulay essays on Clive and Hastings, those central documents of Victorian imperialism, and was inspired by them to write a poem, which he published in *Following the Equator*. (It is worth noting that Macaulay's reputation was in decline by the 1880s, and Twain was now defending him. Arnold had called Macaulay "the Prince of Philistines.") Twain and Macaulay (and Lecky, Macaulay's epigone, whose book Twain made so much use of in *Connecticut Yankee*) were writers in defense of the modern system, while Arnold was in attack on it.

Twain declared himself against literary critics as a group, which is to say, literature-as-a-system. On August 24, 1889, he wrote Howells, about *Connecticut Yankee*, "I'm not writing for those parties who miscall themselves critics, and I don't care to have them paw the book at all. It's my swan-song, my retirement from literature permanently, and I wish to pass to the cemetery unclodded" (*Mark Twain-Howells Letters*, II, p. 610). That sounds highly defensive, and we are not surprised to find that there are two years' worth of entries in his notebooks, and a hundred manuscript pages of a projected reply, with the title, "English Criticism on America," which would have been in effect a self-defense against Arnold.

But the only part that got finished was his famous letter to Andrew Lang of 1889, in which he said,

". . . the critic has actually imposed upon the world that a painting by Raphael is more valuable to the civilizations of the earth than is a chromo; and the august opera than the hurdy-gurdy and the villagers' singing society . . . and the Latin classics than Kipling's far-reaching bugle-note; and Jonathan Edwards than the Salvation Army; and the Venus de Milo than the plaster-cast peddler; the superstition, in a word, that the vast and awful comet that trails its cold lustre through the vast abysses of space once a century, and interests and instructs a cultivated handful of astronomers, is worth more to the world than the sun which warms and cheers all the nations every day and makes the crops to grow. . . . That mass will never see the Old Masters —that sight is for the few; but the chromo-maker can lift them one step upward toward appreciation of art; . . . they may never even hear of the Latin classics, but they will strike step with Kipling's drum-beat, and they will march. . . . I have always catered for the Belly and the Members, not the Head." (*Mark Twain's Letters*, II, pp. 526–527)

Probably it is some such defense which will always have to be made for the adventure novel and for taking an interest in that as literature. But for whom then *did* Twain write?

If Scott and Cooper were read by the responsible class of their societies (the men of power who also took some serious interest in literature, as distinct from the literary class), then Twain was read, or one feels he was read, by the same class in its irresponsible mood. One says that partly because he was a humorist, and it is the job of humor to give expression to irresponsible feelings. Of course he was in the literal sense read by nearly everyone; but above all by the men of action and the men of power. The question is, in which mood did men say, "He's writing for me," or "That's what I wanted to hear said," or "That's just what I would have said"? Applying that test, I would say that Twain wrote for an irresponsible and certainly an unliterary audience.

From *Innocents Abroad* on, Twain was the spokesman for the practical and innovative man, the pioneer, socially mobile, culturally

philistine, emotionally crude. In the *Yankee,* "Raphael was a bird.
We had several of his chromos; one was his 'Miraculous Draught
of Fishes,' where he puts in a miracle of his own—puts three men
into a canoe which wouldn't have held a dog without upsetting. I
always admired to study R.'s art, it was so fresh and unconventional"
(p. 47). He spoke for that class within America, and for America
in that character within the world. And yet his principal heir was
an Englishman who wrote for the responsible class par excellence.

In 1889 Kipling came through America on his way from India
home to England, to begin his literary career. He came to see Twain,
and wrote that he felt the older man's hand on his shoulder as an
honor like being invested with the Star of India. It seems likely that
that was sincere. Kipling had begun in writing by imitating Bret
Harte, and he certainly knew the superiority of Twain to Harte. He
was in many ways fascinated by America, and by the Frontier experience and the types of men and expression it had produced. Many
English critics, and of the sort most favorable to Kipling, had compared him to Twain very early. Andrew Lang wrote Twain a Jubilee
Ode in 1886, and said how he delighted in things under the ban of
"culture." Sir Walter Besant, from whom Kipling learned a lot when
he was beginning, had written enthusiastically about *Huckleberry
Finn* and *The Three Musketeers* and the novel of adventure, in 1898.
Bret Harte and Joel Chandler Harris also were popular in England,
but Twain in fact became the national favorite, succeeding to the
position which Dickens had held. Moreover, Twain returned Kipling's admiration. He admired *Plain Tales from the Hills,* read Kipling's ballads along with Brownings's at public readings, and when he
went to India, saw it through Kipling's eyes. (It is because Twain's
audience and Kipling's were the same in most ways that we must
distinguish them in terms of mood.)

Owen Wister and Theodore Roosevelt

It is typical of Twain's rather paradoxical relation to the adventure
tradition that he, the great writer of the West, played no part in
spreading the cowboy myth. That myth is so important a phase in

the history of the WASP hero and WASP adventure that we must briefly consider it, and relate it to Twain.

In 1895, Theodore Roosevelt invited Kipling to dine with him in Washington, together with Owen Wister and Frederick Remington. Wister had met Remington two years before at Yellowstone Park, and they were working together on stories about cowboys, which Remington was illustrating. Wister had gone to Wyoming for his health in 1885, when he was twenty-five, after Roosevelt had written to him about how wonderful the West was. Like Parkman, Wister suffered from hysterical headaches, and like Parkman, he sought ideas and practices that would harden both himself and his whole class. Wister was a Philadelphian aristocrat and aesthete who had traveled all over Europe by the time he was twenty-two. He wrote his first story about cowboys in a Philadelphia club in 1891, the night some-one said to him that America needed a Kipling of the sagebrush. Thus these men all belonged together; they were collaborating at the task of giving America an adventure hero—one that would satisfy both the democratic and the aristocratic urges of the modern system. They were inventing the cowboy.

For instance, Remington drew a picture which became famous, *The Last Cavalier,* which showed the cowboy as the last variant on the chivalric and cavalier hero throughout the ages. It illustrated Wister's essay, "The Evolution of the Cow-Puncher," in 1895. The essay told the story of a cowboy traveling in the same train with an English peer, and of the instinctive hostility they felt for each other because of the class difference; but the story continued with the peer going to Texas a few years later and adopting the life-style of the cowboy, and revealing himself as fundamentally the same man. "Deep in him lay virtues and vices coarse and elemental as theirs. . . . Directly the English nobleman smelled Texas, the slumbering untamed Saxon awoke in him. . . . Sir Francis Drake was such a one; and Raleigh, the fine essence of Anglo-Saxonism, . . . conqueror, invader, navigator, buccaneer, explorer, colonist, tiger-shooter" (Vorpahl, *My Dear Wister—,* pp. 78–81).

Through the 1870s, cowboys had still been called "herders," and seen as rough, uncouth, barbarous, and violent. Not until the first Wild West Show, in North Platte, Nebraska, in 1882, did the cowboy become a hero; that happened when one of them, called Buck Taylor, caught the eye of a writer, Prentiss Ingraham, who immortalized him in a series of dime novels, beginning 1887. It is he whose work with cowboys is closest to Defoe's with pirates, but his interest in them is less serious. Ingraham first associated cowboys with the semi-Mexican costume so familiar today. Then they were taken over briefly by men of education, above all by Wister.

In 1892 Wister produced *The Virginian*, which redeemed the cowboy both from the dime novel and from the category of uncouthness. Though his Virginian is supposed to get tamed while courting his Bennington schoolteacher, in fact he was a perfect Southern gentleman from the beginning, though one who got up to wild undergraduate pranks. The prefatory note tells the reader that though Wyoming between 1874 and 1890 was very wild, still the Virginian did not speak lewdly to women, and "Newport would have thought him old-fashioned."

The narrator, a civilized man, first sees the other man corralling a pony, and envies the way "he climbed down with the undulations of a tiger, smooth and easy, as if his muscles flowed beneath his skin." The cowboy is a version of the handsome sailor, and is viewed with an even more erotic eye. Then the narrator hears his voice, teasing somebody else, full of lazy charm. And finally he meets the "slim young giant, more beautiful than pictures." At first the cowboy refuses comradeship, because the visitor has been "familiar" with him. Indeed, all the Westerners look askance at the visitor; "Yet I liked the company, and wished that it would like me." In other words, he is on his knees before beautiful young manhood.

But of course the figure we're familiar with from a hundred films, the cowboy who is in a sense Hollywood's major cultural achievement, is not recognizably a knight or a cavalier. Rather like Hawkeye, the Virginian was an attempt to impose a responsible-class profile on an irresponsible-class hero, and the mask fitted only loosely and briefly. Hollywood cut off the literary trappings Wister had attached to the cowboy—though Hollywood has its own gentility.

This is an iconography which has had some curious developments. For instance, it is of some interest that Raymond Chandler said that his private detective, Philip Marlowe, had as antecedents the Virginian and Nick Adams (the Hemingway character). Moreover, when Chandler began writing in 1932 it was for a magazine called *Black Mask*, which then had a masterful editor, Joseph T. Shaw, with a clear idea of his readers. Shaw wrote in 1931 that he pictured the magazine's reader as "a pretty stalwart, rugged specimen of humanity —hard as nails, swift of hand and foot, clear-eyed, unprovocative but ready to tackle anything that gets in the way. ... [a man who] knows the song of a bullet, the soft, slithering hiss of a swift-thrown knife, the feel of hard fists, the call of courage. ... He is vigorous-minded; hard, with a square man's hardness; hating unfairness, trickery, injustice, cowardly underhandedness; ... not squeamish or prudish, but clean, admiring the good in man and woman." Several readers wrote in to say that he must have had Theodore Roosevelt in mind, and they might have added Wister and Remington.

Such was Chandler's original market. And in fact Shaw and Chandler admired each other a lot, and felt in harmony as to their aims in writing. So the cowboy gave birth to his only rival as culture hero, the private detective. He too was a responsible-class culture-hero. Philip Marlowe and the Virginian, Humphrey Bogart and Gary Cooper, turn out to be cousins. Of course, Hollywood introduced modulations and inflections, and modernized the characters, by traits that were, superficially, the reverse of Wister's intentions. The actors were assertively unaristocratic and unchivalric in style. But these changes were in style rather than substance.

It was appropriate that it should be Kipling and not Twain at the Roosevelt dinner. Twain was not in sympathy—as a writer—with this aristocratic kind of adventure hero. Nor did he notably create heroes of any kind in his fiction; which is not to say he had none in real life; but insofar as he drew them (the Yankee is as near as he comes to a hero) they belong to Defoe's type rather than Scott's. But in his relation to them, and other matters, Twain has more in common with Thorstein Veblen, another frontier intellectual and satirist of capitalism, than with Defoe—much less with the well-born Wisters and Roosevelts.

Veblen was essentially a man of heroes, but his worship of them was ironic. He devoted his attention first to the financiers or "pecuniary men" of his society. In *Theory of the Leisure Class* (1899) he said that the ideal pecuniary man was like the ideal delinquent, addicted to sport and gambling, magic and superstition. That book has often been called a saga of the doom of the heroes of America's leisure class. His attitude to them is very similar to that of Norris and Dreiser, amongst contemporary novelists. But in their novels, and in Veblen's own writings about financiers, the irony is almost as bitter, as obsessive, as doom-laden, as it is in the last part of *Connecticut Yankee*. This cannot be called hero-worship in any ordinary sense, even though the writers brood over this figure they have conjured up with quite as much emotional intensity as real hero-worshipers.

Veblen also reminds us of Twain by an idea like this, from *The Theory of Business Enterprise*, "The ubiquitous presence of the machine, with its spiritual concomitant—workaday ideals and scepticism of what is only conventionally valid—is the unequivocal mark of the western culture of today" (*The Viking Veblen*, p. 348). That could be the Yankee himself; and when Veblen looks at the modernization of Germany, he sees it in terms very like those of Twain's novel. "The case of Germany is unexampled among Western nations both as regards the abruptness, thoroughness and amplitude of its appropriation of this technology, and as regards the archaism of its cultural furniture at the date of this appropriation." And he has a footnote comparing the case of Japan. But that cultural furniture*— being the mythos and ethos of the military castes that ruled those countries—turned out to be more important than he (or Twain) expected. Veblen was also like Twain in that bitterness of alienation that almost strangled his voice with irony.

In later life he somewhat overcame, or turned his back on, that self-destructive irony, and in the early 1920s turned to the engineers; his book *The Engineers*, of 1921, said they were the only men who might create a revolution in America, and that a soviet of engineers should be set up. He in part inspired Howard Scott's Technical Alliance, and Technocracy Inc. (1932). This is something we can well imagine Twain taking up, too—or Defoe. In *Imperial Germany*, Veblen had said that the Englishmen who made the Industrial Revolution atrophied man's earlier bent to impute anthropological qualities to everything; and that free institutions and insubordination go with the machine—and thus are incompatible with the feudal and dynastic state which is superimposed on them in Germany and Japan.

The technocratic hero of Twain and Veblen is thus clearly descended from Defoe and Smiles, and distinct from the gentleman cowboy of Wister and Roosevelt; and yet both types were to be found, in real life, side by side at the helms of power.

*Imperial Germany and the Industrial Revolution, p. 83.

Henry Stanley

A historical hero who combined both sorts of trait (though originally and basically of the first type) was Henry Stanley, whose career is absolutely pivotal in the history of the WASP hero, and who was significantly related to Twain. Stanley is a relevant figure for us to look at in several ways. One is as an Anglo-American. He lived in and worked for both countries, and was a citizen of both. Each felt him at times to be somewhat alien, and to belong to the other, and yet both tried to claim him as their own. The history of his reputation illustrates both the irritated animosity between England and America in the '70s and '80s, and the rapprochement of the 1890s, when there were many calls for a reunion of the two countries on imperialist-racist grounds. At that time Senator Beveridge said, "The American Republic is part of the movement of a race—the most masterful race of history—and race movements are not to be stopped by the hand of man. They are mighty answers to divine commands." And he wrote to his friend, M. E. Ingalls, "Never forget that we are the only people on earth whose farmers buy the adjoining farm before they need it. We are of the blood which furnishes the world with its Daniel Boones, its Francis Drakes, its Cecil Rhodes."* Henry Stanley was another of that company, and the focus of much hero-worship, in England and America.

Frank Hird's authorized life of Stanley, published in 1935, says he was "The last of the great adventurers—to use the word in its best and original meaning. . . . His life story was a romance. From the humblest beginning with every disadvantage against him—absolute poverty, friendlessness, his childhood spent in a workhouse . . . not only an explorer of untiring courage and resource, but a great administrator in the creation and management of the Congo Free State" (pp. 11–12). And Marie von Bunsen (who could have married Stanley, and been 'queen of Africa') described him as "one of the tough Conquistador types with the outward habit of a disgruntled farmer and the phraseology and vocabulary of an American journalist" (Hall, *Stanley: An Adventurer Explored,* p. 275). Not a romance-hero, that is, but an adventurer.

*Quoted in T. F. Gossett, *Race: The History of an Idea in America,* p. 318.

Stanley was born a bastard in Wales in 1841, and brought up in a workhouse until he fought the master and ran away. This conclusion to schooling and opening to adventure we have met before; and in Stanley's story we have reason to suspect some romancing. But it seems to be true that his mother, who lived nearby, denied him love; and that he learned piety, cleanliness, and love of order in the workhouse. So that, whatever details he invented, he was indeed very like the Defoe-style self-made man.

In 1859 he sailed as a ship's boy to New Orleans, where he got himself adopted by an English merchant, Henry Stanley, and took his name; very much like Crusoe. He said that Henry Stanley died in 1861, but it seems that in fact the older man broke off relations with him. In any case, he was effectively an orphan again. During the Civil War he served in both the Northern and Southern armies, and worked as a merchant, a sailor, and a journalist. (This variety of activity and flexibility of temperament must remind us of Defoe's own career.) In the last capacity he reported on the Peace Commission to the Sioux in Montana of 1867 and was much impressed with the Indians' calm and bravery. He recommended the Reservations scheme in the *New York Herald* and the *Chicago Tribune,* as the way to settle their problems. Stanley said later that he learned how to handle African natives from watching and listening to Generals Sherman, Henderson, and Taylor deal with Indians.

It was on this occasion that Stanley made Twain's acquaintance, for Twain also was reporting the Peace Commission. Their careers had been not dissimilar. Like Twain, Stanley had worked in San Francisco, Denver, and Central City, as a printer and as a prospector. He was an expert shot with both rifle and six-shooter, and had known both Wild Bill Hickok and General Custer. Later he, like Twain, had something of a career as a lecturer; he was billed as "The American Traveller," wore a uniform he declared to belong to the Turkish navy, and promised to make the muezzin's call to prayer in Arabic on the lecture platform.

1867 was the year he went to work for James Gordon Bennett of the *New York Herald,* one of the most flamboyant figures in a very flamboyant period of journalism. Bennett was exactly the same age as Stanley, and equally ambitious, and soon became jealous of him. But he sent Stanley to report on the war in Abyssinia, where he achieved a major scoop, by getting reports to his paper before any of the British papers got theirs. He got on badly with the British officers, who called him "Jefferson Brick," after the brash American journalist in *Martin Chuzzlewit*—while he thought them effeminate. This was intercaste jealousy—the mercantile against the aristomilitary. But Stanley was more than a journalist, and he knew it. During the war (swimming under fire, capturing an abandoned ship) he had made himself a hero. And now he had found a profession in which his various abilities could all be combined together.

He had always talked of traveling around the world and having adventures. Like Przhevalsky, he liked to take adolescent boys with him. In 1864 he picked up Lewis Noe, a fifteen-year-old shipmate on the *Minnesota,* who traveled with him in Greece, and who later signed a document releasing Stanley from all claims upon him. Edwin Balch was another boy he tried to take on a world adventure. And later he adopted a page, whom he called Baruti (gunpowder), from a cannibal tribe. As in Przhevalsky's case, we find this fondness for boys matched with a shyness with women. On August 1, 1884, he wrote a friend, "I have lived with men, not women, and it is the man's intense ruggedness, plainness, directness, that I have contracted by sheer force of circumstances. . . . The fact is, I can't talk to women. In their presence I am as much of a hypocrite as any other man, and it galls me that I must act and be affected, and parody myself."

Stanley aimed at heroism early. In 1869, while in Madrid to report on the Spanish Civil War, he wrote to a friend, who urged him to take a holiday, describing his achievement so far, and saying, "How have I done all this? By intense application to duty, by self-denial, which means I have denied myself all pleasures, so that I might do my duty thoroughly, and not exceed it. Such has been my ambition. I am fulfilling it. Pleasure cannot blind me, it cannot lead me astray from the path I have chalked out. I am so much my own master, that I am master over my own passions. . . . It is only by railway celerity that I can live. Away from work, my conscience accuses me of forgetting duty, of wasting time, of forgetting my God. I cannot help that feeling. It makes me feel as though the world were sliding from under my feet." We hear there the voice of the Victorian hero, the conscience-driven conquistador. In the Introduction to his Autobiography, he says, "But I was not sent into the world to be happy, nor to search for happiness. I was sent for a special work."

260

Bennett commissioned him to find Livingstone, who had disappeared in search of the source of the Nile in 1866. This was of course
a very American thing to do, very offensive to English sensibility, to
make a newspaper stunt out of the great missionary, England's Christian hero of the whole century—and to presume to rescue him, as if
England could not do so, was doubly offensive. Stanley reached
Zanzibar in 1871, set off into Africa and found Livingstone at Ujiji,
established a filial relation with him, and returned to write *How I
Found Livingstone* in 1872.[5]

He turned his adventures into book form immediately, as
Przhevalsky did, and Stanley had much wider circulation; *Through
the Dark Continent*, 1878, was translated into eight languages simultaneously. His friend Thomas Wallace Knox made a fictional digest
of it called *Boy Travellers in the Congo.* And Stanley himself in 1874
produced a novel, *My Kalulu: Prince, King, and Slave.* The Preface
says it is written for boys. . . . "Those clever, bright-eyed, intelligent
boys, of all classes . . . boys who have a promising future before
them."[6]

From 1879 to 1884 he worked for King Leopold of the Belgians
in the Congo Free State; the reporter and explorer become nation-
builder. He built a fifty-two-mile road from the lower Congo to
Stanley Pool, which made the Congo navigable as an artery of commerce. There he won the title, Bula Matari, the breaker of stones.
A massive bronze statue of him stood beside Stanley Pool until
demolished in the early 1960s. His two-volume *The Congo and the
Founding of the Free State*, 1885, was followed by editions in seventeen other languages.

In London, he and Twain used to stay at the same hotel, and
Twain persuaded him to sign a lecture contract with his own impresario, "Major" Pond. Twain launched Stanley on his lecture career
in Boston in 1886, saying how his own self-esteem sank when he
compared what he had done in his life with all that Stanley had done.
"When I contrast what I have achieved in my measurably brief life
with what he has achieved in his possibly briefer one, the effect is to
sweep utterly away the ten story edifice of my own self-appreciation
and to leave nothing behind but the cellar" (Farwell, *The Man Who
Presumed*, p. 88).

Twain cited Stanley's indestructible Americanism, too. It was like
a breath of fresh air to see "an untainted American citizen who has

been caressed and complimented by half the crowned heads of Europe. . . . He is a product of institutions which exist in no other country on earth—institutions that bring out all that is best and most heroic in a man" (Hall, *Stanley*, p. 272).

It seems likely that this was genuine hero-worship, of a thoroughly modern-system hero; that Twain saw Stanley as a more effective version of himself—as the man who translated their common values into deeds, not jokes. Twain had by then been interested in the other man for some time. In 1872 he had attended the Royal Geographical Society dinner for Stanley, at which Sir Henry Rawlinson had apologized for the Society's behavior to him over the rescue of Livingstone; Twain described it as a manly and magnificent apology, and the occasion must have been a triumph for all adventurers and all frontiersmen. In 1879 he wrote in his *Notebooks*, "Stanley is almost the only man alive today whose name and work will be familiar a hundred years hence" (p. 304). In 1886 Twain tried to get Stanley to write an autobiography and a boys' adventure novel about Africa for his publishing firm. And in 1891 he was to ask Stanley to write a reply for them to one of the books attacking his most recent African expedition.

In 1887 Stanley had set out to rescue Emin Pasha, a European commanding Egyptian troops in Equatorial Africa, cut off after the defeat of Gordon by the Mahdi in the Sudan. This time he took with him a steel boat, 500 Remingtons, 50 Winchesters, and a Maxim. (When he tested the latter, and found it fired 333 rounds in 30 seconds, he said, "It is a fine weapon, and will be invaluable for subduing the heathen.") He had always been fascinated by new machines, and was an inventor himself; like the Yankee, he overwhelmed a hostile native force at one point by building a wooden tower that floated on three canoes, and out of which came a mysterious voice. But of course what was most notable about this ever-increasing weight of equipment was its death-dealing properties. On this expedition he took 800 men with him, and lost 500 of them. He was much blamed for abandoning a rearguard which got massacred.

The commander of that rearguard, Major Barttelot, was a brutal man, who may have been one of Conrad's inspirations in drawing the figure of Kurtz. (Conrad's trip up the Congo took place in 1890, only two years after these events, and he was, by his own account, thinking about them, and about Stanley.) Barttelot apparently gave floggings of three hundred lashes at a time, and looked on with a wide grin. He buried more than eighty of his carriers in less than a year; and hired a body of cannibals to kill and eat another tribe so that one of his men could record the scene.* A good deal was written about Barttelot and the Stanley expedition as a whole, immediately after.

Stanley and his career were a striking embodiment of those forces of adventure and modernization—of the modern world system— which Twain first celebrated and then accused in *Connecticut Yankee*. The moral disapprobation in which he ended was a much more than personal tragedy.

If we compare Stanley with the great British proconsuls in Africa then, Gordon, Goldie, Lugard, Johnson, we shall see how clearly they all belonged to that upper-class, aristomilitary caste we can associate with Wister and Roosevelt.[7] In such men, the sense of self was supported by an imperialist identity which was not, I think, available to Stanley (or Twain). On the other hand, the latter could of course identify themselves as representing the modern world system. And despite the appalling revelations, and the repudiation of that role, to which some of his late writings bear witness, Twain continued to play that role, and celebrate it in others, up to the end. It was only after his death, in 1910, that some more drastic change imposed itself on writers generally.

*Jerry Allen, *The Sea Years of Joseph Conrad*.

Kipling[1]

DURING Kipling's lifetime the modern system crossed the great divide of 1914–1918, after which everyone assumed that the British empire was dying, and everyone in serious literature was openly hostile to it. We have of course found plenty of evidence that they were hostile before, but most characteristically they had expressed their feeling by ignoring the empire as a literary subject. After 1918 they turned more often to it, in aggression. One of the first examples of such writing was also the finest, E. M. Forster's *Passage to India*.

But partly because of that change in climate, and his consequent disappearance from the literary scene, Kipling's career as an adventure writer can be said to have ended with the outbreak of war. We can restrict our view of him to his work as celebrant of overt imperialism and subverter of literature-as-a-system. For the '90s and the Edwardian years were both the time when England threw off the mercantile mask—the aristomilitary caste moving to the front of the Jubilee processions—and the time when literature nearly accepted alliance with that caste and the empire. Kipling made a gallant effort to mobilize sympathetic men of letters (notably the professors of literature) and to reorganize the literary world's criteria of styles and subjects.

He did not engage in literal intrigue to that end. Kipling's energies went into the act of writing almost exclusively; and insofar as he took a hand in action, it was of a patriotic or political kind, not in matters of culture. His efforts to change literature-as-a-system should be compared with Scott's rather than with Dryden's or Coleridge's. But if he is compared with Twain, he will be seen to have made such efforts, and from inside the system. Because there were differences between England and America, Kipling was more literary than Twain. In the English cultural situation, where the responsible class felt it had political power, its sense of cultural responsibility was more acute. Kipling could hope to ally literature to the responsible class, and he invoked a great deal of literary precedent on his side, against the spiritual rebels of literature. (The powerful sympathy of Kipling and Twain for each other, despite this difference in situation, testifies to the essential identity of their spirits.) But the crucial consequence for this study is that Kipling put great artistic intensity into his work, and we are faced with a closely textured and intricately structured oeuvre, which demands more specifically critical attention than my other authors received.

Kim

In that oeuvre, his only successful full-length narrative was *Kim*. Kipling has much more impressive successes in art than the conduct of a full-length romance; and more impressive successes in meaning than *Kim*, charming as that book is. But we can begin with it.

Clearly Kipling was indebted to *Huckleberry Finn* in designing his story. Twain and Kipling were the two great entertainers of the Anglo-Saxon community in its period of overt imperialism, and they helped each other quite importantly in their work. The two books' major motif alone—the idea of giving the WASP public an Irish orphan hero to focus their feelings on—is quite an important one. It subtilizes the strategy and renews the feeling of the adventure tale. And Kipling also makes Kim a Roman Catholic. And culturally speaking an Indian too. Perhaps we should also credit Twain with the idea of substituting a boy for a man as hero, even though there are several other exemplars of that substitution, and several other pressures on Kipling to make it besides precedent. Nevertheless, if many voices in the situation of the writer of English fiction in the '90s—especially one who wanted to celebrate adventure—if many voices combined to command him, "Write for and about boys," still Twain was the one man of genius to have done it.

Then the relationship between Huck and Jim is strikingly like that between Kim and the Lama; drifting along the River is strikingly like traveling along the Road; the episodic, the picaresque, the picturesque, the humorous—the mixture is the same in both books, and behind both narratives looms the idea of the Frontier and of the Empire. There are of course differences, deriving from differences between Frontier and Empire; for instance, the English novel has no dead bodies and no sordid violence; and Kim is perceptibly more adventurous than Huck—there is less debilitating melancholy in his nature; but the likenesses seem more important. Clearly Kipling took more from Twain than from anyone else, though he combined what he took with ingenious devices of his own; like the Lama's quest, which contrasted and intertwined with Kim's in very clever ways; the Chaucerian or Morrisy charm which he gave to the picturesque cavalcade of his personae and places; and so on.

More important, from our point of view, is the godfather motif; the number of adults who care for Kim and in effect adopt him, the Lama, Mahbub Ali, the Sahiba, Hurree Babu. They in effect compete for his affections. At the end, "The Sahiba is a heart of gold," said the Lama earnestly. "She looks up on him as her son." And Mahbub Ali replies rather sourly, "Hmph! Half Hind seems that way disposed" (p. 283). This is on the first level a device for giving the reader, once he has identified himself with Kim, the luxury of feeling loved —not so very important a meaning. But on a second level, we note that these so adoring godfathers are all Indians, of various kinds— Colonel Creighton, for instance, has a cooler relationship to Kim, less personally affectionate and much less adoring. So what we see—and we see it often in Kipling—is the humble affection offered up to a white boy by potent adult figures representing native races.[2] (Two notable cases are the stories "A Sahib's War" and "A Deal in Cotton.") Is *this* an important meaning? Yes, it is in its own terms very richly and convincingly worked out, however many political objections one has to the idea. And this is a development of a motif in Defoe's novels; Crusoe and Singleton have godfathers in this sense, but the range of meaning Defoe extracts from them is much less. (They are not natives, for instance.)

Another motif is the Great Game, and Kim's secret service work. Hannah Arendt says, "What the dragon-slayer is to the bureaucrat [that is, his myth-world predecessor], the adventurer is to the secret agent" (Arendt, *The Origins of Totalitarianism*, p. 216).[3] The phrase "the Great Game" was used about Anglo-Russian conflicts in Asia from the middle of the nineteenth century on. These conflicts generated anxiety, especially by the end of the century. As Jeffrey Meyers points out in *Fiction and the Colonial Experience*, in 1846 2000 miles separated the English frontier from the Russian in Asia; in 1876, only 500 miles, and those occupied by the unstable Amirate of Kabul; the border between Afghanistan and India was "settled" in 1893, that between Afghanistan and Russia in 1895. But fictionally speaking, of course, Kipling plays on the pun introduced by the fact that Kim is still a child. The Game metaphor is always being demetaphorized by its context in the book—Kim is literally only playing games; though of course it is remetaphorized by the matters of life and death involved; the serious meaning emerges from that interchange—from our sense that men are like boys, and vice versa, that politics is like a game, and vice versa—an insight Kipling is very fond of. The characterization of Mahbub Ali conveys the same feeling, and corroborates the phrase "the Great Game."

A somewhat related idea is that of the training of Kim, which is compared to the way that a colt is trained. Given Kipling's ideology, it is of course a most important matter, this making of a boy into a man. Both those terms are heavily loaded in Kipling's usage, and if "boy" is often all that is wonderful, there is another usage of the word, in contrast with "man," which is contemptuous. And the language for describing the rite of passage is predominantly that of horse training. In *Kim* that language is given mostly to Mahbub Ali, who is a horse dealer, and so it seems special to him; but in fact you find it everywhere in Kipling, and it was, for instance, used by his schoolmaster, Cornell Price, about Kipling himself.[4] What this language brings with it is, one, the idea of breaking the colt's will—the fiercer the will, the better, but it must be broken; two, the idea of the boy as animal, the man as human—or divine—the mature adult lives in a world of remote and alienated wisdom; and three, the idea of the man riding on the boy's back—not to imply any direct sexual excitement, but an intimacy of connection which is in some loose sense erotic. It is only when the Lama is hard on Kim, accidentally, that we are aware there is a significant training relationship going on; in the early parts, when Kim merely likes the Lama, and the Lama merely talks wisdom, the relationship does not feel quite real.

In one way the book is clearly a development from Scott, in that its characterization and even action are so fused with 'cultural' or ethnological observation. To meet someone of a different type, religiously, socially, or racially, is an event in itself, to Kim and to the reader. Kipling is very skillful in making these details, potentially so static and informational, effectively dynamic and narrative; the measure of the gulf between this kind of romance and serious fiction of the Great Tradition kind is that here these "external" details matter so much.

In another way, it is clearly a development from Defoe; in that it is informed by the character's glee at his own cleverness. Only instead of a "do-it-yourself" cleverness, this is a "be-it-yourself" kind, focusing on transcultural disguise. We are told on page 160 that the Hindu child's mind could not temper itself to enter another's soul; "but a demon in Kim woke up and sang with joy as he put on the changing dresses, and changed speech and gesture therewith." Kipling asserted (and John Buchan followed him in this) that it was particularly an Anglo-Saxon gift, to be able to imitate every other race.

The serious fictional meaning of this (for of course Kipling has such meanings, being a great artist) is indicated by the imagery of demons and singing—it is being suggested both seriously and playfully that Kim prefers dissimulation to sincerity—the meaning is in the exchange between "seriously" and "playfully." As in the Great Game metaphor, men and boys exchange identities, and this is doubly exciting because of the difference in status between them, dramatized in the training metaphor.

An interesting example of the social power of Kipling's art is the game played by Kim and the Hindu boy, a competition in noting, remembering, and reciting afterward the jewels on a tray. This training in observation is a part of what Kim learns in preparing to become a Secret Service agent. In Ballantyne's *Coral Island* also there is some stress on "powers of observation," and their value in education, and for adventure. (A related phenomenon is the interest in codes and clues—clues for the central character but also for the reader to pick up and interpret—competitively; this is something you find in Jules Verne, Twain, and of course Conan Doyle; an interest serious fiction eschewed.) But Kipling's description of the Game is not only a good deal more vivid, it had a remarkable social effectiveness. "Kim's Game" became a popular social entertainment—not without its more serious intentions—among the class Kipling wrote for. And that was of course the responsible class—the men of action who also cared about literature. Kipling had recreated that constituency. In the '90s indeed, he had attracted also the men of letters, but they left him by the turn of this century. But Philip Mason tells us that people he met at official dinner parties in India, who declared that they didn't read, would add "except of course *Kim.*"

His audience's loyalty to Kipling was very strong, and its character —because they were not habitual readers—might be called unprecedented. Of the two lines of descent of the adventure novel, he clearly has more in common with Scott than with Defoe, in his interest in culture and in his essentially chivalric heroes. And Scott too had of course a very large and loyal audience. But Kipling is unique because such an artist, unique in the intensity with which he combines material from his audience's most familiar experience—the anecdotes of British India, for example—with large poetic and even mythic preoccupations.

For instance, walking is made into an important moral and indeed cultural activity in *Kim.* It is a significant recommendation of the Lama to Kipling's audience that he is a vigorous walker. And climbing is an intensification of walking; this was strongly felt in late Victorian England, where men like Leslie Stephen made Alpine climbing a big thing. "Day after day they struck deeper into the huddled mountains, and day after day Kim watched the Lama return to a man's strength . . . and where he should have sunk exhausted swung his long draperies about him, drew a double-lungful of the diamond air, and walked as only a hillman can. Kim, plains-bred and plains-fed, sweated and panted, astonished. 'This is *my* country,' said the Lama. 'Beside Suchzen, this is flatter than a rice-field' " (p. 230). And the climbing leads to a sense of geography. "Through the speckled shadow of the great deodar-forests; through oak, feathered and flumed with ferns; birch, ilex, rhododendron and pine, out onto the bare hillsides' slippery sunburnt grass, and back into the woodlands' coolth again, till oak gave way to bamboo and palm of the valley, he swung untiring" (pp. 231, 232). As Kipling handles it, and in this he rediscovered the Elizabethans, and was followed by John Buchan and others, geography became a sort of heraldry of imperialism—every mountain and river evokes the excitement of conquest and possession.[5]

That is surely what the reader felt when Kim "watched the wee cows grazing on the housetops, or threw his soul after his eye across the deep blue gulfs between range and range" (p. 233). What is offered is of course romanticism, but beneath surely lies imperialism. "Thus, after long hours of what would be reckoned very fair mountaineering in civilized countries, they would pant over a saddleback, sidle past a few landslips, drop through forest at an angle of 45 on to the road again. Along their track lay the villages of the hill-folk—mud and earth huts, timbers now and then rudely carved with an axe—clinging like swallows' nests against the steeps, huddled on tiny flats halfway down a 3,000-feet glissade; jammed into a corner between cliffs that funnelled and focused every wandering blast; or, for the sake of summer pasture, cowering down a neck that in winter would be 10 foot deep in snow" (p. 232).

The activity for which Kim is being trained is surveying, which brings together the activities of climbing, observing, native disguise, etc., under the aegis of imperialism. It may seem to the modern reader a euphemism to give this name to the secret service of an imperialist power, but in Kipling's time it was at least a general euphemism. And for his readers the survey had quite exact historical references. Captain T. G. Montgomerie was an engineer in the Great Trigonometrical Survey of India who in 1862 suggested to the Asiatic Society of Bengal that a native could get into Tibet and do survey work there, as a move in the Great Game. He chose men in the Indian Educational Service, and some of them became famous in the closed circles of the Indian administration, like Nain Singh, one of Montgomerie's first batch of eight recruits. They got two years' training in the use of the compass and sextant, and in taking an absolutely regular stride, which they counted on the Buddhist rosaries they carried—an adapted version, with only one hundred beads, and every tenth slightly larger. They carried adapted prayer wheels, with a compass and long strips of paper concealed inside them. Their walking-sticks contained a boiling thermometer, their strong box a sextant, and so on. In 1865 Nain and a companion set off to survey the main road to Lhasa, disguised as Bisahari horse-dealers from

Kashmir; and they returned in 1866 with an excellent map, for which Nain got the Gold Medal of the Royal Geographical Society. It is facts and legends of this sort which *Kim*'s first readers brought to their reading.

The figure of the Lama is both Kipling's triumph and his failure. It is a triumph because Kipling is significantly knowledgeable about lamas, and sympathetic with a renunciatory religion. (It is a related point that Kipling treats the Roman Catholic chaplain with more respect than the Protestant; the Protestant element in the White Anglo-Saxon Protestant formula had begun to lose its potency. Chesterton was selling to a large audience the idea of a Roman Catholic Englishness.) Kipling doesn't offer the insights into such religion that a Dostoevsky offers, but his treatment is—up to a point—dignified. And it is quite a remarkable change in the structure of the romance we have been studying that the Lama should have primacy over Mahbub Ali. The latter is after all a version of the Black Prince— an older Chingachgook for a boy Natty. The Lama is something new; as a hero of passivity, he derives from Twain's Jim, but clearly a major difference of status is involved in giving that figure of practical passivity this dignity of cultural background and spiritual insight.

What happens to the romance genre when this figure replaces Chingachgook or Fergus MacIvor as the hero's major tutor? Not very much happens, and that is Kipling's failure. The Lama's powers are circumscribed by the word "spiritual," which is mutually exclusive with the word "practical." His truths are no use in the world. In the end he is quite simply duped as to who Kim is and what he intends to do with his life; in the end it is Mahbub Ali and Colonel Creighton who have trained Kim; it has been good for Kim to have had the Lama's acquaintance in his childhood, and no doubt he will return to see the Lama on holidays and perhaps in retirement, but that is to say that this acquaintance is for him like a convent schooling for upper-class girls—it adds an irreplaceable polish, the true aristocratic je ne sais quoi. For all Kipling's interest in renunciatory Buddhism, the Lama's only function in Kim's life is to be his Mr. Chips. (Of course Kipling intended something more than that; and achieved something more—otherwise there would be no element of triumph in his depiction of the Lama; but the book expresses a deep ambivalence, betrayed in the quite unsatisfactory and merely tricky ending.)

Stalky and Co.

This is both a more characteristic and a more significant Kipling success than *Kim*, because of the aggressive moral realism of the meaning, and because of the corresponding intricacy of the artistic means. It is an unpleasant and difficult book; but a powerful study of authority. Like many other artists, Kipling often makes his best work difficult and unpleasant—though he *could* simply charm and delight, without compromising, as in the *Just So Stories*.

The introductory poem contains a stanza which reminds us of *Kim*, and indicates the continuity between these two of Kipling's books and most of the others—the concern for how boys are trained to be men and Englishmen.

> Servants of the Staff and chain—
> Mine and fuse and grapnel—
> Some before the face of Kings,
> Stand before the face of Kings;
> Bearing gifts to divers Kings—
> Gifts of case and shrapnel.

The boys were trained to be surveyors, but also to be diplomats and soldiers; to treat with kings or to cannonade them. The stress on kings is very characteristic; it blends an ironic contempt with a deep romantic thrill; which fuse in the feeling "I, as an Englishman, am greater than Kings." This is Kipling's version of the anti-imperialist modern world system feeling in Defoe; and despite Kipling's overt love of Empire (unlike Defoe, his imagination turned to ruling, not trading) and despite this being an imperialist epoch in English history, one meaning of "Kings" as Kipling uses it is anti-imperialist. This is after all one of the meanings of his famous poem "Recessional"; that Englishmen should be on guard against the excitements of success and power—though that warning is suffused and subdued by a surge of precisely those excitements.

The crucial difference between Defoe and Kipling is rather in the different ways in which they treat the theme, and induce the excitement, of "how-to-do-it." Both are devoted to that theme, but in quite different ways. Kipling dazzles the reader with technicalities—wants the reader to be excited about things he hasn't understood. Defoe always genuinely wants the reader to understand—to see how the thing is done. There is an element of insincerity in Kipling's cult of expertise, though not in his cult of the expert. And the skills he does really want to explain to us—Kim's and Stalky's skills—are not really trades but tricks. The tradesmen's skills, which Defoe makes so much of, in Kipling take a rather peripheral position—at least in the prose.

The Stalky poem as a whole is a set of copybook maxims; the boys learned to be each "Keen in his vocation" and "To obey their orders," and were "Set to serve the lands they rule (Save he serve, no man may rule)." It was of course Kipling's fate to deal in copybook maxims; he was an artist in service of his rulers; a fate which brought him his characteristic problems as an artist. If we think of other high priests of the copybook gods, like Samuel Smiles, Horatio Alger, Martin Tupper, we shall better appreciate Kipling's achievement. By his time the system of literature, as we have seen, was driven by a motive of opposition to those gods; the aversion felt by Swift and Coleridge and Arnold had been strengthened by sterner principle. Even the realm of imagination as a whole was inspired by an evasion of those maxims. (Though in most cases the imagination evades the kiss of a culture's truisms only as part of a game in which it finally lets itself get caught.) *Stalky and Co.* is a prime example of how Kipling plays that game. In his verse I think he is less successful. The problem one feels with much of it—the problem T. S. Eliot alluded to in his distinction between verse and poetry—is precisely the difficulty of the flat resonances of copybook maxims. More exactly, Kipling's solutions to that problem, which he solves most typically by indicating "savage" and "primitivist" perspectives behind each maxim, demand more from his command of poetic language than he can give. In his fiction, his language has more factual specificity and his structures more dynamic exchange.[6]

We are told in "An Unsavoury Interlude" that, "Outside his own immediate interests, the boy is as ignorant as the savage he so admires; but he has also the savage's resource." And this is a persistent theme; "tribe" is a word often used. Stalky and Beetle and M'Turk, ". . . spun wildly on their heels, jodelling after the accepted manner of a 'gloat,' which is not unremotely allied to Primitive Man's song of triumph," (p. 27) and are seen on page 38, "learning, at the expense of a fellow-countryman, the lesson of their race, which is to put away all emotion and entrap the alien at the proper time." This they do by deceiving one of the masters, and the point is made by the specificity of the analogy—by the credibility of their behavior and by Kipling's analysis of it. (That's the resource he does not command in his verse.) A final example is the West African war-drum they play, a gift from M'Turk's naval uncle, originally made to signal war across estuaries and deltas. ". . . a deep devastating drone filled the passages as M'Turk and Beetle scientifically rubbed its top. Anon it changed to the blare of trumpets—of savage pursuing trumpets. Then, as M'Turk slapped one side, smooth with the blood of ancient sacrifice, the roar broke into short coughing howls such as the wounded gorilla throws in his native forest" (p. 60). And as Kipling evokes behind the boys this somewhat fanciful picture of primitive man, he evokes before them the more realistic image of the people they will be ruling and fighting in their adult careers. Thus he sets boyhood in an imaginative context radically unlike *Tom Brown's Schooldays,* not to mention *Eric*—even less to mention *The Prelude* or *Emile*—but no less valid, imaginatively.

Kipling's heroes set themselves positively against traditional images of school piety and training—against house honor and cricket and so on. (It is quite comic to see his critics, for instance, who feel themselves to be more skeptical than he of Establishment pieties, yet scolding him for blaspheming against these pieties in *Stalky and Co.*) The boys bring to school life a strong disgust for cliches and for the blatant. The most striking case is in "The Flag of Their Country," when the chauvinist M. P. unfurls a flag before them, and unwittingly drives Stalky to disband his cadet corps. Patriotism has been made disgusting. The major activity of the Cadet Corps had been for the boys to learn each in turn to drill the others, and as a part of the drill to shout insults at them in sergeant-major manner; even more, for each to learn to betray no feeling when thus berated. Thus both halves of the story bear upon silence and restraint of expression. The Flag was "a thing shut up, sacred and apart." They had been training themselves in a devotion to it that was profoundly silent, though superficially loud in blasphemies of various kinds. The success of the story resides in the way its form mirrors the intricacies of the moral paradox involved.[7]

The book's central paradox, around which the others are organized, is that of authority. One of the great lessons the boys learn at school is to obey; and yet the heroes are rebels. This is a serious paradox, for obedience is of the essence of the boys' interrelations— Beetle's obedience to Stalky, for instance; and yet Stalky is a real rebel —Kipling once described Stalky's real-life model as displaying "an unaffected contempt" for all the masters at their school. The paradox is mediated through the mechanism of the Headmaster; he represents true authority, which the boys recognize, and he in effect legitimizes their rebellion against the untrue authority of the other masters.* He implements the paradox by imposing punishments on them which are categorically "unjust." What this does is to give irony a role within a system of piety—to give rebellion a role within a system of authority. Kipling builds a very convincing model of how sincerity—and particularly the sincerity of originality and leadership —can be taught; how a model of aggression and resistance can be built into the teacher-student relationship and not destroy it but energize it. The most elaborate fictionalization of this is the story "A Little Prep," in which Stalky out-maneuvers the Head by revealing the latter's secret heroism to the other boys and organizing an outburst of acclamation which is at the same time disobedience, so that the Head can punish them yet again—the piety is saved from blatancy by being interlaced with impudence and punishment.

In the boys' future stands the life of heroism-in-service, most typically in India, on the North-West frontier. It is represented by the old boys who return to the school, and are just as devoted to the Head as they were as pupils. And by the story in which we hear of Stalky's exploits there, where he has "become a Sikh," but where he behaves exactly as he did at school. (And in fact the real-life "Stalky's" career, as Major-General Dunsterville, did parallel the boy's; long after *Stalky and Co.* was published, in the Great War, he led an irregular force from India into Persia, and camouflaged his cars to look like tanks, and so on.) Thus the picture is essentially a triptych; primitive man, the school, and the Frontier; no panels from what literature calls mature life or civilization, needless to say.[8]

*His authority is ideal and potential—as it were, divine—and so the boys don't rub up against it all the time. The school as a whole actualizes that authority, only imperfectly. And at rare intervals *he* actualizes it perfectly, and then we rejoice, to see the divine power we worship made manifest.

Biography and Reputation

As for Kipling himself, he was born in 1865 in Bombay, where his father had just become professor of architectural sculpture in the School of Art, and was as such concerned to preserve native Indian arts. He had been designer to a Burslem potter and then worked as a stone mason on the Victoria and Albert Museum. He was a friend of Edward Burne-Jones and William Morris, and part of the arts-and-crafts movement. During Rudyard's holidays in London as a boy he spent many days in the Victoria and Albert Museum, and the other South Kensington museums, and there is a certain similarity between his work and those collections of exotica and ingenuities from all over the world. So he did not inherit warrior traits genealogically, or biologically—by physical or psychical temperament. His vocation as bard of the Empire was always something of an adventure, almost a paradox, a response to an external idea.

His mother belonged to a group of remarkable sisters, one of whom married Burne-Jones, another Edward Poynter, who became President of the Royal Academy, and another the Baldwin whose son became Prime Minister. Mrs. Kipling seems to have been the most sharp-witted and sharp-tongued of all her sisters, and the writer grew up in a highly competitive but very close family. Both his parents were the children of Methodist ministers, but themselves apostates. Alice Kipling is supposed to have thrown into the fire a devoutly preserved lock of Wesley's hair with the remark, "The hair of the dog that bit us." The example of apostasy from religious to artistic spirituality was probably a powerful heritage for the writer. While living with foster parents in Southsea (having been sent home by his parents at the age of six) he spent holidays with the Burne-Joneses, where the arts and ideal values were one—and where he was happy; while at Southsea, where he was very unhappy, the tone was limitedly moral and religious—what he called "evangelical."

When he left school in 1882, he did not go to the university, which would have been the natural place for a boy with his already developed literary and artistic talents, but to India, where he worked as a journalist, and dined at the Club, and entered the world of the Indian services, with their very strong anti-intellectual group loyalties. Martin Fido has suggested that this was a crucial juncture in Kipling's development; that up to that point he might have developed very differently—into a liberal in politics; and in art a more ordinary sort of aesthete.[9]

But he became instead a cub-reporter on the *Civil and Military Review* and *The Pioneer,* under a short-tempered editor, Wheeler, who "licked him into shape."[10] It is perhaps emblematic that in 1883 he wrote a sarcastic review of Morris's socialist poem, "The Day is Coming." He had turned away from his early idealism. He plunged into Indian life from the angle of a reporter, who was sent by his paper to cover princely ceremonies, cholera outbreaks, bridge-openings, divorce and murder trials—he was very excited when one of his soldier friends was convicted of murder. One of his informants was the original of Mahbub Ali. And Kipling in turn was an informant to General Roberts, the Army's Commander-in-Chief, who asked him what the men in the barracks were thinking, in 1889.

By then Kipling, though only twenty-four, was a famous writer in India. His stories and poems, printed in the newspapers, were collected to form the first six volumes of the Indian Railway Library. That year he came back to England and soon found himself famous. *The Times* published a leading article about his work (probably written by Andrew Lang) on March 25, 1890. In the same year, *Lippincott's Magazine* printed his novel, *The Light That Failed* (in the same twelve months, they also published *Dorian Grey* and *Sherlock Holmes*). And also Henley published Kipling's *Barrack Room Ballads* in his *Scots Observer;* one of which, "Danny Deever," caused the professor of literature at Edinburgh University to tell his students, "Here's literature! Here's literature at last!," waving his copy over his head in excitement. The professors generally were enthusiastic; Dowden, Saintsbury, Quiller-Couch, and also the professorial types among men of letters—Gosse, Lang, Whibley.

Kipling had general as well as instantaneous success. Even the fervent liberals and aesthetes were not united against him. In 1892 Henry James wrote to his brother William, "Kipling strikes me personally as the most complete man of genius (as distinct from fine intelligence) that I have ever known." Lafcadio Hearn in 1897 called him, "the greatest of all living English poets, greater than all before him in the line he has taken. As for England, he is her modern Saga-man; skald, scop, whatever you like . . ." (R. L. Green, *Kipling:*

the Critical Heritage, p. 173). And C. E. Norton, in *The Atlantic,* for January of the same year, wrote "This splendid continuous fertility of English genius, this unbroken poetic expression of English character and life from Chaucer to Rudyard Kipling, is unparalleled in the moral and intellectual history of any other race. . . . He is one of those poets who have done England service in strengthening the foundations of her influence and of her fame" (Green, *Kipling,* pp. 185, 187).

The man of letters who seems to me to confront Kipling in something of the way Matthew Arnold confronted Twain, and Swift confronted Defoe, is Henry James. James was one of the few guests at Kipling's wedding, and in 1891 wrote a long and enthusiastic Preface to an American collection of Kipling's stories called *Mine Own People.* But he always had reservations, and it wasn't long before they became dominant in his judgment. On Christmas Day, 1897, he wrote Grace Norton that he thought Kipling's talent quite diabolically great, and that as a ballad-writer his future might still be big; but one deplored the fact that in prose Kipling could "make use of so little of life." "Almost nothing civilized save steam and patriotism. . . ." And of course neither of those topics were what James really called civilized. "Almost nothing of the complicated soul or of the female form or of any question of *shades. . . .*" James had once thought Kipling might become an English Balzac, but no longer. After 1900 he lost touch with Kipling and with his work.

Thus Kipling soon began to feel the ideological conflict between himself and other writers; deriving not from his politics—not all conservative writers were boycotted—but from the conflict between his subject matter (adventure) and theirs. In essays like "In Partibus," in poems like his attack on long-haired aesthetes in velvet-collar rolls, and in various stories, he expressed a strong unease. And he was soon attacked; notably by Robert Buchanan in "The Voice of the Hooligan" in the *Contemporary Review,* in 1899, Buchanan described Kipling as giving voice to a hooligan imperialism which was driving the old humanitarianism into retreat; he objected for instance to Kipling's depiction of soldiers, asking, "Is General Gordon forgotten?" that we should see the British army in these vulgar terms. But the crucial dates were those of the Boer War; that experience, and the disillusionment with imperialism it brought, marked the end of the liberal intelligentsia's dealings with Kipling.

During the war he served as a war correspondent in South Africa, where he was already a friend of Rhodes, and wrote propaganda for the war effort. Notably, he wrote a ballad about the British soldier for charity, "The Absent-Minded Beggar," which Sir Arthur Sullivan set to music, and which raised £250,000 in contributions for the soldiers. The dissent of the liberals could be seen within his own family, where Lady Burne-Jones disapproved of the war, refused to read Kipling's dispatches, and refused to celebrate the British victories, drawing popular hostility upon herself. Kipling also started a branch of the Navy League where he lived, and built a drill hall and instituted rifle practice. He was convinced that England needed to prepare for war, as was his friend Baden-Powell, who came to live near him. The Scout motto, "Be prepared," had that military meaning among others. Kipling wrote stories for and about the Scouts, and "The Army of a Dream" about a national militia.

Another of Kipling's critics was Wells, the modern Defoe, but he attacked in the name of politics rather than of literature. Indeed, in his *The New Machiavelli* (1911), which is in part a fictional autobiography, Wells says that Kipling was a very great influence on his generation of young men, and cited as his gifts to them a sense of geography (what we would now call geopolitics) and a sense of discipline and devotion which their own Socialist creed could not give them. He goes on to say—and this is only 1911—"Kipling has since been so mercilessly and exhaustively mocked, criticized and torn to shreds—never was a man so violently exalted and then, himself assisting, so relentlessly hauled down." As far as men of letters went, Kipling was by 1911 already beyond the pale.

During the Great War Kipling was a propagandist, and became a symbol of literature-on-the-side-of-the-war-effort. His publishers put out a Services edition of his works, for men in the trenches. After the war he served on the War Graves Commission, and wrote an official history of the Irish Guards, in which his son had served and died. But in 1919 T. S. Eliot reviewed a new volume of his in the *Athenaeum* (May 1) by saying that no one even read Kipling any more—nobody had even a negative opinion about him. He compared him with Swinburne and contrasted him with Conrad. "Mr. Conrad is very germane to the question, because he is in many ways the antithesis of Mr. Kipling." Eliot called Kipling a poet of ideas, in the same sense as Swinburne was, and a poet of Empire; and he made Conrad the model of everything that is to be admired and preferred—the embodiment of the literary imagination.

Then in 1923 Edmund Blunden reviewed Kipling's regimental history of the Irish Guards, and said it was unconvincing, because Kipling had not understood the pandemonium and nerve-strain of war. Praise of Kipling was gradually restricted to the Kipling Society, where his old school friends "Stalky" and "M'Turk" attended meetings into the late 1930s; where ex-colonels still hoped to convince literary critics that "East is East and West is West" was a good poem because it told the *truth*—that that was exactly what frontier officers felt about the marauding tribes they fought and loved.

It is, I think, important to realize *how* the readers who liked Kipling liked him, *what* they liked in him. Philip Mason, in his book *Kipling,* says that he himself was an idolatrous Kipling fan by the time he was fourteen, having identified himself in turn with Mowgli, Kim, and then Beetle. Then as a young man he came to dislike Kipling strongly. Then he got over that dislike. Such a development bears all the marks of a profound educational experience, shaping a reader's mind more powerfully than serious literature often can. And Mason sums up, "No one has had so deep an influence on a whole generation of a certain class as he did. Here was someone who understood the life they were brought up to, their mistrust of politicians and intellectuals, their inarticulate devotion to a cause, the training they had endured, the tenseness that lay beneath the apparently insensitive outer crust, the tenderness they longed to lavish on dogs and children, their nervous respect for those mysterious creatures, women—so fragile compared with themselves, and yet so firmly authoritarian as nurses and mothers" (p. 307).

C. E. Carrington says in his *Life of Rudyard Kipling,* 1956, that his qualification for writing the biography is one he shared with thousands—that he learned to read with *Just So Stories* and the *Jungle Books;* went to school with *Stalky and Co.,* read history with *Puck of Pook's Hill;* and discovered *Plain Tales From the Hills* as his first adult book. In 1914 he formed his ideas of army life from *Barrack Room Ballads* and "The Brushwood Boy," and the story of a centurion's life in *Puck* "strengthened the nerve of many a young soldier in the dark days of 1915 and 1941" (p. 296). In the Preface, he says, "Looking back, I find no other writer who has seen through the eyes of my generation with such a sharpness of observation. I owe far more

to Kipling than to some of the great classic figures of literature.
. . . There is no other writer, great or small, whose work I knew so
well, and I have been often astonished to find how many others, of
all ages, knew him as well as I did. . . ."

From Carrington we also learn that many of Kipling's stories were
based on newspaper items or current anecdotes. "It was his pride to
record traditional army legends, and he took the liberty of a Scott or
Burns in recording them." For instance, "Gunga Din" is based on
the water carrier of the Guides at the siege of Delhi; "Drums of the
Fore and Aft" on an incident in Orme's *History;* and John Chinn
(in "The Tomb of His Ancestors") on James Outram, the friend of
the Lawrences. Thus if Kipling's audience knew his works very
closely, he knew them and their stories just as well.

Carrington tells us that by the time of Kipling's death in 1936, he
had sold seven million volumes in England and eight million in the
United States, and that he remained a best-seller in the 1950s. The
only sharp falloff in his sales, according to R. L. Green, began in
1919, and that was temporary. His popularity abroad is particularly
striking in the case of Russia. An official estimate of 1958 found that
77 million volumes by British authors had been published there since
1918, of which Dickens had written 10 million, Kipling, Doyle, and
Swift 4.5 million each, Defoe, Galsworthy, Scott, and Shakespeare
3.4 million each. And the same year, Russian professors of English
literature on a visit to England declared themselves surprised to see
the importance given to Lawrence and Joyce, and denied to Kipling
and Galsworthy. (This book sketches a point of view which reconciles
their idea of literature with our own.)

Already at the time of his death Kipling's rejection by England's
literature-as-system was obvious. Of the eight pallbearers who bore
him to Westminster Abbey, none was an important poet or novelist
—which was unprecedented for a writer; his eight included the prime
minister, an admiral, a general, and the master of a college.

Of course he continued to be discovered, by individual critics, by
T. S. Eliot, by Desmond McCarthy, by George Orwell, by C. S.
Lewis. But it is significant that the rediscoveries are often announced
in exactly the same terms—each critic starts by assuming a general
prejudice against Kipling; the previous critic's work has disappeared
each time. Thus Desmond McCarthy discovered that Kipling put his
gifts not at the service of the love story, nor of some adventure in

sensibility, nor of worldly success, but (for the first time in literature) at the service of a man's relation to his work; and that this is the significant thing about Kipling. But a few years later C. S. Lewis "discovered" that imaginative literature in the eighteenth and nineteenth centuries omitted, or thrust into the background, what occupies men most, their work, and that Kipling was the poet of work. Apparently there is something about this obvious truth which makes it keep disappearing. It is not by some temporary or inadvertent blindness that men of letters forget about the world of work; it is by a fundamental law of letters. Literature as a whole is turned away from that view. It is comparatively easy for individual readers to twist themselves around and see something that has been left out; much harder for literature to include it. The system exerts a constant pressure, which keeps squeezing Kipling out. Thus the victory in effect remained with Boris Ford, when he attacked T. S. Eliot for his 1941 *Selection of Kipling's Verse.* Ford, writing in *Scrutiny,* said that Kipling's mind was a very crude instrument; seldom if ever in touch with finer spiritual issues; he was of the '90s and suffered the common disability of an artistic decadence, which is "an atrophy of finer feeling." Ford's is not an impressive essay—it discusses Kipling mainly as a way to attack Eliot, by suggesting a similarity between the two, but it carried more weight than Eliot's essay in the world of criticism.

Kipling and the Adventure Tale

Be that as it may, within the tradition of adventure tales, Kipling is surely the greatest writer. But it is disconcerting to have to admit that though Kipling is the greatest writer in this tradition, he makes less use of it than any of the others do. The themes of course are there, but the motifs, and the structuring of the motifs into whole forms, are not. He writes very little book-length narrative of adventure; his heroes are not notable for do-it-yourself skills like Robinson Crusoe, or as observer-participants like Waverley, or as atavisms like Kingsley's or Haggard's heroes. And when romance and adventure motifs *are* to be found in his stories from time to time, they cannot be said to shed much light on their location when connected up with the system we have constructed. The fit is not exact enough to give much pleasure or serve much purpose.

On the other hand, it is not to be doubted, on grounds quite distinct from the recurrence of motifs, that Kipling does belong in this sequence of writers. How could one ever discuss imperialism in literature without making Kipling central? And no one more clearly wrote for the responsible class of the empire, as distinct from, and later as opposed to, the literary class. He named his readers as such. In his Foreword to *The Kipling Pageant* of 1897, he talks of his stories as wares, and says to the captain of the ship carrying them— the editor: "The chief part of our business lies with men who are wearied at the end of the day—certain great captains. They will not bring their womenfolk aboard." And when he died, in 1936, General Sir Ian Hamilton wrote, "His death seems to me to place a full stop to the period when war was a romance and the expansion of the Empire a duty." So completely did he symbolize the concerns of the responsible class.

It is of course possible to point out certain alignments between his work and his predecessors', and he did introduce certain developments. One can see that he uses not the figure of the trader put into circulation by Defoe but its replacement, the figure of the engineer; which brought with it an interest in not only machines but the mechanics of political and social life, too. He expresses that interest brilliantly. One can see that in Kipling's work the figure of the solitary adventurer has been replaced by the figure of the solitary administrator—alone in his heart, but at the center of a complex web of powers and information systems. One can see that in his work the figure of the soldier has been assimilated to other modern system heroes, his chivalric and feudal characteristics modernized. One can see that Kipling, following Twain, introduced touches of the sordid and the horrifying into the adventure framework. All these differences obviously reflect the changes we have studied in the nature of civilization and the British empire, and so ratify and corroborate the scheme of development proposed here.

But observing these features of his work does not lead us to the heart of his achievement—does not seem as important in explaining him as the equivalents were in explaining Defoe and Scott. Finally one must admit the fact of Kipling's recalcitrance from a formal point of view, and build an explanation on that. I have already pointed out that Kipling's intensely literary bent, his genius as a craftsman, perhaps exacerbated by his fate of serving the copybook maxims, led him to reject the given in formal terms. In those terms the adventure romance, and indeed its value-bearing subject matter, is much more easily to be found in Conrad. The way Kipling avoided it was above all by dealing in episodes and fragments. The most obvious evidence of that is that he wrote primarily short stories, in a period when extraordinary prestige and reward attached to the full-length novel. But even as short stories, one must be struck by how fragmentary Kipling's anecdotes are, and how often they are told with a stress on their setting, or on their narrative frame, rather than on their subject.

"The Man Who Would Be King" is a good example. The events and the characters are enacted on the stage of an elaborate theater —the newspaper, the editor, etc.—into which we peer from an odd angle. The effect of this is to stress its character as an anecdote. We don't believe that these events occurred, but we believe that they were told. Kipling's method evokes, very fancifully, a whole series of narratives. What is vaguely but powerfully evoked is the social character of British India, where such anecdotes echoed in the background of everyone's imagination, where everyone was, in a consciously fanciful sense, a man who would be king.[11] Though, since the historical figures whom Carnehan and Dravitt caricature are rather Rhodes and Jameson than anyone Indian, it is in fact everyone in the British empire who had half-acknowledged dreams of that sort.

Or take a story like "The Head of the District," in *Life's Handicap*, or "William the Conqueror." Both of them are very brief anecdotes, which leave the reader wanting to know more—about the persons and events involved, but also caring even more about the genre of life; the administration of such a district, with its multiple layers of nationalities and religions, and the relief of such a famine. Or take the more purely literary case; the Paolo and Francesca story in "Through the Fire" or the Antony and Cleopatra story in "Love o' Women," or the story of Keats in "Wireless" or "The Greatest Story in the World." Here you get the fragment of a well-known poem, play, legend, in some sense concealed in alien material, and made evocative precisely by its fragmentariness and its displacement.

Indeed, it is possible to extrapolate out beyond the use of famous specific stories, and to say that Kipling makes evocative use of familiar fragments all the time. Take for instance "Without Benefit of Clergy," which is as complete a treatment of its people and events as you will find anywhere in Kipling. Even there much of the effect derives from the fact that we recognize the figure of Ameera as a sort of Madame Butterfly. We don't need to hear a full realistic account of her. We say to ourselves "there she is again," and that literary commonplaceness is first cousin to the pathos we feel in Ameera's story—the commonplaceness of her fate in the other sense; that it happens so often. That second commonplaceness, moreover, evokes a third sense, of sad familiarity, associated with the social atmosphere of British India as a whole; one *hears* such stories over and over. This too is an anecdote, whose power of evocation comes from the familiarity of its type; again we don't so much believe that it happened as that it was told. (The Madame Butterfly figure of course turns up often in adventure fiction; in Kipling, one can mention "Lispeth" and "Georgie Porgy.")[12]

Whatever one thinks of that explanation, it is undeniable that Kipling was a hugely successful propagator of the imperial idea and imperial fiction, in England, and abroad. French and Italian critics, before 1914 but also after, often said that England did not appreciate him.[13] In 1934 André Maurois said France could not be expected to get excited about Shaw, having had a Voltaire of their own, but she had had no Kiplings; and told how he had read Kipling when he was sixteen or seventeen, and how *Kim* had affected him more than any other book he read had given him an heroic idea of life.

Rhodes and Imperialism

The most important historical hero of the British imperialism which Kipling celebrated, of course, was Cecil Rhodes, and a significant relation developed between the two men. It was in 1898 that they became friends (at the same time, Kipling forged an alliance with Alfred Milner, another of the great political imperialists of the time). He became Rhodes's wordsmith. "After the idea had been presented —and one had to know his code for it—he [Rhodes] would say: 'What am I trying to express? Say it, *say* it.' So I would say it, and if the phrase suited not, he would work it over, chin a little down, till it satisfied him."* Rhodes designated a house on his estate to be a writers' residence, and it went first to Kipling, who spent several winters in South Africa as Rhodes's guest. Reciprocally, Kipling received inspiration from Rhodes. He said of Rhodes that his personality revealed the spirit of the age; and wrote to him confidentially, "England is a stuffy little place, mentally, morally, and physically." They both criticized men and countries by adventurer criteria. When Rhodes died, it was Kipling who wrote his epitaph, and he was a trustee of the Rhodes Scholarships.

At the same time, it is important to note that Kipling never drew a figure like Rhodes in his fiction. (Perhaps as near as he came to it was the caricature figure of Daniel Dravitt.) Of course, British imperialism in India, which Kipling knew first and best, was quite different from imperialism in Africa; in India, England administered a highly structured and civilized society, and the cultural image of the Englishman there was Roman and proconsular—the weary but selfless administrator, who preserves the peace and the law for the benefit of ungrateful aliens. In Africa England had instead the sense of uninhabited country, and fortunes to be made, and a free hand for speculators, pioneers, farmers—the empire was half a frontier. But almost certainly not this difference but Kipling's artistic conscience warned him away from Rhodes as a fictional subject. In fact, Rhodes was made a character in a good many contemporary novels, as well as innumerable essays and articles and poems, but none that would have satisfied Kipling's artistic taste.[14]

Cecil Rhodes was born in 1853, the son of a clergyman, and one of seven brothers, most of whom went to Eton or Winchester and then to Oxford, but Cecil did not (a link with Kipling). He was a frail, dreamy, introverted boy, bookish and falsetto-voiced and weak-hearted. Like Kipling, he responded to the public idea of Empire rather than to an inherited family identification with it. In 1870, because of his health, he was sent to South Africa to join his brother Herbert. The two involved themselves in gun-running schemes almost immediately, but at the same time, Cecil was working on his exams to enter Oxford, the idea of which he was in love with. He was always fascinated by machinery and gadgets, and by scientific methods, and when the big rush began, he was the first man to use a

*Quoted in C. E. Carrington, *The Life of Rudyard Kipling*, p. 212.

watchmaker's glass to examine diamonds. And there were other such Crusoe motifs to his personality.

He made money immediately and in 1873 entered Oxford, though he had to leave it before taking a degree, to look after his diamond-mine interests. But while there he made friends who were later his allies in African politics—for instance, Sidney Shippard, who became administrator of Bechuanaland when that was acquired in 1884. He was also inspired by Ruskin's lectures celebrating the Empire.[15]

The lectures were what Oxford gave Rhodes in the way of inspiration, but it also gave him a certain leverage in the social prestige of an Oxford gentleman, which he used in his dealings with other South African diamond merchants. And the institution of the Rhodes Scholarships in some sense combined all these aspects of Oxford.

Rhodes drew up his first will in 1877, leaving the fortune he meant to make to the colonial secretary, to fund a secret society (at Oxford he had become a Mason—another link with Kipling). This society was to colonize Africa, the Holy Land, the Euphrates, and South America; to recover the United States, and to set up an imperial parliament. These were the ideas which were gradually modified into the Rhodes Scholarships. In 1893 he founded the Society of the Elect, with W. T. Stead, naming the Jesuits as his models, and with Lords Rothschild and Milner as his associates. The final arrangement was to provide scholarships to Oxford for sixty men from the colonies, one hundred from America, and fifteen Germans (to be selected by the kaiser) each year; men qualified by criteria which combined scholarship with sportsmanship and manliness and moral force. They were to be "the best men for the world's fight."

Rhodes's general ideas were crudely Nietzschean and Darwinist, in accordance with the atavism and saga imagery of his phase of imperialism. "I am a barbarian. I believe with Ruskin that all healthy men love to fight, and all women love to hear of such fighting. . . . I love the big and simple." And, "Expansion is everything. . . . These stars . . . these vast worlds which we can never reach. I would annex the planets if I could" (Millin, *Rhodes,* p. 138). For him, Rome had a positive image, was an inspiration and model for England to follow. He read Marcus Aurelius and Gibbon, compared his own profile to that of Emperor Titus, and for six years kept twenty classical scholars at work translating Gibbon's sources; which cost him £50,000 and ran to hundreds of volumes. He read biographies of Napoleon and hung a portrait of Bismarck in his bedroom. He both participated in the excitement of Empire and spread the excitement—far beyond the limits of England.[16]

In America, Grover Cleveland said, "America would pay $300,-000,000 for Cecil Rhodes" (Gross, *Rhodes of Africa*, p. 417). And Twain, in *Following the Equator* II, called Rhodes ". . . the most imposing figure in the British Empire outside of England. When he stands on the Cape, his shadow falls to the Zambesi. . . . That he is an extraordinary man, and not an accident of fortune, not even his dearest South African enemies were willing to deny, so far as I heard them testify. The whole South African world seemed to stand in a kind of shuddering awe. . . . yet there he stands, to this day, upon his dizzying summit under the dome of the sky, an apparent permanency, the marvel of the time, the mystery of an age, an Archangel with wings to half the world, Satan with tail to the other half" (pp. 376–377).

Rhodes and Kipling were of course figures in the history of the idea of imperialism, as well as in that of the British Empire.[17] We cannot afford the space to study the history of that idea, but it is worth pointing out that their phase of imperialism links up rather strikingly with Carlyle's, though separated by a gap of forty years and more. (During which the quite different meaning of the word we associate with J. R. Seeley had developed. For that matter, Ruskin's idea, Disraeli's idea, Dilke's idea, do not remind us of Kipling half so much as does Carlyle's.) In "Chartism," Carlyle says, "The stream of World-History has altered its complexion; Romans are dead out, Englishmen are come in. The red broad mark of Romanhood, stamped ineffaceably on that Cast of Time, has disappeared from the present, and belongs only to the past. England plays its part . . . and out of Hengst's leather boats what Wellingtons, Washingtons, Shakespeares, Miltons, Watts, Arkwrights, William Pitts and Davy Crocketts had to issue. . . ." (Bodelson, *Studies in Mid-Victorian Imperialism*, p. 28). This is the idea we associate with Kipling and Rhodes; it only needed the politicians' stamp of approval to turn this imperialism into the overt kind. Bodelson points out that Carlyle celebrated the strong man as hero, and the Englishman's great empire of silence, long before Kipling. The saga influence developed gradually, and overbore the mercantile idea. In a sense, all England changed caste

—more exactly, key representatives took on warrior-caste traits. But in fact the changes at the end of the nineteenth century only gave free play to caste-characteristics long culturally suppressed.

Caste

Kipling described *Westward Ho!* as a military-caste school,[18] and it is clear how important an effect it had on him, to be educated in such an establishment and then in the Indian Services environment he went on to. Many of the differences between his fictional sensibility and Twain's—for instance, his idea that Americans were in some sense culturally adolescent—can be traced to that education. What he met in India obviously reinforced that tendency; not so much Indian social formations as the social stratification and caste pride which the English in India had developed there. Literarily, moreover, he found Indian culture a help to expressing that sensibility. Thus in "The Eyes of Asia" he has a Rajput write home from London, "It is not true there is no caste in England. . . . The high castes are forbidden to show curiosity, appetite, or fear in public places. In this respect they resemble troops on parade. Their male children are beaten from their 12th year to their 17th year, by men with sticks. Their women are counted equal with their men. The nature of the young men of high caste is as the nature of us Rajputs. They do not use opium, but they delight in horses, and sport and women, and are perpetually in debt to the moneylender. . . . They belittle their own and the achievements of their friend, so long as that friend faces them. In his absence they extol his deeds" (*The War and the Fleet in Being,* p. 150). The Hindu categories are there only as an indirect means to celebrating the English aristocracy.

Caste thinking is also reflected in Kipling's preference for Muslims over Hindus. This preference was becoming general among Englishmen in India in his lifetime. There were political reasons for this (by making an alliance with this powerful minority, the English split the forces of Indian nationalism) but it was just as much an expression of their spontaneous caste-feeling that Muslims were Kshattriyas (the warrior caste), fiery, proud, gallant. As England came to identify its own interests more and more with its soldiers, it came to value the military caste in other countries too.[19]

It is therefore worth an effort to realize, in terms other than Kipling's own, and on evidence somewhat other, what the characteristics of that caste in England were, and even more—because of the difficulties of the literary reader—what its attractions were. These men (all castes are masculine, but this was a masculine caste) were spirited, commanding, enterprising, simple; above all, commanding. James Morris says, in *Pax Britannica*, page 46, ". . . at that moment of her history, [1897] Britain was settled in the habit of authority—authority in the family in the church, in social affairs, even in politics. It was the last heyday of the patricians . . . the English posture abroad was habitually one of command. To the educated Englishman responsibility came naturally. No other power had been so strong so long. . . ." And it is important to notice there the mixture of political and psychological fact, for that mixture is the essence of caste.

The ideas will best be conveyed by examples. I might begin with a citation from J. A. Froude's *Oceana*, in which he describes enthusiastically Sir George Grey, whom he met in New Zealand. Grey's life, he declares, has been a romance; he began as an officer in the Engineers, then became an explorer in Australia, was at thirty governor of South Australia, then governor at the Cape (and collector of rare books), then governor of New Zealand. There he led the last war against the Maoris—but he is now their beloved white father, their protector, and has collected a volume of their songs and ballads. Grey lived, when Froude met him, on an island he owned, formerly a nest of pirates, now inhabited by people who are his "lieges" and "feudatories." There finally we see how Scott's legends bore on the facts of Empire. "They feel for him what the sons of Ivor felt for Fergus" (p. 311). Grey's is the life of an empire aristocrat, but perhaps too externally described to make clear the psychology of caste.

Winston Churchill's dispatches as a war correspondent, collected by R. Woods as *Young Winston's Wars*, give us a somewhat more personal insight into this temperament. Churchill wrote always enthusiastically about the enemy, and felt all the tragedy of war, even while delighting in the "fine adventures" to be made out of all this misery and ugliness. The note Churchill strikes is developed more fully in this entry by his contemporary, Richard Meinertzhagen.

When war broke out in 1914, this professional soldier who played an important part in developing England's secret service—and who had killed many men—wrote, "I love the naked raw life, bereft of all the trappings and tomfoolery of modern civilization. Wide horizons in thought and vision, freedom and always more freedom, fresh air and exercise and a contempt for Death—that is what I love. Those are the conditions I understand. Must I leave all that behind and without mercy work night and day to kill my fellow men? Must I take part in unrestrained murder?" (Lord, *Duty, Honor, Empire*, p. 281). It is important to grasp the distinctions between different kinds of killing, to do justice to this caste and its role in the national life.

In explaining Meinertzhagen, his biographer quotes a passage from Richard Burton, about returning to the desert, which combines chivalric and atavistic feelings. "At last once more it is my fate to escape the prison life of civilized Europe, and to refresh body and mind by studying Nature in her noblest and most admirable form—the nude. Again I am to enjoy a glimpse of the glorious desert, to inhale the sweet, pure breath of translucent skies that show the red stars burning upon the very edge and verge of the horizon and to strengthen myself by a short visit to the wild man and his home" (Lord, *Duty*, p. 338). Burton, I think, gives one some real insight into the form of manhood which Kipling so admired, and of which England in his time specially made use, needed, and rewarded.

Richard F. Burton (1821–1890) was the son of an Irish colonel who gave him no regular education; when sent down from Oxford in 1842 he set out for India with his bulldog; learned to speak Hindi and Gujerati in Baroda, then moved to Sindh, and got leave to wander the country for three years, learning Arabic, Sanskrit, Pushtu, and native ways of life—an older Kim. He is a prime example of that often-met love of Islam as the culture best suited to the chivalric temperament. Burton wrote a *History of Sindh* in 1851, also a book on falconry, 1852, and another on bayonet exercises, 1853. In 1853 he made a trip to Mecca, disguised first as a Persian mirza, then as a dervish, then as a Pathan. He took an Arab name, which he ever after signed himself by. And this was the story he told in *Narrative of a Pilgrimage to Meccah and Medinah*, published in 1855.

He took the trip as an investigation for the Royal Geographical Society, he says; but also because he was weary of progress and civilization. He is free with his scorn for Hindus, for all educated

Babus, and with his love of all wild races, who are ready to fight. He
translates this into American Frontier terms on occasion. "The free
trapper combines, in the eye of an [American] Indian girl, all that is
dashing and heroic in a warrior of her own race, whose gait and garb
and bravery he emulates, with all that is gallant and glorious in the
white man" (p. 30). His narrative, and his (implicit) characterization
of himself, is very knockabout and even bloodthirsty, against the
Victorian convention. He tells us a lot about a "boy Mohammed" he
picked up who could have suggested Kim; being volatile and astute,
with an acute sense of honor, selfish and affectionate. We are reminded also of Kipling's novel by Burton's eye for racial, religious,
etc., types. And by a kind of cosmopolitanism very like Kipling's.
Burton often mocks England by comparing its manners and morals
to the Orient.

The most striking thing is his evocation and praise of the desert,
the natural habitat of Islam and chivalry.

> In the Desert, even more than upon the ocean, there is present death.
> . . . In such circumstances, the mind is influenced through the body. Though
> your mouth glows, and your skin is parched, yet you feel no langour, the effect
> of humid heat; your lungs are lightened, your sight brightens, your memory
> recovers its tone, and your spirits become exuberant; your fancy and imagina-
> tion are powerfully aroused, and the wildness and sublimity of the scenes
> around you stir up all the energies of your soul—whether for exertion, danger,
> or strife. Your morale improves; you become frank and cordial, hospitable
> and single-minded; the hypocritical politeness and the slavery of civilization
> are left behind you in the city. Your senses are quickened; they require no
> stimulants but air and exercise—in the Desert spirituous liquors excite only
> disgust. (p. 104)

This is a landscape of threnodic militarism, like Haggard's.

What Burton must remind us of also is T. E. Lawrence, and there
is indeed a similarity, though Lawrence was of a type which included
other elements. But it is striking to find how many of the elements
of Lawrence's story, which we shall consider in the next chapter, are
also to be found in Burton; the glamour of the black tents, the natural
aristocracy of the desert, the evil Turkish beys; and the hard and
unsentimental friendships between men.

In 1880 Burton translated Camoens's *The Lusiads,* the sixteenth-
century Portuguese poem in celebration of Vasco de Gama and of
exploration in Portugal's Golden Age. Burton saw himself as another
Camöens, and loved the memory of the romantic age of discovery.

In 1883 he published *The Book of the Sword,* a three-volume study of *l'arme blanche.* And in 1885–1888, a fifteen-volume translation of *The Arabian Nights,* famous for its pornographic explicitness of sensuality.

Burton evokes as completely as anyone the strain of Victorian feeling opposite to the missionary, the liberal, and the man of conscience—the opposite to what Haggard called "the children of light." He creates a voice and an image for the Kshattriya type, unrepresented in Victorian literature, and to be rediscovered in the twentieth century by literary rebels like Evelyn Waugh. But there were in Victorian England many men like Richard Burton, and many more who wanted to be, and among them men of mind and talent. They were the men Kipling expressed and served.[20]

One of the most prominent examples was Colonel Richard Meinertzhagen. Meinertzhagen (1878–1967) was the son of one of the Potter sisters, a nephew to Beatrice Webb, and so born into a ruling caste. Beatrice Webb says in her autobiography, "As life unfolded itself, I became aware that I belonged to a class of persons who habitually gave orders, but who seldom, if ever, executed the orders of other people." This is one aspect of caste, and noted in a very caste manner.

While a boy, Meinertzhagen played the War Game, as did most children of middle- and upper-class families at the end of the century; soldiers, fort blocks, etc., were often permanently set up in a barn, and tactical games of some complexity were played, training the imagination for war; in 1913 H. G. Wells wrote a monograph about this phenomenon. (One might contrast that with the shop-keeping games that merchant-caste children played.) At Harrow, one of his teachers was that Bosworth-Smith whose life of Lord Lawrence I have quoted. He also heard Stanley lecture at Harrow, and met him at his own home, where Stanley said, "If you ever travel in Africa, rule your men with an iron discipline, share starvation and hardship, and never give in." He also met Rhodes, who invited him to South Africa, but his father did not allow him to go. Richard only gradually won permission to make his career in the army, for the Meinertzhagens and Potters had no military traditions. Richard's struggle to follow his vocation was another example of that militarization of English culture at the end of the nineteenth century.

Meinertzhagen was a fine ornithologist, and in love with Nature

generally, although above all a hunter, or, as he himself put it, "obsessed with blood-lust." That was one of the interests he combined
with his military duties in Africa. He began his intelligence work on
the Nandi, a war-like tribe like the Masai, in Kenya. From that he
passed to playing *Kim*-like tricks upon the Germans in intelligence
work, and spying on Russian forts in the Crimea. Like adventure-
heroes in fiction, Meinertzhagen was often in trouble with his superiors in the British army (just like Stalky); at a farewell dinner in
Nairobi, the officers staged a roughhouse afterward as usual, but two
men with grudges set upon him in earnest, whereupon he broke both
their noses with his knee. At the same time, he was a man of great
sensitiveness and self-doubt.

It is important in considering the literature of the time to remember that silent world of soldiers, in which insubordination and violent
hoaxing were often marks of the truest talent and the truest vocation,
and where there was much of the finest intelligence and sensitivity
also. (It is the world Evelyn Waugh tried to enter in the Second
World War.) That world had its readers too. Edward Creasy's *15
Decisive Battles of the World*, 1851, had thirty-eight reprints by
1894; it was followed by Malleson's *Decisive Battles of India*, 1883,
Colonel Whitton's *Decisive Battles of Modern Times*, 1922, and so
on.

Finally, as an example of caste temperament, and caste categories
of thought and feeling, let us look at Leonard Woolf, who at twenty-
eight had 1000 square miles to rule in Ceylon and 100,000 subjects.
Woolf was not a soldier, and indeed belonged to the political and
cultural party opposite to Kipling's, but I think he plainly shared
certain caste-traits with Kipling's heroes. He presents himself in
Growing (published 1961) as melancholy, fond of solitude, fond of
animals, strongly sexed, hot-tempered, a strong administrator who
was complained of but respected by the natives. He competed fiercely
but didn't want to succeed as an officer of the empire. At the end
of his seven years there, in 1911, he was ready, if Virginia Stephen
had not accepted his proposal, to return there, marry a Singhalese,
and bury himself in Hambantola, as a permanent but lower-rank
ruler. These are the traits of a Kipling hero.

What makes this doubly interesting is that he shows us something
of conscious choice and effort in this caste personality. He felt himself

very unlike the Anglo-Indians he worked with. When he first went to Ceylon, he took his fox terrier with him, like Burton two generations earlier, but also a ninety-volume edition of Voltaire. (The first saved him, in the eyes of the Anglo-Indians, from the opprobrium earned by the second.) On the ship going out he learned to improve the social facade behind which he hid his intelligence, and to deal with Ceylon civil servants, and planters. "The process is what is popularly known as 'making a man of him.' It made, let us say, finally a man of me, though the man was, and has remained, three-quarters sham" (p. 37). His real self, he felt, expressed itself only in his letters to Lytton Strachey. But he was made a man, and more deeply than he suggests there.

For in a story he tells about a police magistrate he lived with, called Dutton, one meets the manly Woolf, the aristo-military Woolf, and it is just as striking a presence as the Strachey side of his personality, the Voltairean intellectual from Bloomsbury. Dutton had been described to him in advance as "a bloody unwashed Board School buggar, who doesn't know one end of a woman from another," and "it must be admitted that there was some truth in the portrait" (p. 63). In fact, the portrait Woolf draws is essentially the same. Dutton reminded him of Leonard Bast, in *Howard's End:* and with good reason, for Forster drew exactly the same figure. Dutton read cheap editions of great books, wrote poetry himself—about "fays"—and played the piano badly. His talk of women and love made Woolf "feel slightly sick."

Given a job in England with the post office or the inland revenue, Dutton would have been happy, Woolf says. Because there his colleagues would have been small timid men like himself. "In Ceylon he lived the life of a minnow in a shoal of pike. The basis of his character was timidity, which, as so often, was compensated underneath by boundless self-conceit" (p. 65). He had been a scholarship boy, and had risen above his parents' station in life. "Unfortunately this meant that he was given the kind of education which completely addled his fairly good brain and destroyed every chance of his becoming a rational person. . . . Literature, art, music, poetry, history, mathematics, science, were pitchforked into his mind in chaotic incomprehensibility. . . ." (p. 66). He was denatured by ". . . the undigested, sticky mess of 'culture' which they provided for him. His roots began and ended in Peckham, while his mind was full of Keats" (p. 66). He married a missionary, Miss Beeching, who later complained to Woolf of her husband's impotence.

This is a very Kiplingesque story; this man and Leonard Bast, and Septimus Smith in *Mrs. Dalloway,* are all descended from Kipling's Cockney clerks, like the man in "The Greatest Story." They are drawn the way Kipling drew and saw that figure. The anecdote is full of caste feeling; what little men like this lack is the caste element of temperamental fire and form; they are, to use Hindu terms, Banias trying to be Kshattriyas. Lacking that element of style, that feeling for form, they should never have been given access to the world of the imagination.

Woolf pays tribute to Kipling as the poet of Anglo-Indian society, but grudgingly, and in a way that denies him any insight into men like himself. He says he could never decide whether Kipling had copied colonial society exactly or whether his social world in Ceylon was copying Kipling. "In Kipling's stories and our conversations there was the same incongruous mixture of public-school toughness, sentimentality, and melancholy" (p. 46). But the real Woolf, he implies, did not take part in those conversations. All seven years in Ceylon, Woolf felt he was acting a part; he couldn't really have become an imperialist—"a white ruler of our Asiatic empire."

Woolf could only use Kipling's categories ironically, and yet he could not escape from them. He belonged to Kipling's world, psychologically as well as by situation, and to deny that was in effect to lie. And that seems to be typical of the failure of the English intellectual response to Kipling.[21]

X

Conrad

CONRAD'S reputation as a great modernist began after World War I, after the modern system had entered into its period of self-doubt and general disrepute. The British empire in particular was then accused by enemies both outside and inside the system, and amongst the latter "literature" proved itself one of the most bitter. It is paradoxical, in more than one way, that Conrad should be associated with this process of accusation, but the historical facts are indisputable—he was and is so associated. His critical reputation and literary interpretation have been inseparable from the anti-imperialist ideas general after 1918. Indeed, the critics' interpretations are much more separable from the books Conrad wrote than from those political ideas. But there is another aspect to his importance for us.

From our present point of view, Conrad is a subject of rather similar interest to Tolstoy. First of all because he represents Poland, a country on the periphery of the modern world system, where the sequence and development of that system's ideas was markedly out of phase with England's. And secondly because, like Tolstoy, Conrad used adventure material in fiction and yet identified himself with the most serious ideas of his time; claimed to stand at the very center of literature as a system; and consequently moved the adventure material he used somewhat from its peripheral position in the serious imagination. (Though in Conrad's case what happened was as much that he combined quite crude material of that kind with a mood antagonistic to adventure—so he did not redeem the adventure form —he did not refine the adventure mood itself and separate out what was potentially valuable within.)

I cannot, myself, believe Conrad to have been an intelligence or a talent comparable with Tolstoy. But he was treated as such; he was given an extraordinarily reverential response by the men of letters of his own time and since; and the reason for that misjudgment bears very interestingly upon our argument. It was just because Conrad seemed to bring the adventure tradition to an end by transvaluing it —and because his actual ambiguity could be read as a subtly profound strategy—that literature acclaimed him its champion and in his name triumphed over imperialism and the forces allied to it in English culture. The Empire went into rapid decline after 1918, and England lost its lion's share in the modern world system. Serious literature, so long in resistance, and the children of light generally, felt that they were winning the cultural battle. And Conrad, of all people, was decked out in general's uniform and set to lead the victory parade; though he was at best the Pétain of a literary Vichy.

He was born in 1857, eight years before Kipling, but he was the opposite of precocious; he began life as an author after Kipling, and in his wake. He designed his first books in some sense to fit into an imaginative space defined by Kipling; at least that is what is suggested by something in the Author's Note to his first novel, *Almayer's Folly*, 1895. He says that a woman reader has dismissed books like his, adventure tales of the tropics, etc., by calling them "decivilized"— the standard attack on adventure material. Conrad replies that this is a feminine judgment; in fact the events he tells about are fully real and the characters are men and women like ourselves—"though admittedly they are not the graceful and charming phantoms that move about in our mud and smoke, all refinement and no heart." Such images imply a great deal of Kipling's scheme of ideas; for instance his imaginative geography, with its distribution of reality and unreality, between London and the frontier, between the core countries and the periphery.

Conrad grew up in Poland, where his father was a poet and a patriot, who had suffered exile for conspiring against Russia, the imperial oppressor. The boy grew up in a tradition of political idealism and patriotic indignation, of an aristomilitary kind. Poland in the nineteenth century was obsessed with its loss of sovereignty. Many

Poles, including an uncle of Conrad's, had fought in Napoleon's armies against Russia, and so had taken part in that enormous romance.

Poland became a constitutional monarchy in the sixteenth century; the nobles rose to power, and the peasants were reduced to serfdom, at the same time. Also "the discovery of America paved the way to the second feudal system in Poland, made poor by the imports of gold and silver from the American continent. In contrast, the same era led to the establishment of modern manufacturing plants and industrial enterprises in western Europe, ushering in the period of early capitalism." This is the account of the *Encyclopaedia Britannica*, and it makes Poland a case of Wallerstein's theory of the semiperiphery.

The same is true in political history. The nineteenth century, or the period from 1795 to 1914, is known as Poland's "captivity," after it was divided between Russia, Prussia, and Austria. Throughout the century, Poland had individual exile-patriots, and volunteer legions, fighting against these three countries, or against imperialist tyrants elsewhere.

The first such legion, fighting under Napoleon against Russia, won back Poland's reputation as one of the great military nations. And there were also unexiled patriots, rebelling at home, and often severely punished for doing so, as Conrad's father was. This patriotism was heavily stamped with the character of the aristomilitary caste, which provided most of its leaders, and its expression in literature, which was important to its self-consciousness, was correspondingly romantic, though Christian-Romantic. The literary vocation that Conrad entered was characterized by Scott and not by Defoe.

When the first of the large-scale military risings failed, in 1831, there was a "Great Migration" of Poles to Paris; in which various men of letters played a large part, notably the three poets, Mickiewicz, Slowacki, and Krasinski. Literature (and music) was unusually important in the culture of nineteenth-century Poland, because closely allied to patriotism and rebellion. These three poets taught a messianism according to which the Poles were a Chosen People, called to suffer crucifixion, like Christ, because they had stood for Human Freedom; they must rise again, and when they did, their rising would usher in the reign of justice, liberty, and love. Mickiewicz, in his *Books of the Polish Nation and the Polish Pilgrimation* (1832) had passages like this: "And the nations forgot that they all stem from one

Father, And the Englishman said: my Father is the Ship, and my Mother, Steam. The Frenchman said, My Father is the Land, my Mother the Bourse . . . [But] In proportion as you enlarge and perfect your souls, by so much will you improve your laws and enlarge your frontiers. . . . Do not, therefore, excessively admire the nations which grow fat in prosperity, or which concern themselves mainly with difficult husbandry, or with disciplined organization. . . . The Polish Pilgrim says "Who so would follow Freedom, let him leave his country, and hazard his life" (*Poland*, Schmitt (Ed.), p. 336).

This patriotic and chivalric Romanticism was an important element in Conrad's situation as a writer. It set a standard of extreme idealism, and a model of heroic temperament, to which he responded but against which he also reacted. Of course he was not the first writer to do so, and there were other elements in the Polish literary situation.

We can glimpse his alternatives, and generally the conditions of Conrad's early life through the biography of a slightly older Polish novelist, Henryk Sienkewicz, 1846–1916, who made his career in Polish literature but like Conrad found an international audience. As a boy Sienkewicz read Polish history and biographies of Napoleon, and also *Robinson Crusoe* and *The Swiss Family Robinson;* and dreamed of finding an uninhabited island for himself. Later, he read Scott and Dumas. And then, as a student at Warsaw University, 1865–1871, he read the serious writers of the century, the children of light, Comte, Mill, Darwin, Spencer. This is the paradigm of nineteenth-century education in Europe; a layer of adventure images, upon which in higher education a layer of almost opposite ideas was laid.

In 1863 came another of the great Polish uprisings, and the patriots—especially those in the Great Migration, which clustered in Paris and London, hoped that the liberal powers, England and France, would intervene on their behalf. When they did not, many young people became disillusioned with politics altogether, and even with patriotism, of the old romantic-chivalric kind.

They began to see the Polish past as a shameful story of serfdom, intolerance, and class privilege, and set to work instead for the modernization and rationalization of their nation's life—worked to bring about its entry into the modern world system. This movement is clearly related to Defoe's ideology and sensibility, and versions of it developed in several semiperipheral countries. The Polish version was called "Organic Work." And a natural complement to that was the dream of starting life afresh, in Crusoe-fashion, in the wilderness. Sienkewicz was a friend of the famous actress Modjeska, and her circle, who in 1875 conceived the idea of going to live in America. Sienkewicz's enthusiasm provoked one of the others to exclaim, "Let us all go. We will kill beasts, build huts, make our own garments of skin, and live as our fathers lived" (Giergielewicz, *Henryk Sienkiewicz*, p. 25). They wanted to seek adventures in the jungles of virgin land of the United States, Modjeska tells us in her *Memoirs*, 1910. She saw herself bleaching linen at the brook, as the maidens did in the *Iliad.* Her son wanted to work on the Panama Canal, and that seemed a natural corollary of her vision.

Sienkewicz actually did go to California, and wrote back to the others in 1876, "My attire consists of a flannel shirt, red pants, and a sombrero costing $1. The climate does not require anything else. . . . I got rid of my nerves, my catarrh, my toothache. I sleep like a king. . . . Until now the hardship of this Cossack life only strengthens me. . . . I am as healthy as a bull, much stronger than my red brothers, cheerful and happy. Every morning when I wake up, I remind myself where I am, and I can't restrain a smile of sincere satisfaction." (p. 28.) He lived out those Defoe fantasies and found the experience very strengthening as an adult, but he returned to be a writer in Poland.

As a novelist, he wrote a Scott-like trilogy on Polish history, beginning with *With Fire and Sword* in 1884; and in 1896 published his best-known book outside Poland, *Quo Vadis?*, which had 250 printings in France alone; and in 1905 he won a Nobel Prize. In 1910 he helped introduce the Boy Scouts into Poland; and in 1912 wrote a children's adventure tale that was very successful, and was translated into English as *In Desert and Wilderness.* This is a version of the English adventure, and the literary heir of his American experience. It tells of the adventures of a Polish boy and an English girl in the Sudan and equatorial Africa. Stas Tarkowski, who is fourteen, is fiery, proud, and an expert rifle shot, swimmer, rider, and linguist. Nell Rawlinson, who is eight, is dainty, babyish, with long, golden hair, adored by the natives, and by her black nurse Dinah. Their fathers are both widower engineers working on the Suez Canal; the Pole had fought in the 1863 rising against Russia, been imprisoned in Siberia, and escaped. England is presented as punishing slave dealers all over the world. Gordon is in Khartoum, besieged by the Mahdi, and the children are kidnapped by the latter's agents. They press Stas, with brutal menaces, to renounce Christianity and become a Moslem, but he stands firm. Soon he finds a chance to shoot a lion and his two captors, and the children are free. They wander, lost, through Africa, with their dog, Saba. They pick up Kali, a Black Prince who has been enslaved and who becomes devoted to them. They also free the King, an elephant they find trapped in a ravine, blasting a way out for him by explosives. Then Stas unmasks a fetish man and wins a war for Kali's tribe.

The story is thus a bricolage of motifs from the English adventure novel of the eighteenth and nineteenth centuries, and its interest for us is to show the wholesale way that material was taken over in 1912 by a literature on the periphery of the system. Indeed, that is one interest of Sienkewicz's career as a whole, though the other is the light it throws on Conrad. The latter did not write Crusoe stories or live out Crusoe fantasies or engage in Organic Work; his imagination was too deeply romantic for that; but he was nevertheless influenced by English ideas, and above all by the idea of England.

Conrad had read the literature of France and England as a boy, as well as Polish books. At eleven he declared that all his favorite books were Cooper novels about Natty Bumppo. After that he turned to reading the lives of explorers, from Columbus to Livingstone. The kind of childhood reading he makes particular mention of, in his late essays, is of geography books. He says that Mungo Park and James Bruce were "the first friends I made when I began to take notice— I mean geographical notice—of the continents of the world into which I was born" (*Last Essays,* p. 19). He described himself as a contemporary of the Great Lakes of Africa, in the sense that he could have heard of their discovery in his cradle, and in the later '60s he did his first bit of map-drawing by transferring the outline of the new country of Tanganyika onto a blank map. His idea of Africa was mixed up with images of Mungo Park, Dr. Barth, and above all, Dr. Livingstone—"the most venerated perhaps of all the objects of my early geographical enthusiasm."

This enthusiasm was to lead to a very significant disillusionment when Conrad finally got to Stanley Falls, because that part of the world then could evoke no "shadowy friend or great haunting memory" (Livingstone) but "the unholy recollection of a prosaic newspaper 'stunt' (Stanley) and the distasteful knowledge of the vilest scramble for loot that ever disfigured the history of human conscience" (the Scramble for Africa). The occasion was moreover Conrad's trip up the Congo in 1890, which so disillusioned him with Belgian imperialism, and led to *Heart of Darkness*. That is the curve of Conrad's engagement with the idea of adventure, from boyhood enthusiasm to mature disillusionment. And though one can explain the dynamic of that curve in terms other than the political history of Empire—Conrad's temperament was predisposed to disillusionment on other grounds—still that political history did correspond to and justify his development. Conrad represented and identified with the European conscience as a whole, in that curve.

But like Kipling, Conrad was very conscious of the history of adventure, and its heroes of the past, and often evoked them, in his fiction and elsewhere. In a letter of December 26, 1903, to his friend Cunninghame Graham, he tells of the horrors of the Congo, and says he would like to bury himself in an account of the original Spanish conquistadors, "If only to forget our modern Conquistadores. Their achievement is monstrous enough in all conscience—but not as a great human force let loose, but rather like that of a gigantic and obscene beast. Leopold is their Pizarro, Thys their Cortes, and their 'lances' are recruited . . . of all sorts on the pavements of Brussels and Antwerp" (*Joseph Conrad's Letters to R. B. Cunninghame Graham*, C. T. Watts [ed.] pp. 148–149). But if the Belgians are sordid, the Spaniards must have been romantic, to make Conrad's point. As this suggests, Conrad's imagination was dominated by romance, as distinct from adventure, in all its major categories; even though the idea of modern system values and the corresponding temperament was very important to him, as we shall see.

At the age of seventeen, he told the uncle with whom he lived that he wanted to be a sailor. This not only meant a life of adventure, but a life far from Poland. And in 1874 he entered the French marine service in Marseilles, and socially entered a circle of political conspirators, who promoted the cause of royalty in France and in Spain. In 1878, after either a duel or a suicide attempt, he left France and became a seaman in the English merchant marine, which seems to have always presented itself to him as "unromantic." England and her merchant navy presented themselves in Defoe-like terms to Conrad; as useful, effective, sober, solid, devoted to duty and not to honor;

to service and not to glory. This was an ideal which had been recommended to him (though not as specifically English) by his uncle, and it clearly promised him a stability, by being midway between the two extreme conditions toward which Conrad was drawn—romantic excitement and black pessimism.

Of course England also meant to Conrad a quite romantic kind of adventure-heroism, of which the representative most important to him personally was James Brooke, the White Rajah of Sarawak. Brooke was born in 1803, and so belonged to that early nineteenth-century England which Conrad, writing of Marryat, called a fabulous period of vigorous romance. Romance is always a category in the eye of the beholder, whatever the facts of a particular case, and it is likely that if Conrad had visited Brooke's Borneo as a contemporary, he would have been as disillusioned as he was by the Congo. But as a legend Brooke was very important to him.[1]

On June 15, 1920, Conrad wrote to a Brooke descendant about the Great Rajah, as he called him, "The first Rajah Brooke has been one of my boyish admirations, a feeling I have kept to this day, strengthened by the better understanding of the greatness of his character and the unstained rectitude of his purpose." His correspondent had written to praise *Lord Jim* as the best book ever written about the East Indies, and Conrad continued, "The book which has found favour in your eyes has been inspired in great measure by the history of the first Rajah's enterprise."*

In some sense, the story of the White Rajahs of Sarawak begins with Alexander Hare. (So we gather from Steven Runciman's *The White Rajahs,* Cambridge, 1960.) Alexander Hare was a merchant of Malacca, who worked with the imperialist statesman, Stamford Raffles, from 1811 on, to get Borneo from the Dutch for the British. (At that time, Holland, the imperial power in the East Indies, was nominally the ally of Napoleon and thus the enemy of Britain.) Hare got a private estate of 1,400 square miles assigned him, of which he was sovereign prince, where he kept a palace and a harem. One of the adventurers who joined him there was John Clunies-Ross, a Scots adventurer, who afterward became hereditary prince of the Cocos Islands. Thus Borneo was a happy hunting ground for men who would be kings, from before Brooke's day, and until long after.

*Quoted in Robert Payne's *The White Rajahs of Sarawak.*

In 1815 Java was given back to Holland, and Raffles had to concentrate his schemes on Singapore—and Hare lost his estate soon after. But Brooke read Raffles's essays about British power in the East, and was much influenced by them. He had been born in Benares, where his father was judge of the High Court. Like Clive and Burton, Brooke was rebellious at school, and only found himself when he got to lead some volunteer horse in the First Burmese War in 1825. (Admiral Austen, Jane Austen's brother, who played a part in that war, later played a part in the history of Sarawak, coming there in 1851 to suppress pirates for Brooke.) Brooke criticized the East India Company, and had to resign. He inherited a fortune of £30,000 in 1835, and immediately began preparations to acquire a kingdom in the East. He issued a prospectus, describing Borneo, in 1838, and the next year, arrived there, and gave his help to the Rajah in putting down a rebellion.

In 1841 he was made governor of the province of Sarawak, and in 1846 he published his first book describing what he had done. It had three editions, and made him a national hero in England; but aroused the hostility of Liberals like Cobden and Gladstone, and Radicals like Joseph Hume. (Except for the group around Wakefield and Durham, whose radicalism owed something to French Revolution principles, the Radicals were then anti-imperialist.) A lot of controversy centered around the question of certain pirates, whom Brooke claimed British help in suppressing (on the Rajah's behalf) and of whom the Liberals doubted either the existence or the piracy. (They were wrong about this, it seems, though in general they were right to suspect Brooke of personal imperialism.) Finally, however, Brooke established himself as Rajah of Sarawak, and his nephews and heirs were given the exotic titles of the Tuan Besar, the Tuan Muda, and the Tuan Bongsu. This was one of the great Victorian stories of a Man Who Would Be King, and Conrad embraced the myth enthusiastically.

But because of his divided temperament, with its reversals of sympathy, he relied even more on the unromantic British heroism described before. Moreover he continued to believe in this British style, even during and after his disillusionment with imperialism and romance. We find an essay, "Well Done," of 1918 in which he says "I venture to affirm that the main characteristic of the British men spread all over the world, is not the spirit of adventure so much as the spirit of service. I think that this could be demonstrated from the history of great voyages and the general activity of the race. . . . Yes, there is nothing more futile than an adventurer, but nobody can say that the adventurous activities of the British race are stamped with the futility of a chase after mere emotions. The successive generations that went out to sea from these Isles went out to toil desperately in adventurous conditions. A man is a worker. If he is not that, he is nothing."*

Thus Conrad was really much more old-fashioned than Kipling, closer to both Scott and Defoe, in his understanding of England and her role in the modern world system. While Kipling was describing the transition to Empire, and the rise of the military caste and decline of the mercantile, Conrad celebrated the old-Defoe-style virtues. And his romanticism is closer to Scott than to the saga-atavism that came in after Carlyle, which adapted the chivalric hero to the newer needs of the imperial imagination. Of course, Conrad *had* modern elements to his imagination, but they stood in antagonism to every kind of adventure and political enterprise in general, and left his idea of the British Empire in particular quite old-fashioned and consoling to the general English reader.

The East Indian Trilogy

Conrad began writing fiction by speculating about a man called Almayer or Olmeyer, whom he had met in the East Indies; a failed adventurer. This man was, one might say, the antithesis to Rajah Brooke, and it is significant that the counterpart was the one who really engaged Conrad's creative imagination.

It took him some years to write *Almayer's Folly,* during which time, he says, he was always haunted by the image of that man, and by his social and geographical setting in the Eastern Archipelago. Then his second novel, *Outcast of the Islands,* also has Almayer as a character, and a third novel (not finished until much later), *The Rescue,* has the same general setting, the same themes, and as hero

*In *Notes on Life and Letters,* pp. 189, 190.

Tom Lingard, who is a minor character in the first two. The three books therefore constitute a sort of triology, and a considerable body of work—perhaps Conrad's most sustained engagement with a subject. Lingard (also a character drawn from real life) was a successful adventurer; known as the Rajah Laut, the King of the Sea, or King Tom (Conrad followed Kipling with his play upon the idea of kingship). Almayer (and later Willems in the second novel) is a failure. And it is highly characteristic of Conrad and the writers who followed him that it was the second type that fixed and fascinated their attention.

The British books of this kind had not examined the failures of empire, and one may say that Almayer struck Conrad with the force of a new idea—or of a revolution in ideas. (Kipling's shady men, Carnehan and Dravott, were after all romantically large.) The force naturally came from Conrad's expectations and desires of failure, which had always been there, though hitherto differently named. Conrad saw—and this is why subsequent writers chose him as their godfather—that the Empire was a stage strewn with extraordinary failures, as well as with extraordinary successes. His books are full of examples of human seediness and villainy—Gentleman Brown in *Lord Jim*, Gentleman Jones in *Victory*. These are adventure-villains, the obverse of adventure-heroes, and Conrad delights in them, artistically, with much less equivocation than he does in the heroes.

Almayer marries a Malay girl who had been adopted by Lingard. He does so to win the latter's favor and become his heir. He has a half-caste daughter, Nina, whom he educates as white, but who chooses to be Malay instead and rejects him for being a white adventurer. So in Conrad the themes of adventure and empire are entangled with sex and miscegenation. This complex of themes was only touched on by Kipling, and hardly even that by writers before him, but literature was increasingly under the influence of the erotic movement; and the growing importance of racial theory within the imperialist idea made it a natural development for Conrad to pursue. A further extension of the idea is that Almayer has "gone native"; a phrase which was to inform a good deal of fiction, like Somerset Maugham's, over the next thirty or forty years. Almayer dreams of retiring back to Holland with his wealth, and seeing his daughter triumph in white society, but he gradually slips downhill out of white identity entirely. And in the second novel, this happens to Willems even more dramatically. He too marries to gain favor with a rich man; he too meets his fate in a proud native beauty; but she—her name is Aissa—enslaves him; he does physical work at her bidding, so that his racial identity is really parodied and trampled in the dirt. In various ways like that, Conrad depicts the Empire as a place inhabited by dreams of making it, but by facts of not just failure but total self-destruction.

But besides the character of Almayer, the East Indies islands where he lives are themselves important. (Each area of the empire has an elective affinity for a certain kind of story; Kipling's stories about the imperialism of India are quite unlike Haggard's stories about the imperialism of Africa; and Conrad's affinity is for the East and West Indies.)[2] Archipelagoes are always a favorite site for piracy, and consequently for a many-layered structure of power. In this story of Borneo, for instance, there are Dyaks of various kinds, and tribes subordinate to them, over whom rule Malays (the Rajah Lakamba and Babalatchi); over whom, in some sense, are the Arabs (Abdullah and his nephew Rashid); over whom are the Dutch (including, precariously, Almayer); and then there are the English and the Chinese. These layers do not lie neatly one above the other, moreover, but interweave; and the sense of such complex political situations is one of Conrad's strengths—one sees it again in *Nostromo;* he knew how to put political complexity into fiction, though in static rather than dynamic terms.

The plot is set in motion when Dain Baroda, the Rajah's son from Bali, comes to Almayer and persuades him to sell gunpowder, to make it possible for him to make war against the Dutch. Almayer puts gunpowder into the hands of blacks to use against whites. That is, he sells his white soul. Dain Baroda is a Black Prince, except that he is not subordinate to, or much related to, a white man. His loyalty is to Nina Almayer, and his splendor is erotic rather than political. Nina, who chooses passion and epic in him, is in other ways like Kingsley's Ayancora. The significant new element is Almayer's futile and fumbling betrayal of his race and himself; that is what Conrad and the reader pay most attention to.

Conrad's imaginative mode is much closer to Scott's than to Defoe's. It is highly operatic; people are presented in striking postures and gestures that are held unchanging over several pages, and were very theatrical to begin with. Scenery and costume are given in great detail, and often the action is static, or if it moves, then, as in Cooper, the scene expands sideways, changed by the arrival of more and more characters, rather than by moving forward. In the climactic scene Dain is joined in his hiding place by—one after another—Nina, then Almayer, then Babalatchi, then the Dutch and Taminah. One feels that the central characters, who embody the story, are paralyzed; they ought to move, but they can't; and one feels that about Conrad often.

The new characters he is interested in, figures of decadence and villainy, had been treated by American writers, and in American legend. Conrad in fact treats the Empire as if it were a Frontier in this regard—in the focus of his perceptual interest. Almayer and Willems are not too different from the King and the Dauphin in *Huckleberry Finn;* Gentleman Brown and Gentleman Jones might have turned up in the stories about Davy Crockett and Mike Fink. But aesthetically Conrad was an old-fashioned romantic and had no sympathy (while Kipling had a great deal) for the American and Frontier modes of narrative and characterization; e.g., the use of dialect. So he relies on English-novel techniques—typically Dickensian—for rendering, say, Cornelius in *Lord Jim,* even though those techniques somewhat subvert his purposes by their playful exaggerations.

In these early novels, there is a dream of treasure, in gold and diamonds. There is a sinister hag, Mrs. Almayer. There is a naked corpse, of Dain. There is an explosion, on Dain's brig, while the Dutch are aboard, so that they are killed (Conrad often makes use of such explosions). There is a chest full of the money which Dain paid Mrs. Almayer for Nina. And so on; that is enough to show how lavishly Conrad used the motifs of the adventure-romance; and he continued to do so throughout his writing career.

The Rescue, the third novel of the series, was not published until 1920. The Author's Note says that it was half written in 1898, but put aside because first *The Nigger of the Narcissus,* then *Youth,* then *Lord Jim,* demanded to be written. He says that it was writing the first of these three that gave him the consciousness of mastery first. And it is true that his work then takes an artistic leap forward. But these early and comparatively neglected books are nevertheless interesting, in their own right, and even more from our point of view. The third of them is a failure artistically, but the reasons for its failure are interesting.

In *The Rescue,* Tom Lingard is young, and is presented as a romantic hero; he is explicitly compared with James Brooke, the White Rajah. Conrad says Lingard lacked Brooke's advantages of birth, position, and intelligence, but shared his sympathy for the people of the forests and the sea.[3] This could be a formula for a version of Daniel Boone or Davy Crockett. But in fact Conrad's treatment is theatrical-romantic. Lingard is given a well-shaped head, a beard that burns gold in the sunlight, and a narrow waist. He is engaged in winning a kingdom for a Malay prince and princess when the story opens. Prince Hassim has saved Lingard's life on a previous occasion, and they have formed a Natty-Chingachgook relationship. But their plot is foiled when the schooner of a rich English politician runs aground near their secret meeting-place, and Lingard falls in love with the politician's wife, a Gwendolen Grandcourt-figure. Because of her, he sacrifices everything else, and sails away embittered. All that second half of the book is badly done, but its place in the design of the whole is important from the adventure-myth point of view. Its message is that there are possibilities of heroism, romantic friendship, greatness, out on the seas, which are ruined by the intrusion of representatives of London and civilization.

The whole story is made up from motifs important to the adventure-romance. There is, for instance, a ring that is passed to and fro between Lingard and Hassim, as there is in *Lord Jim.* The Malay princess, Immada, is in love with King Tom, but stands no chance against the English beauty Mrs. Travers, with whom she is often contrasted. This is Madame Butterfly again; the sexual pathos of the inferior race, the triumphalism of the superior. And the heroic heritage of the modern system is invoked often: "Did you follow with your ghostly eyes the quest of this obscure adventurer of yesterday, you shades of forgotten adventurers who, in leather jerkins and sweating under steel helmets, attacked with long rapiers . . ." (p. 96). The triology, being apprentice work, is more in the adventure tradition than the rest of Conrad's fiction. But the later novels work with that tradition's motifs, even as they resist and undermine the spirit of adventure.

Conrad's Later Books

In *The Nigger of the Narcissus* (1897) Conrad introduced a character who was to be important to the further development of adventure. This is Donkin, the evil-spirited man, the nay-sayer; he alone sees through James Wait, the fraudulent Nigger of the title, and he is favored therefore by Wait, and in a sense by Conrad. The author shows himself fascinated by such men, who insistently deny, betray, and sneer at the values other men agree to live by.[4] Melville had been similarly fascinated, and the characters of that kind which the two writers create are a clue to the larger similarity between the latter—that they are both so ambivalent about adventure and heroism. They both affirm and deny those values. Since the surface of their books, the stories they were in a sense commissioned to write, celebrated adventure, we feel that more profoundly they were hostile to it. But it is probably more accurate to say they were ambivalent.

For Conrad's *Youth* (1898) has the ring of conviction, and is an entirely romantic story, entirely affirmative about adventure values. At the end, Conrad/Marlow says, "There was all the East before me, and all life . . . And I thought of men of old, who, centuries ago, went that road in ships that sailed no better, to the land of palms and spices, and yellow sands, and of brown nations ruled by kings more cruel than Nero the Roman, and more splendid than Solomon the Jew" (p. 107). The whole story offers both adventure and romance, strengthening the latter with the former. The unimaginative, unromantic Captain Beard braces the system of shipboard life, the system of the merchant marine, with his integrity, and so safeguards the highly imaginative Marlow (and, we may add, Conrad) against the excesses and collapses that threaten him. (The excesses and collapses later attributed to Kurtz in *Heart of Darkness.*)

And *Typhoon* tells the same fable, in much exaggerated—though wholly successful—terms. The universe throws every horror it has at Captain McWhirr, who represents British ordinariness, and he withstands them. All the metaphysical grotesqueness of life rears up (there are wonderful scenes with the Chinese rolling to and fro, fighting for their dollars while the typhoon is at its worst) but the captain ignores and so masters it. And Jukes, who represents imagination, and Conrad, and the reader, are deeply impressed and grateful. These are, Marvin Mudrick says and I agree, the best of Conrad's work. Mudrick says that that best work was all written in novella form, and all produced in six years. The later and longer novels, so lengthily expounded by the critics, are badly flawed.

The other two fine pieces of that kind are *Outpost of Progress* and *Heart of Darkness.* In the latter, Marlow's first vision of the station, and his walk along the river, his "two hundred mile tramp," are both superb. And indeed the idea of Kurtz is a compelling one; at least it is now, after so many fine critics have lavished their imagination upon him. But it is not at all a realized idea.[5]

And it is still necessary to insist that Conrad, far from attacking English imperialism in the opening pages of this story, is assertively glorifying it.

The old river in its broad reach rested unruffled at the decline of day, after ages of good service done to the race that peopled its banks, spread out in the tranquil dignity of a waterway leading to the utmost ends of the earth. . . . It had known and served all the men of whom the nation is proud—from Sir Francis Drake to Sir John Franklin, knights all, titled and untitled—the knights-errant of the sea. It had borne all the ships whose names are like jewels flashing in the night of time, from the *Golden Hind.* . . . Hunters for gold or pursuers of fame, they all had gone out on that stream, bearing the sword, and often the torch, messengers of the might within the land, bearers of a spark from the sacred fire. What greatness had not floated on the ebb of that river into the mystery of an unknown earth! . . . The dreams of men, the seed of commonwealths, the germs of empire (p. 2).

So when Marlow says, "And this also has been one of the dark places on the earth" (which comes immediately after and is the starting point of the story), the meaning is clearly contrastive and depends on the reader feeling unequivocally how great England has become and still is.

We are told that "The conquest of the earth is not a pretty thing when you look into it too much," but that means that "What redeems it is the idea only." Of course, the idea must not be a "sentimental pretense"; it must not be such ideas as Kurtz has and other non-Englishmen who try to imitate British imperialism; this is Conrad's equivalent for Kipling's "lesser breeds without the law." The saving idea, the English idea, is a tough realism, almost a non-idea, an intellectual silence, like Stalky's silence about the flag; in this story that dour pragmatism is represented by Marlow's rivets. "What more did I want? What I really wanted was rivets, by heavens! Rivets. To get on with the work—to stop the hole. . . . I don't like work—no man does—but I like what is in the work—the chance to find yourself" (p. 23). This element in British adventure—the Defoean element—is symbolized in Towson's book of directions in seamanship. "Not a very enthralling book; but at the first glance you could see there a singleness of intention, an honest concern for the right way of going to work, which made these humble pages, thought out so many years ago, luminous with another than a professional light" (p. 31). This is the ghost of Defoe and Smiles, the spirit of the modern system past. Conrad felt himself very distant, in psychological and historical time, from that spirit, but still celebrated it.[6]

Lord Jim (1900) is, as Mudrick says, and as Conrad's account of the writing makes plain, an overblown short story. It demonstrates the effort it cost Conrad to make a full-scale, full-weight artistic form for his adventure material, which could contain all his ambivalence about it. The story is very like Kipling in its glorification of the English boy; but it is different because Conrad shows his ambivalence. Indeed he makes much of that ambivalence, though he also muffles it in ambiguity. And what spoils Jim as an adventure hero saves him as a modern fiction character.

But he *is* an adventure hero. Like Conrad himself, Jim found his vocation for the sea after a course of adventure reading.

On the lower deck in the babel of two hundred voices he would forget himself, and beforehand live in his mind the sea-life of light literature. He saw himself saving people from sinking ships, cutting away masts in a hurricane, swimming through a surf with a line; or as a lonely castaway, barefooted and half naked, walking on uncovered reefs in search of shellfish to stave off starvation. He confronted savages on tropical shores, quelled mutinies on the high seas, and in a small boat upon the ocean kept up the hearts of despairing men—always an example of devotion to duty, and as unflinching as a hero in a book (p. 5).

He apprenticed himself to all the heroes we have been studying, from Robinson Crusoe on; he affiliated his soul to the genre.

Conrad of course offers us an ironic view of that genre. But he affirms its value. His own affirmations—though the critics have made a big mystery of them—are surely represented by Stein's remarks. "A man that is born falls into a dream like a man who falls into the sea. . . . The way is to the destructive element submit yourself, and with the exertions of your hands and feet in the water make the deep, deep, sea keep you up" (p. 130). This is not a warning against illusion, but against the opposite. One must accept illusion, including the illusion of adventure, one must live in it, interact with it, in order to keep going, to keep afloat. England represented that method in action; Stein might philosophize it, but Captain Beard and Captain McWhirr enacted it. So this is an endorsement of adventure. The adventure idea may seem to us (men of letters) to have betrayed Jim, because it incited him to a heroism he could not achieve, and then to a savage self-punishment. But Conrad meant rather that Jim betrayed it; after all, when he tried harder, or better, with his second leap, the idea yielded itself to him. He became a hero of exactly that kind.

Amongst Conrad's later, larger fictions, *Nostromo* (1904) has received most praise. It has indeed a powerful, Cooper-like sense of geography and history, plus a grasp of politics in places like South America, on the periphery of the system, which no other English novelist could offer.[7] A plot-summary can make the book sound wonderful. Unfortunately Conrad, again Cooper-like, can't make such a plot move forward. These novelists were alike in being profoundly ill at ease with the conventions of their genre.

The story is of a doomed rising, like the story of *Waverley*, but this book is, even sentimentally, on the side of the conservatives. The Negro liberals, the insurrectionary party, are to him quite grotesque. And this is symptomatic of a general alienation from liberalism and from the adventure material, which makes him handle it all clumsily. Also after the Scott model are the operatic heroines, Antonia and Dona Emilia; indeed, they are very close to Waverley's Flora and Rose, but handled clumsily enough to seem more like Cooper's heroines. The best thing is the most modern, the figure of Nostromo, just because that figure expresses Conrad's sense of alienation. Nostromo is the man whose identity it is to belong to the English, to be "our man," their man. This idea sums up all the bitterness of the colonial—the absorption of even virtue by the English. But, as in the case of Kurtz, the idea of the character is quite distinguishable from, and far superior to, its realization.

Despite his alienation, moreover, Conrad was still an imperialist. The confrontation between Captain Mitchell, another of Conrad's comic English captains (comic but better than tragic) and Colonel Sotillo, a caricature of Latin volatility and pretentiousness and pretence, reinforces all the racist stereotypes of imperialism. When Sotillo sees Mitchell's gold watch, he "became so interested that for an instant he forgot his precious prisoner" (p. 269). He had never seen anything so fine, and his officers closed in and craned their necks behind his back. "There is always something childish in the rapacity of the passionate, clear-minded, Southern races, wanting in the misty idealism of the Northerners, who at the smallest encouragement dream of nothing less than the conquest of the earth. Sotillo was fond of jewels, gold trinkets, of personal adornment" (p. 269). So he tries to steal the watch. And everything he does is a racist caricature. He advances one leg, and puts his arms akimbo; he points at his prisoner with a long, almond-shaped nail; he has coal-black ringlets and moustache. Meanwhile, against him, the English Mitchell is absolutely solid.

The novel is made up of adventure-romance motifs. It has treasure —indeed, stolen and buried treasure; it has love—indeed, forbidden love; it has a revolution, a dramatic landscape, a colorful cast, and so on. It is clearly a Scott romance. There is the modern, postimperial bitterness, embodied in Nostromo, of course. That bitterness is spoken out by Martin Decoud, whose pessimistic comments on the hopes that inspire other people are gradually born out by the plot. But it is important to note that Decoud has been completely undermined as an authority, from his first introduction. Despite his pretensions to historical insight, we hear, Decoud "was an idle boulevardier, in touch with some smart journalists, made free of a few newspaper offices, and welcomed in the pleasure haunts of pressmen. This life, whose dreary superficiality is covered by the glitter of the universal blague, like the stupid clowning of a harlequin by the spangles of a motley costume, induced in him a Frenchified—but most un-French —cosmopolitanism, in reality a mere barren indifferentism posing as intellectual superiority" (p. 130). Here again Conrad puts himself firmly on the side of the traditional values and temperament style, British adventure values and styles. So the reader's responsive mood of ruthless irony is again undercut and shattered.

And finally *Victory* (1915) which conveys a strong sense of the ending of the great adventure of the modern system. As in *Nostromo*, an island plays a part, as a place of disaster, where again it is shown —though by a different event—that a man *cannot* live alone. Thus there is a reversal of the *Robinson Crusoe* pattern, with its happy island motif. When islands are places of disaster, adventure is dying, and self-confidence in general is failing. The hero's last words are "Woe to the man whose heart has not learned while young to hope, to love—and to put its trust in life." That affirms adventure, in a yearning and hopeless fashion. But the burden of the book is quite opposite—that salvation lies in the denial of appetite and illusion— though of course salvation does not mean success. "It is not the clear-sighted who lead the world. Great achievements are accomplished in a blessed, warm mental fog . . ." (p. 92). But here, as elsewhere, that scheme of ideas is masked by another, which is almost its opposite. Conrad set the two sides of his temperament fighting, and backed them both equally.

Mudrick says of Conrad that ". . . those of his works which most successfully challenge the nullifying blast of his temperament are tales of the sea" (Mudrick, *Joseph Conrad: Twentieth Century Views*, p. 3). (Tales of the sea being one of the main energizing myths of the modern system.) There Mudrick identifies Conrad's temperament wholly with its impulses to negate. But it seems clear that Conrad felt his division that way himself (set temperament in opposition to faith and duty) and used England and its naval traditions consciously to strengthen his more positive side. In his essay, "Well Done," he says, "The mere love of adventure is no saving grace. It is no grace at all. It lays a man under no obligation to faithfulness to an idea and even to his own self. . . . There is nothing in the world to prevent a mere lover or pursuer of adventure from running at any moment. . . . You find them in mysterious nooks of islands and continents, mostly red-nosed and watery-eyed, and not even amusingly boastful. There is nothing more futile. . . . Adventure by itself is but a phantom, a dubious shape without a heart" (Conrad, *Notes*, pp. 189 and 190). He says adventure but he means romance, and he denies it in the name of modern system values. At other times, as the critics are quite right to insist, he denies the latter quite devastatingly. His ambivalence is total.

Conrad and Criticism

Aesthetically speaking, the really striking thing about Conrad's use of the motifs we have been studying is the clumsy lavishness of that use, the wholesaleness of his acceptance of the form, compared with the discriminations and transformations Kipling imposed upon it. And Conrad's skepticism about the spirit of adventure makes his use of the form more gross and strident. But you would never guess that, reading the critics.

Of course Conrad, like every other writer, made a selection from among those motifs, which made them in some ways his own. But by and large, he followed Scott's selection, especially in his treatment of women; though he introduced, again often in connection with women, motifs and meanings from the modernist imagination, such as those of the erotic movement.[8] And then there is an element of grotesque exaggeration in his writing, which seems to derive from Dickens and other post-Scott rhetoricians. Conrad probably avoided following and learning from Kipling, the real formal innovator in adventure. He seized the opportunity, during the Boer War, to separate himself from Kipling politically, and ever after spoke of the latter as a Patriot—and himself as an Artist. And Henry James, who had repudiated Kipling, embraced Conrad, received him on behalf of literature.

In 1919, as we have seen, T. S. Eliot also embraced him, distinguishing him from Kipling as the sheep are to be distinguished from the goats on Judgment Day; "He is, for one thing, the antithesis of Empire (as well as of democracy); his characters are the denial of Empire, of Nation, of Race almost; they are fearfully alone in the Wilderness." Conrad is great because he is the embodiment of negation. Unlike Kipling, "Mr. Conrad has no Ideas, but he has a point of view, a world." This, clearly, is what makes a serious writer. And modern critics, notably F. R. Leavis in England, have followed Eliot.

Indeed, there is no repudiation by the serious critics for us to discuss. Literature-as-a-system welcomed Conrad, unlike the other novelists in this sequence. This is very understandable; due as it was to the implicit and by no means dishonorable ideology of serious literature. But it was still a fatal error. (This book's approach to literature makes such mistakes less likely; and that is perhaps its main recommendation from a literary-critical point of view.) Conrad is certainly rich in political and psychological insight into the sins and follies of imperialism; insights that open metaphysical depths beneath the adventurer and the reader. But he is not the master of those insights. He equivocates, and often denies them; partly out of artistic clumsiness, partly out of philosophical uncertainty, but also out of genuine ambivalence. Thus the critical enthusiasm for Conrad, like the enthusiasm against Kipling, is not to the credit of the generations that entertained it. Intellectually and aesthetically it was a kind of stupidity or perversity; and judged more generally and ideologically, while one cannot fail to sympathize with the motives behind it, those were surely familiar enough to have been understood and controlled. The failure to do this was especially fatal for Englishmen. Intellectually and aesthetically, England's readers and writers after 1918 were nearly all the children of Kipling, as Eliot and Orwell came to acknowledge, and to deny him in the name of Conrad was in some ways only a fit of pique.

For Americans it was not such a crucial issue. Hemingway acknowledged his debt to Kipling, and that acknowledgment is related to a kind of strength in him which the English writers failed in. Hemingway has heroes; he carries on the development of the WASP adventure; the English writers chose Conrad and rejected Kipling just because the former announced the death of that hero. Indeed, Hemingway's debt was to the imperialist adventure writers, generally. His hero figures, for instance Wilson in "The Short Happy Life of Francis Macomber," owe as much to Edgar Wallace as to Kipling. Wallace's Sanders, who appears in *Sanders of the River,* and other collections, is the same short, sandy-haired man, with the brusque manner and the harsh voice, uneasy with women but sentimental about men. Perhaps via Hemingway, something of Kipling seems to have reached Norman Mailer also in the flamboyant structural and stylistic devices of his journalism. Certainly Mailer's *Why Are We in Vietnam?* is the most distinguished novel using primarily adventure motifs, of modern times; though it follows American and not British models of adventure.

It was above all the love of the male hero which British literature lost or gave up, and which American literature won, after 1918, when the United States took over the cultural leadership. And along with the male hero, we lost a whole range of modes of moral seriousness. That is what the consecration of Conrad has meant. Mailer's novel uses adventure in a critical analysis of imperialism, without losing faith in adventure itself, in a way that British writers have not been able to manage.

XI

In the Trough of the Wave of Imperialism: Adventure Images after 1918

AFTER the Great War, and after Conrad, the adventure form persisted; both as a narrative genre and a style in heroism—its presence permeated English culture after 1918. But the persistence of the form of adventure was no more marked than the resistance to its spirit. At least in the world of literature one can say flatly that England after 1918 was unadventurous; men as serious as Defoe and Scott could no longer write adventures; and the men who could felt the moral support of their audience progressively withdrawn, so that the adventures grew more and more immoral, from Bulldog Drummond to James Bond.

The most typical formal result of combining persistent form with resistant spirit must always be satire; and much satiric or ironic adventure was written, by new writers like Evelyn Waugh or Graham Greene. (However, terms like form and spirit being so slippery, those satires in their way endorsed the spirit of adventure.) And outside literature one can say that the moral and social basis of adventure, its constituency, narrowed. The exploits of a Lawrence of Arabia, and the rhetoric of a Winston Churchill, seemed more the property of a single class than had the heroism of their Victorian predecessors. This too is a matter of persistence and resistance combined.

The Change

The idea of a serious literature of adventure was much expounded by responsible critics at the time of World War I. Arthur Waugh said, "When a people has found its soul, its literature has always found a voice";* and it was in times of war that it found its soul. Of course, in wartime such things are said more easily even by responsible critics. But Leslie Stephen (who died in 1904) "knew many of Mr. Rudyard Kipling's ballads by heart, and shouted Henry Newbolt's 'Admirals All' [about Drake, Nelson, etc.] at the top of his voice as he went about the house or walked in Kew Gardens, to the surprise of the nursemaids and the parkkeepers." And Stephen was a central figure in the system of literature, a serious intellectual and literary critic. But this anecdote reminds us of the change impending at the time of his death. His biographer included the anecdote in his *Life and Letters,* and said it was given him by one of Stephen's daughters—either Virginia Woolf or Vanessa Bell, who did not recite Kipling or Newbolt. Stephen was a man of letters, but he was also a member of the responsible class, and his reading partook of both characters. But his daughters and their readers belonged by intention at least only to the former, and adventure was not their kind of literature.

The change was particularly clear-cut because at the very end of the nineteenth century, and particularly after the scandal about Oscar Wilde and aestheticism, there had been the move to reunite

*In *The Fortnightly,* November 1917.

the two reading publics; it was professors of literature who welcomed Kipling, as we saw, and writers like Chesterton offered to please both publics, with his ballads and his critical essays. (This is the mood John Gross has described and documented in *Decline and Fall of the Man of Letters*.) The split between Defoe and Swift, or between Scott and Coleridge, was declared to be merely local and temporary, not profoundly meaningful. There was a stress upon the Elizabethan age as paradigmatic for literary history, because then the literary class was just as excited and active and brilliant as the military and economic classes. Saintsbury said that when one looked at Elizabethan history, "it must appear that it would have been more odd if Elizabethan literature had not been great than surprising that it was."

I have quoted these comments from *The Literature and Art of the Empire*, which is Vol. XI of a twelve-volume *The British Empire*, edited by Hugh Gunn, which came out in London in 1924. The authors of this volume, Edward Salmon and Major A. A. Longden, say that a literary harvest followed the Armada and another followed Waterloo, and they confidently expect another to follow the Great War. But in fact there was to be no equivalent to Shakespeare and Scott, because the imperialist confidence in England had failed. The fiction that got written in the next decades, including the adventure fiction, expressed revulsion against Empire.

In the 1920s and 1930s, however, the standard poet promoted in schools across England was John Masefield; it was his poems about ships and islands and pirates (and de la Mare's) which English children learned by heart. ("Sea Fever" was the first poem I learned at school.) This was a continuation of late-Victorian literary imperialism. Between 1885 and 1905 ten major biographies of Nelson appeared. (All stressed his dying words, "Thank God I have done my duty.") In 1895–1896, Sir Arthur Quiller-Couch, professor of English literature at Cambridge, brought out his two-volume *Story of the Sea*, full of the old legends: for instance, of the Armada, and the Protestant wind that came up to defeat it and save England in 1588. The same myth of the sea, and ships, and sailing, was taught in the 1920s, in perhaps more conscious and desperate propaganda for the WASP hero than ever before.

And in prose, after Kipling came John Buchan; who was also a tremendously popular writer, and in terms of talent similar to Stevenson; that is, a man of great deftness, and craftsman-talent, but dedicated to adventure and soon repudiated by literature-as-a-system. T. E. Lawrence said that Buchan's books were like athletes racing; "so clean-limbed, speedy, breathless. For our age they mean nothing; they are sport only; but will a century hence disinter them and proclaim him the great romancer of our blind and undeserving generation?"* Lawrence himself, in *Revolt in the Desert,* and in his translation of Homer, and even more in his career, embodied the same idea as Buchan put into fiction. Indeed, it is pretty clear that Lawrence is the man from whom Buchan drew the hero of *Greenmantle.* And, in schools and elsewhere, Lawrence was promoted as England's twentieth-century adventurer, in the 1920s and 1930s. Buchan and Lawrence were the Kipling and Rhodes of postwar England. But in the unsympathetic air of '20s and '30s seriousness, they lacked the power to convince and dominate.

For after 1918, as Lawrence's remark indicated, their idea met stiff resistance, especially in literary men. When Q. D. Leavis compiled her questionnaires for *Fiction and the Reading Public,* asking among other things who leading authors thought their readers were, P. C. Wren (the author of *Beau Geste,* a very popular adventure-romance) wrote, "The bulk of my readers are the cleanly-minded, virile, outdoor sort of people of both sexes, and the books are widely read in the Army, the Navy, and the Public Schools, and the Clubs. . . . Although I now make a good many thousands a year, I still am not a 'professional novelist,' nor a long-haired literary cove. I prefer the short-haired executive type."† By then, such a declaration was much more suicidal for a writer than the equivalent remarks by Scott and Cooper. The responsible class who read the latter two authors, and some part of whom presumably read Marryat and Kingsley, were not to be counted on in the 1930s to swallow that tone, or—except as merest pastime—to read that kind of adventure. So even if Wren had chosen his words better, his declaration would still have meant that he was not trying to please a literate audience at all. The adventure of imperialism had lost intellectual and moral credibility, as it had not done in the nineteenth century, and so Wren's audience, however large in numbers, was essentially a minority.

The end of the war had brought a general revulsion against imperialism. The fifth of President Wilson's Fourteen Points was a demand

*Quoted in Colin Watson, *Snobbery with Violence,* p. 43.
†Watson, p. 222.

for "A free, open-minded and absolutely impartial adjustment of colonial claims." And in close succession came the activities of the Sinn Fein in Ireland, the Bolshevik Revolution in Russia, the foundation of the League of Nations, and the publication of Lenin's *Imperialism*. In India, 1919 saw the first Government of India Act, and then the Amritsar Massacre.*

The men of letters joined in a literary movement in sympathy with this revulsion, whether they were liberals or conservatives politically. The liberal Forster attacked Lord Cromer, one of the heroes of Victorian imperialism, in *The Government of Egypt*, 1921. But the conservative T. S. Eliot, in his 1919 essay, attacked Kipling, and sharply distinguished Conrad from him, as anti-imperialist; indicating the way in which criticism of Conrad, and of literature generally, would go for two generations. Eliot was followed notably by F. R. Leavis—notably and mistakenly, as I have argued. The interest of the mistakenness is that it testifies to the strength of the drive behind it, the drive to find a hero of anti-imperialism who was also a hero of modernism in literature.

The novelists of the next generation continued to write about the Empire, but from an ironic point of view. Besides Forster's great novel, we have Maugham's series of stories, from the group who had begun publishing before the war. And from those who began their literary careers after it, we can pick out George Orwell and Joyce Cary, Evelyn Waugh and Graham Greene, among those who used the imperial setting, and to a considerable extent the adventure genre, but sardonically.

Cary is an interesting case biographically. He went to Nigeria just before the war, and was put in charge of emirates that covered an area as large as Wales. He had been one of six selected from sixty-four candidates for the Administrative Grade of the Civil Service. But he left the Service in 1920, and began writing in the '30s, much influenced by Conrad, and his point of view is anti-imperialist. *Aissa Saved*, 1932, is about the disintegrating effect that Christianity has upon pagan religions; *African Witch*, 1936, is rather like *Passage to India*.

Orwell's *Burmese Days*, 1934, also owes a lot to *Passage to India*, of which it is practically an episode. Orwell served in the Imperial

---

*Jeffrey Meyers brings these facts suggestively together in his *Fiction and the Colonial Experience*.

Police in Burma 1921–1928. Greene and Waugh didn't follow Forster; they knew the empire as travelers and journalists, not as civil servants or conscientious liberals. Nor did they aim at writing great novels; both of them make less use of Conrad than, by ironic reversal, of the Buchan-Mason-Henty pattern of adventure narrative and description. They may be said to have written antiadventures—though one should not confuse that form with Mailer's *Why Are We In Vietnam?*, in which the antagonism is to Empire, not to adventure.

The Persistence

But of course such large changes of mood and image did not occur all together or all at once. There was much conscious resistance to the swing away from adventure and Empire, and much more blind continuance in old paths. For instance, the White Rajahs of Sarawak continued to perform their Lilliputian imperialism until after the Second World War. A Brooke dynasty had been established, and there was as much palace intrigue and unhappiness about inheritance as if it were Rome. The original Brooke disinherited his oldest nephew in favor of the second, Charles; he, who began to reign in 1868, distrusted his oldest son, Vyner, and wanted the next son, Bertram, to be his heir. Vyner in turn disinherited his natural heir, his nephew Anthony, in 1939. The empire might be miniature, but its imperialism was life-size. There was a great deal of excitement about the selection of and the discipline of the young men who went out to serve as officials under the Rajah. And there were always rival adventurers to deal with—Claude Moses and Baron von Overbeck in the second half of the nineteenth century, and in the twentieth century Gerald MacBryan, who became the Rajah's private secretary, and seemed about to inherit the throne. He, in 1935, having married a Malay bride, made a pilgrimage to Mecca as a Moslem, and proposed to become international leader of the Moslems of the East, with Sarawak as his headquarters. (Again we see the attraction of Islam for the military-caste adventurer at the end of our period.) But in 1946 the Brookes finally handed their kingdom back to Borneo, as the British empire in general disintegrated.

MacBryan's trip to Mecca must remind us of England's then most

famous adventurer, Lawrence of Arabia. Lawrence's vision of himself
as hero had affinities with Conrad's vision of heroism—with Lord
Jim, for instance. But Lawrence's youthful reading was dominated
not by sea-adventures, but by medieval romances, especially the
French ones—the *romans d'aventure* of the twelfth century, like
those by Chrétien de Troyes. And he told Liddell Hart, "I also read
nearly every manual of chivalry"; plus Morris and Tennyson's romances and sagas; and he carried a copy of Malory throughout the
Arabian campaign. Morris's work was particularly attractive to him
—as it was to the young Kipling. Lawrence loved *Sigurd the Volsung*,
and in his mind related the saga people it described to the Arabs he
was working with.[1]

He told Hart that as a boy he had dreamed of leading a crusade.
"Naturally, it would be a crusade in the modern form—the freeing
of a race from bondage" (Hart, *T. E. Lawrence*, p. 80). But when
he first got out to the Middle East it was to work on archaeology,
though his job had some connections with the British Secret Service.
The Arab boy Dahoud became his Friday—to whom he later dedicated *Seven Pillars of Wisdom*—and Prince Feisal became his Black
Prince. But though we use terms first associated with Defoe, Lawrence's feeling for these men is like Scott's or Conrad's—much more
romantic. He saw Feisal as representing an older, harder, fiercer mode
of being, deeply alien to his own. Like Kim, and Burton, Lawrence
loved to adopt Arab dress and Arab personality, and to use them to
manipulate his allies and his enemies.

He found the Bedouins "a people of primary colours, or rather of
black and white, who saw the world always in contour. They were a
dogmatic people, despising doubt, our modern crown of thorns."* As
a modern system man, he lacked something, which he found in the
Bedouins. That makes it clear how chivalric-romantic his vision was
—much more romantic than Scott's—even though he sometimes
denies that. "The epic mode was alien to me, as to my generation.
Memory gave me no clue to the heroic, so that I could not feel such
men as Auda in myself. He seemed fantastic as the hills of Rumm,
old as Malory."† He denies any feeling for the epic and heroic, but
obviously in doing so asserts it.[2]

He loved the epic language he could attribute to them, and

*Quoted in Paul Zweig, *The Adventurer*, p. 237.
†Quoted in Zweig, *Adventurer*, p. 235.

could himself use in talking of them. In the Epilogue to *Seven Pillars,* * "There was left to me ambition, the wish to quicken history in the East, as the great adventurers of old had done. I fancied to sum up in my own life that new Asia which inexorable time was slowly bringing upon us. The Arabs made a chivalrous appeal to my young interest, and when still at the High School at Oxford already I thought to remake them into a nation, client and fellow of the British Empire." This is that overexcited language—it arouses the instinctive distrust of the literary reader—which is equivalent to Lord Jim's romantic fantasies. "I meant to make a new nation, to restore a lost influence, to give 20 millions of Semites the foundation on which to build an inspired dream-palace of their national thoughts." Alongside this rhetoric, as in Conrad's Jim, and in Buchan heroes, ran the *Boys' Own Paper* jargon of this letter to a friend, written in the middle of the Rising, "I hope this sounds the fun it is. The only pity is the sweat to work them up, and the wild scramble while it lasts. It's the most amateurish, Buffalo Billy sort of performance, and the only people who do it well are the Bedouin. Only you will think it heaven, because there aren't any returns, or orders, or superiors, or inferiors; no doctors, no accounts, no meals, and no drinks" (Mack, *Prince,* p. 155).

Back at All Souls, Oxford, after the war, Lawrence engaged in undergraduate pranks, while he was made into a national hero by Lowell Thomas, and by Winston Churchill and John Buchan. He was a reincarnation of the WASP adventurer, appearing just when it seemed that hero was vanishing, that option was being denied to Englishmen. Buchan said about him, "I would have followed Lawrence over the edge of the world. I loved him for himself and also because there seemed to be reborn in him all the lost friends of my youth."†

Lawrence responded vividly to his admirers' sense of him. He was the spirit of youth. In a page of his introduction to *Seven Pillars,* subsequently canceled, he wrote, "Yet when we had achieved and the new world dawned, the old men came out again and took our victory to remake in the likeness of the former world they knew." He began to translate the *Odyssey* in 1927. But the tormenting sense of self-betrayal led him to throw away the hero-identity he had so brilliantly built up, by entering the Air Force under an assumed name.

*Quoted by John Mack, *A Prince of Our Disorder,* p. 191.
†From John Buchan, *Memory, Hold-the-Door,* p. 229.

In the Trough of the Wave of Imperialism

Herbert Read said, in reviewing *Seven Pillars*, that Lawrence was not a hero because he was self-conscious. That term means a badly controlled self-consciousness, one that betrays him, by betraying how he shapes himself to suit the expectations of those he presents himself to. That is certainly true of Lawrence, and constitutes one link between him and Conrad's Lord Jim; it is no doubt connected to the self-doubt in both of them; but one must also think of the self-doubt of the epoch as a whole, the resistance of the culture.

Through most of his life he was a figure of romance—a figure out of Scott or at least Conrad, and not out of Defoe or the more interesting side of Kipling. But at the end of his life he became excited about machinery and mechanics. It was now aircraft, and after them speedboats and motorcycles, that absorbed him; and he loved the company of mechanics—because "to them their work alone is real." He was turning away from the personalism of romance. He wrote to another airman, "For thousands of years nature has held this mastery of the last element in her lap, patiently waiting for our generation, and you and I are of the holy ones chosen" (*The Letters of T. E. Lawrence*, p. 725). And to Robert Graves, on February 4, 1935, "I have convinced myself that progress today is made not by the single genius, but by the common effort. To me it is the multitude of rough transport drivers, filling all the roads of England every night, who make this the mechanical age. And it is the airmen, the mechanics, who are overcoming the air" (Mack, *Prince*, p. 331). That was like Defoe's and Smiles's feeling for mechanics and their machines. At that moment—the last in his life, for he died in the following year —Lawrence was reuniting the modernist elements in the heroic sensibility he exemplified.

Finally it is worth considering a woman writer of Lawrence's generation who wrote some acute studies of the epic and heroic landscape which people of his type—and her own—have again and again sought out to support their self-stylization. Her approach was basically aesthetic, but what she says may be associated particularly with the military caste. I am referring to Isak Dinesen, and her two books, *Out of Africa* (published 1938 in the United States), and *Shadows on the Grass* (1961 in the United States). Her father had been an officer in the Danish army (also for a time an adventurer in the States) and she saw her relations to her servants on the model of his to his soldiers. She lived in some sense on a frontier, in Kenya, though her social situation was more that of the plantation South in America; Europeans re-creating for themselves an agrarian aristocracy. She describes her life on her 6000-acre farm, twelve miles from Nairobi, where the views were immensely wide, with great cultural nostalgia. "Everything that you saw made for greatness and freedom, and unequalled nobility" (*Out of Africa*, p. 4). And it was the human landscape she was concerned with as much as the natural. The natives were her servants, but in some sense her superiors. They lived "in life itself, within their own element, such as we can never be" (p. 19). She told her servant, Kamante, tales from the *Odyssey*, and he took them as natural.

And beyond the servants, who were Somalis—a handsome and haughty people—and the agricultural Kikuyu, there were the Masai, a fighting race prevented from fighting, and her portrait of them is one of the most vivid parts of her book. She describes them on page 131 as "a dying lion with his claws clipped, a castrated nation." And on page 135, "They have, to the utmost extent, that particular form of intelligence which we call chic; daring, and wildly fantastical as they seem, they are still unswervingly true to their own nature, and to an immanent ideal. Their style is not an assumed manner. . . . The Masai carriage of the head, with the chin stretched forward, as if he were presenting you his sullen arrogant face upon a tray . . . his bearing makes of him . . . an object for contemplation, such as a statue is, a figure which is to be seen, but which itself does not see . . . faces sleek and swollen . . . neck muscles swell in a sinister fashion, like a cobra, leopard, or bull, a thickness so plainly an indication of virility that is a declaration of war to all the world." This is the Richard Burton sensibility again, the warrior caste of Europe recognizing its equivalent on another continent.

And the English friends she made there, before the First World War, were adventurer figures, from the caste we have studied. Berkeley Cole was a Restoration figure—he had to have champagne sent out to him in the forest, and served in the best crystal, at 11:00 every morning; Denys Finch-Hatton was an Elizabethan—he took her up in his plane. They loved the Masai as she did. The old settlers were untamed, being younger sons of old English families, she tells us. They often formed Hawkeye-Chingachgook relationships with some dark, untamed nomad or hunter; and hunting itself is a love affair with the hunted—for her, most notably, with the lion. Isak Dinesen is a heroine out of John Buchan, a sister to T. E. Lawrence. In the later book, she describes her servant Farah, "a cheetah noiselessly following me about at a distance of five feet, or a falcon holding on to my finger with strong talons and turning his head right and left" (*Shadows on the Grass*, p. 20). She and her servants made up a unity together, Master and Servants. All Africans, she says, are precocious but cease developing early, so the men are like European boys of thirteen to seventeen. This is the best age. "In such young Europeans, too, the code of honour, the deadly devotion to the grand phrase and the grand gesture is the passion urging them on to heroic deeds and heroic self-sacrifice. . . ." They are like the heroes of the Icelandic sagas. "The same ravenous ambition to distinguish themselves before all others and at any cost to immortalize themselves through a word or gesture, lies deep in the heart of the sons of the desert as it did in the hearts of the untamed, salty young seafarers of the Northern Seas" (p. 13). Everything in those sentences is defiantly in the chivalric mode of the military caste; nothing conciliates the mercantile caste and its sensibility. She compares her feelings for "my people" with her father's feeling for his soldiers. He had written, "The love of war is a passion like another, you love soldiers as you love young women-folk—to madness, and the one love does not exclude the other, as the girls know. But the love of women can include only one at a time, and the love for your soldiers comprehends the whole regiment, which you would like enlarged if it were possible." It was the same thing with the natives and her, Dinesen comments (*Out of Africa*, p. 18).

But such sweeping gestures of self-affirmation as hers and Lawrence's were rare in twentieth-century Britain; they were also self-consciously romantic—less in accord with realities in the sphere of politics than the equivalent had been in the nineteenth century. And in the sphere of the arts the dominant mood was ironic or gloomy, dandy frivolous or prophetic grim.

But that mood of negation—negation both of Empire and of the modern system as a whole—dominated all the humanities, in the widest sense of that term. It is symptomatic that anthropology, the study of the primitive peoples on whom empire was imposed, became a field of study central to all modern seriousness. The work of Malinovski and Radcliffe-Brown in England began a movement of thought which both sprang from and strengthened this revulsion.

In the Trough of the Wave of Imperialism

Gradually British sociologists and anthropologists, and those of other countries, ceased to reconstruct the prehistory of civilization, or of the laws of social evolution, in the way which led to self-congratulation by the advanced countries.* Malinovski was strongly influenced by Conrad, in matters of style, and that usually means a temperamental affinity.

After the Second World War

And since 1945 anthropology has been influenced above all by Claude Lévi-Strauss, whose orientation is very antimodern, and whose major points of reference are very close to those of this book. He says, "I have little sympathy for the century in which we are living, for the total ascendancy of man over nature, and of certain forms of humanity over others. My temperament and tastes carry me towards more modest periods when there was a certain balance between man and nature, the diverse and multiple forms of life."† A tribe that eats roots and spiders and wears no clothes may have solved its problems of social organization better than we. Lévi-Strauss dislikes and distrusts the modern world system, made up as it is of progressive-acquisitive-inventive societies, hot and mobile and thermodynamic, like the steam engine. He says we must go back to before Socrates and seize mind before it became our mind; the golden age was the neolithic, before men invented writing and cities. Indeed he is antihumanist. "The world began without the human race, and will end without it." He regards change as proof of impermanence and imperfection, not of energy.

This is clearly the reverse of Defoe's ideology, and announces a complete redirection of sympathies. And other intellectuals have taken up Lévi-Strauss's attitudes. Octavio Paz says mortality is the mediator between culture and nature. It is death that condemns us to culture; an idea which Norman O. Brown has developed at length. And when, in *The Savage Mind*, Lévi-Strauss said, "The ultimate goal of the human sciences is not to constitute, but to dissolve

*See J. W. Burrow, *Evolution and Society.*
†Quoted in *Claude Lévi-Strauss: The Anthropologist as Hero*, N. Hayes (Ed.), M.I.T., 1970, p. 10.

331

man . . . ," that clue was followed by other Paris structuralists. He has made anthropologists the intellectual heroes (wounded heroes) of our time. He describes them as mutilated men—men in revolt against their own society. They go elsewhere to find what is lacking at home; the Golden Age, where sorrows were dissolved by festivities, and men could converse with the Powers. Only by finding and recording that Golden Age can they be reconciled to themselves. (His own life and character were thus reconciled by his practice of anthropology, says Edmund Leach in his essay in *Claude Lévi-Strauss: The Anthropologist as Hero.*)

Thus the anthropologists represent and lead the poets, the pure scientists, and the whole modern movement of silent resistance, within and against Western culture. Lévi-Strauss says, in *Tristes Tropiques,* that law and medicine students are noisy, aggressive, right-wing, while "an arts and science student is characterized by an attitude of refusal towards the demands of the group" (p. 46). For him, teaching and research are "a refuge or a mission," not a training for a profession. And anthropology is the most extreme form of those studies.

In the same book he describes the beginning of his career, in February 1934, when he sailed to Brazil, with a vivid consciousness of following in Columbus's path, but with the hope and meaning of the journey reversed. From Dakar they reached "the fateful latitude 7 north, where in 1498, during his third voyage, Columbus, who was heading in the right direction for the discovery of Brazil, changed course towards the north-west, and so managed, by some miracle, to arrive two weeks later at Trinidad and the coast of Venezuela" (p. 67). (He was then on the edge of El Dorado, which V. S. Naipaul too has been writing about at the same time and in the same mood as Lévi-Strauss; these are the crucial places and journeys for our imagination, now again as they were so long ago.)

Lévi-Strauss describes the Doldrums as "the last mystical barrier between two regions so diametrically opposed to each other through their different conditions that the first people to become aware of the fact could not believe that they were both equally human. A continent barely touched by man lay exposed to men whose greed could no longer be satisfied by their own continent. Everything would be called into question by this second sin; God, morality, and law. In simultaneous yet contradictory fashion, everything would be verified in practice and revoked in principle; the Garden of Eden, the Fountain of Youth, Atlantis, the Hesperides, the Islands of the Blessed, would be found to be true; but revelation, salvation, customs and law would be challenged . . ." (p. 68). The old myths ceased to be energizing—became literary—Crusoe and his epigones displaced them. This chapter, "The Doldrums," is all about Columbus, and about the damage done by the world-wide spread of the modern system.

And, though less authoritative than Lévi-Strauss, England had its prophets of anti-imperialism. Of course World War II brought a revival of the old adventure heroics, which persisted for a few years, and at lower levels of culture. In a book called *British Adventure* (1947) Nigel Tangye says, "It can hardly, however, be disputed that these islands have bred more men and women of adventuresome spirit in relation to population, than any island or continent we may choose." And in a little volume about Gandhi of about this date, Reginald Reynolds introduces him to British boys by describing the port of Porbandar—where Gandhi was born—in terms used by Stevenson or Masefield.

But at the level of significant statement, the writers of England were producing books like Strachey's *End of Empire,* 1960, or Philip Mason's *Prospero's Magic,* 1962.[3] Mason's book is one of a group that take *The Tempest* as a myth of imperialism, and analyze its implications. (Others include Leslie Fiedler's *The Stranger in Shakespeare,* 1972, and D. O. Mannoni's *Prospero and Caliban*—1956 in the U.S.) Mason spent his career in India as an administrator and magistrate (when he returned to England he was shocked to find that Englishmen cheated too) and he analyzes a Prospero complex in himself. It was something he grew up with. His father had been a doctor in the north of England, no grandee, and yet he grew up to regard servants as belonging to another race. He says that before 1914 people would have been shocked to see a maid coming out of the lavatory they used, and the class feeling was reciprocated. Even in the village he grew up in, there were parts where boys of his class were liable to have stones thrown at them. Such racist and class hostility was greatest between 1880 and 1920, he says, because power was being transferred away from the upper class.

But it was his whole culture that was being transformed, including his literature. He says that his boyhood was full of tales of islands, like

333

Peter Pan, and *Treasure Island,* and *Robinson Crusoe,* and *The Tempest.* But now he can't enjoy such tales. The literary critics of his youth, like Quiller-Couch, loved *The Tempest,* and could see nothing in it to offend; because the men of his generation accepted authority—accepted it as theirs. Now we don't. Until recently, Mason says, we all assumed that civilization justified imperialism; the writings of Voltaire atoned for the wrongs done (by the Roman empire) to Vercingetorix. But now we don't. His book is all about the giving up of power, by his country and his class.

The Stracheys had figured at the very top levels of the Indian administration. Sir John was finance minister under Lord Lytton, 1876–1880, Sir Richard presided over the Famine Commission, 1876–1878, and so on. John Strachey's *The End of Empire,* setting out to consider England's relation to the world, now that her empire is being dissolved, professes political hope but expresses historical bitterness. He quotes Engels in *Anti-Dühring,* "Without slavery, no Greek state, no Greek art and science; without slavery, no Roman empire; it is very easy to inveigh against slavery and similar things in general terms, and to give vent to high moral indignation at such infamies. Unfortunately, all this conveys is what everyone knows, namely that these institutions of antiquity are no longer in accord with our present conditions and sentiments." That bitterness about civilization as a whole is inevitably a substratum of the mood in England in this historical moment.

But we are concerned primarily with literature, and with narrative. The form of adventure lived on after the spirit of adventure had died. Sometimes, indeed, the spirit reversed itself, and yet continued to use the old patterns and motifs. Some of the most characteristic fiction of the 1930s in England were the antiadventures of Evelyn Waugh and Graham Greene, in which the Empire and the adventurer were both mocked. (The fact that both writers were also anti-Protestant, and Waugh at least was antidemocratic, is no coincidence.) Like other ironical writings, of course, these books' message was ambiguous. Their form subverted their spirit, and Waugh's adventurer, Basil Seal, though stamped with official disapproval, remained the most vivid and impressive figure in his stories. Waugh never accepted, at the deepest level, England's loss of Empire. He invoked the exemplary heroism of T.E. Lawrence and Winston Churchill in *Put Out More Flags,* and Gerald MacBryan is a putative model for Basil Seal.

Books of that kind still came out in England in the 1950s and 1960s, when Anthony Burgess joined the earlier writers. And we have seen even later than that how the adventure form subverts quite passionately radical intentions, in Pontecorvo's film, *Burn.* In this story of a slave revolt on a West Indian sugar island in the nineteenth century, we find a Black Prince, a romantic landscape (photographed with sadomasochistic sensuousness), and a white adventurer, played by Marlon Brando. Brando is bad but complex, the Black Prince is good but simple; naturally the audience's identification is overwhelmingly with the former. The adventure form carries its own imperialist message, despite the individual artist's intentions.

We are still, in the late 1970s, in the postimperial and anti-imperialist age, but fictional modes are changing away from the simple antiadventure that Greene and Waugh wrote. Amongst the significant new writers there are three names to mention, Doris Lessing, Paul Scott, and V. S. Naipaul. They have accepted the loss of the Empire, as an ideal and as a fact, in ways that Waugh and Greene never did. That loss is their starting point. It is no accident that Lessing and Naipaul are both Empire-born, and their postimperialist and anti-imperialist vision of England is a large part of their intellectual dowry. They have come back to England, to London, part of the huge immigrant movement, as the frontiers of Empire curled up and rolled back. But they have a moral advantage over English writers, by having lived on that frontier, so long veiled from English view. It is significant that they include no element of adventure, and in fact Lessing so avoids the Black Prince figure that she has practically no native characters at all.

In *Guerillas, Guerillas,* Naipaul does use elements of adventure, but steeped in an ultra-Conradian irony, an acid which quite neutralizes their mythic potential. This technique gives him as many artistic problems as it gave Conrad, and Naipaul nowadays is most interesting for "what he wants to say," and so for his nonfiction. In *The Loss of El-Dorado* (1969) he says that, in the Trinidad he grew up in, history was an imperialist fairy tale about Columbus, Raleigh, and the Indians—not about slavery but the abolition of slavery. He tells the story of El Dorado, down into the nineteenth century, in Conradian style, as a sardonic grotesque comedy. But Naipaul has gone far beyond ordinary anti-imperialism; in this story he is sympathetic above all to Raleigh, who "might have been king of the Indians."

Raleigh is his hero, as he was Defoe's. Raleigh's book about Guinea, "suggests mines and gold, spaciousness, enamelled forests, a world in which the senses, needs, life itself, can be extended. The book is part of the world's romance" (p. 86). But what is important in Naipaul, always, is not his affirmation or his argument, but the field of his perception, which is truly prophetic. He tells the story of a Robinson Crusoe figure who arrived in Trinidad in 1593, having spent fourteen months on St. Helena; and he comments that thus Trinidad links the two great fantasies of the New World, Crusoe and El Dorado, Crusoe and Cortes.

Naipaul presents himself as bitterly antiromantic, but nowadays he seems rather bitterly romantic; for his skepticism directs itself above all to all *alternatives* to the modern system. In his most recent book, *India: A Wounded Civilization,* he describes his family memories of Indian life as "a trap door into a bottomless past," and warns everyone against following Gandhi down through that trapdoor. The premodern culture is a form of death in life. Naipaul's vision is still Wellsian, as it was in *A House for Mr. Biswas,* but in reading his last books we think less of *Tono-Bungay* than of *Mind at the End of Its Tether.* The Wellsian vision comes close to madness when what it rests on so denies all its hopes, when technology seems destruction, and Defoe's dream becomes a nightmare.

Paul Scott's *Twilight of the Raj* can be seen as an attempt by the English literary mind to return to the point at which it severed connections with Kipling. For it is not only the setting of his novels which remind us of the earlier writer; it is the thematic subject-matter, the nature of authority and the workings of justice, in a huge empire. His characters—unlike most modern-novel characters—are known essentially in their work, and their relation to that work. But this subject-matter is combined with other things, which derive from the anti-Kipling interregnum, and belong to it in mood; notably, the plot element of an unjust punishment of an Indian who enters into social relations with the English, so like the plot of Forster's *Passage to India,* and the post-Proustian form, with its reverbatory action and reflective analysis, so like Powell's *Music of Time.* Scott may be said to attempt, in fiction, what Orwell attempted in the essay, a reconciliation of Kipling's imagination of responsibility (imagining what power and authority feel like) with anti-imperialist and anti-ruling-class feelings. He re-associates the officer class with a moral seriousness which in post-1918 England has been ascribed instead to the non-officer class. This effort at reconciliation and bringing together is perhaps reflected in the massive size of his novel-series. His form is essentially synthetic, and that is his weakness as well as his strength.

Doris Lessing is a more major figure than either of the two men; largely because she has affiliated herself to the great tradition of the serious novel in English, and tried to give it its modern adaptation. She belongs to a group of writers whose hour has just struck, the women born in the empire, who rebelled against its male ethos as well as against its imperialism and made their fiction out of that rebellion. They were usually daughters of fathers who had failed as adventurers, and mothers who had, in consequence, played a masculine role. In this generation there are Jean Rhys and Elspeth Huxley; in an earlier one, Olive Schreiner and (to some extent) Katherine Mansfield. But Lessing's most important novel for our purposes is not one set in the empire at all, but *Memoirs of a Survivor* (1974) because it is such a dramatic reversal of *Robinson Crusoe* in form. There is no sign of that reversal being conscious, but the writer appeals to anti-Defoe sympathies in her audience. The narrator is a middle-aged woman who looks after a child called Emily Cartwright during a future period when London is breaking down. Machines, services, transport, energy sources, all collapse, fail, vanish. Trade returns to the condition of barter. Primitive skills revive but cannibalism does, too. Emily becomes girlfriend to Gerald, who leads a tribe of boys who live on the street; but he is defeated by a gang of savage kids who grew up in the Underground. If we put the story beside Defoe's, we notice a number of reversals: the survivor replaces the entrepreneur; the sense of an ending replaces the sense of a beginning; a woman replaces a man; staying home replaces going abroad; running down replaces winding up; a disintegrating London replaces Moll Flanders' intensifying London; an empire-originating novelist replaces an empire-oriented novelist. No story could more decisively announce the death of adventure, and the message has been accepted without a murmur, as something everyone agrees to.

Conclusion

I HAVE not been arguing that imperialism is foolish, dangerous, and wrong; and I shall not do so now, though that of course is what I believe. I have argued only that imperialism has penetrated the fabric of our culture, and infected our imagination, more deeply than we usually realize. I thought that the field of literature offered particularly telling examples of this infection, because there, at least in serious literature and serious discussion of literature, we usually feel ourselves remote from imperialism and its influence. In fact, I have tried to show it is rather that we are resistant to that influence, and remote only in the willful sense. All of which takes imperialism for granted, and ignores its political character.

But I do want to point to the background of politics, of practical action. We all, like Marx, want to pass from explaining the world to changing it. First I want to point to the likenesses and differences between that serious-literature, high-culture, resistance to Empire, and other kinds; notably Gandhi's and Tolstoy's more powerful, political and religious resistance. The moral realism and moral scruple, the aversion and recoil from imperialism in all its phases, which work at the motor root of serious literature, work at the root of Gandhi's and Tolstoy's teaching too. But in that teaching they are developed gigantically. Literature turns away from that subject matter and that mode of action, to create in effect an alternative world —often alternative in theme and motif, always in psychic substance —though still a world whose colors are the meanings of this one. Gandhi and Tolstoy began to build with bricks made out of the same materials as the Empire-builders themselves use, trying to take up the same psychic and cultural space as the house we actually live in, trying to displace that house.

Their work is something I shall discuss in the next book in this series, but it connects with some things in this one, because it is

338

related to the literary-cultural resistance, though largely by negation. Tolstoy's Christian anarchism derives some of its interest and authority for us from his participation, as writer, soldier, and citizen, in Russian imperialism; and from his later investment in domestic life and the domestic novel, those standard liberal alternatives to active imperialism, which came to seem to him criminally inadequate. Gandhi was never a novelist, and so does not figure in this book at all. But it was a substantial paradox in Gandhi's anti-imperialism that he invoked the greatness of India's past, and the pride of Indians in their culture—which was of course an imperialist culture. He offered to make India great again, and Indians proud. He even urged them to be violent—in order to fit themselves to renounce violence. (It is not clear to me that he is to be condemned for that paradox. Perhaps he is rather to be admired. Just because practically every kind of political energy can be called imperialist to some degree, we should perhaps *demand* some combination of imperialism with its opposite, and reject only the wrong kinds.)

The life examples of Gandhi and Tolstoy, in that book, will suggest, more powerfully than any arguments I could frame, how imperialism can be resisted passionately, splendidly, tragically. But is there anything to be done less extreme than that, but more vigorous than the mere continuance of traditional culture; any practical and contemporary application of the ideas developed historically and theoretically in this book? What I want to suggest in this last chapter is that there is.

Now that the Empire is definitely dismembered, and England no longer has the lion's share (but something more like a jackal's share) in the world system, it must surely be possible for at least Englishmen to look at the adventure tale differently, to get beyond the persistence and resistance described in the last chapter. It must be possible for them to see it in a different relation to literature-as-a-system, and to see that system in a different relation to culture as a whole. In the more purely speculative sense of "to see" that argument has already been made in the previous chapters, as far as scholarship and theory go, and in the practical criticism of Kipling and Conrad. I have tried to build a new imaginative framework for the adventure tale; and that must remain my book's principal and substantive aim. But I had also a further aim, reaching beyond the limits of scholarship, to provide a platform for a new approach to English literature as a subject of

study—as a part of the national education—something to be substituted for the implicit system I was taught by. That substitution
would be what one could do in the field of literature-in-education
towards a larger cultural change. To promise such a change, even
completely to plan it, I must leave to men like Marx, but anyone may
work toward it.

It is not a question of weaning oneself away from any enthusiasm
for imperialism. That job has been done, as far as humanists are
concerned. The system of literature was always in some sense hostile
to adventure, as we have seen, and after 1918, however the form
persisted, there was a general moral resistance to the spirit. What is
needed, odd though it may seem, is almost the reverse; a general
turning toward adventure in ready appreciation, an unprejudiced
curiosity about and respect for its strengths, an acknowledgment of
our heritage. The way to achieve that—as far as institutional means
go—is to teach the adventure novel in schools and colleges.

I must foresee the objection that to teach these books would mean
not teaching others, and that those, for instance the novels of the
Great Tradition, are of higher literary value. That is true, according
to the traditional—and perfectly valid—meaning of the word "literary." But there are other ideas of literature, and culture, and value.
The adventure novel has one large advantage in seriousness, in that
it deals with that body of historical fact which Simone Weil called
"force." In her essay, "The Iliad or the Poem of Force," she said,
"Only he who has measured the dominion of force, and knows how
to respect it, is capable of love and justice." So the vision of love and
justice of those who turn away from force—as the serious novel does
—is ultimately inauthentic. She studied the *Iliad* in the context of
the German conquest of France, and she chose that poem because
it was about that body of historical fact. Well, so are adventure
novels. They measure its dominion only in the mode of romance, but
that is more than the courtship novel does. That makes them a
satisfactory object of study.

It will be obvious that this argument assigns a large scope to the
critic and teacher; since in themselves, or as usually read, adventures
don't make us think seriously about the dominion of force. But the
critic and scholar took a large scope in presenting the domestic novel
to us too—the seriousness we find in those novels is largely, though
legitimately, due to the serious work done by them. They made

discriminations in them and between them, and brought historical contexts to bear upon them, of great intensity and scope. The difference is just that the adventure novel cannot even seem to have the same *sort* of seriousness as the critics'. The two are on different wavelengths. But Defoe and Scott were of course serious men; and if Jane Austen and George Eliot were more so (which I would dispute anyway) this is clearly not a matter of more or less. It is a matter of the adventure novel's spirit—in all its dispositions of seriousness and lightness—seeming hostile to the critics' spirit. And that hostility can be overcome, I believe, if the critics think about literature—think about the adventures—in a new way.

I need hardly say that the domestic novel should continue to be studied, by students who specialize in the history of the novel. When looked at in connection with the history of Empire and the myth of adventure, that novel will be seen to have new aspects of interest. Take for example Jane Austen's use in *Persuasion* of the contemporary culture-hero Frederick Wentworth, that embodiment of English-navy virtues and charms. Jane Austen had two well-loved brothers in the navy, one of whom played a prominent part in the addition of Burma to the Empire, and the naval officer was her model of manliness. As it happens, Fanny Burney also had such a brother; thus we see one typical relation of the courtship novel (its writers *and* its readers) to the adventurous and imperialist half of England. It was the sisters of the heroes of Empire who wrote and read the serious courtship novel; and whatever their judgments on imperialism, they remained on good terms with their brothers and men like them— even good imaginative terms, as *Persuasion* shows. At the same time, they offered in their novels an alternative to the imaginative world of adventure—something independent of that half of England; while later writers offered a reaction against it. So how to define that novel's relation to Empire is a challenging problem. Thus the study of the courtship novel too can receive a new impetus from this connection. But as for its more general appreciation, its strictly cultural function, one can let people find their own ways to it.

But I mustn't claim that the adventures won't be inferior in certain literary ways. That is unfortunate, but the prize is so large that the price is worth paying; and it means mainly that we must alter the way we teach. These books should not be taught as English Literature, but as what we might call British Studies, by analogy with American

Studies. That is, we should give more attention to each book's cultural function, its circumstances of publication, its readership, its career, and the rewards it brought its author, and *his* career. Defoe, Scott, Twain, Kipling, all participated in so much of the history of their times that they may be said to have embodied it. And then it will make sense, once the adventure novel is at the center of our curriculum, to study the whole phenomenon of publishing, and libraries, and the teaching of literature. Though that has often been proposed over the last fifty years, by critics with a sense of political responsibility, it has never made sense when combined with their sense of literary value, which was apotheosized in Jane Austen. *Her* publishing history had nothing to do with the mass market or the macrophenomena of literature. But replace Austen with Scott, and that sociological background leaps into relevance. For me, a great deal leaps into quite personal relevance.

In the course of my reading for this present book, I came across a sentence that struck me very personally, in Parker T. Moon's *Imperialism and World Politics.* In his book's second paragraph, Moon says, "Every man, woman, and child in Great Britain has ten colonial subjects, black, brown, and yellow." That struck me personally because the book was published in 1926, and I was born in 1927. I was born in the back of a London sweetshop, which had never even known a cleaning woman; but still, *really,* I was born one of those suburban sultans—suburban White Rajahs, Wells and Kipling equally my cradle-sponsors. Of course I had no consciousness of having "coloured" subjects, even in my moments of most serious moral or political reflection. In fact, the more serious I got (as I grew up) the less likely I was to arrive at that consciousness. Who, after all, might have taught me—who, in literature, was saying such things? Kipling—that was precisely the legend beneath his cartoon of the white child adored by native servants. But of course I didn't read Kipling; as it happened, I literally didn't read a word of his in my youth, but even if I had, it would have been in a nonserious way. Seriousness meant, in terms of authors, T. S. Eliot, D. H. Lawrence, F. R. Leavis; in terms of ideas, it meant not dwelling on such thoughts as that I had ten subjects, black, brown, and yellow.

There was of course Orwell, who did want me to cultivate what we might call a Kipling-consciousness, given an anti-imperialist slant. But, at least if we think of the novel, *Burmese Days,* rather than of

Orwell's essays, we must say that even Orwell's effective message was that the whole consciousness of Empire was something infected and pustulent, not something to linger on. This was an effect of the system of literature, which deflected the individual novelist's aim. Not to dwell on such thoughts seems to me a fair enough cartoon-description of the message of all serious literature on the matter. What Eliot and Lawrence and Leavis told me was to think about other things—highly specified and deeply interesting things; but to do so meant, in effect, to ignore the Empire. It meant to think about the story of the sisters and their marriages, from *Religious Courtship* to *Women in Love* (not to mention *The Three Sisters*, Richardson, Austen, James, Flaubert, and Tolstoy). And not to think about the brothers and their adventures, from *Captain Singleton* to *Captains Courageous* (not to mention *The Three Musketeers*, Scott, Kingsley, Cooper, and Karl May).

In intellectual discussion we often assume that to ignore anything is a sin of irresponsibility; but in the context of action, ignorance can be a very positive and constructive policy—to turn away from *x* and concentrate on *y* is perhaps the most effective way of enforcing your judgment of the two. What literature told me (obliquely) was "concentrate your mind and your will on this material; identify yourself with it, embody it, become its representative and champion; that other material is for the minds of another type of person, who will be, in certain ways and at certain moments, your enemy." That was an effective and valuable policy, for the culture and for the individual.

Even in secondary school, I got good marks and high praise for knowing what kind of person Emma Woodhouse was, and why Mr. Knightly was the right man for her to marry. I was valued for having that kind of insight, that kind of knowledge; and as I didn't feel valued for much else, I was grateful for that, and still am. And even if my personal situation had been more favorable, I should still have concentrated myself in obedience upon that psychic material. It was my cultural fate. And I don't and couldn't regret anything so central to everything I have been.

But of course ignorance cannot ever be wholly satisfactory. And now, when we have to *see* it as ignorance, its positive message too familiar any longer to dazzle us, we must look around for some alternative. And we find that historical conditions have changed in such a way that an alternative is available. We are now fifty years away from 1927; nearly fifty from 1930, which George Woodcock tells us was the moment when the Empire—though already on the defensive—achieved its greatest geographical spread.

(We should not let such paradoxes bother us. John Strachey says that it was in the 1950s that England finally found the El Dorado it had been four hundred years in search of—the oil in its Middle East sheikhdoms—much more profitable than India or the West Indies had ever been. Nevertheless the Empire was dead by the 1950s, even if the money still rolled in. That money was not the fruit and flowering of English enterprise, as the golden guineas Defoe handled were—though it was more real, more moral, than the North Sea oil money will be. Sterling was meager and ignoble stuff by the 1950s, good only for consolation, because English culture had shrunk.)

The half century of my lifetime has been a period of national shrinkage and crumbling. If we take my parents' lifetime, the change is even more dramatic. Both were born in 1890, and remember the Diamond Jubilee of 1897, when the Empire included forty-seven separate governments, the navy had three hundred and fifty ships (the next biggest, the French, had only ninety-five) and Englishmen were individually bigger and fitter than other Europeans, according to army recruit measurements—and five members of the Cabinet were over six feet tall, the conventional measurement of great size. Nowadays we don't think of ourselves in such terms.

But that shrinkage and crumbling has affected civilization more directly than culture, the dominant strains in Englishness more than the recessive, the men of Empire more than the men of letters. The balance of power between the two has shifted in favor of literature. And so there is no need for the old defensiveness, the old ignorance. There is no longer need to turn away from the Empire, in that purposive way. It no longer has that power to seduce the young, the glamour of that enormous animal vitality. We can look at it directly, because it's only a moon now, not a sun. We can look up into the heavens, and study it, as a burned-out star, or rather a splendid constellation of stars. We can think about the brothers' story and all it means.

Notes

Chapter I

1. In the first book of this series, *The Challenge of the Mahatmas*, I compared *The Tempest* with *Robinson Crusoe*, and argued for the superior interest of the latter from the present point of view. The two stories have a lot in common, as many scholars have noted, but Defoe's version is what I call an energizing myth; its primary effect on readers is to make them want to go out and do likewise; Shakespeare's story is not energizing in that sense. (John Seelye has made a similar argument, in "Some Green Thoughts on a Green Theme," *Tri-Quarterly*, 1972.)

2. Defoe says, in *A Plan of the English Commerce* (1728), page 53, "I am not at all fond of that modern assum'd style, by which some authors think they do us an Honour, when they call the extended scattered Colonies and Dominions of the English or British Nation the English Empire . . . it is no honour, 'tis enough the King has the opulence of an Emperor, without affecting the title." But on page 113, he says, "the English Nation swelled into an Empire of Nations," under the protection of its navy.

3. When the core countries grew rich, their wealth had a peculiarly virtuous character—the whole nation, or so it seemed to those who loved the modern system, grew rich. In *The Chimera* (1720) Defoe says that in England the people are rich, the government poor; in France it is the other way round. *The Chimera* is a pamphlet on the French economy and John Law's attempts to solve its problems. Frenchmen were eager to sell their public bills and buy into Law's Mississippi Company, Defoe tells us, because those bills ran at a discount of 60 to 63 percent. It is because Englishmen would never do that, Defoe says—because our funds have been made sacrosanct by Parliament—that England will always be in debt, but the English will always be wealthy.

4. Voltaire said in 1735 that the French were the whipped cream of Europe, while England excelled in the more masculine virtues. That was an image Defoe himself had used before, but it is more striking to see it adopted by the disobliged party to the comparison. And if France, so close to being a core nation itself, felt herself at such a disadvantage, one can guess how strong feelings were on the periphery and beyond.

5. Iron, as we see as late as Kipling, was the emblematic metal of the modern world system. As late as 1750 England passed an Iron Act, forbidding colonies to build rolling mills, forges, and processing plants of their own. Iron was to belong to the imperial country. But the attachment had a moral and imaginative character, as well as a prudent and acquisitive one. We put our trust in iron—and we took our pleasure in gold.

And hence gilding was a principal form and emblem of art and luxury, in seventeenth-century Europe as a whole. Braudel has some interesting remarks about baroque art (in his *The Mediterranean*) describing it as an art of propaganda for the Counter-Reformation, created from on top by the friars, for whom Rubens, Caracciolo, Ribera, Zurbaran, Murillo merely executed the paintings. That art too was marked by a profusion of gilding, often of iron. Defoe's writing has an aesthetic character almost opposite to baroque painting, and yet his taste in luxury (that is, his society's taste, in which he participated) has something in common with theirs. What that something is, it seems to me, is shown in the gilded iron of gateways and doors and church ornaments, and the various kinds of inlaid wood and precious stones you can associate with that.

6. Mumford suggests also (on page 70 of *Technics and Civilization*) that the mine

Notes

and its industries are the concrete models of the conceptual world built up by seventeenth-century physics. This is doubly interesting because of the influence which that conceptual model had over the rest of science, and, through that means, over European philosophy. One might point to Hobbes, for instance, as a political philosopher strongly influenced by mechanistic physics; and Hobbes was close to Defoe in several points of doctrine.

7. Saltpeter is potassium nitrate, which occurs in long crystals with a salty taste, and is used in pickling and in pyrotechnic explosions. It occurs naturally, often called niter, as an incrustation on the soil of hot countries like India or Iran, where nitrifying bacteria convert sewage into nitrates. This process has been imitated artificially in Europe. Beds are prepared from humus, dung, animal refuse, wood ashes, and lime, exposed to the air, and moistened with urine and stable runnings. A white film will then crystallize on the windboard side of the beds, and can be scraped off.

8. "Art," in the intenser meanings of that term, is not wholly to be identified with the Brahmin caste, any more than imagination is to be identified with conscience, or religion with morality. In Hindu caste terms, it is the sadhu who seems more analogous with the artist (if we stipulate, again, that we mean the most intense and spiritual kind of artist). Sadhus and Brahmins are two different kinds of holy man, often at cross purposes, and yet also parallel in tendency.

9. Genres that Defoe distrusted—in just the way his whole caste distrusted them —include romance and theater. His attitude to romance, which he believed to be a literary equivalent of Roman Catholicism, will be discussed later in the chapter. Theater I will say just a word about here.

In his *Review* for 1709 he has two essays, one dated August 30 and another September 1, against playhouses and plays. He declares them to be always immodest, bawdy, and blasphemous. He blames the gentry for the tendency of the plays, and proposes to pension off all the players, at the rate of the best salary they ever earned while on the stage, and to raise the money by voluntary contribution. It is evident that he counts on the sympathy of rich merchants, because they are hostile to theater.

10. One can illustrate the distrust the merchant caste felt for the aristocracy from the very early history of the East India Company. While the government was negotiating with the merchants about their charter, it suggested that Sir Edward Michelbourne should sail on their expedition. The merchants objected that they had "resolved not to employ any *gentlemen* in their place of charge"; and requested that they might be "allowed to sort their business with men of their own qualitye, lest suspicion of employment of *gentlemen* being taken hold upon by the generalitie, do dryve a number of the adventurers to withdraw their contributions." (Found by James Mill among the "Minutes of a General Court of Adventurers," and quoted by Reginald Reynolds in *White Sahibs in India,* page 3 of the 3rd edition, London, 1946.)

11. There are of course other definitions of adventure. Paul Zweig, in *The Adventurer,* gives one quite unlike mine. He says that adventurers always flee women, and reinvent themselves as men, in order to find wholly male pleasures; he cites Achilles and Patroclus, Quixote and Panza, as pattern examples. While in our own, domestically inclined, culture, the adventurer has been rejected as a "demonic, half-human personage." This began to happen in the sixteenth century, when romance became precious and frivolous. Robinson Crusoe, Zweig says, is not really an adventurer at all. While Conrad's Lord Jim could become a character in serious literature only because he failed to become an adventure hero—because of his cowardice on the *Patna;* it is Jim's stream of compulsive talk, and the secrets behind that stream, which make him an interesting figure for our culture.

My own point of view is different. I think Crusoe *is* an adventure hero, of modernist adventure—the kind appropriate to the modern world system. About the phenomenon of *Lord Jim,* I must of course agree, but I attribute the phenomenon to a different cause; it is not our culture as a whole which is domestic, but our serious literature. And that split within culture, that specialization of seriousness, is a weakness. Serious culture has to live by reaction against civilization, just as conscience has to live by reaction against the appetitive ego, but the first two must not build themselves private worlds which exclude the second two. As Thomas Mann says, the *Bildungsroman* (he is speaking of *The Magic Mountain*) is the sublimation and spiritualization of the novel of adventure. Insofar as serious writers have turned away from the adventure tale, and its subject matter, the frontier and the empire, they have turned away from an essential part of modern history. I think that turning away has weakened the character of their seriousness.

12. In 1695 Defoe became manager-trustee of a public lottery, of which the prize was £50,000, and in which every ticket was called an adventure.

13. Of course this hostility between military adventure and high culture is not exclusively Western. You find the same thing in India; notably, in the literary interpretations of Krishna and Rama, which make them spiritual heroes, and their battles metaphorical. But then India too was something of an empire-and-not-an-empire, its dominant caste Brahmins.

14. Cortes promised his men fame, or glory, and compared them to the Romans. Even Bernal Diaz, the least romantic of the Conquistadors, boasted of his nobility; he said that he had fought in 119 battles, twice as many as Caesar; and that he, like Caesar, wrote in order that his descendants might know of his exploits. And of course this chivalric style fits Prescott's sense—our sense—of the social fate of the Spanish nobility, and their need for military adventures. Wallerstein says it was noticed at the time that the Reconquista had been giving the nobles employment for many years, and that only the attack on North Africa, and then on Mexico, saved them from unemployment.

In other words, the psychological and sociological facts are in accord with the romance Prescott made out of them. Isabella became queen in 1474, Aragon and Castile were united in 1479, the Inquisition was founded in 1480, and the last Moors were driven off the peninsula in 1492. In that adventure of nationalization, the Spanish military caste played a dominant role. (Indeed, a not insignificant part was played by the military caste from other countries, in the form of knights errant, going on adventures.) When that ended, they were at a loss. The discovery of the New World, at just that moment, brought them a less solid glory (America rewarded merchants better than soldiers) but a more solid wealth.

Seville was then the center of the New World trade, and de Madariaga describes it as "teeming with the most glorious pageant that history had ever seen. The incoming caravels, radiant with the light of the New World; captains, pilots, adventurers, monks, soldiers of fortune, Indian caciques, now stark naked, now dressed in exotic attire with golden rings and headdresses of silver and plumes; slaves, men, women, children, shivering and hungry; gold, gold, gold, . . . the discoverer himself, passing through the streets of Seville at the head of one of his carefully organized processions, richly decorated with popinjays, glittering with golden chains and golden masks of strange design and profile; or perhaps, by contrast, clad in the dark brown frock of a penitent monk of St. Francis, or even, in iron chains, as a proud, shipwrecked, sullen prisoner; waves upon waves of excitement; new lands; banks of pearls; islands to be had for the asking."* How well we recognize that excitement, in the speaker, but also in the thing described, even if we are familiar only with English or American literature. That is

*Quoted in Jon White, *Cortes and the Downfall of the Aztec Empire,* pp. 43, 44.

Notes

the excitement of empire, of the frontier, the excitement of the windfall and the boom.

15. We might take Defoe's account, from his *A History of the Principal Discoveries and Improvements in the Several Arts and Sciences*, (1727) page 273. "From hence Ferdinand Cortez, with at most four hundred foot and four hundred horse, landed on the great continent of America, near La Vera Cruz, marched up sixty miles into the country; fought and beat an army of nearly forty thousand Tlascallans, and after that another of one hundred thousand . . . This handful of men, then extending every way, carried on the Spanish conquests for above two thousand leagues . . ."

16. It is especially interesting to note such slogans in the mouths of those to whom those stories meant fear, not pride. Thus the Mogul emperor, Jahangir, is supposed to have said to the English ambassador, Roe, that one Englishman could beat three Portuguese, and one Portuguese three Hindus. And three centuries later a Chinese mandarin, a governor in Manchuria, told the Russian explorer Przhevalsky (the Russian Stanley) that every Russian was worth twelve Chinese in a fight, and hence there could be no war between the two countries.

17. This story would seem to be archetypical in a loose sense; in that it corresponds to a structure of feelings that recur in many times and places. We shall meet it in Russian literature about the conquest of the Caucasus, for instance, by Pushkin and Tolstoy. The story turns up, in fiction but also perhaps in fact, whenever thoughts of conquest stir men's minds. In 1528 in Florida, John Ortiz, a soldier of Narvaez, was rescued by a chief's daughter; and that is John Smith's story about Pocahontas in 1608. Though in his *Generall Historie* of 1624, Smith claimed to have been rescued by lovely ladies in France also, in Turkey, and in Tartary, which sounds more like fiction.

18. The story has many other motifs important in adventure fiction, of which two must be mentioned. One is the hideous temples of human sacrifice, and their grinning idols—which Cortes' men rolled down the temples' innumerable steps to destruction—and the black-garbed priests running to and fro overhead during the battles. That motif is used often by, for instance, Rider Haggard. The other is the Aztec legend of Quetzalcoatl's return from the ocean, and their duty to yield their empire to him—the legend which worked to the Spaniards' advantage. Fair-skinned men with flowing beards were expected, and they came. Primarily, of course, it was the Aztecs who were deceived by this myth, but there may be a case for saying that the Spaniards and Europeans generally were more largely deceived. There is an unmistakable undertone of gratification in the voices of historians who repeat the story; for the Europeans *were*, after all, in that situation, gods.

Take, for instance, Prescott's perfectly realistic glorification of Spanish arms, when Cortes displayed his troops on a beach before an Aztec chieftain. "The bold and rapid movements of the troops, as they went through their military exercises; the apparent ease with which they managed the fiery animals on which they mounted; the glancing of their weapons and the shrill cry of the trumpet, all filled the spectators with astonishment; but when they heard the thunders of the cannon, which Cortes ordered to be fired at the same time, and witnessed the volumes of smoke and flame issuing from these terrible engines . . . " (Vol. I, p. 189) that finished them off. That is always the mythic moment, when we fire the guns, and the natives flee, or fling themselves flat on their faces. But it is none the less factual for being mythical.

We are dealing with several different kinds of myth; the particular superstition about Quetzalcoatl; the more generally mythic attitude of the Aztecs, who, as Octavio Paz says, experienced all historical events as rites, and the Conquest as a last rite; and then—*our* myth—the extraordinarily evocative spectacle of Spaniard confronting Aztec as contemporary Europeans saw it; which is, I think, the way it must be felt by us today, with much the same intensity of feeling, however differently we value it.

When Braudel says that Mexico and Peru were cultures, not civilizations, and that they were immature, their potentials unachieved, their growths unconsolidated, he is seeing what Cortes saw. So is Parry, when he describes their religion as the sad acquiescent faith of the last great Stone Age culture; or White, saying that they were in the grip of a deep cultural psychosis, their over-ritualized religion the expression of deep fears. We cannot escape from the feelings of that myth ourselves.

19. Macaulay's claim that "everyone knows who strangled Atahualpa" (while they don't know about Surajah Dowlah) may sound exaggerated now, but there is some evidence that the stories of Cortes and Pizzaro were circulating in at least eighteenth-century England. For instance, W. H. Dilworth, whose schoolbooks were used extensively, published a *History of the Conquest of Mexico* in 1759, describing it as "for the improvement of the British youth." In the same year he also published *The Conquest of Peru by Pizzarro and Voyages of Adventure in Florida, especially those of de Soto.* And in 1799 John Britton, later a famous antiquary, published *The Enterprising Adventures of Pizarro.*

20. The cavalry was, in most European armies, dominated by the aristocratic caste, and so out of sympathy with modernist ideology—was, in fact, still chivalric. Of course, that caste supplied the officers to the infantry too. But the latter was part of the modern system, its self-image shaped by that ideology and by its iron, almost mechanical, discipline. Though that was combined, in great soldiers, with a bold inventiveness, independence, and indiscipline; qualities often linked to the aristocratic temperament. One sees that combination at work in the great triumphs of modernist armies like Clive's and Cortes's.

When those two virtues, discipline and indiscipline, were distributed between two modern system opponents, the issue became uncertain. When the rock-like British infantry met sharp-shooters with individual initiative, they were often defeated, as in the American War of Independence, and the Boer War. But as long as a British army (or that of any other European power) faced an enemy from outside the system, they could display amazing courage, devotion, and energy, and defeat immensely larger forces.

Of course, if the enemy did not belong to the modern system, he almost certainly was inferior in military technology. But the victories of the Europeans are not all to be attributed to that technology; and some of the power that technology had seems to have been spiritual. See for instance the paltry number and quality of muskets Cortes took with him, and the immense effect he made with them.

It is interesting to reflect on the very different success which England and Spain met with, when fighting armies belonging to the core states of the modern system. Soon after Cortes's fabulous success against Mexico, Spain struggled in vain against the Dutch provinces for many years, though there she had great advantages in numbers of troops and supplies. And just after Clive's fabulous success against India, England struggled in vain to subdue her American colonies, with again great advantages in numbers and equipment; instead of, as in India, great disadvantages. These differences, whether or not formulated and focused by the mind, worked powerfully on the imagination of all concerned.

21. His purpose is "to consider Britain's relation to the world now that her empire is being dissolved." He calls Clive in India a better example of what empire in general has been than Cortes in Mexico, "because the work of the latter was lost." In any case, the Spanish were antimercantile in style, and would have led the world back to the servile imperialism of antiquity. (Venice and Portugal first established a mercantile imperialism—and out of that grew the capitalist imperialism of England.)

349

Notes

Chapter II

1. The event that the modern system in England recognized as epic, as its foundation myth, like Marathon for Athens or the Great Trek for the Boers, was the defeat of the Armada—the defeat of Catholic Imperial Spain—in 1588. And it is perhaps significant that it was a sea event. Sea fights, especially defensive ones, are easier for nonempires to celebrate than territorial aggressions, like Henry V's invasion of France. (Though Raleigh's report on the Armada, to be found in Hakluyt's *Voyages*, will remind us how bloodthirsty and chauvinist defensive sea fights can be.) This is the story that was being retold by Kingsley and Kipling right up to the twentieth century. Shakespeare, in this as in so many matters, was not centrally of the tradition.

It is worth noting that Shakespeare, and for that matter Marlowe, had neither knights nor merchants among his main characters. He represents neither the military nor the merchant castes. Sidney and Raleigh styled themselves as knights, but in a rather fanciful way; while the sea dogs of Devon, Drake, Hawkins, Grenville, etc., were powerful incarnations of a cross between the two castes. But Elizabethan literature did not respond to that, or only in an idealizing and romanticizing way.

2. J. W. Hunt, in *Forms of Glory*, analyzes the *Aeneid* pictorially, finding three panels in it, each consisting of four books. The first panel, predominantly dark in color, deals with Dido and the fall of Troy. The second, predominantly bright, describes games and troop reviews, visions of Roman glory, and of Augustus. And the third is again about Troy, and the horrors of war. As a whole, therefore, the *Aeneid* brings together conflicting feelings about Rome and empire, to reconcile them in a steadier version.

3. *Henry V* is the climax of Shakespeare's history plays, and there is some reason to suppose that most Elizabethan writers saw that king's story in epic terms. Samuel Daniel, in his poem, *Civil War*, written a few years before Shakespeare's play, says,

> O what eternal matter here is found
> Whence new immortal Iliads might proceed.

And Raleigh said of the English kings, "None of them went to work like a Conquerour, save only King Henry the fifth."

Moreover the play is a sequence of historical tableaux, with a Chorus, prologues, and an epilogue. And it clearly sets out to do what Sidney said epic poetry should do: arouse admiration, inflame the mind, encourage imitation. (It was probably first performed in 1599, while Essex was in Ireland, establishing British empire there.) In other words, this is Shakespeare's structurally imperialist work, as its content confirms.

The play is full of ideas which recur in imperial writing through the centuries to follow. For instance, in Act I, Scene 2, when Ely and Canterbury speak, Ely says that

> . . . my thrice-puissant liege
> Is in the very May-morn of his youth,
> Ripe for exploits and mighty enterprises.

That celebration of the powers of young men runs all through the adventure tales, from Defoe to Kipling. And Canterbury talks of a beehive as a model for the state;

> The singing masons building roofs of gold,
> The civil citizens kneading up the honey, . . .

You will find the same language, as well as the same idea of civilized greatness, in Kipling's "The Mother-Hive."

And the talk about English manliness, especially in war, is very similar to the talk we shall meet in Defoe. The French are made to say that the English are bastards of the Normans, engendered upon a wild and savage stock: their climate is foggy, raw, and dull, and so are they; but this all redounds to their credit. They have no imagination, but great courage. Henry says that when his troops were in health, "I thought upon one pair of English legs, Did march three Frenchmen." But he must not brag; the English style is plain in everything, as we see in his wooing of the French princess. The play's endorsement of war and militarism is unequivocal. In his speech in Act III, Scene 1, Henry says,

> But when the blast of war sounds in our ears,
> Then imitate the action of the tiger;
> Stiffen the sinews, summon up the blood,
> Disguise fair nature with hard-favoured rage . . .
> Now set the teeth and stretch the nostril wide,
> Hold hard the breath and bend up every spirit
> To his full height. . . .

It is no doubt this militarism and the equally unequivocal patriotism which account for the unpopularity of the history plays with men of letters. The Elizabethan audiences were enthusiastic about them, but when Shakespeare's literary reputation revived (among men of letters) at the end of the seventeenth century, the history plays were neglected. It is true that in modern times they have been played more often, but the interest in them has been of a political theory, or history-of-ideas, kind. From a literary-moral point of view they are still largely deplored. Tillyard and Mark Van Doren complain of *Henry V*'s inferiority, and Traversi talks of its pessimism and growing coldness.

4. An interesting example of another social order and the literary form that corresponded to it, is given in Aldous Huxley's *Grey Eminence*. This is the churchman's crusade poem; alternative to both the merchants' adventure and the knights' romance, but closer to the latter. Huxley is talking about Père Joseph, the adviser to Cardinal Richelieu, who in fact tried to launch a real crusade, and more than once; in 1615 with the Duc de Nevers at its head, and later with Wallenstein. His literary form was the epic poem in Latin hexameters. He composed a *Turciad* in 4,637 lines, which was praised by Pope Urban VIII as a Christian Aeneid, but apparently only two copies were ever printed. That is a very poor record to compare with the innumerable editions of *Robinson Crusoe*, and clearly Père Joseph backed the losing horse, literarily and culturally speaking. The Roman Catholic Church, and Latin hexameter poems, were both doomed to defeat by the modern world system. But it is worth remembering that in terms of immediate political effectiveness, he was one of the most powerful men in Europe in his lifetime—which was in the same century as Defoe's. Anyway, Huxley says, "In an age when there were no Westerns or detective stories, the most exciting reading matter an imaginative boy could get hold of was probably to be found in the chronicles of the crusades. To a child of François du Tremblay's times [Père Joseph's natal name was du Tremblay], the infidels occupied the place reserved in the minds of a more recent generation of schoolboys for the Indians. Most men, as they grew up, forgot about the infidels, just as they now forget about the Redskins. Not so François du Tremblay" (page 134).

Huxley gives us a very long cultural perspective there. For by the seventeenth century the Crusades were very old and almost purely legendary, just as the Redskins were by Huxley's time; Redskin stories began in Defoe's time (he was the originator of the twin genre, pirate stories); thus we now stand in the same relation to those stories, so long the energizing myth of the modern system, as Père Joseph stood to the Crusade stories which energized the medieval system. He wrote a new Crusade-poem, and tried to start a new Crusade. I think it more appropriate, as a response to our

Notes

situation, to try to reconsider the dying genre, rather than to revitalize it. But of course I'm a literary critic, not a practical statesman like Père Joseph, who had power at his disposal.

5. I am not suggesting that only, or mainly, knights read these romances; nor that other social orders simply adored or even admired knighthood and chivalry. No doubt much of their reading was purely literary or purely escapist. And the same could be said of the other half of my analogy, the adventure tales that served the merchant caste. The nonmerchant readers did not literally sit dreaming that they were merchants. What seems to be true, in both cases, is that a considerable body of literature was written, tied to one social order, and was read by something like a general reading public. Then what seems probable, what one must assume, is that that reading carried with it something like a general imaginative fealty to, in the one case chivalry, in the other mercantilism, even when the readers' conscious thinking was highly critical of that idea.

6. Lévi-Strauss's account of the Caduveo people in *Tristes Tropiques* suggests that this form of romance, and its connection with a military caste, is not limited to European culture. The Caduveo nobles had paintings stenciled on to their bodies, like our playing cards, and Lévi-Strauss calls them so many Davids, Caesars, Alexanders, and Charlemagnes. They were "like characters in some romance of chivalry, absorbed in their cruel games of prestige and domination . . ." (page 193). The girls among them sometimes followed a warrior, as his page or as his mistress. The women often aborted or killed their children, and adopted others. Extravagantly "noble" in their attitude to life, he says, they produced nothing, relying on others for their upkeep, and living out ideas of courage and magnanimity.

7. Mather's life of Phips is cited by Sacvan Bercovitch in *The Puritan Origins of the American Self,* as deserving to win for Mather the title of "father of the American success story." I give a hint of Phips's story in the next chapter. He was the first governor of Massachusetts under the new Charter of 1692.

8. Protestantism was certainly a very important value to Defoe, and though he inclined to minimize sectarian differences between Anglican and Dissenter, or between Presbyterian and Congregationalist, he had no such feelings about the differences between Protestant and Catholic. Catholicism stood to him for superstition, tyranny, inauthenticity, in religion; and it was inseparable from tyranny, licentiousness, laziness, in the rest of life. And that feeling remained surprisingly strong and constant throughout the life-span of the modern system, at least among its proponents. To take a rather random instance, J. R. Seeley, the most dispassionate and scholarly of imperialists, called the papacy "the burning heart of all human discord," and cherished a life-long passion for Milton as "the Protestant poet"—this in the late nineteenth century. (Seeley's father brought out a pamphlet, "The Pope an Impostor," in 1850, which went into ten editions.) Seeley's was a Broad Church Protestantism, following Coleridge and Thomas Arnold, though more ethical and naturalistic than theirs; it would have been quite congenial to Defoe. (See John Gross's introduction to Seeley's *The Expansion of England.*)

9. This book was quite successful. It had eight editions in five years, and was reprinted many times in the eighteenth and nineteenth centuries, in America as well as England. It was used in the education of the children of George I (Paul Dottin, *The Life and Strange and Surprising Adventures of Daniel Defoe*).

10. Thus one of Hannah More's most famous *Cheap Repository Tracts* was "The Two Shoemakers," about two apprentices, good James Stock and bad John Brown. The *Cheap Repository Tracts,* which contained each a story, a sermon, and some short poems, were written for the sunday schools begun in the 1790s by Robert Raikes.

Three a month were issued between 1792 and 1795, and they sold in tens of thousands. Then the stories were collected and published separately. The most famous was "The Shepherd of Salisbury Plain," about a shepherd with a crippled wife and five children, all of whom accept their misfortunes with exemplary patience. The religious moral had some antirevolutionary bearing, and another tract by More was said at the time to have saved England from a French revolution. Both the stories I summarized are to be found in *Religious Courtship;* which shows again how powerful, how long-lasting, were the currents of thought with which Defoe identified himself. I am tracing only the patterns of one subgenre of his fiction; but the wide sweep of his work as a whole is also relevant.

11. Lewis Feuer's book on the history of science *(The Scientific Intellectual)* in which he argues that science derived from the Epicurean rather than the Puritan tradition of thought, assembles the facts of what I have called the antithesis. The Epicurean tradition clearly *was* very important; and clearly *did* constitute an opposite to Puritanism; and yet out of that opposition between the two emerged a cooperation —science was born, and born bearing the traits of both parents.

12. Edmund S. Morgan, in *The Puritan Family* (New York, 1966) says that the Puritan preachers' favorite figure of speech, for describing God's relation to man and His church—the closest comparison they could find—was always marriage. While Levin L. Schücking, in *The Puritan Family* (1970), reminds us that domestic asceticism was not something new; that eighteenth-century family piety was very close to that prescribed by Richard Baxter in the seventeenth century, and even to the sobriety prescribed by Thomas Brecon (1512–1567). The latter says, in his Catechism of 1560, "to live soberly, should seem to be so purely, discretely, modestly, temperately, and sagely to institute our life, that our consciousness should never accuse us of any evil but testify with us, that we live and do all things godly." (Quoted in Schücking, p. 7.) New Year resolutions were entered into family Bibles, and then re-examined at the year's end. Women were often portrayed as the apostles of gentleness, and later of culture, to men. Mercy in *Pilgrim's Progress*, Schücking suggests, was a first sketch for Pamela.

Schücking says that Elizabethan Puritans were unlike the Baptist communists (whom Troeltsch mistakenly took to be the typical sectaries of that time) just in the importance they gave to the family. Elizabeth did not supply enough preachers to the Anglican churches, and from the 1560s on the conventicles were suppressed, so that Puritans had to make the family the Christian temple. Children were taught by their parents; taught to despise all riches and display, and all idleness and vanity, and all pride and boastfulness. (One recalls Clarissa's motto, "Rather useful than glaring," and the contrast between her and Lovelace in this regard.) Baxter said in *Christian Doctrine* "So that it is an evident truth, that most of the mischiefs that now infest or seize upon mankind throughout the earth, consist in, or are caused by, the disorders or ill-governedness of families." (Quoted in Schücking, p. 56.) And in the eighteenth century this Puritan tradition developed into something more feminist. Fordyce's 1766 *Sermons to Young Women* assigned women the work of missionaries to men, working especially in culture and literature. Goldsmith, in his 1767 *Poems for Young Ladies,* said he had included "such pieces as innocence can read without a blush." And Bowdler brought out his *Family Shakespeare* in 1807. The movement apparently went hand in hand with a feminizing and genteelizing of culture.

13. A passage by Larzer Ziff will explain how Puritanism expressed itself expansively, in colonization and generally on a national and international scale. "A culture of expansion, distrustful of volume as mere resistance, Puritanism asserts a remarkable capacity to reduce the abstract meanings of volume to the precisions of the word and

Notes

to reduce the physical existence of the dimension of space—be it represented by an alien psyche, a wilderness, or outer space itself—to the two-dimensional plane of its technology. Created in response to the expansion of population, trade, and self-mastery in the post-medieval world, it suited the new world superlatively well and will retain its suitability, it is to be presumed, until such time as expansion itself no longer suffices and stasis must be contemplated." (*Puritanism in America*, p. 311.) This shows us the extrovert counterpart to that intense measurement of the minutiae of class, sex, and decorum, which we find in the Puritan novels.

14. Watts was suckled on the steps of a jail in which his father was imprisoned, and at his dissenting Academy heard Cromwell's former chaplain, John Howe, preach. He was in touch with the old Puritanism, and was essentially a man of religion. At the same time, his own career was as chaplain to Sir Thomas Abney, a rich merchant who became lord mayor of London, and one of his paraphrases of the Psalms appeared in *The Spectator.* So he was also a man of the eighteenth century and a man of letters. He is at his most interesting from our point of view when he unites the two identities; in certain hymn stanzas which we can apply to Clarissa, and which help us to understand the spiritual and even religious aura which still clung to stories like hers.

> On earth the usurpers reign,
> Exert their baneful power;
> O'er the poor fallen souls of men
> They tyrannize their hour.
>
> Into a world of ruffians sent,
> I walk on hostile ground;
> While human bears on slaughter bent
> And ravening wolves surround.

15. I have limited myself to the themes of the domestic novel, but more formal characteristics could be related to this set of ideas, if there were space enough. Ian Watt has pointed out, in *The Rise of The Novel,* that Defoe and Richardson were the first great writers to present plots not taken from the literary-mythical heritage; and has explained the implications, that Nature was not completed and unchanging. Their novels implied a growing, changing, progressive universe.

Defoe disapproved of epic, and classical literature, and indeed of myth. Homer, he said, had sung "the Wars of the Greeks . . . from a Reality, into a meer Fiction." (Watt, p. 242.) While Richardson spoke of "the fierce, fighting Iliad," and its responsibility for the militarism of his own times. Indeed, all Watt has to say about formal realism is relevant to this discussion.

I will restrict myself to his quotation from Mrs. Barbauld that Richardson has "the accuracy of finish of a Dutch painter," with the concomitant contrast that Reynolds preferred the great and general ideas of Italian painting to the "literal truth and . . . minute exactness in the detail of nature modified by accident" of the Dutch. This is exactly like the contrast between Richardson and Fielding in serious fiction, and it has quite large implications for the taste that preferred one or the other. Let me point out also that the Dutchness of those Dutch paintings is not irrelevant. Those paintings are the great expression of the modern world system in artistic terms by the Dutch of that period. They correspond to the English novels (which came a little later, just as English supremacy did) and it is worth noting that these painters were not patronized by the rich Dutch of their own time (who preferred classicizing French art), just as the ruling class of England originally despised the novels of Defoe and Richardson.

16. Samuel Smiles, in *Self-Help,* page 300, speaks of Agar's perfect prayer, "Give

me neither poverty nor riches; feed me with food convenient for me," and connects
this with the virtue of living in the middle station, unobserved, not to be seen of men.
Clarissa was the heroine of the modern system's persistent moral scheme.
While Lovelace was brought up by his mother to "bear no control." His tutors were
told he must not know what contradiction or disappointment were. He naturally grew
up very wild and gay; "a young man." He is often described as young, unbroken, his
passions unsubdued. He quotes Milton's Satan, and compares himself. And his friends
are young men with aristocratic names—Belford, Belton, Tourville, Mawbray. Richardson saw the world in terms of the Puritan drama.
17. Smiles says, in *Self-Help*, p. 233, that Wellington was a far greater man than
Napoleon because "Napoleon's aim was Glory; Wellington's watchword, like Nelson's,
was 'Duty'. The former word, it is said, does not occur once in his despatches; the latter
often, but never accompanied by any high-sounding profession."

Chapter III

1. It was around 1680, just as Defoe was coming of age, that the modern business
world was born, J. Sutherland tells us in his *Defoe* (New York, 1958). Fortunes were
made overnight on the 'Change which would have taken forty years of prudent trading
and hoarding. Tradesmen set up coaches, and entertained with silver plate and foot-
men. Stockjobbing, lotteries, and speculation began; coffee houses, the penny post, and
newspapers which appeared two or three times a week, helped all this. Imports rose
from seven millions' worth in 1662 to eleven and a half millions' worth in 1688. Defoe
was so much a part of all this that Sutherland speculates he may have aimed, in the
early part of his life, at becoming lord mayor of London.
2. In *Memoirs of a Cavalier*, the narrator speaks of "the Blackness of those Days,
when Law and Justice was under the Feet of Power; the Army ruled the Parliament,
the private Officers their Generals, the common soldiers their Officers, and Confusion
was in every Part of the Government." (p. 270 of the edition by James Boulton.)
3. It is interesting to study how the Dutch gradually lost their modern system
energy in proportion as they lost their primacy within that system to England. This
is even more striking in the Dutch abroad than in those who remained at home.
Hannah Arendt points out in *Origins of Totalitarianism* that the Boers were the first
Europeans to lose their pride in living in a world created and fabricated by man. "They
agreed to vegetate on essentially the same level as the black tribes . . ." (p. 194). They
employed large numbers of slaves, but their economy was unprogressive, and they
hated the *Uitlanders* above all because they would make South Africa a productive
economy. They had retreated from a thrifty and intensive cultivation to become
herdsmen and hunters. Indeed, there is a retreat—though not in the same direction
—in the New York Dutch whom Cooper depicts in his Littlepage novels.

Appendix to "Defoe and His England"

4. England in Defoe's day, and London more strikingly than any other part, was
newly prosperous. Braudel says that London in 1700 supported 100,000 people out of
trade, but another 100,000 lived off the work done by and for administrative officers,
and for the nobility and gentry who settled around the government.

Notes

It was during these years that such expressions as "Al at Lloyds" became current, lasting in most European languages for two hundred and fifty years, and a clue to much. The firm of Lloyds were underwriters (named after Ned Lloyd's coffee house, established under Charles II) who examined and classified ships and cargoes, and insured them. There was also a growing sector of investors, grouped around the Stock Exchange, while at the other end of the social scale, the East End was already artisan, marine, and semicriminal in its population.

Another clue to that period in England is given by Keynes in his *Treatise On Money* (1930) when he wonders how much Elizabethan England owed to Francis Drake, and Augustan England owed to William Phips. Both these men found and brought to England frontier windfalls once removed. Drake's *Golden Hind* returned from a voyage in 1580 with between £300,000 and £1,500,000, a return to his financial promoters of 4700 percent on their investments, Webb calculates. Queen Elizabeth paid off England's foreign debts with her share, and had enough left over to invest £42,000 in the Levant Company; the profits from which company in turn launched the East India Company. Keynes says that that booty was "the foundation and origin of British Foreign Investment." While William Phips found sunken Spanish treasure off Hispaniola a hundred years later that brought to his stockholders a return of 10,000 percent and much strengthened William III's position on the throne. The boom which began with that windfall ended only with the establishment of the Bank of England, of the Stock Exchange in 1694, and in the following year, the reform of the currency by Locke and Newton.

Among the principal founders of the bank was William Paterson, a friend and associate of Defoe, who was also the parent of the Darien company, an important episode in the history of capitalism and also that in of the Union of Scotland and England. In 1695 Paterson convinced the Scots parliament to launch a company to colonize and trade on the Isthmus of Darien, near Panama, in the general area of El Dorado. The first expedition sailed in 1698, but the company met with determined obstruction by English rivals as well as by Spanish, and so failed, with much loss of life and also of the investments of merchants at home. This caused much bitterness in Scotland. The union was, or included, an act of reparation by England, financially; it set up an equivalent fund of nearly £400,000, of which over half went to pay Darien investors, and the rest went to pay off the Scots' national debt. The failure of Darien also convinced Scottish investors that they could only get their share of trading profits from such schemes by merging Scotland with England. Thus the union was entered into in part as a means to joint mercantile imperialism. There are many such anecdotes, each embodying another aspect of the complex subject, and in most of them Defoe could be named.

We could in fact take our sense of Defoe's England from his own works; and first of all from his *Whole Tour of the Island of Great Britain*, published 1724–1726. As Pat Rogers says in his introduction to the Penguin edition, this is a deeply imaginative book, employing all Defoe's skills as chronicler, polemicist, and creative writer, as well as encyclopaedist. Rogers quotes Christopher Morris saying of this period, "The English were becoming highly immodest about their own political discoveries, their own great men or 'worthies', their own architecture or landscape, and, above all, their own prosperity." Defoe was very well suited to celebrate this new prosperity, and he worked out a literary formula (the tour of the country) which proved highly successful, for other writers as well as for himself. It was the nearest thing to a British epic; verse epics were projected in this period, with titles like *The Brutiad* and *Boadicea*, to rival Virgil or at least Tasso, and some were even written; but more successful was the crop of topographical and historical works, by Camden, Leland, and Drayton, among

356

others. And of these, Defoe's *Tour* was the flowering. Defoe had found the right form, and later writers imitated him.

This was a genre more congenial than epic to the merchant caste, being factual not romantic, and commercial not military. And this specimen, the most successful of the genus, went through nine editions, of which the last appeared in 1779. Samuel Richardson was the publisher of the second and third, and the editor of at least the third. Walter Scott used one of them in writing *Rob Roy*.

In the Preface to Volume I, Defoe says, "This [England] is the most flourishing and opulent country in the world . . ." He exults in the new houses—"and gentlemen's houses"—to be seen everywhere. He gives much detail about the docks and gunyard at Woolwich, and about Rochester, the navy's chief arsenal. He describes with imaginative zest the warehouses and storehouses; "the rope-walk for making cables, and the forges for anchors and other iron-work, bear a proportion to the rest; as also a wet-dock for keeping masts, and yards of the greatest size, where they lye sunk in the water to preserve them, the boat-yard, the anchor-yard . . . the sails, the rigging, ammunition, guns, great and small-shot . . ." (p. 105). His mere lists of material wealth are full of excitement.

Defoe's imagination was vivid but unromantic. When he got to Land's End, he rode his horse into the water, to feel the moment when England stopped; and described the rocks of Cornwall as being cemented together by the ores they contained, to make England strong against the waves. This is his kind of imagination. But he says, in Letter 3, "I shall sing you no songs here of the river Thames in the first person of a water-nymph, a goddess, (and I know not what) according to the humour of the ancient poets. . . . but I shall speak of the river as occasion presents, as it is really made glorious by the splendour of its shores, gilded with noble palaces, strong fortifications, large hospitals, and publick buildings; with the greatest bridge, and the greatest city in the world, made famous by the opulence of its merchants, the encrease and extensiveness of its commerce; its invincible navies, and by the innumerable fleets of ships sailing upon it, to and from all parts of the world" (p. 173). This, he says, will be a "more masculine" manner of speaking. But full of glee, nevertheless.

There is always something new, in England, he exclaims. "New foundations are always laying, new buildings always raising, highways repairing . . . so that as long as England is a trading, improving nation, no perfect description . . . can be given." And in London, "New squares, and new streets rising up every day to such a prodigy of buildings, that nothing in the world does, or ever did, equal it, except old Rome in Trajan's time" (p. 332). (At such moments one sees that Defoe, not Pope, was the true Augustan; and one of his last pamphlets was about London and entitled *Augusta Triumphans*.) "Some have said that there is not less than 100 million of stock transferred backwards or forwards from one hand to another every year."

At the same time he deplores the assemblies, newly in fashion, because they always end in intrigue. In Vol. II, page 231, he says, "They are a plan laid for the ruin of the nation's morals, and which, in time, threaten us with too much success that way." For Defoe, though deeply excited about progress, was full of qualms about luxury. He wanted England to put its trust in iron, not gold (though of course she, and he, would always *take* the latter, too).

In the section on Scotland, he says, "I hope it is no reflection upon Scotland to say they are where we were, I mean as to the improvement of their country and commerce; and they may be where we are" (Vol. II, p. 280). If stock and implements are supplied to the Scots, and if their husbandry is changed, all that is needed is that they stay home and work. But work means enterprise, capitalist enterprise, as emerges in this comment. "I believe they are very good Christians at Kirkenby, for they are in the very letter of it, they obey the text, and are contented with such things as they have. They have all the materials for trade, but no genius to it; all the opportunities for trade, but no inclination to it. In a word, they have no notion of being rich and populous, and thriving by commerce . . . it is to me the wonder of all the towns of North Britain . . . they have the Indies at their door, and will not dip into the wealth of them; a gold mine at their door, and will not dig it" (Vol. II, p. 323). It's a measure of the distance between the two nations in development that Defoe has to say he does not use "merchant" in the Scots sense, to mean a shopkeeper, but in the English sense, "merchant-adventurers who trade to foreign parts, and employ a considerable number of ships" (Vol. II, p. 315).

A Plan of the English Commerce (1728) has an interesting Preface, in which Defoe justifies his book by an imaginative description of the web of commerce as a whole. "The clothier sorts his Wool, dyes and mixes the Colours; the Comb, the Card, the Wheel, the Loom, are all set on Work by his Direction, and he is call'd a Master of his Art, and he is so; but ask him where his Cloths are sold, by whom bought, to what Part of the World they are shift, and who are the last Consumers of them, he knows nothing of the Matter. . . ." (p. vii). This is the imagination of the new society, excited to the point of affirming itself in heraldic images. "The Commerce of the World, especially as it is now carried on, is an unbounded Ocean of Business; Trackless and unknown, like the Seas it is managed upon; the Merchant is no more to be followed in his Adventures, than a Maze or Labyrinth is to be trac'd out without a Clue" (p. ix).

For Defoe, English commerce was primarily the cloth industry, as we shall see, and it is no accident that this was the first trade to be industrialized in England. It is while exploring Defoe's world that the modern reader first becomes aware of his own native landscape, of the factories missing from the England of Shakespeare and Chaucer, and of the driving force of change and progress within Defoe's landscape.

Defoe often urged his countrymen on to imperial and colonial efforts. "There are New Countries, and new Nations, who may be so planted, so improved, and the People so managed, as to create a new Commerce; and millions of people shall call for our Manufacture, who never called for it before" (p. xi). Despised Portugal is taking advantage of this. Five times the amount of European goods that used to go to Portugal's colonies abroad, thirty years ago, are now sent there. But England's trading genius and adventuring temper needs to be revived. We have very few subjects in America, to buy our goods, while "the decayed and indolent Portuguese and Spaniards have many."

Defoe had a very strong sense of national identities, following the cultural plan of the modern world system. Thus the Portuguese (on the semiperiphery now) are decayed and indolent, while the Turks (always outside the system) are enemies to trade, and discourage industry and improvement, and even dispeople the world. "The Mahometans abhor Business and Labour, and despise Industry, and they starve accordingly." And again, "View their condition; they are miserably poor . . . idle, indolent, and starving, . . . and all for want of Trade" (p. 11). And in Russia (on the periphery) workmen hack up a whole tree to get a plank, and sell it no dearer than do Swedes who, by means of saws, get three or four planks from a tree.

At the center of the system, in England, people are at their most shrewd and solid and vigorous. English workmen do more work, and eat and drink more than others. Our workmen's work is strong and substantial in everything they do. But this is not genetic but ethical racism. Defoe says England was not always a center of trade. It had made itself so by effort.

This idea is connected with the gospel of work, the work ethic. ". . . the diligent trading manufacturing World work chearfully, live comfortably. . . . Whereas the unemploy'd World groan out their Souls in Anguish and Sorrow . . . and sink under the weight of their Idleness and Sloth . . ." (p. 29). And this gospel derives from and applies to specifically modern conditions. Defoe tells us that in the past people were divided into Master and Servant, or Lord and Vassal; but now it is Landlord and Tenant—and even in war the long purse is now more effective than the long sword. The merchant caste has triumphed over the military.

England only came to life under those commercial princes, the Tudors. Henry VII set us to manufacture our own wool. Then Elizabeth, "that glorious princess," encouraged her navigators to range the seas "searching the Globe for discoveries, planting Colonies, and settling Factories in all Parts of the World" (p. 99). She "opened all these Doors, she sent out all these adventurers, she planted all those Colonies" (p. 101). Hence developed that English sturdiness, which Defoe describes in terms quite like Shakespeare's in *Henry V.* But the stress on English cloth is Defoe's special contribution, and he makes rich metaphorical use of it.

French cloths look good and deceive the inexperienced buyer, but they lack substance, compared with ours. "But when they came to wear, the consumer presently found the advantage; as the English cloth weighed 20–30–40 lb. a bale more than the French at the scale; so, in the wearing, there was no comparison; the French wore like drugget, rough and woolly; the English like velvet, smooth and solid; the French wore nappy and coarse; the English wore soft and fine; the French wore into rags, and wore out; the English wore firm and lasting, even to the thread; . . ." (*Compleat English Tradesman*, Vol. II, p. 100). Other nations also characterize themselves by their textiles, including the world beyond the modern system. Silks and muslins, for instance, are characteristic of India; exquisite but fragile, luxurious and a touch immoral, as befits an eastern empire. While native tribes show how primitive they are by not weaving at all, but wearing bark or palm-leaf garments.

Thus English broadcloth *is* English character; and the French cloths are an example of the "superficial performances of that nation . . . the real intrinsic Worth of the Goods is found in the English cloths, and in them only. The Czar, the Grand Seignor, the Sophy, and the Mogul, all wear English cloth . . . not too thin for the frozen Laplander, nor too thick for the scorch'd Americans, not too gay for the Men, not too grave for the Ladies."*

This master metaphor, of cloths, weaving, and moral substance, runs all through Defoe. Peter Earle quotes a passage, written in 1713, in which he says the French have "very bright and quick fancy in contriving fashions, figures, and fancies." (Earle, *The World of Defoe*, p. 91.) They are said to be, "whip't cream, froth and surface." Their lack of real prosperity is seen in the wooden shoes they wear. (The English wear leather shoes, and leather is morally like cloth, flexible but durable, expensive but sober.) And the Spanish are proud, the Italians licentious, the Portuguese cringing—all sins against the modern system ethic.

The philosophy of history this leads to is unstable in its evaluation of national "greatness"—of empire. Defoe often compared England with Rome, but his approval of a similarity between them varied. In the *Tour* he hoped that the roads of England might be restored to the perfection they had when the Romans ruled this island. But he also saw a likeness between Rome and France, and that was something he disapproved.

*It is perhaps of interest that in an English pamphlet of 1650, it was said that Dutch cloths will not fail color or be threadbare in seven years' wearing, while the English dressed and dyed their cloth basely (W. J. Webb, p. 134). By Defoe's time, the English were more sure of themselves.

Notes

In contemporary Europe, France and Versailles were Defoe's measure of magnificence, and he quite often invoked it to praise England. But he always condemned the source of that sort of magnificence; Louis XIV was "the august tyrant," and Defoe's hero was Marlborough, our man against Louis. He came to see Rome and France as both military countries—hence empires—and then he saw England as blessedly unlike both.

In *History of the Principal Discoveries, etc.* (1727) Defoe devotes a lot of attention to Rome's enemy, Carthage, and to the Carthaginians' subtlety of wit, and their address in commerce, business, and colonization, which was like the English. Chapter VII is entitled, "Of the encrease of commerce and navigation under the Carthaginian empire, and the check given to useful discoveries, by the success of the Romans against them. Also some probable account, of the first peopling of America by the Carthaginians." They are described as "a people wholly addicted to a search after new discoveries, and boldly venturing into all parts of the world for them" (p. 76). The Romans, on the other hand, were a nation inspired with glory of arms, and puffed up with innumerable triumphs over others, but not at all addicted to the glories of peace, the improvements of the industrious, etc. (p. 124). One begins to sense there his connection of Rome with France, and on the preceding page he had said that the "industrious trading part of the nation has always been beggared and impoverished by the violence and fury of arms. . . ." and "the soldier has always been the plunderer of the industrious merchant. . . ." England had soldiers, and was proud of them; but it was not—and France was—a soldier's country. England (like Carthage) was a merchant's country. (Frenchmen agreed; Bishop Huet a few years later described England and Holland as mercantile countries, and urged France to imitate them therefore.) Thus Defoe was able to define his country and the modern system almost explicitly in the language of caste.

Defoe's journalism was a good deal concerned with French militarism. His *Review* was originally entitled a *Review of the Affairs of France.* On May 31, 1705, for instance, we find him attributing to the French the design of universal monarchy, of empire, and on April 19, 1709, he identified France with Glory, and Louis with arbitrary power. Louis's prodigious designs threatened the whole world.

When Louis was rumored dead, in 1712, Defoe wrote a panegyric on him as God's Scourge upon the world, which is an interesting example of the sort of language used in tribute to heroes one disapproves of; imaginative tribute, moral disapproval. In his *Review,* viii, page 586, "a head capable of the deepest councils; a temper fiery, haughty, magnificent, and to his own subjects dreadful; qualified to reduce the nobility to an abject submission, and the commons to the most profound slavery . . ." That is the language of Milton about Satan, Prescott about Cortes, or Scott about Napoleon. (Quoted by Earle, p. 74.) In *Review,* 111, Defoe wrote "May Lewis XIV be a Memento Mori to men of pride, and show them the emptiness of human glory. Where now are the equestrian statues, the title of august and invincible? Why should one man think to mate the world? Men may say, 'Tis no equal match. But why then has he set himself up a match for the whole world? That pride is punished here—and God has smote him—let us wait, and He will bring him down; for all His works are perfect, and this blow cannot end here." Defoe was one of the first men to use the term and the concept, "balance of power."* His is the voice of the modern world system in

*This, and Defoe's fondness for mechanical analogies for politics (see the machine fable about the Constitution in *The Consolidator*) remind one of Hobbes. Hobbes is often said to have invented the phrase "the balance of power," and the subtitle of *Leviathan* is "The Matter, Form and Power of a Commonwealth." The dynamics of government, the balance of trade, and the circulation of wealth, were ideas the two

international politics, and we can find the same attitude in Scott against Napoleon, and in Buchan against the Kaiser. Whereas in contrast with France he set Holland above all. In the *Review* for Jan. third, 1706, we read "In nations and empires 'tis the same; what infinite crowds of people flock to Holland; cities without number, and towns thick like the houses in other countries, that the whole country seems to be one populous city; people in such multitude that all the land in the country can't find butter and cheese for them, much less maintain them. All this attend upon trade; by trade they possess the world." But trade means objects of real use and value, not luxuries. In 1713 Defoe complained that English trade is much declined from thirty years before, because in place of the cloth manufacturers we used to see in London, we have coffee, tea, drugs, china, and gilded-leather shops, which he considers the same as no-shops.

In *The Compleat English Tradesman* he rejoiced in the fact that 30,000 people are always at work underground in Newcastle to supply London with coal. At the same time, "It is very hard, and a melancholy reflection, to think that wickedness should have got such a root in this nation, and should be so effectually fixed, that it cannot be removed, but at the expense of some part of our trade. . . . It is next to incredible, what a share the luxury of the age has, in the employment of families . . . the greatest empires have always fallen from luxury" (Vol. II, p. 225).

In *The Poor Man's Plea* of 1698 he had talked in more Puritan style, of how luxury got its footing in England under James I; while Charles I established Wickedness by a Law. (He means the Book of Sports, which declared recreation lawful on Sundays after church.) Under Charles II lewdness and debauchery had arrived at a meridian. Now William and Mary were fighting it, by means of the Society for the Reformation of Manners, etc. In Defoe's late work also his tone was less heartily complacent and worldly. In *Augusta Triumphans* (subtitle, "The Way to Make London the Most Flourishing City in the Universe") we read on page 3, "We have been a brave and learned people, and are insensibly dwindling into an effeminate superficial race." He demanded strengthening the watch, and clearing the streets of strumpets, forbidding gaming tables and Sabbath debauches.

But more important for our purposes are the midlife attitudes he expresses in, for instance, the *Essay Upon Projects*, of 1697. He says there that the projecting humor began in 1680, as the monster it now is (though in origin it goes back to Noah's Ark). But it was then (that is, in his own youth) that the joint stock companies for founding colonies began, and they begat stockjobbing; which he describes as a "trade managed with the greatest intrigue, artifice, and trick, ever." These attitudes could be described as ambivalent, but it seems clear that the gleeful component is dominant. At this essay's date he still considers the Romans "the pattern of the whole world for improvement and increase of arts and learning, civilizing and methodizing nations and countries conquered by their valour" (p. 72).

Thus Defoe's nonfiction names the modern world system with great analytical acuteness, though considerable moral ambivalence, and gives a framework to his novels which relates them to the history we are discussing.

5. Vol. I (published 1598) was dedicated to Lord Charles Howard, the admiral. Vols. II and III (published 1599 and 1600) were dedicated to William Cecil, Lord Burleigh, Elizabeth's great statesman. Hakluyt also had dealings with Walsingham, and generally stands midway between the sailors themselves and the bureaucrats. In

men both regarded as of central importance. Hannah Arendt called Hobbes the greatest philosopher of bourgeois politics; of its basis in property, its antitraditionalism, and its process of expanding wealth.

Notes

1589 he was one of the nineteen to whom Raleigh assigned rights in the Virginia Colony. In 1597 he was one of those Cecil consulted about the idea of colonizing Guinea—Raleigh's El Dorado. And he helped to organize the East India Company, which in turn put a copy of his *Voyages* into every one of their ships as ships' stores.

6. It is worth noting that Defoe's attitude to "savages" or "natives" (and the attitude of most adventure writers) swings between this one and the opposite, according to which they are devils, bloodthirsty, obscene, and depraved. What is most striking is not either attitude in itself, but the loose swinging between them. In *Captain Singleton*, as the English pass from one village in Madagascar to another, they pass from a community of angels to one of devils. It is obvious that the natives are seen primarily as "the other," as projections of either the Englishmen's fears or their hopes. But it is worth stressing, in Defoe's case, the willingness to see them in ideal terms. *In Madagascar, or Robert Drury's Journal* (1729) he says "Wherever people have not been corrupted by Europeans, they are innocent, humane, and moral. Men in the state of nature, and considering God as the author of the universe, form no other notions of him, but what are consistent with justice, wisdom, and goodness . . ." (p. 34). Hobbists see men everywhere fighting each other. But there are women and children as well as men; fondness for them is the true state of nature. "From hence arise benign dispositions, softness of temper, and friendships . . ." *Madagascar* is a book whose authorship has not been clearly attributed, but Arthur W. Secord, the Defoe scholar, thinks that the natural philosophy passages are likely to be by Defoe.

7. If the Spaniards cared, this convenient captive tells us on page 403, they would have miners and engineers there, who would find enough gold to enrich the world. "So this land, so fruitful, pleasant, and agreeable, any nation in Europe is free to settle in, for anything we can do to prevent them. We have only the Pope's grant of it. We don't cultivate it."

8. One of the sharpest commentaries on that aspect of the book is to be found in Lewis Mumford's *Technics and Civilization*. His section on "Social Regimentation" has a paragraph on page 42; "The ideal man of the new order was Robinson Crusoe. No wonder he indoctrinated children with his virtues for two centuries . . . [the story] . . . combining in a single setting the element of catastrophe and adventure with the necessity for invention . . . [In the new order Crusoe introduced] . . . Invention took the place of image-making and ritual; experiment took the place of contemplation; demonstration took the place of deductive logic and authority." Despite the geniality of his tone, of course, Mumford is indicting this new order. His book came out in 1934, and is one of those diagnoses of the modern system that were to become increasingly frequent; writers like Mumford too had to turn back to Crusoe, as much as the celebrants of that system.

9. What is at work there is a passion to explain, which is the dominant passion in the book, and controls whatever else Defoe does and intends, and how we react. Insofar as Defoe fails as a novelist, here and elsewhere, fails to interest us in his characters' emotions, and in his characters, it is because of this. It is a possessive and reductive passion, which reduces everything else to backdrop and stage scenery.

10. That may seem rather sweeping, but this does seem to me a case where the ingenuity of scholars has led them astray. The truth about *Crusoe* is so clear, but still so exciting, because so important, that it is merely perverse to turn away toward something less certain. That truth has been discovered time and time again, by all sorts of people. For instance, in 1912, James Joyce, in his lecture, "Daniel Defoe," given in Italian in Trieste, said he had read every line of Defoe, and the only other authors of whom that was true were Flaubert, Ibsen, and Ben Jonson. He called Defoe the first author with English characters and stories. "His women have the indecency of

beasts; his men are strong and silent as trees. English feminism and English imperialism already lurk in these souls which are just emerging from the animal kingdom. The African pro-consul Cecil Rhodes descends in a direct line from Captain Singleton . . ." and *Robinson Crusoe* reveals more than any other book, "The way and heroic instinct of the rational animal, and the prophecy of empire . . . The true symbol of the British conquest is in Robinson Crusoe . . . as Friday is the symbol of the subject races. The whole Anglo-Saxon spirit is in Crusoe; the manly independence and the unconscious cruelty; the persistence; the slow yet efficient intelligence; the sexual apathy; the practical, well-balanced, religiousness; the calculating taciturnity."

At the other extreme of literary sophistication we have Henry B. Jackson's *Robinson Crusoe—Social Engineer* which tells how his discovery of the novel solved, for the author, the whole problem of labor, and opened the path to industrial peace. Jackson says, "Robinson Crusoe is typically Anglo-Saxon in his patient acceptance of fate, and his effort to make the best of it. Crusoe's gospel is the same as that of Kipling. It is the gospel of work and the gospel of courage." Jackson finds in the book, as a blueprint for the future, exactly what Joyce found in it, as an explanation of the past. And he quotes the Victorian, Frederick Harrison; "*Robinson Crusoe* contains, not for boys, but for men, more religion, more philosophy, more political economy, more anthropology, than are found in many elaborate treatises on these special subjects." And that indeed is true understanding the economics, etc., to be of the modern system kind.

Indeed, Lukacs makes the same point very well, from the Marxist point of view, in *Studies in European Realism,* with the help of the following quotation from Hegel about the epic form and ancient culture. "What man requires for his external life, house and home, tent, chair, bed, sword and spear, the ship with which he crosses the ocean, the chariot which carries him into battle, boiling and roasting, slaughtering, eating and drinking—nothing of all this must have become merely a dead means to an end for him; he must feel alive in all these with his whole sense and self, in order that what is in itself merely external be given a humanly inspired individual character by such close connection to the human individual. Our present machinery and factories, together with the products they turn out and in general our means of satisfying our external needs, would in this respect—exactly like the modern state organization —be out of tune with the background of life which the original epic requires" (p. 155). Lukacs goes on to say that this is indeed the problem facing the modern bourgeois novel, and to allow that Defoe solved it. But he insists that Defoe's was "exceptional good fortune" and "an isolated, unrepeatable instance." In fact, of course, it has been repeated innumerable times—at least, that is the argument of this book. But Lukacs was looking for a continuance within his favorite authors, like Scott, Balzac, and Tolstoy, where it is naturally far to seek. (Except in Scott, if you read him in the rather special way I suggest.)

11. He says in this essay that he had intended to write an encomium on money, "as the sum and substance of all human arts, common industry, and the end of life as to this world," but decided it was not necessary. Everyone civilized—even the Americans—realize that gold and silver are the valuable species.

12. The gold and silver lace-man alone provided work for many lesser tradesmen; for instance, wire-drawers, button-makers, thread-spinners, embroiderers, makers of spangles, bugles, fringes, frogs, and tassels; each of which had his own workshop. (This subject is elaborated in R. Campbell's *The London Tradesman,* 1747, pp. 147–154, according to Peter Earle.)

13. In *The Farther Adventures of Robinson Crusoe,* we find a passage that recalls that one, on p. 91. ". . . the echo's rattling from one side another, and the fowls rising from all parts, screaming and making every sort, and several sort of, noise, according

to their kind, just as it was when I fired the first gun that perhaps was ever shot off in that place since it was an island."

I think this makes it clear that Defoe knew and intended the symbolic effect of the original passage; at the same time that effect is artistically naive, compared with similar passages in "literature." Just because it is less under his control, however, it transmits the natural symbolism of the subject more immediately. I want to suggest that that happens quite often in the adventure tales, and that is the sort of aesthetic pleasure they can give, and the sort of aesthetic theory that suits them.

14. Peter Earle points out that Defoe's heroes explore all the land masses left unoccupied by the core states, with the exception of North America—that was left for Cooper. When they venture into the other civilizations of the arena, as Robinson Crusoe does in *Farther Adventures*, his attitude, for instance to China, is fundamentally philistine. It is, incidentally, of symbolic interest to us that Singleton's journey across Africa is more or less the route Stanley was to take in the mid-nineteenth century. Defoe's fantasy was acted out by Stanley over a century later—an example of the history of the modern system.

15. Essentially the same view, with the same distribution of sympathies, was held by the antagonists, the groups opposed to the modern system. Thus Isaiah Berlin describes Russians' sense of Westerners as people "enviably self-restrained, clever, calculating, and fenced in, without capacity for large views or generous emotions." (*Russian Thinkers*, New York, 1978, p. 181.) This is how Crusoe and Singleton and all the white captains emerge, even from Defoe's pen; and the projected counterpart is a Black Prince, passionate, disorderly, and generous.

16. If then Swift established himself at the center of literature-as-a-system, surely this contradicts my earlier theory that literature as a whole allied itself to the merchant caste? There is indeed a contradiction here, but it is in the historical facts themselves. Swift personally was a living paradox and his whole group was "reactionary," and such men and such groups, living contradictions of their society, are often central to literature. Serious literature lives as a (conscious or not) contradiction to the dominant strains in the larger culture, and to the compulsions those strains impose upon writers. So in Defoe's time literature as a whole was allied to the dominant caste, even though its most brilliant and authoritative representatives were in opposition—and were generally praised for being so opposed.

17. W. L. Payne points out, in *Mr. Review* (New York, 1947) that between 1704 and 1713, the years of Defoe's *Review*, Pope and Swift published *The Rape of the Lock*, *A Tale of a Tub*, *The Essay on Criticism*, and *An Argument Against Abolishing Christianity*. And yet the *Review* mentioned no living authors by name. Defoe mentioned only five authors more than once, and his comments on them were standard.

18. Limits-to-growth, and steady-state-economy, have always been the implicit economics and energetics of serious literature. It has not participated in the expansive moods of the culture, and this has been manifest in matters of style as well as of statement. (One of the things meant by "journalist" or other phrases for non-serious writers is that they do so participate.) This is true of both the classical and the romantic phases of serious literature; both are forms of withdrawal, whether—as in the first case —the withdrawal is ironic, contemplative, or aesthetic, or—as in the second—it is nature-worshipping, Christianly compassionate, or erotic. These last alternatives (represented by Wordsworth, George Eliot, D. H. Lawrence) are expansive and assertive in their own way, but it is a way in opposition to the society's. (The last is the most interesting case, because fertility, and so in a sense growth, is one of its values; but still it is self-evident that Lawrence—and Tolstoy, and Hardy—imply a steady-state economics.)

19. The ambiguity derives from lack of specificity. If one is speaking of eighteenth-century literature, then its spirit is Swiftian; if of eighteenth-century culture as a whole, then it is Defoean. The literature reacted against the culture, as is its wont—this is its strength and its weakness. In *Kangaroo*, D. H. Lawrence's representative feels ashamed of himself, in his conflicts with a political leader because he, the man of letters, is so fretful, spiteful, reactive, against the other man's "simple and steady loveliness of spirit."

It is also necessary to be specific about nationalities. In France, eighteenth-century literature—at least the encyclopaedists—expressed less reaction against the mercantile spirit than literature in England. The encyclopaedists found their enemies in the military caste and its ecclesiastical allies. (In many ways they were better heirs to Defoe —they made more of his heritage, intellectually and literarily—than anyone in England.) That was no doubt because the mercantile caste did not dominate French culture as it did English, and so did not need reacting against.

20. Smiles takes his examples from the working class, while Defoe is concerned with the middle class; but both are primarily concerned to dissociate the gentleman-idea from the actual aristocracy. Smiles says the tone of living in England has got altogether too high Boys are given a taste for dress, style, luxuries, and amusements. We see "gingerbread young gentlemen thrown upon the world, who remind one of the abandoned hulls sometimes picked up at sea, with only a monkey on board" (*Self-Help*, p. 290). This is the voice of the merchant caste, mocking the aristomilitary style, and those who affect it.

Defoe's message was essentially the same, though he put more stress on education in the conventional sense. The well-bred are to be envied and emulated, not the wellborn. The oldest sons of well-to-do families are often kept at home, not sent to school or university, and consequently remain big babies.

Defoe also has an eloquent passage on education which illustrates the connection he sees between that and adventure. The reading man "may travel by land with the historian, by sea with the navigators. He may go round the globe with Dampier and Rogers, and know a thousand times more in doing it than all those illiterate sailors. . . . He may measure the latitudes and distances of places by the labours and charts of those who have surveyed them, and know the strengths of towns and cities by the descriptions of those who have stormed and taken them . . . he marches with Hannibal over the Alps into Italy, and with Caesar into Gaul, and into Britain, with Belisarius into Africa, and with the Emperor Honorius into Persia . . . he discovers America with Columbus, conquers it with the great Cortes, and replunders it with Sir Francis Drake . . ." (*Compleat English Gentleman*, p. 226). This is an idea of education in full alliance with adventure; it is notable that it is military as much as mercantile.

Chapter IV

1. Hugh McDiarmid makes the same judgment, with the opposite evaluation. "Scott's novels are the great source of the paralysing ideology of defeatism in Scotland, the spread of which is responsible at once for the acceptance of the Union and the low standard of 19th century Scots literature" (C.M. Grieve, *Lucky Poet*, p. 202).

2. He followed the course of the peninsular war eagerly, unable to sleep when things went ill for England, and was deeply shocked when Jeffrey wrote an article critical of the British action.

3. I use "operatic" to mean the most extreme form of "theatrical." In an anony-

mous review of his own work, Scott observed that he had derived his narrative methods from the theater. And in his comments on *Quentin Durward,* he says that he gave the character Charles of Burgundy the trick of half-drawing his sword because that is a stage tradition in the characterization of Richard III. In fact the characterization and the plots of all his novels move very largely by means of such stage devices. This is another sign of how different romance is from adventure, for there was an antagonism between the mercantile sensibility and theater. Of course, several of Scott's villains have connections with the theater; Scott was something of a Puritan himself. And of course Richardson, a Puritan novelist, made much use of theater traditions. But Scott was theatrical, and Richardson was not, in the sense of inviting the reader to see the grease paint and the prompter.

Appendix to *"Waverley"*

4. There are a few more of the Waverley novels it is worth touching on, in order to amplify points so far only sketched in. For instance, the Introductory to *The Fair Maid of Perth* (1828) shows us Scott's skepticism about, and impulse to mock, the legends he loves. He tells of a Cockney visitor being shown the indelible stains left by Darnley's blood on the floor where he was murdered in Holyrood House. "Two hundred and fifty years, ma'am, and nothing take it away?" the visitor said to the housekeeper showing him around, "Why, if it had been five hundred, I have something in my pocket will fetch it out in five minutes . . . ." And he produced some patented Scouring Drops from his pocket. Scott tells us that the housekeeper screamed as loudly as Mary herself on the night of the murder. The whole anecdote is pure modernism, and could come out of *The Connecticut Yankee,* though Scott then turns around and argues that the bloodstains probably *are* genuine.

In *Old Mortality* Scott depicts the Presbyterian and fanatic, as opposed to the chivalric, side of Scottish life. He was accused by some critics of being prejudiced against the Presbyterians, and certainly he makes their fanaticism particularly terrifying in the scenes of war; in Habbakuk Mucklewrath, the mad preacher, and in John Burnley of Balfour, who murders Archbishop Sharp. Their opponent, Graham of Claverhouse, is a soldier in the grand style, and Scott's very sharp sense of genre distinctions—the very different diction and psychology, etc., can be attributed to different social orders—gives Claverhouse every advantage. Clearly, in the novel, as in life, Scott was hostile to moral and religious intensity; he avoided parsons and preachers socially. When Old Mortality says about the Cameronian sect, "We are the only true Whigs. Carnal men have assumed that triumphant appellation, following him whose kingdom is of this world," Scott appreciates the picturesque effect, but his deeper reaction is one of alarm.

The Pirate is a novel which draws on Defoe for its basic anecdote (and Kipling tells of *his* family acting it out when he was a child). It is set on Zetland in 1724–1725, and the Scots in it have the English role; they are modernist reformers, trying to change the islanders' agricultural methods with a new coulter, spade, and harrow. The islanders themselves belong to a remoter past; they plunder wrecks and give no help to drowning sailors; there is much chanting of Norse runes, and talk of Berserkers, sea-kings, sorcerers, giants, and dwarves. When Clement Cleveland, a pirate, is wrecked there, Minna Troil, a romantic Zetlander, thinks him a sea-king, because he has fought the English. "One of an oppressed race, my father is a Zetlander, or rather a Norwegian," she tells him, "who will not care whether you fought against the

Spanish, who are the tyrants of the New World, or against the Dutch or English, who have succeeded to their usurped domain" (p. 234). And in fact Cleveland grew up on Tortuga, his father being a buccaneer, and he wears flamboyant piratical clothes. But he himself has to warn Minna: "Think not of such visions. Denmark has been cut down into a second rate kingdom, incapable of exchanging a single broadside with England; Norway is a starving wilderness" (p. 235). It is the same lesson of realism, but the historical scope is different, and closer to Defoe's.

Redgauntlet is a novel very close to *Waverley* in pattern, being about a Jacobite revolt. In the Introduction, Scott says that the Jacobite enthusiasm of the eighteenth century is the finest theme imaginable for fiction. The Highlanders were an ancient and high-spirited race, "their character turning upon points more adapted to poetry than to the prose of real life." Their rebellion naturally melts away at the end, when General Campbell brings a pardon from the Hanoverian king to the last group of would-be rebels. Only the fierce Redgauntlet goes into exile with the prince, and he tells his nephew (our representative) that the fatal doom will pass from their house now, because he, the nephew, has chosen the winning side. The family had been "unlucky," everything had gone wrong for it, because it was Jacobite. Now its young heir has sincerely and spontaneously chosen the Hanoverian cause, everything will go right. The moral for Scotland is clear. In the Introduction, Scott says it was Walpole who defeated the rebels—Walpole the representative of Hanoverian commercial realism at its most antiheroic. But Scott is on the Hanoverian side. He says that the great martyr of the Jacobite movement, Dr. Cameron, was in truth a dangerous conspirator.

A basic narrative device in *Redgauntlet* is the division of the narrative center between two young men, Alan Fairford, and Darsie Latimer, who represent Sense and Sensibility. To monitor the events through exchanges between these points of view is of course an eighteenth-century serious-fiction device, perfected by Jane Austen. (The exchanges in *Redgauntlet* are epistolary, another of those devices, but a less relevant one here.) Scott learned a lot from that tradition, and, one guesses, from Jane Austen in particular. Sense, after all, was the moral voice of the modern system; sensibility could be the voice of its alternatives—and would then be dangerous. Colonel Talbot, as a character, and as a function in the plot of *Waverley*, is Austen-like and one of the best done things in that novel.

But Scott also made a considerable contribution to nineteenth-century serious fiction, in *The Heart of Midlothian*. Effie and Jeanie Deans, the contrast between them, and particularly the characterization of Jeanie, are very important models for subsequent novelists. Effie, who takes the wrong turning, and thereafter must hide a broken heart behind a gay facade, is the model for *Bleak House*'s Lady Dedlock, and many other such, while Jeanie must be one of the models for Esther Summerson, the heroine of the same Dickens novel. The characterization of Jeanie translates the Puritanism of her forebears into the kind of virtue suitable to the Victorian novel— as the figure of Clarissa did for the eighteenth-century novel. The theology, the piety, the religious practices dissolve into this decent, quiet, tidy, little figure, strong in feeling but antipassionate, antihedonist, antierotic. Her influence is visible in George Eliot heroines like Mary Garth in *Middlemarch*. And perhaps she may be said to stand halfway between Fanny Price and Jane Eyre; Jeanie introduces the feature of sturdiness so important to the better Victorian heroines. In a similar way, Effie's seducer, Staunton, stands halfway between Lovelace and Rochester. Like Lovelace, he had been overindulged as a boy (his mother was a Creole) and he is associated, like several of Scott's villains, with the stage. In this novel, as in Defoe's *Religious Courtship*, we get a glimpse of the road not taken, the road of serious fiction. Though in fact both Defoe and Scott did contribute significantly to the development of the domestic novel.

Notes

But we must concentrate on the adventure novel, and its association with the themes of empire and frontier.

Quentin Durward treats the material of chivalry in unusually analytic fashion. The Introduction says that in the fifteenth century egotism "was now for the first time openly avowed as a professed principle of action." The feudal system, and the spirit of chivalry "by which, as if by a vivifying soul, that system was animated," began to be abandoned, and the modern system began. Louis XI, who represents the new spirit in the novel, is described thus: "Base enough for any and every useful and political purpose, Louis had not a spark of that romantic ardour, or of the pride generally associated with it, which fought on for the point of honour, when the point of utility had been long gained." That sentence is of course perfectly ambivalent.

And though Louis is compared with Goethe's Mephistopheles, we are also told that he stood, in his antichivalric fashion, for peace, strength, and national unity. In the opening scene, Louis appears incognito, in mechanic-bourgeois dress, and Quentin, the young hero, tells him that were he king, he would throw down the defensive walls and *live*, with breaking of lances and gallant tournaments and feasting with nobles, and dancing with ladies (p. 22). But the progress of the plot, and especially the contrast between Louis and his opponent, Charles the Bold, of Burgundy, makes it clear that the true wisdom is Louis's. (In *The Fortunes of Nigel*, a character like Louis, James I, is drawn with similar care and affection, which rings a good truer than Scott's tributes to flamboyant romance heroines like Elizabeth or Mary Queen of Scots.) The modern system is justified.

A Legend of Montrose has some very striking symbolic contrasts of the old with the new. There is much talk of the purse-proud English, and their new luxury. The silver candlesticks of their domestic dining tables are contrasted with the Scots equivalent, which is a gigantic Highlander standing behind the chair of each guest, holding a drawn sword in his right hand and a flaming torch of bog pine in his left. The claims of the old ways against the new never found a more splendid symbol. The hero, Monteith, has a dash of "the old heroic times' generous romantic chivalry," unlike "the sordid, calculating and selfish modern character" (p. 319). But he retires at the end to a life of privacy, like Waverley, happy in public regard and domestic affection. He accepts the new world. The old world is represented by gigantic Allan M'Aulay, gifted with second sight, cursed with a hatred of the English; he is the son of a woman who was scared out of her wits when her brother's head was set on the table by his murderers; and he is driven by bursts of murderous madness. The contrast clearly teaches the reader to adapt to the modern world.

And finally, *Rob Roy* (1817). The Introduction to the novel says, on page 3, "Rob Roy owed his fame in a great measure to his residing on the very verge of the Highlands and playing such pranks in the 18th century as are usually ascribed to Robin Hood in the Middle Ages. . . . Thus a character like his, blending the wild virtues, the subtle policy, and unrestrained license of an American Indian, was flourishing in Scotland during the days of the Augustan Age, of Queen Anne and George I. Addison, it is probable, or Pope, would have been considerably surprised if they had known that there existed in the same island with them a personage of Rob Roy's peculiar habits and profession." (Defoe, having the same interests as Scott, did know about Rob Roy, in fact wrote about him.) He hated the Union with England. "His ideas were those of an Arab Chief, being such as naturally arose out of his wild education" (p. 18). And Scott also mentions that marriage operations like the rape of the Sabines were then common in the Highlands and in Ireland.

What is notable there is how Scott defines his characters' interest by making comparisons between them and primitive life. The same is true in other novels; a character in *The Pirate* is compared with an Obi woman, and Highlanders in *Waverley* are compared with American Indians. They are conceived with reference to a world-historical contrast between the modern life-mode and its various alternatives. But the imaginative act does not get past a gesture or a hint at that larger meaning.

Rob Roy's hero, Frank Osbaldistone, is another Waverley. His father is a London businessman and a Presbyterian—who disapproves of poetry and theater and Oxford, and everything else feudal or chivalric or romantic. He is, we may say, of Defoe's party. But he is an adventurer, in his modern system way. "Impetuous in his schemes, as well as skillful and daring, each new adventure, when successful, became at once the incentive, and furnished the means, for farther speculation. It seemed to be necessary to him, as to an ambitious conqueror, to push on from achievement to achievement, without stopping to secure, far less to enjoy, the acquisitions which he made" (p. 59). Frank is, in the matter of sensibility, a rebel; interested in literature, he has translated *Orlando Furioso*. So he is ready to be attracted to the romantic alternative represented by his Roman Catholic and Jacobite cousins; one of whom describes Frank's father scornfully as "loving and honouring the King as a sort of Lord Mayor to the empire, or chief of the board of trade." But Mr. Osbaldistone, and Nicol Jarvie, his associate in Glasgow, are on the winning side in the novel; and as usual with Scott, the two senses of winning go together; Frank is brought to see that they are in the right, emotionally, too. Chivalric and feudal values are reconciled with more modern ones, but by means of being subordinated to them.

On page 57, Jarvie says, "But I maun hear naething about honour—we ken naething here but about credit. Honour is a homicide and a blood-spiller, that gangs about making forays in the street; but Credit is a decent honest man, that sits at home and makes the pat play." The way Scott involves Jarvie in adventure despite this philosophy; and the way he makes us like him; were direct models for John Buchan in *Huntingtower*. They were also, more indirectly, modeled on Defoe; in the rough sense that both are comic celebrations of mercantile adventurers—though Scott (and Buchan even more) gives us an aristomilitary perspective on the merchant, which Defoe doesn't. But elements of William, and Moll Flanders, and others, may have entered into the conception of Jarvie. He and Jeanie Deans, in *Midlothian*, are perhaps realizations of the fictional idea that is potential in William—the figure of religious seriousness so designed that the novel-reader can feel sentimentally and humorously fond of it.

5. In "Such, Such Were the Joys," George Orwell says that his prep school, and the slice of English upper-class culture it served, made a cult of things Scottish; ostensibly in the name of the Scots' "plain living and high thinking"; really because holidays in Scotland were the prerogative of wealth. This was the final fate of Scott's imaginative legacy—the mythos and ethos he created for the English ruling class. Not that that mythos in its early period was *radically* different in character, but it was less banal. Other writers of Orwell's generation satirize that Scots piety of the English upper class—Nancy Mitford, Cyril Connolly, and Evelyn Waugh.

6. Scott was born in 1771, and lived through a period in which Scotland enjoyed the sort of industrial development which Defoe had promised her at the time of the Union. Her production of linen doubled during Scott's first thirty years. Cotton boomed, so that Glasgow outgrew Edinburgh. In 1799, when he was twenty-eight, the Carson iron works was founded, which produced the light cannon England used in the Napoleonic wars. Scott welcomed the new prosperity—no man more—but he feared the new class of industrial proletariat, because he wanted to preserve old values (aristocratic but also peasant values, which he wanted the dominant merchant caste to adopt or accept) and he saw revolution as the worst of dangers. At the end of his

Notes

life in 1831, at the polls at Jedburgh, he was reviled by the party that was demanding reforms.

A precocious child, with a phenomenal memory, and a great entertainer, he did not get on with his older siblings, but was fond of his younger brothers, Tom and Daniel; both of whom failed in life rather dramatically. The latter, who went out to the West Indies, showed fear in a moment of stress, and was disgraced. Scott refused to wear mourning when he died a couple of years later. Tom merely went bankrupt, much less of a crime by the gentleman's code, and Scott was not so bitter about it—though of course he lived by the merchant's code too. He felt, late in life, that his touch had been blighting—that no one close to him could flourish.

Scott entered adult life as a lawyer, and David Daiches tells us that the legal profession in Scotland then was the guardian of Scots antiquities. Like other men of his class and profession, Scott saw the Scots law and the Scots church as the last bastions of his country's cultural independence left standing by the Union. It was, Daiches implies, the feeling of the whole legal profession then, that the memory of the old life, the heroic life, should be preserved in documentary and literary trophy-form, since it could not be continued in political form. Certainly Abbotsford, the mock-feudal house on which Scott lavished so much money, was a museum of antiquities and relics; and he tried to establish with his servants there a patriarchal relationship.

He was always a man who played a part. He had an intended personality, even in the most private relationships, which was genial, blunt, hedonistic, lazy. In his *Journal*, in 1829, he commends Lawrence's portrait of him, because it "conveys the idea of the stout blunt carle that cares for few things and fears nothing." But Scott was in fact a slave to his work; and much of his behavior bears the stamp of an anxious and obstinate, sly and secretive man; notably his relations with the Ballantyne brothers, whom he involved in his own ruin, not very honorably. There was a fund of cynicism and pessimism at the bottom of his nature.

He says in his *Journal* (p. 121) that until he was eighteen he felt a passion for solitude and fancy; and having stuffed his head with nonsensical trash, he was undervalued for a time in society. "As I grew from boyhood to manhood I saw this would not do and that to gain a place in men's esteem I must mix and bustle with them. Pride and an excitation of spirits supplied the real pleasure which others seemed to feel in society. . . ." (p. 50). He still really prefers solitude, he says, but accepts worldly values. He admires, for instance, the young, strong, and handsome. "I have perhaps all my life set an undue value on these gifts. Yet it does appear to me that high and independent feelings are largely though not uniformly or inseparably connected with bodily advantages. Strong men are usually good-humoured. . . ." (p. 21).

His literary work, and his literary taste, surely show a clear parallel to this psychological effort, which must of course carry with it a certain insincerity. He said he liked Goldsmith because he "contrives so well to reconcile us to human nature." Earlier in 1829 his Journal contains an entry "In fact, I have very little respect for that dear Publicum whom I am doomed to amuse . . ."; he knows "no publick worth caring for or capable of distinguishing the nice beauties of composition." And in 1831 he declares he is sure mere fear keeps most people from suicide.

Like Byron, Scott denied the sincerity of his own work; Lockhart says he considered literary achievement *far* below practical achievement. To hold this was in effect to deny his own best self, and it is therefore no surprise to find him imitating the world and the aristocracy. He was snobbish about dukes and kings, and the state visit George IV paid to Scotland in 1822 was his great triumph. Of course, this had some advantages for his work. Like Defoe and Twain, Scott refused to withdraw from the world morally, as most writers withdraw. He imitated and participated in his culture's fever of appetite; for instance, the fever of financial credit; in 1825 he failed financially for between £70,000 and £80,000, and though he devoted his remaining years to redoubled writing in order to earn money, he still owed £22,000 when he died in 1832. And if this story begins to remind us of Twain, we can remember also that both men played the king with their families and friends, held court, reigned.

7. Brooks Adams wrote, in *The Law of Civilization and Decay;* "Very soon after Plassey, the Bengal plunder began to arrive in London, and the effect appears to have been instantaneous, for all authorities agree that the 'industrial revolution,' the event which has divided the 19th century from all antecedent time, began with the year 1760 . . ." (Quoted on page 17 of Reginald Reynolds, *White Sahibs in India*). The money also had political effects. In 1767 Lord Chesterfield tried to buy his son a seat in Parliament for £2,500, but found they had all been secured by East or West Indians, for £3,000 or £4,000. Clive's income was estimated to be £40,000 a year by Sir John Malcolm, who wanted, as Macaulay said, to make it out as low as possible (Reynolds, p. 64). Burke said, "Animated with all the avarice of age, and all the impetuosity of youth, they roll in one after another, wave after wave, and there is nothing before the eyes of the native but an endless, hopeless prospect of new flights of birds of prey and passage, with appetites continually renewing for a food that is continually wasting" (Reynolds, p. 10).

8. The alliance of Evangelicals and Utilitarians in Indian policy was typical of much that was happening in 19th century England, which bore on imperialism. Grant and Wilberforce won Parliament over to an Evangelical policy—that England should take responsibility for the morality and religion of India. Wilberforce told Parliament in 1813 that the Hindu divinities were monsters of lust, injustice, wickedness, and cruelty. The Evangelicals had always fought against Enlightenment tolerance and rationalism, and had blamed the French Revolution on the spread of those doctrines. See, for instance, Hannah More, John Thornton, and John Newton.

James Mill, the Utilitarian, also attacked Voltaire's "silly, sentimental infatuation with Eastern despotism." It was in 1819 that Mill's *History of British India* reached Calcutta, and in the same year that he was hired by India House; so we can count his influence as strong from then on. When Lord Bentinck went out to be Governor General, in 1828, he said to Mill, "It is you that will be Governor General."

As a result of these twin pressures, English policy in India altered very considerably. Charles Trevelyan wrote a pamphlet in 1834, justifying the abolition of Fort William, where Oriental Studies had been pursued and employees of the Company been trained, in the spirit of Enlightenment tolerance. It was to Haileybury College in England—a creation of Charles Grant—that trainees were to be sent henceforth, for a more English and Christian preparation. And in 1835 Macaulay wrote his Minute, recommending that education in India be given in the English language, and with reference to English literature. (In religious matters, Alexander Duff was Macaulay's counterpart; he tried to convert the Bengal intellectuals to Evangelical Christianity.)

This concern for education brought together the Dissenters, the Evangelicals, and the Utilitarians—in Indian policy and in other matters. This alliance was in effect the conscience of England throughout the nineteenth century, and it is important to note in how many ways it was a revival of the combination of Puritan and rational interests for which Defoe spoke at the end of the seventeenth century. Grant's concern for continuous self-examination, private religious exercises, and good works, and his sense of life's precariousness, all were clearly Puritan. And this interest, while itself moral, was clearly allied to the merchant and not to the military caste. Thus the dialectic discussed before, as operating at the beginning of the eighteenth century, and affecting

Notes

the history of the novel, was renewed at the beginning of the nineteenth. This was one of the pressures forcing the adventure novel, in both the Defoe and the Scott periods, out toward the periphery of literature—since both the old and the new Puritanisms were antiadventurous.

9. This movement continued. In 1790 two-thirds of America's population of 3.9 million lived within fifty miles of the Atlantic; in the next fifty years 4.5 million crossed the Appalachians; one of history's great migrations, as Michael Paul Rogin says in *Fathers and Children*. In the chapter on Tolstoy and Russia, I shall have occasion to discuss the corresponding migration—eastward—there. It seems likely that the nations that engage in such migrations of conquest and expansion (as opposed to the migrations of misery and slavery such as those caused by Hitler and Stalin) want to hear adventure narratives. All migrations on that scale, whatever their emotional character, are bound to be epic events.

10. Avrom Fleishman says the historical novel began with Scott because "the tension between tradition and modernity first achieved definitive terms in Scotland" (*The English Historical Novel*, p. 38). He is talking about the Scottish school of speculative history, to which Scott belonged. Fleishman reads the Waverley novels as one long sustained history of social institutions.

11. A related development was taking place in the science of man. In the 1840s ethnological societies were founded in most of the capitals of Western Europe and in New York City. They hoped to advise statesmen and administrators, because the modern world system was establishing its power over native populations all over the world, and political, social, and moral problems were arising. In the 1860s, there followed a generation of anthropological societies. At the same time, theories of imperialism and racism were being developed. In France such theories were formulated by Michelet, Thierry, Renan, de Gobineau. Michelet said the French were a free people because of their Gaelic nature, but by the same token needed severe preceptors. De Gobineau was an aristocrat by faith, and feared the degenerative effects of miscegenation. His *Essay on the Inequality of Human Races* (1853) set up divisions between the yellow, the white, and the black. Renan's *Poésie des Races Celtiques* (1854)—its ideas taken up by Matthew Arnold in 1866—allowed the Celts no aptitude for politics. They are all sensibility, individuality, and dream; they are romantic and feminine, worshipers of women and love. English commentators on the Irish, like Kingsley, were more brutal. Charles Dilke, in *Greater Britain*, one of the founding documents of British imperialism, declared that there was a struggle and antipathy between the Anglo-Saxon and the Celt; and he believed "The gradual extinction of inferior races is not only a law of nature but a blessing to mankind" (Vol. I, p. 209). He saw the English as a race of officers, captains, whose destiny it was to command other races. Hannah Arendt says that race and bureaucracy were two ideas discovered in the first two decades of imperialism.

Chapter V

1. In those serious courtship novels, of course, the threatening force, sexual and social, was embodied in aristocrats, not in Indians. That Cooper could ever have written *that* story is hard to imagine. Whenever there was a conflict between Puritans and aristocrats—and Cooper often encountered and imagined such conflicts—he felt himself on the side of the latter.

2. When told to cut down a tree, the brothers stand around it, assertively indolent

and inert. Then one steps forward and buries his axe in the trunk, pauses, and finally brings it down. Only then do the others begin to act, and strip off the branches with showy efficiency. And this sullenness extends to their family relations also. Asa, we are told, had spread a spirit of insubordination among his brothers. And this painfully reminded his father of how *he*, in his youth, had cast off his aged and failing parents.

3. This question of size is clearly symbolic and related to the advancing frontier. In *The Spy* there is a gigantic Virginian, Trooper Lawton. Later there will be gigantic Kentuckians, and then, in other authors, gigantic Texans, and then Californians. While to Englishmen, Americans in general seemed big; also Australians and Canadians. I think it fair to assume that, besides a difference in literal size, certain gestures which claimed size—which extended the literal lines of the body—were practiced by the frontier culture; and were accentuated in loci of confrontation, as for instance when frontiersmen came to the city.

The Frontier was a mythical place; take Boone's Kentucky as an example. Arthur K. Moore, in *The Frontier Mind*, says that Kentucky was the last rumored Paradise to fill large numbers with serious expectation. It was referred to as "the garden of the United States," or (by Moses Austin, in 1797) as the Promised Land, the Goodly Inheritance, the Land of Milk and Honey.

The frontiersmen of Kentucky were typically from Ulster. Of 200,000 people who arrived in the English colonies between 1717 and 1775, one-third were Ulstermen. J. R. Commons has said that these men formed the Western type, which gradually became the American type, in politics and industry. They preferred the small towns inland to the coastal settlements, and soon regressed to a more primitive life-style there. For instance, the men often gave up wearing breeches and took to the Indian breechclout. One of their culture heroes was Simon Kenton, a greater fighter and Indian-killer than Boone, who scalped Indians and stole their horses, in the same way they stole the Americans'. He was put into a novel, *Simon Kenton*, by James Weir, in 1852; but his legend was typically oral and not literary; literature was allied to gentility, and if Daniel Boone was a good deal less genteel than Natty Bummpo, then Simon Kenton was a good deal further out than Boone.

Appendix to "Cooper's Books"

4. Two of Cooper's sea-novels illustrate how much closer he comes to Defoe when he treats of this subject matter. First of all, *The Crater* (1847) which was in fact yet another adaptation of *Robinson Crusoe*—indeed, one of the best—and translated into French as *Le Robinson Américain*. In this nineteenth-century version, Crusoe's island becomes so fertile under his management that it is rapidly colonized, and soon has 379 colonists, with 500 Kanakas to do the manual work. Mark Woolston, the central character, who represents Cooper, becomes governor halfway through the story; but prosperity brings corruption (in the form, notably, of newspapers and demagoguery at the polls) so that Woolston retires in disgust. He soon finds his judgment endorsed by the Almighty, for a convulsion of the ocean bed swallows up the island and its unworthy population. Cooper's story so accelerates and extrapolates Defoe's that it could be read as a nineteenth-century satire on eighteenth-century innocence. But the first half is clearly a romance, in the general spirit of Defoe—though without the striking similarity of tone that we find in the other books to Scott.

The second is *The Sea-Lions* (1849), which was clearly inspired by Franklin's contemporary explorations of the Arctic, and which includes a passage on how climate is affected by the inclination of the earth's axis to the plane of its orbit (pp. 347–351). The heroine couldn't understand the hero's reference to this, so Cooper himself explains it to the reader, showing a passion for science and explanation which is very much in Defoe's line. But even in this book we find him commenting on his characters in aristocratic style. "As for the self-respect, and the feelings of caste, which prevent a gentleman from practising any of those tradesman's tricks, the deacon knew nothing of them" (p. 24).

Thus even in his sea-novels, Cooper spoke with the voice of Scott rather than of Defoe. But we cannot confidently attribute the lower interest of those novels to this one author's caste loyalty, for the sea-novel in general has not been a high genre. (Melville and Conrad, it is true, mated sea material with metaphysical and spiritual profundity, but they did so by crossing genres, and so produced an infertile offspring.) Why the sea material, so closely linked as it was to modern system ideology, did not shape itself—at the high culture level—into the system's central myths, is a question full of interest. That in fact it was Defoe and not Smollett who wrote the great modernist story, and that Cooper's forest novels were more mythic than his sea-stories, deserves discussion.

Cooper's first sea-story, *The Red Rover*, used fictional devices like kidnapings, birthmarks, recognition scenes, which derive from his reading of romances. But he also knew the subliterary sea-stories and sailor legends of England in the eighteenth century, when the sea was the country's great pride, sailors the national heroes, the sailor's life something of a frontier life. Popular sentiment then identified England with the navy, and sailors with liberty of various kinds. Nevertheless, this sentiment was not well represented in fiction or at any high level of culture. It was expressed above all in popular songs, dances, entertainments, operettas, like Charles Dibdin's and Isaac Bickerstaff's—for instance, the latter's *Sailor's Return*, 1760. (Charles Dibdin wrote seventy dramatic pieces, and altogether nine hundred songs, mostly about sailors and the sea. *The Dictionary of National Biography* quotes the remark, "He brought more men into the navy in war time than all the press gangs could.")

There was a gap between all that and literature, except that in fiction there was Smollett; his novels were what nautical fiction meant to Cooper when he began. But Cooper was (together with Marryatt) a significant innovator. Smollett's *Roderick Random* (1748) does indeed carry the motifs of *Robinson Crusoe*, and of other modern world system stories, but its spirit is different. It is an adventure tale, but not modernist adventure. Smollett was basically a picaresque writer, who worked within the limits of a genre, itself clearly fixed within the system of literature. His subversive energy was all spent in satire and "realism"—the harsh, grim, and disillusioning details which are contained by the genre, in its negation of romance. That sets him much further from Defoe than Scott or Cooper were to be. Smollett offers us only a dark-shaded report on experience. *Roderick Random*, for instance, has very little sea adventure, and its sailors are mostly eccentrics; they don't represent their vocation in any ennobling way; the sea episodes take place in a man-of-war, and lack the excitements of individual enterprise; the ship is practically a government institution, to be rendered in the same terms as a prison. And the sea merely a place of dangers.

Prescott praised Cooper* for having animated the ocean with a living soul, unlike Smollett; also because Cooper's ships were small, light, graceful, feminine. He compared Cooper with Byron, who was then usually credited with having made the ocean romantic, as opposed to Smollett, but still real, as opposed to the semifantastic ocean of the romances and of *The Tempest*. Cooper and Marryatt, who between them founded nineteenth-century sea fiction, were, like Smollett, interested in the man-of-

*In *North American Review*, 1832.

war situation, with all its institutional aspects, its incarnation of discipline, but they did not treat it with satirical realism. They—most strikingly, Cooper—treated it in the mode of modernist romance.

In Cooper's novels, the ships are always beautiful, and the sailors are always handsome. Tom Tiller in *The Water-Witch* has "the reckless air and manly attitudes of so fine a specimen of a seaman that he attracted a knot of admirers on the sea-front—with his firm and resolute step, he resembled some fancied sea-god." This handsome sailor, who attracts admirers around him as soon as he steps ashore, reappears in Dana and Melville, and is a very clear example of how modernist adventure could serve the modern world system as propaganda. He puts into the minds of readers the idea of a personal power, a more than ordinary intensity of being, to be attained by becoming a sailor. (That is, I think, how we should understand the eroticism of such portraits, which are strikingly frequent in sea fiction, and strikingly infrequent outside that; this is not "homosexuality," but eroticization as a mode of intensification.)

The sea was the home of freedom within the modern world system, for several reasons. The new trade and the new techniques had first been developed at sea; the new enterprise was essentially oceanic; England, the leading country of the system, was an island; ships and sailors were free of the land, with all its feudal ties. And since freedom was so big a part of the modern system ideology, the ocean was a big part of the modern landscape. And Cooper's America felt it was born to outdo England, in freedom, in seamanship, in adventure, and everything else.

It was quite generally believed that America's destiny lay on the ocean—that she was to continue England's destiny there too, of course supplanting her. In 1813 an American magazine declared that "the glorious successes of our navy have kindled a new and holy spirit of nationality, and enabled the humblest citizen among us boldly to say to the world that he too has a country." And America's part in the defeat of the pirates of the Caribbean and those of the Barbary shore were popular triumphs. By the 1840s, the U. S. dominated the passenger trade between New York and Europe, and its whaling fleet amounted to three-quarters of the world's total. By 1850 the tonnage of the shipping fleet was five times what it had been in 1815. And up to this date it was possible for Americans to see the ocean as their domain in the same sense as the frontier was after that. In 1835 de Tocqueville still prophesied sea power for the U. S. He said that Americans "are born to rule the seas, as the Romans were to conquer the world." And Cooper's *Notions of the Americans* (1828) is full of maritime nationalism. He says the sea is America's manifest destiny—that she is not an agricultural nation. "The great outlet for the rest of the world, the path of adventure, and the only, at least the principal, theatre for military achievements open to the people of this country, is on the ocean" (Vol. II, p. 86).

He puts a stress on adventure. In America the laboring class reads more of adventure than it does anywhere else, and "this is an inducement that stimulates the restlessness of moral excitement . . . which tempt men to quit the land for the water" (Vol. I, p. 337). And sea adventure was naturally linked to nationalism. Cooper's novel *Homeward Bound* and his *History of the American Navy* argued for a big navy, and his novels *Mercedes of Castille* (1840) and *The Two Admirals* (1842) were outgrowths of the *History*. Forest adventure was linked to territorial expansion, and imperialism—uncomfortable thoughts for Cooper. He wanted to see America sailing, and he wanted to write about America sailing. It was events that forced him to enter the forest and deal with all the problems it contained. He tried to deal with them in a sea-captain-like way—insofar as the different myth of the forest permitted that.

One might say that Cooper tried to make linked alternates out of his forest and sea-tales, and the very different heroes he found for each. In the sea-tales, for instance

Notes

Miles Wallingford and *The Crater*, he has military caste heroes and relationships; as also in his Littlepage and Effingham society novels; all are full of young men's strong feelings for other young men of the same caste. The heroes are courageous, commanding, adventurous, sexually ardent (though Cooper can give us only the most conventional account of that ardor) and essentially idle. All this is not true of the forest-tales. Natty Bumppo is precisely not a military caste hero, and this accounts for Cooper's clumsiness in handling him. But when Natty grows old and dies, in *The Prairie*, the caste hero, Captain Middleton, is his heir. (At least, he divides the heritage with the clownish Paul Hover.) And the caste hero and heroine, Oliver Effingham and Elizabeth Temple, are Natty's heirs in *The Pioneers*. In these ways, Cooper tried to assimilate the forest-democracy to the sea-aristocracy; or at least to provide a mechanism of transition from frontier anarchy to hereditary captains.

But Cooper had not the gifts for such a heroic feat of myth-making. The sea material, it seems, would not be allied to the serious mind of the culture, or reward the efforts of the serious artists. Only light reading resulted. The forest material, though immediately more recalcitrant, especially to a writer with Cooper's purposes and loyalties, ultimately yielded more significant fiction.

5. In the Preface to *The Pilot*, page xi, Cooper says about flogging, "With several hundred rude beings confined within the narrow limits of a vessel, men of all nations and of the lowest habits, it would be to the last degree indiscreet, to commence their reformation by relaxing the bonds of discipline, under the mistaken impulses of a false philanthropy. . . .".

6. He was of course a historian himself in his novels—and in a more systematic sense than at first appears. Like Scott, and indeed Dumas, Cooper covered a large area of history in a fairly consistent way. This is the argument of John P. McWilliams, Jr., in *Political Justice in a Republic*. He says that Columbus appears in *Mercedes of Castile* and that each generation thereafter, from 1675 to 1850, is dealt with in one novel each.

7. In *Montcalm and Wolfe*, Parkman said about Pitt, "The middle class, as yet almost voiceless, looked to him as its champion; but he was not the champion of a class. His patriotism was as comprehensive as it was haughty and unbending. He lived for England, loved her with intense devotion, knew her, believed in her, and made her greatness his own; or, rather, he was England incarnate" (Levin, p. 50). And "England sprang into fresh life under the kindling influence of a great man, like Nature reviving at the touch of the sun."

8. He referred to his malady as The Enemy, and made war on it, triumphing over his body. Though his father was a minister, he referred to the clergy habitually as vermin, for his allegiance was not to the Brahmins but to the aristomilitary caste. He said in 1884 that democracy had still to prove that it could give "the world a civilization as mature and pregnant, ideas as energetic and vitalizing, and types of manhood as lofty and strong, as any of the systems it boasts to supplant." He had made an effort to do that himself in 1846, and in the Civil War, he and Motley made such a hero out of Oliver Wendell Holmes, Jr. Later Motley made such a hero out of General Grant, and later still out of Bismarck.

Those heroes were of the WASP race—the race to which the historians themselves belonged—and after the rise of Germany to power they extended the idea to include all Teutons.

Appendix to "Historians"

9. The Spain Prescott described was in the vanguard of political and geographical progress, and exalted by the religious fervor of Queen Isabella. He said that his Spain had set new standards of national unity, royal justice, and efficiency (Levin, p. 32); while Ferdinand defeated the "self-indulgent" Moors, and "stood firm" against the Pope. We hear about Spanish *liberty;* the seaboard was the natural seat of Spanish liberty—though the mountains were too. The Italians were in those days the decadent and over-refined race (Macaulay said the Spanish then were Roman to the Italians' Greekishness).

For Motley, writing about a slightly later period, "Spain still personified . . . chivalry, loyalty, piety; but its chivalry, loyalty, and piety were now in a corrupted condition. The form was hollow and the sacred spark had fled" (Levin, p. 4). Whereas in Holland and England intelligent enterprise had not yet degenerated into mere greed for material prosperity. It still included the love of danger, the thirst for adventure, the thrilling sense of personal responsibility; which "led those bold Dutch and English rovers to circumnavigate the world in cockleshells, and to beard the most potent monarch on the earth, both at home and abroad, with a handful of volunteers" (Levin, p. 4). The Dutch were trained to liberty by their experience of the ocean. They carried with them over the world the seed of religious freedom and the spirit of commerce, industry, and self-reliance.

These national differences are crystallized in, for instance, ship design. The Spanish galleon was "about as clumsy and amphibious a production as could be hoped of human perverseness. High where it should be low—exposed, flat and fragile where elevation and strength were indispensable—encumbered and top-heavy where it should be level and compact, weak in the waist, broad in the stem and stern . . ." (Levin, p. 34). And so on, all of it suggesting that the galleon, and the Spaniards, were not manly. This is typical modern system rhetoric.

Motley was the most blatant of the four, and a glance at the Preface to his book on the Dutch Republic will sum up what I have said so far. That republic was "an organized protest against ecclesiastical tyranny and universal empire"; the Roman Catholic Church was the type of tyranny, while "the splendid empire of Charles V was erected on the grave of liberty." William the Silent was the Washington of the sixteenth century, and his republic instructed the world in "that great science of political equilibrium which must always become more and more important"—the balance of power, to preserve which was, from Defoe on, a prime international concern of the middle class in the core states of the system. "The maintenance of the right by Holland in the 16th century, by Holland and England united in the 17th, and by the U. S. A. in the 18th, forms but a single chapter in the great volume of human fate; for the so-called revolutions of Holland, England, and America, are all links of one chain."

But the chain of progress and modernization was now declared to depend on the character of one race, the Anglo-Saxons. "To all who speak the English language," said Motley, "the history of the great agony through which the Republic of Holland was ushered into life must have peculiar interest, for it is a portion of the record of the Anglo-Saxon race—essentially the same, whether in Friesland, England, or Massachusetts" (Levin, p. 74).

Prescott saw the Spaniards as Visigoths, while Bancroft and Motley found the germs of modern liberty in Teutonic tribal organization. They wrote of the "Germanic" nations that had accelerated the upward march of history. Both studied in Germany, and were sent there on diplomatic missions. Both were friends and admirers of

Notes

Bismarck, and Bancroft of Von Moltke, too. The 1874 volume (No. X) of Bancroft's *History* had two long chapters on Germany and the American colonies. Motley divided the Dutch race between the Celtic Belgae and the German Nervii. The former were inflammable and audacious and vast—" the gigantic Gaul derided the Roman soldiers as a band of pigmies." But they could not sustain a battle as the Germans could. The Nervii were simple, stern, and chaste; while of the Friesians he said, "Those violent little commonwealths had blood in their veins. They were compact of proud, self-helping, muscular vigor." Parkman said the Anglo-Saxon race was "peculiarly masculine . . . peculiarly fitted for self-government." Free institutions would not suit the French, who are excited by opposition, carried away by impulse and passion, running to extremes and to abstractions.

This nationalism and racism constituted a new direction in history-writing. Hume had called the Anglo-Saxons "a rude, uncultivated people, ignorant of letters, unskilled in mechanical arts, untamed to submission under law and government, addicted to intemperance, riot and disorder," who did not deserve "a particular narrative." Much of that phrasing, notably the word "untamed," suggests Hume's general opposition to adventure.

10. The system of political ideas in America corresponded, at some points, to its system of literature. Thus in *Virgin Land,* Henry Nash Smith tells us that there were two main conceptions embodied in the early visions of Empire; the first was essentially a command of the sea, the second a population of the continent. This was a conflict of a mercantilist against an agrarian conception, and in terms of images, a passage to India versus a garden of the world. It was a political issue, and there was a party to promote each image. The leader of the former party was Thomas Hart Benton, who had served under Jackson and saw himself as the heir of Jefferson. The latter party was made up of New Englanders. Politically, this corresponded to the literary division in Cooper, between the novels of the forest and those of the ocean. Both divisions express a deeper agony of decision for America.

But by the middle of the nineteenth century, the end of Cooper's life, the decision was taken. The idea of American empire was aimed at the development of the continent. One of the crucial developments was the railroad. In 1845, Asa Whitney asked Congress for a tract of land sixty miles wide, on which to build a railroad from Lake Michigan to the Pacific. Benton supported him, and began to talk of the Garden of the World, and to see in vision cities rising across the continent, like the Ruins of Empire in reverse. This was an important aspect of the exhilarating American idea—that history could be reversed. In Europe and Asia, one saw the sites of former cities and palaces; here one saw the sites of future such. Benton talked about the great Roman roads, describing his Central National Road; and with the same exhilaration as Kipling showed in describing his Great Trunk Road in *Kim.* A land empire—even if it called itself a frontier—was bound to mean an imperialist ideology. And that took a virulent form in America.

For paradoxically, the crucial difference between the American experience of Frontier and the European experience of Empire, in the first half of the nineteenth century, was that the former became the more imperialist. This change manifested itself in the realm of politics, and the new American politicians were quite different from the old ones. As Richard Yoder says, in "The first Romantics and the last Revolution," between 1810 and 1828 American politics gained a reputation for unsaviness, and men like John Adams and John Quincy Adams, and even more their admirers, turned away from politics towards literature. The New England account of American history became conservative, not expansivist. The Adamses treated the American Revolution as the achievement of national *unity,* above all, and John Quincy at least preferred to praise the Constitution rather than the Revolution. The Romantic writers and artists (Cooper, Irving, Allston, Bryant, Dana, the Channings) came of Federalist families, and were uneasy with·Revolutionary themes. Thus Allston refused to paint the battle pieces in the Capitol Rotunda, and Hawthorne, in *The Grandfather's Chair* (1840) stressed the natural lawfulness rather than the revolutionary fervor of Massachusetts in Revolutionary times. These men found the Adamses more congenial than the new Adams as cultural sponsors. If we try to compare and contrast English experience, we might say that Palmerston had some traits (of imperialist expansion) in common with Jackson as a political leader. But Palmerston worked *with* men like Peel, Russell, Bright, Gladstone, men who belong with Adams—men who were very unlike Jackson. Similarly, the hero of empire contemporary with Boone on the frontier is perhaps James Brooke, the White Rajah of Sarawak. The differences are enormous; that Brooke was born into the military and land-owning caste, and that his exploits took place so far from England and so out of its range, are just two. The effect of these differences, from a literary point of view, was that there was no difficulty for a romance-writer in using the material of Brooke's career, as Conrad in fact did. Brooke fitted perfectly into the categories of romantic adventurer.

11. Everything to do with the battle was enveloped in ideas which associated Jackson with Nature and virtue. Addressing the citizens of New Orleans beforehand, Jackson said, "Inhabitants of an opulent and commercial town, you have by a spontaneous effort shaken off the habits, which are created by wealth, and shown that you are resolved to deserve the blessings of fortune by bravely defending them." He and his followers often spoke of the sudden wealth which had arisen in America since the Revolution, and of the voluptuousness and effeminacy it brought. His troops wore no uniforms, their hair and beards were long, and they observed no external discipline. They fought in Indian style, in small groups, harassing the English.

Appendix to "The American Hero"

12. Boone is of importance to this study above all because he was another incarnation of the same idea as Robinson Crusoe, so that we can learn more about that idea, and what Defoe made of it, by studying Boone and the other American folk heroes.

Boone was born in 1734 to Quaker parents, and in 1742 Count Zinzendorf held a Synod of the Moravians near his house, where Delaware converts to Christianity preached peace to their brethren. (Thus there were in his heritage elements of the same conflict as Cooper dramatized in Natty.) Moreover, according to John Bakeless's *Daniel Boone*, Indians visited the Boone home as friendly neighbors during his childhood; from conversing with them Daniel learned how to think like an Indian— so that when leading other whites against them as an adult, he always knew in advance what the Indians would do. (This idea should remind us of *Kim*, and point up the similarity of Frontier and Empire.) For he grew up a man of war; as a kinsman said he was "ever unpracticed in the business of farming, but grew up a woodsman and hunter" (Bakeless, p. 10). He both changed caste and reverted socially—which helped make him a typical frontier hero. He was the only notably bad speller among the forty-five grandchildren of George Boone. He left school early, after he knocked down the teacher who tried to discipline him. (This story was told of many heroes of empire —for instance, Stanley—and also heroes of romances—for instance, Roderick Random.)

Boone's great fame was earned when he led the settlers into the new land of

Notes

Kentucky. This was land that the English government had reserved to the Indians by the Proclamation of 1763, and so he was involved in many battles against Indians and was captured by them. In fact, he was adopted by the Shawnees as Sheltowee, Big Turtle; his hair was plucked out, all but the scalp-lock, and he was scrubbed by squaws in the river, and painted, and renamed—given an Indian identity. He was sometimes said to be a white Indian. But he escaped, as soon as he could, returned to his countrymen, and led them to drive the Indians out of their land. Still, he was very uneasy with the machinery of white civilization, notably the law; and declared he never wanted to live within 100 miles of a damn Yankee. So when the Spanish governor general of Mississippi, Zenon Trudeau, invited him to move again and settle there in 1795, he was interested. It was a time when Spain was trying to revive her dying empire by inviting in new white settlers, notably disaffected colonists from English or French realms. Many followed Boone to the Spanish Territory, for he was extremely famous as a guide; and there he died in 1820.

His story was told many times in print, and in a way that testifies to innumerable tellings orally. Some of these versions of his character differ significantly from what Cooper (and other responsible-class writers) tried to make out of Boone. In 1832 came John A. McClung's *Sketches of Western Adventure* (Maysville, Ky.). This depicted the West as full of violent adventure, and rejected Eastern versions of Boone as too genteel. McClung even criticized Boone himself for giving too literary and philosophical an account of himself. (In 1818 Boone had told John M. Peek that he had been "a creature of Providence, ordained by Heaven as a pioneer in the wilderness, to advance the civilization and the extension of his country.") *(Sons of Leatherstocking)* The truth, said McClung, was that Boone loved hunting, solitude, and excitement, and was not ordained by Providence or anything else to advance civilization. There were, Richard Slotkin tells us, nine editions of McClung's book, in Cincinnati first, and as late as 1844 (Slotkin, *Regeneration Through Violence*).

Davy Crockett was famous for killing, and for boasting that he had killed when he hadn't. In his autobiographies he describes a shooting-match scene, which he won by putting a spent bullet into the hole left by his first shot, and claiming a perfect double bull's-eye; "Swaggering," he says, "will answer a good purpose at times." But his story is also more full of real violence, and a taste for violence, than Boone's—as for instance the description of the savage fight with a cougar. In Crockett we see the WASP hero as killer. His image was more antigenteel than Boone's—harder to assimilate to Natty Bumppo. Of Irish descent, he grew up on the frontier. His grandparents were murdered by Creek Indians, and a deaf-and-dumb uncle was captured by them, and lived eighteen years in Indian captivity. Davy ran away from home, and spent very little time at school; at fifteen he was still illiterate. He fought alongside Andrew Jackson in 1813, but made his political career in opposition to him; in fact, Crockett's fame was in some sense a publicity invention of the Whigs, who needed a Western man to attract some of the Western vote away from Jackson and the Democrats. He played the role of frontier hero, and played it to the gallery.

His books are full of hints that he may become President, which remind us of the startling new links then being forged in America, between cultural irresponsibility and political power. Crockett became a magistrate first, and in his account of his work one can hear the populism of all his politics. "My judgements were never appealed from, and if they had been, they would have stuck like wax, as I gave my decisions on the basis of common justice and honesty between man and man, and relied on natural-born sense, and no law-learning to guide; for I never read a page in a law book all my life." Elected in 1827, as "the wild man from the West," his speeches, as he reports them, were all style and no content, politically. He refers to Jackson as "the government,"

380

"King Andrew," or "the old Roman," though he keeps his real bitterness for Van Buren, the vice-president.

13. These innumerable dime novels—a tremendous force, at a low cultural level—relay the image begun by Defoe in *Robinson Crusoe*. *Buffalo Bill* (1881) begins with a list of "the strange heroes who loved the trackless wilds . . . who stood as a barrier between civilization and savagery, risking his own life to save the lives of others . . ." It does not name Crusoe—only Crockett, Carson, Boone, and the other Americans; but we have shown ample reason why that line points in the direction of the shipwrecked Englishman. At the level of formula, therefore, the irresponsible class was being given the same idea as the responsible. Of course, other literary elements, in style, incident, characterization, made the total meaning different.

14. This was an American modification that loaded quicker, hit harder, and more exactly, and kept clean longer. Stories about rifles go back a long way. In 1775 the *Virginia Gazette* reported Captain Crescap's 130 riflemen, who could perform incredible feats of marksmanship. One of them could hit a dollar-sized piece of paper on a board 5″ x 7″, held between his brother's knees at a distance of sixty yards.

15. Since I have made narrowly specific allusions to the connection between the American folk hero and Natty Bumppo, I should recall also the broader scope of the former's influence, out beyond America altogether. In Germany, Karl May's version of Natty, Old Shatterhand, with his Indian comrade Winnetou, had enormous influence on German youth at the end of the nineteenth century, as we shall see. In France there was Gabriel Ferry's *Coureur des Bois*, in seven volumes, 1853, which was very popular; and Gustave Aimard's fifty novels of that kind. And in Britain Stevenson says that to him in his youth, "America was to be a promised land," because he had read Aimard's *Loyal Heart, or the Trappers of Arkansas*, *The Pirates of the Prairies*, and *The Gold Seekers*. Ohio was the favorite haunt of Stevenson's imagination, and he says an Englishman thought of America as a young man brought up in an old and rigid circle, and taught to distrust his own instincts, thinks of a family of cousins, all his own age, who keep house together, far from restraint and tradition. This sums up neatly for us the fascination the Frontier hero exerted on the citizen of the Empire.

Finally, let me quote Webb on the frontiersman. "It was his aloneness and the passivity and impersonality of the force against which he moved that explains so much that we in the U. S. have called American. Fundamentally his aloneness meant that man was at last really on his own. He could do in this new environment anything he wanted to do and as much of it as he wanted to do without human opposition. For example, if he wanted to cut down trees, kill game, or navigate streams, he could cut, kill, and navigate without seeking a permit or running afoul of a policeman. . . ." (*The Great Frontier*, p. 34). The hazards he ran were of a different kind—his opponents were the impersonal laws of nature; the risk that the tree might fall on him, for instance. "The fact that this man found his own rewards and punishments and complete self-responsibility for his fortunes, did things to his psychology." The interest of that description is that as well as unifying our folk heroes and Natty, by defining what they have in common, it also points back to perhaps the purest of all embodiments of that idea in Robinson Crusoe. This is the WASP hero in one of his most potent incarnations, the man alone on his island. Webb was not thinking of Defoe, but his remarks make it clear how perfectly that book trained the imaginations of its readers for the tasks which the frontier as well as the empire held ready for them.

Notes

Chapter VI

1. This boomerang effect, and Britain's exemption from it, was discussed by Sir Halford Mackinder (1861–1941) the founder of geopolitics, and theorist of British imperialism. "The separation of the tropical Empire from the European island, although perhaps a source of weakness from the military point of view, has had the extreme advantage, that on the one hand imperial rule in the dependencies has not corrupted freedom at home, and on the other hand those who exercise that rule, go out generation after generation with the spirit of justice and trusteeship ever renewed from their free homes and schools." This quotation, attributed to 1924, is to be found in Bernard Semmel, *Imperialism and Social Reform* (p. 176).

An example of the difference between political conditions in the home country and those in the empire is given by George Dangerfield in *The Damnable Question*. Ireland had a police system, he says, while England itself had justices of the peace (the "gentlemen of the parish"). And while Englishmen *thought* of police systems as something characteristic of European despotisms—of czarist Russia, for instance. Another example is given in Mark Twain's *Following the Equator:* he says that in Australia and Tasmania convicts got fifty lashes for quite small offenses, though England had just repealed the law which allowed up to twenty-five.

2. The idea of importing technical experts from the West into Russia goes back even further than that, and there had even been some practice of it, on a smaller scale. Ivan the Terrible had tried, but met the opposition of the Poles, Swedes, and Lithuanians. In 1547 a hundred and twenty four such experts were turned back at Lübeck, while on their way to Russia. And Sigismund August of Poland wrote to Elizabeth of England in 1567, warning her against strengthening Russia's power by such means. "One supplies them with munitions of war, with arms the use of which they did not know, and what appears most dangerous to me, one procures to them adroit engineers" (John Bowle, *The Imperial Achievement,* p. 18).

3. Nicholas saw the brilliant charge of the Life Guards at Austerlitz, but also the tragic consequences; and the contrast between the two is one of the novel's dominant chords. ". . . of all that mass of huge and handsome men, of all those brilliant, rich youths, officers, and cadets, who had galloped past him on their thousand ruble horses, only eighteen were left after the charge" (p. 304). The dead lay like heaps of manure on the ploughed land.

4. And the occasion, in *The Cossacks,* is the discovery of a dangerous-looking footprint, which is likely to remind us also of Crusoe. Tolstoy had of course read *Robinson Crusoe.* As a boy, and as a father, with his own children, he played games derived from that story. (He also read, and reread, Dumas's historical romances. And he mentions, as an important influence in his early reading, Prescott's *Conquest of Mexico.*)

5. The Russian Formalist, Victor Shklovsky, wrote a book on Tolstoy in 1928, in which he analyzed *War and Peace* as the product of two forces, ultimately irreconcilable, Tolstoy's caste-identity and the novel-form's inherent liberalism. He says Tolstoy intended to glorify the Russian nobility, and to canonize the legend of its heroism during the Napoleonic invasion, but that the tendencies of the novel-genre undermined his intention, and made the meaning of the book more democratic. I see support there both for my interpretation of Tolstoy, and for my theory of genre. Serious fiction was allied to liberalism, as adventure was allied to modernist imperialism.

6. In *The Russian Levites: Parish Clergy in the 18th Century* (Harvard University Press, 1977) Gregory L. Freeze says that the Russian clergy developed a "castelike structure" during the eighteenth century, "as medieval Muscovy became modern

Imperial Russia." He himself hesitates to name it bluntly a caste, though he says that was the general term in mid-nineteenth-century Russia. The official term was *soslovie,* usually translated as estate, and Freeze combines that with caste. He says that the formation of such *soslovia,* out of the medieval social groups called *chiny,* was "a process unique to Imperial Russia; while other European countries were beginning to break apart the traditional estate structure, Russia began to build just such an order of closed social estates" (p. 218). The clergy was the most hereditary and the most separate in juridical status, but the nobility and the merchants were something like castes—and became so in modern times. This is important for us to bear in mind when considering the challenge of Tolstoy's caste-thinking, and caste-thinking in general.

7. In his *Reminiscences,* written near the end of his life, Tolstoy attributed insincerity to his early works, *Boyhood* and *Youth,* on the grounds that they implied a "democratic tendency," which he says he didn't really feel at the time of writing them. That is an example of the sort of insincerity of which he accused Turgenev and the others.

8. It is worth noting that Tolstoy's brother Sergei bought a gypsy girl, and lived with her the rest of his life, having several children by her; that his brother Dmitri bought a prostitute from a brothel and made her his common-law wife; that their father, when sixteen, had a bastard son who became a postilion and who, after the father's death, came begging from his half-brothers (Tolstoy remembered his embarrassment, because the bastard brother looked much more like their father than they did). And finally that Tolstoy himself had a bastard son in 1858, who grew up to be a coachman who worked nearby.

9. On the whole, the Cossacks are much more like American frontiersmen than servants of the British Empire. But one can recognize something Cossack-like in the men John Buchan describes meeting in South Africa. "They were the true adventurer type—long, thin, hollow-eyed, tough as whipcord . . . I took off my hat in spirit to the advance-guard of our people, the men who know much and fear little . . . You can readily whistle them back to the defense of some portion of the Empire or gather them for the maintenance of some single frontier; but when the work is done they retire again to their own places, with their eyes steadfastly to the wilds but their ears always open for the whistle to call them back once more" (*The African Colony,* p. 161).

10. Braudel points out the larger background to the Caucasian wars; that the danger to civilization has always come from either mountain people, like the Caucasians, or the nomads of the deserts and the steppes; the horse and camel people, like the Tatars or the Bedouins. Such men were the war-makers and meat-eaters. They jeered at the men of the settlements, who were often (in Russia, for instance) vegetarian. Islam never securely converted her nomads, the Berbers of North Africa or the Kurds of Central Asia. While sorcery, witchcraft, and vendettas—all such social forms flourished on the mountain tops, in Corsica and Sardinia, and so on. Civilization had to choose, either to excommunicate their mountain enclaves, as China and India did, or to domesticate them by force, as Europe tried to do.

Chapter VII

1. According to Smith, scores of newspaper articles and periodicals and sermons also pointed out the likeness between Lawrence and Cromwell; both men cared naught for appearances, spoke freely, swept obstacles from their paths, worked like heroes, and made others work.

Notes

2. Two more examples of this kind of adventure tale are Michael Scott's *Tom Cringle's Log* (Paris, 1836) and E. H. Trelawney's *Adventures of a Younger Son* (London, 1831). The first, though vigorous and stirring, is formally enchained to Smollett. The second is Romantic; as Byron said, Trelawney was "the personification of my *Corsair*. He sleeps with the poem under his pillow and all his past adventures and present manners aim at his personification" (Quoted in the Introduction to the Oxford English Novels edition of *Adventures.*). One point of interest is Trelawney's masculinism; in this, as in many other ways, he usefully exaggerates tendencies implicit in the adventure and romance forms. He wanted to call the book *A Man's Life*, and when Mary Shelley told him that women would not read the manuscript he showed her, he replied, "My life . . . is not written for the amusement of women . . . it is to men I write, and my first three volumes are principally adapted to sailors. England is a nautical nation . . ." (Introduction, *Adventures*).

3. Max Müller, in his memorial Preface to *The Roman and The Teuton*, described Kingsley as the ideal man. He recalled those ". . . features which Death had rendered calm, grand, sublime . . . How children delighted in him! How young, wild men believed in him, and obeyed him too! How women were captivated by his chivalry!" His funeral in 1875 collected men of all sorts, gypsies and farm-laborers, sailors, bishops, and governors. He will be missed "wherever Saxon speech and Saxon thought is understood."

4. In that message Kingsley was of course very unlike Macaulay and James Mill and the Utilitarians. But his view of India was not so remote from theirs. James Mill's *History of British India* gives a very Hobbesian idea of the state's origin, says J. W. Burrow, in his *Evolution and Society*. The state is seen as a machine, and the civil philosophy is as demonstrable as geometry is. His Books II and III try to determine the stage of civilization reached by native India. His criterion is as follows: "Exactly in proportion as Utility is the object of every pursuit may we regard a nation as civilized." (Quoted in Burrows, p. 45.) In India, of course, he found that many pursuits did not have Utility as their object. So Mill blamed the Orientalist scholars (like Sir William Jones) for inducing the West to overrate Indian culture, which was really very backward. "By conversing with the Hindus of today we in some manner converse with the Chaldeans and Babylonians." Mill, Macaulay, and the Whigs of the *Edinburgh Review*, were very rough in their judgments on the East in general—in conscious dissent from the eighteenth-century high-culture fondness for the exotic. Their line of thought may be associated with merchant-caste low culture—the cultural tendency to which Defoe belonged.

5. Indeed, Dumas's portrait of Richelieu is like Defoe's. Both portraits are composed of phrases like "exquisite subtlety" and "finished art." In the second issue of his *Review*, Defoe described Richelieu as "the most exquisite master of politics, Cardinal Richelieu, whose life and management may hereafter take up a considerable part of these papers . . . the most refined statesman in the world." And writing to Harley, Defoe recommended to the English statesman Richelieu's arrangement of having a series of three offices, each one more secret than the one before, and the third so private that no one was admitted except in the dark (Defoe, *The Letters*, p. 39). Another letter to Harley makes it clear how personally fascinated Defoe was; for he compares himself in Edinburgh, hiring people to betray their friends, with Richelieu. Richelieu was for Defoe what Macchiavelli was for the Elizabethans; and the fascination continued throughout the life of the modern system, as Dumas's success makes plain.

6. That book is credited with beginning the "ethnographic novels" which filled the

penny dreadfuls after 1874. (See Brian V. Street, *The Savage in Literature.*) It is also the book in which Henty describes his trip up river with Stanley.

7. Ballantyne is an interesting figure, in a number of ways. He was son and nephew to the Ballantyne brothers who were close friends of Scott. They printed *The Waverley Novels*, and even copied the manuscripts out so that their employees should not see and recognize Scott's handwriting. Thus he was brought up in the Waverley cult, and was much influenced by it. But at sixteen he was sent out to work in the Hudson's Bay Company, and stayed there six years, 1841–1847. His first book, published in 1848, was entitled *Hudson's Bay;* while his first fiction, published in 1856, *The Young Fur Traders*, had the same setting. Thus he embodied two of the major ideas of Scotland, from our point of view; and from 1856 to 1894 he poured out a stream of very popular boys' fiction, which combined the two, and carried the message of adventure.

8. And this became stronger during his second period, according to Huet's classification. Between 1878 and 1897 his stories were mostly about colonization, and not about the adventures of colonizers but about native rebellions against them. He wrote about the Greek insurrection of 1826, the French-Canadian insurrection of 1837, the Indian Mutiny of 1857, the Bulgarian independence movement, and so on. His work became more literary, and made more reference to Scott. According to Jean Chesneaux *(Une Lecture Politique de Jules Verne)*, there are three main strands to Verne's liberalism. He was in the tradition of 1848; that shows itself in Captain Nemo's gallery of heroes, in *20,000 Leagues Under the Sea*, which included Kosciusko, Botzaris, O'Connell, Washington, Lincoln and Brown. (Compare Defoe's list of Protestant heroes, and Smiles's.) But he was also a utopian socialist, whose heroes work for a scientific and fraternal exploitation of the earth. And he was finally an anarchic libertarian—against the police and for outlaws in general; his books show a strong interest in mutinies, and in islands which are *milieux libres*—alternatives to society.

In the third period, 1898 to 1905, according to Huet, he returned to the subject of voyages, but the mood of his work was much grimmer. *L'Etonnante Aventure de la Mission Barsac*, not published until 1914, tells of Henry Killer's wonderfully efficient settlement in Africa called Blackland, which makes use of ingenious ideas devised by the scientist Marcel Camaret, but works by slave labor. This is a dystopia, and all the enthusiasm for science of the earlier books has gone sour.

Of these three periods, the most important from our point of view is the first. Besides the titles already cited, it is worth mentioning *Les Enfants du Capitaine Grant*, 1867–1868, a three-volume odyssey about those children in search of their captain-father, who was shipwrecked while founding a Scots colony in Patagonia. The theme must remind us of Defoe, and it is worth noting also the fondness of Verne for captains. After Captain Singleton and Captain Roberts, we have to wait until Verne began writing to meet such a concentration on this figure in fiction. The story of Captain Nemo, 1870, owes more to Dumas in the revenge motif, and is more politically motivated. Nemo is an Indian prince in disguise, and he sinks a British cruiser as part of his revenge. But *L'Ile Mystérieuse* (1873) is closer to the Crusoe pattern; an engineer, a journalist, a seaman, and a child are wrecked together, and are saved by the expertise of the engineer. He is an American called Cyrus Smith, who has as much skill of hand as ingenuity of mind, and they name the place Lincoln Island. It is, Chesneaux says, an Anglo-Saxon parable, a hymn to work.

9. Take for instance Andrew Lang, who played a large literary role, as the friend of Twain, Kipling, and Haggard, and who edited the Border Edition of Scott. In his introduction to *Ivanhoe*, 1894, Lang defended Scott thus—against Ruskin: "Perhaps

Notes

Mr. Ruskin was never a boy. Scott, like Thackeray, had been a boy, and never forgot that happy company of knights, ladies, dragons, enchanters, all the world of Ariosto . . ." Lang's identification of boyhood with chivalry was of the first importance in the history of children's literature. So was his identification of romance with self-indulgence, in opposition to intelligence and criticism. He continues, "We cannot all be old and melancholy . . . There shall be cakes and ale, though all the critics be virtuous, and recommend stuff 'rich in heart-break'. Still shall the greenwood trees be green . . ." That pouting whimsy was so often employed by Scots writers that it comes to seem inherently Scottish.

Chapter VIII

1. Justin Kaplan has pointed out how many features *Connecticut Yankee* shares with that standard adventure-romance of the period, *King Solomon's Mines;* a wicked shaman, an eclipse, a love affair, a climactic battle, and a clash of cultures. (Kaplan, *Mark Twain and His World,* p. 146.)

2. In 1877 he wrote about Germany, "What clean clothes, what good faces, what tranquil contentment, what prosperity, what genuine freedom, what superb government!" The Germans seemed to be applying modern system values to life, under Bismarck, and it was a natural corollary that they should appreciate Twain's humor so enthusiastically. His works were brought out there in six volumes between 1874 and 1878, and he was a favorite German author. It was known that the Kaiser himself loved *Life on the Mississippi.*

3. There were many sides to that character, and several of them ugly. There was a Frontier racism, which one hears sometimes in Twain; in, for instance, this sentence from *Roughing It.* "The Bushmen and our Goshoots are manifestly descended from the self-same gorilla, or kangaroo, or Norway rat, whichever animal-Adam the Darwinians trace them to" (p. 132). And some of Twain's animus against Cooper was his Frontiersman's contempt for the Noble Red Man image which Cooper had carved in the service of the responsible culture of America.

It may be relevant, in this connection, to point out that the road and the ride West Twain describes in *Roughing It* are very like the road and the ride (from Charlestown to Johannesburg in South Africa) which Gandhi describes in his *Autobiography.* It was on this journey that Gandhi came up against brutal racism, and received his decisive call to political action. He was humiliated for being an Indian by a coach-driver who was a "man of power" exactly like those Twain celebrates. The road to Johannesburg was one of the Great Transport Roads of South Africa. "It was all Romance, the first form of Romance," says a 1914 description, *The Old Transport Road,* by Stanley Portal Hyatt. Johannesburg, which had a population of 40,000 in 1893, but 160,000 by 1904, was (like some California cities) called "the central sin-spot of civilization." (See Hamilton Fyfe, *South Africa Today,* 1911.) Gandhi himself remembered its citizens as always running, never walking, and everyone as being obsessed with gold. It was therefore a typical mining and bonanza town, just like those Twain knew; among the street names were Gold, Quartz, Banker, Claim, and Nugget. (Gandhi called the Transvaal the El Dorado of the Western world.)

The similarity between Frontier and Empire comes out in an American's description of Pretoria, where Gandhi spent a year (Poultney Bigelow, *White Man's Africa*). "It was about noon; the sun was broiling down as it does in Texas; the broad, dusty streets reminded me of an average prairie town west of the Mississippi, and this impression was further heightened by noting great freight wagons drawn by sixteen oxen, and scrawny mustangs galloping about, with sunburnt, shaggy Boers astride them" (Quoted in C. D. S. Devanesan's *The Making of the Mahatma*, p. 248). This was Twain's environment, including incidents like that in which Gandhi was involved. Twain saw, and indeed described, many such incidents. But he identified—not unambivalently, of course—with the drivers, not with the insulted and injured.

4. Twain asks his readers to share his own humiliation before these figures of violence—his own doubt of "civilized" values when in their presence—and it is notable how clearly American Studies still mirrors that doubt and embarrassment. I don't (any longer) think that simply a weakness in American Studies. I now think the self-confidence of critics who do not embody these doubts unreal. But there is no doubt that it considerably hampers work in that field. I can take a couple of examples of the embarrassment I mean from Henry Nash Smith's tributes to Twain. First from his introduction to *Mark Twain: 20th Century Views.* "This is the kind of veneration that railway conductors and gifted Irishmen in bars might feel for generals or prizefighters; it is not their usual attitude towards men of letters. The fact is that in the popular conception Mark Twain was not a man of letters . . ." (p. 2). The second from *Mark Twain: the development of a writer,* where he says that the humorists' diction contrasted with that "considered appropriate for the upper ranges of literature," just as vernacular values contrasted with those of "accredited spokesmen for American society." All kinds of unprinted quotation marks flutter around the phrasing of those passages, announcing an embarrassment about "men of letters" and "American society," and for that matter "the people"; an embarrassment which debilitates the argument, since those are the crucial concepts it employs.

5. The serious mind of England was furious. The Royal Geographical Association, which had been preparing an expedition with the same purpose, said Stanley's story was all lies. The Brighton meeting of the British Association in 1872 invited Stanley to speak, but openly disbelieved what he said.

The English response shows how staid the English mind had become; how completely the puritan-merchant mind had subdued itself in its alliance with the aristocracy; had formed an establishment. But it is important to note that Americans didn't believe Stanley either, though their disbelief was less disapproving. Even in New York, such was the atmosphere of journalism then, it was confidently asserted that Stanley was writing his reports, locked up in a hotel room somewhere in the city; and for a long time no one really believed them. "Dr. Livingstone, I presume?" was a broad joke from the beginning, at the popular as well as more sophisticated levels of culture. The whole affair, but especially the contempt of the English establishment, deeply upset Stanley. It is a vivid case of Anglo-American mutual hostility.

Ill-feeling continued. When his dispatches were published, a year later, the *Saturday Review* said that Stanley described bloodshed with relish; and accused him of carrying too far "the American method of treating savages." (Here we see Empire dissociating itself from Frontier.)

But public opinion changed toward Stanley. In 1873 he reported the Ashanti war, in Africa, and made friends with G. A. Henty in the course of it. The latter commemorated their travels together in his popular *By Sheer Pluck.* When Livingstone died, Stanley was commissioned by the London *Telegraph* to continue exploring the lakes which the former had been investigating, in search of the source of the Nile. The disreputable newspaperman became the famous explorer. In 1875 he persuaded the King of Buganda to let Christian missionaries into his territory; and that was the first step in the process which resulted in the addition of Kenya and Uganda to the British Empire.

Notes

About this time, the other kind of complaint about him began to get louder. By his own account, his expedition in Buganda killed thirty-three natives and wounded one hundred—Stanley himself shot fifteen. He began to be called the modern Pizarro. Sir John Kirk, the British consul at Zanzibar, said that Stanley had kicked a man to death. It was also a cause of scandal that Stanley made alliance with Arab slave traders. The latter went west across Africa in his footsteps. In 1889 one of their raids destroyed a hundred villages and killed thirty thousand people. Being an explorer did not mean a career in pure science, or pure adventure; it meant conquest and often war.

6. The novel is dedicated to those suppressing slavery, but its interest is part adventurous, part (innocently) pornographic. The story is about Selim, a white-skinned Arab lad from Zanzibar, slender and girlishly beautiful, who is awakened from childishness to boyishness by the challenge of the American consul's son. "Nazarene lads are bolder and more manly than we," he says; much to his audience's gratification. So he gets a rifle, and goes to Africa, with his two slaves, to find adventure. There he himself gets enslaved by blacks, and often flogged, until he is befriended by Kalulu, prince of the Watuta. The latter is a "type to make the marble forms of Phidias blush; body, arms, and limbs were unmistakably magnificent in shape . . . a perfect youthful Apollo . . . [with] surpassing grace of movement and manly beauty" (p. 137). Selim's skin, on the other hand, is soft and smooth, and he has lustrous orbs, and quite often his clothes are taken off. The two become fast friends, and Stanley compares them with David and Jonathan. "What boy, of any nation, in any public school, has not some friend who is as dear to him as a born brother?" (It was of course predictable that one aspect of so large a cult as that of "the boy" in nineteenth-century England should bear this sexual character; a general judgment must be that that character makes itself felt quite rarely.)

7. Gordon was the most remarkable of these proconsuls, and as a personality he cannot be said to be typical of anything, with his religious mysticism and unworldliness. But his career was typical, in some ideal-type sense, of British imperialism then; as a troubleshooter, first in China, then on the Danube, in the Sudan, in India, in South Africa, in Palestine, and again in the Sudan; where he finally died, to become one of England's great military martyrs.

More typical is Sir George Goldie (1846–1925). He was born into a wealthy aristocratic family, ran away from Woolwich Military Academy to Egypt, and lived three years in the Sudan with an Arab mistress (and was always interested in the idea of rebuilding a Sudanese empire). Having come back to England, he again eloped, this time with the family's governess, to Paris in 1870, and married her reluctantly in 1871. He was a domineering presence, an atheist who read Ibsen and Wagner. In his own words, "All achievement begins with a dream. My dream, as a young child, was to colour the map red. In 1877 I left England (largely to escape from personal entanglements) to explore the interior of Nigeria. On the journey back I conceived the ambition of adding the region of the Niger to the British Empire." He had first gone there in 1875, to look after the interests of a firm which belonged to his family. In 1879 he took over the other English firms that traded there, and in 1886 got a royal charter to develop Nigeria, and led wars against the Nupe and Iloria in 1896. Frederick Lugard and Mary Kingsley, the explorer, were his allies in imperial politics.

Lugard was born in India in 1858, where his father was an Evangelical missionary. He acquired Uganda and organized Nigeria for the empire, and actually became governor of Hong Kong, and then of Nigeria. His biographer, Margery Perham, says of his caste identity, "It was a double sense of caste in that he felt himself to belong to a class within his nation and to a nation within Africa, both of which he believed, had the code of noblesse oblige." Back in England, he always dressed for dinner, even in those last years of his life when that was an old joke. She says he was "the supreme type of that imperialism which had long been the pride of his country and was now judged, by the major part of humanity, as something very near a crime."

Finally, Sir Harry Johnston, 1858–1927, known as the Prancing Proconsul, because of his oddity and gaiety. He was very small and young-looking and vivacious, a gifted artist, linguist, botanist, and zoologist. But he set up the new country of Uganda in 1899. He fought his battles under a huge white umbrella, and dressed his Sikh constabulary in white, yellow, and black, and put the same colors on his notepaper.

These heroes had a less Carlylean style in heroism than the Lawrence brothers, and the Indian army men generally—as embodied in them, the Empire is perceptibly more modern. But they were all men whose sense of self was supported by an aristocratic caste identity.

Chapter IX

1. Kipling is an obvious subject for any study of imperialism in literature, or of the great popular novelist, or of the WASP hero, or of caste psychology. Nevertheless, in coming to Kipling I face a double challenge, both aspects deriving from his being more purely and intensely an artist of literature than the other writers we have considered; being quite possibly, as T. S. Eliot said, the greatest man of letters of his generation. This means on the one hand that he is very inventive and "original," so that his work doesn't fit simply into the patterns I have been drawing; on the other it means that he deserves and demands a quantity of exposition and analysis which, within the limits of this book, I can't afford to give him.

The impulse to give him that is also strong because he, much more than the other adventure novelists, has been badly treated by critics. I am not thinking of the hostile essays—there are plenty of acts of repentance, too—the significant bad treatment is silent and general, is manifested as much in neglect as in anything else, is the work of an inhibiting prejudice in the mind of nearly every literary reader.

There is a resistance to Kipling which is an extreme example of the hostility to literature and the adventure tale that we have been studying; extreme because of Kipling's politics. The feeling against him is the by-product of reasoned convictions which I would never call prejudices in themselves; but their by-product is a disturbance of literary judgment. You may decide that that prejudice is a small price to pay for valuable convictions—and certainly I have small hope of undoing the prejudice by an argument—but ideally it must be possible to both cherish one's political convictions and see Kipling as a great writer about imperialism.

2. Of course Kim was in effect a native boy too, and one element in the English audience's fondness for him was that Kipling evoked their memories of such boys on his behalf. They said, "I knew a boy just like Kim." Independently of Kipling, they had focused their fondness for India on nimble, impudent, mischievous Indian boys of that kind—as opposed to Indian girls or adults. This bias was not felt merely with "natives"; it was a striking feature of late Victorian culture, that its emotional focus was on boys. We have seen that children's literature turned to the service of boys, in the middle of the nineteenth century, and that serious writers devoted their talents to that kind of writing. And something similar could be seen happening in other features of the culture, besides literature. At no other time could a play like *Peter Pan* have had the extraordinary success it had in London. This aspect of *Kim* is another example of Kipling's gift for taking material from the

Notes

very surface of his audience's mind, and fitting it to his serious artistic purposes.

3. Hannah Arendt has several perceptive and sympathetic things to say about Kipling in her *Origins of Totalitarianism*. "The author of the imperial legend is Rudyard Kipling, its topic is the British Empire, its result the imperialist character . . . and chivalry, nobility, bravery, answered the legend's call "And" Imperialism was a chance to escape a society in which a man had to forget his youth if he wanted to grow up" (pp. 208 and 210).

4. He told him, "You needed a tight hand in those days," and Kipling goes on to speak (in *Something of Myself*) of "the necessary wrench on the curb, that fetches up a too-flippant colt." While later, in India, his newspaper "chief" "took him in hand and broke him." Kipling says, "For three years or so I loathed him," but does not even need to add that later he valued the discipline he had received. And in *The Complete Stalky and Co.* there is a poem, "The Centaurs," which is about the training of young colts by Chiron, their stern preceptor.

5. The word "great," the capitalization of nouns like Road and River, and Mountain and House, and the use of phrasing evocative of the Bible or Shakespeare, and a whole corpus of such devices, Buchan inherited from Kipling. For instance, in *The African Colony*, there is a chapter about the Cape–Cairo Road, entitled "The Great North Road"; in which we read of the romance inseparable from all roads, and of a river that "pours a stately flood through the low coastlands to the sea" (p. 161). Buchan was very skillful at this sort of thing. Toward the climax of *Prester John*, the hero writes, "Behind me was heathendom and the black fever flats. In front were the cool mountains and the bright streams and the guns of my own folk." (He has escaped from territory held by insurgent blacks.) He goes on to quote "Night's candles are burned out." It would be impossible to evoke in fewer and simpler words the major sanctions of his high culture—Shakespeare, the Bible, *Pilgrim's Progress*, hill-climbing in Scotland; or to ally those ideals to the facts of imperialism—as represented by "the guns of my own folk"—more tactfully.

6. Also in essays. During the Great War, Kipling gave some remarkable talks of that kind, one to the Guards Cadet Corps in 1917, called "The Magic Square," on the primitive origins of military drill, and another to junior naval officers in 1918, called "The First Sailor," on the primitive origins of ships and sailing. (Both are to be found in *A Book of Words*.)

The idea of primitivism had definite political affiliations. Liberals believed that man had developed past his primitive ways, and should be *ashamed* of any traces of them in his mind. For instance, J. A. Hobson says in his *Imperialism* (1902), "Imperialism is a depraved choice of national life, imposed by self-seeking interests which appeal to the lusts of quantitative acquisitiveness and of forceful domination, surviving in a nation from early centuries of animal struggle for existence. Its adoption as a policy implies a deliberate renunciation of that cultivation of the higher inner qualities . . . etc." (p. 368). This book is a very important context in which to find such a declaration. Hobson's interpretation of imperialism, based on the history of South Africa and the Boer War, began the theoretical development of that concept which was taken up by the Left everywhere. Lenin, Luxemburg, and Kautsky, all made use of Hobson.

He said that the diamond merchants of the Rand had caused the Boer War, and the military imperialism was capitalism's natural mode of expansion; and that such imperialism was essentially like the Roman kind, and would create servitude and license, overcentralization and parasitism, even in England. His theory, arriving in the context of the general moral revulsion against the British part in the Boer War and the Belgian part in the Congo, carried a lot of conviction against Kipling's party. And

390

it is important to note how the idea of primitivism belonged to that conflict. Gandhi, for instance, developed Hobson's idea; literature—at least, the ideology of the great writers, like Eliot, Pound, and Lawrence—unconsciously followed Kipling.

In Kipling's party, or in alliance with him, we must put Karl Pearson and his "science" of eugenics. Pearson was a socialist; but he wanted a "warrior-chieftain" to lead his socialist state. He and Francis Galton proposed a Jihad (to be conducted by means of eugenic controls) against customs and prejudices that impaired the physical and moral qualities of the English race. Women should be sexually free, but politically confined to the kitchen and the nursery. And it is important to remember that both Shaw and Wells were eugenists for a time.

7. We can measure the effect of Kipling's fictionalization of this theme if we look at his essay on the same subject, "An English School," of 1893. (In *Land and Sea Tales*.) The school motto was "Fear God and Honour the King" and the hymn sung on the last Sunday of every term was "Onward Christian Soldiers"—the favorite stanza being, "We are not divided, All one body we, One in hope and doctrine, One in charity." There we glimpse the United Services College as more ordinary celebrants of its virtues would have described it. And of course he saw it that way, too. He quotes the poem the school sent to the Queen (written by himself, though he doesn't say so).

> Such greetings as should come from those
> Whose fathers faced the Sepoy hordes
> Or served you in the Russian snows
> And, dying, left their sons their swords.
> For we are bred to do your will
> By land and sea, wherever flies
> The Flag, to fight and follow still,
> And work your Empire's destinies."

Those are the copybook maxims that echo behind the slang and the cynicism of *Stalky and Co.*, and whose resonance makes it an extraordinary book.

Appendix to *"STALKY and Co."*

8. Most of Kipling's works deliver the message, "harness your imagination in the service of your society," and not all are intricately structured. Some deliver that imperative as crudely as you might think—reading literary critics—Kipling always wrote. But even those books are pungently flavored and full of literary interest. Let me cite a few cases.

In *Letters of Travel*, 1892–1927, we find an early essay, "Captains Courageous," which says on page 83, "There's a man in Yokohama who in a previous life burned galleons with Drake. He is a gentleman adventurer of the largest and most resourceful —by instinct a carver of kingdoms, a ruler of men on the high seas, and an inveterate gambler against death. . . ." There we see how Kipling (like Twain) would put his imagination at the service of the successful businessmen he met—his splendidly historical and poetic imagination.

On page 90 of the same book, he says, "A man who has *lived* . . . has heard the Arabian Nights retold and knows the inward kernel of that romance which some little folk say is vanished. Here they lie in their false teeth, for Cortes is not dead, nor Drake, and Sir Philip Sidney dies every few months if you knew where to look. The adventurers and captains courageous of old have only changed their dress a little and altered their employment to suit the world in which they move. Clive came down from

Notes

Lobengula's country a few months ago protesting that there was an empire there, and finding very few that believed. Hastings studied a map of South Africa in a corrugated iron hut in Johannesburg ten years ago . . ." There we might say that Kipling is serving the politicians, if one calls Rhodes a politician. "The others, big men all and not very much afraid of responsibility, are selling horses, breaking rails, drinking sangaree, running railways beyond the timber-line, swimming rivers, blowing up tree trunks, and making cities . . ."

Thematically, therefore, Kipling wrote about and for adventure. And his writing had a more aggressive edge against other themes and values than previous adventure writers. Thus he wrote in an essay about and from Canada in 1908, "A People At Home" (pp. 141–142), "I wonder sometimes whether any eminent novelist, philosopher, dramatist or divine of today has to exercise half the pure imagination, not to mention insight, endurance, and self-restraint, which is accepted without comment in what is called 'the material exploitation' of a new country" *(Letter of Travel)*.

A somewhat similar idea is expressed in a story, "A Conference of the Powers," of 1890, in *Many Inventions*, in which a group of young subalterns meet the great novelist, Eustace Cleever—who may be a partial portrait of Henry James. When this man of letters looks at these men of action, Kipling notes that, "The line of the chin-strap, that still showed white and untanned on cheekbone and jaw, the steadfast young eyes puckered at the corners of the lids with much staring through red-hot sunshine, the slow, untroubled breathing, and the curious, crisp, curt speech, seemed to puzzle him utterly (p. 28)." "Him" being the Jamesian novelist, whom we may take to represent literature. "To me," the latter said softly, "The whole idea of warfare seems so foreign and unnatural, so essentially vulgar, if I may say so, that I can hardly appreciate your sensations" (p. 29). When one of them, called "The Infant," tells him about Burmese dacoits who crucify their victims—Cleever "could not realize that the Cross still existed." These young subalterns deal with such facts daily; they have all killed enemies, all enjoy fighting, and all like their enemies. The novelist's mind is "stretched" by them and his soul "over-awed." When the Infant says modestly that he has only seen Burma, Cleever adds, "And dead men, and war, and power, and responsibility." After the encounter he says that no one would sing (that is, write novels) if he could kiss (that is, fight wars).

(I haven't meant to imply, even by silence, that Kipling was not occasionally vulgar —in the way that last quotation shows. But I think readers often find him vulgar when it is his subject matter that embarrasses them, and it is their own ideological squeamishness that is at fault.)

The poem "To the True Romance," in the same volume, says,

> Thou art the Voice to kingly boys
> To lift them through the fight,
> And Comfortress of Unsuccess
> To give the Dead good-night.

(The language is, as in Kipling generally, chivalric-romantic, rather than Defoe-plain. There are plenty of facts in Kipling, but they are subsumed in mythic patterns.)

This kingly-boy side of Kipling's work receives one of its most full-scale treatments in "The Brushwood Boy," 1895, interesting also as a simpler kind of failure than is at all common in Kipling. George Cotter is the perfect English upper-caste boy, responsible for the tone of his school; where the "wise and temperate" Head has led him to see how men and boys are "all of a piece," and that he who can handle the one will control the other. When he joined his regiment, "he bore with him from school a character worth much fine gold . . ." *(A Kipling Pageant, p. 350).* ". . . his training had set the public school mark upon his face, and had taught him how many were the 'things no fellow can do.' By virtue of the same training he kept his pores open and his mouth shut." He boxed his men into obedience and devotion to him. One sees here something Kipling usually conceals, or expresses more discreetly, his love of young Englishmen of "the right type." It was indeed a social passion of the time, which you meet in many writers, and which often seems quite cannibal in its relish of their physical charm. Kipling usually avoided describing his hero directly; for instance, in "A Sahib's War," we hear the narrative of a Sikh servant about his young master—who is dead before the story begins—and our sense of the young Englishman's beauty is suggested only by the ugliness of the three Boers whom the Sikh fiercely sacrifices to his memory—a fanatical preacher, his fat wife, and his idiot son.

George Cotter is, one may say, a prince of the copybook maxims. Kipling for once has tried to introduce no reactive moral realism, no unpleasantness. He is what English mothers then wanted their boys to be. The other element in this characterization is yet more romantic—that he dreams, and in his dream life roams an entirely different country from the banal one of every day. Sexless in real life—when his mother tucks him up for the night, she can tell he's never been kissed—his destiny is to meet a girl who dreams of the same world he does. Thus their eroticism can all take place in that dream world, and in this world they are just Girl and Boy, which is how they address each other. This is Kipling-as-Barrie, and the vision of England, embodied in George's home, is equally as golden and unreal as the characterization. It is all rose gardens and white peacocks and "the shadow of the old house lay long across the wonderful English foliage, which is the only living green in the world. 'Perfect! By Jove, it's perfect.' Georgie was looking at the round-bosomed woods beyond the home paddock, where the white pheasant boxes were ranged; and the golden air was full of a hundred scents and sounds" (*A Kipling Pageant*, p. 364). The same sense of England's beauty, as something rich and perfect, valuable and vulnerable, can be found in "They," 1904, and "An Habitation Enforced," 1905. In the first, the house is built of weather-worn stone, with mullioned windows and rose-red tile roofs, yew topiary, and "a great still lawn." There is a great rose-grown gate and a heavy oak door sunk deep in the thickness of the wall. (Heavy, deep, and thick are often key words in this kind of writing.) In the second, some Americans buy an old house and learn how to live in it, and thereupon they get over their nervous problems and are able to have a child. (This suggests the connections the culture felt between this kind of expensive beauty and a therapy for exasperated nerves and impaired fertility.)

The ineptitudes of "The Brushwood Boy" are embarrassing rather than interesting. But *The Naulahka*, the novel Kipling wrote with his American brother-in-law, is interesting, even though not very successful. It combines material from the Frontier (from Twain's world) with material from the Empire. The story opens with Nick Tarvin and Kate Sheriff in Topaz, Colorado. She is the daughter of a railway engineer, but was converted to religion and social work at school, and wants to go to India to help Indian women, who are nothing but their men's chattels. He is a real estate and insurance agent, who "believes" only in Topaz, a man who habitually lies and tricks his competitors, but who has surrendered his conscience to Kate, and is willing to obey what she says are its laws (p. 21).

> The Law whereby my Lady moves
> Was never Law to me
> But 'tis enough that she approve
> Whatever Law it be.
> For in that Law and by that Law
> My constant sourse I'll steer;

Notes

> Not that I heed or deem it deed
> But that she holds it dear.

Kipling tells us that "men to whom life is a joke find comfort in women to whom it is a prayer." (p. 21.) Nick is a "nervous, bony, loose-hung man, with a kind, clever, aggressive eye, and a masterful chin" (p. 23). Elected to the state legislature, he tells the other legislators dry and laconic anecdotes in Abraham Lincoln fashion.

Kate goes to India as a medical missionary, and Nick follows her to the court of an opium-addict maharajah. There he dams a river, trains the maharajah's son to be manly, and makes the maharajah laugh. Another Connecticut Yankee, he dominates the splendid and jeweled court by his gunplay and his skill in horse-breaking. "It made him tired to see the fixedness, the apathy and lifelessness of this rich and populous world, which should be up and stirring by rights—trading, organizing, inventing, building new towns, making the old ones keep up with the procession, laying new railroads, going in for new enterprises, and keeping things humming" (p. 121). He has a putative romance with Sitabhai, the most beautiful of the maharajah's wives, a Morgan le Fay character, who says, "If you were a king and I a queen, we would hold Hindustan between our two hands" (p. 277). She throws a knife at him and he responds with a kiss upon her lips. Here the story works out some of the implications of *Connecticut Yankee* which Twain turned away from. Kipling wrote a poem on the same theme.

> Strangers drawn from the ends of the earth, jewelled and plumed were we
> I was the Lord of the Inca Race, and she was the Queen of the Sea.
> Under the stars beyond our stars, where the veinless meteors glow,
> Hotly we stormed Valhalla, a million years ago.

This is the same vein of feeling as Haggard's *She* develops—the Anglo-Saxon hero's feeling that for a man like him there must be something better waiting than an Anglo-Saxon woman.

Kipling felt a generous, though not uncomplicated, admiration for America and the Americans; a much more romantic feeling than he had about Englishmen. He felt that America was still boyish, and shirked discipline, shirked moral realism and responsibility. So in *Something of Myself* he wrote, "I never got over the wonder of a people who, having extirpated the aboriginals of their continent more completely than any modern race had ever done, honestly believed that they were a godly little New England community, setting an example to brutal mankind" (p. 441). But in *From Sea to Sea,* he says, "Wait till the Anglo-American-German-Jew—the Man of the Future—is properly equipped. He'll have just the least little kink in his hair now and again; he'll carry the English lungs above the Teuton feet that can walk forever; and he will wave long, thin, bony, Yankee hands, with the big blue veins on the wrist, from one end of the earth to the other. He'll be the finest writer . . . etc." (p. 109). Americans were for him an intensified version of Australians or Canadians, and almost citizens of the Empire.

On the whole, Kipling's attitude toward America was very similar to Stevenson's, who said in *From Scotland to Silverado* that an Englishman thinks of America with envy; that there is a hostility between them, because tomorrow belongs to the Americans—"for us, England and yesterday." This was, I think, a very widespread feeling in England at the end of the nineteenth century, and it could be connected with the split we have discussed between Empire and Frontier. (It is worth noting, also, some striking parallels between Kipling and Stevenson, biographically and literarily; that they both married American women, older than themselves, and somewhat managing

394

and maternal; that their books were family enterprises—Kipling's father providing illustrations to his books, Stevenson's son-in-law doing the same for his—; that they sprinkled verses, that looked like quotations, through their narratives, as part of a way to bring literature into forced alliance with adventure; and so on.)

Whereas Kipling's tone about Englishmen at home tends to be this of *Letters on Leave*, "A Death in the Camp." "Above that they seem to be, most curiously and beyond the right of ordinary people, divorced from the knowledge of the fear of death . . . because they have everything done for them they know how everything ought to be done . . . little trifles like colonial administration, the wants of the Army, municipal sewage, housing of the poor, and so forth. Every third common need of average men is, in their mouths, a tendency or a movement or a federation affecting the world" (p. 184). On the next page he complains of a man who "knows all about the aggressive militarism of you and your friends; he isn't quite sure of the necessity of an Army; he is certain that colonial expansion is nonsense; and he is more than certain that the whole step of all our Empire ought to be regulated by the knowledge and foresight of the working man . . . (p. 185) . . . You mustn't treat any man like a machine in this country, but you can't get any work out of a man until he has learned to work like a machine . . . (p. 197) . . . I honestly believe that the average Englishman would faint if you told him it was lawful to use up human life for any purpose whatever. He believes that it has to be developed and made beautiful for the possessor" (p. 190).

This vein of thought, Kipling's most interesting but most shocking, is again expressed in "Drums of the Fore and Aft," 1888, his story about a green regiment that broke under fire, and how two drummer boys rallied it by playing "The British Grenadiers." ". . . wherefore the soldier, and the soldier of today more particularly, should not be blamed for falling back. He should be shot or hanged afterwards—to encourage the others—but he should not be vilified in newspapers, for that is want of tact and waste of space . . . (*A Kipling Pageant*, p. 101). . . . Speaking roughly, you must employ either blackguards or gentlemen, or, best of all, blackguards commanded by gentlemen, to do butchers' work with efficiency and dispatch . . . and God has arranged that a clean-run youth of the British middle class shall, in the matter of backbone, brains, and bowels, surpass all other youths. For this reason, a child of 18 will stand up, doing nothing, with a tin sword in his hand and joy in his heart until he is dropped" (p. 103).

If this were an evaluative account of Kipling's work, I should spend a long time on stories like "The Bridgebuilders," 1905, which is a very remarkable confrontation of the myths of India with the antimyths of the modern world system. The Hindu gods have caused the Ganges to flood and beat against the great bridge which Findlayson has just built. The burden of the story is the question whether the white man's gods are merely another embodiment of the multiform Indian gods, or whether they represent something new in the world; and there is some real strength of feeling and sharpness of sight on both sides.

But I have space for nothing more than *Puck of Pook's Hill*, 1905, and its continuation, *Rewards and Fairies*, 1910. These are retellings and dramatizations of key episodes in English history, narrated by Puck to two modern children of the age of Kipling's own. Kipling had often been reproached—by Chesterton, for example—with writing about England as if he were a foreigner, without knowing it from inside. In serious fiction, this was the age of Hardy, dominated by a powerful mood honoring English ruralism, and these stories are in some sense Kipling's contribution; nonimperialist, nonindustrial, nonmechanical; quietist, cyclical, fertility-oriented. Kipling accommodates his older, somewhat opposite interests to these, and the two make a rich mixture. Here the primitive origins of modern customs are much more gently evoked

Notes

—though "The Knife and the Naked Chalk" and "Cold Iron" do that very beautifully —and it is the historical origins which interest him.

Most important from our point of view are the stories about the Roman centurions and the Saxon and the Norman brothers-in-knighthood. These are important because of the powerful use Kipling makes of a motif we noted in Dumas; the confrontation between young men—here a pair each time—and an older man who represents a cold and in some ways sinister wisdom. Sir Hugh and Sir Richard face deAquila, small and crooked-nosed, bitter and wise and responsible. Parnesius and Pertinax face Maximus, the great Roman general, who offers the former greatness in return for a cruel but politic deed. (The implicit identification of England with Rome is an important step in the development of that theme—since as late as Kingsley the identification was fought off as sinister. It is negotiated by stressing the frontier character of the Roman settlements—the Great Wall is, as Kipling describes it, a frontier town—and that of course implies an identification with America too.) The young men love each other, fight and compete against each other; the old man is spiritually alone and rather sinister, but imposes his will upon them, the will of civilization; it is an implicitly emotional, in some sense an erotic, transaction, but much more metaphorically so than the equivalent in *Kim.*

Kipling was a great metaphorician, a great artist of allusion. This is to be noted particularly in his language, which alludes to various areas of experience and expertise. One direction is indicated by the language of the Bible and the sagas; another is the language of trades and crafts; another is the language of sports and military affairs. But the allusion is not only a matter of vocabulary, it is also a matter of concept and factual detail, description and characterization, all of which are likely to be extremely compressed, complex, and suggestive. In *Puck* the allusion is predominantly historical and literary in direction, and the book is a triumph of vivid and richly intricate evocation of the English past. In this aspect of his work Kipling is quite worthy to be put beside Scott and Shakespeare. These stories are in fact Kipling's Foundation Epic; except of course that these are short stories and at an opposite extreme from the epic poem in most formal terms; that paradox—the fragmentariness of Kipling's form, combined with the monumentality of his themes—is something I must return to.

The motif of iron runs through *Puck of Pook's Hill;* it is introduced in the first story, of Weland's sword, which is given to Hugh the Saxon. "Knights of the Joyous Venture," an adventure tale which uses most of the motifs we have been following, describes how Hugh and Richard sell iron in Africa, and get gold and ivory in return. "A Centurion of the 30th" also has lots about iron. And *Rewards and Fairies* begins with "Cold Iron"; a story in which a fairy child becomes human, at the age of sixteen, when he finds a slave-ring of iron, and fastens it round his own neck. Thus one of the most important motifs in the modern imagination received careful literary treatment, at the climactic moment of the system's career.

9. He went to the United Services College, the school depicted in *Stalky and Co.* In *Something of Myself* he describes it as a caste school, meaning the military caste. Seventy-five percent of the boys, he says, were born outside England, and hoped to follow their fathers into the army. In "An English School" he says, "and so the men she made went out to Boerland and Zululand and India and Burma and Cyprus and Hong Kong, and lived and died as gentlemen and officers" (*Land and Sea Tales,* p. 562). And indeed, in 1914, of his schoolmates, Godby was commanding the New Zealand forces, Maclaglan led a brigade of Australians, Rimington was chief engineer in Mesopotamia, and Dunsterville (the original of Stalky) was to lead an expedition into North Persia. (Carrington, *Life of Rudyard Kipling.*)

10. In a talk given to a naval club, in 1908, he said, "One is influenced forever by

one's first commission, and mine threw me among disciplined men of action—the Indian services—where men were required to live under authority and act under orders." And in *Something of Myself* he said that at the club in India he met, "none but picked men at their definite work."

11. This theme of kingship, and this way of playing with it, runs through all the adventure genre. In *A General History of the Pyrates*, 1724, Defoe says the Madagascar pirates had slaves and seraglios, and came out to meet Woodes Rogers, "attended like Princes; and since they actually are Kings de facto, which is a kind of Right, we ought to speak of them as such." But their clothes were worn out; "their Majesties were extremely out at the elbows"; and he left them in "a great deal of dirty State and Royalty . . . and if Ambition be the darling Passion of Men, no doubt they were happy. One of these great Princes had formerly been a Waterman upon the Thames . . ." (pp. 61–62).

That is the satiric-realistic stress, such as we find in Twain's "The Duke and the Dauphin." It is really quite continuous with the more romantic stress we can hear in this passage from John Buchan's *Salute to Adventurers* (1915), a romance which sums up an unusual number of these motifs. Andrew Garvald, a Scots merchant, has helped an Indian find his kingdom in Virginia in the 1680s, and so this king, Shahlah, urges Garvald to ride west with him, and give up trade for kingship. "While the blood is strong in the veins shall we ride westward in the path of a king?" Garvald reflects, "I might be a king over a proud people, carving a fair kingdom out of the wilderness, and ruling it justly in the fear of God. These western Indians were the stuff of a great nation. I, Andrew Garvald, might yet find that empire of which the old adventurers dreamed." But in fact he chooses the quieter destiny, the white man's way, marriage, and trade.

12. I have argued in another essay, "Our Turn to Cliché," that English literature after 1918 is characterized by a marked preference for quotation, allusion, and cliché. I cite Virginia Woolf and Graham Greene as particularly notable among novelists for the importance of this device in their work. (The essay is to be found in my *Trans-Atlantic Patterns*.) It now seems to me that they learned this art—though they are not so expert at it as he—from Kipling. If so, this unacknowledged debt is a neat example of the general ingratitude of modern English literature; they have claimed Conrad as father while owing more to Kipling—for this seems to me a very significant debt, establishing the important terms of reference for all criticism.

13. The other European countries had followed England in adding territory during these years. Hannah Arendt says that in two decades the British added 4.5 million square miles and 66 million people; the French 3.5 million square miles and 26 million people; Germany 1 million square miles and 13 million people; Belgium 900,000 square miles and 8.5 million people. Such countries needed stories of Defoe's or Kipling's kind.

In the decade before 1914 there were French novelists who wrote about Algeria with some of Kipling's ideas and techniques; for instance, Robert Randau (*Colons*, 1907, and *Explorations*, 1909), who depicted France as a land of ideas, Algeria a land of action, and made much of the regenerative effects of close contact with the soil. There was also Louis Bertrand, who compared the English with the Romans, the French with the Carthaginians, turning Defoe's idea to France's advantage. In those years, Barrès, Maurras, and Seillière were all saying that France had become overcivilized and needed more force and violence, which she could find in colonization. Pierre Mille (1865–1960), who had lived in London and admired the English, and translated Kipling, wrote stories around a character, Barnavaux, who was like Kipling's Irish soldier, Mulvaney.

Notes

In Germany the colonies promised an escape from the pressures expressed in Willkomm's *Die Europamüden*, of 1838, says Hugh Ridley, in "Germany in the Mirror of Its Colonial Lit." (*German Life and Letters*, July 1975.) The colonies felt free from the pressures of class that troubled Germany, a freedom which attracted the army but also the civil service and the peasant farmers. Frenssen's *Peter Moors Fahrt Nach Südwest* was very popular. Hans Grimm (1875–1960), who had lived in England and South Africa, wrote *Volk Ohne Raum*, 1926, which sold 750,000 copies, and became an officer of the Colonial Service. Mille also was an authority on French colonial matters, and both followed Kipling's naturalist-aesthete line, though Mille's landscapes are lyrical, while Grimm's are utopian; but Mille approved miscegenation (and native culture) while Grimm repudiated it. Germany also had some women writers about colonial life; Frieda Von Bulow, in love with Carl Peters, in *Tropenkoller*, depicted colonial life as making every German an aristocrat. And in *Ludwig v. Rosen*, 1892, she showed that colonial life offered a hardness, passion and archaic quality that would redeem even effete aristocrats. Frieda Kraze's *Heim Neuland* had a heroine who sought sexual liberation until she found, in the colonies, that that would reduce her to the level of the natives.

It may be appropriate here to describe the phenomenon of Karl May, also. He bore no known relation to Kipling, but he belonged to Kipling's era, and bore a very important relation to the Anglo-Saxon adventure hero. Karl May (1842–1912) wrote forty volumes of Western adventures, translated as a whole into twenty other languages; 24 million volumes by him have been sold in Germany, and 2.5 million of *Winnetou* alone. Winnetou is the son of the chief of the Mescalescou Apaches, who becomes the blood brother of Old Shatterhand, a German adventurer on the American frontier with a blond beard, etc., who could fell both man and beast with a blow of his fist.

May wrote in the first person, and was photographed wearing Shatterhand's costume—fringed leggings and hunting jacket, two revolvers and a bowie knife, a gun on his back and one in his hands. In various ways May encouraged his readers to believe that he *was* Old Shatterhand; he built himself a Villa Shatterhand with his profits. (He was in prison for fraud and theft—on other charges—early in his career.) He had at one point earned a living writing soft-core pornography, and these books are full of idealized homosexuality. But there is a surface ideology of Christian knighthood—Shatterhand converts Winnetou.

But May's interest lies in his success. *Der Spiegel* called him recently a Praeceptor Germaniae, and the greatest influence on German youth between Goethe and Mann; there is an annual Karl May Festival at Bad Segeburg. Hitler recommended him to his general staff, and Einstein and Schweitzer both acknowledged his moral influence. Georg Grosz wrote in his autobiography "The reading of these books awakened in the youngster a yearning—that secretly exists in practically every German—for distant lands and exotic adventures. (These books could well have been the result of the ardent propaganda of the time for German colonial expansion.) Yes, indeed, we certainly had a warm place in our hearts for our great, blond, German-American hero, Old Shatterhand, who with one blow of a clenched fist could lay low a horse, not to mention a contemptible traitor.... Winnetou was one of the ideals of the German youth of my day. He actually became a national hero, even more famous than his renowned colleagues, Uncas and Chingachgook, because there was something 'German' about him." This is a particularly vivid case of a general phenomenon, the infection of other core countries with the virus of Anglo-Saxon adventure.

14. Amongst novels about Rhodes, we can mention Gilbert Parker, *The Judgement House*, 1913. Sarah Gertrude Millin, *The Jordans*, 1923. Morley Roberts, *The Colos-*

sus, 1899. Antony Hope, *The God in the Car.* G. Skeleton, *Dominion,* 1925. F. B.
Young, *City of Gold,* 1937–1939. And Stuart Cloete's trilogy, beginning with *Turning Wheels,* 1939.

15. Ruskin said "There is a destiny now possible to us, the highest ever set before
a nation to be accepted or refused. We are still an undegenerate race; a race mingled
of the best northern blood. We are not yet dissolute in temper, but still have the
firmness to govern, and the grace to obey . . . will you, youths of England, make your
country again a royal throne of kings? . . . And this is what England either must do,
or perish: she must found colonies as fast and as far as she is able, formed of her most
energetic and worthiest men . . . if we can get men, for little pay, to cast themselves
against cannon-mouths for love of England, we may find men also who will plough
and sow for her, and who will behave kindly and righteously for her, and will bring
up their children to love her" (R.A. Huttenback, *The British Imperial Achievement,*
p. 101).

16. At the same time he much admired the Boers for their pastoralism, and thought
of himself as in some ideal sense a farmer. He worked hard for Anglo-Boer unity, and
admired Kruger. His plans might have succeeded but for the discovery of gold in the
Transvaal, which led indirectly to the Jameson Raid in 1895.

In relation to black Africa, on the other hand, he was simply expansionist. In 1888
he signed a treaty with Lobengula, which gave the latter £100 a month, 1,000 Martini
rifles, 100,000 rounds of ammunition, and a gunboat. The Aborigines' Protection
Society had warned Lobengula, but he thought he was signing away a mine, not a
country. The charter was delivered to him by a contingent of Royal Horse Guards,
who galloped up to the kraal in silver breastplates and plumed helmets, escorting a
coach emblazoned with V. R. (Victoria Regina) and drawn by eight silver-caparisoned
mules. In 1889 the British South African Company was chartered—on the rumor of
the discovery of King Solomon's mines in Mashonaland. In 1890 his 186 Pioneers
(some of them Boer) began their march north there and to Matabeleland, using
dynamite and naval searchlights to strike terror into the Zulus. Each of the Pioneers
was promised 3,000 acres and 115 gold claims. Rhodes told them, "You have the proud
satisfaction of knowing that you are civilizing a new part of the world. Those who fall
in that creation fall sooner than they would in an ordinary life, but their lives are better
and grander" (Huttenback, p. 112).

17. In fact, Lenin, in his *Imperialism* (1916), quotes from a speech of Rhodes of
1895. "I was in the East End of London yesterday and attended a meeting of the
unemployed. I listened to the wild speeches . . . in order to save the 40,000,000
inhabitants of the United Kingdom from a bloody civil war, we colonial statesmen
must acquire new lands to settle the surplus population, to provide new markets for
the goods produced by them in factories and mines . . . If you want to avoid civil war
you must become imperialists."

18. Many public schools had some connection with the army. In 1830, 12 percent
of the boys leaving Harrow and Rugby joined the forces; in 1850, 27 percent; though
it fell off later—in 1880 it was only 14 percent, but it is worth noting that nearly all
of those reached the rank of colonel or above. And some schools had very strong
military traditions. Cheltenham sent out 4,237 boys between 1841 and 1910, and
1,896 served in the forces; while Clifton had much the same record (Ellis, *The Social
History of the Machine Gun,* p. 101).

19. The link with the aristocracy, and the social career of the military caste, can
be traced to some degree in Army Lists. In France the Revolution drove aristocrats
out of the army, but they returned after 1815. The more they were pushed out of the
economic and political life of nineteenth-century France, the more they took over the

Notes

army—and later on, the empire. (Their other field was diplomacy, where aristocrats could serve their country while hating their government, hating the French state.) In 1875, out of the 365 cadets at the military academy of St. Cyr, 102 had "de" before their name. In Germany at about the same time, 65 percent had "von" before theirs. That proportion sank, but in 1914 it was 53 percent for officers above the rank of colonel. In England, in 1875, 50 percent were from the aristocracy-plus-the-gentry. (I take all these estimates from "Officers and Gentlemen" in Ellis, *The Social History of the Machine Gun.*) And Army Regulations breathed the spirit of chivalry—with a concommitant hostility to technology. The French regulations, according to Ellis, said the army must always take the offensive, must always charge, and cavalry must be the army's real strength. And there was a cult of the well-bred horse. The British Cavalry Training Manual of 1907 said, "It must be accepted as a principle that the rifle, effective as it is, cannot replace the effect produced by the speed of the horse, the magnetism of the charge, and the terror of cold steel."

20. Hannah Arendt points out in *Origins of Totalitarianism* that imperialism gave a new lease on life to social structures which would otherwise have collapsed; and we might add, psychological structures. She says that the educated classes everywhere welcomed it, for that reason, though governments often fought against it. All the parliamentary parties, in England, France, and Germany, collaborated in imperialist programs sooner or later; and it was Englishmen in the colonies, or thinking about the colonies, who were the most patriotic-militant. The effect of all this on psychological structures—mediated via school, notably—was to promote the development of leaders, commanders, captains. This is how the Kshattriya caste, to which Kipling belonged, and for whom he wrote, was propagated. In India itself, that caste almost certainly owes its origin to a similar imperialist situation.

21. This is the idea I hinted at in the first footnote to p. 285. The Bloomsbury sensibility (and in this it was only typical of most kinds of English sensibility after 1918) declared itself the very opposite of Kipling's, in feeling for words and for personality, in taste in letters and in life generally, as well as in politics. And yet the only significant writer who owed nothing to Kipling, or practically nothing, was D. H. Lawrence. I say "practically nothing" because Lawrence's primitivism, and its political corollaries, are not totally unlike Kipling's. But on the whole, Lawrence did indeed choose Hardy and not Kipling as his godfather. But his colleagues did not. This is immensely important for understanding the cultural conflicts of England over the last fifty years.

Chapter X

1. Brooke was important to adventure enthusiasts generally. I have already mentioned his appearance in the dedication to *Westward Ho!*. And when Borrow said it was a crown of glory to carry the blessings of civilization and religion to the barbarous, he asked, "But who has done so in these times?" and answered himself, "Only Rajah Brooke." And A. P. Wallace said the Dyaks looked up to Brooke as to a supernatural king.

2. One of the likenesses between the two locations is indicated by the legends of treasure. In *Almayer's Folly* we are told, "The coast population of Borneo believes implicitly in diamonds of fabulous value, in gold mines of enormous richness in the interior. And all those imaginings are heightened by the difficulty of penetrating far inland, especially on the north-east coast, where the Malays and the river tribes of

Dyaks, or Head-hunters, are eternally quarrelling." This is very similar to the situation in Costaguana, in *Nostromo*, and in the historical Guinea, where European adventurers (like Raleigh) were drawn further and further on by such stories among the native population. There is no reason to declare that Conrad was drawing an analogy by this coincidence. A safer conclusion to draw is that in fact Europeans' imaginations all over the world were set aflame by contact with the already burning sparks of adventure and ambition of native imperialism.

3. On page 1, Brooke is described as being "a true adventurer in his devotion to his impulse—a man of high mind and of pure heart." Conrad's language blends adventure with romance. Brooke, we are told, "recognized chivalrously the claims of the conquered; he was a disinterested adventurer, and the reward of his noble instincts is in the veneration with which a strange and faithful race cherish his memory."

4. *Victory* (1915) presents adventurers as villains. The main villain, Gentleman Jones, is a sort of Gilbert Osmond of adventurer, while the hero, Axel Heyst, is in retreat from the world, and is the opposite of an adventurer. Conrad's sympathies lie with him, though they are, as ever, ironic. Reflection is a pernicious habit, as Stein had said in *Lord Jim*, and Axel is too reflective and clear-sighted.

5. Jeffrey Meyers, in *Fiction and the Colonial Experience*, says that Kurtz should be associated with Rimbaud, who wrote home from Abyssinia in 1888 in exasperation against the natives he had to deal with. "Obliged to chatter their jibberish, to eat their filthy messes, to endure a thousand and one annoyances that come from their idleness, their treachery, and their stupidity." Meyers makes no suggestion that Conrad was thinking of Rimbaud, only that both men were at the same moment passing through the same experience—one of the many deaths of the nineteenth-century liberal imagination. Certainly, given the imaginative ascendancy achieved by both Kurtz and Rimbaud in the 1920s and 1930s, in England at least, it behooves us to keep them bracketed in our minds.

6. For instance, in 1898 he wrote about Marryat, the sea-novelist he was emulating, "To his young heroes the beginning of life is a splendid and warlike lark, ending at last in inheritance and marriage . . ." (Notes on *Life and Letters*, p. 53). Marryat wrote when the century was young, and Conrad was conscious of writing when it was old. He was also conscious of being an artist, a sophisticated Romantic artist, as Marryat was not. "There is an air of fable about it . . . [Marryat's world] . . . It is the beginning and the embodiment of an inspiring tradition . . . His figures move about between water and sky, and the water and the sky are there only to frame the deeds of the Service" (p. 54). Conrad of course paid great attention to the water and the sky in themselves. Marryat's heroes "do not belong to life; they belong exclusively to the service. And yet they live; there is a truth in them, the truth of their time; a headlong, reckless audacity, an intimacy with violence, an unthinking fearlessness, and an exuberance of vitality, which only years of war and victories can give" (p. 54). Marryat's books, as well as his heroes, drew vitality from those years of war and victories. But the truth of Conrad's times is very different, he implies.

Conrad feels himself further from such figures, and his own heroes, than Kipling does from his subalterns, but it is not a distance of unfamiliarity. Conrad has known the sailors he writes about. It is a distance of alienation—while Kipling embraced his heroes, Conrad felt his inner self very remote from his. His Captain Beards and Captain MacWhirrs are incredible, incomprehensible, phenomenal. He compared Marryat with Cooper and noted that the latter was more concerned—like himself—with Nature and with Art. Conrad, of course, felt himself much more the artist and the metaphysician than either.

However, Cooper and Marryat also served their countries' navies, and Conrad no

Notes

doubt saw himself as like them in that. At least he often endorsed that service of theirs. "Perhaps no two authors influenced so many lives and gave so many the initial impulse towards a glorious or a useful career." And he was something of a recruiting agent himself. In *A Mirror of the Sea* (1905) he said, "The British navy may well have ceased to count its victories. It is rich beyond the wildest dreams of success and fame. . . . It is too great for mere pride" (p. 185). Of course, his fiction is more ambivalent.

7. *Nostromo* is of particular interest because, according to Jerry Allen in *The Sea Years of Joseph Conrad,* the setting Conrad had in mind was Colombia, a setting that combines memories of Raleigh's search for gold in the sixteenth century with a reference to Theodore Roosevelt's 1903 promotion of the secession of the province of Panama, in order that America might dig the Panama Canal. Thus the story links sixteenth-century El Dorado with twentieth-century technology. For instance, the San Thome mine which Gould works had been abandoned by the Indians; just as the mine at San Thome mine which Raleigh sought was filled in by the Indians, to save themselves from rapacious adventurers. Costaguana is Raleigh's Coast of Guinea.

In 1876, when he was eighteen, Conrad had sailed from Marseilles to Martinique and on to Colombia, and his ship was carrying a cargo of arms to help the conservative side in the revolution then taking place, just like the one he described in *Nostromo.* The story of El Dorado could not fail to have excited his imagination, then or whenever he heard it. In fact the legends are told by Santiago Perez Triana in one of his books, and Triana was the Panamanian Minister to London and the man Conrad drew as the character Don José in *Nostromo.* Triana tells how de Quesada led seven hundred Spanish soldiers in search of the gold in 1536, and how Raleigh followed de Quesada. It is one of the great stories of the second half of the sixteenth century, and of modern imperialist adventure.

8. This is very half-hearted. Charles Gould, the representative Englishman of *Nostromo* is made out to betray his wife, by caring more about his mine; but this, like Jim's betrayal of Jewel, is little more than a rhetorical device in Conrad. Perhaps because Conrad had blended the material of the serious novel with that of adventure, he quite often makes such a point against his adventurers; a diagnosis of just the kind that D. H. Lawrence was to make the starting point of his philosophy of eroticism (see Lydia's account of her Polish husband in *The Rainbow*). But Conrad clearly has no sense of eroticism as a serious idea by which to live. He merely makes a point against his adventure heroes, because he is uneasy with their heroism.

Chapter XI

1. Morris's *The Well at the World's End* (1898) is an extraordinary evocation of stripling eroticism, which was very popular with the whole generation before 1914, according to Paul Fussell, in *The Great War and Modern Memory.* Here the adventure component in romance is quite melted out by the heat of sexual fantasy. The young hero is loved by everyone, typically older women, who hold his hands, kiss his lips, weep to look upon him—he lets one cut a lock from his thatch of golden curls. The monk of Higham laughs to see him sleepy and naked in the morning, and the carline of the Castle of Abundance says, "Far would many a Maiden run to kiss thy mouth, fair lad," —whereupon he "laughed gaily" and went into the hall with her. The adventures are nothing but hazy episodes in the heat of erotic excitement. Nothing could be further from Defoe's kind of story. Its relevance to our interest is just that it shows the tribute that Edwardian culture paid to the young man figure. But it is notable also that the

story's various representatives of the commercial impulse—called "chapmen"—are all scorned. The story is clearly romance, but of the sexual-fantasy kind.

2. He thought of his father as having been lord-like in Ireland, in his first marriage —before being carried off and subdued by Lawrence's Puritan mother. As an old woman, the latter went out to China as a medical missionary, with her older son, Robert—at a time when T. E. Lawrence was serving in the Air Force in India. Thus there was a caste drama in the family, like a *Pamela* in which Mr. B. escaped literal marriage (but underwent everything else); the mother, lower class, Puritan, and dominant; the father, upper class, amoral, and subdued. Naturally, this affected the way Lawrence saw himself. He described himself in a letter to Mrs. G. B. Shaw in 1925 as being two people: "Naturally the very strong one, Say 'No,' the Puritan, is in firm charge, and the other poor little vicious fellow can't get a word in, for fear of him" (John E. Mack's *A Prince of our Disorder*, p. 403). This suggests why Lawrence chose the chivalric style so decidedly.

3. Among American books on similar topics, one might cite John Seelye's *Prophetic Waters* as having a similar character. Seelye for instance calls the explorer, La Salle, an American Kurtz; he describes how in 1680 La Salle found the fort he had established (Fort Frontenac) deserted by the men he had left in it; while the boat which was to have carried him down the Mississippi had a "Conradian graffito" scrawled across it: *"Nous sommes tous sauvages."*

Bibliography

The primary purpose of this bibliography is to name the editions I used, so that the reader can find my page references. Secondly, I want to identify more fully books cited only glancingly. And finally, I name some books just because I am so indebted to them. But this principle has not been followed consistently, because of the counter-principle —that a full list of everything I'd used would be too long.

Allen, Jerry. *The Sea Years of Joseph Conrad.* New York, 1965.
Arendt, Hannah. *The Origins of Totalitarianism.* New York, 1966.
Bakeless, John. *Daniel Boone.* New York, 1939.
Bercovitch, Sacvan. *The Puritan Origins of the American Self.* New Haven, Conn., 1975.
Biglow, Poultney. *White Man's Africa.* New York, 1898.
Billington, James. *The Icon and the Axe.* New York, 1966.
Bird, R. M. *Nick of the Woods.* New Haven, Conn.: Yale University Press, 1967.
Birukoff, Paul. *Leo Tolstoy, His Life and Works.* New York, 1906.
Bodelson, C. A. *Studies in Mid-Victorian Imperialism.* London, 1924.
Bonner, William. *Captain William Dampier.* Stanford, Calif., 1934.
Borrow, George. *The Bible in Spain.* London, 1906.
    Lavengro. London, 1906.
Bosworth-Smith, R. *Life of Lord Lawrence.* New York, 1885.
Bowle, John. *The Imperial Achievement.* New York, 1975.
Braudel, Fernand. *Capitalism and Material Life 1400–1800.* London, 1974.
    The Mediterranean. London, 1972.
Buchan, John. *African Colony.* Edinburgh, 1903.
    Prester John. Popular Library, New York, 1973.
    Salute to Adventurers. London, 1915.
Burrow, J. W. *Evolution and Society.* London, 1966.
Burton, Richard. *Narrative of a Pilgrimage to Mecca and Al-Medinah.* London, 1879.
Butterfield, Herbert. *The Whig Interpretation of History.* New York, 1951.
Cammaerts, Emile. *Discoveries in England.* London, 1930.
Campbell, Lily B. "English History in the 16th Century," in *Shakespeare's Histories: 20th Century Views,* ed. Waith.
Carrington, C. E. *The British Overseas.* London, 1968.
    The Life of Rudyard Kipling. New York, 1956.
Cawley, R. R. *The Voyagers and Elizabethan Drama.* Boston, 1938.
Chesneaux, Jean. *Une Lecture Politique de Jules Verne.* Paris, 1971.
Christian, R. F. *Tolstoy's War and Peace.* Oxford, 1962.
Christie, J. A. *Thoreau as World Traveller.* New York, 1965.
Conrad, Joseph. *Almayer's Folly.* Kent Edition, New York, 1925.
    Heart of Darkness, Typhoon, and *Youth,* in *Three Short Novels.* New York, 1960.
    Lord Jim. New York, 1968.
    Mirror of the Sea. Kent edition. New York, 1925.
    Nigger of the Narcissus. Kent edition. New York, 1925.
    Nostromo. Signet Classic, New York, 1960.
    Notes on Life and Letters. London, 1925.
    Outcast of the Islands. Kent edition. New York, 1925.

Bibliography

The Rescue. Kent edition. New York, 1925.
Victory. Kent edition. New York, 1925.
Cooper, James Fenimore. the Leatherstocking Tales in the Iroquois edition, New York, 1906, except for those listed below.
    The Chainbearer. New York, 1856.
    The Crater. Cambridge, Mass., 1962.
    The Deerslayer. New York, 1963.
    Notions of the Americans. New York, 1913.
    The Pilot. New York, 1859.
    The Pioneers. New York, 1959.
    The Prairie. New York, 1964.
    Satanstoe. New York, 1859.
    The Sea-Lions. New York, 1856.
    Wyandotte. New York, 1856.
Crockett, Davy. *Davy Crockett's own story as written by himself.* New York, 1955.
Dana, R. H. *Two Years Before the Mast.* New York, 1909.
Dangerfield, George. *The Damnable Question.* New York, 1976.
Darling, Richard L. *A History of Children's Book Reviewing in America.* New York, 1968.
Defoe, Daniel. "Appeal to Honour and Justice," in *The Shortest Way With Dissenters and Other Pamphlets.* Oxford, England, 1928.
    The Complete English Gentleman. London, 1890.
    The Complete English Tradesman. London, 1841.
    Captain Singleton. London, 1973.
    The Chimera. London, 1720.
    Conjugal Lewdness. Gainesville, Fla., 1967.
    An Essay Upon Projects. London, 1697.
    The Family Instructor. London, 1841.
    The Four Year Voyage of Captain Roberts. London, 1726.
    The Farther Adventures of Robinson Crusoe. London, 1925.
    A General History of the Pyrates. Columbia, S. Car., 1972.
    A History of the Principal Discoveries and Improvements in the Several Arts and Sciences. London, 1727.
    Impartial History of the Life and Achievements of Peter Alexandrovitz. London, 1723.
    The Letters, G. H. Healey (Ed.). London, 1955.
    Madagascar. London, 1890.
    Memoirs of a Cavalier. London, 1972.
    New Voyage Round the World, in *Duncan Campbell.* London, 1725.
    A Plan of the English Commerce. London, 1728.
    The Poor Man's Plea. London, 1698.
    Religious Courtship. Edinburgh, 1803.
    The Review. ed. A. W. Secord. New York, 1938.
    Robinson Crusoe. London, 1963.
    A Tour of the Whole Island of Great Britain. London, 1928.
Dekker, George, and J. P. McWilliams. *Fenimore Cooper: the Critical Heritage.* London, 1973.
Devanesan, C.D.S. *The Making of the Mahatma.* New Delhi, 1969.
Dinesen, Isak. *Out of Africa.* New York, 1938.
    Shadows on the Grass. New York, 1960.

Dottin, Paul. *The Life and Strange and Surprising Adventures of Daniel Defoe.* New York, 1929.
Earle, Peter. *The World of Defoe.* New York, 1977.
Edwardes (Lady). *Memorials of Herbert B. Edwardes.* London, 1886.
Elliott, J. H. *The Old World and the New 1492–1650,* Cambridge, 1970.
Ellis, John. *The Social History of the Machine Gun.* New York, 1975.
Emerson, R. W. *English Traits.* Boston, 1856.
Farwell, Byron. *The Man Who Presumed.* London, 1958.
Fenn, G. Manville. *G. A. Henty.* London, 1907.
Feuer, K. B. *The Genesis of War and Peace.* New York, 1965.
Feuer, Lewis. *The Scientific Intellectual.* New York, 1963.
Fleishman, Avrom. *The English Historical Novel.* Baltimore, Md., 1971.
Froude, J. A. *Oceana.* London, 1886.
Fussell, Paul. *The Great War and Modern Memory.* New York, 1975.
Giergielewicz, M. *Henryk Sienkiewicz.* New York, 1968.
Gleason, Abbott. *European and Muscovite.* Harvard University Press, Cambridge, Mass., 1972.
Gossett, T. F. *Race: the history of an idea in America.* Dallas, 1963.
Grieve, C. M. *Lucky Poet.* London, 1943.
Gross, Felix. *Rhodes of Africa.* London, 1956.
Guillen, Claude. *Literature as a System.* Princeton, New Jersey, 1971.
Haggard, H. Rider. *Allan Quatermaine, King Solomon's Mines, Nada the Lily.* Macdonald Illustrated Edition. London, 1949.
Hakluyt, Richard. *Voyages and Discoveries.* London, 1598.
Hall, James. *Letters from the West.* London, 1828.
Hall, R. *Stanley; an Adventurer Explored.* Boston, 1975.
Harcave, Sidney. *Years of the Golden Cockerel.* New York, 1968.
Hart, B. Liddell. *T.E. Lawrence, in Arabia and after.* London, 1934.
Hayden, John O. *Scott: the Critical Heritage.* New York, 1970.
Henkin, Leo J. *Darwinism and the English Novel.* New York, 1940.
Herzen, Alexander. *My Past and Thoughts.* New York, 1968.
Hill, H. *Mark Twain: God's Fool.* New York, 1973.
Hirst, F. W. *The Political Economy of the War.* London, 1915.
Hodgson, Margaret T. *Early Anthropology in the 16th and 17th Centuries.* Philadelphia, 1964.
Howard, Michael. *War in European History.* London, 1976.
Huet, Marie-Hélène. *Histoire des Aventures Extraordinaires.* Paris, 1973.
Hunt, J. W. *Forms of Glory.* Carbondale, Ill., 1973.
Huttenback, R. A. *The British Imperial Achievement.* New York, 1966.
Huxley, Aldous. *Grey Eminence.* New York, 1941.
Jackson, Henry W. *Robinson Crusoe—Social Engineer.* New York, 1922.
Johnson, W.R. *Darkness Visible.* Berkeley, Calif., 1976.
Joyce, James. *Daniel Defoe.* Buffalo, N.Y., 1964.
Kaplan, Justin. *Mark Twain and His World.* New York, 1974.
    Mr. Clemens and Mark Twain. New York, 1966.
Kingsley, Charles. *The Heroes.* London, 1868.
    The Roman and the Teuton. New York, 1891.
    Westward Ho!. New York, 1934.
Kipling, Rudyard. "An English School," in *Land and Sea Tales.* London, 1923.
    Book of Words, Burwash edition. Garden City, N.Y., 1941.

Bibliography

From Sea to Sea. Burwash edition. Garden City, N.Y., 1941.
Kim. New York, 1959.
A Kipling Pageant, Garden City, N.Y., 1935.
Letters on Leave, in *Uncollected Prose.* New York, 1941.
Letters of Travel. New York, 1941.
Many Inventions. Burwash edition. Garden City, N.Y., 1941.
The Naulakha. New York, 1891.
Something of Myself. Burwash edition. Garden City, N.Y., 1941.
Stalky and Co., New York, 1959.
The War and the Fleet in Being. Burwash edition. Garden City, N.Y., 1941.
Kisch, H. M. *A Young Victorian in India,* E. A. W. Cohen (Ed.). London, 1957.
Kliushevsky, V.O. *Peter the Great.* London, 1958.
Koebner, Richard. *Empire.* London, 1961.
———— with H.D. Schmidt. *Imperialism.* London, 1964.
Krause, Sidney J. *Mark Twain as Critic.* Baltimore, Md., 1967.
Lane, Michael. *Introduction to Structuralism.* New York, 1970.
Laqueur, Walter. *Guerilla.* Boston, 1976.
Leach, Edmund. "The Legitimacy of Solomon," in Lane, *Introduction to Structuralism.*
Lensen, G.A. *Russia's Eastward Expansion.* New Jersey, 1964.
Lévi-Strauss, Claude. *Tristes Tropiques.* New York, 1977.
Levin, David. *History as Romantic Art.* Stanford, Calif., 1959.
Longworth, Philip. *The Cossacks.* New York, 1969.
Lord, John. *Duty, Honor, Empire.* New York, 1970.
McWilliams, J. P. *Political Justice in a Republic,* Berkeley, Calif., 1972.
Macaulay, T.B. "Lord Clive" and "Warren Hastings" in *Essays.* London, 1907.
Mack, John E. *A Prince of Our Disorder.* Boston, 1976.
MacShane, Frank. *The Life of Raymond Chandler.* New York, 1976.
Marryat, F. *Masterman Ready.* London, 1937.
Mason, Philip. *Kipling.* New York, 1975.
———— *A Matter of Honour.* London, 1974.
———— *Prospero's Magic.* London, 1962.
Maurois, André. *The Titans.* New York, 1957.
Meigs, Cornelia, Eaton, Anne, and Viguers, Ruth Hill. *A Critical History of Children's Literature.* New York, 1953.
Meyers, Jeffrey. *Fiction and the Colonial Experience.* Rowman and Littlefield, Totawa, N.J., 1973.
Millin, S.G. *Rhodes.* London, 1933.
Moon, Parker T. *Imperialism and World Politics.* New York, 1928.
Moore, Arthur K. *The Frontier Mind.* Lexington, Ky. 1957.
Morgan, Edward S. *The Puritan Family.* New York, 1966.
Morris, James. *Heaven's Command.* New York, 1968.
———— *Pax Britannica.* New York, 1973.
Moskowitz, Sam. *Explorers of the Infinite.* New York, 1973.
Mott, Frank L. *Golden Multitudes.* New York, 1947.
Mudrick, Marvin. ed. *Conrad: 20th Century Views.* New Jersey, 1966.
Mumford, Lewis. *Technics and Civilization.* New York, 1934.
Naipaul, V.S. *The Loss of El Dorado.* New York, 1969.
Nef, John U. *War and Human Progress.* Cambridge, Mass., 1950.
Novak, Max. *Defoe and the Nature of Man.* New York, 1963.

O'Connor, John J. *"Amadis de Gaul" and Its Influence on Elizabethan Literature.* New Brunswick, N.J., 1970.

Orwell, George. "Such, Such, Were the Joys," in *A Collection of Essays.* New York, 1970.

Pace, Antonio. *Benjamin Franklin and Italy.* Philadelphia, 1958.

Parker, Alexander A. *Literature and the Delinquent.* Edinburgh, 1967.

Parkman, F. *The Oregon Trail.* Madison, Wis., 1969.

Parry, J. H. *The Age of Reconnaissance.* Cleveland, 1963.

    Trade and Dominion. New York, 1971.

Paton, James. *The Story of John G. Paton.* New York, 1896.

Payne, Robert. *The White Rajahs of Sarawak.* London, 1960.

Petit, Paul. *Pax Romana.* Berkeley, Calif., 1967.

Philbrick, Thomas. *James Fenimore Cooper and the Development of American Sea Fiction.* Cambridge, Mass., 1961.

Plum, H.G. *Restoration Puritanism.* Chapel Hill, N. Car., 1943.

Prescott, W.H. *The Conquest of Mexico.* New York, 1913.

Raeff, Marc. *Michael Speransky.* The Hague, 1969.

    Peter the Great. Boston, 1963.

Rayfield, Donald. *The Dream of Lhasa.* Athens, Ohio, 1977.

Reynolds, Reginald. *White Sahibs in India.* London, 1946.

Ridley, Hugh. "Germany in the Mirror of Its Colonial Literature," *German Life and Letters.* July 1975.

Robinson M.B. "The House of the Mighty Warrior . . . ?" in Lane *Introduction to Structuralism.*

Rogers, Pat. *Grub Street.* London, 1972.

Rogin, M.P. *Fathers and Children.* New York, 1975.

Ross, John F. *Swift and Defoe.* Los Angeles, 1941.

Runciman, Steven. *The White Rajahs of Sarawak.* London, 1960.

Salmon, Edward, and Longden, Major A. A. *The Literature and Art of the Empire.* London, 1924.

Schmitt B.F. (Ed.) *Poland.* Berkeley, California, 1945.

Scholes, Robert. *Structuralism and Literature.* New Haven, Conn., 1974.

Schücking, Levin L. *The Puritan Family.* New York, 1970.

Scott, Walter. *The Fair Maid of Perth.* Sterling Edition, Boston, 1892.

    The Journal, W.E.K. Anderson, (Ed.). London, 1972.

    The Legend of Montrose. Sterling Edition, Boston, 1892.

    The Pirate. Sterling Edition, Boston, 1892.

    Quentin Durward. Sterling Edition, Boston, 1892.

    Rob Roy. Century Edition, Edinburgh, 1870.

    The Surgeon's Daughter. in *A Legend of Montrose.*

    Waverley. New York, 1969.

Seeley, J.R. *The Expansion of England.* Chicago, 1971.

Seelye, John. *Prophetic Waters.* New York, 1977.

    "Some Green Thoughts on a Green Theme," *Tri-Quarterly,* 1972.

Semmel, Bernard. *Imperialism and Social Reform.* Cambridge, Mass., 1960.

Simmons, E.J. *Tolstoy.* Boston, 1946.

Slotkin, R. *Regeneration Through Violence,* Middletown, Conn., 1973.

Smiles, Samuel. *Character.* London, 1878.

    Lives of the Engineers. London 1874.

    Self-Help. London, 1958.

    George Stephenson. Boston, 1858.

Bibliography

Smith, H.N. *Mark Twain: the development of a writer.* Cambridge, Mass., 1962.
Mark Twain: 20th Century Views. Englewood Cliffs, N.J., 1963.
Virgin Land. Cambridge, Mass., 1950.
Sombart, W. *Luxury and Capitalism.* Ann Arbor, Mich., 1967.
Spiller, R.E. *Fenimore Cooper.* New York, 1931.
Stevenson, R.L. *From Scotland to Silverado.* Cambridge, Mass., 1966.
Strachey, J. *The End of Empire.* New York, 1960.
Street, Brian V. *The Savage in Literature.* London, 1975.
Sumner, B.H. *Peter the Great.* London, 1950.
Survey of Russian History. London, 1944.
Swift, J. *Gulliver's Travels,* in *Works,* ed. W. Scott, vol. XII.
Thaden, E.C. *Conservative Nationalism in 19th Century Russia.* Seattle, Wash., 64.
Thomas, Henry. *Spanish and Portuguese Romances of Chivalry.* London, 1920.
Thompson, J.W. *A History of Historical Writing.* New York, 1942.
Tolstoy, Alexandra. *Tolstoy: A Life of My Father.* New York, 1953.
Tolstoy, L.N. *The Cossacks and the Raid.* New York, 1961.
Hadji Murad, in *Posthumous Works,* Vol. I, New York, 1920.
War and Peace. New York, 1966.
Tolstoy, Sonia. *The Diary of Tolstoy's Wife.* London, 1928.
Traversi, Derek. *Shakespeare: The Roman Plays.* Stanford, Calif., 1963.
Trelawny, E.J. *Adventures of a Younger Son.* New York, 1974.
Turner F.J. *The Frontier in American History.* New York, 1953.
Twain, Mark. *Connecticut Yankee.* New York, 1963.
Following the Equator. Author's National Edition, New York, vol. XV.
Life on the Mississippi. Stormfield Edition, New York, *Letters,* Stormfield.
New York
Mark Twain-Howells Letters. Cambridge, Mass., 1960.
Notebooks and Journals. Berkeley, 1975.
Roughing It. Stormfield Edition, New York,
Van Dijk, Tenn A. *Some Aspects of Text Grammars.* The Hague, 1972.
Veblen, Thorstein. *Imperial Germany and the Industrial Revolution.* New York, 1915.
The Viking Veblen, Max Lerner (Ed.). New York, 1948.
Vorpahl, B.M. *My Dear Wister -.* Palo Alto, Calif., 1973.
Waith, Eugene M., ed. *Shakespeare's Histories: 20th Century Views.* Englewood Cliffs, New Jersey, 1965.
Watts, C.Y., ed. *Joseph Conrad's Letters to R. B. Cunninghame Graham.* Cambridge, 1969.
Wallerstein, Immanuel. *The Modern World System.* New York, 1974.
Ward, J.H. *Andrew Jackson.* New York, 1955.
Watson, Colin. *Snobbery with Violence.* London, 1971.
Watt, Ian. *The Rise of the Novel.* Berkeley, Calif., 1957.
Webb, W.J. *The Great Frontier.* Boston, 1952.
Weil, Simone. *The Iliad; or the Poem of Force.* Pendle Hill, 1956.
White, J.M. *Cortes and the Downfall of the Aztec Empire.* New York, 1971.
Wolff, Tatiana. *Pushkin on Literature.* London, 1971.
Woolf, Leonard. *Growing.* London, 1961.
Ziff, Larzer. *Puritanism in America,* New York, 1973.
Zweig, Paul. *The Adventurer,* New York, 1974.

Index

Index

Index

Index

Index

Henty, George Alfred, 33, 221–23, 233, 385, 387
Herder, Johann Gottfried von, 172
Heroes and Hero-Worship (Carlyle), 209
Heroes or Greek Fairy Tales for My Children, The (Kingsley), 218
Herzen, Alexander, 35, 125, 131, 165, 166, 171, 178, 179, 192, 195
Hetzel, Jules, 225–26
Hickock, Wild Bill, 259
Highland Rogue (Defoe), 99
Hill, H., 249
Hird, Frank, 258
Hirst, F. W., 10
Historians: Cooper and, 153–54, 377–79; Scott's influence on, 121–26; *see also specific historians*
Historical adventurers: of modern empire 27–36; *see also specific historical adventurers*
Historical novels: Scott's influence on, 121–26; *see also specific historical novels*
History of the Reign of the Emperor Charles V, The (Robertson), 123
History of England, The (Macaulay), 124
History (Froude), 125
History of Historical Writing, The (Thompson), 122
History of Civil Society (Ferguson), 123
History of the American Navy (Cooper), 375
History of the Military Transactions of the British Nation in Indostan, A (Orme), 113, 281
History of the Principal Discoveries, A (Defoe), 73, 348, 360
History of the United States, A (Bancroft), 153, 378
History of the World, The (Raleigh), 72
Hitler, Adolf, 372, 398
Hobbes, Thomas, 346, 360n–61n
Hobson, J. A., 390–91
Hodson, William, 209
Hogarth, William, 94
Holland, Josiah G., 251
Holmes, Oliver Wendell, Jr., 250, 376
Homer, 45, 113, 156, 174, 323, 354
Homeward Bound (Cooper), 375
Honoria Lawrence (Diver), 210

Hope, Anthony, 399
Horace, 43, 44
House for Mr. Biswas, A (Naipaul), 336
"House of the Mighty Hero or the House of Enough Paddy?, The" (Robinson), 56
House of the Wolfings, The (Morris), 219
Howard, Lord Charles, 361
Howard, Michael, 13, 14
Howard's End (Forster), 295
Howe, John, 354
Howells, William Dean, 245, 251
"How to Read the Gospels" (Tolstoy), 185
Huckleberry Finn (Twain), 246, 253, 265–66, 309
Hudson, Henry, 213
Huet, Marie-Hélène,, 226, 385
Hugo, Victor, 126
Hume, David, 117, 122, 153, 155, 378
Hume, Joseph, 305
Hunt, J. W., 350
Hunter, Sir William, 223
Huntingtower (Buchan), 369
Hutchinson, G. A., 223
Huttenback, R. A., 399
Huxley, Aldous, 351
Huxley, Elspeth, 337
Hyatt, Stanley Portal, 385

Icon and the Axe, The (Billington), 182
Iliad (Homer), 84, 340
"Iliad or the Poem of Force, The" (Weil), 340
Impartial History of the Life and Actions of Peter Alexandrovitz, An (Defoe), 182–83
Imperial Achievement, The (Bowle), 6
Imperial Germany (Veblen), 240, 257
Imperialism, *see* Empire; Modern empire
Imperialism (Hobson), 390
Imperialism and World Politics (Moon), 342
India: A Wounded Civilization (Naipaul), 336
Ingalls, M. E., 258
Ingraham, Prentiss, 254–55

418

Index

Index

421

Index

Mille, Pierre, 397, 398
Millin, Sarah G., 287, 398
Milner, Alfred, 285
Milton, John, 40, 64, 156, 209, 352, 355
Mind at the End of Its Tether (Wells), 336
Mine Own People (Kipling), 278
Mir Jaffir (Indian prince), 32
Mirror of the Sea, A (Conrad), 402
Mirsky, D. S., 181
Mitford, Nancy, 369
Moby Dick (Melville), 87, 140
Modern empire, 3–36; Arendt on, 400; capitalist adventure and, 20–27; caste and (*see* Caste); Cooper and, 129–32; dating, 5–7; energizing myth of, 3–4, 7, 345; Belgian, 239, 258–63, 303, 387–88; French, 397–98; German, 167, 168, 239–40, 256–57, 397–98; historical adventurers of, 27–36 (*see also specific historical adventurers)*; Kipling and, 285–89, 389–400; modern world system and, 7–14, 345; resistance to, 338–44; Russian (*see* Tolstoy, Lev); Scott and, 118–20
"Modest Proposal, A" (Swift), 90
Modjeska, Helena, 301
Moffat, Robert, 120
Moll Flanders (Defoe), 51, 70, 73
Moltke, Count Helmuth von, 378
Monikins, The (Cooper), 156
Montalbodo, Francanzano, 38
Montcalm and Wolfe (Parkman), 153, 376
Montesquieu, Baron de la Brède et de, 122
Montezuma, 27, 29, 30, 32, 88
Montgomerie, Capt. T. G., 270
Moon, Parker T., 342
Moore, Arthur K., 159, 373
Moore, George, 125
Moore, Tom, 112
More, Hannah, 352–53, 371
Morgan, Edmund S., 353
Morris, Christopher, 356
Morris, James, 114, 218, 232, 290, 326
Morris, William, 276, 277, 402
Morse, Samuel, 239

Moses, Claude, 325
"Mother-Hive, The" (Kipling), 350
Motley, John Lathrop, 31, 153–55, 376, 377–78
Mott, F. L., 245
Mr. Midshipman Easy (Marryat), 214–15
Mrs. Dalloway (Woolf), 296
Mudrick, Marvin, 316
Mullah, Kazi, 194
Müller, Max, 384
Mumford, Lewis, 12, 345–46, 362
Music of Time, The (Powell), 336
My Dear Wister (Vorpahl), 254
My Kalulu: Prince, King and Slave (Stanley), 261
My Past and Thoughts (Herzen), 178
Myth: energizing, 3–4, 7, 345; structuralist approach to, 55–57; *see also* Adventure narratives; *and specific titles*

Nabokov, Vladimir, 175
Nader (Félix Tournachon), 227
Nada the Lily (Haggard), 231–32
Naipaul, V. S., 332, 335
Napier, Sir Charles, 120, 208
Napoleon I, 7, 152, 299, 355; as historical hero, 25, 27, 35–36; in popular literature, 231; Rhodes and, 287; Scott and, 101, 111, 361; Tolstoy and, 169, 176, 196
Napoleon III, 192, 225
Narrative of a Pilgrimage to Meccah and Medinah (Burton), 291
Narvaez, Pánfilo de, 348
Naulahka, The (Kipling), 393–94
Nechaev, Sergei, 180, 196
Nef, John U., 11
Nelson, Horatio, 152, 322, 355
Nevins, Allan, 153
Newbolt, Henry, 222, 223, 321
New Family Instructor, The (Defoe), 70
New Machiavelli, The (Wells), 279
Newman, Cardinal, 110
Newton, Sir Isaac, 205, 356
Newton, John, 371
New Voyage Round the World, A (Defoe), 71–74, 85
Nicholas I, Czar, 165, 178

Index

Index

Index

THE PELICAN HISTORY OF ART

EDITED BY NIKOLAUS PEVSNER

Z I

PAINTING IN BRITAIN 1530 TO 1790

ELLIS WATERHOUSE

ELLIS WATERHOUSE

PAINTING IN BRITAIN
1530 TO 1790

PENGUIN BOOKS
MELBOURNE · LONDON · BALTIMORE

Penguin Books Ltd, Harmondsworth, Middlesex
Penguin Books Inc, Baltimore, Maryland, U.S.A.
Penguin Books Pty Ltd, Melbourne, Victoria, Australia

★

Text printed by R. & R. Clark Ltd, Edinburgh
Plates printed by McLagan & Cumming Ltd, Edinburgh
Made and printed in Great Britain

★

TO

C. H. COLLINS BAKER

WHO FIRST AROUSED IN ME AN INTEREST IN
BRITISH PAINTING

★

CONTENTS

CONTENTS

Notes will be found at the end of the chapter
to which they refer

LIST OF PLATES

ACKNOWLEDGEMENTS

ANYONE who has tried to see or to study British painting will know that my largest and deepest debt is to the great number of private owners who have allowed me to see their pictures, either by making their houses accessible to the public, by lending their pictures to public exhibitions, or by yielding benevolently to the importunity of a stranger. That part of our national heritage in painting which dates from before the nineteenth century is still very largely to be seen in its original and gracious natural setting, the private home, which ranges from the Royal Palaces to the country Manor house. These houses and their contents are our national glory, and their steady disappearance before the sapping operations of the Treasury is rapidly becoming our national shame. To all these owners who have allowed their pictures to be seen and reproduced here my greatest debt of gratitude is owed.

This wide dispersal of the material for the history of British painting – assisted by our national apathy – is the reason for its neglect by serious students and for the backward state of our knowledge of it. Its historian is not merely the latest of a long line, gleaning the chaff which may have escaped his forerunners who long ago established all the principal dates and the detailed lines of development of individual artists. There is still a great deal that we do not know, and hardly a week has passed since I began writing this book in which a new picture has not turned up or a signature and date been read which has modified previous conceptions. I am not apologizing for the tentative character of this book, but, as it is one of a series which includes much more richly cultivated ground, it is perhaps well that the ordinary reader should be made aware of the state of scholarship on the subject – and be encouraged to make further research and find the author wrong.

The bibliography and footnote references must provide the acknowledgements for the dead and for the living who have gone into print, but certain friends and helpers must not go unmentioned. It was C. H. Collins Baker who first guided my interest in British painting: and this book is the slow outcome of the interest and enthusiasm for which he, more than any other, is responsible. Of those of a later generation I am most indebted to John Woodward, who has not only drawn many pictures to my attention, but has read the proofs and drawn attention to my ambiguities and errors. Others who have been especially helpful are W. G. Constable, Oliver Millar, John Steegman, and Mary Woodall. For particular kindness in securing photographs and permissions for reproduction I am indebted to the National Trust, the National Gallery, the National Maritime Museum, the Governors of Christ's Hospital, the Manchester City Art Gallery, Messrs Christie's and Messrs Sotheby's; and to the Frick Collection in New York.

PART ONE

PAINTING UNDER THE TUDORS

CHAPTER I

HENRY VIII AND THE GENERATION
OF HOLBEIN

THE year 1531, in which the Convocation of Canterbury recognized Henry VIII as the Supreme Head of the Church in England, can conveniently be taken to mark the close of the medieval period of art in England. By 1535, at any rate, most of the old religious themes in painting were proscribed and the painter was no longer able to exercise his art in what had been the most fruitful field of subject-matter for artists in Europe for a thousand years. A taste for pictures of classical mythologies had not been imported as yet from Italy, and a new and national tradition of painting had to grope its way to birth by exploring the only outlet which remained, the field of portraiture. We can best estimate the nature of this subject-matter from the finest surviving monument of Pre-Reformation figure style, the windows of King's College Chapel, Cambridge, which were set up between 1515 and 1531. If Henry VIII had been endowed with any of the qualities necessary for a royal patron of the arts, a wonderful opportunity was to hand for welding the painter's art to the service of a Protestant kingdom. For, by the end of 1532, Hans Holbein, who had paid an earlier visit of a year and a half to London, had come to settle in England for the remainder of his life, driven by economic necessity to seek fortune in what seemed a hopeful and prosperous kingdom as a change from the meagre prospects for a great artist in a city, such as Basel, torn by the religious disturbances of the Reformation. Holbein, conscious of his prodigious abilities, came to the Court of Henry VIII as a speculation, as Leonardo and Bramante, two generations before, had come to the Court of the Sforzas at Milan. His powers were frittered away to as little purpose as Leonardo's were by his royal patron, but, by the time of his death in 1543, he had left few fields of art in England untouched. On painting, where there was little native tradition, his influence was less than on the art of the printer or goldsmith, perhaps also less than his influence on architectural decoration. But 'modern' painting, in any serious sense (as opposed to 'medieval' painting), may properly be said to begin in Britain with Holbein's second and final visit in 1532.

Portrait Painting in England before Holbein

The remains of portrait painting of the period before Holbein's arrival are somewhat more meagre than has hitherto been supposed, since the 'Lady Margaret Beaufort' in the

National Portrait Gallery (allegedly of 1460/70) has proved to have another head beneath its present surface. There is, in fact, no portrait known of before 1500 (apart from a few miniatures in books) which can reasonably be supposed to be taken from the life. We have, however, record of the fleeting visits of two foreign portrait painters of distinction in the early years of the sixteenth century, each upon one of those matrimonial occasions between sovereigns which were the chief means of familiarizing one nation with the portrait art of another. In 1505 a painter who can, with reasonable confidence, be identified as the Flemish-trained Michel Sittow (1469–1525), Court Painter in succession to Isabella the Catholic and to Margaret of Austria, accompanied Hermann Rinck, the agent of Maximilian, King of the Romans, on an embassy to offer to Henry VII one of Maximilian's daughters in marriage. On 20 October 1505, as the inscription on the picture (National Portrait Gallery) states, he painted Henry VII at the order of Hermann Rinck, and the portrait can be traced, with considerable probability, in the 1516 and 1524 Inventories of Margaret of Austria.[1] What may be an earlier portrait of Henry VII, probably taken also from life (Irving T. Bush, New York: formerly Earl Brownlow), could be by a Flemish or a British hand. It has been wildly associated[2] with the second recorded visit of a foreign painter, that of Jean Perréal (c. 1460–1530), Court Painter to Louis XII of France, who came to London in September 1514 in connexion with Louis' marriage to Mary Tudor, sister of Henry VIII. Certainly a prototype of this kind of Henry VII was in England, since other early versions survive in English collections.

It is with more or less pedestrian copies of standard royal portraits that native painters in England seem to have been mainly occupied during the opening years of the sixteenth century. It is possible (but has not yet been seriously explored) that something of the same sort also existed in Scotland. There is little evidence for date in the surviving examples, and stylistic criteria are not of much avail where comparative material is lacking and the paintings are of more or less subaesthetic character. There is documentary evidence that series of portraits of kings (or, at least, of 'images' of kings) were known in England as early as the fourteenth century, and certain late fifteenth-century images of this kind (the named king being *Athelstan*) belong to the Society of Antiquaries in London: but the only serious evidence for dating such works as survive is that some of the repainted examples at Windsor are presumed to be identical with those mentioned in the 1542 and 1547 Inventories[3] of the collections of Henry VIII, where they seem to have been regarded with the respect due to works of some antiquity. In general style these are more or less similar, and the latest born of the sitters is Prince Arthur (d. 1502), portraits of whom are not likely to have been in much demand any length of time after his death. Such serial portraits were undoubtedly produced right up to the end of the sixteenth century and probably, with very little change of style, well into the seventeenth century, so that the status of other examples or series which survive must await a detailed technical examination which has never been attempted. The chief groups which survive (all different in serial compositon and none complete) are in the possession of the Duke of Northumberland, the Marquess of Salisbury, the Society of Antiquaries (once in the Paston family's possession), and a remarkable series which was at Southam

Delabere until the sale, by Sotheby's, 11 June 1947; a few of this last group, and some others, are in the National Portrait Gallery. An example in relatively pure condition, with a reasonable chance of being an early example of this class, is the 'Henry VI' (National Portrait Gallery, 2450; Plate 1A). Journeyman work of this kind is to be met with also in France and the Low Countries, and there is nothing specifically British about this kind of image.

The only painter's name which can, in fact, be associated with such portraits is that of a Fleming, Joannes Corvus, whose two surviving works appear to be only very little more individualized than these images of dead sovereigns, although he is generally presumed to have had access to his sitters – but even this is by no means certain. It is generally accepted, and seems probable, that 'Joannes Corvus Flandrus' – as his name once appeared on the frames, both now destroyed, of 'Bishop Foxe' at Corpus Christi College, Oxford, and 'Princess Mary Tudor' at Sudeley Castle – is the latinized form of Jan Rav, who matriculated into the Painters' Guild at Bruges in 1512; of 'Jehan Raf, painctre de Flandres', who painted a map of England for François I in 1532, and a 'pourtraict de la ville de Londres' for the same King in 1534 (which possibly implies his presence in England before that date); and of 'John Raven, born in Flanders' (but not described as a painter), who acquired naturalization in England 13 May 1544. It is also generally but more rashly accepted that the 'Foxe' may date c. 1518 (or before 1522, which is a date which appears on a variant portrait of Foxe of a similar type at Sudeley Castle) and that 'Mary Tudor' (from her age of thirty-four, which was also recorded on the lost frame) dates c. 1530. But neither of these portraits has the air of being taken from life, and it is at least equally likely that they are copies by Corvus (perhaps of the 1540s) of earlier paintings, and that Corvus is an unimportant artist, the accidental preservation of whose name has lent him an artificial interest. A much more distinguished artist of the same presumed class is the painter of 'Margaret, Countess of Salisbury', c. 1532/5 (National Portrait Gallery; Plate 1B).

Painters other than Holbein in the Service of Henry VIII

The English work of Holbein is best considered in immediate precedence to that of his successors, and it will be best to consider first the other names of painters, for they are still little more than names, which occur in the Household Expenses of Henry VIII. It can be stated at once that Henry VIII was not a considerable patron of the art of painting. It was tapestries which were the chief artistic adornment of the walls of his palaces, and on which he spent relatively large sums. He could not, however, avoid employing painters, and those who served him can be divided into two distinct classes, the Serjeant Painters and those who otherwise formed part of his household. The Serjeant Painters [4] do not, at first, properly fall into the province of a history of painting. But, as names are few at this period, and we know those of the Serjeant Painters, attempts have been made at various times to attribute existing works to them. They were extensively employed in the multifarious painting works needed on special and festive occasions, and the preamble to the patent of Robert Streeter in 1679 as Serjeant Painter gives the fullest account of their charge: 'Serjeant Painter of all our works as well belonging to our royal palaces and houses as to our Great Wardrobe as also within our Office of Revels as also for our Stables, ships and vessels, barges, close barges, coaches, chariots, caroches, litters, waggons and close cars, tents and pavilions, Herald's Coats, trumpets, banners and for funerals to be solemnized.' The first of them was John Browne, whose patent of appointment dates 11 January 1511/12: Browne died in December 1532, but a reversionary grant of office (dated 19 June 1532) had already been given within his lifetime to his successor, Andrew Wright: Wright was succeeded by Anthony Toto (grant dated 26 January 1543/4), who died in 1557/8, but seems to have abandoned the exercise of his office by 1554. Toto is the only one of these who must, on present knowledge, be also considered as a painter of pictures, but reference should perhaps be made to a fine portrait of a lady, dated 1536 and by a Flemish painter, on which an inscription has been read as 'AW' and dubiously interpreted as the signature of Andrew Wright (Earl of Darnley Sale, 1 May 1925 (50), as by Mor; now in Lord Lee's estate destined for London University).

The painters who appear in the surviving volumes of the household books of Henry VIII are Luke Hornebaud (Horneband, Hornebolte, etc.), Gerard Hornebaud, Vincent Vulpe, Anthony Toto, and Bartholomew Penni: there is also Nicholas da Modena, who was certainly an artist of some kind, but may perhaps not have practised painting. Nothing that was painted by any of them for Henry VIII can be identified with the remotest probability, and the only one of them of whose work it is permissible to speak with any conviction is Gerard Hornebaud, who appears in the accounts for 1528 to 1531 but seems probably to have returned soon afterwards to his native Ghent, where he was dead by 1540. He appears to have been a distinguished manuscript illuminator and cannot be associated with any other class of work. Luke Hornebaud, however, must certainly have been a painter of real importance and was held in the highest esteem, being paid always a higher salary than Holbein himself (55s. 6d. a month) from his first appearance in the household accounts in 1528 until his death in May 1544.

Luke Hornebaud came from a large family of Ghent artists, and seems to have been born, presumably at Ghent, about 1490/5: he matriculated into the Ghent Painters' Guild in 1512 and came to England some time between 1523 and his first appearance in the household accounts in October 1528. On 22 June 1534 he was made a denizen and appointed painter to the King. There our detailed knowledge of him ends. Vulpe, certainly an Italian, was employed mainly in the same kind of tasks as the Serjeant Painters, and the attribution to him of the series of gay pageant pictures at Hampton Court, 'The embarkation of Henry VIII from Dover, 1519', 'The Field of the Cloth of Gold', 'The meeting of Henry VIII and Maximilian', etc. – which were probably ordered and painted in the Low Countries – is certainly inacceptable.

We ought to be on surer ground with the other two Italians, Penni and 'Toto', who appear almost inseparably together in the accounts, for we have independent confirmation of their background from Vasari. Bartolommeo di Michele Penni was born in Florence in 1491, the brother of Gianfrancesco Penni and (apparently) of Luca Penni, both better known High Renaissance artists: he is first documented in the household accounts, with Toto, in 1530, became a denizen in 1541, continued to receive his quarterly wages in 1547/8, and was probably dead by 1553. He was probably less important than 'Toto', whose real name was Antonio di Nunziato d'Antonio. The latter was a pupil of Ridolfo Ghirlandajo and acquired the nickname of Toto del Nunziata in Florence, where he was born 8 January 1498/9. On 28 September 1519 he signed a contract at Florence with Torrigiano to remain with him for four and a half years and to exercise his art in Italy, France, Flanders, England, Germany 'or anywhere else in the world' for a certain salary. Torrigiano was the Italian sculptor employed on the tomb of Henry VII, but he in fact finally left England soon after 1519. It is probable, however, that Toto had by then come to England (probably with Penni) and it is a fair hypothesis that he was employed by Wolsey, since it is immediately after the fall of Wolsey (October 1529) that Toto and Penni first appear in the royal service.[5] Toto was made a denizen 26 June 1538: his New Year gifts to the King, probably of his own painting, include a picture of the 'Calumny of Apelles' on New Year 1538/9, and a 'Story of King Alexander' at New Year 1540/1. In January 1543/4 he became Serjeant Painter (perhaps the first 'artist' to hold that appointment) and he seems to have retained that appointment until about the accession of Queen Elizabeth, since he died 1557/8. We have to imagine his style as a watered version of Florentine style of about 1510/20, perhaps modified by prolonged experience of the Netherlandish Mannerist style, but the little we know about him is valuable since it gives a clue to the existence of some other kind of painting than portraiture at the Court of Henry VIII. One specimen survives of the kind of ambitious subject picture, in a mixed Flemish and Italianate style, which we may imagine to have been in vogue in London in the middle of the sixteenth century – the 'Judgement of Solomon' in the Hall of the Middle Temple.

Of other contacts with artists independent of Holbein it is worth mentioning that 'one Ambros Paynter to the quene of Navara' (possibly Ambrosius Benson) visited the King at Eltham on 13 June 1532;[6] and the painter of the 'Henry VIII' at Hampton Court (of which a repetition belongs to the Merchant Taylors' Company), who is conceivably rather than probably Joos van Cleve, is also to be reckoned with. It is generally accepted, but is far from certain, that the inscribed scroll held by the King in this portrait (from St Mark xvi. 15) alludes to the publication of Miles Coverdale's English version of the Bible in 1536.

Holbein in England

The development of Holbein's style does not belong to the history of painting in England, but some account of his art in its mature form is necessary for the understanding of the work of his successors in Britain. He was born in Augsburg 1497/8 and trained there and, by the time he settled in Basel in 1519, he had paid a short visit to North Italy (in particular to Lombardy) and, like Dürer before him, had fused something of the spirit of the Italian with that of the Northern Renaissance. He is the great artist of the Northern humanist movement, which had its centre in Basel round the personalities of Erasmus (whose work he illustrated) and the printer, Froben, for whom he designed a very large number of woodcuts. Had it not been for the troubles caused by the Reformed religion at Basel, which drove him to seek employment in England, he might well have become a great religious painter. As things turned out, his mature painting was mainly in the field of portraiture, where he remains unsurpassed for sureness and economy of statement, penetration into character and a combined richness and purity of style.

In 1526, just before his first visit to England, he had painted the small 'Venus' and 'Lais' (both at Basel) which reveal a knowledge both of Leonardo and of Raphael. He thus arrived in London in the autumn of 1526 the heir of all that was best and noblest in European art. He came with a letter from Erasmus to his friend Sir Thomas More, written from Basel. 'Here', says Erasmus, 'the arts are freezing, he is coming to England to scrape some angels together' (*ut corrodat aliquot Angelatos*) – which leaves one in no doubt that the journey was prompted by economic necessity rather than by any higher motive. The glamour, for Erasmus at any rate (who may well have advised Holbein to this move), of the early years of Henry VIII had not yet evaporated: the years when Erasmus's pupil, Lord Mountjoy, later tutor to the young Prince Henry, had written to his old teacher (1509): 'Our King is not after gold, or gems, or precious metals, but virtue, glory, immortality.' That so much promise could have come to so little fruit was more than the optimistic Erasmus could believe, but More, while saying to Erasmus in reply 'your painter is a wonderful man' adds 'I fear he won't find England as fruitful as he had hoped'. Nor did he, but it would appear that the prospects seemed to him better than at Basel. This first visit lasted only until the spring or early summer of 1528 and his patrons for portraiture were drawn only from the small group, of which More was the most conspicuous, who were in touch with the international humanist movement: 'Archbishop Warham' 1527 (Louvre); 'Sir Thomas More' 1527 (Frick Gallery, New York; Plate 2); 'John and Thomas Godsalve' 1528 (Dresden); and the astronomer 'Niklaus Kratzer' 1528 (Louvre). His major project on this visit was the lost (perhaps uncompleted) group of 'The family of Sir Thomas More' 'in watercolours', of which there remains a diagrammatical drawing at Basel and a later life-size copy in oil at Nostell Priory; and drawings from the life for seven of the heads are at Windsor. This group of drawings ranks among the supreme masterpieces of portraiture and surpasses in quality the more schematic and more rapidly executed drawings of Holbein's later English years. The sanguine assumption that so great a painter could not have been in England and enjoyed the patronage of one so close to the Court as More without some royal patronage has led to the general acceptance that a certain 'Master Hans' who had a share in the decoration of the banqueting house erected at Greenwich in February 1527 for the reception of the Ambassadors of François I, was Holbein. But Hans (or John) is among the commonest names and there is nothing whatever to support the supposition.

The few English portraits of this first visit are more elaborate in their pattern and artistry than the later English group and they have no successors in the work of Holbein's following in England. That of 'Sir Thomas More' may be taken as a standard for their style. Except for the work of Titian nothing of the same Senatorial dignity of presentation was being produced in European portraiture at this time, but the means – predominantly linear – are the exact opposite to Titian's. The figure bulks largely in a clearly defined space whose cubical volume is deliberately reduced by a curtain – in the closely similar

'Sir Henry Guildford' 1527 at Windsor, the same effect is produced by a drawn curtain on a rod, and in the companion 'Lady Guildford' 1527 in St Louis a column with a transverse tiebeam serves the same purpose; features, hands, and the carriage of the body are all used to convey character with equal effect, and the whole work has a Shakespearean profundity and seems to convey the full image of a European personage. The very maturity of the style must have made such portraits seem strange in England to all but the international humanist circle, and, when Holbein came to London again, his style became more unadorned for English sitters.

After four more uneasy years at Basel, Holbein was back in London by the end of 1532 and he died in London between 7 October and 21 November 1543. The patrons of his earlier visit were dead or had fallen into disgrace, and it was the merchants of the Hansa Steelyard in London who were his first patrons. He painted for their Hall, about 1533/5, two large allegories in grisaille on a blue ground, executed in tempera on linen, of the 'Triumph of Wealth' and the 'Triumph of Poverty'. The two pictures left England in the seventeenth century, were last heard of in 1691, and are now known only from drawings and engravings. Other than portraits these were the most important work of a more or less permanent character which Holbein painted in England, but no echo can be traced of their influence on later British painting.

The chief portraits of the members of the Steelyard were painted in London in 1532 and 1533 and are now at Berlin, Windsor, New York, Brunswick, and Vienna. The most elaborate is the 'Georg Gisze' 1532 (Berlin), and in this and 'The Ambassadors' (National Gallery), which was his major work in 1533, it looks as though he were deliberately trying to show off his powers of imitation, perhaps to catch the unsubtle appreciation of the Court.

The first Court official he is known to have painted on this second visit to England was 'Robert Cheseman' 1533 (The Hague). It was perhaps not long afterwards that he painted 'Thomas Cromwell' (Frick Gallery, New York), and the first of Henry's Queens that he certainly painted was 'Jane Seymour' (Vienna; Plate 3), whose portrait probably dates soon after her marriage in May 1536. From that time onward he was on the official pay-roll of Henry VIII's Household.

The portrait of 'Jane Seymour' may be taken as the standard for Holbein's second English style. The figure is no longer seen (as was the 'Sir Thomas More') as displacing with its bulk a recognizable section of space: it approaches rather to a flat pattern, made alive by a bounding and vital outline. Reynolds, speaking from an eighteenth-century standpoint, speaks of a kind of defect in the background of pictures, which 'have the appearance of being inlaid, like Holbein's portraits which are often on a bright green or blue ground'.[7] This analysis is very just, but, rather than criticize this effect, we should seek to inquire into the reasons for this change of style. It may be due to the specific taste of the English Court, to a changing trend in European painting, to the conditions under which the painter worked, or to a combination of all three of these causes.

There is no doubt that Henry VIII never appreciated Holbein's potential capacity as an artist. He probably esteemed him chiefly for being, in the words of the British Ambassador at Brussels in 1538, 'very excellent in making Physiognomies', and he sent him to foreign Courts in 1538 and 1539 on the (to him) immensely important task of painting possible wives for himself. In March 1538 Holbein was at Brussels to paint Christina of Denmark, 'Duchess of Milan' (National Gallery), and in 1539 he was at Düren to paint 'Anne of Cleves' (Louvre). In the case of the Duchess of Milan we know from the Ambassador's dispatches that he had only one sitting of three hours, and yet the completed full-length picture is one of the most vital and lively portraits ever painted. In this one sitting he may be presumed to have made only a drawing – such as exist in the wonderful series of portrait drawings at Windsor – and notes of colour: the portrait was later elaborated in the studio without further direct access to the sitter. Similar conditions may well have prevailed with most of his aristocratic English sitters, and, in the Windsor collection, which perhaps represents more or less what was in Holbein's studio at the time of his death, we have the one living element which went to the building up of those elaborate pieces of jewellery and dress which some of his later portraits seem to be. This tendency to flat pattern, with elaborate dresses and aloof, inscrutable features, persisted in England right into the reign of James I, but it is uncertain whether it was imposed on the artist by the taste of his patrons or was a convention dictated by his limited access to his sitters. At the same time it should be noted that Court portraiture in other European centres was developing on similar lines, with a plain background and an emphasis on costume and silhouettes. The work of Cranach at the Court of Saxony and of Bronzino at Florence shows exactly the same tendency, in this respect, as Holbein's later English portraits, and a parallel change of style is found in the work of Hans Eworth after he settled in England.

Holbein's first portraits of Henry VIII seem to date from 1537, the year in which he was commissioned to paint in fresco upon the wall of the Privy Chamber in the Palace of Whitehall the commemorative group of Henry VIII and Jane Seymour with Henry VII and Elizabeth of York. The date was to be seen on the original, as can be seen in the small copy made by van Leemput, in 1667, which is now at Hampton Court. The original perished in the Whitehall fire, but, by a miracle, a part of the original cartoon survives at Chatsworth (Plate 4). The cartoon represents a slightly different version of Henry VIII's head, which was turned full face in the final work. Everything but the architectural detail of this group must have been dictated to Holbein. What went on in the Privy Chamber is not known, but it was certainly accessible to visitors: we know from van Mander's account in 1604 that the image of the King made a somewhat overwhelming effect, and the whole painting and its pattern is an almost medieval 'painted document', with the figures centred round a text which was designed to compare Henry VIII not unfavourably with his father and to glorify the House of Tudor.

The head of the King in the cartoon was used also for the only other certain portrait of Henry VIII by Holbein which survives: a small picture on a very different scale (formerly Earl Spencer: now Thyssen collection, Lugano) in the style of Clouet's portraits. This form of portrait is rarely to be paralleled in Holbein's work, but it has a probable companion in the 'Jane Seymour' at The Hague.

No other major works for the King are recorded, but Holbein was engaged, at the time of his death, upon a large painting which must certainly have had royal approval – a picture commemorating the granting of a charter in 1541 by Henry VIII to the Barbers and Surgeons, who were recombined into a single society on this occasion. This is an even more medieval work in spirit than the Whitehall fresco and the whole pattern of the picture must have been dictated by Holbein's patrons. As Wornum has remarked, 'the principle of the composition is somewhat Egyptian', for the King is shown much larger than the assembled Barber-Surgeons, behind whom he is seated. This work was certainly left unfinished at Holbein's death and has suffered so much from fire and repaint that no serious estimate of it is possible without a technical examination. It must always, however, have lacked any of the Renaissance serenity which Holbein could have given to such a scene. The noble miniature in grisaille on vellum at Windsor of 'Solomon and the Queen of Sheba' (where Solomon is unquestionably modelled on Henry VIII) – which could well have been, as has been supposed, a study for a projected wall decoration – shows what Holbein's powers in this kind of composition might have been, if untrammelled by medieval-minded patrons. But the Barber-Surgeons picture (the only major historical picture ever commissioned by one of the Livery Companies of the City of London) was no doubt intended as a visible historical document rather than as a work of art. With a king who had lately dealt so casually with ecclesiastical charters, it was as well to have some more remembrancing evidence than the document itself. In later reigns such need was no longer apparent and the springs of art patronage in the City dried up.

All that remains otherwise of Holbein's work for the English Court is the marvellous series of portrait drawings at Windsor (after some of which tracings or copies seem to have been made, and from these later painters of more modest talent produced paintings, such as the 'William Fitzwilliam, Earl of Southampton' at Cambridge, which bears the date 1542); a small number of portraits of Henry's Queens; of the young 'Prince Edward' (c. 1538/9: Washington), and an equally small number of portraits of persons attached to the Court. Holbein continued, however, to paint the German merchants of the Steel-yard, and his incidental drawings touch and influenced all the arts and crafts of the day, lettering, binding, architectural decoration, metalwork, and armour.

For later English painting the important and vexed question arises of what studio, what assistants and pupils, Holbein had in England. Certain later portraits of the King of two main types, one represented by versions at Rome (Corsini) and Windsor, the other by many versions in English collections of which the best are at Warwick Castle and Castle Howard, are plausibly assumed to go back at least to a Holbein drawing. Other contemporary variant 'copies' exist (such as the Liverpool 'Henry VIII' (Plate 5), the different 'Henry VIII' at Belvoir, and the Woburn 'Jane Seymour') of very good quality, which cannot, however, be accepted as from Holbein's own hand. These imply the existence of pupils or assistants trained to a high level of craftsmanship, and these cannot have dispersed at once, on Holbein's death in 1543, without a trace.

Holbein's immediate Following

It is when we look for the independent work (apart from copies) of this presumed group of direct assistants that the material seems to be surprisingly scanty. A distinct influence from Holbein is traceable in the later work of the two most distinguished painters of the next generation (both of them foreigners), Gerlach Flicke and Hans Eworth, who will be treated in due course: and there is a general air of the patterns which Holbein introduced in the small number of distinguished portraits, by hands which must at present remain anonymous, which can be dated from the later 1540s and throughout the reign of Edward VI. But the number of such pictures which show anything like the accomplishment one would expect from a direct pupil is exceedingly small. An 'Unknown Lady' (Plate 6B) in the Fitzwilliam collection at Milton Park is one of the best examples; a few pictures which pass under Holbein's name (such as the 'Edward VI' in New York) come under this heading; a few others can be named[8] and it is probable that more will turn up in the course of time.

In the National Gallery in London can be seen a good example of each of the two types of Holbein follower: the 'Unknown Man' of 1545 by John Bettes is the unique work of a painter whose technique is in the Holbein tradition, while the portrait of 'William, Lord de la Warr', of about 1549, is the work of a painter strongly influenced in pattern and style of presentation by Holbein, but without a trace of his technical elegance.

Of John Bettes we know only that his signature in French ('faict par jehan Bettes Anglois'), cut from the original, is now pasted on the back of the picture in the Tate Gallery, which is dated 1545: and that he was paid for making certain miniature portraits in 1546/7 for Queen Catherine Parr.[9] The addition of *Anglois* to the signature might be taken to suggest that the picture was painted abroad. Another John Bettes, a pupil of Hilliard, is recorded as a miniaturist at the end of the century.

The same character of uniqueness attaches to the Windsor portrait of 'Princess Elizabeth' of about 1546 (Plate 7B). This is a work of great refinement of execution in which a certain French elegance is conceivably to be detected. Two years earlier her elder sister, Mary, had been painted, and in Mary's Privy Purse Expenses for 1544 appears the entry: 'pd. to one John that drue her Grace in a table' (i.e. picture). This portrait has not been identified with any degree of plausibility, and 'John' might be Corvus or Bettes or Eworth (for Hans = John), or with equal probability some as yet unidentified painter.

NOTES TO CHAPTER I

1. G. Glück, *Burl. Mag.*, LXIII (Sept. 1933), 100 ff.

2. M. Goldblatt, *The Connoisseur*, CXXIII (Mar. 1949), 9, where it is supposed that Perréal was copying an earlier picture.

3. W. A. Shaw, *Three Inventories of Pictures*, Courtauld Institute Texts, 1 (1937).

4. For the Serjeant Painters see W. A. Shaw, *The Connoisseur*, XXXI (1911), 72–81.

5. R. W. Carden, *Proceedings of the Society of Antiquaries*, XXIV (1911/12), 179–85.

6. (Sir) Harris Nicholas, *The Privy Purse Expenses of King Henry VIII . . .* (1827), 221. For an attempt to identify this Ambrose with the brother of Jean Clouet, see G. Glück, *Aus drei Jahrhunderten euro-*

päischer Malerei (1933), 254 ff.

7. Notes on Dufresnoy's *Art of Painting* in *The Works of Sir Joshua Reynolds*, ed. E. Malone (1797), II, 250. I owe this reference to Dagobert Frey, *Englisches Wesen im Spiegel seiner Kunst* (1942), 245, where there is a valuable discussion of Holbein's change of style.

8. Another picture of this small class is Mr H. E. M. Benn's 'Portrait of a Lady' (R.A. 1950/1). An 'Unknown Man', dated 1546 in the Besançon Museum as 'School of Holbein', also deserves consideration, but may be nearer to Flicke.

9. Erna Auerbach in *Burl. Mag.*, XCIII (Feb. 1951), 45.

CHAPTER 2

HOLBEIN'S SUCCESSORS AND HANS EWORTH

WITH the death of Holbein in 1543 and of Luke Hornebaud in 1544 the Household of Henry VIII was left without any considerable portrait painter. Until very recently we have been in the dark about what followed, but the researches of Dr Erna Auerbach[1] have lately revealed that these painters were succeeded by Guillim Scrots (Scroets), who has hitherto lived but a shadowy existence in the history of art as 'Guillim Stretes'. I have no hesitation in accepting Dr Auerbach's equation of Scrots and Stretes.

Guillim Scrots (Stretes)

Scrots, a Netherlander, was appointed *peintre en titre* to Queen Mary of Hungary, the Regent of the Netherlands, in 1537, and must clearly have been trained in the style of the official portraiture of the Hapsburg Courts. Probably by 1545, and certainly by 1546, he had entered the service of Henry VIII as King's painter with the annual salary of £62 10s, which was much higher than any painter of the Household had received before. It is clear that the King was determined to spare no expense in getting the most up-to-date painter, with the best European Court pedigree, that money could buy. He did not choose carelessly, for, although Scrots was not a painter of high creative or imaginative gifts, he knew all the latest fashions, and a series of portraits appeared at the English Court during the next few years which could vie in modernity with those produced anywhere in Europe, even by painters of much greater natural distinction. Scrots disappears from the scene in the summer of 1553 and it is probable that he left the country about the time of the accession of Mary Tudor.

It would certainly be rash (as well as stylistically inconsequent) to ascribe all the portraits of distinction produced between 1544 and 1553, which cannot definitely be given to other hands, to Scrots. But we may fairly surmise that it was he who gave the impetus which produced the remarkable series of full-length portraits which was painted during these years, and a certain number of pictures can now be quite plausibly associated with his name. Two of the most interesting full-lengths can, however, hardly be by him, the 'Sir Thomas Gresham' dated 1544 at the Mercers' Hall, and the 'Young Man in Red' at Hampton Court. To understand their unusual qualities a short account of the full-length portrait in Europe is necessary.

The full-length standing portrait, which was later to become one of the types of picture most constantly and most happily exploited by British painters, owes its origin to Germany. It first appears there early in the sixteenth century, and characteristic early examples are the portraits at Dresden of Duke Henry the Pious of Saxony and his wife, which are dated 1514. Its first appearance in Italy is Moretto's 'Unknown Man' of 1526 in the National Gallery, but it did not become current in Italy until Titian, in 1532, in direct imitation of Seisenegger's 1532 'Charles V' at Vienna,[2] painted his own version of the Emperor, now at Madrid. In 1533 Holbein, in his double portraits of 'The Ambassadors', at the National Gallery, painted his first experiment in this vein, which he followed later with the 'Duchess of Milan'. It is not until the 1540s (e.g. 'Cristoforo Madruzzo' 1542 in the Stillman collection in New York) that even with Titian the standing full-length becomes anything but exceptional, and it is a curious fact that, by about the same date, it showed signs of having taken root in England, which was otherwise decidedly backward in the arts in relation to the rest of Europe. The Mercers' Hall 'Sir Thomas Gresham' of 1544 is closer than any other of these portraits in spirit to Holbein, including the meticulously painted skull at the sitter's feet, and it can hardly be attributed to Scrots. It is possible, however, that it may have been painted abroad, since we know that Gresham was often in the Low Countries, where he sat to Moro on at least three different occasions. But the same can hardly be said of the 'Young Man in Red' at Hampton Court (Plate 8), which has superficial affinities with the 'Lord de la Warr' at the National Gallery and is equally unlike the portraits which are plausibly identified as the work of Scrots. This 'Young Man in Red' is not only unique in England, but anticipates anything else in Europe so far known as being the first standing full-length silhouetted against a wide horizon, with a spreading landscape below. It has, however, certain affinities with the curious painting in the National Portrait Gallery (No. 1300) in which a panorama and a portrait of 'Edward VI' can only be seen on looking into a cylindrical mirror. This is still dated 1546 and was once inscribed on its original frame (as recorded by Vertue, 1, 54) 'Guilhelmus pingebat'. It would be unreasonable not to suppose that this was the work of Scrots, since we now know that he was in England in 1546, and it may well be that he was showing off his cleverness in this picture to Henry VIII in the same sort of way that Holbein may have been when he painted the curious perspective distortions in 'The Ambassadors'.

Scrots's full stature first appears in a series of full-length portraits, most probably slightly posthumous and commemorative works,[3] of 'Henry Howard, Earl of Surrey' (Plate 9), who was executed for treason in the winter of 1546/7. Two plain full-lengths are at Knole and at Parham; a similar picture with fancy corners is at Castle Howard; and another, figured under a very elaborate Mannerist arch, is at Arundel. These conform to an Italian rather than to a German pattern, and their closest parallel is with the work of Moroni, but Moroni's portraits of this character do not, as at present traced, begin before 1554. The circumstantial evidence for their being by Scrots is considerable, and his Hapsburg training would be sufficient to account for their Italianate air, for we know that Mary of Hungary particularly admired the work of Titian.

Scrots was continued as King's Painter, with the same high salary, under Edward VI, and Dr Auerbach has shown[4] that there is very good reason to suppose that he was responsible for the type of full-length portrait of 'Edward VI' which was especially used for the furtherance of political propaganda abroad. A document of 1551 makes it plain that Scrots had painted two 'great tables' (i.e. full-length portraits) of Edward VI, which had been sent to Ambassadors abroad. There exists circumstantial evidence to connect these great tables with the principal type of full-length 'Edward VI', which is most accessibly represented by the picture at Hampton Court which was acquired from the Hamilton Palace sale as by Holbein. Negotiations were on foot in 1550/1 for a marriage between Edward VI and the eldest daughter of France, and a portrait of the young King had been sent over by September 1550 as a present to the French Queen. A French hostage in England in 1550, the Vidame de Chartres, had obtained leave 'to take away the King of England's painter to execute portraits of the King of France and other great personages' in 1551. The two portraits of Edward VI now in France (in the Louvre and at Roanne) are both of the same type as the picture at Hampton Court, and another version, often mentioned by hearsay in the earlier literature, which was at the sale from Southam Delabere by Sotheby's 11 July 1947, lot 76, has a laudatory inscription in English, Latin, and Greek, which suggests that it was made 'for export' to any foreign country in which at least one of these languages would be understood. From all these circumstances it is reasonable to suppose that this pattern of 'Edward VI' can be associated with Scrots, and Dr Auerbach has shown that the pattern seems connected with the Seisenegger of the 'Archduke Ferdinand' of 1548 at Vienna, so that this deliberate blending of the Holbein formula with that in fashion at the Hapsburg Court may be taken to indicate a conscious attempt to keep pace with current artistic trends on the Continent. This tendency is in marked contrast with what we shall find in the reign of Queen Elizabeth.

Scrots, however, can hardly be associated with the most distinguished of the portraits of 'Edward VI' (Plate 7A), the long three-quarter-length at Windsor, which is also perhaps of about 1550. This is of high technical excellence and has an individual flavour of its own, with certain affinities to the Holbeinesque 'Henry VIII' at Rome. The stance of the boy King is certainly based on the Holbein image of his father in the Whitehall fresco, but it is in reverse. This was no doubt insisted upon by the King's advisers, who were concerned to show, in the official portrait, that Henry VIII's policy remained in force. But by cutting the figure below the knees, the painter has contrived to give the King something of the decent timidity of youth – as becomes apparent if it is compared with certain full-length extensions of the design (as in pictures at Petworth and in possession of the Osborne family, where the King is shown standing before a canopy of state), which are of less good quality and have an air of swagger and bravado which the Windsor picture altogether lacks. The accessories at Windsor – the caryatids and medallion in relief of Marcus Curtius on the column base to right – all indicate a painter in touch with the Mannerist style prevailing in other European Courts. These would all point to Scrots if we could reconcile the handling with that of the full-length portraits. Unless the latter are all studio productions this view would be difficult to accept.

Gerlach Flicke

Almost exactly contemporary with Scrots was another foreign painter, Gerlach Flicke (a name corrupted into 'Garlicke' in the Lumley Inventory).[5] He was a German from Osnabrück and can be traced in England from 1547 until his death in London in 1558. He signed and dated in 1547 a distinguished portrait of an 'Unknown Nobleman' (Plate 6A) (usually precariously identified with the 13th Lord Grey de Wilton) which was bequeathed in 1941 by the Marquess of Lothian to the Edinburgh Gallery. This is wholly in the Westphalian style, such as may be met with in the tom Ring workshop, but the signed 'Archbishop Cranmer', which is hardly later than 1548 (National Portrait Gallery), shows that Flicke had modified his style in the direction of the Holbeinesque. The only other certain work[6] is a battered little diptych of 1554 with small portraits of himself and a fellow prisoner (for he was in gaol) named Strangeways: this seems to lack any distinctive style. We know that Flicke was a Roman Catholic, but the changes of official religion in the middle of the sixteenth century seem to have had little effect on the practice of such painters as we know.

Foreign Visitors under Queen Mary

The only tangible figure whose career as an artist we can follow at all closely in the mid sixteenth century is Hans Eworth, who worked uninterrupted throughout the reigns of Edward VI, Mary, and Elizabeth. Toto remained Serjeant Painter at the beginning of Mary's reign, although he appears to have retired from practice by 1554, when Nicholas Lyzarde exercised the functions of Serjeant Painter, to which office he was fully appointed 10 April 1556. Lyzarde remained in office until his death in 1571 and presented a picture of the 'Story of Ahasuerus' at New Year 1558 (the drawing for which is perhaps in the British Museum as de Heere), but nothing else to the point is known about him or about his successor, William Herne (Heron), who held the post from 1572 until 1581.

During the Marian restoration of the Catholic religion a certain amount of religious painting reappears in the churches, but only slight and battered remains have been recovered from later whitewash, and there was not time, during these troubled four years, for anything like a tradition to be revived or formed. One painter of European note, whose work left its impress on the development of Eworth's style and is therefore best considered before him, did pay a flying visit to England about the time of Mary's marriage to King Philip of Spain in 1554 – Antonio Moro (Anthonis Mor van Dashorst). Moro (c. 1517/20 – 76/77) was the leader of the new style of portraiture which prevailed in the Hapsburg Courts, a style which was calculated to accord with the increasing formality in Court etiquette. Starting from the basis of Titian's portraits of the Spanish kings, he drained out of them all the warmth and colour and perfected a reticent, rather marmoreal type of 'historical' portrait – the northern counterpart to the style of Bronzino. Before his visit to England he had visited Rome, Madrid, and Lisbon, as well as the Spanish Courts in the Netherlands, where he worked mainly, and he is the last international painter of high repute to visit England in the sixteenth century, except for Zuccaro, whose visit was nearly as short as his own. The only portraits actually known to have been executed in London by Moro in 1554 are the signed and dated paintings of 'Queen Mary', of which there are originals at Madrid; Fenway Court, Boston; and in the Marquess of Northampton's collection (Plate 10A). But a number of English portraits exist, probably dating from Mary's reign, which show a very close imitation of his style, such as the 'Lord Maltravers' (d. 1556) at Arundel Castle, and the 'Edward,

Lord Windsor' on loan from the Earl of Plymouth to Cardiff.[7] There is no need to postulate a later visit of Moro to England in 1568, for the 'Sir Henry Lee' of that year (National Portrait Gallery) and the later portraits of Gresham may well have been painted in the Netherlands. It is sufficient to note that examples of Moro's work, specimens of the most 'advanced' of current European styles of portraiture, were available in England.

There was certainly nothing in the nature of a stampede of foreign painters of religious and subject pictures to come to England at the time of Mary's revival of the old religion, but record exists of one painter from Antwerp who did come to London in such hope of patronage about 1555 – Cornelis van Cleve.[8] But he went mad about the time of Elizabeth's accession and had to return home in 1560. Nothing certain of his work survives.

Hans Eworth (Ewouts)

With Hans Eworth we tread on less uncertain ground, and he is the first painter of respectable stature, working for more than a brief period in England, whose development we can follow step by step with the aid of signed and dated works. His signature takes the form HE, but his name is spelt in the documents in a bewildering variety of ways – Haward, Eeuwouwts, Eywooddes, Evertz, Evance, Huett, and perhaps Suete, are some taken at random. He was born in Antwerp, matriculated in the Antwerp Guild in 1540, and can be traced in London from 1549 (possibly from 1545) until 1574. This span of thirty years is covered by upwards of thirty signed and dated works at present known. Only the earliest of them, a small panel of a 'Turk on Horseback' (Plate 11B) against a landscape (Earl of Yarborough), dated 1549, is not in any way a portrait, but there is record of a 'Mars and Venus', which bore his signature, at Gunton Park in the eighteenth century; he perhaps made a drawing of 'David and Saul' in 1562 (Earl of Ancaster MSS., as 'Haunce the drawer'); and he was employed on mythological figures for the Office of the Revels 1572/4.

Eworth was not of a stature to originate a style for himself: he is one of those secondary painters, a class especially useful to the historian, who reflect with great versatility the changes in the taste of the patrons for whom they work. In his first portraits, of 1550, we can see the robust and bourgeois style he learned at Antwerp, where a landscape rich in incident or allegory gives information about his sitters. By 1554 he had achieved Court patronage and changed to a more sober and reticent style of presentation, and the rival manners of Holbein and Moro can be seen at work in him: in the reign of Elizabeth we find him tending sometimes towards the furniture-and-costume piece, where pattern takes the place of style, and, in one instance, venturing into the alembicated world of allegory with which the Queen's poets surrounded her complex personality.

The two earliest dated portraits, both of 1550, are in many ways the most interesting of Eworth's works, since they introduce something new into the field of portraiture in England. They represent two filibustering toughs, uncle and nephew, who were planning a joint expedition to Morocco in 1550, when the younger, Sir John Luttrell, died of the sweat. The elder is 'Captain Thomas Wyndham' (Earl of Radnor), a bluff personage caught in a moment of repose from the battlefield. A camp and soldiers are visible in the background: he is resting against a tree with his powder flask round his neck, two gun barrels behind his head, and his helmet ready to put on. It is almost an 'action' portrait, altogether alien from the aloof and timeless figures we have so far had to record. The companion portrait of 'Sir John Luttrell', at Dunster Castle (Plate 12), is no less lively and even more curious. Allegory is included in the presentation, which is deliberately designed to illustrate the verses which are inscribed on the picture: 'More tha[n] the rock amydys the raging seas / The consta[n]t hert no da[n]ger dreddys nor fearys'. Sir John is naked and wading, waist-high, in raging seas with a ship broken by storm and lightning in the background, the survivors being overwhelmed in little boats. On his wrists are bracelets inscribed in Latin: 'Money did not deter him, / nor danger wreck': and he gazes up confidently to a vision where a naked figure of Peace in the sky succours him, with more remote attendant figures who hold his spear, his armour, his charger, and his money-bags. Their exact import is obscure, but doubtless specific, and there seems an allusion to his dual role as warrior and merchant adventurer. These allegorical figures are in the style of Jan Massys or Frans Floris and exactly follow the contemporary Antwerp tradition. They perhaps give a clue to the kind of subject picture which was current in England at the time.

A few years afterwards, about 1553, Eworth painted 'Mary Tudor' (Plate 10B), for the picture in Sir Bruce Ingram's collection is surely Eworth's unsigned masterpiece rather than by another hand. In this he has gone back to Holbein for inspiration, especially to the earlier Holbein where the figure is seen in a clearly defined space. The minute and beautiful painting of the jewels and the meticulous, yet soft, modelling of the face reveal an almost feminine talent working in Holbein's robust idiom. In 1554 (the year of Moro's visit) he painted the Queen again (Society of Antiquaries, London), in a more iconic fashion against a plain curtain; and the echo of Holbein is at once strong and confused in the 'Lady Dacre' (Plate 11A) of about 1555 at Ottawa. A Holbeinesque portrait of her deceased husband hangs on a curtain behind and the robust figure seems to be aiming at the solid and full presentation of Holbein's earlier style. Yet for all the wealth of accessories in the room the background gives the effect of a flat arabesque. By 1559, in the double portrait of the 'Duchess of Suffolk and Adrian Stoke' (Colonel Wynne-Finch) each of the two figures is conceived in the style of Moro, but with a richer feeling for arabesque and an anticipation of the Elizabethan costume-piece, while the background is a plain glossy black with the date and the ages of the sitters inscribed across it in gold as in Holbein's latest works. What seems to have been the traditional early Tudor Court style has been effectively superimposed upon the more robust and bourgeois style of Eworth's earlier period.

In the companion portraits of 1562 of 'Thomas, Duke of Norfolk' (Lord Rothschild) and of the 'Duchess of Norfolk' (Lord Braybrooke, Audley End) Eworth had graduated towards the new 'costume-piece' style which was to be characteristic of Elizabethan art. The two pictures are conceived as forming a single unit, each set before one-half of a continuous armorial tapestry. The likenesses are distinguished, but the figure is not otherwise of prevailing importance, and the charm of the pictures lies in the generally flat effect of all-over pattern. The background of Eworth's later works is more often plain, but a flat arabesque is usually the main element in their effect.

Two works, however, of particular interest fall outside this category. The 'Henry, Lord Darnley and his Brother' (Plate 13) of 1563 at Windsor has full-length figures, but measures only 25 inches high, so that the spirit of the picture is that of a large miniature or limning – and the miniature, as will appear, was to be at the head of painting fashions in the latter years of Elizabeth's reign. Since the recent cleaning of the life-size version of this picture at Holyroodhouse, which is dated 1562 but is unsigned, we can see that the Windsor picture is only a copy of the latter, and the Holyrood picture, which is in a 'waterwerf' technique on fine linen (as Holbein's original of the More family group is reported to have been), is not altogether convincing as the work of Eworth. It is by a hand no less distinguished, however, and suggests the surprises which may yet be in store when Tudor portraiture is studied in earnest. Another very able painter was also using the large miniature scale in the 1560s, as the two Kirkby portraits (Nos 107 and 111 in the R.A. Winter Exhibition of 1950/1) reveal, and it may prove that this scale was popular with the country gentry, while the larger scale was normal for the Court.

Eworth's final[9] style is fully Elizabethan in spirit and is revealed in the 'Queen Elizabeth confounding Juno, Minerva and Venus' (Plate 14) of 1569 at Hampton Court, an elegant piece of flattery to the Queen, no doubt on a programme laid down by a literary patron. It is a Judgement of Paris in modern dress, with Elizabeth as Paris, who surprises the God-desses by awarding the apple to herself. Variations on the same theme occur in literature,[10] but later than 1569. The figure style of the Goddesses, which is much inferior in refine-ment to that of the portraits of the Queen and her two ladies-in-waiting, remains identical with that in the allegorical portion of the 'Sir John Luttrell' of 1550 (Plate 12). Mytho-logical compositions in the same style are not uncommon and, unless signed, are ascribed to unknown Flemish Mannerists. It may well be, however, that such compositions, painted in England in the sixteenth century, are at present unrecognized rather than non-existent. A certain example is the 'Ulysses and Penelope' at Hardwick Hall dated 1570, which is already recorded in the house in an Inventory of 1601. Such a picture might even be by Eworth himself.

NOTES TO CHAPTER 2

1. Erna Auerbach, *Burl. Mag.*, XCIII (Feb. 1951), 46 ff.

2. G. Glück, 'Original und Kopie' in *Festschrift für Julius Schlosser* (1927), 224 ff.

3. I have given the evidence at length in the Catalogue of the R.A. Winter Exhibition, 1950/51, under No. 51.

4. Erna Auerbach, *Burl. Mag.*, XCI (Aug. 1949), 221-2.

5. The Lumley Inventory of 1590, best published by Sir Lionel Cust in *Walpole Society*, VI (1917/18), 15 ff., is the most important artistic document of the sixteenth century. Apart from furniture (much of which is illustrated in gay drawings), it gives a list of portraits which made up the greatest of English sixteenth-century portrait collections, considerably richer than that of the Crown. It preserves the names of a number of painters who were first identified by this means, and belongs to the Earl of Scarbrough.

C

6. Reproduced in *The Connoisseur*, XLV, 163–4. A few unsigned portraits can reasonably be associated with Flicke, but the fourth 'signed' work which appears in the books is impossible to accept, although the attribution can be traced back to an Inventory of the 1720s. It is a Clouet school portrait of the 'Duc de Nemours' belonging to the estate of the late Marquess of Lothian, on to which an ingenious hand, probably of the early eighteenth century, has painted 'G. Fliccus'. Its divergent style has led to several ingenious hypotheses.

7. This may well be by Moro himself. As Lord Windsor was a Roman Catholic and lived latterly much abroad, it need not have been painted in England.

8. Known to earlier literature as 'Sotto Cleve', he was the son of the better-known Joos van Cleve and was born in 1520 and died 1567. The venerable tradition that he was a portrait painter has been exploded by L. Burchard in *Mélanges Hulin de Loo* (1931), 53 ff.

9. Pictures later than 1569 by Eworth are rare and uncertain: there are unimportant portraits of unknown ladies of 1571 (at Chequers Court) and 1573 (Hon. Michael Astor), but the full-length 'Lady Sidney' at Petworth, alleged to be dated 1573, shows an earlier style of costume, and the two portraits of 1578 at Long Melford have nothing whatever to do with Eworth, although they appear in all the official catalogues of his work.

10. The literary references are given by F. A. Yates in *Warburg Journal*, x (1947), 60 ff.

CHAPTER 3

PAINTING IN THE ELIZABETHAN AND JACOBEAN AGE

Painting in the Reign of Queen Elizabeth

THE career of Hans Eworth penetrates some twenty years into the reign of Elizabeth, which is that period of painting in Britain to which least serious study has been devoted. There is no lack of portraits, even of dated portraits, but the general level of work is of an even mediocrity, executed in the main, it would seem, by small factories rather than by painters with a personal style of their own. The records of Elizabeth's reign, more numerous than those of Henry VIII's, have been published much less fully: the painted portrait on the scale of life seems to have been less esteemed than earlier in the century, and there was no attempt to keep abreast of current trends in European style. Many of the new nobility of the age, which set high store by sculptured tombs (such families, for instance, as the Spencers and the Heneages, whose tombs are among the most memorable of the period), have left no painted portraits in this century, and it is not until about 1618 that a change comes over the portrait taste of the nobility.

For it must be noted that, however momentous historically may have been the change from the dynasty of the Tudors to the Stuarts, with the union of the Crowns of England and Scotland, there is no change in pictorial style until towards the close of the reign of James I, when the precocious taste of Charles, Prince of Wales, began to make itself felt. As in architecture, therefore, we can fairly speak of a 'Jacobethan' style in portraiture, and the studios which were flourishing in the later years of Queen Elizabeth's reign continue unchanged under James I. It is thus convenient and appropriate to consider these groups of portraits, which centre round the Gheeraerts and de Crits studios, under the title of 'Jacobethan portraiture'.

Another point is fundamental to a consideration of Elizabethan painting, which is that, as at no time later, the art of miniature (called 'limning' at this time) far surpasses in quality and contemporary esteem all other forms of painting. Alone of painters in Elizabeth's reign, Hilliard and his rival, Isaac Oliver, are worthy to be named as contributors to the age of Shakespeare. It was these miniaturists whose practice and aesthetic were valid for this age, and the historian of painting in Britain must accord them a degree of attention which the art of the miniaturist does not require in later centuries. Whether Hilliard and Oliver also practised painting on the scale of life is not at present known for certain. There is not any established connexion between Elizabethan painting on the scale of life and Elizabethan miniatures.

Painters' Names under Elizabeth

As the result of a misunderstanding of venerable antiquity most Elizabethan portraits which to-day bear any label at all are ascribed to Federico Zuccaro (Zucchero). There is no justification for this, as will be seen when we come to consider Zuccaro among the occasional foreign visitors to England. One native painter alone, George Gower, deserves separate attention, and is beginning to take on tangible contours, but the names of a considerable number more are known from two main contemporary sources – the Lumley Inventory of 1590, already mentioned, and Francis Meres' *Wit's Commonwealth*, part ii, 1598.[1] Among these disembodied names we may select those around which there is some chance that patient research may be able to assemble groups of works: for one or two of them a beginning has already been made.

The Lumley Inventory of 1590, which has served to enable the reconstruction of Flicke and Eworth, mentions also 'the famous paynter Steven', Seigar, and Hubbert. Of these, 'Steven' alone is a tangible personality at present, and he has been satisfactorily identified with Steven van der Meulen, who matriculated into the Antwerp Guild in 1552, was living in England in 1560, and was naturalized here in 1562. Two of the portraits mentioned in the Inventory, the 'John, Lord Lumley' 1563, and its companion of 'Lady Lumley', remain in the possession of the Earl of Scarbrough and are at Lumley Castle to-day. There is also a high degree of probability that van der Meulen is the 'Master Staffan' who went to Sweden in 1561 and painted Eric XIV at the time of the negotiations for a marriage between King Eric and Queen Elizabeth, and a full-length of Eric XIV at Gripsholm has been plausibly identified with this portrait.[2] In the Lumley portraits, van der Meulen appears as a rather less forceful echo of the style of Eworth.

Of 'Seigar' (probably the name should be Segar and the painter was connected with, or identical with, Sir William Segar, Garter King-at-Arms, or his brother Francis) nothing certain is known, but his portraits are praised in a contemporary poem. Hubbert reappears (as Hubbard) in Lord Northumberland's accounts for 1585/6 (Syon MSS.) as receiving the very large sum of seventeen pounds, in two payments, for a portrait of 'Madam Dundragoe'. One further name, of those listed by Meres, is worth mentioning since that too can be connected with a payment: Arnolde. In 1565/6 'Arnold' received a payment of £4 6s 10d for a portrait of Sir Henry Sydney (Penshurst MSS.), and, in 1572/3, in the accounts of the Office of the Revels, John Arnolde, the Keeper of the Vestures, made a payment of ten shillings to 'Arnolde the Paynter' for 'the picture of Andromedas'.

Meres mentions also a painter 'Lockie', and the name of Locky (Lockey), with the christian names of Richard, Rowland, or Nicholas, reappears variously in the literature and as a signature on the Nostell Priory version of Holbein's More family group (with the date 1530) and on a portrait of Bishop King engraved by de Passe (about 1620). We are at present completely in the dark about the painter or painters of that name. Another of Meres's names, 'Hieronimo', can, however, be fairly confidently equated with Hieronimus Custodis, an Antwerp painter, by whom three signed portraits are known, each bearing the date 1589 – a rather feeble 'Sir John Parker' (Hampton Court), 'Giles Lord

Chandos' (Woburn – a larger, unsigned version was formerly at Nuneham), and 'Lady Elizabeth Bruges' (Woburn). This last is both tender and delicate and reveals Custodis as one of the most attractive painters of this class. His widow remarried in London in 1593.

George Gower

With George Gower[3] we come at last to a native English painter, somewhat unexpectedly a man of gentle birth, who seems, from at least 1573 until his death in 1596, to have been at the top of his profession of portrait painter. He was grandson of Sir John Gower of Stettenham (Yorks.) and may conceivably have been the George Gower who became a Freeman at York 1555/6, with the profession of 'merchant'. Our certain knowledge of his personality (and of the social and economic background of a painter of this age) derives from his 'Selfportrait' (Milton Park; Plate 15A) dated 1579. In the background is a pair of scales, in one of which the painter's coat of arms is outweighed by a pair of dividers, the instrument of the painter's craft. The implication that even a gentleman might turn for his living to painting is further emphasized by some crabbed verses. Their gist, in modern English, seems to be that, though youthful indiscretions had enticed Gower alike from the practice of arms and 'virtue' (? = virtù), he thanks God for the gift of being able to paint, a gift which he long neglected. But now 'Skill revives with gain' and he is enabled to lead a restful life by practising with the pencil, which he supposes is all for the best! Two other portraits, of 'Sir Thomas Kytson' and 'Lady Kytson' (Lately bought by the Tate), both dated 1573, can be securely identified as by Gower from accounts. Round these three works, which are not without a decided individuality in style and are distinct from the Eworth tradition, another group of Elizabethan portraits should one day fall into place. One can confidently accept Mr J. W. Goodison's attribution of two other portraits of 1573 in Lord Middleton's collection.[4] What still, however, remains uncertain is which of the portraits of 'Queen Elizabeth' are to be attributed to Gower, for he seems at one time to have been in a fair way to have a monopoly of official portraits of the Queen, apart from miniatures. He was appointed Serjeant Painter 5 July 1581 for life, and a draft patent exists of 1583/4, which would have granted him the sole right of making portraits and prints of the Queen, with a similar right to be granted to Hilliard for miniatures. This patent was never executed and the draft may have been an enterprising scheme on the part of Gower and Hilliard to get a monopoly for themselves, but it presumably implies that Gower had already painted the Queen and that the portrait had been approved.

Portraits of Queen Elizabeth

Unfortunately research into the exceptionally difficult subject of the portraits of Queen Elizabeth is not sufficiently advanced for us to make a legitimate guess about which of them may be by Gower. But the subject of the Queen's portraits is so central to any understanding of late sixteenth-century English portraiture that the present state of knowledge must be summarized.[5]

The subject must be approached both from a historical and from an aesthetic angle. Historically the position seems to be that the Queen, for some years after her accession, was unwilling to sit to a painter, in spite of the demand which existed for her portrait. There exists a draft proclamation of 1563 in William Cecil's handwriting to prohibit the making of unauthorized likenesses until the Queen should sit officially to 'some coning person mete therefor', but Elizabeth is not known to have approved this proclamation, and one cannot point with certainty to a portrait of her as Queen earlier than the allegorical group of 1569 by Hans Eworth. The Hilliard miniature at Welbeck (and its variant in oils on a large scale at Warwick Castle) is generally dated from the later 1560s, but there is no specific evidence for this. Both are more or less medieval in iconographic pattern and seem to derive in type from the miniatures in the opening initials of the Plea Rolls:[6] these have no successors. It is not until 1572 that a dated Hilliard portrait of the Queen is known – the miniature in the National Portrait Gallery – and it is not until 1573 that any substantial payment to Hilliard is recorded, so that it may be accepted as probable that it was about 1572/3 that Hilliard was appointed limner and goldsmith to the Queen. It is also from this same period, the middle of the 1570s, that the large portraits of the Queen begin to date – the one holding a rose in the National Portrait Gallery (190); the closely related picture with the Pelican Jewel (coll. E. Peter Jones, destined for Liverpool); and the finest of all, the 'Cobham' portrait (Plate 16A) in the National Portrait Gallery (2082). The impulse behind this series seems to have been the close contact during the 1570s with the French Court and the French marriage project. Their 'aesthetic' is that of the miniatures of Hilliard, which will be discussed later. Also, perhaps, before 1580 is the portrait of the Queen holding a colander (symbol of maidenhood), of which the prototype is at Siena. All these show a certain preoccupation with facial likeness and the idea of the 'cult image' has not altogether ousted the idea of portraiture, but, in the Siena picture, the mysterious conceits in Italian show a tendency to translate the portrait into the strange world of Emblem literature.[7] The portrait with an ermine at Hatfield probably also belongs to the 1580s, but before the Armada; and it is probably only after the defeat of the Spanish Armada in 1588 that the more legendary portraits of the Queen begin. By that time the Queen's features were certainly showing signs of age and she wore a wig of a colour unknown to nature. As her portraits of this time were distributed with politic discrimination and were intended as pledges of loyalty and as symbols of state and power, some sort of cult image was required. It is from these years that date the pictures which Walpole sufficiently describes as showing 'a head of hair loaded with crowns and powdered with diamonds, a vast ruff, a vaster farthingale, and a bushel of pearls', and of which Sir Henry Hake has written:[8] 'The origin and growth of the legend of Elizabeth is written in the succession of her portraits which become more fantastic and magnificent as her reign and legend advance.'

The portrait most obviously connected with the defeat of the Spanish Armada is that at Shardeloes (of which there is a second version at Woburn) with the Armada in the background. This may probably be dated soon after 1588. For the early 1590s there is another reasonably established date in the portrait from Ditchley (Plate 18), bequeathed by the late Viscount Dillon to the National Portrait Gallery, which is traditionally reported to have been a gift to commemorate a visit of the Queen to Ditchley in 1592. The hieratic quality of this image is extremely striking. It looms against a stormy sky like some protecting and avenging deity, and stands upon – or rises out of – a tapestry map of England, with the Queen's foot resting exactly upon the spot where Ditchley lies. Another image of the same class is the full-length portrait at Hardwick, in which the naturalistic animals on the embroidered dress are strangely at variance with the mask-like face.

Something of the aesthetic of these portraits will have become apparent from this historical account of them. The common principles by which the historian of painting is accustomed to judge Western portraiture of the Renaissance do not apply. Likeness of feature and an interest in form and volume have been abandoned in favour of an effect of splendid majesty obtained by decorative pattern, and the forms have been flattened accordingly. The Queen's astonishing wardrobe and the politic skill with which she used it alone made this anachronism in Elizabethan portraiture possible. James I inherited the wardrobe as well as the style, but the Elizabethan legend, which gave vitality to both, was incommunicable, and it is not surprising that it took some fifteen years for a new tradition to begin to develop.

Nicholas Hilliard

The painters of Queen Elizabeth's surviving portraits on a large scale were not artists of technical or intellectual gifts. These were reserved for the Queen's limner and goldsmith, Nicholas Hilliard, a native of Exeter, born about 1547, who died in 1619 at the age of seventy-two. He is now known to have painted 'in greate' also, but nothing has been identified with certainty. Painters in miniature are normally a byway which the historian need hardly consider in the general account of a school of painting. But Hilliard is the central artistic figure of the Elizabethan age, the only English painter whose work reflects, in its delicate microcosm, the world of Shakespeare's earlier plays. It is an Italianate world,[9] whose presuppositions about art, the theory of art, and the artist's title to distinction are derived from Lomazzo and Alberti and from Baldassare Castiglione's idea of the 'Gentleman'. Hilliard's art has also close formal connexions with the art of the French Court, which Hilliard is known to have visited in 1577/8. It is supreme in its orchestration of the non-representational and purely decorative elements in the Elizabethan style, as may be seen by comparing what is perhaps Hilliard's masterpiece, the 'George Clifford, Earl of Cumberland' (National Maritime Museum, Greenwich; Plate 19), with its almost exact contemporary, the Ditchley 'Queen Elizabeth' (Plate 18). Hilliard's work is most nearly paralleled by some of the finest of Persian miniatures, but Hilliard has an additional quality which is no less surprising than his virtuosity in arabesque – a prodigious gift of psychology. This he could not exercise in his miniatures of the Queen, but in his *Arte of Limning*,[10] written about 1600, he gives some account of his aims and practice which explains what Mr Pope-Hennessy has finely called the 'tantalizing intimacy' of the best of his miniatures of private persons. Hilliard describes[11] how the 'curious drawer' must watch and, as it were, catch 'these lovely graces, witty smilings, and these stolen glances which suddenly, like lightning, pass and another countenance taketh place'; how he must note 'how the eye changeth and narroweth, holding the sight just between the lids as a centre, how the mouth a little extendeth both ends of the line upwards, the cheeks raise themselves to the eyewards, the nostrils play and are more open, the veins in the temple appear more and colour by degrees increaseth, the neck commonly erecteth itself, the eyebrows make the straighter arches, and the forehead casteth itself into a plain as it were for peace and love to walk upon'. Such are the refinements at which Hilliard's art was aiming, and which it achieved at its best. The painters on a larger scale, all inferior artisans, were aping an art whose springs they did not understand, and this perhaps explains the unsatisfactory character of most Elizabethan portraiture. With the death of Queen Elizabeth the understanding of these subtleties died too and the more prosy reign of James I saw the rise to popularity of the miniature style of Hilliard's younger rival, Isaac Oliver, whose aims were a realistic likeness attained by the use of shadow. Of the portrait painters in large, only Gower may have had some understanding of Hilliard's style: their names are joined in the draft patent of 1584 and the legend on Gower's 'Selfportrait' (Plate 15A), already quoted, suggests a similar preoccupation with Hilliard's about the social status of the artist. The more popular Flemings were craftsmen and did not aspire to be anything else.

Visiting Foreign Painters

None of the few foreign painters who worked in England for a year or so was important for the development of painting in Britain, but mention should be made of Lucas de Heere, Cornelis Ketel, and Federico Zuccaro. De Heere and Zuccaro are chiefly of interest owing to the reckless play which has been made with their names by those anxious to find an attribution for Elizabethan portraits.

Lucas de Heere (1534–84) was a distinguished painter from Ghent, mainly of subject pieces and historical decorations. He was a pupil of Frans Floris and his style (which cannot be controlled from surviving examples) was probably much the same as that of Hans Eworth. He also worked at Fontainebleau on designs for tapestries, and it is this connexion with the French Mannerist school which makes his presence in England (as a victim of the Duke of Alva's proscriptions) of possible significance. He was here from 1568 to 1577, but no surviving painting can be associated with his name.[12] He was, however, perhaps the teacher of the most prolific portrait painters of the next generation.

Cornelis Ketel (1548–1616) was a native of Gouda and, like de Heere, also worked (in 1566) at Fontainebleau. He was in England from 1573 until about 1581, in which year he had finally settled in Amsterdam. He was both a portrait and a history painter, and, like Holbein before him, found his first clients in the German merchants of the Hansa Steelyard. A young English merchant, whose name van Mander gives as Pieter Hachten (possibly a Hatton and a kinsman of the future Lord Chancellor), bought from him an allegorical picture, with figures larger than the scale of life, of 'Force overcome by Wisdom and Prudence', of which he made a present to Sir Christopher Hatton. This introduced Ketel to Court circles and he is reported to have painted a portrait of Queen Elizabeth in 1578 for the Earl of Hertford.[13] Half a dozen signed portraits with dates from his English period have so far been traced,[14] and it will be seen from the 'Unknown Youth of sixteen' of 1576 (Hon. Clive Pearson, Parham; Plate 15B) that there is little to distinguish his style at this date from the later work of Eworth. Unfortunately his most ambitious portrait of these years, the 'Sir Martin Frobisher' 1577 (Bodleian Library, Oxford), is too ruined to provide a sure criterion of his style.

With Federico Zuccaro (c. 1543–1609) we reach a name of far greater contemporary distinction. On Titian's death in 1576 (soon after Zuccaro's visit to England) Federico Zuccaro was probably the most internationally famous of Italian painters, and he is certainly one of the central figures of the Roman Mannerist school which exercised such a profound influence on the style of painting in the Mediterranean world. It might seem as if another Holbein had come to England, and, had he really stayed here the four years which have been alleged from the time of de Piles up to the present century, it is quite possible that the current of British painting might have flowed more in consonance with the main stream of European style. In fact, however, he arrived in England late in 1574 and he was back in Italy by the autumn of 1575.[15] All that he is recorded with any certainty to have painted in England are full-length portraits of Queen Elizabeth and the Earl of Leicester:[16] all that survives is the pair of drawings for these in the British Museum[17] (Queen Elizabeth; Plate 20B). His name, taken in vain, is to be found on the labels in most of the great houses of England.

The Development of Series of 'Historical Portraits'

We have seen how portraiture seems to begin with series of portraits of kings, some of them perhaps imaginary. By the close of the century other series, of lesser personages, had begun to come into being, and it will be convenient to deal once for all, at the birth of the type, with that recurrent phenomenon in British collections, the imaginary historical portrait, examples of which, mistaken by later ages for works contemporary with the sitter, have periodically been introduced to confound the history of art. First after kings, perhaps, came series of portraits of religious reformers (all more or less contemporary) and an interesting correspondence has been published,[18] giving an account of how one Christopher Hales, as early as 1550, was seeking to collect portraits of the Zürich reformers for the adornment of his library. But the crucial example of a series of largely imaginary portraits is that of the Constables of Queenborough Castle which Sir Edward Hoby had painted in 1593 for the Hall of the Castle of which he was then Constable. These began with Edward 'III' (Queen's College, Oxford) and 'John of Gaunt' (now at Badminton) and continued up to Sir Edward himself. They all centred round a portrait of Queen Elizabeth, and the whole scheme was explained in some appropriate (but obscure) lines in Latin, followed by the date 1593.[19] This series was already dispersed by 1629, but most of them passed through the sale of Sir John Tufton in 1686 and sixteen were, in Vertue's time, at Penshurst, where two remain. On the portrait of 'Thomas Fitzalan, Archbishop of Canterbury' (one of the two remaining at Penshurst), Vertue read correctly a monogram which appears to be LCP (or a combination of these letters), which he surmised, in the privacy of his notebook, to be the signature of Lucas Cornelisz de Kock, a painter otherwise unknown who is stated by van Mander to have come to England in the early years of the sixteenth century. Hence examples of this series of portraits, now widely scattered, have periodically been dated a century too early.

In this last decade of the sixteenth century, which saw the creation of the imaginary portraits of the Constables of Queenborough Castle, another kind of imaginary portrait also begins to come in—the College Founder's portrait. At Oxford these were the creation of a Dutch painter, Sampson Strong, alias Starkey (c. 1550–1611), whose abundant activity can be traced at Oxford from 1589 until his death.[20] He is found working also at Christ's Hospital, Abingdon, where there is a portrait, almost certainly from his hand,[21] of a benefactor who died in 1424, which is a work of pure invention. A parallel group of portraits exists at Peterhouse, Cambridge.

The Flemish Studios of the Jacobethan Period

Towards the close of the 1540s the full-length portrait seems to have fallen out of favour, and it is not impossible that it was restored to favour by the two full-lengths of the Queen and Leicester painted by Zuccaro in 1575. Of the very few such pictures before that date, such as the 'Unknown Man' 1571 at Petworth, and the two Eworth portraits (also at Petworth) of 'Sir Henry Sydney' and 'Lady Sydney' of 1573 (?), both the pattern and the style are still Holbeinesque. After 1575 a change in style takes place and full-length portraits become more frequent, at first of great persons, such as 'Sir Christopher Hatton' (Earl of Winchilsea) and the Earl of Leicester. The Ketel of 'Frobisher' 1577 is one of the first of the series, and, by about 1590, the full-length 'costume piece', with a single figure or, on occasions, family groups, had become the most typical and characteristic form of English portrait. From 1590 to about 1625 a great number of these costume pieces were executed. There are splendid series of them at Woburn, Penshurst, and Welbeck, and a number of dispersed examples come from Wroxton and Ditchley. Most of them to-day are covered with dust and grime and give a false effect of what they were meant to look like. But when they can be seen cleaned – as can the dozen at Redlynch (Margaret, Countess of Suffolk) – they glow with the enamelled brilliance of a formal *parterre*. There is nothing like them in contemporary European painting, and, although they should be classified perhaps with the decorative rather than with the plastic arts, their qualities deserve respect. It is customary, but probably incorrect, to associate most of these with the name of Marcus Gheeraerts.

They seem, in fact, to be the product of several closely associated workshops of Flemish painters who were interconnected by marriage. The two main dynasties are the families of De Critz[22] and Gheeraerts,[23] and connected with these are Robert Peake and the miniature painter, Isaac Oliver.

A goldsmith of Antwerp named Troilus de Critz settled with his family in England, where he became a denizen in 1552. Of his children, John (born probably before 1552; died 1642) became a pupil of Lucas de Heere (1571), was a painter on his own and travelled in France as a protégé of Walsingham in 1582: by 1598 he was one of the best-known painters in England and he stepped into the office of Serjeant Painter (at first jointly with Leonard Fryer, who had succeeded Gower in 1596) almost immediately after the accession of James I in 1603. He still held that office at the time of his death in 1642. In 1610 Robert Peake was associated with him in the office of Serjeant Painter. The eldest of this John de Critz's sisters, Susanna, married in 1571 the elder Marcus Gheeraerts, a historical and decorative painter and engraver from Bruges, who was a refugee in England from 1568 to 1577: a younger sister, Magdalen de Critz, married in 1590 her elder sister's stepson, the younger Marcus Gheeraerts (1561/2–1635/6). One of the daughters of Susanna de Critz and the elder Gheeraerts, Sara, became in 1602 the second wife of Isaac Oliver. It may well not be far from the truth if we suppose that the four painters, John de Critz, the younger Gheeraerts, Peake, and Oliver, were the leading figures in a small factory or factories which produced the costume pieces of this age. The few paintings which can be firmly associated with one or other of these names do not enable us, by stylistic analysis, to separate out the various hands.

The crucial document for John de Critz is a bill of 1607 for various portraits painted for the Earl of Salisbury. They include a portrait of James I and several of the Earl himself: one of the latter was for the Ambassador at Venice, who was Sir Henry Wotton. In a letter of 22 June 1609[24] to Lord Cranborne Wotton explains how he has had a mosaic made from this de Critz portrait in Venice, and the mosaic, which is still at Hatfield, serves to identify the de Critz type of portrait of the first 'Earl of Salisbury'. It may be provisionally suggested that most of the early portraits of James I and Anne of Denmark issued from the de Critz workshop, and there is a payment for such pictures in 1606 which were sent to the Archduke of Austria. An accessible example is the 'James I' dated 1610 at Greenwich (Plate 21A), which differs only in small particulars from the one dated 1606 which was formerly at Nuneham Courtenay.

It is probable that the elder Marcus Gheeraerts was never a portrait painter. If he did paint portraits his name can only be associated with a small panel (18 × 15 in.), in a dainty, almost miniature technique of 'Queen Elizabeth' (Welbeck; Plate 20A) on which the signature 'M. G. F.' was discovered during cleaning c. 1890. But if, as seems probable, this is a painting of c. 1590, it is more likely that it represents the early style of the younger Gheeraerts. Vertue[25] records a letter at Penshurst in which the name of 'Gerrats' was associated with a portrait group which can be identified with the 'Barbara, Lady Sydney and six children' (Plate 17), correctly (but by a later hand) dated 1596, at Penshurst. In 1611 he is styled 'his Majestie's paynter' and there are payments in 1611, 1613, and 1618 for various portraits of the royal family. The ruined 'Camden' of c. 1620 (Bodleian, Oxford) has a signature and there are two full-lengths of 1625 of 'Sir William Russell' and 'Lady Russell' at Woburn, one with a signature. These hardly agree in handling with the dainty little bust of 'Lucy, Countess of Huntingdon'[26] (late Sir George Leon, Bart), which is authentically signed and bears the date 1623. In short, the personality of Gheeraerts remains an enigma.

Unlike the others of this group, Robert Peake was, so far as is known, an Englishman and he was not involved in the family interconnections of de Critz and Gheeraerts. But his training must have been on the same lines, and it would be plausible to suppose that they all first learned the art together under de Heere. Peake first appears in the accounts of the Office of the Revels, in which, from 1576 to 1579, he is paid as one of the minor painters working for William Lyzarde. By 1598[27] he is in good employment as a portrait painter and is described as painter to Prince Henry in 1609. In 1610 he was joined with John de Critz in the office of Serjeant Painter: perhaps de Critz did the portraits of the King and Peake those of the Princes (the payments known suggest something of the sort). At any rate, a full-length portrait of 'Prince Charles' (Plate 21B), for which Peake received payment in 1613, in the Cambridge University Library, is one certain work. A group of four portraits of the de Ligne family,[28] all dated 1616, appeared to me to be certainly by the same hand, and a rather damaged portrait called 'Lady Arundel'[29] bears the date 1622 and a monogram RP (R in reverse), which is presumably Peake's. The lace patterns in all six pictures are very nearly identical, and that may well provide a clue for identifying Peake. A signed 'Man' of 1593, lately acquired by the Earl of Wilton from Melton Constable, gives the clue to his earlier style.

It is by the application of the Morellian method to costume and accessories that we have the best chance at present to differentiate the hands in these pictures – a favourite carpet, or a trick of lighting the folds of curtains. Two examples from the wonderful series at Redlynch, the 'Countess of Stamford' (Plate 23) and the 'Countess of Suffolk' (Plate 22), will serve to illustrate the possibilities in this direction.

The fourth artist who must be considered in this group is Isaac Oliver, a Frenchman rather than Fleming, for he came as a child to England from Rouen in 1568 and died in London in 1617. He is only known for certain as a miniaturist, who learned his dexterity of hand from Hilliard, but belongs in style to the post-Elizabethan spirit. He was possibly in Holland in 1588 and certainly in Venice in 1596, and his means of obtaining likeness in his miniatures are the European ones of light and shade and modelling in the round, which Hilliard evaded. Although Hilliard retained his official position under James I and Oliver played a subordinate role, Hilliard's star waned with the death of Elizabeth and his fire dried up. It is Oliver's miniatures which give us the most living portraits of the reign of James I and prefigure the style of the next generation. The literary evidence that he painted on the scale of life is not clear, but not negative. A comparison of his miniature of the '3rd Earl of Dorset' (Victoria and Albert Museum; Plate 24), signed and dated 1616, with the life-size portrait of the same sitter at Redlynch, with the date 1613, shows at least what an Oliver in large would look like. There are also figure drawings of religious and historical subjects by Oliver in an Italianate Mannerist style.

Although Oliver has not the extreme refinement of Hilliard's psychological approach to his sitters, his best miniatures show a sense of character which is wholly lacking in most of the large-scale costume pieces. There are a few life-scale portraits, however, which seem to belong technically to this Jacobethan age (rather than to the generation of Mytens and Johnson) which capture the qualities of the miniaturists. The portrait called 'Frances, Countess of Essex' (Welbeck; Plate 26A) shows the power of tender penetration and shy perceptiveness of which this style was capable, combined with a miniaturist's finish and a Mannerist elaboration of pattern. It is hard to believe that such a picture is not Oliver on the scale of life.

Two pictures exist which are rather more than mere group portraits, and which can be associated with this Flemish style – the 'Visit of Queen Elizabeth to Blackfriars' 1600 at Sherborne Castle[30] and the two versions (National Portrait Gallery and Greenwich) of the 'Conference of English and Spanish Plenipotentiaries' 1604. Of neither is the painter known.

Beginning of Landscape and Genre: Wall Paintings

Topographical landscape in drawings and watercolour is to be found in the sixteenth century, but only one oil picture is so far known (at any rate of moderate distinction) which shows an English scene and combines landscape and genre – the 'Wedding at Horsleydown in Bermondsey',[31] signed by Joris Hoefnagel, at Hatfield. Hoefnagel (born Antwerp, 1542: died Vienna, 1600) was a miniaturist and topographical draughtsman as well as a painter, and there is room in his much-travelled career for a visit to England about 1569. The picture is unique as showing a bourgeois scene in a recognizable English setting, and the style is a competent derivation from the Brill-Brueghel manner. But the picture seems to have remained without successors in England.

Secular wall paintings from the sixteenth century do exist, but they are mainly decorative, and the work of local house-painters. An exception is the series from Hill Hall, Essex,[32] now in the Victoria and Albert Museum, which are pedestrian imitations after tapestries from Raphael school designs. It will be sufficient to have mentioned the existence of this class of work.

Painting in Scotland

There were portrait painters in Scotland before the union of the two Crowns under James I in 1603: but they were fewer than in England, and infinitely less of their work survives. To set against the great series of portraits of Elizabeth, there is not one of the surviving authentic portraits of Mary, Queen of Scots, which was executed during her stay in Scotland. Whether the battered painting at Hardwick of 'James V and Mary of Guise' (1540) is contemporary it is no longer possible to say: but Mary of Guise brought with her from France Pierre Quesnel, who became the father, while resident of Scotland, of two distinguished portrait painters who later worked in France. The first 'paynter to the King' was a certain Arnold Bronkhorst who was appointed to that office on 9 September 1580,[33] and a bill survives for a full-length and a half-length portrait of the young James VI and a portrait of Buchanan. In June 1581 there is also a payment in the Lord Treasurer's accounts to a certain Adriaen 'Vanson' for portraits of the King and John Knox sent to Beza in 1580 and engraved in his *Icones*.[34] It remains uncertain whether any of these names can be associated with the portraits of the King as a boy and youth which survive (National Portrait Gallery, etc.).

A specifically Scottish type of picture, without parallel in England, is what one may call the 'vendetta portrait', designed to keep alive the memory of an atrocious deed. The earlier of the two known is the 'Darnley Memorial Picture' (showing the young James VI at his father's tomb) at Holyrood, of which there is a second version at Goodwood.[35]

This appears to have been painted in London in 1567 by a Brussels artist, Levinus Voge-larius, but it was assuredly a Scottish commission. The other is the most gruesome pictorial document of the age, the life-size portrait of the corpse of 'The bonnie Earl of Moray' (Earl of Moray, Darnaway Castle; Plate 26B) as it lay in state in 1591, with all the ghastly wounds of Huntly's vengeance meticulously depicted. The formal qualities of this paint-ing are superior in energy and realism to the contemporary English costume piece, and it remains an effective reminder of how little we know of the painting of this period. Some-thing about its facture suggests the work of a professional herald painter.

NOTES TO CHAPTER 3

1. A list of known names is given in W. G. Con-stable and C. H. Collins Baker, *English Painting of the Sixteenth and Seventeenth Centuries* (1930), 34–5.

2. See W. G. Constable in *Burl. Mag.*, LXVII (Sept. 1935), 133–4.

3. The reconstruction of Gower, from which the information in the text is taken, is by J. W. Goodison in *Burl. Mag.*, XC (Sept. 1948), 261 ff., where the documents are published.

4. Published in Burlington Fine Arts Club, *Ex-hibition of late Elizabethan Art* (1926), plates vi and vii.

5. The foundations of a study are to be found in F. M. O'Donoghue, *A Descriptive and Classified Cata-logue of Portraits of Queen Elizabeth*, 1894, and a useful attempt at a summary chronology (on the basis of costume) is F. M. Kelly in *The Connoisseur*, CXIII (1944), 71 ff.

6. Dr Auerbach has been engaged on the study of the plea roll initials.

7. On the column is inscribed: 'Stanco riposo e riposato affanno'; on the globe: 'Questo vedo e molto'; and on the colander: 'A terra il ben – mal dimora in sella'. The most famous of the Hatfield portraits belongs to the same world of Emblems: the Queen holds a rainbow, over which is written 'Non sine sole Iris', and she wears a dress patterned with eyes and ears, presumably to show the universality of her intelligence, but there may also be more esoteric allusions, since Leicester was nicknamed by her 'Eyes'.

8. 'The English Historic Portrait: Document and Myth', offprint from *Proceedings of the British Academy*, XXIX (1943), 8.

9. The best account of Hilliard's style is in Mr John Pope-Hennessy's *A Lecture on Nicholas Hilliard*, 1949, with the essence of which I am in entire agree-ment, although I would question some of the sug-gestions about the origins of Hilliard's style. The rest of what is known about Hilliard and many illustra-tions are to be found in Mr Graham Reynolds's *Cata-logue of the Hilliard and Oliver Exhibition*, Victoria and Albert Museum, 1947: see further, correspond-ence in *The Times Literary Supplement*, 9 Aug. 1947, and 25 Sept. 1948, and Dr Auerbach's article in *Burl. Mag.*, XCI (June 1949), 166 ff., where she gives the evidence that Hilliard, in 1598, agreed to paint 'a faire picture in greate' of Queen Elizabeth.

10. Published in *Walpole Society*, I (1912).

11. *Arte of Limning*, 23–4; I have simplified the spelling.

12. From Vertue's day until 1912 the signature of Hans Eworth (*HE*) was supposed to be that of de Heere, and this error should be allowed for in all that relates to portraits in what is otherwise the best ac-count of what is known of de Heere – Sir Lionel Cust, 'A notice of the Life and Works of Lucas d'Heere', in *Archaeologia*, LIV (1894).

13. This would normally have descended to the Duke of Northumberland, but it can hardly be the small head at Syon House, which has affinities with the portrait at Siena of about the right date.

14. A list in Constable and Collins Baker, *op. cit.* 37.

15. These dates are to be deduced from the most complete synopsis of all the documents relating to Zuccaro which has so far been published, in Werner Körte, *Der Palazzo Zuccari in Rom*, Leipzig (1935), 70–9.

16. Raffaello Borghini, *Il Riposo*, 1584, p. 573 (Book IV, p. 143, of the Siena edition of 1787), who says: 'in Inghilterra fece il ritratto della Regina Elisa-betta, e quello di Milord Lostrè [*sic*] suo favoritis-simo, ambedue interi, e grandi come il naturale'.

17. No painting closely related to the drawing of the Queen is known, but there is a large panel of Leicester (79 × 43 in.) which is clearly based on the drawing but shows him in different armour. This was formerly in the Duke of Sutherland's collection at Trentham and last appeared in Anon. (Mrs Otto Kahn) sale, Christie's, 28 July 1939, lot 60: it was not an original by Zuccaro.

18. P. Boesch in *Zwingliana*, IX (1949), 16 ff.

19. The legend about these portraits and their supposed connexion with Lucas Cornelis was started by Vertue (II, 51–2) and canonized by Walpole (ed. Dallaway/Wornum, I, 65) on the strength of 'an itinerary by one Johnston' [*sic*]. On purely stylistic grounds it was exploded by Sir Lionel Cust in the introduction to the Exhibition of Early English Portraits at the Burlington Fine Arts Club, 1909, pp. 49–50, but its most recent victim was S. H. Steinberg in *Burl. Mag.*, LXXIV (Jan. 1939), 35–6, and it is enshrined in Thieme-Becker. It can be exploded on securer grounds by consulting Walpole's misnamed source, Thomas Johnson's *Iter Plantarum Investigationis Ergo Susceptum*, 1629 (S.T.C. No. 14703).

20. The documentation of Strong is to be found in Mrs R. Lane Poole, *Catalogue of Oxford Portraits*, II, xi ff.

21. Arthur E. Preston, *Christ's Hospital, Abingdon* (1929), 36 ff.

22. Full documentation in Mrs R. Lane Poole, 'An outline of the history of the De Critz family of painters', in *Walpole Society*, II.

23. Mrs R. Lane Poole, 'Marcus Gheeraerts, father and son', in *Walpole Society*, III, publishes the documents. This is followed by an article on Marcus Gheeraerts by Sir Lionel Cust, which is rich in illustrations but almost devoid of critical value.

24. Logan Pearsall Smith, *The Life and Letters of Sir Henry Wotton*, I, 460: the mosaic is illustrated, I, 452.

25. Vertue, V, 75. This letter does not appear among the published Penshurst MSS., Sir Robert Sydney to Lady Sydney of 26 Jan. 1596/7 (Hist. MSS. Commission, Penshurst MSS., II (1934), 230) refers to this picture, but does not name the painter. Two portraits at Penshurst also have 'Marc Garrard's' signature: the attribution is probably correct, but the 'signatures' seem to have been put on by Sartorius when restoring the pictures in 1748.

26. Exhibited R.A., 1938 (11), and reproduced in the Album of the Exhibition.

27. The few documents known on Peake are summarized in A. J. Finberg, 'An authentic portrait by Robert Peake', in *Walpole Society*, IX, 89 ff.

28. Two pairs of companion portraits of a father and mother and a boy and a girl. They appeared (as 'Jamesone') in the T. S. Pearson-Gregory sale, 18 June 1937, lots 21 and 22.

29. Sir Gerald Chadwyck-Healey sale, Sotheby's, 21 July 1943, lot 48.

30. A full account of this historically very interesting painting, by the Earl of Ilchester, is given in *Walpole Society*, IX.

31. Best illustrated in *Burl. Mag.*, XXXI (Sept. 1917), 89, where the article by F. M. Kelly is only valuable for dating the costume not later than 1570.

32. For this whole subject and the bibliography, see F. W. Reader, 'A classification of Tudor domestic wall painting', in *The Archaeological Journal*, XCVIII (1941), 181 ff.

33. The documents are published in *Archaeologia Scotica*, III (1831), 312–13.

34. See James Drummond, *The Portraits of John Knox and George Buchanan*, Edinburgh, 1875 (from *Transactions of the Antiquarian Society*, 10 May 1875), p. 7. An Adriaen Johnson, 'picturemaker', became a denizen of London, 29 Oct. 1550.

35. Sir James L. Caw, *Scottish Portraits*, I (1902), plate x.

PART TWO

PAINTING UNDER THE STUARTS, UP TO THE REVOLUTION OF 1688

CHAPTER 4

THE PRECURSORS OF VAN DYCK

THE beginnings of a change of style in portraiture – away from the Elizabethan 'costume piece' and in the direction of contemporary practice in the Courts of Northern Europe – are hardly to be discerned until the year 1617, some fourteen years after the accession of James I. The hundred years which follow can properly be considered as a single unit by the historian of art, and can conveniently be described as 'the age of the Stuarts', although the period ends rather with the death of Sir Godfrey Kneller in 1723 than with the passing of the Stuart dynasty in 1714 with the death of Queen Anne. The painting of this age falls naturally into four subdivisions: the precursors of Van Dyck, the age of Van Dyck and Dobson, the age of Lely, and the age of Kneller. It will make for clarity, in the present state of knowledge, if they are treated separately.

The Precursors of Van Dyck

Three painters from the Low Countries, all trained abroad, make their appearance in Court circles in England nearly simultaneously, in 1617 and 1618: Paul van Somer, Abraham van Blijenberch, and Daniel Mytens. The year 1618 also marks the beginnings, in so far as present knowledge goes, of the finest British-born portrait painter of the generation before Van Dyck – Cornelius Johnson. The boundaries between the work of Mytens and the work of Johnson are still imperfectly defined, and the style of all these painters seems to depend on the contemporary school of portraiture at The Hague, which centres round the personality of Mierevelt (1567–1641).

Paul van Somer (Paulus van Someren)

Van Somer is perhaps a little more archaic in style than the other painters named when we first meet his certain work in 1617. But, by 1620, he is abreast of Mytens and Johnson. So little is known of him that extreme caution must replace the rather reckless use which has been made of his name in recent years. He was born in Antwerp about 1577/8: in 1604 van Mander mentions him as working at Amsterdam with his elder brother, Bernard, with a reputation both as a portrait and as a history painter: in 1612 and 1614 he was living at Leyden: he is recorded in passing at The Hague in 1615 and at Brussels in 1616, and he had settled in London by December 1616.[1] He was buried at St Martin in the Fields 5 January 1621/2. His working life in England amounts, therefore, to little more than five years, but he seems to have been employed by the Crown almost at once. The huge full-length at Windsor of 'Queen Anne of Denmark (Plate 27), with a horse', a Negro groom, five Italian greyhounds and a view of one of the royal palaces (believed to be Oatlands), is fully signed and dated 1617. Although the painting of the face is only a little freer than the painting of the Gheeraerts and de Critz group of portraits, the general air and grandiose arrangement of the picture suggest something of a more European world, and the ribbon which floats in the sky bears the Italian legend *La mia grandezza dal eccelso* (perhaps an assertion of Divine Right). Paul van Somer could conceivably have studied in Italy – as his brother is known to have done – but no close parallel to this fashion of portrait has yet been noticed. At Windsor is also a battered '3rd Earl of Pembroke' signed and dated 1617.

A respectable tradition gives to van Somer four head-size portraits of 'Elizabeth, Countess of Exeter' and her three daughters, in the possession of the Marquess of Ailesbury, which bear either the date 1618 or a picture of the famous comet of that year; and tradition, as well as an old inscription, gives to him two half-length pictures dated 1619 in the same collection – the '2nd Earl of Devonshire with his Son' and the 'Countess of Devonshire with her Daughter', which are entirely harmonious in style with the 'Anne of Denmark'. They are very close to the work of Mytens, but stand a little more limply and with less physical assurance. In the same years he is recorded in documents as working for the Earl of Rutland and the Earl of Dorset, and, for the years 1619 to 1621, there are records of official payments for portraits of the King, the Queen, Prince Charles, and for a copy of a portrait of Prince Henry (d. 1612).[2] A single signed and dated portrait reveals to us his later style, 'Thomas, Lord Windsor' 1620 (lent to Cardiff by the Earl of Plymouth), a finely drawn and painted head, a little more tender in its interpretation of character than Mytens, and a little broader in handling than the contemporary early work of Johnson. A very handsome full-length 'Countess of Oxford' of *c.* 1621 (Marquess of Ailesbury) is also inscribed as by van Somer. Cleaning and opportunities for throwing a strong light on to dark pictures will probably round off our knowledge of van Somer before many years have passed.

The same is hardly to be anticipated for Abraham van Blijenberch, of whom our knowledge is extremely scanty. From documents we know that he was taking pupils at Antwerp in 1621/2, and we can feel reasonably confident that he paid a short visit to England, probably about 1618. This is to be deduced from the facts that he painted a portrait of Charles, Prince of Wales[3] and that his portrait of 'Robert Ker, Earl of Ancrum' (Marquess of Lothian's trustees) is dated 1618. His other known portrait of an English sitter, the signed half-length of 'William, 3rd Earl of Pembroke' (Earl of Powis), shows him to have been the hardly distinguishable peer of Mytens or van Somer of about 1618.

Daniel Mytens

The career of Mytens was prolonged in England until after the final arrival of Van Dyck and brings us into contact with the chief patrons of the arts in the golden age of collecting: Thomas Howard, Earl of Arundel, King Charles I, and, in a lesser measure, George Villiers, Duke of Buckingham. At this time in England (and perhaps at no other) collecting and the patronage of the living painter went hand in hand. The artistic programme of Charles I, which he may be said to have taken over from the Earl of Arundel, was to align and marry the tradition of art in Britain to the European tradition. In this he succeeded and British painting has never been the same again. But the first inspirer of this aim was Lord Arundel and he was more or less directly responsible for introducing into England the three artists who most contributed to this end: Mytens, Inigo Jones (in architecture), and Van Dyck. Mytens is by far the least of these, but he is not an inconsiderable figure.

Daniel Mytens was born at Delft; in 1610 he matriculated in the Guild at The Hague, which leads to the plausible suppositions that he was a pupil of Mierevelt and was born about 1590; he was still at The Hague in 1612, when he made his first marriage; he is next documented in August 1618, when he writes to Sir Dudley Carleton from London in excellent English[4] and is described in a letter from Carleton to Arundel as 'your Lordship's painter'; in 1618 he had not yet succeeded in doing a portrait of Prince Charles, but he seems to have been introduced to James I about 1619, and official payments for portraits ordered by the Crown begin in May 1620 (a payment for the portrait of the 'Earl of Nottingham' now at Greenwich); on van Somer's death he succeeded as Court portrait painter, and payments for portraits of James I and Prince Charles begin in 1623 (presumably, therefore, painted in 1622). He was more particularly favoured by the Prince (perhaps through Arundel's influence), but was granted a pension of £50 a year for life by James I on 19 July 1624 'on condition that he do not depart from the realm without a warrant from the King or the Council', which clearly reflects the royal misgivings over Van Dyck's departure after his abortive visit in 1620/1. On 22 August 1624 Mytens was made a denizen 'by direction of the Prince', and the same month he was granted the lease of a house in St Martin's Lane, also by the Prince's directions: this lease was enrolled on 30 December 1624 through Sir Henry Hobart, Prince Charles's Chancellor (d. 1625), who had sat to Mytens for his portrait 22 December 1624.[5] King James died in March 1625 and on 30 May 1625 Charles I appointed Mytens 'Picture Drawer to the King': on 10 August 1626 there appears among the Acts of the Privy Council a 'passe for Daniell Mitten, his Majesty's picture drawer, to goe over into the Low Countries and to remaine there for the space of six months'. This must surely have been an inspired journey so that Mytens could refamiliarize himself with the latest fashions in Flemish portraiture, and the work he did on his return shows that he had studied to good advantage. Thereafter payments for royal portraits are continuous until after the arrival of Van Dyck in England in the spring of 1632. Such payments in fact continue until May 1634, but no certain royal portrait by Mytens is known after 1633. At what date Mytens finally returned to Holland is obscure, but the pass for him to go to the Low Countries 'with his truncks' is dated 12 September 1630, and that for his wife, with three children and two maids and 'to take with them their truncks of apparel &c' is dated 11 May 1631.[6] In 1637 he was living at The Hague acting as one of Lord Arundel's many agents for his collections,[7] and he seems to have died there before 1648. No paintings are at present known which date after his departure from England.

There is a bust of the 'Third Earl of Southampton' at Althorp which appears to bear Mytens' genuine signature and the date 1610, and is entirely consonant with the style of Mierevelt. The next pictures which can be ascribed to him with reasonable certainty are the pair of life-size full-lengths at Arundel Castle of 'Thomas Earl of Arundel' (Plate 29) and his 'Countess', which can, with every probability, be identified with those mentioned as already painted in the letter of 1618. There is still a certain stiffness about the figure of Lord Arundel, but the hands have a quality of flesh and blood which had been lacking in earlier portraiture in England, and there is a certain breadth and 'impressionism' about the painting of the ruff which distinguishes this picture from the meticulous portraits of bits of lace and linen which had prevailed hitherto. The setting of the portrait also has a precise localization which marks it off from the earlier groups of portraits, for it is in the Sculpture Gallery of Arundel House and shows the first large-scale invasion of the Mediterranean world into England, that collection of Roman sculpture which led Horace Walpole to call Arundel 'the father of *virtù*' in England. In the Greenwich portrait of the 'Lord High Admiral the Earl of Nottingham' (paid for in 1620: repetitions at Nostell Priory and in the Nottingham Gallery), the typical Mytens formula is established. The bulk and weight of the man are presented as never before in English portraiture, but character is achieved at the expense of elegance. This last defect (if such it be) is more apparent in the earliest of the portraits of 'Charles Prince of Wales', that dated 1623 (but not signed) at Windsor, in which one feels at once that the sitter is faithfully but not flatteringly represented.

It was in 1623 that Prince Charles and Buckingham made their impulsive visit to Spain to woo the Infanta, which was attended with artistic consequences almost as important as its political consequences were trivial. In Spain Charles came under the influence of Venetian painting of the High Renaissance and, in the Spanish royal portraits from the hand of Titian, Rubens, or the young Velazquez, he saw for the first time what eloquence of authoritative persuasion could reside in a royal image. If Charles's impassioned collecting of 'Old Masters' and the purchase of the great Mantua collection can be directly traced to this experience of the Spanish journey, so too can his search for a painter who would understand and fulfil his royal needs. Such a painter he finally found in Van Dyck, but he attempted at first to convert Mytens to his purposes. Soon after his accession he made him his painter and sent him to the Low Countries to study the latest fashions in Court portraiture. And the results were rewarding. There is an elegance, where possible also an air of romance, about Mytens' full-length portraits painted in the years immediately after his return from the Low Countries. It has often been said that, in these, he anticipates Van Dyck, but it is more likely that he visited Antwerp and drew his new inspiration from the same springs at which Van Dyck was feeding his more precocious and courtier-like talent.

Mytens' most notable works of these years are the 'Duke of Buckingham' 1626 at Euston Hall (repetitions at Milton Park and elsewhere), the 'George, Lord Baltimore' 1627 (Wentworth Woodhouse; Plate 32), and the wonderful portrait of the 'First Duke of Hamilton' 1629 (lent by the Duke of Hamilton to Edinburgh; Plate 31), which is the great masterpiece of pre-Vandyckian portraiture in England.

It does not – as has generally been supposed – seem to have been altogether from Rubens that Mytens derived this new inspiration. In 1625 Rubens had painted that equestrian portrait of Buckingham in the full Baroque style which perished by fire in 1949 with the Earl of Jersey's pictures: the 1626 Mytens of the same sitter has no tincture of this style, but rather a certain Spanish gravity. The 'Lord Baltimore' of 1627 has this in an even more marked degree and is only comparable (allowing for a difference in degree of genius) with the contemporary work of Velazquez. Velazquez is known to have painted a sketch of Charles in Madrid in 1623, which is now lost, and it may well be an echo of this work which accounts for the gravity of 'Lord Baltimore'. There is a payment in 1625 to Mytens for a copy of 'Titian's great Venus', and the profound influence of Charles I's collection of Venetian pictures on those painters who could gain access to it begins to operate from this moment. The 'Duke of Hamilton' of 1629, with its wonderful harmony of silver against a clear, silvery, blue curtain, shows a feeling for colour which was entirely Mytens' own, as well as his power of romantic interpretation with a favourable sitter.

But his time from 1629 onwards was mainly taken up with royal portraits, and the sitters were not favourable to Mytens' genius. What Charles I and Henrietta Maria really looked like it is no longer possible to say, since Van Dyck has transmitted to posterity his 'official' image. But we know that neither was tall nor graceful, and it is clear that Mytens' powers of imagination were insufficient to the task of ennobling propaganda. There are three principal types of Mytens 'portraits of the King – the type in red (of which there is a signed and dated original of 1629 in New York and a rather hard studio copy of 1631 at Greenwich): the type in grey (of which there is a studio version dated 1631 in the National Portrait Gallery): and the type in Garter Robes (of which there is an original dated 1633 at Wentworth Woodhouse (Plate 32) and others at Balcarres and the St Louis Museum). It will be sufficient to compare this last with the 1636 Van Dyck of 'Charles I in Robes of State' (Plate 33) to appreciate where the King found Mytens lacking. There are payments also for several Mytens portraits of 'Henrietta Maria with the dwarf Jeffrey Hudson' (a subject which inspired Van Dyck to one of his most triumphant impositions), but no certain example is known.[8]

This factory production of royal portraits is a phenomenon which persists from now onwards, and the difficulty of estimating a painter from such works – even when they are of high quality – has recently been proved in the case of Mytens. There is a payment in 1630 to Mytens for 'his Majesty's picture at large with a prospect, and the Crown and the Sceptre, in a scarlet embroidered suit', and such a picture (the only one known with a prospect) exists at Chatsworth. It is an exact version otherwise of the signed Mytens type in New York, but the penetrating eye of Mr Oliver Millar[9] has lately noticed that it is signed by Cornelius Johnson and dated 1631. Johnson therefore must have been devilling for Mytens at this date with hardly distinguishable fidelity, and there are portraits, such as the double bust figures of the King and Queen at Welbeck,[10] before which it is impossible to feel certain which of the two was the painter.

There remain a number of full-length portraits, some of them of real distinction, which cannot be allotted to any of the painters so far named, although they mostly masquerade under the name of one or other of them. Cleaning and research into early accounts may well bring back a number of forgotten painters of this kind to our knowledge, and one such has, in fact, been rediscovered in recent years – John Eycke, whose signature, with the date 1630, appears on a full-length of the 'First Lord Fitzwilliam'[11] at Milton Park, where there is also a companion portrait of Lady Fitzwilliam. He may well be the same as 'Mr. Yeekes the picture drawer', who received £4 for a posthumous portrait of Lady Crane in Sir Henry Hobart's accounts for 1 May 1624 (Norfolk Record Society).

Cornelius Johnson (Jonson)

It is in single heads, however, rather than in full-lengths that the beginnings of what may perhaps be called a native British tradition can first be discerned. The first unquestionable master of these is Cornelius Johnson, a British-born subject (since he was baptized in the Dutch Church at Austin Friars 14 October 1593), although his father had come to London as a refugee from Antwerp and his more distant forebears hailed from Cologne. He has received much praise as an all-British product and as the first to seize (as only an Englishman could) upon that shy and retiring streak in the English temper, whose presence in a portrait is a sure sign of native English art. It would probably be more true to say that he was a painter beautifully sensitive to individual character and wholly without any private national temper, for the portraits he painted in Holland after his retirement from the Civil War in 1643 are as thoroughly Dutch in temper as his English portraits are English.

We have no clue to his training, which is as likely to have been Dutch as English. It was certainly not unusual for a young Englishman to be apprenticed in Holland to learn painting in the early years of the seventeenth century.[12] His first signed work, a portrait of an 'Old Lady' dated 1617,[13] looks like a Dutch work and a Dutch sitter. His undoubtedly English work begins in 1619, and we can trace his career year by year, in a succession of signed and dated works[14] until 1643, when his wife's fears at the outbreak of the Civil War led him to retire to Holland. His pass for leaving the country is dated 10 October 1643 and he settled first at Middelburg. Later he is found working at Amsterdam and at Utrecht, and he died at Utrecht 5 August 1661.[15]

His portraits of 1619/20 mark a new departure in style in England, and it will be well to analyse a typical (if unusually attractive) example, the 'Susanna Temple'[16] (Plate 34B) dated 1620. It has the air of an Isaac Oliver miniature in large and it may well be that Johnson had learned of a miniaturist (although his own miniatures, which are in oil on copper, hardly begin before 1625). The feigned oval surround, which Johnson sometimes paints as if it were a marble frame in these early works, emphasizes the oval form, as in a miniature, and the paint has a high enamel and the colours often a bright glossiness which may well derive from the same source. All the resources of the artist are put into the head, and, unlike our view of Mytens, it is by his heads that we remember Johnson. He certainly began by specializing in heads and had already achieved mastery in that form by 1619. The earliest three-quarter length with hands that has been identified is the earliest of his portraits of Lord Keeper Coventry[17] (a constant patron) dated 1623. In this the hands and pose are still relatively clumsy but, in the 1627 three-quarter length of the same sitter in Lord Brabourne's collection, he can be seen to have learned from Mytens and even to be copying the Mytens form of hand. By 1631 (as has been noted in the Chatsworth Charles I) he is actually doing an almost indistinguishable copy of a Mytens. He seems to have been rewarded by being sworn 'His Majesty's servant in ye quality of picture maker' on 5 December 1632 (after Van Dyck's arrival, and perhaps to supply the defection of Mytens, who was unwilling to play second fiddle to Van Dyck). Even as early as 1632 something of Van Dyck's air has begun to creep into his sitters, as may be seen from the charming 'Lady of the Kingsmill family' 1632 (Plate 34A), formerly at Longford Castle and now in the collection of the Hon. Mrs Clive Pearson at Parham. But Johnson, in such pictures, takes from Van Dyck only as much as he can assimilate, and Van Dyck's rhetoric is muted down into a formula adapted to the domestic rather than the public portrait. In these years Johnson's heads have often a lovely silvery tone. In his rare (or rarely identified) full-lengths, which, by what is perhaps more than an accident, are scarcely ever signed, he imitates the patterns and trappings of Van Dyck's portraits more closely and with less of his own particular charm. Fairly certain examples are the portraits (dated 1638 but not signed) of Thomas Earl of Elgin and his Countess at Redlynch Park. It seems possible from these that a number of pictures which now pass under the name of Van Dyck or his studio may be from Johnson's hand.

So sensitive was Johnson to the changes of taste and fashion that his latest English works, such as the 'Sir Robert Dormer' 1642 (Plate 35A) (now in Mr T. Cottrell Dormer's collection), betray a close kinship in style to Dobson. In all these changes of style, except perhaps in that revealed in his first works about 1620, Johnson follows rather than initiates a trend in taste, but he retains his liking for the feigned stone oval to the last and he keeps that freshness of approach to his sitter's personality which is his greatest virtue.

English Contemporaries of Johnson

Johnson's technical excellence and high qualities as a draughtsman of a head mark him off from the general level of contemporary work, but vast numbers of portraits exist which belong generically to the same style of portraiture. A very few such pictures bear signatures and it is possible from some of these for the first time to get a glimpse of the activity of painters working outside London. A single portrait of an 'Unknown Man' 1636 in a Welsh collection[18] is signed by an equally unknown Edward Bellin: the full-length of Lord Keeper Williams in the muniment room of Westminster Abbey is dated 1624 and signed 'J.C.', and this painter might be the same as the 'J. Carleton 1635' whose name is traditionally attached[19] to three heads of members of the Danby family at Swinton Park, which suggest a provincial Cornelius Johnson. In the possession of Mrs Vaughan Morgan in London (1938) was a portrait of a lady signed 'T. Jones fecit' and dated 1628. Two portraits have been published[20] which bear the letters IO in monogram and are dated 1637 and 1641: these may well be by the same hand, and the signature not an attempt at clumsily forging the signature of Isaac Oliver (d. 1617), but the suggested identification with John Osborne, the English craftsman in whalebone and horn who settled in Amsterdam, is sufficiently improbable.

As further evidence for what little is known of the lesser painters of this period a few disembodied names may be listed: William Larkin who is paid for two portraits in 1617/19 (Duke of Rutland MSS.) and who had painted a portrait of Lord Herbert of Cherbury before 1610;[21] amongst the Naworth Castle accounts[22] portraits are mentioned by one Heskett in 1621 and by Charles Barker in 1629 and 1633 – these latter were certainly painted on the spot; Evelyn's *Diary* under 1626 records that his picture was 'drawn in oil' at his father's house at Lewes 'by Chanterell, no ill painter'; and a list of such names could presumably be very considerably extended.

More interesting than any of these are two contemporaries of Johnson who are each mainly familiar to us by a more ambitious work: John Souch and David des Granges. John Souch was a Chester painter. In 1616/17 he is recorded in the Roll of Freemen of the City of Chester as prentice to Randle Holme, the herald painter who was Deputy of the Office of Arms, and he himself received a prentice at Chester in 1636.[23] A signed portrait by him of a Cheshire sitter was in the Puleston sale 18 December 1933, lot 16, but his chief surviving work is the remarkable group of 'Sir Thomas Aston at the deathbed of his first wife' 1635 (Manchester; Plate 36).[24] This is obviously, in many ways, the work of a herald painter. The figures are treated more or less as symbols and are not arranged in a grouping at all closely imitated from nature: the first Lady Aston appears, in an altogether medieval way, both as a living portrait and as dead in the same picture. But the heads are clearly studied from the model and are treated in the same spirit as Johnson treats his heads.

David des Granges is relatively well known as a miniature painter of secondary importance. His family came from Guernsey, but he himself was born in London either in 1611 or 1613[25] and survived until the 1670s. A portrait on the scale of life, in style like an inferior Johnson from the 1630s, is at Wemyss Castle, and another life-size (49 × 40 in.) portrait of a 'Lady and child', dated 1661, was in the sale at Mottisfont Abbey in 1933. But his one memorable picture can be precisely dated to 1637 or 1639,[26] the group of the 'Family of Sir Richard Saltonstall' (Plate 37) and his second wife taken at the time of the birth of one of his last two children. This was formerly at Wroxton Abbey, where it traditionally bore an attribution to des Granges, and was acquired in 1933 by Sir Kenneth Clark. It is gay in colour – salmon and silver are the prevailing notes – and tender and domestic in interpretation, the only thing of its kind at present known to rival Johnson in those endearing qualities of interpretation for which he is most justly admired.

The closest in style of all these minor painters to Johnson, though far beneath him in gifts, was Gilbert Jackson, whose active career can be traced from 1622 to 1640.[27] About twenty signed and dated portraits by him have been found and others can often be recognized by his liking for dresses of strong grass green (often with garish vermilion bows) and a way of painting lace which makes it look as though soaked in water. He is less addicted than Johnson to the painted oval and altogether inferior in drawing. Although based on London it seems possible, from the distribution of certain groups of portraits by him, that he travelled the country and settled in various districts for months at a time – Wales in 1631/2 and Oxford 1634/5. His most important portrait is the 'Lord Keeper Williams' 1625 at St John's College, Cambridge. Very close also to Johnson in many ways is George Jamesone, who must be considered under painting in Scotland.

Sir Nathaniel Bacon

The only truly native English painter of real distinction of the generation before Van Dyck was an amateur, Sir Nathaniel Bacon. He was born in August 1585 and was buried at Culford on 1 July 1627. He painted only for his own family and his works had no influence on his contemporaries, and four of the half-dozen paintings which survive are portraits of himself. By far the most remarkable is the full-length at Gorhambury (Plate 28), which shows the gifted amateur in his study (rather than his studio) and reveals an interest in painting accessories and still life that is repeated in 'The Cookmaid' in the same collection. He also painted, in a miniature on copper, the first British landscape (Ashmolean, Oxford), which is a curiosity rather than a work of art, and records survive of classical subjects. The portrait at Gorhambury (c. 1620) reveals some study abroad, and the silver-grey and lemon colouring of parts of it indicate Utrecht as the source, and probably Terbrugghen as the painter who inspired it.

Foreign Painters contemporary with Johnson

Foreign visitors among the portrait painters are less numerous than might have been expected. An attractive painter, otherwise unknown, signed a picture of 'Lord William Russell and his Dwarf' 1627 at Woburn Abbey as 'Johanes Priwizer de Hungaria'; in 1628 Gerrit Honthorst was in England for some months, apparently on trial as official Court portrait painter, for he was made a denizen 28 November 1628 and granted a pension for life as 'the King's servant', but he returned to Holland in December 1628 after painting a few portraits such as the 'Duke of Buckingham and Family' (Buckingham Palace) and arranging for the large composition for Hampton Court, which was executed in Holland. Hendrik Pot painted Charles I (Louvre) in London in 1631, and a number of well-known painters were in London for short periods: Sandrart (1627), Hannemann (for a number of years), Ter Borch (1635), Lievens, etc.; but nothing is known of their work in England. Sir Balthasar Gerbier[28] (1592–1667) may have painted a few portraits, but was chiefly occupied with other business; Nicholas Lanier (1588–1666), whose interesting 'Selfportrait' is in the Examination Schools at Oxford, was mainly a Court musician and agent for picture collecting; George Geldorp, who came to England about the time of Charles I's accession, is documented as the painter of two admirably prosaic full-lengths of the second Earl of Salisbury and his Countess at Hatfield,[29] but he seems soon to have developed into an artistic impresario, dealer, and pimp, and, although he survived the Restoration and was mixed up with art and artists all his life, there is little evidence that he did much painting himself – he died in 1665. There is finally Cornelius de Neve (who has been wrongly confused with other Neves or de Neves working in the 1640s or 1650s), by whom there is a portrait signed and dated 1626 (National Portrait Gallery, Reference No. 1346) and a double full-length of Lord Buckhurst and his brother of 1637 at Knole: the former of these may well have been painted in Holland and is typical of The Hague school.

Painting other than Portraiture

In the Low Countries the first quarter of the seventeenth century saw the birth of an immensely rich and various school of landscape painting, but there was nothing comparable in England. The very word 'landscape' was a Dutch importation into England in this century for something which had to be imported from abroad. A few views of British scenes exist, however, pretty certainly by Flemish workmen, in the tradition of topographical draughtsmanship. Among the most notable are a pair of views of the river at Richmond in the Fitzwilliam Museum, Cambridge, which were ascribed in the eighteenth century to the Antwerp painter, David Vinckeboons, but which bear no resemblance to his signed works. These perhaps date from the 1620s, and there are rather similar views of Pontefract Castle at Windsor and at Northwick Park. Clearly dated 1630 is the handsome view of 'Old London Bridge' at Kenwood signed by Claude de Jongh (d. 1663), and another such view is said to be dated 1650.[30] The Antwerp painter Alexander Keirincx (1600–1652: in England called 'Carings') was in the employ of Charles I and is documented in England 1640/1: he practised the style of landscape created by van Coninxloo, which very rarely bore much relation to natural scenes; and another Antwerp painter, Adriaen van Stalbemt (1580–1662) was in England in 1633 and signed (together with J. van Belcam) a 'View of Greenwich Park' (Windsor) with small figures of Charles I and his Court. The 'River Thames from above Greenwich' (Plate 41) is also the subject of the solitary landscape worthy of the name which can be allotted to these years. It is in Captain Sir Bruce Ingram's collection and can be dated about 1635. It is painted in the broad panoramic style of Hollar's etchings, and, if we knew that Hollar ever practised in oil, an attribution to him would hardly be wide of the mark.

Figure subjects are even rarer. There is occasional evidence that country workmen still used some of the old Catholic repertory (except for the persons of the Gospel story) in decorative panels, as in the heads of the Prophets and Sibyls at Chastleton House, which perhaps date about the middle of the reign of James I. Sir Nathaniel Bacon, no doubt imitating his foreign models, is said to have painted pictures of Ceres and Hercules and the Hydra, but the only Northern artist who can seriously be mentioned in this connexion is Francis Cleyn.

Cleyn was born at Rostock in 1582 and spent some years studying in Rome and Venice, where he absorbed impartially most of the prevailing styles. He then became Court painter to Christian IV of Denmark and a number of historical paintings from his hand survive in the various Danish royal palaces.[31] He settled in England in 1625 and became chief designer for the Mortlake tapestry works, which supplied the equivalent of historical paintings for the royal palaces. His most remarkable designs, which were executed in tapestry, are the 'Hero and Leander' series of which the finest examples survive in the Swedish State collections, but he seems also to have turned his hand to paintings and some of the unattached full-length portraits may prove to be from his hand. On the strength of his work in Denmark one may accept Dr Margaret Whinney's attribution to him of the three canvases from the 'Story of Perseus' let into the ceiling of the Double Cube Room at Wilton.[32] This seems to have been set in place after 1654. Cleyn was buried at St Paul's, Covent Garden, 23 March 1657/8.

Italy, however, was the great seat of historical painting and Charles I succeeded (after a failure with Guercino) in persuading one Italian painter of distinction to settle in England, Orazio Gentileschi. Gentileschi came to London in 1626 and can be documented here up to 1631, and it is probable (but unverified) that he died in London about 1638. Two of his easel pictures survive at Hampton Court, and the ceiling of the Hall at Marlborough House is pretty certainly that which he painted for the Queen's House at Greenwich. Yet another of the pictures of his London period may be the handsome 'Rest on the Flight' recently acquired for the Birmingham Gallery.

Painting in Scotland

A considerable number of portraits survive in Scottish collections, dating from about 1620 onwards, which were assuredly painted in the Northern Kingdom, but the only name which can confidently be associated with any of them before the middle of the century is that of George Jamesone. Jamesone is an almost exact Scottish counterpart to Cornelius Johnson, although he was neither so sensitive a draughtsman nor so perceptive an observer of character. He is also particularly difficult to judge to-day, since the medium with which he painted was usually so frail that most of his surviving portraits are mere travesties of what they once were. One of the very few which can still give some impression of his style is the 'Marquess of Montrose' 1629 (Plate 35B) at Kinnaird Castle, and Jamesone's surviving works are all of more or less the same character – except for a late and battered 'Selfportrait' (Countess of Seafield) which shows the painter in his studio with pictures ranged upon the walls, which include a Seapiece and a large Mythology. Apart from this we have no evidence that he painted such things.

Jamesone came from Aberdeen: on 27 May 1612 he was apprenticed to one John Anderson at Edinburgh,[33] a painter whose work is unknown. About 1619/20 he appears working on his own at Aberdeen in a style akin to Johnson: he came to Edinburgh in 1633 for the visit of Charles I (whom he painted), and he visited Italy the same year without any appreciable alteration to his style. From 1634 he worked mainly at Edinburgh, or travelled round Scotland, and he died at Edinburgh late in 1644.

Jamesone is only certainly known from busts or half-length portraits and there is not convincing evidence that any of the whole lengths which are ascribed to him are from his hand. The 'Erskine' portrait in the Edinburgh Gallery is too damaged for judgement, the 'Lord Spynie' at Balcarres is by a different, and perhaps superior hand, and the 'Conversation piece' at Tyninghame does not agree with his usual style. Nearly all Scottish portraits of this period tend to be ascribed to him, but it is better to withhold judgement

43

in the present state of knowledge, and some of the most distinguished portraits which bear his name (such as the 'Earl of Melrose' – later First Earl of Haddington – at Tyninghame) seem to be by a more competent painter trained in the Miereveld tradition.

On the evidence of a portrait in the Edinburgh Gallery which is alleged, on very slender evidence, to be a 'Selfportrait' by a painter named Scougal, a fourth Scottish painter of this name has found his way into the literature. This is a picture in the Mytens tradition of the 1630s or early 1640s, but there is no documentary evidence for a painter of the name of Scougal until the second half of the seventeenth century – nor has any other picture of this period been met with in Scotland which seems to be by the same hand.

NOTES TO CHAPTER 4

1. For van Somer's dates see A. Bredius, *Künstler-Inventare*, III, 807 ff.; and VII, 210 ff. It has always been assumed by British writers, without evidence, that he came to England about 1606; but cleaning has shown that the 'signature' G(?) *van Somer London* on a picture dated 1611 at Gateshead is not genuine: see J. Steegman in *Burl. Mag.*, XCI (Feb. 1949), 52 ff., where the 'Lord Windsor' of 1620 is published.

2. Historical MSS. Commission (Duke of Rutland MSS.): *Diary of Lady Anne Clifford*, ed. V. Sackville-West, 1923, 105 and 107; Mrs C. C. Stopes in *Notes on Pictures in the Royal Collections*, ed. Lionel Cust (1911), 86.

3. W. Noel Sainsbury, *Original Papers relating to Rubens, etc.* (1859), 355, identifying 'Yor highness' as probably James I, but Charles, Prince of Wales, seems certain.

4. Published in W. H. Carpenter, *Pictorial Notices of Van Dyck and his Contemporaries* (1844), 176–7; and reprinted in Mary F. S. Hervey, *The Life of Thomas Howard Earl of Arundel* (1921), 143 ff.

5. MS. Account Book of Sir Henry Hobart from 5 Oct. 1621 to 29 June 1625 bequeathed by the 11th Marquess of Lothian to the Norfolk Record Society, under 22 Dec. 1624 – 'To Mr Daniell Mittens the picture drawer by the hands of Sr John Hobart in parte of payment for ye drawing of yr Lorpps picture 005/10/0'.

6. Mrs C. C. Stopes in *Burl. Mag.*, XXII (Feb. 1913), 280.

7. Mary F. S. Hervey, *op. cit.* 404–5.

8. A possible candidate is the picture in the Duke of Leeds sale, 20 June 1930, lot 45, as Van Dyck.

9. *Burl. Mag.*, XC (Nov. 1948), 322.

10. Reproduced in *The Studio*, May 1948, 136.

11. *Burl. Mag.*, LXXIII (Sept. 1938), 125, where two other signed portraits are noted.

12. On 29 Apr. 1613 Michael Austin, an Englishman, resident in London, apprenticed his son, Nathaniel (otherwise unknown), to Jan Teunissen at Amsterdam to learn painting (*Oud Holland*, LII (1935), 288).

13. Anon. sale, Christies', 28 May 1948, lot 174, as Van Vliet, but clearly signed CJ in monogram and dated 1617.

14. There is a preliminary catalogue by A. J. Finberg in *Walpole Society*, X. Finberg lists about 175 portraits up to 1643, when Johnson left England, and I have notes of about a further 60, so that Johnson is the first British painter of whose work a considerable portion has been identified. He usually signs his pictures with some form of the initials CJ.

15. Catalogue of the Centraal Museum, Utrecht, 1933.

16. T. Pearson-Gregory sale, 18 June 1937, as 'A Lady of the de Ligne family', but it can be identified from R. White's engraving as Susanna Temple, afterwards Lady Thornhurst and Lady Lister.

17. Sir R. L. Hare, Bart, sale, 1 Mar. 1946, lot 63.

18. *Burl. Mag.*, XC (July 1948), 204.

19. J. Fisher, *The History and Antiquities of Masham, etc.* (1865), 171.

20. Prince Frederick Duleep Singh, *Portraits in Norfolk Houses*, II, plate at p. 40 as '? John Osborne'; and A. C. Sewter in *Burl. Mag.*, LXXVI (July 1940), 25, as Cornelius Johnson.

21. *Autobiography of Edward, Lord Herbert of Cherbury*. There seems no reason to identify this with the

picture in the National Portrait Gallery. An Eliza-
bethan-looking portrait of 'Mrs Turner' is called
Larkin in an eighteenth-century inventory of pictures at Claydon.

22. Lord William Howard's account books for
Naworth Castle in *Surtees Society*, LXVIII (1877),
182 ff.

23. *Lancashire and Cheshire Record Society*, LI, 118,
where his name is misprinted as 'South'.

24. C. H. Collins Baker in *The Connoisseur*, Mar.
1948, reprinted in the N.A.C.F. Report for the year
1947.

25. Basil S. Long, *British Miniaturists* (1929), 123.

26. The sitters are Sir Richard Saltonstall (1595-
1650), his second wife, Mary Parken (married 1633),
and the children surviving at the birth of either
Bernard (b. 1637) or Mary (b. 1639).

27. Mrs R. Lane Poole, *Catalogue of Oxford Portraits* II (1925), xxv ff., gives the references for many

of them; see also Catalogue of the exhibition of
Historical Portraits at Cardiff, 1948.

28. Basil S. Long, *British Miniaturists*. There is a
long account of him in Walpole's *Anecdotes*.

29. C. H. Collins Baker, *Lely and the Stuart Portrait Painters*, II, 112.

30. Mrs Hilda F. Finberg in *Walpole Society*, IX,
47-8 for de Jongh and other early landscape painters;
also Colonel M. H. Grant, *The Old English Landscape
Painters*, I and II (n.d.), III (1947), where all that is
known about early landscape painters is copiously
related.

31. For documentation and illustration of Cleyn's
work in Denmark see Francis Beckett, *Kristian IV og
Malerkunsten*. Copenhagen (1937), 43 ff. (There
exists an offprint in English of this chapter.)

32. *The Archaeological Journal*, CIV (1948), 172.

33. Register of Apprentices of the City of Edinburgh, 1583-1666, *Scottish Record Society* (1906), 98.

CHAPTER 5

THE AGE OF VAN DYCK AND DOBSON

THE dominant figure in Northern Baroque art is Rubens, and England was not exempt from his pervasive influence. He had painted the Earl of Arundel first in 1620 and the Duke of Buckingham (in Paris) in 1625, and he was already something of a legend in English Court circles by the time of Charles I's accession. Toby Matthew, writing from Brussels to Sir Dudley Carleton as early as 1620, says, 'his demands are like ye Lawes of Medes and Persians', and it seems possible that he was already marked out as the painter of the ceiling of the Banqueting Hall at Whitehall (the building of which was finished in March 1622) as early as 1621. He finally visited England, on a diplomatic mission, from 5 June 1629 to 6 March 1630. During these months he was as much fêted as an artist as he was as a diplomat and Charles I knighted him on 21 February 1630. During this stay he painted the picture of 'St George' (Buckingham Palace) in which Charles I appears as St George and Henrietta Maria as the Princess and the background is a view of London. He also presumably made final arrangements on this occasion for the ceiling of the Banqueting Hall, of which the separate elements were painted on canvas at Brussels and were completed by 1634. They finally reached London in December 1635 and were installed in the ceiling in March 1636.

The ceiling of the Banqueting Hall is the one full Baroque painted decoration in England, and, although it has remained *in situ* up to the present century, it has never received the attention that it deserves. Recent opportunity for close examination shows that a considerable number of the major figures are executed by Rubens himself, and the whole invention gives proof of prodigious vitality and decorative power. But it was set in place at a time when the shadow of the coming Civil War was already beginning to obliterate all thoughts of grandiose projects, and it has remained the least fruitful and the least studied of the surviving great works inspired by the patronage of Charles I.

Sir Anthony Van Dyck

It is with Van Dyck that the name and fame of Charles I and the glamour of the Royalist cause are indelibly bound up. We are perhaps no longer able to judge dispassionately to-day how much the common verdict of men, and even 'the judgement of history', on Charles I and his times owe to the poet and magician whose name was Van Dyck. The extraordinary treatment which he received from the King makes it clear that his value as a propagandist in the cause of absolutism was fully appreciated, and he was treated, as no painter had been before, by the high aristocracy of England as an equal.[1] A weighty element in the secret of the style of his English portraits – a style which has no real parallel in British painting until the time of Lawrence – is that he painted his sitters, in all the fabulous glamour of Cavalier costume, as an equal.

The details of Van Dyck's development as an artist are no part of the history of British painting. He reached England fully formed. But his influence has been so immense that, as was the case with Holbein, we must not omit him (as has been usual), but treat him as an integral part of the tradition of British painting and seek to analyse his character as an artist. Much detailed study has been made of his earlier work, but a proper study of the portraits he painted in England is still a desideratum[2] and no attempt can be made here to fill the gap.

Van Dyck was born at Antwerp 22 March 1599 to a prosperous middle-class family. He was an infant prodigy and was apprenticed to van Balen when he was eleven; before he was nineteen, in 1618, he was entered in the Antwerp Guild as a Master. By that date he had absorbed, with mystifying precocity, everything which the flourishing contemporary Antwerp school could teach and he was in a fair way to rivalling Rubens himself, on whose

doubt owe it to this fact

visit of a few months to
of James I. In February
eight months, to go and
rvice. It remains obscure
for his subsequent history
at least the eight months
Italy by the latter part of
gering longest at Genoa
mmand of all the know-
to the formation of his
ning of April 1632.
ven Van Dyck's style an
ch he could not have got
s and Van Dyck was a
ife and energy, and Van
rmal reticence in aristo-
traits, but he found little
bourgeoisie on his return
as an essential element in
ern and practice of Titian,
yck's Italian sketch-book
rity of Titian full-lengths
ail of Van Dyck's English
, as in the 'Strafford with
Woodhouse), Van Dyck
the group absurdly called
chiavelli').
as at once forgiven and he

[handwritten card:] Best Wishes for Easter 1953

was treated by Charles with extraordinary favour. A house was provided for him in Blackfriars (i.e. outside the liberties of the City of London and thus outside the jurisdiction of the Painter-Stainers Company). Before July 1632 he was appointed 'principalle Paynter in ordinary to their Majesties' with a pension of £200 a year; he was knighted on 5 July 1632; he was given by the King a gold chain and medal on 20 April 1633; and the King and Queen frequently made personal visits to his studio. He never became a denizen, but the King attempted to secure his permanent residence in England by finally arranging, 1639/40, his marriage to an English lady of noble origin. No artist had received such favours before.

Van Dyck died in London 9 December 1641. Even during his official residence in England he had spent some time abroad. He was away a whole year in Antwerp from early in 1634, and he made visits of some months to Antwerp and to Paris in 1640 and 1641. His whole active career in England lasted for less than eight years and his activity during that time must have been almost incessant, even though his patrons were limited to the royal family and to the immediate circle of the Court. In his English portraits he created – or brought to light by sensitive observation – a new world which has imposed its authority on the imagination of Europe. How much, we must ask, of this world had an objective existence? For it is often held against Van Dyck that he falsified the truth of appearances and hopelessly corrupted an honest British tradition in portraiture which was beginning to be formed.

Van Dyck's Portraits of the Royal Family

Such an inquiry may best begin by considering the portraits of Charles I and Henrietta Maria, for evidence on whose features (at any rate on the King's) we have ample comparative material by other artists. It was for the painting of royal portraits that Van Dyck was encouraged to come to England, they were his principal task during his first few years in London, and it was because of their success that the King made much of him. A number of Privy Seal Warrants[3] survive for payments to Van Dyck for specific work, and there is a bill from Van Dyck, which must date from 1638, for work done and not then paid for. From these it appears that, in the first four months of his residence in London (by 8 August 1632), Van Dyck had completed: portraits of the King and Queen separately; the group (now at Buckingham Palace, but falsified by later enlargements) of the King, Queen, Prince Charles, and Princess Mary; four portraits (presumably repetitions from stock) of the Archduchess and members of the House of Orange; a companion Emperor to the series of Titian emperors from Mantua; and repaired one of the Titians. Another nine portraits of King and Queen were completed before May 1633 and these may well not include the equestrian portrait with M. de Saint-Antoine (at Buckingham Palace) which is dated 1633. These nine portraits came to £444 and by February 1636/7 there is a payment of £1200 for additional pictures, one of which was no doubt the King in Garter Robes at Windsor, dated 1636, and another the group of the three elder children (Windsor). Finally, we have the bill of 1638 which itemizes twenty-two portraits, including the splendid 'Charles I with Groom and Horse' (Louvre) and the group of the five children at Windsor. With such a series of Van Dycks judiciously distributed to friendly royalty abroad and to loyal supporters at home, it is not surprising that the King never, of his own free choice, sat seriously to another painter after Van Dyck's death.

As far as truth of feature goes Van Dyck's portraits of the King are in sufficiently faithful agreement with those of him by Mytens and Johnson. In the most exacting of all, the view of the King's head in three positions (Plate 38A), painted about 1636, to be sent to Bernini in Rome to enable the sculptor to make a bust of the King, Van Dyck comes off triumphantly. It is in the full-length portraits and in the use of Baroque accessories that Van Dyck's gifts of elegant interpretation (and thus, by implication, of 'falsification') appear. Neither the King nor the Queen was tall and perhaps neither was altogether graceful, and Van Dyck certainly slides over these difficulties. We may allow the last word on this point to be with Sophia of Bavaria (later the Electress of Hanover), who saw the Queen when she came to Holland in 1641 and wrote: 'Van Dyck's handsome portraits had given me so fine an idea of the beauty of all English ladies, that I was surprised to find that the Queen, who looked so fine in painting, was a small woman raised up on her chair, with long skinny arms and teeth like defence works projecting from her mouth....'

Van Dyck also added new overtones of authority to the most grandiose of his portraits of the King, of which perhaps the noblest is the 'Charles I on horseback' in the National Gallery (Plate 39). This is perhaps inspired by the equestrian 'Charles V' by Titian and the implications of the equestrian portrait (a novelty in English royal iconography) were all with the commanders of victorious armies. The King was no doubt as much responsibl for this absolutist element as was Van Dyck, but it is in such pictures that we find, for the last time for a century, painting done in England fully in line with the most advanced contemporary European tradition.

Van Dyck's Portraits of the Court

It was not, however, his royal portraits but his portraits of the British aristocracy which left such a profound bias on the direction of British taste. The revolution which Van Dyck effected can best be appreciated by the form in which the theory of portraiture was canonized in the early eighteenth century by Jonathan Richardson: 'a good portrait, from whence we conceive a better opinion of the beauty, good sense, breeding and other good qualities of the person than from seeing themselves, and yet without being able to say in what particular it is unlike; for nature must be ever in view'. We can perhaps go a little further than Jonathan Richardson in analysing in what particulars Van Dyck's portraits are unlike.

It is not for nothing that Waller speaks of Van Dyck's studio as a 'shop of beauty'. The beauty specialist is concerned with studying the temperament of the individual and advising how that can best be exploited along the lines of prevailing taste. Van Dyck had precisely this sensibility, which he directed not only towards individuals but towards nations and classes of society. It is usually possible at a glance to guess whether a portrait by Van Dyck represents a Genoese nobleman, a burgher of Antwerp, or a member of one of the princely houses of Northern Europe. Given the national temper and the national costume, he devised a series of patterns appropriate to these various classes. The individual appears only in the features of the face, which Van Dyck studied and drew with meticulous fidelity. A certain absence of strong character was presumably not uncommon at the Court, but Van Dyck was equal to interpreting a strong character in a woman, such as the 'Frances, Marchioness of Hertford' at Syon House (Plate 40A), or a thoroughly unpleasant one, such as the 'Lady Castlehaven' at Wilton (Plate 40B). For each shade of character he adopted an appropriate technique and no great painter has shown a greater variety of handling in his heads. He rearranged the standard trappings of the Baroque portrait, the damask curtain, the pillar, or the truncated column, with corresponding sensibility, and, on the rare occasions when he painted a poet rather than an aristocrat – as in the 'Killigrew and Carew' at Windsor (Plate 38B) – he prescribes for himself a different kind of pattern. It is needless to add that these personal subtleties escaped his countless imitators. But his poses, his hands, and his dresses became the fashion-plates of the contemporary artist, and an important source for their wide circulation was the series of etchings by Hollar published in 1640 as 'Ornatus muliebris anglicanus', a number of which echo (with a great loss in elegance) some of the poses of Van Dyck's portraits.

Van Dyck's Work apart from Portraiture

On the information of Sir Kenelm Digby, Bellori (1672, pp. 261–2) gives a list of religious and mythological paintings executed by Van Dyck for British patrons during his English period. Of these little or nothing survives, but a 'Cupid and Psyche' (which is not mentioned by Bellori) remains at Windsor. As with most great artists whose living is perforce gained mainly from portraiture, the desire was ever recurring to display his powers on some ambitious scheme of public decoration. About 1638 Van Dyck had sufficiently interested the King in a project of decorating the walls of the Banqueting House with scenes illustrating the History of the Order of the Garter for him to be required to make some sketches. A brilliant sketch in grisaille, for one wall, in the collection of the Duke of Rutland, is all that survives of this project. It shows the King in the centre and a procession of all the Knights of the Garter, and is conceived in emulation of Veronese. But the King could not afford to finance the scheme and this disappointment may have played a part in causing Van Dyck to seek, as he certainly was seeking during the last years of his life, suitable employment away from the English Court. In spite of his great collections and his undoubted love of art, Charles I was unable to employ his one great painter to the full capacity of his powers.

Van Dyck's Studio and his immediate Following

The question of Van Dyck's studio remains profoundly obscure. Apart from a statement, which probably refers to Edward Bower, that he was at one time 'servant to' Van Dyck, there is no evidence (contrary to what is often said – of Dobson for instance) that any British painter of consequence learned directly from Van Dyck. The names of his assistants that we know, J. de Reyn and David Beek, are Flemings, and he probably preferred to have Flemish workmen, trained in the same studio tradition as he had been himself, to help him in the subordinate work on his portraits and to execute replicas. That a considerable number of replicas of different sizes could be ordered at one time we know from a letter of Strafford's,[4] but the great number of inferior repetitions which appear to-day to be more or less contemporary, were probably painted after Van Dyck's death by professional copyists such as Belcam, van Leemput, and Simon Stone. Of these, van Leemput, (d. 1675 and known as Remée), certainly painted original portraits as well as copies. On the other hand, an enormous number of portraits exist which date from about 1638 to 1650 and which are closely modelled on Van Dyck, so closely that the individuality of the painter is obscured. It has occasionally been suggested in recent years that these may be by Weesop, a painter who came to England about the time of Van Dyck's death and left in 1649, but there is not a shred of evidence for this, and Weesop's signed 'Execution of Charles I' (Earl of Rosebery) disproves it. We can only recognize at present that the imitators of Van Dyck form a numerous and nameless tribe, whose works spread the more obvious elements of Van Dyck's style far beyond the limited aristocratic circles for which he had worked himself. A great many such works are 'traditionally' called Van Dyck to-day in the houses where they hang.

Van Dyck's few portrait groups, of which the most notable is the huge 'Pembroke family' at Wilton, had no immediate following. For an artist so accomplished in the single figure they are all curiously awkward and clumsily designed.

Painters of the 1640s uninfluenced by Van Dyck

The influence of Van Dyck did not succeed in pervading the work of all his contemporaries, even of all those who were employed about the Court. The elder John de Critz, who was appointed Serjeant Painter about the time of the accession of James I, has already been noticed in the last chapter. He continued to hold that office until his death in 1642, but was only employed by the Crown on decorative work and restoration. Two at least of his sons, John the younger (born before 1599) and Emmanuel (born between 1599 and 1609), were early associated with him in the office of Serjeant Painter, to which the younger John succeeded by warrant dated 18 March 1641/2. This John fell fighting at Oxford soon after his appointment and we know nothing of his work, but a group of portraits survives in the Ashmolean Museum at Oxford which there is good reason to suppose is by a member of the de Critz family and slightly less good reason to suppose is by Emmanuel.[5] All are portraits of persons related to the de Critz family and one is a portrait inscribed by an eighteenth-century hand as 'Oliver de Critz', 'a famous Painter' (but nothing else is known of his painting); the others are all of the Tradescant family and that of 'Hester Tradescant and her Stepson' is dated 1645. With them can be associated the portrait of 'John Tradescant Jr' in the National Portrait Gallery, but no other absolutely convincing attribution to the same hand has been found. In style this group of pictures looks forward perhaps to Gerard Soest, but its antecedents are mysterious. Two of the pictures are, in a minor way, masterpieces, fine in quality and original in interpretation – 'John Tradescant with a spade' (Plate 44B) and 'John Tradescant and his friend Zythepsa'

(Plate 43). There is a seriousness, a meditative sadness, about both these pictures, akin to what we shall find in Dobson but without Dobson's romantic Cavalier overtones. No doubt this is a reflection that the times were out of joint, but the painter has risen to the occasion and shown himself a master of the poetic possibilities of portraiture. Tradescant's Cabinet of Rarities was well known and the still-life of shells in his portrait with Zythepsa is an allusion to this, but the shells have been endowed with more than the value of a mere decorative accessory and their collector's love for them has been conveyed by the painter in his making them appear as a third personality in the portrait group. Emmanuel de Critz lived on until 1665, but all that we know of his later practice is that he copied a Lely for Pepys in 1660 – a sad decline.

Connected by marriage with the Tradescant and de Critz families (his mother had remarried John de Critz the younger), and in style with the group of portraits called Emmanuel de Critz, was Cornelis de Neve (or Le Neve), perhaps related to the painter who has already been mentioned among the contemporaries of Johnson. A portrait in the Ashmolean Museum at Oxford, which came with the Tradescant portraits, is inscribed 'Mr Le Neve / a famous Painter' and is probably a selfportrait of about 1650: in the same collection is a portrait of Nicholas Fiske, which is conceivably by the same hand and is dated 1651 and signed 'CDN'. Le Neve is mentioned in Sir Edward Dering's accounts for 1648 and 1649,[6] and Evelyn mentions him casually in 1649: the last that is recorded of him is that he painted a portrait of Elias Ashmole in 1664, which is now at Merevale Hall.

Traces survive of two other painters, not altogether dissimilar to one another in style and both equally distant from Van Dyck, who were active in the 1640s and most probably executed their few works at present identified when travelling the country. Of each a single group of works from one year only is known for certain. T. Leigh is found in North Wales in 1643. He signed, in a flowing hand,[7] five portraits of members of the Davies family of Gwysaney and Llanerch, and all are dated 1643. Two are now in the Cardiff Gallery, of which the female portrait is a ruin, but the 'Robert Davies' (Plate 42A) and the three still at Gwysaney (Major Davies-Cooke) show a competent painter trained in a tradition akin to Cornelius Johnson. It is possible, but needs further exploration, that he may be the Thomas Leigh who signed, in 1656, a receipt for a posthumous portrait of Robert Ashley in the Middle Temple.

The second painter, akin to Leigh but a little more awkward in style, seems to have borne the initials 'IW'. In the possession of the Pochin family at Barkby Hall in Leicestershire are four portraits[8] signed 'I.W.F.' and dated 1648. Nothing further by the same hand has been traced.

A versatile artist, perhaps more of the journeyman class, Richard Greenbury, also deserves to be mentioned. His career overlaps Van Dyck's stay in London at both ends, and we find him as copyist, restorer, glass painter, and as executing painted altar-hangings.[9] He was apparently a Roman Catholic but was already employed by the Crown in 1622/3 for a portrait of James I (perhaps a copy): the last date we have for him is 1651. He followed Sampson Strong at Oxford and painted a portrait of the Founder for Magdalen in 1638, and did other work about the College, but he also copied old masters for the King and the competent copy of Dürer's portrait of his father at Syon House is a surviving specimen of his work. There is record of a lost work, a large canvas showing the cruelties of the Dutch at the Amboyna massacres in 1623, which he painted for the East India Company for purposes of propaganda, and which was so fearsome that it had to be destroyed. He appears to have been able to turn his hand to any class of painting or restoration and his career throws light on the lost corners of art history in England at this time.

William Dobson

Aubrey, who knew him, quite rightly called Dobson 'the most excellent painter that England hath yet bred'. He is, in fact, the most distinguished purely British painter before Hogarth. He was born in London in 1610, the son of a Master of the Alienation Office: his father was of a respectable St Albans family who had wasted his estate by luxurious living. Dobson is said to have inherited this tendency to extravagance, but he was forced to learn the business of painting in order to earn his living. Richard Symonds, who no doubt learned it from Cleyn himself, wrote in his notebook in 1653 that 'Mr Clein was Dobson's master and taught him his art'. From Cleyn he inherited much of the tradition of the Italian High Renaissance and a leaning towards the Venetians, and through Cleyn he could presumably gain access to study, and perhaps copy, some of the Venetian paintings in the royal collection. Without such training we should have to postulate that he had been to Italy, for Dobson's style is nearly independent of Van Dyck and could not have been learned from Van Dyck. It is probable that he copied Van Dyck too, and a copy has been reported of Van Dyck's 'Earl of Arundel and Grandson' with Dobson's signature (formerly in Major Baker-Carr's possession). Until this reappears it is better to suspend judgement, for there is no other evidence of any nearer connexion between Dobson and Van Dyck. We know nothing whatever of Dobson until 1642 (at the earliest), when the Court had moved to Oxford. Van Dyck had died in 1641 and John de Critz, the new Serjeant Painter, was killed in the fighting at Oxford. Dobson seems to have filled in a makeshift way something of the gap caused by both deaths, but there is no evidence that he was ever appointed 'Principal Painter to the King' and only the unsupported note of an eighteenth-century antiquary (Oldys) that he was Groom of the Privy Chamber and Serjeant Painter. He seems to have been active partly at Oxford and partly in London during the period 1642 to 1646 and he was buried at St Martin's in the Fields in London 28 October 1646. He painted the official portraits of the King's children and members of the royal entourage at Oxford during these years, but the King does not seem to have sat for the completion of his own portrait.

The work of these last four years is thus all that we know of Dobson and between fifty and sixty paintings are at present traced. Of these, only two are full-lengths, four are double portraits or groups, a few are single heads, and by far the greater number are half-length portraits with hands. A particularly mature and splendid example of this last class is the 'Endymion Porter' in the National Gallery (Plate 47), which is valuable for the analysis of his style as it can be compared with a portrait of the same sitter by Van Dyck (in a double portrait) in the Prado.

The spirit of Dobson in this portrait is altogether more robust and less consciously elegant than the spirit of Van Dyck. The hands are larger and more solid, the texture of the paint rough and impasted and not smooth, the figure bulks larger because nearer to the plane of the picture's surface. Van Dyck uses his Baroque accessories, the pillar and the curtain, for purely decorative ends: Dobson employs a more learned and specific repertory of such accessories. A colossal bust of a poet in the background, and a relief, perhaps representing the Arts, in the lower foreground, are clearly intended to have some sort of relevance to the person represented. And such accessories are almost habitual with Dobson. 'Sir Charles Lucas' (at Corsham and Audley End), 'Sir William Fermor' (Duke of Portland), the 'Marquess of Montrose' (Duke of Montrose), the picture called 'Sir George Carteret' (Greenwich), and the 'Sir William Compton' and 'Earl of Northampton' (both at Castle Ashby), all have enigmatic classical reliefs or similar accessories in the background. This practice is altogether unknown to Van Dyck and rare in Europe in the seventeenth century, although it had become more or less standard by the time of the manuals for painters which were popular at the end of the century (e.g. Gerard de Lairesse). Its origin, however, and the source from which Dobson, probably through Cleyn, derived it, was Italian sixteenth-century manuals, particularly Lomazzo, who had been translated into English in the sixteenth century. In his *Trattato dell' arte della pittura, etc.*, Book VI, chapter 50, Lomazzo says, 'First you must consider the quality of the person who is the subject of the portrait, and, according to that quality, give the portrait its appropriate symbol'. Dobson's style is thus learned as well as aristocratic and relies much more than Van Dyck's on the intellect of the spectator.

In what is perhaps Dobson's masterpiece among single portraits the accessories are less enigmatic – the 'Charles, Prince of Wales' in the National Portrait Gallery of Scotland (Plate 46). The boy soldier is seen with his page, with a battle raging in the background, and a jumble of military trophies on the ground from which emerges a hideous mask of Envy and Civil War. The figure is deliberately cut off at the knees (as Van Dyck would never do) to give weight and moment to it, and the difference between Dobson and Van Dyck can nowhere be better observed.

This learned, latinizing, and allegorical aspect of Dobson's art is most fully (and least happily) exemplified in the only[10] subject picture by him at present known, an 'Allegory of the Religious Wars in France' (T. Cottrell-Dormer).[11] The invention here is presumed to have been largely Sir Charles Cotterell's, but we know that Cotterell and Dobson were close friends, and the picture is evidence of the cultured and allusive world with which Dobson associated. As a picture it is far from satisfactory and it reinforces the suspicion that Dobson, although a master of the half-length portrait, was ill at ease in full-lengths. The only two of these known, 'Sir William Compton' (Castle Ashby) and the 'Earl of Peterborough'[12] (Drayton House, signed and dated 1644), are much more dependent on Van Dyck models for pattern than one would have expected, and they show considerable uneasiness in the treatment of the lower half of the human figure.

Dobson's greatest originality, however, is shown in his few group arrangements of half-length figures. Two of these are among the finest and most interesting British paintings of the first half of the century, and neither has any close parallel among works of this age. The group of 'Prince Rupert, Colonel Murray and Colonel Russell' (Plate 45), which belongs to Lord Sandys, can almost be described as a 'historical conversation piece' on the scale of life. It depicts an incident during the Civil War when Colonel Russell was persuaded not to abandon the Royalist cause and the three men are about to drink to this decision, Colonel Murray dipping a Royalist cockade into the glass. There is about all Dobson's portraits – nearly all of which portray men prominent in the royal cause – a look of romantic heroism, as of the fated defenders of some precious heritage, but this group surprises the kind of decision which gave rise to such a look, and this psychological element in his portraiture, which is far removed from the aristocratic aloofness of the Van Dyck tradition, is what marks Dobson off from all his contemporaries.

The other group is more enigmatic and shows 'Dobson, Sir Charles Cotterell, and Sir Balthasar Gerbier' (Albury Park (Plate 48)). The painter is the central figure and he seems to be being rescued by Cotterell from some temptation put forward by Gerbier. It is at least possible that this group also signifies a conflict of loyalties of the same sort as the other, but one more personal to Dobson himself.

Pictures akin to Dobson

A considerable number of portraits survive from the 1640s which show a decided kinship to Dobson but do not seem to be from his hand. But their number is very much smaller than the number of those which reflect the more prevailing style of Van Dyck. Dobson is not known to have had any pupils and the name of no other painter is recorded with any reputation comparable to the quality of one or two portraits whose attribution has hovered unsatisfactorily between Van Dyck and Dobson. The most remarkable of these is the 'First Earl of Denbigh' (Plate 51), originally at Hamilton Palace, which was presented by Count Seilern to the National Gallery in 1945. It is far beyond what we know of Dobson's powers in a full-length portrait, and yet the style is decidedly nearer to Dobson than to Van Dyck. As it is recorded as by Van Dyck in an inventory of the 1640s it may have to enlarge our knowledge of Van Dyck himself. Another portrait of a kindred character, also with a suggestion of the Orient about the background (there are pyramids and a crocodile), is the 'Sir William Paston' (a half-length) at Felbrigg.

Henry Stone

Confusion prevails over the paintings which can be ascribed to the only known English contemporary of Dobson whose name might be put forward as the possible painter of Dobsonesque pictures – Henry Stone. The main facts of his life are known.[13] He was baptized in London 15 July 1616 and died there 24 August 1653. On his tomb, which was set up by his brother, John, it is categorically stated that he 'passed the greatest part of 37 years in Holland, France, and Italy'. We know that he returned to England from Italy in 1643 and that he was apprenticed as a young man to his uncle, the Dutch painter, Thomas de Keyser, at Amsterdam. This would give him perhaps ten years abroad before 1643, so that we can reasonably assume that he was out of the country for a considerable period also between 1643 and his death in 1653.

The literary tradition fails altogether to conform to this. According to this,[14] 'one Stone' worked for Van Dyck; he was a pupil of Michael Cross, who was sent by Charles I to Spain to copy the Titians in the Escorial, and he perhaps accompanied Cross to Spain; in 1652 'Mr Stone who copies' showed Richard Symonds the pictures in Suffolk House; he 'was an extraordinary copier in the reigns of Charles I and II'; he was generally known as 'Old Stone'. Since the days of Vertue this Old Stone who specialized in copies has been equated with Henry, son of Nicholas Stone the sculptor, but only the blind desire of the blind to follow the blind can justify the equation.

We now know, however, from an account at Woburn dated 1661,[15] that the Stone who copied Van Dycks was a certain Simon Stone who worked on until after the Restoration, so that the way is clear for considering independently the work of Henry Stone, who may conceivably have painted some of the puzzling Dobsonesque portraits.

There is, in fact, a portrait of this character at Stoneleigh Abbey (a repetition is at Lamport), which is decidedly Dobsonesque and rather foreign in style and bears an old inscription (it is hardly a signature), 'H. Stone F. 1649'. From this portrait of 'Thomas Lord Leigh' (Plate 44A) it should be possible to recover some knowledge of the true Henry Stone.

Edward Bower

Dobson and Stone were more or less independent of Van Dyck, and the former at least was the leading painter on the Royalist side. When we come to those who worked for sitters on the side of Parliament it is curious that we should find a much stronger dependence on Van Dyck models. Bower, in fact, in a contemporary letter of Lord Fairfax,[16] is stated to have been servant to Van Dyck. This must have been before 1638, which is the first date known for him. He came very probably from the South-West, perhaps Devonshire, and he picked up in Van Dyck's studio (where he can in no sense be considered to have been a 'pupil') enough of the machinery of picture-making to enable him to produce provincial imitations. He probably painted Lord Fairfax at Bath in 1646 and he was certainly in London at the time of the King's trial in January 1648/9, when he made drawings of the King from life, as he sat at his trial. From these he produced at least three slightly different paintings which were popular with the copyists for a number of years. They are more historically poignant than competent as works of art, but Bower seems to have enjoyed a certain prestige in the City of London from then until his death in January 1666/7.

Robert Walker

There would, on grounds of style, be more reason to surmise that Walker, the much inferior counterpart to the Royalist Dobson on the Parliamentary side, may have actually been a pupil of Van Dyck. The date of his birth is unknown and the only material on which to base a supposition of his age and early training is his 'Selfportrait' (Plate 50B) in the Ashmolean Museum at Oxford. This very interesting picture is signed and gives evidence of a degree of sardonic wit in Walker which one would not have guessed from his other known works, for it is a deliberate parody of Van Dyck's 'Selfportrait' (Plate 50A) in the collection of the Duke of Westminster. Van Dyck displays himself with a good deal of arrogance, as the object of royal patronage. He stresses the gold chain which the King had given him in April 1633 and he points to the sunflower, a symbol of royal patronage, which is turned towards him. Walker converts the image into a straitened and upright design (he is always prone to exaggerated verticals) and he points, not to a sunflower, but to a statuette of Mercury, the patron of vagabonds and thieves. If the Van Dyck was perhaps painted about 1633/4, and the Walker was only a year or two later and shows a man of some twenty-five to thirty, we can suppose Walker born between 1605 and 1610. He seems at any rate to have been in independent practice by 1639, if his signature and the date have been correctly read on a picture of 'Cardplayers' in the von Rechberg collection at Donzdorf.[17] The latest certain date that we have for him is 1656: he was possibly still alive in 1658, and he is generally supposed to have died a little before the Restoration.

The rather Italianate kind of joke shown in the Oxford 'Selfportrait', the subject of the picture of 1639, and the fact that Richard Symonds in 1652 quotes Walker's opinion about the effect of rolling them on pictures painted on the canvas favoured in Italy, make plausible Mr Collins Baker's suggestion that he studied in Italy. We certainly know that he did copies of Titians in the royal collection and his connexion with Titian's patterns is sometimes even closer than Van Dyck's. He is next heard of in 1648, when John Evelyn sat to him for the very curious portrait now on loan from the Evelyn family at Christ Church, Oxford. This is perhaps the least English-looking portrait painted in Britain during the seventeenth century and must have been directly intended by the sitter to give him the air of an Italian virtuoso. For it is a sort of parody of a typical Italian picture of the 'Penitent Magdalen'! We may surmise that Evelyn would have chosen a painter lately in Italy for the execution of this curious whim. By 1649, however, we find Walker painting Cromwell[18] and the *peintre-en-titre* of the new régime. We can gather by implication from the arrangements for Cromwell's funeral, that he had no 'official painter'.

Walker was kept busy during the first years of the Protectorate painting portraits of Cromwell (N.P.G., Leeds, Althorp, etc); and a certain number of portraits of other prominent personalities of the time are so entirely consonant in style with these that we need not hesitate to ascribe them to Walker. One of the best is the 'Colonel Hutchinson' at Milton Park (Plate 49A), which is of exceptional interest for being accompanied by a companion portrait of 'Mrs Hutchinson' (Plate 49B) which can safely be treated as a norm for Walker's female portraits. Just as the Cromwell portraits all derive from Van Dyck patterns, the 'Colonel Hutchinson' is deliberately imitated from Titian's 'Allocution of the Marquis of Vasto' now in the Prado, and it is a significant reflection that the official Commonwealth portraits should all echo the designs of absolutist Court painters. On the other hand, no full-length and no equestrian paintings of Commonwealth personalities are known.[19]

Two signed and dated portraits of 1656 survive – an 'Unknown Youth' belonging to the Shirley family in Ireland and the '2nd Duke of Somerset' at Syon House. Both betray a flagging hand and a continued dependence upon the models of Van Dyck. The truth is that, even during the Commonwealth period, the rising star of Lely had eclipsed in popular patronage the artist favoured by the Protector. Walker is also known to have painted 'Philosophers', which we may imagine to have been in the vein of Ribera.

Isaac Fuller

Although he lived on long after the Restoration, Isaac Fuller is best considered with Dobson and Walker. He may well have been older than either, but there seems no sound evidence for placing his birth, as is often done, in 1606. He studied in France under François Perrier, presumably before Perrier's second visit to Italy (1635/45), and he was working at Oxford in 1644, at the same time as Dobson. After some years at Oxford he became established in London, and closed a steadily more besotted existence on 17 July 1672. His work of 1644 and that of 1670 show common qualities, a sort of fierceness of approach and *bravura* of execution, which, combined with his known fondness for the bottle, has led the Bodleian 'Selfportrait' (Plate 52B) to be absurdly labelled as 'painted when drunk'! It was clearly painted when in full control of a lively hand and an original mind, and makes us regret that so little of his work is known to survive to-day.[20]

A portrait at Ecton of the poet 'John Cleveland' (Plate 52A) bears on the back a label saying that it was painted at Oxford in 1644, and there is eighteenth-century tradition to support the attribution. It is something new in British painting, and shows a new tendency from which Lely was to learn. The quiet pose and gestures of Van Dyck or Dobson have given way to something more vivid and expostulant, and it may be instructively compared with a picture such as the Bourdon 'Selfportrait' in the Louvre. The face is executed with a certain careless dash and shows an unquiet spirit, and the same characteristics appear in the 'Edward Pierce' at Sudeley Castle, painted some years after the Restoration. The only other certain works of importance which survive are three variations of a self-portrait. The earliest is perhaps that in the Bodleian, signed and dated 1670, in which the plain dark cap he was originally wearing has been altered – entirely in the interest of the design – into a singular dark crimson headpiece. In the variant in the National Portrait Gallery a bust is placed instead of the drawing and the picture is converted more into a 'virtuoso portrait'; in that at the Queen's College, Oxford, Fuller's son has been added behind. These are a striking anomaly for their time, with the scale deliberately a little larger than the life. They are a faint echo of Rembrandt's later selfportraits, and as nearly out of touch as those are with the prevailing taste.

Fuller's work other than portraiture is lost. He did some religious painting at Oxford and decorated a large room at the Mitre Tavern in Fleet Street with a series of life-size figures of classical divinities in which Vertue thought the Bacchic figures the best. From his description[21] we can still picture with some vividness the 'fiery colours' and the prominent marking of the muscles. One is reminded, for the muscles, of Perrier's engravings after the Antique. Some large historical paintings of the adventures of Charles II after the Battle of Worcester, which once adorned the Irish Houses of Parliament, are said to have survived, at least until recent times, in the possession of the Earl of Roden in Ireland.

The names of a few painters are known whose style may be distantly associated with Fuller. William Sheppard is known by several versions of a single portrait of Thomas

Killigrew, painted at Venice in 1650, of which the original is perhaps at Dyrham. From Venice Sheppard seems to have gone to Rome, but was back in England before the Restoration. A portrait of the '3rd Earl of Downe', datable to 1658, was last in a sale at Sotheby's 17 February 1937 (77) and was signed 'Betts f.' This had a ruggedness reminiscent of Fuller, which was not repeated in a portrait of 'Lady Humble'[22] signed 'John Betts 1660' (formerly in John Lane collection), which is dominated by the style of Lely. In the Examination Schools at Oxford is a portrait signed 'Ro. Fisher Pinxit' and dated 1655, whose bold and rough facture suggests a direct connexion with Fuller: and the same remarkable collection includes a portrait of 'Christopher Simpson' engraved as by J. Carwarden in 1659. Carwarden is mentioned in 1636 and a signed portrait by him, dated 1658, was in a sale 5 May 1927, lot 86. He may have been the composer John Carwarden. In the Autobiography of the Rev. Henry Newcome (Chetham Society, XXVI, 97) there is reference to a painter named Cunney working at Manchester in 1658, and another provincial portraitist who has left more extensive traces is Edward Mascall. He was the son of an embroiderer at York, where he was born about 1627, and where he was admitted a Freeman in 1660. His works, ranging in date from 1650 to 1667, were found mainly in the North of England (two were at Hornby Castle, one at Wykeham Abbey, and one at Lowther Castle), but two, one of 'Mary Edgcumbe' 1658, were among the pictures destroyed by bombing at Mount Edgcumbe. His work has an austere Puritan cast which is not without distinction.

Painting other than Portraiture

Little survives of landscape which can be associated with the years from 1630 to 1660. Certain drawings, apparently of English scenery, are ascribed to Van Dyck and have a surprising freshness of approach, and there is a solitary oil painting at Chatsworth (with little figures partly cribbed from Rubens) which shows something of the same spirit. This is traditionally ascribed to Inigo Jones (1573–1652) and, if it be his, it is unique. It agrees well enough, however, with the style of Frans Wouters (1612–59),[23] a pupil of Rubens who came to London in 1637 and was made 'Painter to the Prince of Wales'. Wouters was back in Antwerp by 1641, but he painted one or two landscapes in England (in the style of Rubens and not from nature) and an admirable example from the collection of Charles I remains at Kensington Palace.

Another pupil of Rubens, Abraham van Diepenbecke (1596–1675), was probably in England as early as 1629, when he painted a dozen pictures of horses (now at Welbeck) for the Earl of Newcastle, some of them with views of the Earl's houses in the background. These pictures make Diepenbecke the theoretical father of sporting painting in England, a genre which was to develop increasingly with the eighteenth century.

A negligible future was before another kind of painting which had a certain vogue in England at this time – the architectural interior. The younger Hendrik van Steenwyck was already settled in London in 1617 and he appears to have remained in England until his death about 1649. Only one English continuator of the same tradition is known, a certain Thomas Johnson,[24] whose working life is known to extend from 1651 to 1685.

His single surviving original work is more poignant as an historical document than important as a work of art – a view of the interior of Canterbury Cathedral in 1657 with figures of Puritans destroying the stalls and the stained glass. It reveals unexpected possibilities and Johnson is reported in 1685 as showing to the Royal Society a number of views that he had taken in the neighbourhood of Canterbury.

Painting in Scotland

There is no lack of names of painters in Scotland at this time, nor lack of portraits, but there is a lack of identification of the painters of portraits between the death of Jamesone in 1644 and the emergence of the first certain member of the Scougal family. The most prominent of the painters who took prentices at Edinburgh during this period are John Sawers (Sewers) who took eight prentices between 1595 and 1649 and whose son-in-law, Joseph Stacie, took a prentice in 1656: one Telfer (Tailfier) also was taking prentices between 1647 and 1663.

NOTES TO CHAPTER 5

1. This is sufficiently demonstrated by the astonishing draft of a letter of 1636 from the Earl of Newcastle to Van Dyck among the Welbeck MSS. (R. W. Goulding and C. K. Adams, *Catalogue of the Duke of Portland's Pictures* (1936), 485).

2. The best short general account and collection of illustrations is that by Gustav Glück in the *Klassiker der Kunst* series, 1931, which altogether supersedes the earlier volume in the same series by Emil Schaeffer. But Glück was not very familiar with British collections, and several of the most remarkable groups of works by Van Dyck in this country (such as those belonging to the Dukes of Bedford and Northumberland, and Lord Leconfield) are hardly represented at all. A much fuller list of his English portraits, made with only a slight attempt at separating originals from copies, is in Sir Lionel Cust's *Anthony Van Dyck* (1900).

3. Published in full in W. H. Carpenter, *Pictorial Notices* (of Van Dyck, etc.) (1844), 66 ff.

4. Lady Burghclere, *Life of Strafford* (21 Jan. 1636), II, 19.

5. For all the documents and illustrations on the de Critz family, see Mrs R. Lane Poole in *Walpole Society*, II.

6. *Notes and Queries*, First Series, I (12 Jan. 1850), 161. He has been confused also with Jerome Neve (*Latine* Nyphus), who painted two large pictures of his own family in a Vandyckian style, which are now at Petworth. There is no reason to believe that this Neve worked in England. He seems to have married about 1625 and had eight children with obviously unEnglish names. A signed portrait by Cornelis de Neve, dated 1647, is said to be at Long Melford.

7. The version of the *Robert Davies* at Gwysaney and a detail of the signature are reproduced in *Burl. Mag.*, XC (July 1948), 204 and note.

8. All four are published by A. C. Sewter, *Burl. Mag.*, LXXVII (July 1940), 20 ff. I do not agree with the attribution there to the same hand of the portrait of 'Lord Hussey' – a posthumous imaginary portrait, of which another version is at Doddington Hall, Lincs.

9. He appears wrongly in the *D.N.B.* as *Robert Greenbury*. The best and fullest account of him is by Mrs R. Lane Poole in *Catalogue of Oxford Portraits*, II, xv ff.

10. Others are mentioned by earlier writers, but the *Decollation of St John* from Wilton is only a copy after Stomer.

11. Published by Oliver Millar in *Burl. Mag.*, XC (April 1948), 97 ff.

12. Reproduced in *Burl. Mag.*, LII (Feb. 1928), 94; and in N. Stopford-Sackville, *Drayton* (1939).

13. The documentary information about the Stone family (mixed up with a good deal of mythology) is to be found in W. L. Spiers, 'The

Note Book and Account Book of Nicholas Stone,' *Walpole Society*, VII.

14. The sources for the 'literary tradition' are the addendum to the 1706 edition of R. de Piles, *Art of Painting*, p. 463, and the various references in Vertue (see Vertue Index).

15. Gladys Scott Thomson, *Life in a Noble Household* (1937), 290.

16. What little is known or to be guessed about Bower, and the bibliography for the evidence, is published in the *Burl. Mag.*, XCI (Jan. 1949), 18 ff.

17. Mentioned in the article, signed B. C. K., in Thieme-Becker.

18. The thorny subject of the portraits of Cromwell is treated at greatest length, but not exhaustively, in *The Portraiture of Oliver Cromwell*, reprinted from *Biometrika*, XXVI, by K. Pearson and G. M. Morant. There is unconfirmed tradition that the Walker portrait of 'Cromwell' (based in design on Van Dyck's 'Sir Edmund Verney') which descended to Mrs Polhill-Drabble (last in Anon. sale, 2 Nov. 1945, lot 78) was a wedding present to Bridget Cromwell and Ireton in 1646: a similar picture at Burghley House is alleged to have been given to Lord Exeter in 1647. But Mr E. S. de Beer has shown, on historical grounds, that a demand for portraits of Cromwell did not arise until about 1649, when he had gone to live at Hampton Court and was developing into a personage, and the date 1649 is found on the two versions of the Walker design with a page at the left (taken from the 'Lord Newport' in Van Dyck's double portrait at Petworth) at the National Portrait Gallery and at Leeds (from Naworth). The third and latest design, with the page at the right, is documented as 1655/6 by Walker's receipt for £24

published in Pearson & Morant, *op. cit.* 77. The Florence portrait and the one at Birmingham are Lelys of 1653/4: see *Historical MSS. Commission, 6th Report*, 1877 (MSS. of Miss ffarington of Worden), 437b, and E. S. de Beer in *History*, XXIII (1938/9), 132. Mr Collins Baker has introduced a red herring by supposing that the 'Great Duke' mentioned by Walpole was the Duke of Marlborough, when he was the Grand Duke of Tuscany.

19. An apparent exception is the full-length Lely of 'Monk' at Chatsworth. But Monk himself was an exception, and it is my impression that the head in this has been superimposed upon an earlier picture.

20. Beyond those pictures mentioned in the text a little 'Head of a Girl' at Dulwich alone has a seventeenth-century attribution to Fuller. His name appears occasionally in eighteenth-century MS. catalogues, as at Dunham Massey and Exton Park, but I cannot reconcile the smooth texture of the two portraits from Exton published by A. C. Sewter in *Apollo* (Mar. 1941), 62, with what we know of Fuller.

21. Vertue MSS., i (*Walpole Society*), XVIII, 101-2.

22. Published by C. H. Collins Baker, *The Connoisseur* (July 1917), 127.

23. The best treatment of Wouters is G. Glück, *Rubens, Van Dyck und ihr Kreis* (1933), 222 ff.

24. The view of Canterbury belongs to Mr W. D. Caröe and is reproduced as plate xxxvi of the Catalogue (1924) of the Exhibition of British Primitive Paintings, 1923. Another picture with an elaborate architectural interior and figures, signed and dated 1658 and formerly in the Erskine of Linlathen and Woodward collections, is only a copy of a Vredeman de Vries at Hampton Court.

CHAPTER 6

THE AGE OF LELY

Sir Peter Lely

FROM about the year 1650 Lely had the largest practice of any portrait painter in the kingdom, but his name is as indissolubly connected with the years after the Restoration in 1660 as that of Van Dyck is with the reign of Charles I. He was the first painter after Van Dyck to attain to anything like the same position of public eminence, and Charles II appointed him his Principal Painter and, on 30 October 1661, granted him a pension of £200 a year 'as formerly to Van Dyck'. His style, infinitely less subtle and less personal than Van Dyck's, left a deeper impress on British painting, and we can trace back to Lely, and perhaps no further, the main themes of later British portrait painters and the establishment of a sound, well-grounded, unimaginative tradition of studio practice which has dogged official portraiture in Britain to our own times. He is the first painter in England by whom an enormous mass of work survives. For it would not be difficult to make a catalogue of four or five hundred pictures more or less painted by Lely himself, and the number of studio replicas and copies runs into thousands.

Lely's style is matter for the historian rather than for the student of the genius of the creative artist. In mere executive ability he was perhaps equal to Van Dyck. His drawing could be impeccable, he was capable of lovely colour, and he has hardly been surpassed in his painting of the texture of silks and satins. In the power of rendering the sleepy voluptuousness which was fashionable at the Court of Charles II (and elsewhere in Europe at the time) he was unrivalled. But he altogether lacks that flame of personal genius, that power of creating as well as recording an image, which warms the imagination when we contemplate a masterpiece by Van Dyck or Dobson. His style is international rather than English, and one or two portraits by Jan Mytens in Holland or Bourdon in France are scarcely to be distinguished from Lelys. Although he never left England after he had made his name, and although his portraits were hardly to be seen abroad, Sandrart, who had never seen a Lely painting, records his great reputation and reveals the secret of his success in a little poem[1] which begins:

Was reimet sich auf wahre Kunst?
Herr Lilli saget: Königsgunst.

(What rhymes with true art? Mr Lely says: 'The favour of Kings'.)

Lely's family name was van der Faes and he was born on 14 October 1618 at Soest. Though his family was Dutch he happened to be born at Soest in Westphalia rather than at Soest in Holland.[2] He was trained at Haarlem under Pieter de Grebber and became a Master in the Haarlem Guild in 1637. Nothing is known of his work before he came to London and the date of his arrival is uncertain. There seem to have been rival traditions in the eighteenth century that he came over (a) for the marriage of William of Orange and

Princess Mary, which took place in 1641, (b) in 1643. I think 1643 the more probable date,[3] and it is likely that Geldorp, who had been concerned in Van Dyck's coming over in 1632, was concerned in Lely's arrival also.

At any rate Vertue was told by the veteran painter Isaac Sailmaker (1633–1721) that Lely 'wrought for Geldorp in his house' on his first coming over and that the young Sailmaker was employed there also. This might well be about 1643/5. Vertue also reports that Lely first painted landscapes and history pieces on coming to England, and only later turned to portraiture, and, in another passage, Vertue refers to early Lely portraits which were in the style of Dobson or Fuller. The most likely candidate for an example of Lely's first phase is the 'Blind harper' at Althorp (Plate 42B), which has always borne an attribution to Lely and is strongly reminiscent of what we know of Fuller.

As a painter of portraits Lely first comes into prominence in 1647 and no certain portrait by him of an earlier date is known. During some months in 1647, when the King was at Hampton Court he was visited by his children who were in the custody of the Earl of Northumberland, and Lely painted for the Earl the curious and rather moving group of Charles I and the Duke of York (Plate 54A) now at Syon House. This picture is without parallel in Lely's *œuvre* and shows something of the same psychological interest as was noticed in Dobson's groups.

At this time (1646/7) when the three younger of the royal children were in the care of the Earl of Northumberland, he also commissioned from Lely a portrait group of them, now at Petworth (Plate 54B), which, although more tender in interpretation than is usual with Lely, shows for the first time some of the new elements he was to introduce into fashionable portraiture. In addition to Van Dyck's column and curtain Lely has introduced a very elaborate Baroque fountain and cherub and he has set the figures well inside a gently wooded parkscape. The only Van Dyck portrait which anticipates these motives is the picture called the 'Countess of Carlisle' at Windsor, which may well have been taken by Lely as the starting-point for this 'portrait in a landscape' which was to become a dominant theme in British painting until the end of the eighteenth century. It is significant that this particular Van Dyck is more charged with voluptuous overtones than any other of his English works. The patronage of the Earl of Northumberland may well have given Lely his first opportunity to study Van Dyck, and it is worth recording that the two finest Van Dyck copies which traditionally bear Lely's name – the 'Algernon, Earl of Northumberland' (Syon House) and the 'Anne, Countess of Bedford' (Count Bentinck, Middachten) – are both after originals which then belonged to Northumberland (originals now at Alnwick and Petworth).

At about the same time we also find Lely associated with so strong a Royalist as the poet Lovelace, who might almost be described as serving Lely as a press agent. On the group at Syon House Lovelace wrote his poem 'See what a clouded Majesty...' and it is curious to find what element in the portrait he selects for admiration, for it is a quality which Lely speedily eliminated from his portrait style. 'The amazed world', says Lovelace, 'shall henceforth find / None but my Lilly ever drew a Minde.' On 18 October 1637 both Lovelace and Lely were together made free of the Painter Stainers' Company and Lely made a drawing of 'Lucasta' – a *decolletée* lady at full length, with a scoop – for the

1649 edition of Lovelace's Poems. A painting in a similar style which must be of this date is the 'Henry Sidney' (later Earl of Romney) at Penshurst (Plate 55), where there is a group of Lely portraits of about 1650. The boy (b. 1641) is seen walking in a landscape with a dog, in a costume which might be described as 'pastorally classical'. He is extremely conscious of the spectator and the tranquillity of Van Dyck has given place to movement, Van Dyck's gracious ease is replaced by something of affectation, and there are un-equivocal overtones of the voluptuous. It should be added that it is also splendidly painted and has a captivating resonance of soft colour, and it is worthy of remark that this confection was produced in the first years of the Commonwealth. It is the direct ancestor of certain portraits of children by Reynolds.

Another poem by Lovelace, *Peinture. A Panegyrick to the best Picture of Friendship, Mr Pet. Lilly*, which must have been written during the early 1650s, makes it clear (amid a great deal of obscure jargon) that Lely was painting a number of mythological subjects at this time, and it is probably correct to date in the middle 1650s such pictures as the 'Europa' at Chatsworth and the 'Sleeping Nymphs' at Dulwich, the latter of which seems almost a foretaste of Etty. A much copied picture, 'The Duet' (Plate 61) (which often goes under the bizarre title of 'Anne Hyde and her Music Master'), now in Lord Dulverton's collection, is actually signed and dated 1654. It is Metsu done over in terms of Van Dyck.[4] Up to the time of the Restoration, when he had no time for anything but portraits, Lely probably produced a steady stream of such subject pictures, which seem to have found a ready market in the austere days of the Commonwealth and Protectorate.

In 1651 Lely even made a bid with Parliament for employment as a historical painter. The proposal, in which Lely was associated with those dubious characters, Gerbier and Geldorp, was to decorate Whitehall with oil pictures of all the memorable achievements since the Parliament's first sitting. The scheme came to nothing, but is an indication of Lely's adaptability to the immediate political scene, a quality less admired at the moment than it has been in the past. At any rate he made a good deal of money during the Commonwealth and began that collection of pictures and drawings, one of the finest non-princely collections in Europe, whose sale after his death was the first of the spectacular picture auctions of the modern world. By the time of his death he was in possession of no less than twenty-five first-rate pictures by Van Dyck and his collection of old master paintings and drawings made unnecessary for him a visit to Italy and must have turned his studio into an academy for young painters, whose fruits can hardly be estimated.

Where the materials from which to select are so ample it will be best to consider only a relatively small number of his portraits, and such only as can be rather closely dated. At the beginning of the 1650s Lely received £5 for a head-size and £10 for a half-length, and the payment, on 21 April 1651, for the half-length of 'Lady Dering' (now at Parham Park; Plate 53B) occurs among Sir Edward Dering's accounts.[5] A companion picture of her sister, 'Lady Finch' (from Burley-on-the-Hill), now belongs to Judge Beckett, and the two provide a norm by which to date portraits in this style. The pose is tranquil and derived from Van Dyck: so too is the texture, tone, and painting of the draperies; but the ladies are more embowered in a rocky forest, a little more modishly pastoral than is normal to Van Dyck – and, in one, the ubiquitous Cupid fountain appears. A splendid example of the male portraits of about the same date[6] is the 'Sir William Compton' (Plate 53A) at Ham House, long called a Dobson in spite of Lely's signature. In this, as in other portraits at Ham of the same period, Lely is certainly dependent on Dobson's temper for his own interpretation. Where he had no models, however, as in his rare child portraits, he could contrive a pretty fancy without imitation – as in the '3rd Duke of Somerset and Lady Elizabeth Seymour' as babies, c. 1652/3 (formerly at Savernake). By 1653 he was painting portraits of Cromwell for the various foreign Ambassadors, an example of which is now at Birmingham: and he shows that he could adapt himself to the requirements of dowdiness in the 'Ladies Anne and Arabella Wentworth' of about 1653/4 at Wentworth Woodhouse. The extreme limit of his austere Commonwealth style appears in 'The Perryer family', signed and dated 1655, at Chequers Court – five gloomy people who appear to be waiting for the end of the world in the presence of an over-lifesize bust. Busts of this character[7] are a common feature in Lelys up to the time of the Restoration, when they vanish altogether. A glimpse into Lely's relations with his sitters is to be found in Dorothy Osborne's correspondence[8] in October 1653, where she writes of a portrait of herself that 'Mr Lilly will have it that hee never took more pains to make a good one in his life' but 'that was it I thinke that spoiled it; he was condemned for making the first hee drew for mee a little worse than I, and in making this better hee has made it as unlike as tother'. It is almost as if we had surprised the exact moment at which Lely decided to abandon a scrupulous truth to feature (at least in female portraits) to flattery. He never looked back.

Although Lely perhaps worked only in his London studio after the Restoration, he did not disdain in the 1650s to visit 'gentlemen's houses'[9] in the role of a travelling painter. It may have been when in Suffolk about 1655 that he met Hugh May (son of Sir Humphrey May) who appears in the disguise of Lely's 'servant' on a pass for travel to Holland which was granted to both of them on 29 May 1656. May's later activity as an architect is still little studied, but he and Lely between them seem to have cornered a good deal of the royal patronage to artists at a later date and it is at least possible that both made contact with the exiled Court on this journey to Holland in 1656. Lely's immediate recognition as the official painter after the Restoration and certain obscure financial transactions with the Crown at a later date suggest that, on this visit to Holland in 1656, Lely may have embarked on a policy of 'reinsurance'. He was back in London by 1658, if Vertue read that date correctly on a portrait of the dwarf painter, Richard Gibson (also with a colossal bust), which seems to have been the original of the picture now in the National Portrait Gallery; and at least three large portrait groups can be dated with some certainty to the very end of the Protectorate. The largest and most accessible, the 'Hales family' at the Guildhall, presents certain difficulties of dating, but 'The family of the 2nd Earl of Carnarvon' (Sir John Coote, Bart; Plate 56) can be closely dated to 1658/9 and the 'Family of Sir John Cotton, Bart' (Miss Brewis, Oxford) is inscribed with the date 1660. The Carnarvon group is signed and includes one of the gigantic busts, and is a repertory of Lely's style just before the Restoration. These groups are more judiciously disposed than any comparable works by Van Dyck, and are the forerunners of a kind of picture which was to remain fixed in the British tradition. Parallel with these are two 'fancy conversation pieces' with figures on a smaller scale, of which the most famous is the group wrongly called 'The artist and his family' in the late Lord Lee's collection. These are probably un-identified subject pieces and should be classed rather with the Chatsworth 'Europa' than with the portrait groups.

With the Restoration Lely became Principal Painter and his output became incessant. He veered over at once to a new style which accorded with the taste of the Court and which he had no occasion to alter for the rest of his life.

By 1660 Lely's prices had advanced to £15 for a head and £25 for a half-length: in 1671 he put them up to £20 a head, £30 a half-length, and £60 for a whole-length. The latter seems to have remained constant, but in 1678 he was charging £40 for half-length portraits. To cope with the vast influx of work he needed an extensive studio organization, for his time for sittings was soon booked up days in advance and sittings began at least as early as 7 a.m. Perhaps his most valuable assistant was John Baptist Gaspars (d. 1692), a native of Antwerp who came to England in the 1640s and painted 'postures' successively for Lely, Riley, and Kneller, as well as executing a number of copies: the backgrounds, ornaments, and draperies were often painted by Lankrink (1628–92), another Antwerp artist, who was also in independent practice as a landscape painter: Joseph Buckshorn (Bokshorn) often painted his draperies: and many other lesser names are known. At the end of his life he perhaps had some assistance in accessories from the young Largillierre. We can best picture the method of the studio and understand the various degrees of 'originals' which issued from it by comparing it with that of Rigaud, from whose *Livre de raison* we have the fullest available documentation of a busy studio practice of this kind. Studio method was now, perhaps for the first time in England, in line with continental practice.

The fertility of Lely in finding new variations of pose for ladies of assured or easy virtue, and for men whose appearance after 1664 was rendered increasingly monotonous by the perruque, is remarkable. But these poses, or 'postures', all have in common a Baroque element which is lacking in the postures of Van Dyck and Dobson, and whose beginnings have been noticed in Fuller. They tend to be restless, the figures are often in movement, and the hands are eloquent, either in repose or in gestures which, to modern eyes, are often far from elegant. The ladies draw closer to them a scarf which is falling from their shoulders, they make play with a glass bottle or a globe or a pearl necklace, they cool their hands at a Baroque fountain, they draw up their sleeves preparatory to dipping their hands in water, or they seem to point to mysterious assignations in the distant groves. The men are more static, but they too cannot keep their hands still. By at least 1670 Lely had formalized these poses into numbered series and his executors' accounts have all the postures numbered. An entry such as '58 Lord Arran (ye Ladie 57)' reads like a dress-maker's catalogue. But, in spite of this realistic attitude towards his job, Lely never became slack (as Kneller did) in his own practice. He was for ever refining the subtlety and dexterity of his technique, and those of his latest portraits which he troubled to paint with his own hand carry all the resources of his considerable powers to their highest pitch.

Two famous and accessible series of portraits sufficiently indicate his style in the 1660s – the 'Windsor Beauties' (at Hampton Court) and the 'Flagmen' at Greenwich. Between them they show the extreme limits of his powers in voluptuousness and austerity. The spirit of the Windsor Beauties is best indicated by de Grammont:[10] 'The Duchess of York wished to have a gallery of the fairest persons at Court: Lely painted them for her. In this commission he expended all his art; and there is no doubt that he could scarcely have had more beautiful sitters.' An example with a very characteristic 'posture' is the 'Elizabeth, Countess of Northumberland' (Plate 58B). Pepys first saw the series in place in 1668 and calls them 'good, but not like'. They are perhaps the most characteristic of Lely's work, but are far surpassed, to modern taste, by the series of Admirals at Greenwich which were being painted 1666/7. Of these the 'Sir Jeremy Smith' (Plate 57A) shows Lely at the summit of his powers of drawing, painting, and interpretation. In such works Lely's splendid prose borders upon the poetry of the great masters.

At rare moments, with a favourable sitter (preferably, perhaps, not an Englishman), Lely could attain even to something of this poetry. The 'Van Helmont' at the National Gallery (Plate 57B), which can be securely dated to about 1671, has about it the repose of the philosopher and makes us assume that the postures of Lely's English sitters were required by their own rather than the painter's taste. A little later, in a more modish but still charming vein, is the picture which probably represents 'Lady Barbara Fitzroy' (Plate 58A; b. 1672), once at Ditchley and lately acquired by the York Art Gallery. This has the dazzling prettiness and colour of Lely's latest style.

Lely has been dwelt on at this length because he is, for the historian of painting, by far the most important figure working in England in the seventeenth century. He established the types of portrait which prevailed until the romantic period, and his business-like pliability to the taste of his sitters established a tradition which was first to be attacked by Hogarth. He was knighted 11 January 1679/80 and he was buried in St Paul's, Covent Garden, 7 December 1680. His place as Principal Painter in Ordinary was not filled until March 1684/5, when Antonio Verrio was appointed 'in place of Sir Peter Lely deceased'.

Lely's vogue was not seriously rivalled by any of his contemporaries, although the clique which surrounded Queen Catherine of Braganza sought, about 1664, to spread the report that Huysmans 'exceeded' Lely. The general view of contemporaries can be taken from Pepys, who visited Wright's studio after Lely's in 1662 and remarks, 'Lord! the difference'; and in 1667 Pepys notes that Lely's 'pictures are without doubt much beyond Mr Hales's, I think I may say I am convinced: but a mighty proud man he is, and full of state'. Among his contemporaries there are four who deserve particular attention, Hayls, Soest, Wright, and Huysmans.

John Hayls (Hales)

Probably the oldest of these, and certainly the most elusive and the least important, is Hayls. We have no knowledge of his nationality, but he certainly worked with Miereveld in Holland before the latter's death in 1641. He only comes alive to us in the pages of Pepys's *Diary*, and the portrait of 'Pepys' in the National Portrait Gallery is certainly a version of one he was painting in 1666. This is perfectly consonant in style with the portraits of two of the younger children of Montague Bertie, 2nd Earl of Lindsey (Charles and Bridget), which were formerly at Uffington and retained an attribution to 'Hales'. They must date about 1653 and there is some likelihood, from a note in one of Richard Symonds's notebooks, that Hayls was in Rome in 1651. Other early attributions to Hayls remain puzzling.[11]

Gerard Soest (Zoust)

Soest is a more tangible figure and a better painter than Hayls, and his style is sufficiently mannered to make him one of the most easily recognizable of portrait painters. He was probably older than Lely, since Flesshier, who knew him well, thought him near eighty at his death, 11 February 1680/1. He is supposed to have come from Lely's own birthplace, Soest in Westphalia, which would be a curious coincidence. Campo Weyerman (a dubious authority) mentions a Joachim van Soest, by whom he certainly means this artist, who came to London in 1644, and there is reasonable circumstantial evidence, from the 'Earl and Countess of Bridgewater' at Welbeck, that he was here before 1650. A signed group in the National Portrait Gallery, inscribed (certainly incorrectly) 'Sir Thomas and Lady Fairfax' (Plate 59), is a marriage portrait of the middle of the 1650s and has a grace and tenderness about it which is quite distinct from Lely. It has also a deliberate sense of pattern and composition, independent of its portrait content and based on large, sweeping, curves, which was always to be characteristic of Soest. By the Restoration his manner had become fixed, and a portrait of an 'Unknown Lady' (Plate 62B) formerly in the Twisden collection at Bradbourne is an epitome of his later manner. The dress is a deep and striking cherry red: the drapery forms a series of flowing curves, independent of nature and forming folds as if made of thin plates of zinc. The whole figure is slightly pneumatic, with large and pulpy hands, which never quite clutch the object to which they are attached. These elements remain constant with Soest and give a certain mannered fascination to his work, though the legend was insistent in Vertue's day that Soest did not succeed with portraits of ladies. But he is hardly ever uninteresting and a portrait such as 'Major Richard Salwey' (Salwey collection, Overton House), signed and dated 1663,[12] comes near to rivalling Lely's 'Flagmen' of nearly the same date. Soest, however, never approached Lely's vogue, and, in 1667, when Lely charged £15 for a head, Soest's charge was only £3. Yet this was his best period, in which he must have painted the 'John, 2nd Marquess of Tweeddale' (Yester House; Plate 62A), as can be deduced from the 'Persian Vest'[13] the sitter is wearing. This also is signed and a dazzling display of gay colour, notably salmon and silver. The same short-lived costume effectively dates what is undoubtedly Soest's masterpiece, the signed group of 'Cecil, 2nd Lord Baltimore, with a Child and a Negro Page' (Plate 60) now the property of the State of Maryland. In this the basic pattern is deliberately modelled on the much earlier formula of Mytens,[14] with whose portrait of the 1st Lord Baltimore it was doubtless designed to match. But this imposed austerity is compensated for by a luxury of incidental detail, which makes it one of the most fascinating portraits painted in England in the seventeenth century. There is a flavour of the eccentric and of the true artist about Soest, which makes us regret that he was born to such prosaic times. In later life he seems to have explored other modes than portraiture, and certain fancy portraits of ladies with musical instruments have been noted (formerly at Coombe Abbey) and there is a justifiable temptation to ascribe to him other works which are not strictly portraits. A remarkable and pretty certain example has lately been acquired by the Boston Museum.

Jacob Huysmans (Houseman)

Huysmans is a much less tangible figure and remarkably few pictures can be identified with absolute certainty as his work. He is almost certainly the Jacob Huysmans, a native of Antwerp, who was apprenticed to Frans Wouters at Antwerp in 1649/50. He was perhaps a Roman Catholic and it may well be that much of his work in England consisted of religious and historical works, for Vertue reports that 'the most famous piece of his performance' was over the altar of Queen Catherine's Chapel in St. James's. It is certainly with Queen Catherine of Braganza that he is chiefly identified to-day, and Vertue also reports that he called himself Her Majesty's painter. The Queen's supporters seem to have cried him up for a time as the rival of Lely, about 1664, perhaps soon after his coming to England. In that year (26 August) Pepys saw in his studio the 'Duchess of Richmond in Man's Attire' (Windsor) and the two most ambitious portraits which remain to us to-day of Queen Catherine of Braganza – the 'Queen as S. Catherine' now at Gorhambury, and 'Queen Catherine as a Shepherdess' at Windsor (Plate 64). This elaborate confection is the fullest epitome of Huysmans' style, which is more nearly allied to what one may call the Continental Catholic Baroque than Lely's Protestant idiom. It is full of allegorical reference. The Paschal Lamb was the Queen's emblem and the Cupid is probably an allusion to the child of whom she was, in 1664, hopefully expecting to become the mother. In the background other Cupids disport themselves, and one, who is flying, recurs in other Huysmans (the 'Coke family group' (Plate 63) and Mrs Granville's 'Anne Granville'.)[15] The ducks and large weeds in the foreground anticipate Wissing, and the colour also, with its metallic lustre and the sharp, tortured folds, is wholly unlike Lely. With a view to annoying the Queen, the Duchess of Cleveland had Lely paint her in a very similar pose, in a picture now known only from Sherwin's engraving; but the opposite of this, Huysmans deliberately imitating Lely, has yet to be proved and it is better to reject from Huysmans' work the various versions of the Duke and Duchess of York which now tend to be ascribed to him.

Huysmans' most important picture, and the only one signed with his name in full, is the group of 'Four Children of John Coke of Melbourne' (Marquess of Lothian; Plate 63), in which flowers, sheep, waterfalls, and a Cupid riot unrestrained.[16] No more Baroque group was painted in England. But his signed 'Izaak Walton' at the National Portrait Gallery shows that he was equally capable of severe restraint in the Dutch manner. The only later dated works known are 'Father John Hudleston',[17] signed and dated 1685, at Hutton John, and a portrait of 'Izaak Walton Junior',[18] of 1691. He died in London in 1696 and had never been a serious rival to Lely.

Huysmans' was the best, but not the only example of the French style. Its extreme example was only a visitor to London, Henri Gascars. Just as Huysmans was pushed by the Catholic clique around the Queen, Gascars was pushed by the Catholic supporters of Charles II's sister, the Duchess of Orleans. It is even not unlikely that he was a French agent.[19] He came to London about 1672 and was extremely favoured by the Duchess of Portsmouth: he left soon after Princess Mary had married the Prince of Orange, and Louis XIV, in consequence, ceased his payments to the King (1677). He is next found, in 1678, painting the Commissioners for the Peace Treaty at Nijmegen, which certainly looks suspicious. He is abundantly represented at Goodwood, but his most outrageous attempt to introduce the French mode is the 'James, Duke of York, as Lord High Admiral' at Greenwich (Plate 65), which appears as Gascars in James II's Catalogue. His ladies and children wear torrents of lace and simper in the most Frenchified manner, and it is not surprising that his engraved group of the daughters of the Earl of Warwick was sold from Burley-on-the-Hill 20 June 1947 (73) as by Mignard.

Michael Wright

Far and away the most interesting and serious of Lely's contemporaries and possible rivals was Michael Wright. Not only was he the only one of them who was British born, he also showed the greatest promise, had the best opportunities, and seems to have had a considerable practice. At least sixty of his works are now known which can be closely dated, and a good many more are convincing attributions, for his style is easily recognized. At his best he is a portrait painter of high distinction, and, unlike his contemporary painters in England, he had come into direct contact with the best painting that Europe was producing in his own time. Yet his promise never fully materialized, and a number of important problems about him remain unsettled. Even his name and his origins are obscure.

The tradition since Vertue's day has been that he was a Scotsman. Vertue had the information from Alexander Nesbit, himself a Scotsman, who was born at Leith in 1682. But an unnamed, no doubt non-juring, source independent of Nesbit and curiously circumstantial, told Thomas Hearne[20] in 1715 that Wright was born in Shoe Lane in the Parish of St Andrew's, Holborn; that he was converted to the Roman Catholic faith by a Scottish priest and taken to Scotland, and thence to Rome. He cannot be traced in the Registers of St Andrew's, Holborn, but he is presumably 'Mighelle s[on of] James Wryghtt' baptized 25 May 1617 in St Bride's, Fleet Street, and his appearance as a youth in Edinburgh is certain, for he was apprenticed to George Jamesone on 6 April 1636 as 'Michaell (Wright), son to James W., tailor, citizen of London'.[21] What he did when his apprentice days were up (about 1642) is not known, but his presence in Italy in 1647 is to be inferred from an etching of a 'Madonna, after Carracci' which is signed 'Michael Ritus'. We know from Orlandi that he was enrolled a member of the Academy of St Luke at Rome in 1648,[22] and he appears in the list of members given by Missirini, as 'Michele Rita, inglese' (not 'scozzese'). He was the only British painter so enrolled in the seventeenth century, and the fact that he was a Roman Catholic can be taken as certain. In the Academy at Rome he came into direct contact with the most distinguished artists of the Mediterranean world at this time, not only the native artists, Algardi, Bernini, and Salvator Rosa, but the very cream of European painting (outside the Dutch). Among the foreigners listed in the Academy of St Luke in 1651[23] appear 'Claudio Melan, Gioachino Sandrart, Nicolo Pussino, Diego de Silva Velazquez, Michaele Rita, pittore inglese'. To have seen Poussin and Velazquez plain is more than was given to any other British painter, but Wright seems only to have made himself master of the superficial qualities of the Roman Baroque.

The trouble seems to have been that, in Rome, Wright became an impassioned antiquary as well as a painter, and perhaps his scholarly and social interests always made painting with him something of a pot-boiling side line. Hearne's informant reported that Wright 'was very well versed in the Latin Tongue, and was a great master of the Italian and French', and also that he 'made himself known to the most celebrated Antiquaries (in Rome), who had a respect for him, and were very ready and willing to communicate their Knowledge to him'. We know from Vertue that many of his gems and coins were later bought by Sir Hans Sloane, and from Evelyn (6 May 1664) that he had a collection of rare shells. It is also corroborated by Torriano[24] that he made a considerable name for himself in Italy, but the only possible evidence for pictures done in these years is the record of a copy of Van Dyck's 'King Charles in three positions' (Plate 38A) (then in Bernini's possession), which appeared in an eighteenth-century sale, and a signed 'Cleopatra' at Welbeck, probably the copy of a Guido. Again according to Hearne's informant, Wright then went into Flanders and became Antiquary to the Archduke Leopold William,[25] and it was perhaps as the result of the Archduke's resignation of his position as Governor of the Netherlands in 1656, that Wright decided to return to England. His first dated work[26] is the small panel (wholly uncharacteristic of the painter in size and material) of 'Elizabeth (Cromwell), Mrs Claypole' (Plate 66A), signed and dated 1658, in the National Portrait Gallery. The sitter died in 1658 and I have no doubt that the picture is posthumous, but it is not, as might be supposed, satirical.[27] The fact that it is on a small panel makes it at least possible that it was painted in Flanders.

'Mrs Claypole' is perhaps the most Italianate portrait painted in England in the seventeenth century. It is a mass of Italian emblems and seems to indicate the most deliberate and unblushing toadying to Cromwell, who was Mrs Claypole's father. The relief in the lower left corner shows Minerva issuing from the brain of Jove and has the legend 'Ab Jove incrementum', which presumably refers to Mrs Claypole's relationship with Cromwell. The tower and laurel are symbols of Chastity, of which the tower represents its incorruptibility, while we know from Ripa that a branch of laurel accompanies the figure of Matrimonial Chastity. It is signed 'I. MRitus', and, for the next twenty years, Wright fitfully puts 'J', 'Jo.', 'Jos' (for Johannes) before the Michael of his signature. No explanation of this is forthcoming unless it signifies his repudiation of the Roman faith. During his London career he was patronized to some extent by Catholic families (there are several examples of his work at Arundel and Wardour Castles), but by no means exclusively so. On the other hand, his selection for the post of Steward of the Household to the Roman Catholic Earl of Castlemaine on his Embassy to the Pope in 1685 suggests that he had never abandoned his faith. Already in 1659 he was called 'the famous painter' by Evelyn in his *Diary*, but he never contrived to modify his style according to the prevailing Court taste and, in consequence, he always played second fiddle to Lely. He was, in fact, at the height of his powers in 1659 when he signed and dated the 'Colonel the Hon. John Russell' at Ham House, a picture which shows a revival of the style and spirit of Dobson.

Throughout the 1660s Wright produced a series of portraits in this Dobsonesque vein. His men look as if they were fighting for a cause, and his women look as if they were of gentle birth. Occasionally, as in the 'Sir Robert Rookwood' of 1660 (formerly at Hengrave Hall), he even adopts Dobson's trick of a classical figure in the background. A characteristic (but unsigned) example is the picture at Wardour Castle which perhaps represents the '3rd Lord Arundell of Wardour' (Plate 66B).[28] The pattern is original and the whole conception of the portrait has a quality of nobility to which Lely never attained. Perhaps with proper patronage Wright might have expanded his powers to their true stature. Instead he was compelled to imitate the Lelyesque, if he was to secure Court patronage. His 'Duchess of Cleveland'[29] (Earl of Lisburne), signed and dated 1670, shows how he tried to add something of his Roman learning to an imitation of Lely's voluptuousness, but it does not bring out those qualities in the sitter which were her chief capital. He did, however, do some work for the Court. In 1667 he painted the child 'Duke of Cambridge' (Buckingham Palace and Belvoir) and he also painted a ceiling (now destroyed) for Whitehall. It may have been these commissions which led him to place 'Pictor Regius' (or some such formula) after some of his signatures after 1668. No official appointment to justify this signature has as yet been traced.

It is conceivable (but unproved) that Wright visited Scotland between 1662 and 1665. The few dated works of these years are of Scottish sitters – the 'Countess of Cassilis' 1662 at Yester (an unsigned companion of her husband is at Culzean), and 'Sir William Bruce' 1665, in the Scottish National Portrait Gallery.

At any rate, Wright was back in London and busy from 1667 to 1669 (at least a dozen pictures from these years are known), and, in 1670, he was considered the next best painter after Lely. On 19 April 1670 the Court of Aldermen of the City of London[30] decided to have the portraits taken of the Lord Keeper and the various Justices of the Common Pleas and King's Bench and Barons of the Exchequer, who had assisted in the difficult adjudications occasioned by the Great Fire of London. After (it is reported but not documented) a failure to agree with Lely, who insisted that the sittings should be at his studio, on 27 September 1670 a Committee was appointed to decide on a painter. The names of Wright, Huysmans, and Hayls were recommended to the Committee, but Wright was decided upon and payments to him begin 28 February 1671. Between 1671 and 1675 Wright painted twenty-two full-length portraits at £36 each, which remained (in, for the most part, sadly restored condition) in the Guildhall until the recent war. Now there are only two survivors in a fit state to be hung in the Library. These were perhaps Wright's most considerable works and the series by which he was famous to his contemporaries. While he was painting them he also did important work for one of the Aldermen who was responsible for his appointment, Sir Robert Vyner. He painted for Vyner in 1672 the full-length 'Prince Rupert' which, after curious vicissitudes, has found its inappropriate home in the hall of Magdalen College at Oxford: and in 1673 he painted the 'Family of

Sir Robert Vyner' (Studley Royal; Plate 67), the most ambitious of his later works, which shows a tendency in the accessories towards the French taste.

Continental models, French or Dutch, seem in fact to have been the sources from which Wright sought inspiration in his later years. About 1676 we first find him putting his sitters into pseudo-Roman attire, as Maes was doing and other Dutch painters, and some of his backgrounds have a distinctly French air. The most original picture of these years is the 'John Lacy in three roles' at Hampton Court, one of the earliest actor pictures and the ancestor of one of the great genres of British eighteenth-century painting. This appears to be dated 1675 beneath its present grime, and it is tempting to associate with it, as Mr Collins Baker has done, the so-called 'Highland chieftain' (Plate 68) in the Scottish National Portrait Gallery, of which Lord Brocket and Lord Forteviot have other versions. This may well be Lacy as 'Sawney the Scot', but the accuracy of the costume has led to the suggestion of more grandiloquent names. It remains, in any case, the earliest and one of the best portraits in Highland dress. At the end of the 1670s Wright seems to have visited Ireland, and a picture dated 1679 is at Malahide Castle. He was back in England by 1683.

From 1685 to 1687 Wright was back in Rome as Steward of the Household to Lord Castlemaine's singularly fruitless embassy to the Pope, and he occupied his time in writing an account of it in Italian, of which a very entertaining translation in English was 'printed for the author' in 1688. He seems to have done no painting in Rome and such portraits as are known of the members of the embassy while in Rome are the work of Tilson or others. This diplomatic absence proved fatal to Wright's portrait practice, for it was precisely during these years while he was away that Kneller consolidated his position as Lely's successor. No work certainly dated after his return has been traced,[31] and a note in Vertue (v, 14) shows Wright selling his books in 1694. Hearne's informant gives a picture of Wright forced to sell all his collections to pay his debts and then falling into a decline, and Vertue gives good authority for the staetment that he died in 1700 and was buried at St Paul's, Covent Garden (no longer, it is to be presumed, a Catholic). The only possible entry in the Registers is 'John Right' who was buried 23 February 1699/1700.

In his best work Wright is much more sensitive to the *nuances* which make up a character than is Lely: and the ladies in his portraits do not all look like one another. It may well have been these virtues which weighed against his popularity, for the ladies represented by all the really successful portrait painters up to and including Hudson, although the fashionable appearance differs from one generation to the next, all seem to have enjoyed looking as much alike as possible. Wright's Catholic background may also have limited the number of his clients.

By what may be no more than an accident it was another Roman Catholic painter who approached most nearly to Wright in the scrupulous honesty of his presentation of character – Pieter Borsselaer. He was a Dutchman and is documented as painting chimney-pieces at Middelburg in 1684 and 1687, but he was working in England in the 1660s and 1670s.[32] Little of his work is known, but what survives shows a distinguished and severe sense of character, particularly with elderly sitters. His portrait of 'Sir William Dugdale' (Merevale Hall) is signed and dated 1665 and is accompanied by a portrait of 'Lady Dugdale'. There is a kinship with Soest in the form of the hands and a certain melancholy seems to pervade all his portraits. In December 1673 'Petrus Busler, Lymner' of St Peter-le-Poor, Broad Street, was indicted for recusancy and the same charge appears in 1678 and 1679 for a Petrus Busler of St Gregory's, though he is styled 'generosus' and not 'lymner' under these dates. It is probable that he returned soon afterwards to Holland.

Lely's immediate Pupils: Greenhill, Wissing, etc.

We only hear of Lely recommending to the King the work of painters (such as Verrio and Roestraeten) who were not portraitists and thus were not likely to rival his own monopoly. Most of his own pupils were kept tied closely to the studio and were engaged in executing copies directly after the Master, or the accessories in his own pictures. A few of these emerged as portraitists on their own after Lely's death, but only one pupil of Lely's earlier time achieved independence – John Greenhill – and he predeceased his master.

Greenhill is an interesting figure as one of the few British-born painters of this age who showed real promise, but his career was cut short by dissipation. He came from a family of substantial yeomen of Steeple Ashton, Wilts., and was probably born at Salisbury (where his father became Diocesan Registrar). The date of his birth is usually given as 1644/5 on the slender ground that his younger brother, Henry, is known to have been born in 1646: but he may well have been born about 1640, or even earlier. He went to London as a young man to become Lely's pupil and his apprentice years were at any rate over by 1665 when he signed and dated a 'Portrait of a Mother and Child'.[33] Style and hair-dressing in this picture of 1665 exactly agree with the 'First Mrs Cartwright' at Dulwich (Plate 70B), signed 'J. G.', which we would be unable to date on other grounds. In the Cartwright bequest to Dulwich there are four portraits authenticated as by Greenhill from Cartwright's list of 1687: a head of the Duke of York, Cartwright's first wife's picture 'like a shepherdess', a portrait of Greenhill himself, and a 'Man with a Bald Head'. This last (No. 374) is signed 'J. G.' and could well be an actor's portrait in a character part, and it is significant that it is wholly unlike Lely. The other two pictures at Dulwich now called Greenhill are presumably not by him, as they are not so called in the 1687 list. But the four certain examples may be taken as a standard for Greenhill's early style of c. 1664/5, and are nearer to Soest than to Lely. In 1667 Greenhill did his one known etching, a portrait of his brother Henry: and it is not until about 1673, when we next meet him for certain, that his imitation of Lely is very close. The 'Seth Ward, Bishop of Salisbury' (Salisbury Guildhall) was commissioned from Greenhill in October 1673; and a portrait of 'Sir John Oxenden, 2nd Bart' (Lady Capel Cure sale, 20 November 1931, lot 33) is dated 1673 as well as signed. The 'posture' in the latter is one Lely was using about 1670/1 and the picture is hardly to be distinguished from a Lely studio work. Later still, Greenhill escaped from this servitude to Lely and was branching out with a style of bust portrait which anticipates Riley, when death overtook him, 19 May 1676.

Only three portraits are known of this last phase of Greenhill, which is much the most interesting – the 'Captain John Clements' at Greenwich (which has always been ascribed to Greenhill); another portrait of a 'Naval Officer' at Greenwich (Plate 70A), with *JG* in a monogram, which was sold at Lord Kinnaird's sale, 21 June 1946 (71), as 'Admiral Grenfelt' by Sandrart; and a portrait of Thomas Weedon, with a similar monogram, in the Earl of Ellesmere sale, 18 October 1946 (93). The last suggests a possible date, as it may be a marriage portrait of 1675,[34] so that this group would represent Greenhill's final style. There is something sturdy and solid about these pictures which foreshadows the style of the generation which succeeded Lely, of which Greenhill would seem to be the pioneer. The Cartwright portraits showed that Greenhill was already associating with players at the outset of his career, and it was this association which was his undoing. The society he kept in his latter days is sufficiently indicated from the fact that Mrs Behn (for whom he nourished a passion) and Lord Rochester wrote poems on his death.

The most important of Lely's later pupils, who emerged into independence on his death in 1680, was Willem Wissing. Like Greenhill he too died in his thirties, just as he was developing a style of his own: but it was a style neither sturdy nor restrained. The essential facts about Wissing's life can be extracted from the fulsome Latin of the monument put up to his memory by John, Earl of Exeter, in St Martin's, Stamford.[35] He was born at Amsterdam in 1655, was a pupil of Lely, and had spent some time in France. His early training took place at The Hague, whence he came to England in the latter part of 1676 and he presumably entered Lely's studio at once. In the accounts of Lely's executors he appears as one of the assistants and it may well not have been until after Lely's death that he went to France, where he picked up a passion for metallic flowers, huge weeds, and a generally frenchified line in accessories. Dated works in England begin to be numerous in 1684 and he certainly painted 'Charles II' (St James's Palace). On the accession of James II he found particular favour with the new King and was sent to Holland in the summer of 1685 to paint the Prince of Orange (signed versions at Penshurst and St James's Palace, etc.). On his return he painted the whole royal family, and mezzotints after a series of 'originals painted by Mr Wissing' are advertised in the *London Gazette* for 19/23 August 1686. But his chief patrons during his last years (1685–7) were a group of allied families in Lincolnshire and the surrounding counties. His first patron in the group was Sir John Brownlow, whose wife he painted at full length in 1685: this is still at Belton together with the portrait of the infant 'Elizabeth Brownlow' (Plate 71B) surrounded by a veritable shrubbery of exotic weeds. The same tendency appears in other children's portraits of this date and in a number of full-lengths (Grimsthorpe Castle and elsewhere). Finally Wissing was taken up by the Earl of Exeter, and he died at Burghley while painting what is certainly his masterpiece, the young 'Lord Burghley' with dog and gun (Plate 71A), which is still at Burghley House. Wissing has been damned by recent writers as the apex of vulgarity in seventeenth-century portraiture, but this last picture of his (which is finer than the mezzotint suggests) shows him working in the tradition which runs from Van Dyck to Reynolds, and he might well have developed into a painter of distinction. All his known work was crowded into four years and he was at least as popular as Kneller during these years. His death left the way open for Kneller's all too undisputed supremacy.

Of the other personalities involved in Lely's studio after his death we know little. The man who finished most of the pictures seems to have been Sonnius, of whom little more is known than that Roger North called him 'old and touchy' in 1687. One of Lely's chief hands, however, must have been Thomas Hawker, who, apparently in hopes of succeeding to Lely's practice, took over Lely's house and studio from 1683 to 1685, but had finally to be ejected for insolvency. There is a full-length in robes of the 'First Duke of Grafton' (Euston Hall), of about 1680/1, which is engraved as by T. Hawker, and the signature 'Tho Hawker Pinxit' appears on a charming oval bust of the boy '3rd Earl of Rochester' at Hinchingbrooke, of about the same date. Both these owe everything to Lely and have nothing individual about them. The only other known work is a group of 'Five children of Theophilus Leigh', about 1696, at Stoneleigh Abbey, whose signature once read 'THawker fecit'. This shows an adaptation of the Lely manner to the Kneller style and has a certain rustic charm. The same Hawker, presumably, was living in Covent Garden and patronized by the Leighs' kinsman, the future Duke of Chandos, in 1700 and 1701. There is no evidence to equate him with the 'Edward Hawker, painter' who is recorded by Vertue as alive in 1721 aged about eighty. But a Thomas Hawker was buried at Covent Garden 5 November 1699.

The most devoted follower and copyist (she was hardly the pupil) of Lely was Mary Beale. Born Mary Cradock, she was baptized at Barrow, in Suffolk, where her father was the incumbent, 2 March 1632/3. In 1651 she married Charles Beale and she was already, it would seem, an amateur painter. She decided to become a professional about 1654, when she settled in Covent Garden.[36] Nothing certain, however, is known about her work until about 1671. From that year to 1681 we have transcripts of several of her husband's diaries, which cover six years and give a record of her work. About 140 portraits are recorded for these six years, a number being copies after Lely, and a goodly proportion of the sitters being clerical. Enough of her work has been identified to show that, with the exception of an occasional portrait of a sympathetic sitter, she was a drab and unoriginal follower of Lely's manner – at any rate after 1670. She particularly affected heads in feigned stone ovals adorned with fruit in stone. She was buried at St James's, Piccadilly, 8 October 1699.[37]

Among Lely's professional copyists should be mentioned Theodore Russel (Rousel), baptized at London 9 October 1614 and at first a pupil of his uncle, Cornelius Johnson, and later of Van Dyck. He specialized in neat, small-scale copies of Van Dyck and, later, of Lely, and survived until 1688/9. A female amateur who painted her own portrait in the style of Lely and also did small-scale pictures, both portraits and mythologies, was Miss Anne Killigrew,[38] who died in 1685 aged twenty-four.

Minor London Painters

Bare mention must suffice for a few painters known only from occasional works. One Robert Mallory, a City painter (documented *c.* 1653–88), was perhaps the vendor rather than the painter of the 'Walter Pell' which hangs under his name in the Hall of the Merchant Taylors Company. William Trabute of St Anne's, Blackfriars, by whom there is a signed portrait of 1670 in the Oldswinstead Hospital, Stourbridge, was indicted for recusancy in 1673, and a portrait, said to be signed and dated 1677, is reproduced in *The Ancestor*, XII, 17. Thomas Sadler, whose parents married in 1645, is best known for his signed portrait of 'John Bunyan' of 1684, and another portrait, of 'Mary Bryan', signed and dated the same year, belonged to Sir Bryan Godfrey Faussett; Walpole, on good authority, says he was a friend and pupil of Lely and took to miniature painting in his later years. Matthew Snelling (working 1647 to 1672) was also mainly a miniature painter, but a very feeble portrait of 'Dr Baldwin Hamey' belonging to the Royal College of Physicians (to which it was presented by his nephew in 1700) has always been ascribed to Snelling, although his initial is now given as 'J'.

Painters in the Provinces

By the latter part of the seventeenth century it was becoming increasingly frequent to find a portrait painter established in the larger provincial towns. A few examples may be given for widely separated areas. In York, which developed a considerable artistic life of its own at the turn of the century, a portrait painter named Comer was settled for a number of years. Charles Beale mentions him on a visit to London in 1677 and there are bills for his work at Welbeck dating 1683 and 1685. At Welbeck a group of full-length portraits in the style of a scholar of Lely can be associated with the bills. Moving across the country to Cheshire, a portrait painter, Thomas Gomersall (Gumerson), said to be of Chester, was married at Wrexham in 1670,[39] and was living at Wrexham in 1671 and at Shrewsbury in 1675/6: in 1682 and 1683 there are payments to him for portraits in the Chirk Castle accounts. A Jeremias Vandereyden, a pupil of Hannemann at The Hague in 1658, received payments (Belvoir MSS.) in 1675 and 1676 for work for Lord Roos, and was buried at Stapleford, Leicestershire, 17 September 1695, under the name of 'Jeremiah Vanroyden'. Among the Salisbury Corporation accounts[40] there are payments in 1672 and 1683 to Christopher Gardiner of Bristol, painter, and some of his uninspiring works survive. At Oxford, thanks to Mrs Lane Poole's researches,[41] rather more is known. The tradition of Sampson Strong was carried on by John Taylor, who became Mayor in 1695. He was perhaps living in London in the Parish of St Botolph, Bishopsgate, where he married in 1655, but his Oxford residence and activities begin about that year, and he continued at Oxford for forty years, doing portraits for the City, the University, the Colleges, and Christ's Hospital, Abingdon, a good many of which survive. Mention should also be made of James Gandy (1619–89), who is said to have settled in Ireland about 1661 and had a good practice there; I have never seen a documented example of his work.

Occasional Foreign Visitors

A few foreign painters of a more ample reputation worked for periods of varying length in England. There is little to justify the interesting legend of Rembrandt's brief residence at York in later life, but one of Rembrandt's pupils, Samuel van Hoogstraeten (1627–78), worked in London from 1662, until the Great Fire of 1666 led him to return to Dordrecht. The only portrait so far known from these years is that of 'Thomas Godfrey' (Sir Bryan Godfrey-Faussett), signed and dated 1663, but he made a name for himself by ingenious perspective inventions. Pepys admired one of these (19 January 1663) in Mr Povy's closet, and that is probably the 'Perspective of a Corridor' dated 1662 at Dyrham Park (Glos.), where there is also another very large 'Perspective of a Court Yard'.

Benedetto Gennari (1633–1715), a nephew of Guercino, was taken into the employment of Charles II and much employed on religious painting for the Crown, for which the Queen's Catholic Chapel made considerable demands. He reached England in September 1674[42] and remained until the Revolution of 1688. A good many of his mythological paintings, authenticated by the James II Catalogue, are still among the store-rooms at Hampton Court. In 1687 he was painting various pictures for the Chapel at Whitehall and he completed the 'Nativity' for the High Altar in 1688: all of which were paid for out of the Secret Service money of James II. He also painted a great many portraits of leading figures about the Court, most of which remain to be traced. But his Italian style left no traces in England.

Nicolas de Largillierre (1656–1746), although he belongs to a later European generation, should be mentioned here, since he was one of the latest recruits to Lely's studio. After entering the Antwerp Guild as Master in 1672, he came to London in 1674, an accomplished fruit and flower painter. It was in Lely's workshop that his talents as a portraitist first developed, and he probably remained attached to it until Lely's death in 1680, although he painted a few portraits on his own in England, which are only known from engravings. A signed 'Still-life' of 1676 was in Lord Darnley's sale, 1 May 1925 (40): and 'Two Bunches of Grapes', signed and dated 1677, belonging to Mr Lugt at The Hague, show great delicacy and accomplishment. These mark the beginnings of still-life painting in England, a genre which never found much favour. Largillierre left London for Paris in 1682, impelled by the Test Act, but he returned for a short visit in 1685/6 to paint the new King and Queen. Mezzotints after these are advertised in the *London Gazette*, 9/13 December 1686. He carried something of the spirit of Lely to France, but left no mark of his own on British painting.

The still-life tradition, in a rather original vein, was also successfully practised by Pieter Roestraeten, a native of Haarlem and son-in-law of Frans Hals. Born about 1631, he was apparently in London by 1666, and at first painted scenes of peasant genre. There are half a dozen of such pictures, signed and dated between 1672 and 1676 at Ugbrooke, showing a Surgeon, a Cobbler, a woman plucking a turkey, and other domestic scenes. But Roestraeten's main forte was a new kind of still-life, in which wrought plate, silver, or ivory tankards, and the like, form the main ingredients. These are not uncommon in moderate size, and an enormous example, dated 1678, is at Chatsworth. He was buried at St Paul's, Covent Garden, 10 July 1700.

Another Dutchman, the Leyden painter Edward Collier, did variations on this kind of still-life with letters, gazettes, globes, and so on. He appears to have been in London for a short time about 1695/8, and the last known date for him is at Leyden in 1706. It should be remarked that Dutch painters seem to have done still-life arrangements of this kind in Holland with English letters and newspapers – presumably for the English market. Lord Lothian seems to have been a particular patron of this kind of painting, for there remain at Newbattle Abbey examples of Roestraeten and Collier and the solitary signed 'Flower Piece' of B. Ferrers (d. 1732) done in Britain on a short visit and dated 1695 (or 97).

History Painting

Vertue records the names of a number of history painters of whose works no trace remains to-day; but decorative history on walls and ceilings, which was to expand to real importance in the hands of Verrio and Laguerre, finds its beginnings in the personality of Robert Streeter, who left no branch of painting untried and would have been a universal genius had he been endowed with the requisite talent. Pepys speaks of his 'perspectives', and these may have been pictures in the vein of Hoogstraeten, but his main reputation was for landscape and history. The traditional date of his birth is 1624 and he died early in 1679. He was certainly trained abroad, already had a high reputation in England by 1658, and was appointed Serjeant Painter by Charles II at the Restoration in 1660 – presumably as the most handy, British-born, painter-of-all-work available. The Earl of Bedford bought a landscape from Streeter for his bedroom (presumably for a chimney-piece) in 1660 for £4 10s (Woburn MSS.) and the one landscape by him known, the 'View of Boscobel House' (Hampton Court; Plate 72), which appears as by Streeter in the James II Catalogue, may well have been painted not long after the Restoration. It is not pure topography and shows some of the resources of art, and must count as the first respectable ancestor of the 'country house portrait' which was to become a popular genre in the eighteenth century. Two rather nondescript 'Prophets' exist at St Michael's, Cornhill,[43] but the most important of Streeter's surviving works is the ceiling of the Sheldonian Theatre at Oxford, painted in 1668/9. A variety of allegorical figures appropriate to the building are arrayed in the heavens, from which they spread their benign influence. Mosaical Law, the Gospel, History, Divine Poesy, Mathematics, Astronomy and Geography, Architecture, Rhetoric, Law, Justice, Physic, Logic, Printing, and Truth are the principal figures, and the whole is disposed with at least the science of the painters of the Italian or French baroque. The execution may be unselect and the whole ceiling be a very minor example of a form common enough in the rest of Europe, but it is not in the least amateurish in compositional resource. But though the fashion may have been set by Streeter, it was more profitably and amply exploited by foreign visitors whose reputation it is difficult for us to understand to-day.

Landscape

There was no shortage of landscape painting in England at this time, but nearly all of it was of poor quality and most of it was unrelated to the English scene. Lankrink, who painted backgrounds for Lely, continued painting landscapes in the style of Gaspard Poussin or Francisque.[44] He was buried at Covent Garden 11 July 1692. Jan Loten (d. 1681) painted scenes in the Dutch taste; Robert Aggas (d. 1679) had a considerable reputation, and one of his works remains in the Painter-Stainers' Hall: other names have been preserved by the piety of Colonel Grant, and one may add, for landscape painters in the provinces, the record of one Thomas Francis, who was painting 'landscapes for chimney pieces' at Chirk Castle in 1672.

Apart from Streeter, however, the only two names of note are Hendrick Dankerts and Jan Siberechts. Dankerts (whose elder brother John was a history and portrait painter and also worked in England) became Master in The Hague Guild in 1651 and accompanied his brother to Italy in 1653. He married his first wife in the Catholic Chapel Royal in London 24 October 1664 and was thenceforth a good deal employed by the Crown. Hampton Court and the back passages of Windsor still contain a number of his landscapes. He specialized, however, in views of famous places which he turned out to pattern. In 1669 he did for Pepys views of Windsor, Whitehall, Greenwich, and Rome, and the Earl of Bedford bought from him in 1675/6 'a landscape of Plymouth and the citadel there and parts adjacent' for £10. No doubt he had made drawings on the spot, which he kept as his stock-in-trade for turning out to order views of famous places. He left England about the time of the Test Act in 1678 and died in Amsterdam apparently early in 1680.

Jan Siberechts is at times a good deal more interesting.[45] He was baptized at Antwerp 29 January 1627 and was a fully formed lansdcape painter when he came to England some time between 1672 and 1674, perhaps on the invitation of the Duke of Buckingham. He too was a Catholic and one of his daughters was employed in making lace for the Queen's pious purposes. He remained in England until his death, which traditionally took place in 1703. Although the bulk of his paintings executed in England are simply landscapes in the Flemish style with Flemish peasants, occasionally a hint of the English scene creeps in. There is, however, a group of paintings which show him as the first professional exponent of the 'country house portrait'. As early as 1675 and 1676 he painted views of 'Longleat' which still belong to the Marquess of Bath, he painted Chevely in 1681 (now at Belvoir Castle), and in 1694 he was summoned to Chatsworth to paint the old house before it was demolished. This picture only survives in what is probably a later copy by Richard Wilson, but a drawing at Amsterdam inscribed 'By Chatsworth in Derbyshire 1694' is the first fresh and sincere view of one of the wilder pieces of British scenery done by a competent artist and without any attempt to Italianize the scene. In 1695 he painted for Sir Thomas Willoughby a more or less topographical view of 'Wollaton Hall and Park' (Lord Middleton), and a number of other pictures, one of which (undated), a 'View of Nottingham and the Trent' (Plate 73), has claims to be nearly the beginning of British landscape painting. He must have travelled extensively in these years, for there is a 'View of Nannau Hall and Park' in Cardiganshire dated 1696; another view of a country house, dated 1697, was in the Wanstead sale in 1822; and in 1698 he signed his last known work, a panoramic prospect of 'Henley on Thames'.[46] This aspect of Siberechts has been neglected in favour of his better-known and more conventional pictures, but he has better claims than anyone to the title of the 'father of British landscape'.

Sporting Painting: Francis Barlow, etc.

It is refreshing and unexpected to come upon so simple and honest a painter as Francis Barlow in a period such as this. There is about him that tinge of amateurishness which clings to so much of the best British painting, married to faithful observation of nature and to honesty. In one of Thomas Rawlinson's notes he is felicitously called 'a happy painter of birds and beasts', but he is a little more than that, though birds and beasts were his main subject. He was probably (as he calls himself) a Londoner, but an early tradition (found in Peck's *Desiderata Curiosa*, 1732) calls him 'Barlow of Lincolnshire'. The date of his birth is uncertain, but he was probably born in the 1620s and he first emerges as an etcher in some illustrations to Benlowe's *Theophila*, 1652. The text on the portrait title-page of that book (which was perhaps also engraved by Barlow) curiously enough uses in his praise the same expression of approval as Lovelace has used of Lely in 1647: 'Where others' art surpast you find / They drew the body, he the mind'. As early as 1653 Richard Symonds records that he received £8 for a picture of fish, and Evelyn in 1656 (*Diary*, 1908 ed., p. 188) calls him 'the famous painter of fowls, beasts and birds'. A typical example is 'An Owl mocked by small Birds' (Plate 74), one of a pair of overdoors at Ham House, of which the companion (which is much damaged) is signed and dated 1673. No doubt it lacks the elegance of Baroque pattern with which Hondecoeter orchestrated his arrangements of fowls, but it is not without a feeling for design and it reveals that loving observation of animal structure and character which was to achieve its greatest exponent in Stubbs. Barlow must have watched with close attention all manner of creatures. In the half-dozen, mainly vast, canvases in Lord Onslow's collection[47] which Evelyn saw at Pyrford and one of which is dated 1667 there is a veritable anthology of wildfowl and waterfowl, as well as a frieze of closely characterized hounds. There is a lively picture at Parham of a hound holding on to the leg of a flying gamebird, and among a group of Barlows at Shardeloes (one of which seems to have on it the date 1696) there are carp and a huge pike, as well as a charming full-length portrait of a boy. His most ambitious and remarkable painting, however, is the large portrait of 'Arthur, 3rd Viscount Irwin' (Temple Newsam House, Leeds; Plate 69), which, though unsigned, is assuredly by Barlow and must date about 1700. He stands loading a gun in a brown rocky landscape, amid closely observed plant forms. A dog, a hare, a pheasant, a woodcock, a flight of duck and other birds all form part of the picture. Perhaps Barlow did not do very many paintings (not many are known), for he could never resist crowding them with animal life. His drawings, mainly for engraving, and his own etched illustrations are numerous and cover many fields of sport untouched by his known paintings. He is the real father of British sporting painting and one of its more distinguished exponents.

A contrast to Barlow is provided by the Rotterdam painter, Abraham Hondius, who had travelled in Italy before he settled in London about 1666. He died in London about January 1695, and painted all manner of subjects, but specialized in animal scenes, usually of some savagery. His technical equipment was far superior to Barlow's and he had a considerable sense of Baroque design, but there is a lack of humanity and of loving observation about all his animal paintings, which, by comparison, throws Barlow's virtues into relief.

Finally, one should mention the first appearance during this period of a minor form of portrait painting which was long to remain next in popularity with British patrons after the portraits of their immediate family – the painting of their prize-winning animals. An obscure portrait painter named Otto Hoynck, from The Hague, where he became a

Master in the Confrérie in 1661, came to England, where he became 'painter to the Duke of Albemarle.[48] He is last recorded in an Amsterdam document (perhaps his will) of 1686, but the point of interest about him is that he signed a picture of a greyhound (Sir Archibald Buchan-Hepburn sale, 23 February 1934, lot 138) which was the winner of Lord Shaftesbury's collar in 1671 and of the Duke of Albemarle's collar in 1672. The picture is dated 1675/6 and is the first example of its class at present known.

Miniature Painters

Although the absolute pre-eminence which miniature painting achieved in the time of Hilliard was not maintained throughout the seventeenth century, the miniaturists of Lely's day were sufficiently important to require attention here. From the close of the century they can be omitted from a general history of painting in Britain.

Peter Oliver, the eldest son of Isaac Oliver, was born about 1594, and was buried in St Anne's, Blackfriars, 22 December 1647. Although a competent painter of portrait miniatures, he was of nothing like the importance of his father, and he specialized in miniature copies after Italian paintings. More remarkable was his near contemporary, John Hoskins, whose first signed works date from the 1620s. Hoskins emerges from the style of Isaac Oliver and had evolved, by the time of his death on 22 February 1664, a new style parallel with Lely's style in portraiture. He has not yet been altogether disentangled from his son, another John Hoskins, but, as no dated works by either are known from after 1664, it is almost certain that the elder Hoskins was the only one of the two to count. The elder Hoskins was limner to Charles I, who granted him in 1640 an annuity of £200 a year for life – but he must already have been, by that date, employed by the Crown for a number of years. His real importance lies in the fact that he was the uncle and teacher of Samuel Cooper, who stands, with Hilliard, as one of the two greatest British painters in miniature. Cooper, like Hoskins before him, executed a number of miniatures which were reductions in little after portraits by Van Dyck or others, but the great bulk of his work was clearly from direct sittings. After the end of the century the work of the professional miniature painters became more and more a matter of reproducing large paintings by others in little.

Samuel Cooper is a somewhat mysterious figure. He was born in 1609 and died in London on 5 May 1672. After Van Dyck he was certainly the most widely cultivated artist of his age in Britain, and he had the biggest international reputation in his own day of any British painter. His prices were at least on a level with Lely's and we know that Pepys, in 1668, paid Cooper £30 for a miniature of his wife, without the frame. Cooper is generally supposed to have worked with Hoskins at least until 1634 and he is known to have travelled extensively on the Continent. These travels must be fitted in before 1642, when the dated series of his works begins. In the 1640s he painted Royalists and Parliamentarians alike and his portraits of Cromwell and his near associates are much the most distinguished likenesses of the chief figures of the Commonwealth. This did not prevent his being appointed limner to Charles II; and he painted most of the chief persons of the Restoration Court. Many of his miniatures are thus of the same sitters as Lely and we may compare the interpretation of the two artists. There can be no doubt that Cooper is always the better artist when any qualities of refinement are called for. His talent has a feminine delicacy about it, it is a wood-wind instrument by comparison with Lely's brass.

The next generation is best represented by Thomas Flatman (1635–88), a gentleman by birth and education, and Lawrence Cross (or Crosse), who died in 1724, aged over seventy.[49]

Painting in Scotland

An otherwise unknown painter who signs himself L. Schünemann appears to have been working in Scotland in the later 1660s. A portrait of 'Lady Margaret Hamilton', signed and dated 1666, was in the Hamilton Palace sale in 1919,[50] and the Scottish National Portrait Gallery has a signed 'Duke of Rothes', probably painted soon after he became Lord Chancellor in 1667. The several painters of the name of Scougall, however, seem to have been the leading portrait painters in Scotland at the time, although there is some confusion about them. A more or less putative John Scougall, whose supposed 'Self-portrait' is in the Edinburgh Gallery, has already been mentioned among the contemporaries of Mytens. But it may well be that this portrait is rather later than it looks and is by the first of the Scougalls for whom there exists anything like a historical documentation – David Scougall. He appears under date 17 May 1672 in Sir John Foulis of Ravelston's Account Book, and two gentle and rather timid little companion portraits of the 'First Marquess of Lothian' and the 'Marchioness of Lothian', now in the Scottish National Portrait Gallery, are dated 1654 and that of the lady is inscribed (rather than signed) 'Dd Scougal'. These do not agree at all in style with the accredited works of John Scougall.

John Scougall, who was known in later life – to distinguish him from his son, George – as 'Old Scougal', is a fairly clear figure and was the leading portrait painter resident in Edinburgh during the last quarter of the century. He died at Prestonpans in 1730 at the age of eighty-five and he probably gave up painting about 1715. The first certain reference to him[51] is in the accounts at Penicuik House for November 1675: 'To John Scougall for 2 pictures £36' (i.e. £36 Scots = £3 sterling). These pictures can fairly confidently be identified with the portraits of (presumably) 'Sir John Clerk, 1st Bart' (Plate 75A) and 'Lady Clerk' (Plate 75B) still at Penicuik. They are his best and most sensitive portraits at present known and I am inclined to see in them something of the influence of Michael Wright, who was perhaps in Scotland in the 1660s. Among the Wemyss Castle accounts are three for portraits signed by John Scougall in 1692, 1694, and 1697, and his name occurs several times in Lady Grisell Baillie's Household Book[52] from 1696 to 1705. Among the pictures at Mellerstain which descend from Lady Grisell are several inscribed in a hand of the 1720s 'Scugal P.' or 'Old Scugal P.' – 'Mrs Kirktown' 1694, 'Rachel Baillie' 1696, 'Grisel and Rachel Baillie' as children 1698, and 'Patrick, Lord Polwarth' 1700. These are much harder and more perfunctory than the Penicuik pictures and we must assume that Scougall's quality steadily deteriorated as his age advanced. He worked for the Glasgow Town Council in 1708/12 and 1715, painting portraits of Kings and Queens which are mainly feeble copies after stock designs by Kneller. From 1715 to 1724 there are various payments to his son George Scougall, whose style is almost beneath consideration. Portraits in the style of John Scougall are fairly numerous in Scottish collections, but some of them are probably by David Paton.

David Paton is best known as a miniaturist. Copies of plumbago miniatures after Samuel Cooper of Charles II, dated 1668 and 1669, are at Ham House and Drumlanrig, and the Duke of Hamilton possesses three frames, each containing five plumbago miniatures, which are signed on the mounts 'David Paton fecit 1693. Edinburgh'. But he also painted in oils, as early engravings testify. The original of the engraved 'Thomas Dalyell' (d. 1685) appears to be the picture at The Binns, and the original of the engraved 'Sir John Nisbet' (d. 1687) is at Winton Castle. This latter is very close to Scougall in style. The last date at present known for Paton is a receipt among the Wemyss Castle accounts, dated 26 March 1697, and signed 'David Paton, Leith'.

A journeyman painter, for whom mention is almost more than sufficient, Jacob de Wett, contracted in 1684 to paint one hundred and ten (largely legendary) Kings for Holyroodhouse, where they remain. And he did similar work at Glamis Castle 1688/9.

NOTES TO CHAPTER 6

1. Joachim von Sandrart, *Academie der Bau-, Bild- und Mahlerey-Künste von 1675*, ed. A. R. Peltzer (1925), 355.

2. It has been fashionable in recent years to plump for Soest in Holland and to treat Houbraken's evidence as an invention. But Lely, on his naturalization in 1661/2, called himself of the Dukedom of Cleve, which presumably involves Soest in Westphalia: see *Publications of the Huguenot Society*, XVIII (1911), 82.

3. Houbraken and others say he came over in the train of William of Orange for the marriage in 1643: but the marriage was in 1641. The two portraits of the Prince and Princess said to have been painted on this occasion have been identified with: (a) the originals of two portraits in the Earl of Crawford's possession, one of which is by or after Hannemann, while the other is ten years later than 1641; (b) pictures conveniently signed 'P. van der Faes' of which a 'Princess Mary' is published in *Burl. Mag.*, LXXXII (Apr. 1943), 100, signed 'Peter van der Faes 1641', and a 'Prince William', signed 'Van der Faes Pinxt. aet. 26', was in a sale at the Anderson Galleries, New York, 21 Jan. 1927, lot 85. I do not believe in either of these. The only other evidence for Lely being in England before 1643 was the date of '1642' said to be on the head of 'James, Duke of York' at Syon House, but this has turned out to read 1647.

4. Lely's subject pictures have been so wholly and undeservedly neglected in the literature that a few more may be noticed here. A favourite subject was 'Susanna and the Elders', of which an early version (before 1650?) is at Birmingham, and later versions at Burghley House and in the Neeld sale, 13 July 1945, lot 98, as Victoors; in the reserves of the Louvre is an 'Atalanta & Meleager'; in the Baroda Gallery a 'Judith'; a 'Boys blowing Soap Bubbles' was in Earl Fitzwilliam's sale, 11 June 1948, lot 38; and a curious 'Idyll' was lent to R.A. 1938, no. 46, by the late Sir Edmund Davis. The only post-Restoration 'subject pictures' are those which represent the lighter ladies of the Court as 'Venus' (at Penshurst and formerly at Lowther Castle) or as the 'Magdalen' (at Kingston Lacy). For many illustrations see R. B. Beckett, *Lely*, 1951.

5. *Notes and Queries*, First Series, I (12 Jan. 1850), 162.

6. For my reasons for dating this *c.* 1651 see *Burl. Mag.*, LXXXVI (Feb. 1945), 51.

7. No explanation of these busts is available, but they are so disturbing that later owners painted the busts out in the two portraits of the 'Earl of Essex' and 'Lord Capel of Tewkesbury' after the Cassiobury sale in 1922. The latter has now found a home in the Metropolitan Museum, New York, and the bust has re-emerged to view.

8. *Letters of Dorothy Osborne to Sir William Temple*, ed. G. C. Moore-Smith (1928), 106.

9. For Lely visiting houses near Bury St Edmunds (near to the Mays' house at Boxted) see Roger North's *Lives of the Norths*, 1890 edition, II, 273.

10. *Memoirs of the Count de Grammont*. Translated by Peter Quennell (1930), 190.

11. Mr Collins Baker reconstructs Hayls from certain pictures at Woburn, relying on the list in Vertue (II, 40), where the artists' names are given 'on the authority of some who pass for judges in painting'. The one traceable picture categorically called Hales in that list is 'Colonel John Russell', a picture of about 1645/8, which may well be an early phase of Hayls. The 'Ladies Diana and Anne Russell' of *c.* 1655/6 is hesitantly called 'perhaps not Vandyck but … Hales', but this charming and Vandyckian picture is hard to reconcile with the more solid projection of the Uffington portraits of *c.* 1653. At Lacock a 'Sir Gilbert Talbot' is mysteriously labelled 'Hayles 1679' but looks a good deal earlier. There is also a puzzling monogrammist, *JH*, who seems to have worked in Cheshire and Lancashire, 1647–62 (see M. R. Toynbee, *Country Life*, 15 Sept. 1950, 840 ff.).

12. Reproduced in the Album of the *Exhibition of 17th Century Art in Europe*, R.A., 1938.

13. For the style and dating of the Persian Vest see E. S. de Beer in *Journal of the Warburg Institute*, II (1938), 105 ff.

14. The '1st Lord Baltimore' was painted by Mytens, but the original found its way to Wentworth Woodhouse. The version sold, with the rest of the portraits of the Lords Baltimore, from Windlestone, at Sotheby's, 26 July 1933, may well have been a copy by Soest. This too now belongs to the State of Maryland.

15. Reproduced in Roger Granville, *The History of the Granville Family* (1895), 406.

16. Mr Collins Baker wrongly calls them the children of Thomas Coke. They are in fact Thomas Coke (1674–1727) and his brother and sisters: the Cupid in the sky represents Francis, who died an infant in 1680: see J. Talbot Coke, *Coke of Trusley* (1880), 71.

17. Reproduced in *Country Life*, 26 Jan. 1929, p. 122.

18. Reproduced in *The Fishing Gazette*, 13 Dec. 1924.

19. Gascars was born in Paris *c.* 1634/5 and died in Rome 1701. He was *agréé* at the French Academy 1671; in London *c.* 1672–7; in Holland 1678/9; received a Member of the French Academy 1680; and set off on further travels in 1681. A life-size portrait of one of the Estes at Modena is dated 1681; he worked for a time at Munich; was at Venice 1686; and finally settled in Rome, where an altar-piece by him survives in Sta Maria dei Miracoli.

20. *Remarks and Collections of Thomas Hearne*, V (Oxford Hist. Society, 1901), 112–13, under date 14 Sept. 1715. Hearne calls him William, but his informant, where he can be checked independently, seems to have known more about Wright than any of Vertue's sources.

21. Register of Apprentices of the City of Edinburgh, 1583–1666, Scottish Record Society (1906), 213.

22. (P. A. Orlandi), *L' abecedario pittorico*, p. 329, of the Naples edition of 1733. Walpole's misprinting of the date as 1688 has misled some subsequent British writers. M. Missirini, *Memorie per servire alla storia della Romana Accademia di S. Luca* (Rome, 1823), 472.

23. G. J. Hoogewerff, *Bescheiden in Italië*, II (The Hague, 1913), 130.

24. See *Journal of the Warburg and Courtauld Institutes*, VI (1943), 217 ff.

25. Corroboration of this is given in a reference, for which I am indebted to Mr E. S. de Beer: the *Journal of Constantin Huygens, Jr.*, First Part (1876), 361–3.

26. If we are to believe Vertue (I, 50; II, 66), a portrait of the 'Duke of Norfolk' was at Norfolk House in 1718 dated 1656, but the 'pictor regius' in the signature makes this date very hard to believe in, and the picture is not to be found at Arundel to-day, though there are other Wrights there. It is, of course, possible that Charles II in exile may have given Wright cause to call himself 'pictor regius'.

27. The justification of this statement is in the fact that the picture comes from collateral descendants. It was acquired from the Earl of Chichester, and Walpole saw it in possession of Thomas Pelham of Stanmer, whose wife was a great-granddaughter of Mr Claypole's sister, Frances. Walpole also saw another version at East Horsley in 1764 (*Walpole Society*, XV, 61).

28. The identity of the sitter is extremely obscure. In addition to the one at Wardour (where there are three other examples of Wright), there is a similar picture at Deene Park called 'Hon. Edmund Brudenell', and a third, formerly at Abbotsford, has lately been most improbably christened 'Sir Philip Stapleton'. A bust version, to which no name is attached, also exists in Essex.

29. Reproduced in *Burl. Mag.*, LXXXVIII (Sept. 1946), 226.

30. For clearing up the tangle of the Guildhall Wrights I am deeply indebted to Mr Raymond Smith, Librarian of Guildhall, and Mr P. E. Jones, Deputy Keeper of the Records. Mr Collins Baker, misled by Evelyn's habit of adding later notes to earlier entries in his *Diary*, has wrongly divided the series into two and dated some 1662. For the sad decision to preserve only two, see *The Times*, 18 Nov. 1949, p. 6. Reproductions will be found of the 'Earl of Nottingham' (wrongly captioned as his father) in A. I. Dasent, *The Keepers of the House of Commons* (1911), 176; and of 'Sir Timothy Littleton' in F. A. Inderwick and L. Field, *Report on the Inner Temple Pictures of Judge Littleton and Sir Edward Coke* (1896), 8.

31. There is a story about a Wright who applied in vain for the post of King's Limner in Scotland about 1700. This may well be Wright's nephew (of the same name), about whom nothing certain is known beyond the fact of his existence. Four feeble Kneller studio pieces of *c.* 1700, formerly at Melville House, Fife, are the only possible traces of him I have come across.

32. For Borsselaer see C. H. Collins Baker in *The Connoisseur* (Sept. 1922), 5 ff., where most of his known works are illustrated: but it should be observed that several of the portraits at Bisham Abbey now labelled 'Bursler' or 'Burslee' are clearly not by him. A 'Portrait of a widow' at Amsterdam, signed and dated 1664, was bought in London. For the references to the 1670s see *Catholic Record Society*, XXXIV (1934), 157, 212, 221, and 238.

33. Exhibition, Burlington Fine Arts Club, *The works of British-born artists of the seventeenth century* (1938), Exhibit 12, lent Mrs E. Durham. Mr Collins Baker's account of Greenhill is confused by an unusual proportion of inacceptable attributions. The date of the Cartwright portraits at Dulwich remains a mystery, which is only the more baffling with the evidence on the Cartwright family provided by Miss E. Boswell in *Modern Language Review*, XXIV (1929), 125 ff.; and G. E. Bentley, *The Jacobean and Caroline Stage* (1941), II, 402 ff.

34. Thomas Weedon, later a Gentleman of the Privy Chamber to Charles II, married at Westminster Abbey, 24 Apr. 1675.

35. For the full text see Rev. Peter Whalley, *The History and Antiquities of Northamptonshire* (1791), II, 583. The evidence for Wissing's arrival from The Hague in 1676 is in J. H. Hessels, *Archives of the London Dutch Church: Register of Attestations, etc.* (1892), 106.

36. This transpires by implication from a letter of 1 Feb. 1654 from Bishop Duppa to Sir Justinian Isham among the Lamport MSS., for whose communication I am indebted to Sir Gyles Isham, Bart.

37. The correct date was published by Elizabeth Walsh in *Burl. Mag.*, XC (July 1948), 209.

38. See Sir Lionel Cust, *Burl. Mag.*, XXVIII (Dec. 1915), 112 ff.

39. *Chirk Castle Accounts (continued)*, 1666–1753, compiled by W. M. Myddelton (1931), 158 and 161.

40. C. Haskins, *The Salisbury Corporation Pictures and Plate* (1910), 15.

41. Mrs R. Lane Poole, *Catalogue of Oxford Portraits*, I (1912), xxvii ff.; II (1925), xiii ff.

42. Gennari's own account of his activities remains unpublished in the Biblioteca Comunale dell' Archiginnasio, Bologna, MS. B.344.

43. Reproduced, as well as the central portion of the Sheldonian ceiling, in the *Burl. Mag.*, LXXXIV (Jan. 1944), where there is a summary of what is known about Streeter.

44. For what is known of Lankrink see *Burl. Mag.*, LXXXVI (Feb. 1945), 29 ff.

45. T. H. Fokker, *Jan Siberechts*, Brussels, 1931.

46. Reproduced in *Country Life* (6 Feb. 1948), 277.

47. The four large ones are reproduced in W. Shaw Sparrow, *British Sporting Artists* (1922), from which the main facts about Barlow and his engravings can be extracted from a disorderly mass of speculation. The same writer first published the date of his burial in *The Connoisseur* (July 1936), 36 ff.

48. *Oud Holland*, L (1933), 179.

49. For further information on British Miniaturists see Basil S. Long, *British Miniaturists* (in dictionary form), 1929; R. W. Goulding's Catalogue of the Welbeck Miniatures, published as vol. V of the *Walpole Society*; and *British Miniaturists* by J. Graham Reynolds (1952).

50. Duke of Hamilton sale, 6 Nov. 1919, lot 18, as 'L. S. Gunemans'; it reappeared correctly catalogued in a sale 12 May 1929, lot 141.

51. The 'Lady Marchmont' at Mellerstain inscribed 'Scugal P. 1666' is in a costume of the 1690s and is presumably an error for 1696. One of the two portraits of 'Sir Archibald Primrose' in the Earl of Rosebery's collection appears to be dated 1670, but the attribution to Scougall is only traditional.

52. *The Household Book of Lady Grisell Baillie*, 1692–1733, Publications of the Scottish History Society, New Series, I (1911).

PART THREE

THE AGE OF KNELLER AND ENGLISH BAROQUE

CHAPTER 7

THE DECORATIVE PAINTERS FROM VERRIO TO THORNHILL

ALL the great movements in European painting during the seventeenth century passed Britain by. The expansion of the Baroque style took place largely in Catholic countries, but Rubens had left a noble example of it in the ceiling of the Banqueting Hall at Whitehall. The coming of the Commonwealth left it without a successor. The realistic movement associated with the name of Caravaggio had sent one of its best painters, Orazio Gentileschi, to the Court of Charles I – in vain. The classic art of Poussin was unknown in Britain and those great controversies between the adherents of Poussin and those of Rubens which enlivened Paris at the close of the century had no echo in London. But the Court and the nobility who looked to France for the guidance of taste were aware that it had become fashionable for the staircases and ceilings of houses to be covered with vast mythological or allegorical paintings, and, by the time Baroque painting had lost its initial fire and faded into decorative platitude, it was introduced, in this watered form, into the British Isles. A beginning, by a native painter, has already been mentioned – Streeter's ceiling in the Sheldonian Theatre at Oxford. Its better-known foreign practitioners were not more distinguished artists than Streeter. Of a number of names two still linger in the public consciousness, immortalized by Pope's sufficient account of the kind of wall or ceiling that they decorated – 'where sprawl the Saints of Verrio and Laguerre'.

Antonio Verrio

Verrio perhaps counts as the most heavily remunerated painter in Britain up to the time of Sir John Millais. It suggests some reflections on the British character that he is also one of the worst. In a grandiloquent inscription on one of his (now destroyed) paintings at Windsor Castle he calls himself a Neapolitan and 'of no humble stock'. By a considerable stretch 'Neapolitanus' could imply that he was born at Lecce, in the toe of Italy, and it has been cheerfully accepted that he was born there about 1639 since the statement was first made by de Dominici, one of the least reliable even of Neapolitan writers. There is certainly a tradition to-day at Lecce of one or more painters named Verrio who sought their fortune outside the Salentino – and came to a bad end – but I am not convinced that the two paintings at Lecce now called Verrio are early works of the painter who came to England. De Dominici mentions a ceiling in the Pharmacy of the Jesuit College at Naples which was signed and dated 1661 by Verrio, but this has vanished. In the later 1660s Verrio was working at Toulouse,[1] and two altar-pieces by him survive in the Toulouse Museum; in 1671 he was *agréé* at the Paris Academy, and it is probable that he came to England the same year at the instigation of Lord Arlington. If the entry in Evelyn's *Diary* for 16 October 1671 is not a later addition, Evelyn saw, at Lord Arlington's house on that day, the first work Verrio did in England. It too has vanished. On 5 May 1675 Verrio became a denizen and his first royal employment is said to date from 1676, although the published warrants do not begin until 31 October 1678. From then until the Revolution of 1688 Verrio was in continuous employment by the Crown and received something like five and a half thousand pounds for work done at Windsor Castle, as well as several 'bounties' from the Secret Service money and payments from the same source (after 1685) for his subsidiary role as gardener at St James's Palace. Details of his work for Windsor and (after 1686) for Whitehall can be extracted from the Calendars of State Papers (Domestic) and Calendars of Treasury Books. The most illuminating is a warrant dated 16 November 1678 that there be no molestation to 'several foreigners, being painters and other artists employed in paintings and adorning Windsor Castle', for being Popish recusants. These are named as 'Antony Verrio and Frances d'Angely his wife, and John Baptiste and Francis their sons: Michael Tourarde, Jacob Coquet, – Lanscraon, Bertrand du Mailhey, painters employed by Verrio: René du Four his apprentice ... etc.'; later is added, 'Antonio Montingo, a painter of flowers employed by Signor Verrio at Windsor Castle'. Evelyn saw the work being done on 23 July 1679 and speaks of 'that excellent painter, Verrio, whose works in fresco at the King's Palace at Windsor will celebrate his name as long as those walls last'. From 1680 he was being paid at the rate of £200 a year, and, by Royal Letters Patent dated 30 June 1684, Verrio was appointed 'our chief and first painter', and with all rights and privileges belonging to that post 'as amply as Sir Peter Lely, late deceased, or any other held the same'. Only the most meagre fragments remain of the work at Windsor and none of the work at Whitehall, which occupied most of Verrio's time until he was turned out of his house and employment at St James's after the Revolution and Riley and Kneller were jointly sworn and admitted as chief painter in December 1688.

Verrio at first refused to work for William III and his name disappears from the Treasury Books from 1688 to 1699. His chief employment during these years was at Chatsworth[2] – where he painted the Great Staircase in 1690, the State Dining-room 1691/2, the altar-piece for the Chapel 1693, and the ceiling of the present Library in 1697/8 – and at Burghley. He was certainly a member of the Earl of Exeter's household at Burghley House in 1694 and he was probably engaged on the vast wall spaces which he covered there from 1694 to 1697. In 1699 a new period of royal patronage begins and he was employed at Hampton Court and Windsor from 12 June 1699 until at least 1704. Soon afterwards his eyes failed and he was pensioned by Queen Anne. He died at Hampton Court 15 June 1707.

His work can be sufficiently seen on the Great Staircase at Hampton Court, which includes most of the gods and goddesses of Olympus; on the ceiling of the State Bed-chamber there, with paintings emblematical of sleep; and in 'Mars reposing on the Lap of Venus' (Plate 77A) on the ceiling of the King's dressing-room. All these were completed shortly before 1702 and make us wonder why on earth Verrio was so greatly admired. In quality, liveliness, and imagination he was surpassed by Laguerre.

Louis Laguerre

Verrio was a pretentious, vulgar, and extravagant personality, but Laguerre was the reverse. He was also the better painter. Born in Paris in 1663, he worked for a short time with Lebrun and came to England at the age of twenty in 1683/4 with Ricard, an archi-tectural painter whom he assisted for some years. Together they worked for Verrio at Christ's Hospital in 1684, and in 1689 they were both at Chatsworth, where between 1689 and 1694 they painted the Chapel, the ceilings of a number of the State Rooms, and the Painted Hall. Between 1691 and 1695 Laguerre was working at Sudbury Hall.[3] Although Verrio monopolized most of the royal commissions (Laguerre only did some grisailles at Hampton Court for William III), there was ample scope for Laguerre in country houses. He painted much at Burghley and the learned programmes which he affected – due probably to his early training under the Jesuits – can be gauged from the text for the decoration of the Ballroom at Burghley which is preserved in Peck's *Desiderata curiosa*. Among much other work he is recorded at Devonshire House in 1704; painting Marlborough's battles at Marlborough House in 1713; and, probably about the same date, doing his masterpiece, the Saloon at Blenheim. From about 1711 he came up against his more pushing rival, Thornhill, who had learned, so Vertue reports, much of his art from Laguerre: and the better commissions tended to go to Thornhill. From about 1714 he did a good deal of work at Canons, and he died in London 20 April 1721. During his last years he gave himself more to portraiture and history painting than before, but little work of this kind is known to survive.

A number of lesser figures of the historic style need only be mentioned. Gerrard Lans-croon (d. 1737), in 1678 an assistant of Verrio, painted at Burley-on-the-Hill in 1712; Pierre Berchet (1659–1720) came to England in 1681 with the architectural painter Rambour, and also worked first for Verrio and later on his own; another such was Nicholas Heude who alone carried this style into Scotland. He was a French Protestant from Le Mans, who had been *agréé* at the Paris Academy in 1672 and came to England in 1683 as an assistant to Verrio. The Duke of Queensberry is said to have brought him to Scotland, but his only surviving works are two signed ceilings – an *Aurora* and another allegorical figure subject – at Caroline Park near Edinburgh. He died in indigence at Edinburgh in 1703.

The other decorative and historical painters who were active in Britain before the pre-dominance of Thornhill can be divided into two groups, the invasion from France, patronized by Ralph Montagu (later first Duke of Montagu), who had been special Ambassador in Paris from the 1660s onwards; and the invasion from Italy, centring round the personality of Pellegrini, who was brought over to England by another Montagu, Charles, Earl (and later first Duke) of Manchester, when he was Ambassador at Venice.

The Duke of Montagu's Artists

Ralph Montagu was building the first Montagu House in Bloomsbury in 1675, 'in the French taste', with Hooke as architect. This was decorated with mythological paintings by Verrio, but the house was destroyed by fire in January 1685/6. Lord Montagu (as he had then become) at once set about building a new house, and, as a zealous supporter of French art, he selected a French architect, Puget, in 1687, and introduced a number of French decorative painters. The chief of these were: Charles de la Fosse (1636–1716), who was at work here only c. 1688/90 and returned to France on Lebrun's death in 1690; Jacques Rousseau (c. 1626–94), a pupil of Swanevelt who had also studied in Italy, and specialized in landscapes with architecture and figures in a manner derived from Poussin; and Baptiste Monnoyer (1634–99), one of the most distinguished painters of flowers, who had worked for Lebrun at Versailles. Both the last two painters did canvases (Plate 78) for the decoration of Montagu House until its completion about 1692, and many of these remained in the collection of the Duke of Buccleuch until they were sold 1 November 1946. A number of Monnoyers from Montagu House still survive at Boughton. Five architectural landscapes by Rousseau remain as *superportes* at Hampton Court, but he is not known to have done other work. Flower-pieces by Monnoyer are not uncommon in the older British collections, although his name is used generically for pictures which are not from his hand. He is commonly known as 'Baptiste'.

Another French painter of a younger generation, James Parmentier (1658–1730), was also employed as assistant in the work for Montagu House. He had visited England first in 1676 but later went to France and Italy and settled here only in 1680. In 1688 he did work for Montingo (Verrio's flower painter) and for Berchet and Henry Cooke (d. 1700), both minor history painters. In 1689 he worked for Closterman and began to assist Rousseau at Montagu House, where he continued until 1692. In 1694 he worked for William III in Holland at Het Loo, but he was back and settled in Yorkshire by about 1700/1, where he did work at Hull, York, and elsewhere – history paintings, altar-pieces, or portraits. He is mentioned occasionally by Thoresby's Yorkshire correspondents (Thoresby Society, XXI, 192) and settled in London on the death of Laguerre in 1721, but did not meet with much success. He died in London 2 December 1730. By accident we can reconstruct his career from Vertue's notes, so that he can be taken as typical of a class of painter of whose movements in general we know little. His altar-piece at Hull is deplorable.

In the 1690s Montagu was also doing much decorative work at Boughton, and for this he employed another French history painter, Louis Cheron (c. 1655–1725), who came to England about 1695 after study in Rome, where he had made many drawings after Raphael. Cheron's watered Marattesque style can be seen on several ceilings at Boughton and he was working also at Chatsworth 1699/1700, but his importance rests on the fact that he was much concerned in the instruction at the two drawing academies started in London in 1711 and 1720, in which his teaching along Roman lines had a considerable influence on the younger generation of painters, Vanderbank, Highmore, etc., who had never visited Italy. He died in London 26 May 1725.

The Italian Invasion

It is a comfort to turn from these depressing minor Frenchmen to the Venetian painters who came over a generation later, Pellegrini and the two Ricci. They were not great painters, but they were masters of an easy, fluent, decorative style which it is still a pleasure to look at, and they brought with them something which was badly needed in England at the time, the breath of one of the most civilized (perhaps even over-civilized) cities in Europe. The history of the best in British painting in the eighteenth century is largely the history of the assimilation by British painters, for the first time, of the best that Italy had to offer, and the first appearance of Italian painters in England at the beginning of the century is an important symptom.

Although not the oldest of them, Gianantonio Pellegrini (1675–1741) was the first to arrive. He had been a pupil of Sebastiano Ricci at Venice, and married one of the sisters of Rosalba Carriera. In 1708 the Earl (later Duke) of Manchester, then British Ambassador at Venice, returned to England, where Vanbrugh was engaged in adapting his house at Kimbolton. With him he brought Pellegrini, whose versatility and lightness was well adapted to go with that passion for the heroic and gigantic which was an element in Vanbrugh's style. Pellegrini did not paint much at Kimbolton, but what he did was charming – some wall-paintings of a Roman Triumph, a staircase fresco with a Moorish trumpeter and some musicians on a balcony (Plate 77B), a niche with a chained monkey and a parrot on a perch, and a few ceilings with Cupids, in addition to a large canvas of the Duke's children. He also painted the Duke of Manchester's London house (now destroyed) and Vanbrugh found much work for him at Castle Howard, where he painted in 1712 the cupola of the Great Hall, which was destroyed by fire in the 1940s. There is also a fascinating canvas of girls round a table at Castle Howard, and the method of wall decoration by canvases let into the wainscoting was what he practised at Sir Andrew Fountaine's at Narford, where the most varied selection of his work remains to-day. 'Thetis Bringing the Infant Achilles to Chiron', 'The Rape of Europa', 'Nessus and Dejanira', 'Hylas', 'Minerva and Arachne', 'The Death of Lucretia', and 'Medor and Angelica' are among the subjects painted at Narford, and the lightness and facility of the style remind us for the first time of the Mediterranean world. Pellegrini was involved in the foundation of the Academy in London in 1711, but he left for Düsseldorf in 1713, and was back only for a short visit c. 1718/19, after which he went to Paris. An Italian pupil of his, Vincenzo Damini, did some feeble painting in Lincoln Cathedral in 1728, but returned to Italy in 1730.

The two Ricci, Sebastiano (1659–1734) the uncle, and Marco (1676–1729) the nephew, are more important for the history of painting in Venice than they are in England. The elder tempered the style of Veronese with a Rococo idiom and was the forerunner of Tiepolo, and the younger was the pioneer of the fantastic landscape which came to full perfection in Guardi. Marco Ricci came to England first with Pellegrini, in 1708, but he soon returned to Venice and brought back with him (*c.* 1709) his uncle, who had been Pellegrini's master. In England the two Ricci sometimes collaborated, Sebastiano painting the figures and Marco the landscapes, and also worked independently. The fresco of the 'Resurrection'[4] in the semidome of the apse in Chelsea Hospital Chapel is Sebastiano's surviving masterpiece. It has a Rococo verve and a feeling for decoration and movement which were altogether new. Two large mythologies by him, 'Diana and her Nymphs' and 'The Triumph of Venus', still hang on the stairs of Burlington House. A wave of nationalist feeling, fanned by Thornhill, prevented Ricci getting the commissions for Hampton Court and for St Paul's, and the two Ricci left England about 1716 (when they are recorded at Paris) soon after Thornhill had started work on St Paul's. Easel pictures painted by one or the other, or by the two in collaboration, are at Chatsworth and Welbeck, but the great series of works by both in the royal collection comes from Consul Smith and was painted after the two had finally returned to Venice in 1720.

About the time the Ricci left England, in 1716, another Venetian painter, Antonio Bellucci (1654–1727), came to London from Düsseldorf. He belonged to an older tradition than Sebastiano Ricci, deriving his style rather from Padovanino and Luca Giordano and having no tinge of the Rococo about him. He remained only until 1722. The best of his works to be seen in England to-day is a vast canvas of 'The Family of Darius before Alexander' in the Ashmolean Museum at Oxford. A rather feeble 'Adoration of the Shepherds' and a 'Deposition' from his hand also remain at the sides of the altar in the Church at Whitchurch, Edgware, commissions from the Duke of Chandos.

Sir James Thornhill

Baroque decorative painting in Britain culminated, however, in the personality of Thornhill, an Englishman, born of good Dorset stock at Melcombe Regis in 1675. His early training is obscure, but certainly included a good deal of practical knowledge of architecture. Vertue makes clear that he thinks Thornhill derived most of his pictorial style from Laguerre, and this may well be true. He seems to have succeeded Verrio and Laguerre at Chatsworth, where he was working about 1707. He came into prominence as a historical painter under Queen Anne just at the time Verrio died, and his first major commission about which we have knowledge was the decoration of the Painted Hall at Greenwich (Plate 76), where his work was started in 1708 and dragged on rather fitfully until 1727. It is his best and most visible work and has an energy and gusto which reveals the lesson of Ricci as well as the schooling of Laguerre. A number of lively drawings for the scheme are in the British Museum, but their vivacity is hardly carried through into the finished work. The scheme at Greenwich is of particular interest since some of the main themes to be depicted were from recent or contemporary history, such as 'The Landing of William III' and 'The Landing of George I'. Thornhill was thus faced with the problem of how much truth to appearances was consistent with the grand manner, and the issue was complicated for him by the fact that he had a

THE DECORATIVE PAINTERS FROM VERRIO TO THORNHILL

natural bent towards closely observed genre.[5] On a drawing in the British Museum for the latter subject is a revealing list of 'Objections that will arise from the plain representation of the King's landing as it was in fact and in the modern way and dress'. These objections were: that it was night, that no ships were visible, but only small boats, which would make a poor show in the composition; that the nobles who were actually present were, many of them, in disgrace at the time of painting, and that it would be difficult 'to have their faces and dresses as they really were'; and that the King's own dress on the occasion was not graceful 'nor enough worthy of him to be transmitted to posterity'. Finally there was a vast crowd 'which to represent would be ugly, and not to represent would be false'. Thornhill chose not to be 'ugly' and to represent the King's dress 'as it should have been rather than as it was'. The problems which beset the painter of scenes from contemporary history have never been more clearly analysed, and this clear thinking sufficiently reveals Thornhill's native instinct towards realism, which marks him out from his foreign predecessors.

The final result certainly shows that Thornhill had at least as considerable knowledge of the Italian repertory of decorative expedients as his foreign rivals. His abilities were various and extensive, and paintings by him of every class, from landscape to religious history, are listed in his sale after death, but very few examples of the minor categories have so far been identified. Three portraits, dated 1710, are in the Master's Lodge at Trinity, Cambridge, and others, a little later, are at All Souls', Oxford. But he is hardly known to-day outside his grandiose decorations, although his sketch-book, made on a journey in 1711 to Holland and Belgium, shows at least as great an interest in architecture as in painting, and his name was put forward in 1719 for the post of Surveyor to the Board of Works. He was also loud in pushing himself forward and imposed his predominance, partly by underground political channels and the support of the Earls of Sunderland and Halifax, during the early years of the Hanoverian dynasty. He was working at All Souls', Oxford, in 1713/14; in 1715 he painted the ceiling of the Prince's Apartments in Hampton Court, and when, in the same year, the question came up of who should get the commission for painting the cupola of St Paul's, he was given the job against Laguerre and Ricci. Ricci, disappointed of Hampton Court and St Paul's, left the country, and there seems to have been a current of nationalist feeling which Thornhill fanned and profited by. In this, as in other things, Hogarth followed in his father-in-law's footsteps.

Thornhill began the eight huge grisaille 'Stories from the Life of St Paul' in the cupola on 1 May 1716 and they were completed in September 1719. But he was doing many other works at the same time, in addition to carrying on at Greenwich. In 1716 he was still at work on the ceiling of the Great Hall at Blenheim, which commemorated the Duke's victory at Blenheim. In 1717 he visited Paris. In 1719 he signed the 'Stories from the Aeneid' at Charborough Park. His period of greatest prosperity runs from 1716 to 1723. He succeeded Kneller in 1716 as head of the Academy which had been founded in 1711, but it is doubtful if this first Academy lasted for more than a further year or two. In June 1718 he was sworn 'History Painter to His Majesty', and on 8 March 1720 he succeeded Thomas Highmore as Serjeant Painter, was Master of the Painter Stainers'

Company, and was knighted on 2 May. In 1722 he was elected M.P. for Melcombe Regis, but his desire to be everything overreached itself and Lord Sunderland's death the same year affected his progress. The rising arbiter of taste was Lord Burlington and his protégé was William Kent, and Kent's appointment in 1723 to decorate Kensington Palace was the turning-point in Thornhill's painting career. It was a turning-point in the history of taste in England also.

William Kent (1685–1748), whose name is justly honoured in the history of architecture and subsidiary arts, need not be taken seriously as a painter, though he had studied painting under Luti in Rome 1714/15, where he had first met Lord Burlington. The alliance of Kent and Burlington begins in London in 1719, with Kent finishing the painting which Ricci had left uncompleted at Burlington House, but Lord Burlington gradually saw that his friend's talents lay outside the field of history painting and in the direction of the picturesque enlivenment of architecture. What was happening in England was what had happened earlier in France, where the heroic style of Le Brun, to which we may parallel that of Thornhill, gave way to the Rococo modes in which the painter played a minor and more subordinate part to the architect and decorator.

The South Sea Bubble of 1720 also no doubt played its part in chastening the style of building and decoration. Soon after the work at Greenwich was completed in 1727 Thornhill was engaged in a lawsuit with Mr Styles of Moor Park over payment for the work he had done there. In 1729 Vertue notes that he had 'no great employment in hand' and he devoted his later years to making copies of the Raphael cartoons at Hampton Court, which were still in his possession at his death on 4 May 1734. In the obituary notice in the *Gentleman's Magazine* he was described as 'the greatest History Painter this Kingdom ever produced', which was probably true enough, since competition was slight. His name and fame left as a legacy that bias towards the Grand Style, from which Hogarth never escaped, with which Reynolds was tinctured, and which was only finally exorcized by the suicide of Haydon. Thornhill remains the least studied in detail of the eminent names in British painting.

Jacopo Amigoni

The final collapse of the patronage for large-scale historical decoration is shown in the case of the last of the distinguished Italian visiting painters, Jacopo Amigoni, who worked in England from 1730 to 1739. He painted several London houses, now demolished, but his best surviving work is the series from the 'Story of Jupiter and Io' at Moor Park, where he succeeded to Thornhill after the latter's quarrel with Mr. Styles. These are very accomplished examples of Venetian Rococo – the best is 'Mercury Presenting the Head of Argus to Juno' (Plate 79) – but they show a new departure in decoration which had been anticipated by Pellegrini at Narford on a smaller scale. They are large canvases let into the wall instead of frescoes, but taking up the space that wall-painting would have done. The principle, but not the scale of canvas, was to become the norm. Gradually the role of the painter became more and more subordinate and painting was used only for chimney-pieces and superportes – exactly as had happened in France. But the great bulk of these decorative pictures were the work of journeymen hacks and cannot find a place in a general history of British painting.

Amigoni did a fairly good business in large canvases of mythological subjects, but he was finally forced, like all the native British painters, to eke out his livelihood with portraits. These he diversified by the introduction of Cupids, whenever possible, but examples survive of a more prosaic vein.[6] His most remarkable English portrait is the full-length of 'Lady Sundon' at Melbury, which has a distinctly foreign air. He married an Italian, Antonia Marchesini, at the Catholic Chapel Royal on 17 May 1738, and departed the next year for Paris and Venice, ending up in the more congenial atmosphere of Madrid, where he was Court Painter.[7]

NOTES TO CHAPTER 7

1. For Verrio's Toulouse period see *Biographie toulousaine* (1823), II, 480–1.

2. Francis Thompson, *A History of Chatsworth* (1949).

3. *Country Life*, two articles in July 1935.

4. Reproduced, after its recent cleaning, in *Illustrated London News* (22 Oct. 1949), 637.

5. E. Wind, *Journal of the Warburg Institute* (1938), 122 ff.

6. The engraved 'Sir Thomas Reeve' is published by T. Borenius in *Burl. Mag.* (Jan. 1939), 39.

7. There is a summary of what is known of his English work in C. H. Collins Baker and Muriel Baker, *Life of the Duke of Chandos* (1949), 284–5. The Duke of Chandos was surprised at Amigoni wanting to do his pictures on canvas – but he belonged to the old school.

CHAPTER 8

PORTRAITURE IN THE AGE OF KNELLER AND HIS IMMEDIATE SUCCESSORS

John Riley

WHEN Lely died at the close of 1680 no immediate appointment was made to the post of 'chief painter'. It may well not then have been obvious who would succeed to the fashionable portrait practice of Lely from the three or four possible candidates. The young foreigner Kneller was beginning to come into favour, but his star was still only in the ascendant; Michael Wright had serious claims but could hardly be called fashionable; John Riley had perhaps established a fair name for himself among the middle classes; and another young foreigner, Wissing, was beginning to become known. We have seen that it was not until 1685 that the appointment was made, and it then went to Verrio, perhaps from motives of economy (since Verrio was already in receipt of £200 a year from the Crown), but the uncertainty as to who was the right portrait painter for the job persisted and was solved by a compromise after the Revolution of 1688, when Verrio was turned out and, in December 1688, John Riley and Godfrey Kneller were jointly 'sworn and admitted chief painter'. In the meantime Wissing had died, and Wright, by his absence at Rome, had lost any fashionable support.

John Riley had for a time been a pupil of Soest, and he was born in 1646. One of his scholars told Vertue that Riley was a man 'of established reputation' in 1680, but he seems to have been little noticed by the great world before Lely's death and we are still without any certain clue to his early style. From 1680 until his death in London 30 March 1691 a fair number of portraits survives which can be documented by engravings, diaries, early inventories, or nearly contemporary inscriptions that they are by Ryley, Royley, or Royle, as his name was indifferently spelt. He did his best with the great world which he was called upon to paint, taking over from Lely some of his poses and even his posture-painter, Gaspars, who was later taken over by Kneller: but there is evidence of his diffident and uncourtierlike temperament, and the native Riley is only plainly apparent in the one or two pictures he painted of persons in the humbler walks of life. Curiously enough, the two chief of these are fully signed and are amongst the most sympathetic portraits of this depressing period – the 'Scullion' (Christ Church, Oxford; Plate 81) and the portrait at Windsor of 'Bridget Holmes' (Plate 80; dated 1686), the venerable housemaid to James II, in her ninety-sixth year. There is a faint friendly air of parody about this latter work which could never have been anticipated from Riley's official manner. The curtain and Baroque pot suggest the grand manner and the old woman is wielding her mop as if it had been a general's baton, and is directing it against a mischievous page boy. It is obvious that Riley was most at home below stairs, and the portrait at Kensington Palace of 'Mrs Elliot', the King's nurse, for which we have the evidence of the Queen Anne Inventory[1] that the head only is by Riley and the rest by Closterman (i.e. *c.* 1689/91), confirms this.

This collaboration with Closterman probably began when Riley was appointed chief painter. The two artists formed a partnership and shared expenses. They also shared equally the profits of whole-lengths (at £40 each) and half-lengths (at £20 each): but for heads only (at £10 each) Closterman received only 30s. and Riley pocketed the rest.[2] It is indicative of the nature of Riley's practice at this time that Closterman did very badly from the arrangement. Typical examples of this dual control are the three half-lengths of the 'Misses Bishopp' at Parham of about 1690, in which the qualities which make Riley a portraitist of some distinction have almost evaporated.

This distinction is one of temper rather than of painting. His best male portraits have a haunting, shadowed melancholy, from which the vulgarity of Lely's style has been drained away: and his few women's portraits have a shy and gentle aspect. The Woburn 'Mr and Mrs John Howland', probably painted at the time of their marriage in 1681, illustrate both these characteristics. At Althorp is a 'Lady Spencer of Offley and her Son John', which can be dated by the sitter's diary to October/November 1683, in which this air of shyness is almost embarrassing. In men's portraits he was more successful, and the 'Elias Ashmole' 1683 (Ashmolean Museum, Oxford), 'Sir Charles Cotterell' 1687 (Cottrell-Dormer collection), or the 'Duke of Lauderdale' (Plate 86A) at Syon House, are fine examples of his power of probing character of a grave and melancholy cast. But it should be added that this melancholy may be as much mannerism as penetration, for it is found also coupled with a discordant gaiety of draperies in the full-length portraits (*c.* 1686/7) of two of the Brownlow Baronets and their wives at Belton. In his royal portraits Riley was at his least characteristic: certified examples are at Oxford (Ashmolean and Bodleian Library – some of the latter very bad) and at Althorp.

One of Riley's fellow pupils under Soest is identifiable in William Reader, son of a clergyman at Maidstone, who lived for a time in a nobleman's house in the west of England and fell upon evil days, ending them in the Charterhouse (Vertue, IV, 83). The nobleman seems to have been the Earl of Aylesford, and a number of Reader's portraits appeared in the Aylesford sale 23 July 1937. Portraits signed by him are known dated 1672 and 1680. They are extremely rustic and primitive, but the hands and drapery folds clearly betray Soest's training.

Riley's historical importance lies partly in the fact that he was the teacher of some of the most important portraitists of the next generation – Murray, Gouge, and Richardson. Through the last, who became Riley's ultimate heir, the line runs through Hudson to Reynolds.

Sir Godfrey Kneller

Riley's partner in the office of 'Principal Painter' after the Revolution was Godfrey Kneller, who assumed the whole office on Riley's death in 1691, was knighted on 3 March 1691/2 and was created a baronet 24 May 1715. This honour was conferred by George I, the least art-loving and the least British of our Sovereigns, and it raised the official painter to a position of social eminence unequalled until it was surpassed by

Queen Victoria when she conferred a peerage on Lord Leighton. There can be no doubt that Kneller was the dominant artistic figure of his age in England. His mature portrait style reflects with relentless objectivity the fashionable world under the reign of three Sovereigns with no leanings towards the arts. The downright shoddiness of much of his enormous output is a mirror of the cynicism of his age, but he had a wonderfully sharp eye for character, could draw and paint a face with admirable economy, and maintains, even in his inferior work, a certain virility and down-to-earth quality which is refreshing after the languishments of the age of Lely. He was one of the first to concentrate on the portrait as a document concerned with the likeness of a historical personality rather than as a work of art. The art historian may shake his head over him, but the historian must rate the vast series of portraits that Kneller left behind him as a most precious aid to his studies. A hundred years later a rather similar artistic personality appeared in Raeburn.

Godfrey Kneller was born in Lübeck, either in 1646 or 1649.[3] He studied under Bol in Amsterdam, perhaps about 1666, and is alleged to have come into contact with Rembrandt in his latter days. From Holland he went to Italy. In Rome he encountered Maratta[4] and Baciccia, the leading native portrait painters of their time; in Naples he is alleged to have worked with some success, and in Venice too, where Bombelli was the leading portraitist. No trace of his work has been found in Italy, and there is little to show from these Italian contacts in his first works after he settled in England in 1674. A 'Philosopher' of 1668 (Lübeck), probably painted before his Italian journey, is like the work of a pupil of Bol such as Cornelis Bisschopp, and the so-called 'Admiral Tromp' of 1675 (Antony House), which is the first known picture of his post-Italian phase, is entirely in the spirit of Bol, which remains the dominant influence in the portrait of his first English patron, 'Mr Banks' 1676 (Bastard collection, Kitley). But a change comes over his style about the time that he was introduced to Court. He first painted Monmouth's Secretary, 'Mr Vernon', in 1677 (National Portrait Gallery) in a soft smudgy style recalling Maratta rather than anything English or Dutch, and this led to his painting Monmouth himself. If the 'Duke of Monmouth' (Plate 82) at full length at Goodwood, of about 1677, is by Kneller, as is traditionally supposed, it is his first masterpiece and explains his introduction to the King and his sudden rise to popularity. But there is a curious gap in our knowledge of Kneller from 1678 to 1682. Not more than two or three portraits are known.[5] In 1683 Kneller emerges with something approaching his mature style – which is markedly different from his works of 1677 – and hardly a year passes from then until his death from which at least half a dozen signed and dated works cannot be named. There is room for a visit abroad from 1677 to 1683 (as Mr Collins Baker has suggested) – perhaps for two visits, with a return to London in between. Nothing else would so easily account for the assured quality of Kneller's style in 1683 in contrast to his rather timid beginnings, and I would accept, as a provisional hypothesis, that this was what happened, although Vertue has no knowledge of it.

By 1685 Evelyn, in his *Diary*, was calling Kneller 'the famous painter'. Wissing's death and Wright's absence in Rome in 1685 may have had something to do with it, but Kneller himself, with his keen eye to the main chance, was no doubt the chief reason. His style in 1683 – unlike that of 1677 – is based on Lely. He uses, with very slight modification, many of Lely's poses, and he adopts the same unquiet gestures: but he stiffens up the backbone of the figures in his portraits. The 'Sir Charles Cotterell' (Plate 84B) of 1683 and the 'Edmund Waller' of 1684, both at Rousham,[6] have this new, more rigid pose, and a picture such as the 'Duchess of Portsmouth' (Plate 83) of 1684, at Goodwood, although it represents one of the most languorous personalities of the age, has a military rigidity of bearing if compared with Lely's various full-lengths of the 'Duchess of Cleveland'. At times during these early years Kneller even shows something of the same sensitive penetration of character and melancholy as Riley – as in such an unusual and noble work as the 'Philip, Earl of Leicester' (Plate 84A) of 1685 at Penshurst: a sad and disappointed old man, his disquiet shown by a use of diagonals that was altogether outside Lely's canon. Kneller is an artist who can be usefully judged only by his exceptional and outstanding works, which are sufficiently numerous to make it plain that they are not happy accidents but really represent what he would have been capable of had the times been favourable to the sensitive use of his talents. One may cite as examples of these before the end of the century (all certified by signatures and dates): the 'Chinese Convert' 1687, at Kensington Palace, which he himself considered his masterpiece; 'Mrs Dunch' 1689, at Parham Park, an uncompromising study of an elderly lady; 'Anthony Leigh as "The Spanish Friar" ' 1689 (National Portrait Gallery), one of the first actor's portraits in a character part; the 'Duchess of Marlborough and Lady Fitzhardinge' (Plate 87B) 1691, at Blenheim, a most admirable study of two great ladies playing cards; 'Dr. Burnet' 1693, at The Charterhouse, friendly and grave and sober, and wholly lacking in irrelevant frills, comparable to the undated 'Mrs Richard Jennings' and 'M. de St Evremond' at Althorp; and the 'Matthew Prior' 1700 in the Combination Room at Trinity College, Cambridge. This is a gallery of something close to masterpieces judged by any standards of portraiture, and of much richer variety than could be produced from any fifteen years of Lely's activity.

Like Lely, Kneller is probably best known by certain series of portraits. Kneller's Hampton Court Beauties, dating from the years immediately after 1694, are at full length and cannot compare in voluptuousness with Lely's Windsor Beauties: his series of Admirals at Greenwich, dating from the first decade of the eighteenth century (with some companion portraits by Dahl) do not reach the same high level as Lely's Flagmen, although a picture such as the 'Sir Charles Wager' of 1710 has an energy and directness of a kind Lely never achieved: but Kneller's Kit Cat series, which has now happily found a home in the National Portrait Gallery, not only surpasses any group of portraits by Lely in historical interest, but includes some masterpieces of direct painting and incisive portraiture, which are the legitimate ancestors of Hogarth and Gainsborough and much of the best British portraiture in the eighteenth century.

The best of Kneller's later work, after 1700, is concentrated in the Kit Cat series. These forty-two portraits, all but one of the size of about 36 × 28 in. (which has become known from them as the Kit Cat size and has the advantage of showing both head and one hand), were painted between 1702 and 1717, and represent the members of the Kit

Cat Club, which has been described as the Whig Party in its social aspect. In most of these Kneller took more trouble with hands and drapery than usual, and some of the heads – such as the 'Sir Samuel Garth' (Plate 85B) – are among the most brilliant he ever painted. For variety of character, though mostly seen within the equalizing frame of the periwig, they are quite splendid and reveal in Kneller a knowledge of the human mind which one would not have guessed from the many tales of his prodigious vanity. The fatuous libertine 'Lord Mohun', the pensive, almost feminine, melancholy (which led to his suicide) of the 'Earl of Scarbrough', the superciliousness of the young 'Duke of Grafton', 'Sir John Vanbrugh's' consciousness of success, are all admirably portrayed; and in the portrait of old 'Jacob Tonson' (Plate 85A), who commissioned the whole series, Kneller took the trouble to add some subtlety of design and produce something which was a work of art as well as a portrait.

The last date on any of the Kit Cat series is 1717 and Lord Nottingham, writing in that year to his daughter,[7] says: 'Sir G. Kneller shall draw me as you propose unlesse upon viewing some of his later pictures we find what I have been told that his eyes fail him as well they may at his age'. But his eyes lasted well enough until his death on 19 October 1723, and his last portrait of 'Alexander Pope' (Viscount Harcourt), painted in the year of his death, shows little diminution of his powers.

In 1711 Kneller became first Governor of the first Academy of Painting to be set up in London, and he showed keen interest in the Academy until he was replaced as Governor in 1716 by Thornhill. In this way he helped to impose a sound studio tradition on the next generation of painters, and he set the tone which was to prevail in British portraiture for at least a generation after his death.

It may well be also that Kneller's own studio practice, which was comparable to Rigaud's in France, had a demoralizing influence on contemporary portraitists. His studio was a model factory. Kneller himself would draw the face from his sitter and transfer it to the canvas, while the rest, as often as not, was finished off by a multitude of assistants. There was a specialist for perukes, for draperies, for lace, for architectural backgrounds, for the landscape, and so on. The names of a number of Kneller's assistants are known, but few attained to independent distinction.[8]

Lesser Portrait Painters

Of the considerable number of names[9] of portraitists which are known for this period, a few were of sufficient repute or promise to deserve more than a passing reference. They may be taken alphabetically.

Johann Baptista Closterman was a personality and certainly played a fairly prominent social role. He has already been mentioned in connexion with Riley. Born at Osnabrück about 1660, he was a pupil of François de Troy at Paris in 1679 and came to London in the early 1680s. For the last years of Riley's life (up to 1691) he painted draperies, hands, and accessories for Riley and a considerable number of Rileyesque portraits survive which can be generically called Riley-Closterman. One of the best, in which Closterman's participation is documented by an early inventory, is the 'Mrs Elliot' at Kensington

Palace. He also completed the works left unfinished in Riley's studio. During the 1690s he was taken up by the Duke of Somerset and the group of 'Seven Children of the Duke of Somerset' at Syon House was one of his most important commissions. He went to Spain in 1696, just after he had completed the huge group at Blenheim of the 'Duke and Duchess of Marlborough and their children', and he had probably already, before his departure, formed a connexion with the Earl of Shaftesbury, that enlightened but eccentric patron of the arts who was looking for a pliable painter who would execute his own philosophic ideas. It is not certain whether his full-length portrait of the 'Earl of Shaftesbury' (used as an engraving to the 1723 edition of Shaftesbury's *Characteristics*) was painted before or after his travels. In Madrid, as is certified by a letter of 12 November 1698, he painted his masterpiece, the full-length of the 'Hon. Alexander Stanhope' at Chevening (Plate 88). There is evidence in this that he had at least troubled to look at Velazquez's portraits. In 1699 he was at Rome, where he painted Maratta from the life, and he was probably back in England by the end of 1702. At Belvoir is a signed 'Marquess of Granby' of 1703, but he seems to have painted less in his later years and taken more to picture-dealing. He was buried in London 24 May 1711. His later style derives wholly from Kneller and is well exemplified by the engraved 'Duke of Argyll' in the Marquess of Lothian's collection at Melbourne Hall.

By contrast Thomas Hill was a painter of some refinement. His dates are generally given as 1661 to 1734, but the date of his death (at Mitcham) may perhaps have rather been 1724. A dozen or so engravings are known after his portraits, and the few that survive[10] – several of them of his friend 'Humphrey Wanley' – are all original and refreshing in a stereotyped age. Vertue (who knew him) records that he learned drawing from Faithorne and painting, presumably about 1678/9, from Theodore Freres, so that his work does not automatically belong to the Lely, the Riley, or the Kneller style. He also seems to have been something more like an English gentleman than most contemporary portrait painters, except Tilson, whose friend he was. Hill's engraved 'Sir Henry Goodricke' of about 1695, which was in the Castle Howard sale, 18 February 1944 (49), as a Lely, is nearer to Michael Wright in colour and temper than anything else. On two separate occasions, the first perhaps soon after 1700, the second in 1720, he stayed at Melbury and painted a number of pictures for the Strangways family, including a huge group of 'Mr and Mrs Thomas Strangways and their eight Children'. The signed 'Susanna Strangways' (Plate 87A) at Melbury of about 1705 has a gentleness and refinement hardly to be found in any other portrait painter of the time.

A real gentleman painter, however, was Hugh Howard, born in Dublin 7 February 1675. As a younger son he had to earn his living and he accompanied the Earl of Pembroke in 1696 on his travels through Holland and Italy. In Rome he decided to professionalize what had before been an amateur talent and he became a favourite pupil of Maratta. He also, like Wright in Rome before him, became an art expert and in 1700 he 'brought home what the Italians call *la virtù*, and we a taste and insight in building, statuary, music, medals, and ancient history'.[11] At first this stood him in little stead and he had to practise portrait painting, first at Dublin, and later in London – a documented example, very like Closterman in style, is the 'Sir Justinian Isham' of 1710 at Lamport. But he married money in 1714 and his antiquarian knowledge recommended him to the Duke of Devonshire, who secured him the post (9 November 1714) of Keeper and Register of the Papers and Records of State, whereupon he abandoned 'the mechanical, though genteel' art of painting. On 18 June 1726 he succeeded Dartiquenave as Paymaster of the Royal Palaces, and he died, a very rich man, on 17 March 1737/8 – one of the first of the enriched 'experts'.

Edmund Lilley, who was buried at Richmond (Surrey) 25 May 1716, enjoyed considerable patronage in the reign of Queen Anne.[12] There is an engraving after a portrait of 'Queen Anne' dated 1702, another huge 'Queen Anne' signed and dated 1703 is at Blenheim, and another of 1705 was in Lord Clarendon's collection. A signed portrait of some distinction is 'Edward Tyson' at the Royal College of Physicians. The last recorded date at present on any of his pictures is 1707.

Henry Tilson was one of the most promising of the lesser portrait painters. Born in London in 1659, he was son of Henry Tilson of Rochdale, Yorks., and grandson of a Bishop of Elphin. He was at first a pupil of Lely and may then perhaps have veered into the orbit of Kneller. In 1685 he accompanied Dahl (who will be considered later) to Paris (1686) and to Italy. They spent most of their time in Rome, where Tilson is said to have made a name for himself by doing crayon copies of the Old Masters. A crayon portrait of 'Francesco Giuseppe Borri', done in Rome in 1687, is in the Hansteen collection in Oslo,[13] and a small oil portrait of 'Hon. Thomas Arundell', done in Rome in 1687 and formerly at Wardour Castle, belongs to Mr R. J. A. Arundell. These are both in the Roman rather than the British tradition. In 1689 he had returned to London with Dahl and was developing a style very similar to Dahl's, when he cut short his life by suicide about 25 November 1695. A signed portrait of 'Master William Blathwayt' 1691 at Dyrham, and a signed 'Mrs Howell' 1693, formerly at Padworth,[14] and some portraits of his own family known only by old photographs, are all that remain of his later work at present identified. But they are enough to show that he promised better than most of his contemporaries.

John Vandervaart, born at Haarlem, probably in 1653, came to England in 1674 as a painter of still-life and small landscapes with figures. From about 1685 to 1687 he painted draperies for Wissing and then set himself up as an independent portrait painter, in which he had only moderate success. Typical late works are the 'Mr and Mrs Robert Bristow' of 1713 at Squerryes Court. About 1713 he largely abandoned original work for restoring and expertise and there is an account of his later activities in Vertue, III, 32. He was buried at St Paul's, Covent Garden, 30 March 1727.

The Verelst Family

So much confusion attends the scattered published references to the several painters of the name of Verelst, that it is better to treat them all together, although the last continued his activities into the middle of the eighteenth century. Sifting a good deal of conflicting evidence,[15] I would sort them out as follows. Two sons of a painter at The

Hague (who never came to England), Peter Verelst, finally settled in England. The elder son was Harman Verelst, who became a member of The Hague Guild in 1663, worked later at Amsterdam and Paris, and went to Vienna in 1680, where he became Painter to the Emperor. When the Turks besieged Vienna in 1683, Harman came to England, and his earliest portraits in England, all dating from 1683, are found in East Anglia. In the later 1690s he probably worked a good deal in Yorkshire, and he died in London in 1702. He was a competent portrait painter in the Closterman style. His younger brother Simon, baptized at The Hague 21 September 1644, seems to have come to London as a flower painter in 1669 and is mentioned as newly arrived in Pepys' *Diary* 11 April 1669. Although he seems to have painted a certain number of portraits in the 1680s – a fairly certain example is the extremely odd 'Marquess of Lothian' in the Scottish National Portrait Gallery – he was already showing signs of insanity by 1691 and spent his latter years painting enormous roses and other aberrations proper to a flower painter. He died in 1710. Harman's son Cornelius (1667–1728/9) seems to have been a flower painter and nothing of his work is known. Harman's daughter Maria (1680–1744), known as 'Mrs Verelst', specialized in small oil miniatures, of which examples are to be seen at Welbeck and Penshurst, and also painted rather pedestrian portraits on the scale of life, of which several examples are at Mellerstain, dated 1725. The next generation is represented by what are probably two sons of Cornelius Verelst: John, who is probably 'Mr Verelst, a noted Face Painter', whose death is recorded in the *Gentleman's Magazine* under 7 March 1734, and by whom I have seen signed and dated works ranging from 1706 to 1734; and William, whose painting career begins just after John's death, in 1735, and who seems to have died *c.* 1755/6. William's work will have to be considered in passing under the painters of Conversation Pieces, but John has a smooth, unflattering style, making his figures look a little as if made of rubber, which makes him easy to recognize.

The Swedish Portrait Painters – Dahl and Hysing

Kneller's only serious rival in public patronage was the Swedish painter, Michael Dahl. Born in Stockholm on 29 November, probably in 1659, he learned the essentials of the international Baroque portrait style under Ehrenstrahl. He left Sweden for further study abroad in July 1682 and came first to London, where he seems at once to have entered into Kneller's orbit, and may even have assisted him. In 1685 Dahl and Henry Tilson, who has already been mentioned, travelled through Paris to Italy, where they remained for three years, visiting Venice and Naples, but mainly settled in Rome, where Dahl painted 'Queen Christina of Sweden' 1687 (Grimsthorpe Castle). They left Rome in November 1688 and came via Frankfurt back to London (March 1688/9), where Dahl finally decided to settle. He formed close friendships with the Swedish diplomatic personnel in London and seems to have been successful from the start in securing sufficient patronage. About 1696 he succeeded Closterman in the good graces of the Duke of Somerset and did a good deal of work at Petworth from that date until 1720. His Petworth Beauties of the later 1690s compare very favourably with Kneller's Hampton Court Beauties and may well have been planned in conscious rivalry. There is a softer, gentler, more feminine character about them than about Kneller's, and Dahl's colour at this date has a corresponding softness and tenderness. About the same date he was first patronized by Prince George of Denmark and Princess Anne, and, after the accession of Queen Anne in 1702, he painted a number of the presentation royal portraits. His Admirals at Greenwich, painted *c.* 1702/8 in a series to which Kneller also contributed, are the best index of his powers and of the difference in his outlook from Kneller's. 'Sir Cloudesley Shovell' (Plate 86B) and 'Sir James Wishart' are perhaps the best examples, and there is a genial and friendly quality about the interpretation which is distinct from Kneller's straining after more heroic or more forceful characterization. There is never any of Kneller's bravado and vulgarity about Dahl, nor was there in his private character, but it becomes increasingly difficult after about 1715 to distinguish between an ordinary Kneller and an ordinary Dahl. After Queen Anne's death in 1714 Dahl's patronage from the Court ceased, but this did not bring any corresponding loss of patrons among the nobility and gentry, the Law, and the Church. For the ten years after Kneller's death he was probably the most busily employed portraitist, but old age made him give up painting about 1740 and he died 20 October 1743, having outlived the fashion of the style to which he had kept. A 'Holy Family' at Stockholm, although certainly made up of portraits, is the only example, and a pretty one, of his style outside straight portraiture which is known to survive.

Except for changes in the fashion of dress and the fact that plain backgrounds or interiors take the place of the Lelyesque rocks and trees, Dahl's pattern and style carry on the tradition of the late seventeenth century right up to the time when the young Reynolds began to learn the craft of painting. His gentle style suited old-fashioned and conservative persons, and his one pupil of any importance, Hans Hysing, carried the style on for another decade. Hysing (Huyssing) also was born in Stockholm, where he was apprenticed to a goldsmith for three years from 1691, but he later took to painting and came to England in 1700, where he lived with Dahl until about 1725, although he was practising on his own long before that date. In the Earl of Ducie sale 17 June 1949 were eight whole-length portraits, all by the same hand, one of which was signed and dated by Hysing 1721. The postures are perhaps a little more awkward than Dahl's and Hysing never attains the faint quality of personal charm beneath the formal and conventional presentation which is to be found in Dahl's best work, but otherwise he is a faithful disciple. He died in London 1753.

The Generation after Kneller

This period is the most drab in the history of British painting. The one lively personality that it includes is Thornhill, who was predominantly a decorative painter and the successor to Verrio and Laguerre, as well as being the father-in-law of Hogarth. In portraiture the leaders were Richardson and Jervas, but neither of them deserves to give his name to the age in the same way that Lely or Kneller have done. Horace Walpole, speaking from a consciousness of the defect of the later (and, to our minds, greater) age which succeeded it, makes a penetrating statement to account sympathetically for the barren prosiness of Richardson's style. 'The good sense of the nation' he says 'is characterized in his portraits. You see, he lived in an age when neither enthusiasm nor servility were predominant.' This hits unkindly the defects of the qualities of the great age of British painting, but it finely describes the background of those painters who belonged to a younger generation than Kneller and were active at the time of his death in 1723. Vertue (III, 12) gives a convenient list of 'Living painters of Note in London' in 1723. A few of the older, such as Dahl, Vandervaart, and Parmentier, have already been mentioned in the previous chapter. It is the older members of the group, who flourished before the explosion of Hogarth in about 1730, who must be dealt with now.

Riley's Pupils: Richardson, Murray, etc.

It is a curious fact that Riley, perhaps the least prominent of the successful painters of the generation after Lely, but the only one of them who was born an Englishman, should have been the lineal father of the strongest tradition in eighteenth-century British painting. He was the teacher of Richardson, who, in turn, was the teacher of Hudson and Knapton, and Hudson was the first master of Reynolds. From Kneller only Jervas came forth, though the younger painters of this period learned much of their craft from the academy which both Kneller and Richardson were instrumental in founding in 1711, and from its successors.

Jonathan Richardson, who was born in 1665, was the oldest of this new generation. He came to independent practice rather late, having first been apprenticed to a scrivener, and he worked with Riley as his pupil for the last four years of Riley's life, about 1688 to 1691. It was in Riley's studio, by his own account, that he first happened upon the works of Milton, and the most interesting thing about Richardson is, in some ways, that he had a bent for learning and for the theory of the arts, and his published writings (dating from 1715 onwards) had a much more vivifying influence than his painting. These writings fired the young Reynolds to be something more than an 'ordinary' painter. From them we get the clue to understanding what Richardson was driving at, and to what Vertue means when he says Richardson 'studies a great manner' and describes his style as 'more sedate' than that of his contemporaries.

Richardson must have been in considerable practice before 1700, but the only portrait I can point to as in all probability his and from this time is the 'Lady Catherine Herbert and her brother Robert' at Wilton of c. 1698/1700. In this the prevailing style is that of Riley, but Kneller also counts for something. In later works – except for a few self-portraits, in which he shows a greater liveliness – the likeness to Kneller evaporates, and a more solemn and mask-like piece of prose results. Signed examples are uncommon, attributions frequently wild, and not many of the engraved portraits can at present be identified. But Walpole's judgement that 'he drew nothing well beyond the head' is unjustified. He was certainly at his best in men's portraits, and certain examples of his mature style which are more or less accessible are: 'Lord Chancellor Cowper' c. 1710(?) at Panshanger (Plate 89); the '1st Marquess of Rockingham' 1711 (St John's College, Cambridge); 'Robert, Earl of Oxford' 1712 (Christ Church, Oxford); 'Matthew Prior'

1718 (Welbeck); 'Charles, Earl of Sunderland' 1720 (Althorp); 'Lord Carmichael' 1726 (Scottish National Portrait Gallery); 'Sir Hans Sloane' 1730 (Bodleian); 'Richard Hale' (d. 1728), of whose portrait there is a replica by Richardson himself of 1733 in the Royal College of Physicians, London; 'George Vertue' (Plate 90B) 1738 (National Portrait Gallery). This last is as good a piece of solid and incisive prose as one could wish for, with a plain, British directness such as Kneller lacks: and 'Sir Hans Sloane', Richardson's noblest experiment in the grand manner, is a handsome and entirely individual work. We are on less certain grounds in estimating Richardson's female portraits. There is a signed and dated full-length of the 'Duchess of Roxburghe' 1716 at Floors Castle, and there are busts of 1720 and 1722 at Mellerstain, which have a weight and manner quite unlike the work of Jervas. Finest of all is the full-length 'Lady Mary Wortley Montagu' at Sandon.

Richardson's prices in 1718/19 were 10 guineas for a head and 20 for a half-length (double Dahl's prices), and he had raised his scale by 1730 to 20, 40, and 70 guineas. In December 1740 he publicly announced that he had given over business, but he continued his literary studies, latterly in collaboration with his son Jonathan Richardson the younger (1694–1771), who also did a little painting, but who specialized in the new study of 'connoisseurship'. In addition to his literary bent, Richardson possessed the classic collection of Old Master drawings, worthy to rival, in its separate way, with Lely's collection of paintings and drawings of the century before.

The career of Riley's other pupil of some consequence, Thomas Murray, who was reputedly of Scots extraction, is almost the exact opposite to Richardson's, whose elder he was by two years. He was born in 1663 and apparently had some training under the last of the de Critzes before entering Riley's studio. He was in independent practice at the age of nineteen, when he did full-lengths, now at Welbeck, of the Duke and Duchess of Albemarle. But this lofty patronage was followed by humbler work and he is found in 1695 and 1697 doing posthumous likenesses of benefactors for Oxford Colleges (Queen's College and St John's), and, in 1697, also doing replicas of Kneller's royal portraits for the Merchant Taylors' Hall. Unlike Richardson the best of his known work seems to have been done before 1700, and in a style very close to Riley's. A signed 'Mrs Vernon' of 1692 was in the Ratcliffe sale 28 July 1938 (20) and is one of his few identified women's portraits, for, like his master and like Richardson, he does not seem to have excelled with ladies. One of his most attractive works is the young 'Sir Edward Smyth', signed and dated 1699, in Sir Algernon Tudor-Craig's possession, and the likeness to Closterman may perhaps be accounted for by what Vertue tells us of his using other hands to paint his draperies, landscapes, etc. After 1700 he pursued a prosperous business among the clergy and the professions and in academic circles, maintaining an even level of dullness in most of his portraits but with rare and happy exceptions. Several examples are at Queen's College, Oxford, and there is a 'Sir Isaac Newton' of 1718 at Trinity, Cambridge, which is a little above his average. By astute parsimony he had accumulated a fortune reputed at £40,000 at the time of his death on 1 June 1735, so that his practice must have been large although his portraits are rather infrequently to be found to-day, at any rate with his name attached to them.

Lesser members of Riley's school, whom it will be sufficient to mention, were: Anthony Russell (*c.* 1663–1743), one of Vertue's most assiduous informants, but none of whose works have been traced – unless a monogrammed Bishop Burnet of 1691 in the Scottish National Portrait Gallery be his; and Edward Gouge, who died of hard drinking 28 August 1735. Portraits by Gouge of 'Sir Roger and Lady Hudson' were in Miss Oswald Smith's sale 13 February 1948 (2) and were of sufficient individuality to make attributions to him of other nameless portraits possible. He also painted a ' Polyphemus' and some copies after Guido and Cignani for Lord Egmont.[16]

Charles Jervas

The name of Jervas (pronounced, and often spelled, Jarvis) would have been more wholly forgotten than it is, if this astute painter, who married money, had not cultivated by his hospitality the society of men of letters. But as it crops up frequently in the correspondence (and even in the poetry) of Swift and Pope, and as the *Tatler* (4 April 1709) refers to 'the last great Painter Italy has sent us, Mr Jervase', and as Jervas painted many of the portraits of his literary friends, he is still fitfully remembered. He was born in Ireland, traditionally about 1675. For a year (probably 1694/5) he studied in London with Kneller and made copies of the Raphael cartoons at Hampton Court, which he sold to Dr George Clarke of All Souls, who financed his travel to Italy. Although recorded in Dublin in 1698, he was in Paris in 1699, where he drew a head of 'Prior' in crayons, which is now at Welbeck, and he had finally settled in Rome (presumably after travelling in North Italy) by the beginning of 1703.[17] He was back in London by the beginning of 1709 and seems to have become famous overnight. Except for a few visits to Dublin and a collecting visit to Italy in 1738/9, he remained in London until his death on 2 November 1739.

While we know Richardson best from his men's portraits, we know Jervas best from those of ladies. His patrons were at once in the highest ranks of society as well as in the literary world, and we know that, as early as November 1711, he was painting the Duke of Marlborough's daughters and Lord and Lady Strafford.[18] His women all look astonishingly alike and resemble a robin or one of the birds of the finch tribe. They languish rather more than Kneller's female sitters and often affect one hand up to their heads, and certain favourite poses (a 'shepherdess', etc.) are repeated. At his best Jervas has a pleasant soft and flowing quality to his silks and satins, which is rare in this age, and which he no doubt learned from the Van Dycks and Titians that he assiduously copied. He was appointed Principal Painter to the King 25 October 1723, in succession to Kneller, an impulsive act of George I, partly from pique at Dahl's refusal to paint a royal baby.[19] George II continued him in this office, but although his royal portraits did not please, he was much patronized at the end of his life by Sir Robert Walpole. A good and sufficient example of his work is the 'Jonathan Swift' (Plate 91B) at the National Portrait Gallery.

Just as Richardson was a dull painter for all his learning, Jervas was a dull painter for all his serious study of the Old Masters. In his sale (11 ff. March 1739/40) were life-size copies by himself after many of the most famous English Van Dycks, as well as of many of the most famous Italian pictures. Yet the light of the Italian genius, which was to transform the style of the generation of Reynolds and Wilson, seems to have shone in vain on Kneller and Jervas, perhaps because they approached the great works of the past with imperfect humility.

Painting in Scotland

Kneller's equivalent in Scotland was undoubtedly John Baptist Medina, who was knighted by the Lord High Commissioner in Scotland in 1706. He was of a Spanish family, born in Brussels about 1659 and trained there under Du Chatel, and he came to London in 1686 as a painter of history, landscape, and portraits, but only his portraits are known. He seems to have specialized in Scottish sitters and a portrait of 'George, Earl of Melville', signed on the back and giving Drury Lane as his address, is in the Scottish National Portrait Gallery. It differs in style from Kneller only in its less firm drawing and in the preference, which Medina always showed, for arrangements in dark rose and blue. About 1688/9 Medina settled in Edinburgh and did a thriving business in portraits for the rest of his life. His charges were £5 a head and £10 a half-length, and his works can be seen in abundance in most older Scottish collections. An accessible group of about thirty oval portraits, including a 'Selfportrait' 1708 (Plate 90A), which is perhaps Medina's masterpiece, is in the Surgeons' Hall at Edinburgh. These are Medina's more modest equivalents to Kneller's Kit Cat series. He died 5 October 1710 and his practice was carried on by his son, who was using his father's postures and costumes far into the eighteenth century. Medina was also the teacher of William Aikman, the most distinguished Scottish portraitist of the next generation.

If Medina corresponds to Kneller, Aikman may fairly be held to be the equivalent in Scotland of both Richardson (for his men's portraits) and Jervas for his women's portraits. Son of the laird of Cairney, where he was born 24 October 1682, he must have had some powerful bent towards painting, for he sold the family estate to travel abroad and improve his art. Examples can be seen at Penicuik House of his portraits of about 1707, when he had studied under Medina only, and of soon after his return to Edinburgh in 1712, after several years in Rome and a visit to Constantinople. There is a gain in assurance but no evidence, in the later work, of anything which only Italy could give him. As with most of the painters of this period, his 'Selfportraits' are the best, of which there is a good example at Edinburgh (Plate 91A). He painted assiduously in Scotland from 1712 until about the date of Kneller's death in 1723, when he migrated to London in search of wider fields. In London he moved in the same literary circles as Jervas, and had a fair practice among the Scots in London, but ill-health soon set in and he died 7 June 1731. With Richardson he counts as the best portraitist of the generation which followed Kneller's death, but his masks are Scottish masks and Richardson's are English, and that is the only difference between them.

The first painter of Scottish origin to have begun to break away from this deadening tradition in the direction of Hogarth is Jeremiah Davison (c. 1705?–45). He seems to have got his training in London and was given facilities for copying from the royal collection.

His main practice was in London, but he made a profitable visit to Scotland under the patronage of the Duke of Atholl. His work is still too little explored to define the limits of his gifts, which were considerable.

NOTES TO CHAPTER 8

1. Communicated to me by Mr Oliver Millar.

2. Mr Collins Baker, *Lely*, etc., II, 43, curiously misunderstands this arrangement.

3. For a discussion of the evidence see Martin Davies' *National Gallery Catalogue of the British School* (1946), s.v. Kneller.

4. Maratta painted visiting Englishmen in Rome, and these portraits, like Batoni's at a later date, may not have been without their influence in England. Important examples are the full-lengths of the 'Earl of Sunderland' and the 'Earl of Roscommon' (both of the early 1660s) at Althorp; 'Sir Thomas Isham' 1676 at Lamport; and the bust of 'Charles Fox' at Melbury and the '2nd Marquess of Tweeddale' at Yester.

5. For 1678 I can only point to a 'Duke of Monmouth' at Bowhill, 'Lord David Hay' at Yester, and the 'Marquess of Tweeddale' at Floors Castle. The 'Earl of Nottingham' in the Hanbury sale, 20 June 1947, lot 62, is engraved as 1681.

6. Both are illustrated in Collins Baker, *Lely*, etc., II, 76 and 80.

7. Pearl Finch, *History of Burley-on-the-Hill* (1901), I, 221–2.

8. Among them are: John Jacob Bakker (perhaps the 'I. Baker' of Simon's mezzotint of the 'Sir Stephen Fox' of 1701 at Melbury) who was painting draperies for Kneller in 1697 and whose name appears on feeble copies of royal portraits formerly at Melville House; the old Marcellus Laroon (1653–1701/2), father of the better-known painter of the same name, by whom there is a 'Lord Lovelace' 1689 at Wadham College, Oxford, and 'William Savery' 1690 at Plymouth; two brothers named Edward and Robert Byng whose sketch-books are in the British Museum, of whom Edward seems to have been Kneller's most trusted assistant at the time of his death, while Robert was working on his own, in a style wholly derived from Kneller, as early as 1697 and as late as 1719; James Worsdale (*c.* 1692?–1767) alleged to have been a natural son of Kneller, whose faithful copy, dated 1731, of Kneller's 'Duchess of Buckingham' is at Mulgrave Castle; in 1733 he was painting royal portraits for the Nisi Prius Court at Chester

Castle; in 1735 he had settled in Dublin, but returned to England in the 1740s and was made 'Painter to the Board of Ordnance'.

9. An alphabetical list of some of them is: Joseph Brook of Bury St Edmunds (working 1690–1724, probably died before 1728), who had a good business in Suffolk doing originals and copies; Wolfgang William Claret (d. 1706, will published in *Burl. Mag.*, XXXV, 87–8), a miniaturist as well as a painter, in England from at least 1679 and probably came from Brussels; Charles d'Agar or de Garr (born Paris 1669), son of Jacques d'Agar, later Court Painter in Denmark, he had a fashionable practice in London from at least 1705 until he committed suicide in May 1723, but his works are hard to distinguish from the general run of Kneller imitations, when they are not certified by engravings; Simon Dubois (1632–1708), a Dutchman, long resident in Rome, who was in England from 1681 and was made a denizen 8 May 1697; William Gandy (buried at Exeter at a ripe age, 14 July 1729), a Devon painter whose work is said to have given hints to the young Reynolds – see Collins Baker, *Lely*, etc., II, 56 ff.; Garrison, a painter working in the Wigan-Preston area *c.* 1713, by whom there are signed works at Balcarres; J. Hargrave, working from 1693 to 1707; Frederick Kerseboom, or Casaubon (Solingen 1632–London 1692/3), who had studied in Antwerp and Paris and spent fourteen years in Rome, two of them as pupil of Poussin – there are engravings of Poussinesque history-pieces by him done in London, and signed English portraits exist from 1683; his nephew Johann Kerseboom (d. 1708) is known by engravings as the painter of a few English portraits; Samuel King, working 1693/5; James Maubart (d. 1746), who specialized in copies of portraits of poets and groups of children enriched with sprays of honeysuckle; Garret Morphey, an Irish Catholic (d. Dublin 1715/16), who was working in Yorkshire 1686/88; Henry Peart (d. a little before 1700), who mainly copied Van Dyck and Lely; William de Ryck (1635–97), an Antwerp painter who was working in England in the 1690s; and finally the Dutchman, Willem Sonmans of Dordrecht, who came to

England in the early 1680s, and is interesting because he normally spent term time at Oxford and worked the rest of the year in London, where he died in 1708. All these painters show slight individualities of style, but all except Morphey and de Ryck were swallowed up by the prevailing Kneller fashion.

10. See a note on Hill in R. W. Goulding and C. K. Adams, *Catalogue of the Duke of Portland's Pictures* (1936), 449.

11. *Diary of the 1st Earl of Egmont* (Hist. MSS. Commission, 1920), I, 224–5.

12. There is an unexpectedly well-informed article on him in the *D.N.B.*

13. Reproduced in Jens Thiis, *En ukjent Norsk Kunstamling*, Oslo (1941), 37.

14. Darby Griffiths sale, at Padworth Place, by Winkworth, 26 ff., Sept. 1933, lot 577, illustrated as Wissing.

15. The crucial source for disentangling the Verelst family is the obituary notice of Harry Verelst, Governor of Bengal, in the *Gentleman's Magazine*, 1785, II, 920.

16. For a list of sources for Gouge see C. H. Collins Baker and M. I. Baker, *Life of the Duke of Chandos* (1949), 86 n.

17. Oxford Historical Society, *Collectanea*, II (1890), 403 ff.

18. *The Wentworth Papers*, ed. J. J. Cartwright (1883), 213 and 279.

19. Lord Egmont's Diary (see note 11), III, 275.

CHAPTER 9

MARINE PAINTING : LANDSCAPE : OTHER GENRES

Naval Painting – the van de Veldes

THE first serious infiltration of the great Dutch school of painting which had grown up throughout the seventeenth century occurred in a severely practical way. Willem van de Velde the Elder, who was born at Leyden in 1611, had been employed since the time of the first Anglo-Dutch war in 1652 as the official Dutch war artist for the various sea-fights which took place between the Dutch and English navies. He accompanied the Dutch navy into battle and made countless drawings on the spot, and he elaborated a new technique for more permanent painted records, which would not lose the spontaneity of the drawings. This was to draw in black paint (in emulation of Indian ink) on a prepared vellum-coloured ground, and these large grisailles are the main feature of his art. He also painted shipping pieces in oil (of which there are examples at Greenwich), but he was essentially an official war artist and historical precision of delineation is the prime element in his paintings. For this reason, one must suppose, his powers were desired in the service of the British navy, and in 1673, in the middle of the third Anglo-Dutch war, upon what inducement we do not know, he simply changed sides and settled in England with his son, Willem van de Velde the Younger. In 1674 father and son were given official appointments under the English Crown to take and make 'draughts of seafights', and they were provided with a studio in The Queen's House at Greenwich. The elder van de Velde never stepped out of this role as the recording artist for the navy until his death in London in 1693, but the son added many of the more peaceful graces of art to his official gifts and became the ancestor of a school of sea-painting in England.

Willem van de Velde the Younger, who was born at Leyden in 1633, no doubt learned the rudiments of art and the drawing of ships from his father, but he was also a pupil of Simon de Vlieger, an artist for whom the moods of the sea were as interesting as the details of the ships upon it, and who had more of a landsman's sense of the picturesque than old van de Velde. The younger Willem continued his pictures of naval battles and portraits of single vessels, but he also painted sea pieces, usually on a smaller scale, for the mere pleasure of the marine subject. He remains the uncontested master of tranquil marine painting, with a lovely sense of pearly tone, and the tradition which he established in England was continued unaltered in essentials, in the work of Monamy, Scott, Brooking, and many lesser names, until Turner, at the end of the eighteenth century, troubled the waters by the intrusion of romantic heroics. He died at Greenwich 6 April 1707 and can be admirably seen at the National Maritime Museum, but the formation of his style belongs to the history of Dutch rather than of English painting.

The English Imitators of van de Velde

Direct pupils of van de Velde are not known in England, but his first important imitator, Peter Monamy, born in Jersey probably about 1690 (the usual date of c. 1670 seems much too early) is called, in the Latin inscription on the engraving made from his portrait in 1731, 'Painter of Ships and Marine Prospects, second only to Van de Velde'. He too can be well studied at the National Maritime Museum and he had caught the tone of his exemplar's style very well. But his knowledge of the sea was much less than his knowledge of ships and there is a faint air of calico about much of his water. His seafights, also, were, in the main, reconstructed arrangements of earlier battles, done to order, and even his later scenes of contemporary naval actions (from about 1739 onwards) were probably not done from study at the time. His smaller pictures were made for dealers and, at the time of his death, 1 February 1748/9, he does not seem to have been in a good way of business. A lesser echo of Monamy is Robert Woodcock (c. 1691-1728), a musician of ability who took to painting copies of van de Velde in 1723, but committed suicide in 1728.

The painter, however, who earned, and not inappropriately, the title of 'the English Vandevelde' was Samuel Scott (1702?-72), who will be discussed at greater length as a painter of London views. Although he is recorded as only having once been to sea, his first phase as a painter is wholly in the van de Velde tradition, studies of men-o'-war and sailing vessels in a calm, rather loosely strung together into a pattern which shows that he had not at first mastered van de Velde's sense of design. His earliest known picture,[1] which is of this kind, is dated 1729, and another, dated 1732, is at Parham Park. In 1732, he also collaborated with George Lambert in painting views of the East Indies Settlements (in what was until recently the India Office), and joined Hogarth and others on a jovial trip, to whose illustration he contributed a marine view. But his best work of this class was commissioned by the Earl of Sandwich and Lord Anson to record the naval actions of 1745. In 'The Engagement between "The Lion" and "The Elizabeth", 1745' (Hinchingbrooke; Plate 95A – the Marquess of Bute has a closely similar picture painted for Lord Anson), which Horace Walpole called 'the best picture Scott ever painted';[2] and 'The engagement between the Blast Sloop and two Spanish Privateers, 1745' (late Sir Sidney Herbert – signed and dated 1747), Scott shows a mastery of tone and a rather dramatic sense of pattern, which differentiates him from van de Velde and reveals him as a master in his own right. After Canaletto's arrival in London in 1746 Scott seems to have turned, almost for good, to views of London or reaches of the river, which were presumably more popular and more lucrative.

The last of the marine painters of this generation, and the one with most active experience of the sea, was Charles Brooking, by whom there are several signed examples at Greenwich. His career was cut short by death, under the age of forty, in 1759, soon after the Treasurer of the Foundling Hospital had discovered his work in a dealer's shop and promised him some patronage. There is a poetry of tone and a sense of fresh breeze about his few surviving works, which show that he had the promise of becoming the best sea-painter of the century. The success, which might have been his, went to a Gascon, Dominic Serres (1722–93), who became a foundation R.A. and received most of the commissions for sea pieces.

The Landscape Tradition from Wyck to Lambert

The Dutch father of the first English landscape tradition may probably be found in Jan Wyck. His father, Thomas Wyck (c. 1616–77), was a specialist in pictures of alchymists, oriental harbours, and such exotics, who had visited England in the 1660s and painted some London views, but his main work was done in Holland, where Jan was born, presumably at Haarlem, 29 October 1652, according to the inscription on Faber's mezzo-tint of his portrait by Kneller. Jan spent most of his working life in England and was famous for his battle pieces (especially for pictures of the 'Battle of the Boyne') and for subjects with broad panoramas, in which horsemen and (sometimes) portraits were combined. He seems also occasionally to have painted sporting groups, and it was during the later 1690s that he was the teacher of John Wootton, the first artist who was to popularize the sporting picture in Britain with something like the same level of distinction and success as the portrait painter. Jan Wyck died at Mortlake 26 October 1700.[3]

A painter who worked at times in collaboration with both Wyck and van de Velde was Gerard Edema (1652–c. 1700), a versatile painter of picturesque landscapes. He had been a pupil of van Everdingen, the first artist to introduce Scandinavian scenery into Dutch painting, and he himself travelled as far afield as Norway, Newfoundland, and Surinam, but he was based on London from about 1670 and he died at Richmond in Surrey. His work is lively and decorative, with a tendency towards the bizarre and the 'picturesque', of which he was one of the earliest exponents in England. It can be seen on a vast scale at Chatsworth and in a number of little pictures at Althorp. Lesser Dutchmen who settled in London in the 1670s were Adam Colonia (1634–85), who painted the figures, and Adriaen van Diest (1655/6–1704), who painted the landscapes, in works of collaboration. Van Diest is also known as a minor portraitist and genre painter, but he had a name chiefly for the decorative landscapes which were part of the house furnishing of the time.

Apart from these more or less imaginative artists, a certain amount of landscape painting was being done at the close of the seventeenth century by the professional topographers. Leonard Knyff (1650–1721) was a masterly topographical draughtsman of bird's-eye views of gentlemen's parks, and John Stevens, who died 6 October 1722, worked at times in the same vein in painting. In addition to small decorative landscapes done for dealers, he painted a series of vast views of Hampton Court, Herefordshire, which were in the sale at the house in 1925. One of these is now in the possession of Viscount Hereford.[4]

The elder Jan Griffier (c. 1645–1718), a Dutchman who came to London about the time of the Great Fire (1666), but spent the years of the turn of the century in Holland and Germany, painted a number of topographical landscapes in a style based on

Siberechts, but his chief work was in imitation of earlier painters, and his importance lies in the fact that he was the father of two painters who were among the first decent topographical artists, with a bent for real landscape, that worked in England. The two younger Griffiers have not been fully disentangled. Their names were Robert, allegedly born in England 7 October 1688, who died about 1750, and Jan II, who was working in England in the 1730s and 1740s. A 'Regatta on the Thames' (Plate 92) in the collection of the Duke of Buccleuch is clearly signed R. Griffier and dated 1748, and suggests that the artist had not neglected to look at Canaletto (who visited London in 1746), and prospects of Windsor and London signed Jn. Griffier are at Milton Park, while views of Billingbear and Audley End, dated 1738 and 174(2?), also signed by Jan Griffier, are at Audley End. All these are enlivened by little figures, but the basic style is topographical and not that of Gaspard Poussin or stage designing, which was the alternative landscape tradition which obtained in England in the first half of the eighteenth century. Lesser exponents of the same style can be unearthed from the pages of Colonel Grant.

The rival landscape style, a more artificial one, can be best seen in the work of John Wootton, whose repute as a sporting painter has thrown into the shade his considerable contribution to the landscape tradition. It has been suggested that he was the John Wootton who was baptized at Snitterfield (Warwick) 16 September 1683, but he was probably born rather earlier, if we may believe the evidence of a drawing of 1694, in which he contributed figures to a landscape by Siberechts. In the later 1690s he was a pupil of Jan Wyck, with whom he collaborated in one or two battle pieces, and at a much later date, presumably the early 1720s, the third Duke of Beaufort (to whose great-aunt he had been page)[5] paid for him to travel to Rome. It was presumably in Rome that he fell under the spell of Gaspard Poussin and Claude, the two classic masters whose work was to become so highly appreciated by British collectors in the middle of the century, and, on his return in the 1720s, Wootton introduced Gaspardesque landscapes into the British tradition. There are good examples of such pure landscapes at Temple Newsam, but he not infrequently introduced a classic backdrop into his sporting pictures, which form the major part of his work.

Wootton will be treated more at length under Sporting Painters, but his landscape experiments are important because he became the teacher of George Lambert, and because the Gaspardesque style which he introduced was at the bottom of one aspect of Gainsborough's poetic landscape style. Direct imitations of Gaspard did not lose their popularity until the birth of the great naturalist school of British landscape painting at the close of the century, and the predominance of the Gaspardesque idea was one of the most powerful obsessions with which the naturalist school had to contend.

George Lambert, who was born in Kent in 1700 and died in 1765, has been rightly claimed by Mr Collins Baker as the painter best qualified to be called 'the father of English oil landscape'. As early as 1722 Vertue notes him as a young painter of promise who was imitating the style of Gaspard Poussin and Wootton. He was still producing very handsome 'variations on a theme of Gaspard' in the later 1740s, but it is not for such works that he most deserves to be esteemed. In 1727 his portrait by Vanderbank was done in mezzotint by Faber (no doubt partly as an advertisement) with the inscription 'Chorographiae Pictor', which is presumably meant to mean that he took portraits of actual scenes, and in 1732 he collaborated with Scott in the pictures of the East Indies Settlements (India Office).

It is about the middle of the 1730s, however, that we first begin to learn his true form in a set of pictures of 'Westcombe House, Blackheath' (Plate 96), which are now at Wilton. Tradition relates (and there is no reason to doubt it) that the figures in these are by Hogarth, and the shipping, in one of them, by Scott. We thus find Lambert ranged from the start with the progressive party, and the pictures are the first portraits of a Country House, which are not of purely topographical interest but show an eye for picturesque arrangements and involve an awareness of the idea of landscape gardening – of which William Kent was the first great master – which had such a hold over British taste in the eighteenth century. In a sense, the greatest English landscapes of the century are not the works of Lambert or Wilson or Gainsborough, but the gardens of Rousham (as they once were) and of Stourhead (as they are to-day). British landscape painting before the romantic period is founded on the same artificial principles as British landscape gardening, and it is significant that Lambert, about the time he painted the views of Westcombe House, became the chief scenery painter at Covent Garden, and the kind of picturesque artifice which was appropriate for the stage is also at the bottom of Lambert's views of gentlemen's seats. Three views of 'Chiswick Villa' (Duke of Devonshire) are dated 1742, with figures – as always with Lambert – by another hand. In these the stage convention and artificial nature are married to perfection, and the same spirit, with a vaster stage and a greater command of atmosphere, is found in the two 'Views of Copped Hall'[6] of 1756, which reveal in their skies a kinship with Richard Wilson. Lambert also painted the simple English rural scene, but in studied arrangements, which suggest a little the backdrop for the stage. These were perhaps a little more 'stock designs' than has been supposed, for the most famous of them, the big landscape dated 1757 at Foundling Hospital – which he presumably presented to that institution as one of his best works – is a repetition of a small picture of 1753.[7] But Lambert was the first native painter to apply the rules of art to the English rural scene, and, in this sense, Wilson followed him.

Canaletto and Samuel Scott

In the early 1740s the War of the Austrian Succession considerably interrupted the steady stream of British Milords and gentlemen who travelled round Europe and spent a good deal of money on the arts. British painters at home began to launch out in the 1740s into other forms of art than portraiture, hoping to catch some of the money which had been going to foreign painters, and, as the obverse to this situation, Antonio Canaletto (1697–1768), who had relied very largely on the British visitor to buy his steady output of views of Venice, decided in 1746 to visit England himself. It was clearly a case of the Mountain coming to Mahomet, and it is sufficient to remark that there is hardly a single Canaletto painting of any importance in any of the public collections of Italy.

An introduction was effected at once to the Duke of Richmond, and Canaletto began his English period with the two lovely 'Views of London from Richmond House' (Plate 94B) 1746, which are now at Goodwood. He never painted better pictures in his life. The enchantment of Venetian sunshine was still upon him, the weather when he was painting them must have been fine, and the two most sparkling views of London that have ever been achieved were produced, sprinkled with little figures as alive and full of London character as his Venetian figures had been alive with the *genius loci*. He later painted many admirable London prospects, but he never recaptured the same sparkle. His contemporaries related that he painted best what was before his eyes, and the grey British skies and masses of trees, with both of which he was unfamiliar, must have filled his horizon. He found good patrons later in Sir Hugh Smithson (later Duke of Northumberland), in the Duke of Beaufort, and the Earl of Warwick, for whom he painted their country seats. But he was never at home with the English scene, as he was, before and after, with Venice. His English views have been fully catalogued by Mrs Finberg, and all show a high level of even accomplishment.[8] There are many drawings as well as paintings among them, and Canaletto's method was to build up a repertory of drawings, from which he would later elaborate his picture in the studio. Sometimes he seems even to have painted views from other people's drawings (presumably Samuel Scott's), showing work under construction as it was before his own arrival in London. Except for a period of eight months in 1750/1, when he was back in Venice, Canaletto remained in England until 1755. When he left, the vogue had been established for London views, especially reaches of the Thames, diversified with characteristic figures. The heir to this new fashion was Samuel Scott.

Scott's beginnings have already been described in the account of the English followers of van de Velde, and there is no evidence to hand that he was known as anything but a marine painter at the time of Canaletto's arrival in London in 1746. He does, however, appear to have done some topographical studies of London in pen and wash which can be dated, on archaeological grounds, as far back as 1738. It appears to have been Canaletto who created the demand for this kind of picture, and Scott veered over to the new fashion and was in good practice by 1748.

Scott learned a good deal from Canaletto, but he was not a base imitator. His true quality, more even than with most British painters, has been obscured by the mass of feeble copies and imitations which pass under his name. He diversified his views with little figures, sometimes gay and amusing ones, but he did not seek to give them Canaletto's almost factitious sparkle. Like Canaletto he kept a repertory of drawings, from which he produced painted versions and repetitions, either with alterations only in the figures – as in two versions of identical size of 'The Building of Westminster Bridge' of which that in the Bank of England (formerly Lord Hatherton's) was being painted 1748/9, while that at Herriard Park is signed and dated 1750; or with enlargements and additions, as in the Bank of England 'Old London Bridge' 1748/9, whose composition was varied and extended in 1749 to fit as an overdoor in Longford Castle. He is at his best when he can combine, as Canaletto could not, the view of the London waterfront with the marine style of van de Velde, as in Lord Hambleden's huge 'Tower of London' 1753 (Plate 93). In all these the watery quality of the English atmosphere is rendered with a feeling very different from Canaletto's Venetian brilliance. Scott, in fact, for all his amateurishness (when compared with Canaletto), has converted a foreign fashion into a native product. At times he even achieves an unexpected grandeur and solemnity of design, as in Lady Lucas's 'An Arch of Westminster Bridge' (Plate 95B), of which another large version is at Felbrigg. In the 1750s Scott settled at Twickenham, where he painted various prospects, and he made a first visit to Bath in search of health in 1760. He finally left the London area in 1765 and, after a short stay at Ludlow, where he painted some inland views, settled at Bath until his death 12 October 1772.[9] It is unlikely that he painted much in his later years and certainly no change came over his style after the 1750s.

Amongst imitators it will be sufficient to have mentioned Francis Harding (died before 1767) who is mentioned by Vertue already in 1745 as an able imitator of Pannini and Canaletto, and W. James (exhibiting 1761–71), the sedulous ape of Scott.

Landscape in Scotland

The classical landscape tradition penetrated also to Scotland. A family, or firm, of decorative painters named Norie, whose dynasty died out only in 1845, practised the Gaspardesque mode from the middle of the eighteenth century.[10] The founder of the family was James Norie the elder, born at Knockando (Morayshire) in 1684, who died a Town Councillor of Edinburgh 11 June 1757. His son, the younger James (1711–36), and a younger son, Robert (who lived to 1766) were joined with him in business, and a number of decorative landscapes, presumably by this family, remain in some of the older houses in Edinburgh. Documented examples are four upright pictures, signed 'R. Norie 1741', in the Duke of Hamilton's apartments at Holyrood. These show a blend of Gaspard Poussin and Pannini in style, although one may be intended to represent the 'Falls of the Clyde'. As teachers of Alexander Runciman and Jacob More, in the former of whom native Scottish landscape begins, the Nories can be considered the modest founders of a tradition.

Popular Genre and Scenes from Common Life

It was a Dutchman too who first introduced paintings of what one may call popular genre into England, a field which was to be richly elaborated by Hogarth. Egbert van Heemskerk has been little noticed,[11] and he did not work for the patrons of high art. Born at Haarlem 1634/5, he can be traced in Holland until the end of the 1660s. He was trained in the tradition of painting boors and scenes from the tavern, of which Brouwer (whose works he copied) was the greatest exponent. Coming to England, probably in the 1670s, he developed as his speciality the illustration of scenes from the life of the people, in which he displays a keener eye for character and the savour of the scene than he does skill in execution. His works are realistic and rude rather than caricatures, and some of them were doubtless indecent. But Vertue tells us that, about the time that

Hogarth was beginning to form his genre style, Heemskerk's works were 'in vogue among waggish Collectors & the Lower Rank of Virtuosi'. They are, in fact, symptoms of the times. Among his more important pieces are several pictures of 'Quaker Meetings' (Hampton Court; Powys Museum, Welshpool, etc.), and a very lively 'Election in the Guildhall, Oxford' (Plate 94A), signed and dated 1687, which is now in the Oxford Town Hall. This last is not an unworthy precursor of Hogarth's scenes from common life, but it is ingenuously and shrewdly observed and not loaded with Hogarth's satirical counterpoint. Heemskerk died in London in 1704.

This tradition was carried on, at the same level of low life, by Joseph van Aken, who came to England in the second decade of the eighteenth century and died 1749. Although best known as the most employed drapery painter of the 1730s and 1740s, he painted a number of genre scenes from common life, ranging in date from about 1720 to 1740.[12] These are works produced in the studio, in which the same figure, or group of figures, reappears in different arrangements, and they are of more sociological than artistic interest. Peter Angillis (1683/5-1734), who worked in England from 1712 to 1728, specialized in genre in which piles of vegetables play a large role, but his scenes do not often have a specifically British background, although he is known to have painted Covent Garden. His affinities are with Claude Gillot in France.

Covent Garden is also the subject of several pictures by a painter of Spanish origin who married in London in 1729, Balthazar Nebot.[13] His 'View of Covent Garden' 1735 (Woburn Abbey) to some extent combines in anticipation the style of Scott's London views with figures which owe something to Hogarth, but are wholly lacking in satirical overtones. Nebot's best work deals with the London scene, but, in later life (1754 and 1762) he is also found painting views of Fountains Abbey.

Painting of Birds, Still-Life, etc.

Francis Barlow had no successors in his faithful interpretation of native bird and animal life, but a bird and beast painter named Cradock, whom Vertue and Walpole call Luke, but the burial registers Marmaduke, was buried at St Mary's Whitechapel, 24 March 1717. He had some reputation, and a picture of 'Poultry and Ducks' by him is at Knowsley. A more tangible foreigner of the same class is the Hungarian, Jakob Bogdany, who specialized in exotic fowls and did a good deal of work for William III, both in England and Holland. There is a large collection of his work at Kew Palace, and he died at Finchley in 1724. A Fleming from Antwerp, Pieter Casteels (1684-1749) seems later to have had the largest business in bird painting from the time of his coming to England in 1708 until he retired from painting to make designs for calico in 1735. He popularized the style of Hondecoeter, but without anything of the same kind of Baroque swagger in his patterns. His pleasantly composed arrangements of hens, doves, and ducks, sometimes with a peacock to give them an air, are still to be met with fairly frequently, but they are an offspring of Dutch art without anything to suggest that they were painted in England.

NOTES TO CHAPTER 9

1. Published by Mrs Finberg in *Burl. Mag.*, LXXXI (Aug. 1942), 201 ff.

2. *Walpole Society*, XVI, 49.

3. *Ibid.*, XXI, 34.

4. Reproduced in John Steegman, *The Artist and the Country House* (1949), plate 2.

5. Sir Osbert Sitwell, *Burl. Mag.*, LXXX (Apr. 1942), 88.

6. Reproduced in J. Steegman, *op. cit.*, plates 22 and 23: one of the views of 'Chiswick Villa' is plate 12, and there is a good selection of topographers' views of country-houses.

7. P. C. Manuk sale, 17 Dec. 1948, lot 76.

8. Mrs Finberg in *Walpole Society*, IX and X.

9. The best short factual account of Scott is in Mrs Finberg's article, *Burl. Mag.*, LXXXI (Aug. 1942), 201 ff.

10. *James Norie*, privately printed, Edinburgh 1890, for a Wehrschmidt-Norie marriage.

11. F. Saxl in *Journal of the Warburg and Courtauld Institutes*, VI (1943), 214 ff.; and H. S. Rogers in *Oxoniensia*, VIII and IX (1943/4), 154 ff.

12. Ralph Edwards in *Apollo*, Feb. 1936, 79 ff.

13. Colonel M. H. Grant, *The Old English Landscape Painters*, III (1947), 7.

PART FOUR

HOGARTH AND THE PRECURSORS OF THE CLASSICAL AGE

CHAPTER 10

INTRODUCTORY

THE shadow of Kneller hung over painting in Britain during the long years of Whig Government with a persistency which rivalled that of the political predominance of Sir Robert Walpole. It was not that there was no opposition to it, but that that opposition, whose focal point was Hogarth, failed to attain the authority to impose itself. The successful portrait painters, and their wealthy patrons, seem to have subscribed to Walpole's motto: *Tranquilla non movere*. It seems, therefore, at a first reading, as if the young Reynolds, when he settled in London in 1752 after returning from Italy, took the town by storm with an entirely novel style, and soon imposed his own predominance on the tomb of Kneller's reputation. Reynolds's biographers have encouraged this view and Northcote tells the amusing story[1] of John Ellis, the last survivor of Kneller's pupils, coming to see Reynolds's portrait of 'Marchi', and saying 'Ah! Reynolds, this will never answer! Why, you don't paint in the least degree in the manner of Kneller'; and finally, unable to give any good reasons for his objection, crying out in a great rage 'Shakespeare in poetry, and Kneller in painting, damme!' and immediately running from the room. But a closer examination of the tangled and little studied skein of painting from about 1729 to 1749 shows that Reynolds was not so remarkable an innovator as he has seemed. Rather, he was fortunate in coming to maturity in the opposition school, when the major battles had already been won, and when society was ripe for a change. A genial address and great pliability of disposition, gifts which had been denied to Hogarth, helped him to win and to hold his new predominance. It is the story of what happened to painting in the reign of George II which made this possible, that must be related here.

We can follow in much closer detail than heretofore what was happening in the art world of London from the Notebooks of George Vertue, which begin just about the time of the death of Kneller and end just before Reynolds is ready to step onto the scene. Amid the welter of minute facts, Vertue occasionally pauses to reflect, and he notes in 1732 that 'Art flourishes more in London now than probably it has done 50 or 60 years before'. In 1737, after speaking with approval of the style of Teniers, Watteau, 'and some of those Flemish Masters of the Scholars of Rubens', he adds, 'and indeed some painters lately here, have studied that pencilling, touching manner, with great Success and freedom of composition which is likely to carry a merit with it of a lasting duration'. In December 1738 he remarks that 'whatever advances the Art of painting has made in

England since I have taken notice of it – is neither getting nor looseing. That is, instead of Sir Godfrey Kneller, who then stood paramount, now we have several painters who draw and colour masterly.'

Such observations made at the time are very precious, but Vertue was an accumulator of the raw facts of history, and in no sense a historian. He never puts down observations, probably he never reflected, upon the larger issues which lay behind the changes which were taking place. One of the most considerable of these was that the British genius, after one of its phases of inspissated insularity, was going through one of its periodical spells of catching up with the European tradition – absorbing, while affecting to despise, it. When Fielding,[2] in his introduction to *Tom Jones* (1749) describes his general bill of fare as human nature which he will at times 'hash and ragoo ... with all the high French and Italian seasoning of affectation', he might be describing, with a dash of mockery which was already becoming old-fashioned, the spirit in which Reynolds set out for Italy in the very year the words were written. Hogarth's attitude is exactly like Fielding's: he devoured, with Gargantuan voracity, anything which France and Italy had to offer (usually through the medium of prints) but insisted that the foreign executant should be despised and only the British painter patronized. At the height of Vanloo's popularity in London, in 1741, Hogarth, doubtless in exasperation, signed his 'Portrait of a Man' at Dulwich 'W. Hogarth Anglus pinxt'.

It was no new thing for a British painter to journey to Italy. The change which occurs in the middle of the eighteenth century is a change in what the painters did when they got there. Howard had been a pupil of Maratta in the 1690s and had acquired a knowledge of *virtù*, but his portraits show no sign of Italian influence. Jervas showed equally little evidence of profiting by his Italian studies; Kent in 1714 was a pupil of Benedetto Luti, whose portraits are an inferior parallel to Kneller's; and the favourite teacher for foreigners in Rome in the 1730s was Francesco Imperiali. Young painters would eke out their money by copying Old Masters, usually perhaps of the Bolognese school, for visiting Milords, and they would absorb some knowledge of Greco-Roman sculpture, but perhaps their chief aim would be to form a profitable association with some wealthy British visitor, who would patronize them on their return. Certainly there was no systematic study of the Great Masters, and in particular of Raphael and Michelangelo, who now become the chief objects of study. A new direction to the studies, both of patron and painter, was given by the publication by the two Richardsons, in 1722, of *An Account of some of the Statues, Bas-reliefs, Drawings and Pictures in Italy*, a very creditable volume which listed judiciously what was most to be admired and the grounds for such admiration. It certainly played a great part in the growth of connoisseurship among British collectors, and it was probably as often to be seen in the hands of the young British painter in Rome. Most of the leading portraitists of the younger generation studied in Italy and their return is duly chronicled by Vertue. Pond came back to England in 1727, Knapton in 1732, Slaughter (from Paris and Flanders) about 1733, Giles Hussey in 1737, Hoare in 1738, Ramsay in 1738, Edward Penny in 1743. For the older generation the Italian journey was to some extent made up for by the various academies which were active in London from the first foundation of that of which Kneller became

Governor in 1711, where Italian painters (such as Pellegrini) and those who had studied in Italy (such as Cheron) participated. The history of the several academies is not altogether clear. Thornhill succeeded Kneller in 1716 as the Governor of the 1711 Academy, but it is doubtful if it still survived in 1720, when Vanderbank and Cheron were instrumental in founding another. This too did not last for many years, and Thornhill, in the winter of 1724/5, opened an academy in his own house. Hogarth inherited the apparatus of this at Thornhill's death in 1734 and it was reorganized on 'democratic' lines and survived until the foundation of the Royal Academy in 1768, which took over its paraphernalia. The artist in London was thus much better placed than he had ever been in the preceding century. There was, however, nowhere for him to exhibit his pictures except his own studio. The first attempt to remedy this position was made, on the initiative of Hogarth, at the newly established Foundling Hospital, to which a number of painters, during the 1740s, presented works of portraiture, history, and landscape, which were available to the inspection of inquiring visitors. The sense of a body corporate of artists thus took gradual shape during the reign of George II and blossomed out in 1760 into the Society of Artists, and was finally canonized in 1768 by the establishment of the Royal Academy.

The full marriage of the British tradition with the Italian Grand Style was not, however, fully solemnized until the time of Reynolds. It was prepared for by a series of flirtations with the French style, which was much better calculated to undermine the formality of the Augustan age. Peace with France established at once much closer communication between the two countries and the coming and going of painters and engravers from France was much greater than is usually realized. In 1720 Raoux paid a visit to London of some months, and the dying Watteau was also in London during 1719 and 1720; from May to November 1724 Antoine Pesne paid a visit from Berlin, and Mercier probably settled in London about 1725. Numerous engravers had been settled here for some years: in 1722 Vertue lists Dorigny, Baron, Dubosc, Dupuis, and Le Blond, and the traffic in prints from France was considerable. Most important of all was Gravelot, who worked in England from 1732 to 1746 and profoundly influenced both painters and engravers in the direction of elegance. Probably Hogarth himself, and certainly Highmore, show the influence of Gravelot, and Hayman and the young Gainsborough (in his figures) are saturated with Gravelot's art.

Although at the level of the Court there was a marked divergence between British and French taste, the middle classes of the two countries approximated more and more in their likes and dislikes, and the enthusiasm which greeted Samuel Richardson's *Pamela* (1740) in France initiated the period when the products of British culture, now well established at home, began to make themselves known abroad. Diderot was familiar with the work of Hogarth and Hogarth probably played a considerable part in the formation of *la peinture morale* in France, for which Diderot proclaimed such passionate affection. The 'small conversation' or 'conversation piece' was probably introduced via France by Mercier and the French pastoral was imitated in England by Nollekens. Even the recovery of some popularity for the history subject, for which there was almost no demand in 1736,[3] may in part be claimed to be due to the French engravers and the fashion for illustrated editions of standard authors which spread to England from France. One of the first of such books was Tonson's *Racine* (1723), with plates by Louis Cheron. By the beginning of the 1740s the idea of pictures illustrating literary subjects had spread to English painters, and Vanderbank's small paintings of the 'Story of Don Quixote' bear dates from 1731 to 1736. Harmer's edition of Shakespeare with Hayman's illustrations was published in 1744 and contemporary paintings by Hayman of Shakespearean subjects exist. Highmore's pictures which were made for the illustration of Richardson's *Pamela* were engraved in 1745 and Hayman was painting at about this time the decorations for Vauxhall Gardens, in some of which the invention of Gravelot is documented. Hogarth's 'novels in paint' may be mentioned here in this context, but belong to a class by themselves. Thus the reign of George II will be seen to be the formative period for British history painting which makes such a vast outcrop in the later part of the eighteenth century.

French influence also counts for much in the introduction of a painterly texture, what Vertue calls 'the pencilling, touching, manner' which is so conspicuous in Hogarth and gives life to the portraits of his slightly older contemporaries, Vanderbank, Highmore, and Dandridge, although Kneller himself was not immune from this virtue. The most conspicuous difference between the two schools of portraiture in this transitional period is between those who descend from Kneller and the contemporary French tradition, who apply their paint in such a way that it is a pleasure to look at, and those, such as Hudson, Pond, Knapton, and lesser figures, who descend from the tradition of Riley and Richardson and despise the surface graces. It is an irony that the young Reynolds should have been apprenticed to Hudson, and the difference between them which led to a friendly separation may have been in part due to Reynolds realizing that he was learning in the wrong school.

In addition to these influences from abroad certain changes were coming over society during these years and the class of patrons for portraiture was expanded to include the increasingly prosperous and educated middle classes. For the newly rich there were, and always have been, painters who would cater for their affectations, but there was a demand also during these years for a genuine and informal style which would reflect, not the formal and masklike image of the Augustan period, but the human and informal graces of men and women whose hearts were touched by the 'sensibility' reflected in Richardson's *Pamela*, and whose practical good nature found its outlet in works of philanthropy such as the establishment of the Foundling Hospital. Hogarth's 'Captain Coram' (Plate 101), painted for the Hospital, is the most splendid monument of this style and it is reflected in nearly all his portraits, as well as in those of Highmore after the early 1730s. Highmore's 'Mr Oldham and his Friends' (Tate Gallery; Plate 107), of the 1740s, shows the length to which this new informality could reach. It is reflected also in Court circles, as the result of that curious animosity which persisted throughout the Hanoverian dynasty between the King and his eldest son. Frederick, Prince of Wales (1707–51), whose virtues were more apparent in his appreciation of the arts than in other walks of life, signalized his opposition to his father by patronizing experiments in portraiture as far removed as possible from official formality. Mercier became his official painter soon after his arrival in England (from Hanover) in 1728, and painted, in 1733, the very singular 'conversation' of the Prince and his sisters (who were then hardly on speaking terms) making music in the gardens at Kew (National Portrait Gallery): and the large Du Pan group of 1746 at Windsor of the 'Princess of Wales and her Children' (Plate 111) is the first deliberately domestic royal portrait painted in England. During the reign of George II the domestic virtues gradually triumphed until they were canonized by the example of the Court under George III. The nature of the accompanying change in portraiture can be most clearly seen when we reflect that a Lely or a Kneller Duchess is usually represented as plucking a blossom of syringa or slapping her knee with a rope of pearls, while Reynolds frequently represents sitters of the same quality engaged in embroidery or the making of lace.

A brief chronological survey of the main changes in fashion, as they are reflected in Vertue's notes, combined with what seem to-day the most important painting achievements of the time, will properly precede an account of Hogarth and his contemporaries. Just before Kneller's death, in 1723, and at the outset of his notes on living artists, Vertue gives a list of the painters then in the public eye. Nearly all the portraitists have already been mentioned in the earlier chapters and the only new names are: Thomas Gibson (c. 1680–1751), a follower of Kneller, of whom nothing further need be said; John Vanderbank, and Enoch Seeman; in the same year he notes the first appearance of the young Highmore. John Smibert, who was soon to leave for the New World, is added in 1724. In 1727 Gay's *Beggar's Opera* was produced with great success, not least because it contained much covert satire on the Walpole administration: and it is significant that Hogarth first appears as a painter in 1728 in a picture taken directly from the stage performance of that work. About the same date the 'Conversation Piece', with small-scale figures, in an intimate setting, perhaps introduced by Mercier 1725/6, first becomes popular. Dandridge, Hogarth, Charles Phillips, and Gawen Hamilton are the names which are first associated with this new genre, and with the allied small-scale whole-length single figure. The scale made this a cheap form of portraiture and it is significant that those who were successful in this form turned away from it as soon as they could to the more remunerative field of life-size portraits. In 1730 Vertue mentions Vanderbank's drawings for 'Don Quixote' and his paintings on this theme date 1731–6. Jeremiah Davison puts in an appearance in 1731, Marcellus Laroon in 1732, and the same year Vertue notes that art flourishes more in London than it had for fifty years. It was in 1732 also that Hogarth's first series of moral stories in paint, 'The Harlot's Progress', appeared in engraving: the first pictures designed for mass reproduction and to appeal to all classes. Hudson, who was later to be the most prosperous of the snob portraitists, is first mentioned in 1733. In 1735 Hogarth's copyright act, immediately followed by his engravings of 'The Rake's Progress', marks a step forward in the artist's status, and the first of an invasion of foreign portraitists, drawn to England by the prosperous condition of the arts, appears in the person of the Cavaliere Rusca. His visit was short, but he returned in 1738, and, in the meantime, Soldi had arrived about 1736, Van Loo in 1737 – with prodigious success – so that Allan Ramsay, who had returned from Italy in 1738, described his London success in a letter of 1740 as 'I have put all your Vanloes and Soldis and Ruscas to flight and now play the first fiddle myself'. In 1737 Vertue first notes the prosperity of Joseph van Aken, who painted the draperies (and most, except the face) for a considerable number of portrait painters. This had reached such a pitch by 1743 that van Aken seems to have worked at least for Highmore, Hudson, Knapton, Pond, Ramsay, Dandrige, Wills, and Winstanley, and, as Vertue says, 'puts them so much on a level that it is very difficult to know one hand from another'. On his death in 1749 he seems to some extent to have been succeeded by a younger brother, and the van Aken problem makes certain questions of connoisseurship in this period extremely tricky. The incorporation of the Foundling Hospital in 1739, followed by Hogarth's presentation to the Hospital in 1740, marks the beginning of a period in which the principal painters of the newer school, led by Hogarth, sought scope for historical and religious subjects, and Highmore, Hayman, Wills, Casali (who arrived in England in 1741) presented religious works to the Hospital, while others, including Richard Wilson and the young Gainsborough, presented landscapes. In the 1740s a national school of painting had at last reached maturity, and the new tendencies were well on the way to winning the field. In 1740 Jonathan Richardson retired from the practice of painting and devoted himself to literary studies, an example which was to be followed in later years by several of those who had helped to make possible the final victory of Reynolds – Ramsay, Highmore, and Hudson. The central figure of the period is undoubtedly Hogarth, who must be treated first. The lesser figures, both older and younger, can be grouped around his achievement.

NOTES TO CHAPTER 10

1. J. Northcote, *Supplement to the Memoirs of . . . Sir Joshua Reynolds* (1815), xvii.

2. I have stolen this apt quotation from T. S. R. Boase's article in the *Journal of the Warburg and Courtauld Institutes*, x (1947), 91.

3. T. Atkinson, *A Conference between a Painter and an Engraver* (1736), quoted by T. S. R. Boase, *op. cit.* 88–9.

CHAPTER II

HOGARTH (1697–1764)

HOGARTH was far and away the most significant artist of those who were the first to owe their technical training to the academies which had been founded in London in the second decade of the eighteenth century. But he was neither a typical nor a model product of those academies, since he relied all his life on a prodigious visual memory rather than on drawing from the thing or person before him, and his first training had been under Ellis Gamble, a professional engraver of arms on silver plate. Alone of the painters of consequence of his generation (or the next) – if we except Hayman – he had been brought up in the world of engravers, and this was to affect his art in more ways than one. The overloading of ornament which was in fashion for engraved plate at this time encouraged Hogarth's naturally flamboyant fancy, and gave him a facility in its expression which could hardly have been acquired by a more academic training in drawing. It also, however, encouraged spirited improvisation rather than studied composition, and led to his overcharging some of his compositions with more figures and matter than they could reasonably bear. The London engravers, many of whom were of French origin, were in closer touch with the Continent than the painters, and it was through the brisk trade in engravings that the ideas and compositions of the great classics of painting became current outside their own country, while the same trade served for the circulation of prints of scenes from common life and of illustrations to works of history and romance. The young Hogarth seems to have devoured everything of this kind that he could get a sight of, storing in his visual memory everything from the formulas of Raphael and the vivid idiom of Callot to the lowest, but sometimes effective, awkwardness of cheap Dutch broadsides. It is this apparent faculty of having swallowed whole a popular illustrated encyclopaedia which makes Hogarth appear to-day, when scholars have painfully detected his 'borrowings', a prodigy of learning. But it is likely that his use of this vast visual repertory may rather have been to some extent subconscious. None the less, it is the stuff from which many of his pictures are formally derived.

Hogarth was a man of pugnacious and self-assertive temperament, one of the first English painters of note who could be called a 'character'. He ceaselessly publicized his activities, had no scruples about being consistent, and was something of an opportunist. His propaganda in his own favour has been sufficiently successful for him to be glibly called, in one British history of painting after another, 'the father of British painting'. It will be apparent that this is nonsense, and the false claims of the Hogarth legend have done a good deal to obscure the real claims of Hogarth the painter. In order to follow the course of his career with sympathy, it is necessary to understand the general lines of his ambition, which remained constant throughout his life. He tells us himself that it was the works of Thornhill at St Paul's and Greenwich which fired him to be a painter. Not so much, perhaps, the glamour of the works themselves as the fame and distinction which surrounded the artist who had done them – a knighthood, the position of King's Painter, and the reputation of having earned a name in history painting, the highest flight in the current hierarchy of art in European esteem. His ambition was quite simply to succeed Thornhill and become heir to all his successes, and he died a disappointed and rather embittered man because he had failed. He pursued his ends with something of the engaging *naïveté* of a (quite imaginary) African native who would eat a white missionary on the assumption that he would thus become possessed of the white man's knowledge and powers, and it never occurred to him that Thornhill's position was largely due to the aptness of the times in which he lived to support a history painter of his class, and that the times had changed. He began by marrying Thornhill's daughter (1729), and he carried on very vocally a strong nationalist line (which had played some part in Thornhill's success) and attacks on the 'Old Masters', while, all the time, pillaging the old and modern masters of half Europe for his own compositions. All these elements in his character[1] are apparent in his work.

He must also have been endowed from heaven with a gift for handling the medium of oil paint. There were two schools of painting among the portraitists of the time, the one descending from Kneller, which included the more progressive younger artists, Vanderbank, Dandridge, Highmore, Gawen Hamilton, and Hogarth, in which the actual texture of the paint surface counted for something; and the other descending from Riley, and including Richardson and, later, Hudson and Ramsay, in which a smooth texture, without 'pencilling', was favoured. But the Kneller-Vanderbank tradition was quite insufficient to account for the lovely and dainty use of paint which is found in Hogarth right at the beginning of his career. It is something nearer to Watteau or to Jean-François de Troy than to anything in England, and it remains a mystery how Hogarth can have come by it. His very first paintings, a series of repetitions of a scene taken from *The Beggar's Opera*, which was then playing to crowded houses, were done in 1728/9 and are something completely new in British painting. They would not look out of place among a collection of works by Lancret and Pater, and it is impossible to avoid the conviction that Hogarth had seen something more intimately French than the work of Mercier. With a mind of such quick visual response a single picture might have been enough.

'The Beggar's Opera' (Hever Castle; Plate 98), which shows the scene as it was presented on the stage, was so successful that Hogarth was commissioned to make three or four repetitions of it, which show slight variations. He had to invent nothing, so that the scene is not overloaded, and his visual method enabled him to present the incident with the vivacity of a moment in a real drama. It made his name as a painter of lifelike portraits on a small scale, and he soon had to turn this reputation to account, since his marriage to Jane Thornhill in 1729 forced him to earn a living seriously by portraiture, and the small-scale group or conversation piece, introduced by Mercier about 1725/6, was in its early popularity.

A good many single figures of 'conversation' size and small conversations date from 1729 to 1733 and one or two are as late as 1738, but the mode was not sufficiently remunerating for the labour involved and Hogarth abandoned it as soon as he had struck another and more profitable vein. Only one or two of the more ambitious examples need be considered, and it is worthy of remark that those which take place indoors are always more successful than those which have a landscape background. Hogarth's sympathy was always with man and cities rather than with 'nature', with which he probably had little patience, and his conversations are always better the nearer they approach to a scene on the stage. With characteristic ambition he tried, very early in the series, to paint a conversation of more participants than those of any of his rivals, and Vertue notes that 'The Wollaston Family' (Plate 97) 1730, now on loan to the Gallery at Leicester, created a considerable stir. No less than seventeen persons are arranged in the room, in two groups, which are somewhat naïvely bound together by a gentleman whose gesture has no psychological relevance but to introduce one group to the other. There is evidence of alternative arrangements of some of the figures showing through the more transparently painted afterthoughts and it is characteristic of Hogarth that, even in so ambitious and difficult a composition, he did not work it all out in a drawing first, but improvised as he went along. In 'The Assembly at Wanstead House' (Philadelphia), painted 1729 to 1731, there are no less than twenty-four figures, but the composition is a good deal less ingenious, and the figures at the back are crowded in, in something approaching desperation. It was the vivacity of the stage which inspired Hogarth and, when once he could combine the stage and a conversation piece, as in the 'Children playing *The Indian Emperor* before an audience' 1731/2 (Earl of Ilchester; Plate 99), he produced his masterpiece in this vein. The scene on the stage is itself a sort of heroic version of that which he had depicted in 'The Beggar's Opera' (Plate 98), and the sideways view of stage and spectators gave him an opportunity for a second group of equal vivacity with the first. Hogarth hardly ever later displayed the rich resource of his powers of picture-making to better advantage, and the picture must count as the first real masterpiece of small-scale figures in British painting. It is also as good as anything of the kind painted in France, and there is a tenderness in the observation of the children which had to wait for Gainsborough to rival it.

About 1731 Hogarth painted half a dozen pictures which were engraved in 1732 with the general title of 'A Harlot's Progress'. The originals perished in the fire at Fonthill in 1755, but their importance as the first of a new class of picture, with which Hogarth's name is perhaps to-day most generally associated, requires that the genesis of this new mode should be considered. Vertue, writing at the time (in 1732), not only reveals their immediate success, when he calls the series 'The most remarkable Subject of painting that captivated the Minds of most People, persons of all ranks and conditions, from the greatest Quality to the meanest', but indicates their accidental genesis. He says that Hogarth began with a single picture, without any intention of painting a series. He was then advised to make a companion to it, and then 'other thoughts increased and multiplied by his fruitful invention', so that he painted six in all. This smacks of the truth and is so true to our other knowledge of Hogarth's character that it is difficult to disbelieve. The type of picture grew out of what he was doing at the time, small-scale stage groups and conversations. The difference in 'A Harlot's Progress' is that Hogarth invented the drama himself as well as painted the scene, and it is characteristic of his mind that he should have invented the drama as he went along and not worked it out carefully in advance. In his later years, when he wrote his autobiographical notes, and in the light of his later works of the same kind, Hogarth describes in relation to this series what were no doubt his final intentions in later pictures of this class. 'I therefore turned my thoughts', he says, 'to a still more novel mode, *viz.* painting modern moral subjects, a field not broken up in any country or in any age... I wished to compose pictures on canvas, similar to representations on the stage; and farther hope that they will be tried by the same test and criticized by the same criterion ... In these compositions, those subjects which will both entertain and improve the mind, bid fair to be of the greatest utility, and must therefore be entitled to rank in the highest class.' The reasoning in the last sentence is characteristically Hogarthian and false. But Hogarth at least makes clear that these pictures must be judged as the work of a dramatic writer and a moralist, as well as the work of a painter. No doubt the triple intention overloads his canvases and obscures at times (too often) their purely artistic virtues, but the historian of art should take what he is given and seek to give an account of it, and not complain that it is not something else. By engraving this series Hogarth's art penetrated into every class of society and the engravings were immediately pirated. This provoked Hogarth to action, and his next preoccupation was to get an act passed which would ensure the copyright in the engraving of his works to the artist who had created them. This act was passed shortly before Hogarth issued his second series of moral fables, the eight pictures of 'A Rake's Progress', which were engraved in 1735 and have now found a home in the Soane Museum (London).

We have no means of telling what the painterly quality of the 'Harlot's Progress' series was like. That of the 'Rake's Progress' is extremely uneven. At times it reaches the highest degree of exquisite paint and at others it is merely perfunctory. The reason is presumably the simple one that, since the engravings were to be the lucrative element, and Hogarth neither hoped to sell (nor succeeded in selling) the original paintings at even a decent price, the paintings themselves could be skimped. This is no doubt reprehensible, but Hogarth's importance is twofold: his importance in the technical tradition of painting, and his importance in the popularization (or vulgarization) of the works of the contemporary artist. At any rate, the two Progresses deflected him for a time from his remoter goal of becoming the great history painter of the time, but the engravings of 'A Rake's Progress' brought him in enough money to enable him to work more along lines in which he was interested himself than on the lines on which he could get commissions. He had also drunk deep of the sweets of being a castigating moralist, and his mind was by nature directed towards philanthropy. It is characteristic of the man that he contrived to turn his energies in a direction which would combine the interests of a philanthropist, a moralist, and a painter.

Thornhill's death in 1734 re-awoke Hogarth's ambition to shine as a history painter, although he had so far had no experience in that branch of art beyond having possibly painted one or two figures for his father-in-law. Commissions for historical work were not forthcoming, so Hogarth devoted much of 1735 and 1736 to painting huge compositions of 'The Pool of Bethesda' and 'The Good Samaritan' for the staircase of St Bartholomew's Hospital, of which he had recently become a Governor.

The Old Masters had been generously (and judiciously) pillaged for these vast works, but Vertue reports that they were by everyone judged to be more than could have been expected from Hogarth. Their chief shortcoming is perhaps their lack of monumentality.

They have the air of compositions planned on the scale of conversation pieces and then enlarged. They did not provoke any commissions and Hogarth had to suppress again, for a time, his desire to shine as a history painter, and turn once more to popular genre for engraving – such as the 'Four Times of Day' (two at Grimsthorpe Castle, and two in the National Trust collection at Upton House). At the same time, having inherited the apparatus of the academy which Thornhill had held at his own house, Hogarth promoted a new academy, which, under more democratic management, survived until the formation of the Royal Academy and its Schools in 1768.

Hogarth now turned for a further livelihood to doing portraits on the scale of life, a task to which all British painters had to turn their hand if they were to prosper. After a few experiments with his family and friends he characteristically again appeared before the public with an ambitious portrait, which, with interested generosity, he presented to the Foundling Hospital. This was the seated full-length of 'Captain Coram' (Plate 101), that noble and benevolent man who had secured a charter for the Foundling Hospital in 1739. Coram was a friend of Hogarth's and Hogarth became one of the first Governors of the Hospital, to whom he presented the portrait in 1740. At the same time, under Hogarth's inspiration, the Foundling Hospital built up, during the first ten years of its existence, a connexion with the best artists of the day, who presented to it examples of their work, which were exhibited in rooms to which the public had certain access. In this way Hogarth contrived to set in motion the machinery which was to lead to the formation of the Royal Academy. The portrait of 'Captain Coram' is one of the great landmarks in British portraiture. It was at once the most original portrait to have been painted for at least half a century in Britain, and one of the first to be more or less on public exhibition.

Even its subject-matter was to a large extent new.[2] It is not an aristocratic portrait painted for a palace, nor even a full-length to fit in with the family series in the house of a country gentleman. It is, as it were, a 'state portrait' of a middle-class philanthropist, painted to form (as it remains) the principal ornament of a benevolent institution. It was painted with affection to keep Captain Coram's name in remembrance, and the aspect of his character which is stressed is not his birth, nor the social status to which he has climbed, but his good nature. The man himself smiles out at us from the canvas. He is no longer a type with individual features, but an individual in his own right, whose character is reflected in those features.

'Captain Coram' is not, of course, the first portrait in which these elements appear. Hogarth himself had shown the way to middle-class portraiture of this kind before, and all the more progressive artists of his generation, most of all Highmore, had been escaping gradually, from about 1730, from the tyranny of the social mask. But 'Captain Coram' is the first portrait of this class which partakes also of the nature of a 'state portrait'. Dr Antal has convincingly shown that Hogarth deliberately modelled himself on Rigaud's portrait of 'Samuel Bernard' (with which he would have been familiar from Drevet's engraving), and toned down that full Baroque presentation of a prosperous financier into something which had lost all the overtones of arrogance, while it retained to the full the feeling of dignity. Considerable resources of art were, in fact, needed to give dignity to the squat figure of the old naval captain without straying from the truth of appearances, and it is a gauge of Hogarth's powers as a creative and intellectual artist that he has married his new subject-matter to the European tradition. Old-fashioned painters and old-fashioned sitters might go on for many years in the old tradition, but the vanguard of British painters, who were to make British portraiture the most impressive in Europe in the next generation, took their lead from 'Captain Coram', and Hogarth himself never had occasion later to turn his forthright vision to such monumental purposes.

The five years from 1740 to 1745 are those during which Hogarth was most active as a portrait painter on the scale of life. Among the most typical and accessible examples are the 'Unknown Man' of 1741 at Dulwich, signed 'W. Hogarth *Anglus*', no doubt as a dig against the great temporary popularity of Vanloo in London; the 'Mrs Salter' of 1741 or 1744 in the National Gallery; and the 'Graham Children' of 1742, in the Tate Gallery. 'Mrs Salter', on its more modest scale, is worthy to rival 'Captain Coram'. This unclouded directness of apprehension of character is more remarkable in a woman's portrait than in a man's, and the sparkle of life in the face and in the mere paint as well suggest that Hogarth had refreshed his experience of France. This makes the reading of the date as 1744 the more likely; for Hogarth visited France in 1743, where he must have seen in the Salon the work of the only other great European middle-class painter of the time – Chardin. That love of the texture of paint, which is part of Chardin's means of transforming common things into symbols of an ideal world, is nowhere more apparent in Hogarth's work than in 'Mrs Salter' and in the greatest of his series of modern moral subjects, the six pictures of 'Marriage à la Mode' in the National Gallery, at which he was working from 1743 to 1745.

The 'Marriage à la Mode' series is incomparably superior to 'A Rake's Progress', and not merely because it was designed to appeal to, and to castigate, a higher level of society. The engravings probably had the same appeal to all classes of persons, but Hogarth, to judge from the loving beauty of their execution, seems to have hoped that the original paintings might in this case appeal to a collector of a superior class. And well they might. The top-heavy piling up of pictorial wisecracks, which makes the earlier series so tiring to read, has here given place, in the best of the series, to a lucid economy of order and design, no less rich in satirical counterpoint. George Barnfield has given place to Molière. 'Scene II: Early in the Morning' (Plate 102) is not only a miracle of psychology, and a brilliant exercise in the comedy of manners, it is also one of the most captivatingly lovely paintings of the English school. In Fielding's already quoted words from the 1749 introduction to *Tom Jones*, here is human nature which Hogarth has contrived to 'hash and ragoo with all the high French and Italian seasoning of affectation'.

In June of 1745 Hogarth, who had spared nothing of self-advertisement, held a sale of the various painted originals for his popular engravings. The result was a failure, and it became clear that contemporary paintings of modern moral subjects could not compete in value with quite secondary Old Masters. At the same time the building of the Foundling Hospital was completed and Hogarth turned again to his original ambition of history painting and to organizing the more progressive artists into helping to decorate the Foundling Hospital. Four large religious histories were presented to the Hospital during the next few years by their painters, Hogarth, Hayman, Highmore, and the Rev. J. Wills.

Hogarth's own contribution was 'Moses brought before Pharaoh's daughter' (1746), and this was followed by his one more-or-less public commission for a history picture, 'Paul before Felix' 1748 at Lincoln's Inn, in which the Raphael cartoons are the obvious inspiration. These do not enhance his reputation.

Profiting by the excitements of the Forty-five he also painted 'The March of the Guards towards Scotland', in which the vein of the modern moral subject was blended with political satire in a way which broke new ground in the field of the subject-matter of painting. The possession of this also fell to the Foundling Hospital as the result of an ingenious but rather unsuccessful attempt to get a good price for the picture by raffling it. A second experiment in the same genre, the fruits of an unsuccessful attempt to visit Paris in 1748, was 'O the roast beef of old England!' or 'Calais Gate' (National Gallery; Plate 103), in which the pictorial and satirical qualities are admirably fused. This also made a highly successful print but did not find an immediate purchaser. After this, however, Hogarth retired more or less from painting until he had completed his polemico-theoretical work, *The Analysis of Beauty*, which was published in 1753. It has a greater importance in the history of European art theory than in the history of British painting, and does not contribute very much to the direct understanding of Hogarth's style. It reinforces, however, the impression of Hogarth's wide and intelligent knowledge of the work of foreign artists.

When Hogarth re-emerged as an active painter, about 1754, the star of the young Reynolds was already in the ascendant, and the 'new style', to which Hogarth himself had contributed so much, had won the day. But Hogarth himself was not in the line for fashionable commissions and he was not in busy practice during the last ten years of his life. Nor was he one of those to whom old age brings a lucid wisdom, with a corresponding enhancement of the creative powers. The four pictures of his last series, 'An Election' (Soane Museum, London), painted about 1754, show a return to the overloaded narrative style of 'A Rake's Progress'; and the vast 'Triptych' which he painted in 1756 for St Mary Redcliffe, Bristol, shows no advance in monumentality over the religious compositions painted for St Bartholomew's Hospital. Even 'The Lady's Last Stake' of 1758/9 (now in the Albright Art Gallery, Buffalo), though not unworthy to compete with the 'Marriage à la Mode' series, shows no progress beyond them and must have seemed, at the time it was painted, to be an attractive survivor of the style of the 1740s. His one novel experiment, the 'Sigismunda' of 1759 (Tate Gallery; Plate 104), was undeservedly greeted with laughter and abuse. It was a perfectly serious attempt to show that an English painter could produce as good a work in the Bolognese manner as many of the old masters of that school for whose pictures British collectors were then paying enormous sums. In that aim, it must seem to unprejudiced eyes to-day, it has succeeded; it is at least as distinguished a work of art as the Furini of the same subject, whose spectacular auction price had led Hogarth to the experiment. Had Hogarth sought to sell it as an Old Master, instead of as a creation of his own fancy, it might well have been a success.

It is in certain sketches or studies, not made for the public eye, that Hogarth in his last years still reveals to us to-day that he had lost nothing of his freshness of vision – 'The Shrimp Girl' (Tate), and the wonderful 'Hogarth's Servants' at the National Gallery

(Plate 105). In the six heads in this latter picture, painted with tenderness and sympathy, without a thought of public praise or blame for the finished work, with no desire to point a moral, we can see Hogarth's natural gifts at their most unclouded. He seems to set before us a group of characters for a story as innocently charming as *The Vicar of Wakefield*. In this, and in a few portraits such as 'Captain Coram' (Plate 101), we can see how much of the Goldsmith in Hogarth was lost in his public parade of the Fielding element in his character. Private pictures of this kind are not those which make Hogarth important in the history of British painting, but they must none the less be numbered among the small company of great masterpieces of the British School.

Hogarth's place in the broader panorama of European art is probably greater than that of any other British painter, and it is hardly related to his importance within the British school. His modern moral subjects lie behind the growth in France of *la peinture morale* of which Greuze was the most fashionable exponent. Their ramifications extend towards David and Goya. But in British painting, which is our concern, Hogarth's art has always been respected, but has never been dynamic.

NOTES TO CHAPTER 11

1. By far the best account of Hogarth's artistic character, which is bound up with his private character, is in A. P. Oppé's introduction to *The Drawings of William Hogarth* (1948). The bulk of Hogarth's paintings is illustrated and catalogued in R. B. Beckett, *Hogarth* (1949). For biographical material the 1907 edition of Austin Dobson's *William Hogarth* is still the best source.

2. Dr Antal's valuable essay, 'Hogarth and his Borrowings', in *The Art Bulletin*, XXIX (1947), 36 ff., has suggested several of my remarks in this connexion.

CHAPTER 12

HOGARTH'S CONTEMPORARIES

ALTHOUGH the historian must inevitably focus his main light upon the lively personality of Hogarth, there was a group of slightly older painters, who had a more considerable fashionable practice as portraitists and who were tending, more or less independently, in the same forward direction. They would doubtless have been highly displeased at being categorized as 'Hogarth's contemporaries', and a critic of that age would have been no less surprised at the description. George Vertue, speaking in 1731 (III, 54) of the leading artists, after calling Dahl, Richardson, and Jervas 'the three foremost Old Masters', goes on to the next class of those that studied in the academy under Kneller, and he names Hogarth last in a group which includes Vanderbank, Highmore, and Dandridge, all of whom were in good practice before Hogarth started oil painting. All three belong to the group which was interested in the texture of the paint surface, and all three are candidates for the authorship of pictures which have strayed incorrectly into the lists of Hogarth's works.

John Vanderbank

Vanderbank died, from the aftermath of debauchery, 23 December 1739. He was probably the oldest of the group, although Vertue, who knew him well and thought that he had the greatest promise (though it was not fulfilled) of any painter of his time, says that he was 'not above forty-five' when he died. But he is perhaps to be identified with the John Vanderbank 'born at Paris in France: son of Arnold Vanderbank by Mary his wife' who was naturalized 11 April 1700.[1] This would make him old enough to have taken the initiative with Cheron, another Frenchman, in founding a second academy in 1720, and his certainly signed works begin, on present knowledge, the same year.[2] From 1723 one can point to signed and dated works for every year of his life. In pattern they are not often strikingly original, but they are hardly ever banal, and Vertue (III, 57) makes clear that it was Vanderbank who started, in 1732, the fashion of using a Rubens costume for portraits of ladies.[3] The faces are admirably drawn with the brush in the free, painterly style which is characteristic of Hogarth also, and which Vertue calls 'a greatness of pencilling'. His masterpiece is perhaps the 'Queen Caroline' (Plate 100) of 1736 at Goodwood, which conveys something of the indomitable personality of the then dying Queen, and is the first vivid portrait of British royalty since the Revolution of 1688. Outside of portraiture Vanderbank is at present known only by twenty small scenes illustrating *Don Quixote*,[4] which range in date from 1731 to 1736. These too are first cousins to Hogarth in their fresh, if slovenly, use of paint, and are amongst the earliest examples of painting with a literary source in England, a genre which was to have a considerable expansion during the eighteenth century.

Joseph Highmore

Highmore was, in temperament, the exact opposite to Vanderbank. He was a man of 'habitual temperance' and lived to the ripe age of eighty-eight, having been born in London 13 June 1692, and dying in retirement at Canterbury 3 March 1780, on the eve of the romantic period. He had by then long given up the practice of painting, a characteristic of those of the earlier generation who survived into the new world of Reynolds and Gainsborough. He was a man of letters and had first been trained to the Law, but he spent his leisure hours at Kneller's academy 'where he drew ten years'. His clerkship expired in 1714 and he began painting as a profession in the following year. A portrait of 1721[5] and an accomplished etching of a man in profile, dated 1723, are all that is at present identified of his work before 1728, but from 1728 onwards his career can be followed, year by year, in a series of signed and dated portraits until his retirement from practice and to Canterbury in 1762.[6]

The development of Highmore's art runs closely parallel to that of Hogarth in its formal elements, and even to some extent in its social implications. But it is entirely without a bias towards the satirical, the comic, or the moralizing. The writer of Highmore's obituary tells us that 'he had a tender, susceptible heart, always open to the distresses of his fellow creatures and always ready to relieve them', and, if we may liken Hogarth to his friend Fielding, we can best understand Highmore by considering him the parallel in painting to his friend, Samuel Richardson, whose portrait he painted and whose work he illustrated. As in Hogarth we begin to find a friendly warmth creeping into his portraits from the beginning of the 1730s, a directness in the interpretation of character. Its progress may be measured, to take examples from accessible collections, by comparing the 'John Whitehall' of 1731 at Birmingham, with the 'Mrs Perry' of 1739 at Penshurst. The small full-length of 1750 of 'Samuel Richardson' (National Portrait Gallery; Plate 108) has a genial quality which amounts almost to an introduction, and it is this geniality, which has as its complement a certain tender and almost feminine quality, which marks the difference between Highmore and Hogarth.

In the twelve paintings illustrating Richardson's *Pamela*, which are now divided between the Tate Gallery, the Fitzwilliam Museum at Cambridge, and Melbourne, and were engraved in 1745, Highmore can be seen working in a vein superficially comparable with Hogarth's in his 'Marriage à la Mode' series. But the difference of spirit and intention is considerable, much greater than the difference in quality. Highmore is illustrating, and not *telling* the story. The French daintiness of handling is common to both series, but the corresponding daintiness in feeling is Highmore's alone, although it is to be reckoned with in painters such as Hayman in their work of the middle of the 1740s. A comparison of Highmore's 'Pamela telling a Nursery Tale' (Cambridge; Plate 106) with the 'Children building Houses with Cards', engraved in 1743 as by Hayman after Gravelot's invention, shows the same spirit at work and suggests the source of the influence – Gravelot. The importance of Gravelot, who was a draughtsman and engraver rather than painter,[7] can hardly be over-estimated in this connexion. He was the prime sponsor of the rococo and

French manner, which did much to break down Augustan formality, and reached its purest English flowering in the early work of Gainsborough. Of the older generation it was Highmore who felt this influence most and corrupted it least. In Hogarth's hands it became something like a French dish attempted by an English cook.

In 1746 Highmore was one of those who presented a religious history picture (under Hogarth's stimulus) to the Foundling Hospital, and his 'Hagar and Ishmael', which harks back somewhat to the style of Lely, is the most agreeable of the series, and Highmore is recorded as having painted four or five other history pieces of the same character.

We probably do not as yet know the full gamut of Highmore's art. The writer of his obituary says that he painted more 'family pieces... than anyone of his time', but hardly any have been identified, and his single conversation piece on the scale of life at present known was only re-identified by Dr Antal[8] after it had been acquired by the Tate Gallery on its own merits as by an unknown hand. This 'Mr Oldham and his Friends' (Plate 107), probably painted in the 1740s, considerably enlarges our knowledge of Highmore's possibilities. In style it is perhaps nearer to Mercier (who will soon be discussed) than to Hogarth, but it has an English quality and informality which Mercier lacks, and it picks up a thread in the British tradition which had been lost since the time of Dobson's more heroic 'Conversations'. Here the figures seem to have stepped from the pages of Sterne rather than of Richardson. Character is conveyed as truthfully as by Hogarth, but with less rude directness, and Highmore's softer modelling allows for the play of shades and gradations, of suggestions rather than statements, which Hogarth's brusque method rejects.

Bartholomew Dandridge

Dandridge[9] was baptized 17 December 1691 and was probably working as late as 1754. In his normal portraits on the scale of life he differs little in style from Vanderbank, except that he has rather less bravura of touch, but his groups and single figures on a smaller scale are more interesting, and Dandridge must count for something in the development of the conversation piece. As with Hogarth and Highmore the series of his recognizable works begins with 1728. What is especially interesting in Vertue's account of Dandridge is the fact that he seems to have made something of an art of organizing the grouping of his conversations, making little models of the figures to enable him to study the play of light and shade. This is something quite different from Hogarth's more slap-dash method of improvisation and the difference can be clearly seen by comparing 'The Price Family' (Plate 110) of about 1728[10] (Metropolitan Museum, New York), which is pretty certainly by Dandridge, with Hogarth's Wollaston group of 1730. Dandridge has grasped the principles of Rococo style, which Hogarth never did.

The same decorative preoccupations can be seen in two later groups, 'The three Noel Girls' (formerly at Stardens) of about 1740, and 'Mr and Mrs Clayton and their Daughter' at Squerryes Court, of about 1754. It is apparent, too, and there seems to be something French about it, in the small-scale equestrian portrait of 'Frederick, Prince of Wales' 1732 in the National Portrait Gallery, and in one or two other pictures of the same category.

Minor Painters

Of the lesser fry, other than painters of conversation pieces, many names are known and many more portraits survive on which the signature of some otherwise unrecorded painter can give a moment's interest to the curious student. We know enough of the eighteenth century – as we hardly do as yet of the seventeenth – to feel sure that they need no mention in a general history. A few artists, however, deserve mention, though not always for the same reasons. The least of these is John Smibert (1688–1751?), a native of Edinburgh who had studied in Rome and was beginning to make a name for himself in London before he accompanied Bishop Berkeley to Bermuda in 1728, whence he migrated the following year to Boston and became the founder of the independent portrait tradition of New England. The best of his pre-American works is the 'Sir Francis Grant' (Lord Cullen; Plate 114A) of about 1725/6 in the Scottish National Portrait Gallery.

The two less expensive portrait painters at this time who had a good practice in copying as well as in original portraits were Enoch Seeman and Isaac Whood, both of whom carried on the style of Richardson without yielding to the blandishments of the new style. They perhaps specialized in the more old-fashioned clients, and Whood (1688–1752) had considerable connexions in antiquarian circles and was kept in employment for many years (largely on making copies) by the Duke of Bedford. Enoch Seeman (1694–1745) was a native of Danzig who came young to London and was in good employment by 1717. He was accurately categorized by the Duchess of Marlborough in a letter of 1734:[11] 'Seeman copies very well, and sometimes draws the faces like', but uncommissioned works, such as the 'Selfportrait' at Thirlestane Castle, show that he was not as uniformly pedestrian as he seems. His last major commission, 'Lady Cust and her nine Children' at Belton, of 1743/4 is specifically known to have been given to Seeman because Hogarth persisted in asking too high a price.[12] Enoch's brother Isaac Seeman, who survived until 1751, was also a portrait painter, but does not seem to have had a considerable practice.

Two much abler and more attractive painters, both probably of the generation born before 1700, are best mentioned here, as the work of both is sometimes confused with that of Hogarth. Of G. Beare no documentary reference has been found, but it is probable that he was working in the West Country. His signature is known on some ten portraits ranging in date from 1744 to 1749, two of which (both of 1747) – 'Thomas Chubb' and 'Francis Price' – are in the National Portrait Gallery. They show a friendly directness not unworthy of Hogarth, and Beare's 'Jane Coles' at Ven House, a child with a doll and a cat and a basket of fruit, is so Hogarthian in the texture of the paint as well that it has twice been exhibited as by Hogarth although plainly signed and dated 1749 by Beare. The other painter is George Knapton (1698–1778), who will be mentioned also among the painters in crayons. After seven years with Richardson and three on his own in London, he spent a further seven years in Italy from 1725 to 1732. Nothing is known of his work and little of his activities before 1736 when he became a foundation member of the newly formed Society of Dilettanti, with the official title of Painter to the Society. Between 1741 and 1749 he painted a remarkable series of portraits[13] of members of the society in a variety of fancy dress (except for the Duke of Bedford), which shows that he was in touch with the principal patrons of portraiture in the country. From at least 1737 he had a large practice in doing crayon portraits, but his work in oil is rather infrequent, though hardly ever without some originality or distinction. One of the prettiest is the engraved, but undated, 'Lucy Ebberton' at Dulwich, and typical examples of his best work are the 'Earl of Burlington' 1743 (Chatsworth), 'The Hon. John Spencer and his Son out Shooting' 1745 (Althorp; Plate 109), and the huge group of 1751 at Marlborough House of the 'Princess of Wales and her Eight Children'. In 1763 Knapton resigned his place in the Dilettanti Society and appears to have given up painting. As far as our knowledge goes he did little after the early 1750s. His latest dated work at present known is the 'Wathen Family' at Birmingham of 1755.

NOTES TO CHAPTER 12

1. Publications of the Huguenot Society, XVIII (1911), 302.

2. No. 2034 at the National Portrait Gallery, which is signed 'V.p./1712' and assigned to Vanderbank, is more probably by John Verelst.

3. For the later popularity of this mode, which was taken up by the drapery painter Van Aken (who was also employed by Vanderbank), see J. Steegmann in *The Connoisseur* (June 1936), 309 ff.

4. The paintings were in the Heldmann sale at Worton Court, Isleworth, 13 Mar. 1939. A number of quite different drawings also exist.

5. J. W. Goodison in *Burl. Mag.*, LXXII (Sept. 1938), 125.

6. The main source for Highmore's biography is the obituary notice in the *Gentleman's Magazine* (1780, pt. I), 176–9.

7. Gravelot tried his hand at painting too, but his one certain 'Conversation Piece' (see *Gazette des*

Beaux Arts, Feb. 1932), the 'Augustus Hervey saying farewell to his Wife' 1750, at Ickworth, has nothing of the elegance of Highmore or Hogarth.

8. *Burl. Mag.*, XCI (May 1949), 128 ff.

9. Our present information about Dandridge, and a preliminary list of his works, is given in C. H. Collins Baker, *Burl. Mag.*, LXXII (Mar. 1938), 132 ff.

10. The attribution and dating are Collins Baker's, *op. cit.*, but the circumstantial evidence is convincing. An additional fact is that Robert Price was born in 1717.

11. Gladys Scott Thomson, *Letters of a Grandmother* (1943), 136.

12. Lady Elizabeth Cust, *Records of the Cust Family*, Second Series (1909), 247, 250, 260, and 261.

13. All twenty-three are reproduced either in (Sir) Lionel Cust, *History of the Society of Dilettanti* (1898), or in Sir Cecil Harcourt Smith, *The Society of Dilettanti* (1932).

CHAPTER 13

CONVERSATION PIECES AND FANCY PICTURES: MERCIER AND HAYMAN

TOWARDS the close of the 1720s there came into fashion what was for England a new kind of picture, which is to-day called the 'Conversation Piece'. The essence of such pictures is that they represent a number of persons, a family or a group of friends, with a certain degree of informality and at ease among themselves, not stiffly posed for the benefit of the painter. They may be represented in their homes or in their gardens and the figures should be small in scale, generally some twelve to fifteen inches high. The eighteenth century applied the term 'a conversation' to all informal groups, whether small in scale or on the size of life, and whether the figures were portraits or productions of the painter's fancy, but to-day the term is restricted in general use to small-scale portrait groups.

The genre was not uncommon in Holland in the seventeenth century and in France in the first quarter of the eighteenth, but it acquired a special character of its own only after its introduction into England, not for reasons connected with art but because of the structure of English society. It is not an aristocratic form of portraiture, and it is no accident that it begins to appear at precisely the time when the formality of British portrait style begins to yield under the softening influence of more natural manners. When the middle classes, often with large families, began to wish to have their portraits painted, a kind of picture was inevitably evolved which was adapted to relatively small houses. For figures on this modest scale a correspondingly modest price per head could legitimately be demanded, so that economic and social considerations combined to promote the vogue of the conversation piece. On the other hand the more ambitious painters, whose early reputation had been made in this kind of small-scale group, Hogarth, Mercier, Dandridge, and Charles Philips, all found later that this genre was insufficiently remunerative and sought to graduate into portraiture on the scale of life. A few others, such as Arthur Devis, settled comfortably into a routine of steady employment in portraiture on this scale for middle-class patrons, either in groups or in single figures of corresponding size.

Among the earliest of British conversation pieces must be counted 'An English Family at Tea' (National Gallery 4500, on loan to the Victoria and Albert Museum), which is generally dated, on grounds of costume, to about 1720. This is only a step removed in style from the genre pictures of Joseph van Aken, and it would not be at all surprising if the picture turned out to be by van Aken himself. But something more modish – and the conversation piece, though rarely aristocratic, is almost invariably modish – first appears in a picture by Philip Mercier, which is dated 1725. So much confusion prevails over Mercier, especially over his beginnings,[1] that he must first be considered at some length. As he has claims to be among the founders of both the conversation piece and the fancy picture, he deserves more attention than he has received.

Philip Mercier

Philip Mercier was the son of a French Huguenot tapestry worker who had migrated to Berlin, where Philip is said to have been born in 1689. He studied in the Berlin Academy under Pesne, who gave a French bias to his art. Vertue, whose account of Mercier's earlier years is all we have to go on, writes in a language which is susceptible of several interpretations. It may be that Mercier paid a *first* visit to England about 1711, bringing with him a portrait of the infant Prince Frederick (b. 1707), but met with no success. At some time he studied in Italy and in France and he was making etchings after Watteau in 1723/4. Whether he made these in London or Paris is far from clear, but there is no serious evidence to justify the constantly repeated statement that he was Watteau's host in London in 1720. His first dated painting is a conversation piece, signed and dated 1725, in the collection of Lord Rothermere, which certainly does not look as if it had been painted in England.[2] As it descended in the family of Baron Schutz, a prominent Hanoverian figure at Court from the time of the accession of George II, and as much points to its having been painted at Hanover, we may provisionally place Mercier's effective arrival in England between 1725 and 1726 when he painted 'Viscount Tyrconnel and his Family' (Plate 115) in another conversation piece at Belton House.[3] This amusing picture is the first modish conversation piece at present traced in England. But it is exceptional in that it is almost wholly French in style, is aristocratic in intention, and includes a figure of the painter himself, who is shown drawing the others in their recreations. Mercier, however, did not need to continue to practise in this vein since, in 1728, the young Frederick, Prince of Wales, reached England from Hanover and took his old Hanoverian friend into favour. Mercier was appointed Painter to the Prince of Wales 6 February 1728/9, Page of the Bedchamber on 6 March, and Library Keeper 26 January 1729. In 1728 he painted full-lengths of the three Princesses, which were given by the Queen to Lord Grantham, and he was kept busy during the next few years with portraits of the 'Prince of Wales' (of which the best is in the National Portrait Gallery; Plate 114B), with occasional conversation pieces of the royal family such as the (perhaps maliciously intended)[4] 'Frederick, Prince of Wales and his Sisters at Concert' 1733 (National Portrait Gallery), and possibly with catering for some of the Prince's less edifying pranks. It may have been in the latter role that he finally quarrelled with his royal master about 1736/7, and was deprived of his Court appointments. But he had also established a considerable Huguenot connexion, notably with Sir Thomas Samwell of Upton,[5] and he settled down for a time as a portrait painter in Covent Garden, and to the creation of a new kind of genre, which one may call 'fancy pictures'.

Vertue, in 1737, gives, in his confusing English which shows a brave attempt to find words for something new, an account of these fancy pictures – 'pieces of some figures of conversation as big as the life: conceited plaisant Fancies and habits: mixed modes really well done – and much approved of'. Nine of these, ranging in theme from 'A Venetian Girl at a Window' to 'A Recruiting Officer' were engraved by the younger Faber in 1739. Hogarth's pioneer work no doubt counts for something in these, and they were probably designed to make money by the engraving rather than as paintings, but the subjects are intended only to please and have no moral or satirical connotation, and they are quite literally works of fancy.

By 1740 (when he signed and dated the huge conversation piece at Thorpe Hall) Mercier had retired to Yorkshire, where he had a good practice for some years in portraits on the scale of life, often full-lengths. Good examples, of 1741 and 1742, are in the York Gallery, at Temple Newsam and at Burton Agnes. He also travelled further afield. He may have been in Scotland in 1745: in 1747 Vertue mentions a brief visit to London to sell pictures of 'The Five Senses' as well as a short visit to Ireland: in 1750 his presence in Edinburgh is attested by a receipt at Wemyss Castle.

In 1751 Mercier returned to London, and his latest dated portrait that I have seen (of 1752) shows that he was master of the new style. But the competition of the rising generation was too much for him, and he all but settled in Portugal in 1752. His later years in London were largely occupied in producing fancy pieces for the engravers, of which Houston scraped a good number 1756/8. Few of the originals are in accessible collections, and some are very feeble, but the 'Girl with Kitten' at Edinburgh (engraved 1756) suffices to show how strong a French tincture his art retained to the last.

Mercier was hardly a genius, but his pictures have passed under the names of Hogarth and Watteau, and he was a restless and mobile personality of a decided artistic character. That character was markedly French and his most original productions were widely diffused in popular engravings. He deserves closer study than he has received as a constant, if unspectacular, French influence in the formation of the British style. He and Gravelot both count for something in Hayman. The style of his fancy pictures was taken up by Henry Morland: and it was later carried on by Gainsborough, under whose name at least one of Mercier's pictures has constantly passed.

Old Nollekens and Young Laroon

Two minor figures deserve passing mention, who worked in something of the same tradition as Mercier. Joseph Francis Nollekens (1702–48), the father of the well-known sculptor, was a native of Antwerp, who is stated to have been a pupil of both Watteau and Pannini. He came to London in 1733, where he worked at first for Tillemans, but later built up for himself a fairly good independent practice in small fancy pictures and galant genre in decidedly distant imitation of Watteau and Pater. His best patron was Earl Tilney, and the list of his works in the sale of Lord Tilney's heirs at Wanstead House in 1822[6] provides the best catalogue of the kind of fancy subject, with figures on a small scale, which was popular in the 1730s and 1740s. A genuine conversation piece (said to be from Wanstead) at Northwick Park, if correctly ascribed to Nollekens, suggests that he was capable of better things than the usual run of his imitations of Pater.

The younger Marcellus Laroon (1679–1774), whose father has been noticed as a follower of Kneller, amid the diversions of a busy and hectic life, which included the stage, the army, and a good deal of general roistering, produced a number of paintings (and more drawings) of the same character, mainly during the 1730s and 1740s. One or two portraits by him are known, but most of his paintings are works of fancy, sometimes pastoral, sometimes of low life, and sometimes inspired by the stage. His 'conversation pieces', of which the Duke of Buccleuch's 'Musical Party' (Plate 112B) is one of the best examples, appear also to be works of imagination. But all his pictures are original in technique and lively in drawing. Many have the appearance of stained drawings, and all have a suggestion of tapestry rather than of oil paint about them. They are also curiously un-English and may owe something to his stay in Venice.

A third foreign practitioner of the conversation piece was the Swiss Barthélemy Du Pan (1712–63), who was in England from 1743 and returned to Switzerland about 1751 (after a visit to Dublin). When Mercier had fallen into disfavour with Frederick, Prince of Wales, Du Pan, in 1746, painted the large group of 'The Children of the Prince of Wales' (Plate 111) at Windsor, which carried on the same tradition as Mercier, and set a new fashion in the treatment of portraits of royal children, which was to lead on to Zoffany and Copley.

Arthur Devis and his Forerunners

The conversation piece, and the single portrait on the same small scale, found their first contented specialist in that comfortable painter, Arthur Devis. But Devis was in no sense a pioneer. His limited vogue, 'limited' in the sense that his patrons were mainly drawn from the rising middle classes, was led up to by certain minor predecessors, in addition to Hogarth and Dandridge. In the early 1730s, when the conversation piece first became fashionable and before it had acquired its middle-class flavour, it was Charles Philips (1708–47) who was popular in the highest circles rather than his abler contemporaries. His vogue with the aristocracy lasted during the years 1732 to 1734, in which he painted groups of doll-like families, usually in an elaborately wainscoted interior, for the Earls of Albemarle, Fitzwilliam, Northampton, and Portland, and doubtless for many more. By 1736 the aristocracy no longer favoured this kind of group and Philips had graduated to portraiture on the scale of life, in which he was merely an inferior Mercier. During this same period also, Gawen Hamilton[7] (1698–1737) was considered by Vertue to be, in some ways, superior to Hogarth, and his portrait group of 'An Artists' Club in London 1735' (National Portrait Gallery; Plate 112A)[8] shows more vividly than any other picture the worldly condition of the more successful and conservative artists of the time. Both Philips and Hamilton painted, alongside their groups, single figures at full length on the same scale, a diminutive kind of portrait which gained increasing popularity with the growing number of persons who lived in rooms which were neat but not spacious. Other painters, too, occasionally strayed into the conversation genre, such as Peter Tillemans (d. 1734), the sporting and topographical artist, who was Devis's first teacher and painted the children of his best patron, Dr Cox Macro; and Willem Verelst, whose 'Family of Mr Harry Gough' 1741 (Elvetham Hall) makes one hope that other conversations from his hand will be discovered. But Arthur Devis was the first painter who found in portraiture on this scale a means of making a constant livelihood throughout pretty well the whole of his career.

Arthur Devis (1711–87)[9] was born at Preston and was the son of a man who became a

Town Councillor there. He thus sprang from the kind of level of society which was to find most satisfaction in his work. He appears to-day as a rather refreshing figure in a sequence of painting which is dominated at one end by Augustan formality and at the other by the high rhetoric of Reynolds. He is a 'discovery' of the twentieth century (even of the 1930s) and his fascination for the social historian has led him to be a good deal over-rated in recent writing on English painting. He was a very minor figure in his own day and had no influence on the future, but he was prominent among the successful group of painters who were not 'out of the top drawer', as may be inferred from his becoming President of the Free Society of Artists in 1768, just as all the more forward painters were going over to the newly mooted Royal Academy. A letter of 1764/5 from Lord John Cavendish to his sister (Welbeck MSS.) shows vividly what the aristocratic patrons thought of his powers. The 4th Duke of Devonshire had offered his picture to his old tutor and had left the choice of a painter to him, and the tutor 'desired it may be painted by one Mr Devis of Queen Street, because he makes all his pictures of a size, which suits his rooms better than those of other painters: I am much afraid it will be frightful, for I understand, his pictures are all of a sort: they are whole lengths of about two feet long; and the person is all ways represented in a genteel attitude, either leaning against a pillar, or standing by a flowerpot, or leading an Italian greyhound in a string, or in some other such ingenious posture.' The Duke was prepared to submit, but would not pass any criticism on the picture in order not to be held responsible for any absurdity which might result. And a contemporary pamphlet on the Exhibition of 1762 (*An Historical and Critical Review*) remarks of one of Devis's portraits (No. 65) 'Dog like a pig. Leather breeches the principal object.' After this warning contemporary note, we can allow ourselves with a clear conscience to yield to the undoubted charm with which the kindly passage of two centuries has invested Devis's works. The world they picture is so secure.

Devis is reported to have first studied under Peter Tillemans (d. 1734), who was a master of panoramic landscape, as can be seen in his numerous views of Newmarket Heath. It may well be that he began with the intention of becoming a landscape painter, as his younger brother, Anthony Devis (1729–1816), an altogether minor person, remained for the whole of his long life. His first known work is an imitation of Pannini, dated 1736; but by 1742, when he was already settled in London, he was an accomplished painter of conversations and small portraits. Dated works of this character range from 1742 to 1764. By that date he was eclipsed in his speciality by Zoffany, and so spent his later years experimenting with painting on glass and acting as a restorer. During the twenty years of his heyday his style scarcely alters, and very nearly the whole man can be read in a single example of each of his two characteristic types of picture. 'The James Family' 1751 (Tate Gallery) is an excellent specimen of his conversations. The setting is a spreading parkland, with the suggestion of a distant village, and one has the impression, common to all his outdoor scenes, that it is always afternoon. This spreading park, in which the tradition of Tillemans still lingers, is inhabited by its proprietor and his family. A certain sense of ownership of all that the eye surveys, of his park, his wife, and his children, is one of the elements which no doubt helped to make Devis's works popular with the gentlemen who paid for them. In accordance with this intention the various individuals and objects (chairs, vases, and distant pavilions) are itemized, as if in an inventory, and given an allotted portion of space to themselves. The figures do not in fact 'converse', but present themselves, however formally linked by hand or gesture, in turn, in a sort of timid isolation, which has an air of charming *naïveté*. And a feeling for colour, at once tender and gay, takes away what might otherwise seem an excessive display of interest in 'property'. This effect is too constant in Devis for it to have been unconscious, and we must count him as a master of middle-class social overtones. Just as the English middle classes had no parallel in Europe at this time, Devis too had no parallel among contemporary European painters, and his wood notes are among the most purely native in English painting.

In his single figures he is rather less at ease. He is too fond of the ingenious and genteel postures which roused the misgivings of the Duke of Devonshire. A particularly engaging example, full of character in spite of its genteel absurdity, is the 'Unknown Young Man' (Plate 117) of 1761 at Manchester. He stands by a reading-desk and seems to have been surprised while practising to an invisible audience his powers as an orator. It is pictures like this which give Devis something of the charm of a minor novelist, and, however slender his claims to distinction may be rated by the historian of art, he will always rank high in the affections of the historian of manners. It should be added that his name is often, at present, used in vain for a mass of less competent work by contemporaries who are still unidentified. None of them comes near to the quiet peace of Devis's settings or to his nice appreciation of social values.

Francis Hayman

Hayman is historically the most important of this group of painters: he is also the most versatile. It has been pointed out by Mr T. S. R. Boase[10] that he was 'the meeting-place of two schools, the continental and the English', but he was the meeting-place also of much more than that. His career touches at some point all the various traditions which went to make up the medley of English painting and draughtsmanship in the middle of the eighteenth century, and he had a large finger in every artistic pie of the time.

Born at Exeter in 1708, he survived until 1776. He was first employed as scene painter at Drury Lane and became a master in the field of popular subjects which he was one of the first to use for easel pictures. When he first swims into our ken as an artist, in 1741, it is as a ceiling painter, presumably in histories (though no works of this kind are known to survive) – and this no doubt partly accounts for Edwards's statement, which would otherwise seem surprising, that he 'was unquestionably the best historical painter in the kingdom, before the arrival of Cipriani'.[11] By 1744 he was busy in several roles. He collaborated with Gravelot in the designs and engraving for Hanmer's *Shakespeare*, which appeared that year: he had started work for Jonathan Tyers on large paintings for the pavilions and boxes at Vauxhall Gardens:[12] and he was one of the most active promoters, again with Gravelot (and with James Wills), of the academy in St Martin's Lane. He was as much a part of the engraving world as Hogarth was, and his familiarity with 'histories' can be gauged from the fact that he was employed for the engravings to Congreve,

Milton, Pope, Don Quixote, and for Dodsley's portraits, and he was still doing new engravings for Shakespeare as late as the 1770s – and this leaves out of account an un-catalogued number of occasional frontispieces. He was one of those who presented, in 1746, a history picture 'The Finding of Moses' to the Foundling Hospital. He was active in the negotiations which led to the formation of the Society of Artists in 1760 and he was President of the Society from 1766 until 1768 when he seceded to the new Royal Academy, of which he became a founder member and, in 1771, Librarian. His closest links are with the two leading figures of the older generation, the very British Hogarth and the very French Gravelot, and with one of the most original native geniuses of the younger genera-tion, Gainsborough, who pretty certainly worked with him and Gravelot in the later 1740s. He is, as it were, the funnel through which the traditions of stage decoration, of Hogarth, and of Gravelot pass and mingle, to emerge refined in the early style of Gains-borough. During the later 1740s, while Hogarth was in semi-retirement, Hayman bore his mantle, and his output during his most active decade (1745–55) includes religious histories, painted illustrations to Shakespeare, scenes from the stage, fancy pictures, some of the earliest unaffected scenes from the common life of the people, sporting pictures, conversation pieces, as well as portraits on the scale of the conversation piece and on the scale of life. No other painter of his day could show such variety.

There is a reverse side to this rather glowing picture; the important figures in the history of art need not all be great painters, and Hayman is one of those who were not great. Horace Walpole, who was too much alive to his defects, says unkindly that he was 'a strong mannerist, and easily distinguishable by the large noses and shambling legs of his figures', and we may guess that Walpole was thinking of the conversation piece of his own father, 'Sir Robert Walpole in the Painter's Studio' (National Portrait Gallery; Plate 120B), in which these defects are more than usually to be discerned.

This picture, which cannot be later than 1745, may serve as a standard for Hayman's style, although his more pleasing conversations normally take place in the open air. It is at the opposite pole from the conversations of Devis. The figures are much larger in scale and they are linked together in what may legitimately be called 'conversation'. In none of Hayman's groups are there any overtones of pride of possession in family or land. The features of Hayman himself also deserve attention, for we can understand what Walpole means by calling Hayman a 'strong mannerist', when we rediscover this rather plebeian, or equine, face leering at us as the Princess in the 'Finding of Moses' or frowning at us as Hamlet in the pictures from Vauxhall Gardens. Even in a fancy picture such as Mrs Christie-Miller's 'Girl at a Spinning Wheel', or in scenes of low comedy such as the 'Lecherous Friar' (Musée Magnin, Dijon – as Hogarth), it is the same smug face, and Hayman is one of the most easily recognized of painters.

But Hayman's importance is independent of these defects, and so is the charm of a number of his works. It is no mean achievement to have painted one of the earliest scenes from Shakespeare,[13] 'The Wrestling Scene from *As You Like It*' (Plate 119), which presum-ably dates from about 1744, when Hanmer's *Shakespeare* was published; and it is evidence of the fertility of Hayman's invention that, although he had designed an engraving of the same scene, the painting is altogether different from the engraving. It is a genuine illustration, and not imitated from the stage scene, although the style of stage scenery is clearly involved, especially in the light key of colour. We may suppose that the four Shakespearian scenes which Hayman painted for the Prince of Wales's pavilion at Vauxhall, probably in 1744/45, were of the same character.

Hayman's work at Vauxhall,[14] for which he painted a variety of large pictures from about 1744 to 1760, must have been more constantly before the public eye than any other painting of the time in London. It blended the tradition of stage scenery with the 'historical' style, and ranged in theme from the pure pastoral to subjects from the story of the Seven Years' War, with contemporary portraits. The most interesting pictures were canvases, measuring about five by eight feet, which adorned the alcoves which studded the various walks. A few were of scenes from Shakespeare or from contemporary novels, but most were simple pictures of rustic games or folklore scenes. Two of these, 'Sliding on the Ice' and 'The Dance of the Milkmaids on Mayday' (Plate 118), were acquired by the Victoria and Albert Museum in 1948. They are something new in theme for British painting, just as the commission for them was something new in British patronage, and they mark the beginning of a tradition which reached its height in Wilkie and continued vigorously through the nineteenth century. They are a sort of London equivalent, on a popular and rustic level, of what Boucher was doing in France. The difference is that they are studied from common life, and the ornamental element 'with the high French seasoning' is superadded upon something which is quite down to earth. Exactly the same character belongs to Gainsborough's Ipswich pastorals of the middle 1750s. But it is Hayman who must count as the creator of this specifically British form of a continental genre.

The style of Hayman's landscape backgrounds is sometimes so curiously similar to early Gainsborough that we may be permitted to wonder whether Gainsborough did not in fact sometimes paint them for him in the later 1740s. We know that his backgrounds were often by other hands,[15] and there can be no doubt in my mind, in spite of much argument against the thesis by Mr Whitley, that Hayman in his early Vauxhall period was the formative influence on the young Gainsborough.

After 1755 Hayman would seem to have done rather little painting, and that mainly of large historical or religious subjects. Perhaps mercifully for his reputation, none of these are known to-day.

Bare mention should also be made of the Rev. James Wills, an agreeable minor painter in Hayman's orbit in the 1740s. He has been mentioned as active, with Hayman and Gravelot, in running the St Martin's Lane Academy in 1745, and his 'Little Children brought to Christ' 1746, was the fourth of the large religious works presented to the Foundling Hospital by their painters – the other artists being Hogarth, Highmore, and Hayman. It is perhaps more religious in feeling than the others and it is very close, in places, to Hayman's figure style. A conversation piece of the 'Andrews Family' 1749 (Fitzwilliam Museum, Cambridge; Plate 120A) is also close to Hayman, but more loosely constructed and less 'conversational'. But Wills did not prosper as a painter and he joined the Church, dying Vicar of Cannons in 1777.

NOTES TO CHAPTER 13

1. The traditional account of Mercier and his relation to Watteau, which I believe to be altogether unfounded, is given in E. Dacier and A. Vuaflart, *Jean de Jullienne et les graveurs de Watteau au XVIIIe siècle*, I (1929), 100 ff.; and R. Rey, *Quelques Satellites de Watteau*, Paris (1931). See also P. Wescher in *The Art Quarterly*, xiv (1951), 179 ff.

2. Reproduced in the *Catalogue of the Arts Council Exhibition of English Conversation Pieces of the Eighteenth Century*, 1946, exhibit 6. The picture, which was in the J. Pierpont Morgan sale, 31 March 1944, has wrongly been called 'A party on the terrace of Shotover House', which it in no way resembles. It does, however, come from Shotover House, where it had descended from the Schutz family, and is first recorded in the sale at the house by Farebrother, Clark, and Lye, 26 Oct. 1855, lot 663.

3. It is signed but not dated, but must have been painted between Lord Tyrconnel's being made K.B. in 1725 and the death of William Brownlow in 1726 (see Lady Elizabeth Cust, *Records of the Cust Family*, Second Series 1909, 191–2).

4. Ralph Edwards in *Burl. Mag.*, xc (Nov. 1948), 308 ff.

5. For a list of the Merciers at Upton see Baker's *History of Northamptonshire* (1822/30), I, 226. The most remarkable was a large convivial group mentioned in Dallaway's notes to Walpole (ed. Wornum, II, 319 note 1): this reappeared at Christie's, as 'English school', 17 March 1939, lot 88. See *Journal of Warburg and Courtauld Institutes*, xv (1952).

6. The list is accessibly published in J. T. Smith's *Nollekens and his times* (1920 edn, ed. W. Whitten), II, 41 note.

7. Mrs Finberg in *Walpole Society*, vi, 51 ff.

8. The painters who appear in the group are Dahl, Hysing, Hamilton himself, Wootton, Kent, and Goupy, and there are the engravers George Vertue and Baron, Rysbrack the sculptor, and Gibbs the architect.

9. Sydney H. Pavière, 'The Devis Family of Painters' in *Walpole Society*, xxv, 115 ff. This has been expanded in Mr Pavière's monograph on Arthur Devis, 1950.

10. *Journal of the Warburg and Courtauld Institutes*, x (1947), 91.

11. E. Edwards, *Anecdotes of Painters...* (1808), 51.

12. For what is known of the Vauxhall paintings see Prof. L. Gowing's forthcoming study in the *Burlington Magazine*.

13. Anonymous sales, 19 Nov. 1948, lot 131, and 28 July 1950, lot 173, in both cases as by de Troy. The only earlier Shakespearian pictures are two of Hogarth's less characteristic paintings of c. 1730.

14. A description of Vauxhall in 1760, with a list of the paintings, is conveniently reprinted in Leslie and Taylor's *Life and Times of Sir Joshua Reynolds* (1865), I, 327 ff. Prof. Gowing has made a full study of the Vauxhall paintings which will appear in the *Burlington Magazine*.

15. W. T. Whitley, *Artists and their Friends in England 1700–99*, I, 219.

CHAPTER 14

FASHIONABLE PORTRAITURE TO HUDSON AND RAMSAY

In December 1737 there arrived in London the Frenchman Jean-Baptiste Vanloo (1684–1745), who had already had a certain vogue in Turin and in Paris. He arrived at a very opportune moment, when Richardson and Dahl were in their decline and before the emergence of a new generation of fashionable face painters. After a few months, says Vertue, 'a most surprising number of people of the first Quality' sat to him, and he became the rage. It is not easy for us to-day to see why, for he had none of the graces of the art of France. One of the first portraits which made his name was that of 'General Dormer', signed and dated 1738, which is still at Rousham. In it we see the style of Richardson seasoned with a little of the high French affectation. The pose is a little less placid and easy, hands and arms make a little for elegance: draperies and the tablecloth curl into a little more Frenchified folds – and that is about the whole difference. But Vanloo is important, because it is this tinge of modishness which he introduced into the Richardson formula which marks the change between Richardson and his son-in-law, Thomas Hudson. Vanloo remained in London in good practice until the autumn of 1742. His success perhaps also contributed to the rise to temporary prosperity of another foreigner, the Italian Andrea Soldi (c. 1703–71), who had been in England since about 1735. His portraits of around 1740 have the same cosmopolitan air as Vanloo's, which seems to be what English sitters liked, but they become increasingly English with advancing years. He is at his best in a few large groups such as the 'Thomas Duncombe and Family' 1741 (Earl of Feversham), or the musical group of 'The Family of Sir Thomas Head' 1750 (on loan to Aston Hall, Birmingham). We can judge of the predominance of Vanloo and Soldi at this time from the young Ramsay's letter of 1740, in which he says: 'I have put all your Vanlois and Soldis...to flight'. He mentions no English rivals.

The English fashionable painters during this trough period were, in fact, unusually poor. But mention should be made of Arthur Pond (c. 1705–58), a pupil of Vanderbank who had returned from Italy in 1727, and had made a certain name for himself as a crayon portraitist and a much greater name as a virtuoso. In oil portraits he is usually uncommonly feeble and his highest level is his 'Richard Snow' 1738 (Fitzwilliam Museum, Cambridge). But he has been credited in recent years with the charming group of 'A Lady winding Wool and a Gentleman drawing'[1] (National Trust, Upton House), which would make him a lesser figure of some interest. On purely stylistic grounds, however, it seems likely that this is by Pieter van Bleeck (1697–1764), a painter of portraits and theatrical groups, usually of quite modest ability, who painted at least one certain work of real distinction, the 'Mrs Cibber as Cordelia' c. 1755 (on loan to the Stratford Memorial Theatre).[2]

Thomas Hudson

To these lesser fry succeeded Thomas Hudson (1701–79), the son-in-law of Richardson and the heir of what one may call the Riley tradition. We can watch his gradual emergence in the pages of Vertue's notebooks. Vertue first mentions him in 1733; by 1738 he is still not listed as among the 'principal painters'; but he is in full swing by 1741; and by 1744 he was thought to have the fullest run of employment in town. The large number of his surviving works, and the fact that the young Reynolds was his pupil from the end of 1740 to 1743, have led to his being one of the few names of painters familiar to those who believe that British painting begins with Hogarth and Reynolds, and he has a little niche in all the standard books. It is doubtful if he deserves this eminence, and he is altogether inferior to such a painter as Highmore. Hudson may fairly be described as the last of the conscienceless artists, of whom Lely was the first in England, who turned portraits out to standard patterns and executed comparatively little of the work themselves. The drapery painter counts for a great deal in Hudson, first Joseph van Aken (who died in 1749) and then van Aken's younger brother. Hudson and Ramsay are linked in this respect, and they were Joseph van Aken's executors: but whereas Ramsay must rank as one of the major formative influences on British painting of the age of Reynolds, Hudson, for all that he was Reynolds's teacher, counts for nothing at all.

It is a very curious fact that, for all his undoubted reputation by 1740, it is not possible at present to point with any certainty to a Hudson portrait painted before 1745[3]. His immense vogue, on present experience, seems to have been about 1746 to 1755, when the young Reynolds began to make his name. Certainly one of his best pictures, and one on which he probably took more trouble than usual – since it was more or less for public exhibition – is the full-length 'Theodore Jacobsen' 1746, which he presented to the Foundling Hospital. It is sound and solid and conservative, but the learned accessories are out of Hudson's usual canon, and a more typical example of his style is the 'Admiral Byng' 1749 at Greenwich (Plate 116). This is straightforward and solid, with no graces and no nonsense and no poetry about it. The drapery was no doubt put in by the drapery painter and the shipping in the background by a marine specialist. For young men there were more elegant poses, sometimes the holding of a mask: for ladies there were several standard poses in studio costume, complete with pearls. There is an even hardness and roundness of modelling to the faces, and a corresponding hard metallic glitter to the satins. The impassive masks of Richardson are only slightly modified and the draperies have a tinge of the Rococo which was due to Vanloo, and the personality of the painter hardly appears. This is all the more conscienceless since we know, from a very few experiments, that Hudson was not altogether incapable of something better. The engraved 'Charles Erskine' of 1747 (Edinburgh Gallery) is a surprising essay in the vein of Rembrandt, and Hudson could attempt with some felicity a rather playful group such as 'Sir John and Lady Pole' 1755 (Antony House; Plate 113). Towards the end of the 1750s he went into prosperous retirement before the rising star of Reynolds, but occasionally painted a portrait, if specially commissioned, such as the full length of Sir William Browne 1767 at the Royal

College of Physicians. In this the texture of the paint in a few places shows that he had deigned to look at Reynolds, and the lighting is suggestive of the new style, but those are the only concessions to modernity.

Allan Ramsay

Hudson's style is nearly invariable and his portraits never show any traces either of a sensitive approach to his sitter's character or of a refined perception. Ramsay's lowest standard is almost indistinguishable from Hudson's normal, but this is comparatively rare: at his highest he is often a worthy rival to Reynolds, and he continued refining his art up to the time, in the middle 1760s, when he more or less abandoned painting. Although a dozen years younger than Hudson, his known career begins well before we know Hudson's. No certain Hudson is known before 1745, but one can name thirty to forty Ramsay portraits before that date. He may thus be considered as belonging to Hudson's generation. At the same time, although his working career was over before the foundation of the Royal Academy, his finest and most familiar portraits stand comparison with the works of the first generation of Academicians. He is the only portrait painter (and he painted nothing but portraits) who belongs equally to both worlds, and he and Hogarth, in their very different ways, are the two pioneers who broke the ground for the age of Reynolds. The difference between these two can be easily assessed by pondering Northcote's remark on a Ramsay portrait of 'Queen Charlotte' (now at Cullen House) of the early 1760s: 'It was weak in execution and ordinary in features but the farthest possible removed from anything like vulgarity. A professor might despise it, but in the mental part I have never seen anything of Van Dyke's equal to it.'[4] It is what Northcote calls 'the mental part' which is the keynote to the new style, and it was something which had been largely lost to British painting since Van Dyck. He means by it not only everything which goes into making a portrait into a picture, but also the whole process of interpreting character in terms of form, colour, and tone. Ramsay was sometimes lazy about the mental part, but the stuff of it was in him. One should add that, although Ramsay was particularly qualified by sympathy and experience to interpret the Scottish physiognomy, his importance lies in his contribution to the development of the English School and not in the small part he played in the development of painting in Scotland.

Born in Edinburgh in 1713, the son of the writer of *The Gentle Shepherd*, Ramsay somehow picked up the rudiments of drawing in Scotland before passing a few months in Hysing's studio in London in 1734. His father's friends, the Clerks of Penicuik (Sir John had studied drawing under Mieris, and his son, the architect Sir James, had been a pupil of Imperiali), probably account for his early training much more than anything he learned under Hysing, and, when he went to Italy in 1736, he could draw a head in the manner of Richardson. From 1736 to 1738 he worked in Rome with Francesco Imperiali and in Naples with the aged Solimena (1657–1747), and it is what he got from these two masters, a novel air of life and breeding and a feeling for the composition of a portrait, which led to his immediate success on his return to Britain.

Francesco Fernandi, called Imperiali, is for the inquirer one of the most elusive Roman painters of his time. His patronage by Cardinal Imperiali enabled him to live a sort of black-market career outside the fold of the Roman Academy of St Luke, and the official biographers of Roman painting have therefore all been silent upon him. His art is of Marattesque derivation and he specialized in teaching foreigners, and it is probably significant that his one known Italian pupil was Pompeo Batoni (1708–87), who was to specialize in portraits of British gentry and nobility travelling abroad.[5] There is a certain complementary quality in the art of Batoni and Ramsay: the air of cosmopolitan breeding which the young traveller learned to like from Batoni in Rome, could be best obtained from Ramsay when he had returned to London. From Solimena Ramsay learned what Lord Chesterfield called 'the graces'. There is a drawing of a girl's figure at Edinburgh on which Ramsay has written: 'From a picture of Solimena in his own house 1737', which is perhaps taken from the 'Jacob and Rachel' now at Venice. Ramsay has shown no interest in the flaming Baroque element in Solimena's style, but has copied a figure, gracious and feminine, in line with his own special talent – and he has laid special emphasis on the movement of the hands. In the great collection of Ramsay drawings at Edinburgh, which comes from the painter's studio, there are more than a hundred studies of hands – hands which indicate grace and character. This new approach to portraiture Ramsay may well have owed in considerable part to Solimena, whose few recognized portraits are the most lively that were being produced in Italy at the time. A single dated portrait of this period survives, the 'Samuel Torriano' 1738 at Mellerstain (Plate 122A), in which the hand and the drapery and the head all play an equal part in building up the character. Were it not signed, it might well have baffled attribution, but the kind of trouble which Ramsay has taken to make the portrait into a picture gives a foretaste of his later method.

By 1739 Ramsay had settled in London. Although he made fairly frequent visits to Edinburgh up to about 1755, he always remained based on London, where even a Scotsman would pay more for his own portrait than he would in Edinburgh. By 1740 he was writing complacently to a friend: 'I have put all your Vanlois and Soldis and Ruscas to flight and now play the first fiddle myself'. Hudson in fact was his only serious competitor in the 1740s, and, in 1746, Ramsay matched Hudson's gift of his portrait of 'Theodore Jacobsen' to the Foundling Hospital with his own gift of the full length of 'Dr Mead' (Plate 121), a far more accomplished work, in the European 'grand style'. Here, for the first time in the century, we come upon a portrait which shows that the painter had profited to the full by a training in Italy. It lacks the intensely English temper of Hogarth's 'Captain Coram' (Plate 101), but it has altogether escaped from the English awkwardness of Hudson, and the 'grand style', about which Reynolds has so much to say in his *Discourses*, has been introduced into British portraiture. Even the secret, which has generally been considered one of Reynolds's own specific contributions, that this style can be achieved by the adaptation of classical models to modern portraits, was anticipated by Ramsay. In his 'Norman, 22nd Chief of Macleod' 1748 (Dunvegan Castle; Plate 124) Ramsay has adapted the 'Apollo Belvedere' to a portrait walking by the seashore, as Reynolds was to do in his 'Commodore Keppel' 1753/4 (Greenwich; Plate 125), which made his reputation. Ramsay has been even bolder than Reynolds was to be, for he has put his Apollo into tartan trews! With such evidence it is impossible to escape from the conclusion that the marriage of the Italian grand style to British portraiture was primarily the achievement of Ramsay.

These high lights in Ramsay's work of the 1740s, though they must be picked out by the historian, are not altogether characteristic of his output. His work in this decade is more curiously uneven than that of any of his contemporaries, and this has delayed the recognition of his importance. It was no doubt due to the extraordinary pressure of demands upon his brush. An able Scottish painter working in London, skilfully advertised by his father in Edinburgh, brought about at once a demonstration of the loyal solidarity of his fellow countrymen. In his first year in London he had painted the dukes of Argyll and Buccleuch and the duchess of Montrose, and the number of his portraits of Scottish sitters in the 1740s is very large. To get through the work he had recourse at once to the drapery painter and he shared van Aken with Hudson and many lesser men. The results were sometimes extremely perfunctory, but there is evidence from his drawings that Ramsay used the drapery painter with a greater sense of responsibility than his contemporaries.

Ramsay differs from all the other major British portraitists of the century in his use of drawings. Reynolds's drawings (other than quick sketches from the compositions of others) are rare and slight and hardly ever related to his portraits: Gainsborough's drawings are independent works of art and also hardly ever made with a specific portrait in view. Ramsay's are mainly studies of pose and costume, when they are not studies of hands: the face is usually left blank, but he took the greatest trouble with graceful arrangements of dresses and hands, as well as with arrangements of the figure. A number of these have on them what seem to be instructions to the drapery painter, and, as far as can be judged by comparison with van Aken's own drawings (many of which found their way into Ramsay's studio and are still catalogued at Edinburgh as Ramsay's own), whereas other painters sent their portraits to van Aken to be dressed up in one of his own genteel arrangements, Ramsay sent his with specific instructions and an accompanying drawing. In this way, even while having recourse to the drapery painter, Ramsay built up a new repertory of natural and graceful arrangements to supersede the stock models of the earlier generation.

Ramsay might well have been content to rest on his laurels in the 1750s if it had not been for the competition caused by the emergence of Reynolds about 1754. Alone of the portraitists of the earlier generation Ramsay rose to the occasion and his 'Lord Drummore' 1754 (Colstoun; Plate 126), with its new lighting and 'modern' sense of the weight and presence of the sitter, shows him competing with Reynolds with some effect. It was probably a feeling that he must refresh his knowledge of Italy, whence Reynolds had lately returned, rather than the reason usually given of the difficulties over his second marriage, which led to his second visit to Italy from 1755 to 1757. But this time he sought a different source of inspiration. He drew at the French Academy and he made studies, not from those examples of the grand style which had so much influenced Reynolds, but from such models of gracefulness as Domenichino's frescoes in S. Luigi dei Francesi. It may well be that his admitted masterpiece, the 'Portrait of his Wife' (Edinburgh; Plate 123A) dates from these years, before which one must echo Northcote's already quoted remark (on another picture) that it is 'the furthest possible removed from anything like vulgarity'.

It may be that Ramsay had felt that it was precisely this quality, which, with a delicacy akin to his own, we may call 'an absence of vulgarity', that was lacking in Reynolds's early style, and that therefore it was one on which he should concentrate himself. It certainly prevails in his later works which may be said to begin with this portrait of his wife. The figure is set a little distance in from the picture frame, a muted light, with silvery or greenish shadows, prevails in the flesh tones, and more attention than ever is given to the hands. Horace Walpole, with keen penetration, sums up the contrast which was felt between Ramsay and Reynolds in 1759, when he says: 'Mr Reynolds and Mr Ramsay can scarcely be rivals; their manners are so different. The former is bold and has a kind of tempestuous colouring, yet with dignity and grace; the latter is all delicacy. Mr Reynolds seldom succeeds in women, Mr Ramsay is formed to paint them.' Reynolds soon took steps to learn from Ramsay in this respect, but the judgement was true at the time it was made.

Immediately on his return to London in 1757 Ramsay became involved in a new source of patronage which was profoundly to affect his later output. Another Scottish patron, Lord Bute, engaged his services to paint full-lengths of himself and the young Prince of Wales (both at Mount Stuart), which are the introduction to the great series of full-lengths of his second style. At Mount Stuart too are 'Augusta, Princess of Wales' c. 1758, 'Lord Mount Stuart as a Harrow Archer' 1759, and the most original achievement of his later time, 'Lady Mary Coke' 1762. This muted harmony of silvery white satin and soft dark green exhales a gentle poetry and tender reticence which convinces the imagination however little it may accord with what we know of the tempestuous character of the sitter. It is one side of Van Dyck recreated in eighteenth-century terms, and, in what Northcote would call 'the mental part' of it, it surpasses Van Dyck.

Ramsay's portrait of the Prince of Wales found favour, and when the Prince succeeded in 1760 as George III Ramsay was commissioned to paint the official portraits in spite of the fact that John Shackleton (a decidedly minor person who died in 1767) was King's Painter. He also painted several versions of Queen Charlotte and the demand for repetitions of these pictures was so extensive that he gave up outside commissions except for particular friends.[6] Although he was at the height of his powers and some few of his private commissions of these last years – the '6th Earl of Coventry' 1764 (Earl of Coventry) and 'Lady Holland' 1766 (Melbury) – are among his finest portraits, he seems to have been content to turn his studio into a factory for the repetition (by assistants) of royal portraits Much of his later life (he did not die until 1784) was devoted to literary pursuits, and no certain painting is known from his hand after 1769. He refused a knighthood and had no connexion with the Royal Academy, though he retained the friendship of the President. No satisfactory explanation has ever been given of this change of heart, but an accident to his arm, at some unspecified date, may have had something to do with it. At his best he certainly ranks among the major figures in British portraiture.

William Hoare

William Hoare of Bath (*c.* 1707–92) may reasonably be linked with Ramsay's name since he too was a pupil of Imperiali and is said to have become a friend of the young Batoni in Rome. Hoare went to Italy with Giuseppe Grisoni (1699–1769) in 1728, and stayed there some nine years. Grisoni was an Italian portraitist of some merit – as his 'Colley Cibber' at the Garrick Club shows – and was Hoare's first master, so that it is curious that Hoare should never have shown himself to be anything but a prosy and competent follower in the line of Richardson. He had settled in Bath by 1738 and was the leading portraitist there in oils and crayons until the arrival of Gainsborough in 1759, who took away a good deal of his custom. He was a favourite in the families of Pitt, Grenville, and Pelham and a considerable portion of his recognized work consists of repetitions of portraits of that political clique. In 1769 he became an Academician, but ceased exhibiting after 1779. It is possible, since the bulk of his work in oils remains unrecognized, that the present estimate of his quality is too low, and there is an original sense of colour, sound drawing, and a considerable feeling for personality in his 'Mrs Richard Jesser' (of the end of the 1740s) in the Bristol Gallery. At any rate it compares very favourably with Hudson's work of the same period. His group of 'Three Sons of the 9th Earl of Lincoln' (Duke of Newcastle) of the middle 1760s has the mechanics of Hudson but a fresh perception of life and youth in the heads, which almost amounts to charm. But he never, as Ramsay did, accepted or understood the new style.

Thomas Frye

Thomas Frye (1710–62), an Irishman who came to London in the middle 1730s, also deserves mention. Some of his earlier portraits have been mistaken for Hogarth's, and his later work is more advanced than Hudson and has been confused with Ramsay. But his practice of painting was discontinuous, as he founded and managed the Bow porcelain factory from 1744 to 1759, and spent much of 1760 producing rather singular portrait mezzotints in imitation of Piazzetta drawings. He also painted miniatures in addition to full-lengths, both life-size and on conversation scale. He is never uninteresting, but too little of his work has been traced to give a positive account of his style.

Portrait Painters in the Provinces

A number of painters who worked in provincial centres in what is loosely called 'the Hudson style' deserve a passing notice. Knowledge of them is probably at present very incomplete, but several were in quite good practice in East Anglia and in the Lancashire–Cheshire areas. Norwich in particular seems to have been a profitable area for portrait painters. A certain D. Heins, of German origin, was working there from about 1725 until his death in 1756, and his son, John Theodore Heins (1732–71) continued his Norwich practice, but migrated to London in 1767. Both Heinses painted sound, solid, portraits on the scale of life as well as occasional conversation groups. Thomas Bardwell (1704–67) too, a native of Suffolk, who achieved some reputation in London in the 1740s and 1750s, was settled in Norwich until his death and had an extensive Norfolk clientèle. In the Lancashire-Cheshire area one can point to James Cranke (1707–80), a 'self-taught' artist, who formed his style by copying Hudson; James Fellowes, whose activity can be traced from 1711 to 1751; and Henry Pickering, who returned from Italy about 1745 and was active in and around Liverpool until 1760. Pickering's full-length of Sir Rowland Wynn 1752 at Nostell Priory is not inferior to the best of Hudson's efforts. In Somerset too we can trace a fairly abundant activity for one painter, Richard Phelps, who can be traced from 1729 until 1785. He too painted entirely in Hudson's manner and can be studied at Dunster Castle and Crowcombe Court. It is probable that further exploration would bring to light many other names, but these are sufficient to give an indication of the sort of work which was being carried on in the provincial centres.

NOTES TO CHAPTER 14

1. British Art Exhibition, R.A. 1934, Memorial Catalogue No. 75 and plate xxiii.

2. Published in *Journal of the Courtauld and Warburg Institutes*, x (1947), 92.

3. Indistinguishable (almost) from Hudson's portraits are half a dozen at Sandon which are documented by a bill as being by James Crank, 1745.

4. Quoted from Sir James Caw's essay on Ramsay in *Walpole Society*, xxv, 79.

5. For a preliminary census of Batoni's portraits of English sitters see John Steegman in *Burl. Mag.*, LXXXVIII (Mar. 1946), 55 ff.

6. A long letter of 1766 to the Duke of Portland explaining Ramsay's position as official portraitist, in spite of Shackleton's right of office, is published in R. W. Goulding and C. K. Adams, *Catalogue of the Duke of Portland's Pictures* (1936), 470–1.

PART FIVE

THE CLASSICAL AGE

CHAPTER 15

INTRODUCTORY

JUST as the reign of George II was the formative period of British painting, the first thirty years of the reign of George III can be called the 'classical' age. The same loose, but convenient terminology entitles us to call the period which begins in the 1790s and coincides with the French Revolution and the early poetry of Wordsworth the 'romantic period'. Lawrence, Fuseli, Blake, and the beginnings of Girtin and Turner are the prime elements of this later period, and their names will start another volume. But a number of survivors of the earlier style lived on until as late as the 1820s and can properly be treated here, while the chief interest of other figures who died in the 1790s lies in their role as forerunners of romanticism. The classical age did not end and the romantic begin at any moment of time to which the historian can point his finger, yet the year 1789 stands out as the watershed between these two periods. Gainsborough had died in 1788 and Reynolds went blind in 1789, and in the latter year the young Lawrence, who had first exhibited in 1787, showed his 'Queen Charlotte', which is now in the National Gallery. We can certainly say that the strength of the classical age was over. Yet of two almost exact contemporaries, Rowlandson and Blake, the former must be treated in this volume, while the latter must await the next.

The beginning of the classical age can be defined more closely. The year 1760 was marked not only by the accession to the throne of a young king who was sympathetic to the arts – and no one with a vestige of artistic feeling had sat on the throne since the revolution of 1688 – but by the first public exhibition of the newly incorporated Society of Artists. From that year onwards at least one, and latterly more, public exhibitions of pictures were held, so that young painters could see and study the work of their elders and good or bad work could become a subject for public discourse. It is true that public criticism of the exhibitions was slow in developing and the field was mainly occupied by the scurrilous works of 'Peter Pindar' and 'Anthony Pasquin', but the *Morning Post*, under Bate-Dudley's editorship, in the 1780s began to take a serious interest in painting, and other papers have short and sporadic notices of the exhibitions. George Vertue's notes on contemporary painters, which are the gossip of the studio, give way to literary sources of a different kind, and it is rather from the gossip of the collecting classes, such as Horace Walpole's letters, that we have to estimate the contemporary view of art and artists. This is not a gain in factual wealth, but it is evidence of the higher esteem in which art was held.

The man who had done, and who continued to do, most to raise the status of the artist in this way was Sir Joshua Reynolds.

Year by year, from 1760 to 1789, Reynolds exhibited his most important portraits and historical compositions. And year by year, from 1769 until his eyesight failed, he read at the annual prize-giving of the Royal Academy Schools a *Discourse* which reinforced and supplemented the lesson of his paintings. The theoretical background against which the painting of the classical age must be considered is to be found in Reynolds's *Discourses*. No one, not even the President himself, altogether lived up to this high standard, and one of the main interests for the historian is to watch the gradual breakdown of these principles but their dominance is not in doubt. It was against them that the more reflective of the romantic painters consciously reacted, and this reaction can be seen in its most violent and instructive form in Blake's petulant and angry comments in the margin of his copy of the *Discourses*.

Reynolds, who was conscious that a native school was only beginning in his own time was all for high art. He had a keenly developed economic sense and he probably felt as strongly as Hogarth the fact that British connoisseurs, apart from portraits, would spend their money only on foreign paintings. The classic story to illustrate this point of view in the 1760s is that related by Northcote of one of the many collectors who went to see with such enthusiasm West's 'Pylades and Orestes'. When asked by his son why he had not purchased a picture he spoke of with such praise, he replied: 'You surely would not have me hang up a modern English picture in my house, unless it were a portrait?' It was this attitude Reynolds sought to undermine, not, as Hogarth had tried, by satire and invective, but by an elaborate process of intellectual sapping. By first marrying the portrait to the tradition of history painting he hoped gradually to educate public taste into considering history pictures a natural thing for a British artist to paint and for a British collector to buy. It cannot be claimed that he was successful, although a considerable number of the huge quantity of history paintings produced during these thirty years did in fact find private purchasers.

The opportunity of exhibiting their pictures in public after 1760 was not an unmixed blessing for British painters. We know from one or two engravings what these public exhibitions were like, and they are horrifying by modern standards. The walls would be plastered with pictures arranged like the components of a jigsaw puzzle, with the frames touching one another. There would be as many as six rows of small pictures, and those full-lengths which were given the best position 'on the line', would have the toes of the figure about on a level with the eye of a tall spectator. Nothing but trumpet tones would be heard in a display of this kind, and this sufficiently accounts for the fact that Ramsay, whose style in the 1760s was of a deliberately shadowed and feminine kind, never exhibited in public, and that Gainsborough, after a final quarrel in 1784 over the hanging of his pictures, abandoned the Academy and held exhibitions in his own painting room. It was in this way that the 'exhibition picture' was born, an unnatural genre which has been the curse of painting ever since the foundation of academies. In Reynolds's own work of the 1760s there is a clear distinction between his portraits for public exhibition, such as the 'Duchess of Hamilton' at Port Sunlight, and those for private commissions, such as

'Countess Spencer and Daughter' at Althorp (Plate 132). After the opening of the first Academy in 1769 Reynolds hardly painted a picture which was not planned to be capable of being shown in public, and this accounts for the preference many people feel to-day for the more informal portraits of his earlier years.

The Society of Artists quickly got out of hand. At first anyone who sent in a picture was entitled to have it shown, and the first exhibitions, for all that they included some very distinguished pictures, were flooded with a torrent of trivialities which would hardly find admission to-day to a Parish Bazaar. It was too late to formulate a rational principle of admission and exclusion, and the justification for the foundation of the Royal Academy in 1768, to which most of the best artists from the Society of Arts seceded in 1769 – which those who did not, or were not invited to, considered a betrayal – was that it was necessary to begin all over again and to be able to exclude the absurd. The first Academy exhibition was very high-minded indeed and contained only 136 items, but the number had increased to 245 the second year, and by 1788 it had increased to 656. A great deal of a very low standard was admitted to these early exhibitions, but they did succeed in keeping out such items as 'A basket of flowers – in paper' and miscellaneous objects in wax and needlework. It was no doubt this feeling of the need for keeping a high standard of formality which excluded Stubbs and Gilpin, as mere 'sporting painters', from the first Academy, but this rigidity was soon relaxed and the Academy then, as ever since, has tried to provide accommodation for the greatest possible number of exhibitors who reach a certain level of competence, so that they could profit by the unquestioned prestige of its exhibitions.

The emergence of various classes of picture during these years will be noticed in subsequent chapters, which deal with the work of the various artists, but it may be useful to summarize here the main landmarks in chronological order. To the first public exhibition, in 1760, Reynolds had sent his 'Duchess of Hamilton as Venus' (Port Sunlight), a picture shamelessly designed to be hung high and to delude the eye into being a history picture: it won enthusiastic praise. In 1761 Hogarth sent his 'Sigismunda' (Tate; Plate 104), which was openly called a history piece in emulation of the Seicento: it was greeted with howls of execration. Zoffany's first theatrical conversation appeared in 1762, and Gainsborough's first landscape in 1763. In 1764 the young Benjamin West exhibited his first classical history picture and aroused great interest (but no commissions), while Edward Penny's 'Death of Wolfe' (Plate 168A), perhaps because it was so unheroic in character, passed unnoticed. In 1765 came Wright of Derby's first 'candle-light picture', and, about 1766, the conversation piece, hitherto reserved for the middle classes, was reintroduced into the fashionable world by some royal commissions to Zoffany. The earliest of these were not exhibited, but the fashionable conversation piece probably owes its twenty years' vogue to the new passion of the royal family for domesticity. In 1767 a young Scottish painter, John Runciman, just before his early death, painted in Rome a picture of 'King Lear in the Storm' (Edinburgh) which is the first herald of literary romantic painting. In 1768, just when the quarrels and negotiations which led to the foundation of the Royal Academy were seething, Sawrey Gilpin, a sporting painter who had hitherto been content with horses, began his series of 'Gulliver and the Houyhnhnms' to show that sporting painters could tack on to the history waggon too. The year 1769 was sufficiently marked by the first Academy, in which those painters who were permitted to exhibit, were on their most solemn behaviour, and it is interesting that one of the few pictures praised by the contemporary Press was Gainsborough's 'Lady Molyneux', which was one of the few which had made no concessions to the prevailing solemnity. This high tone was somewhat relaxed in 1770. In 1771 West's 'Death of Wolfe (Plate 168B), in contemporary costume (but with no attempt at historical truth) showed that there was a keen public interest in heroic pictures of modern events and that it was no longer obligatory to dress all heroic figures in antique costume. In 1773 Reynolds showed his first fancy picture in a lighter vein, the 'Strawberry Girl', and for the years 1773 to 1775 the Academy suffered its first temporary defection of a major kind through Gainsborough not troubling to exhibit. Both Reynolds and Gainsborough, at London and Bath, had a scarcity of sitters at about this time and Gainsborough came up to London in 1774, a date which marks the decline of Bath as a second seat of artistic patronage, for Wright, who tried to settle there in 1775, could not make a living. The same years mark the arrival of an interest in 'medieval' histories: Alexander Runciman had completed his Ossian ceiling at Penicuik House in 1773, and West exhibited at the Academy in the same year his 'Death of Bayard', in which Salvator Rosa is a predominant influence. At the Society of Arts at the same time Mortimer was showing 'Banditti' and pictures of wandering soldiery which also owed their inspiration to Salvator. In 1775 came the first direct attack on Reynolds and on his method of cribbing from the Old Masters to enhance the distinction of his portraits. This was Nathaniel Hone's picture of 'The Conjurer', which was excluded from the Academy on the grounds of impropriety, as the female assistant was supposed to resemble Angelica Kauffmann. In 1776 Romney set up in Cotes's house in Cavendish Square and became a third among the fashionable portraitists in London. At the same time the interest in the South Seas was at its height, Reynolds exhibited his portrait of 'Omai' and Hodges his views taken on the expedition to the South Seas. Tilly Kettle too, in the preceding years, had been sending back portraits of native princes from India and the field of subject-matter at the Academy was taking on imperial proportions.

The critical period for the ideas of high and classical endeavour, with which the Academy had started, occurred about ten years after its foundation. From 1777 to 1783 Barry was at work on his paintings for the Royal Society of Arts, which are the one major project, that came to fruition, which was the logical outcome of Reynolds's theories. They were coldly received, and pictures of a quite opposite character were making the Academy interesting. A tepid breeze from France was felt in the rather *risqué* pictures of ladies in bed which Peters was painting just before he turned to the Church in 1778, and Copley's 'Brook Watson and the Shark' (Plate 172) of 1778 was the direct antithesis to everything that Reynolds had preached. In 1779/80 Copley painted his 'Death of Chatham', a naturalistic rendering of a strictly contemporary event which anticipated the later work of Jacques-Louis David.

In the 1780s the constricting influence of the Italian Seicento, and even of Raphael and Michelangelo, was on the wane. Reynolds himself, after a visit to Flanders, absorbed a good deal of the influence of Rubens; Gainsborough's fancy pieces, of which the first was exhibited in 1780, aroused an interest in scenes from common life which was quickly followed by the younger generation. Opie, who first exhibited in 1782, showed 'The School' in 1784, and the domestic pictures of Wheatley and Morland began to make their appearance. The fashionable conversation piece came to an end with Copley's 'Sitwell Family' of 1787, and the young Lawrence started to exhibit the same year.

The later 1780s and 1790s were the heyday of the history picture, but it was a history picture of a very different kind from anything Reynolds had recommended. The introduction of 'period' costume on to the stage (and of a 'period' unknown to history) had corrupted the purity of the classical tradition, and although some painters clung to the old formulas, most of the contributors to Boydell's Shakespeare Gallery (begun in 1786), Macklin's Poet's Gallery, Macklin's Bible, Bowyer's Historic Gallery, and other such ventures, adopted a convention from what one can only call 'public theatricals'. It was no more than a step to the purely romantic convention of Fuseli, who had begun to exhibit in England in 1775. For the history picture Fuseli stands as Lawrence stands to portraiture, and with the full emergence of these two lively and impressive figures the classical age of British painting is over.

CHAPTER 16

SIR JOSHUA REYNOLDS (1723–92)

THE name of Reynolds has recurred fitfully in earlier chapters. He can be said to have given it to an age as no one since Kneller had done. He was the intimate friend of Burke, Dr Johnson, Garrick, and Goldsmith, and he was no stranger to Horace Walpole. Just as we cannot picture the age of Charles I without doing so through the eyes of Van Dyck, we cannot picture the splendid years of the third quarter of the eighteenth century, when Britain was so rich in statesmen, soldiers, sailors, founders of empire, lawyers, and men and women of literature, the arts, and the stage, except through the eyes of Reynolds. There is more affinity in nervous temperament between Van Dyck and Gainsborough – and in the tender loveliness of their mere painting – but in everything else Reynolds must be accounted the eighteenth-century equivalent of Van Dyck. Like Van Dyck he came to maturity at an opportune moment in the development of art, as heir to the struggles of an earlier generation. Rubens, with great intellectual effort and against a weight of conservative opinion, had created the 'modern' European style of the seventeenth century, and Van Dyck fell heir to it: Hogarth and, in a much lesser degree, Ramsay had created the 'modern' British style of the eighteenth century, and Reynolds was born at the right moment to fall heir to it. He was also endowed by nature with a rational intellect of a high order, and he had a power of phlegm which was denied to Van Dyck.

Anyone who seeks to estimate the qualities of Reynolds must take into account his virtues both as a painter and as an historian. It is easier to criticize him as a painter. He was curiously insensitive to draughtsmanship, if by 'draughtsmanship' we mean only a feeling for the beauty of line, a quality which Gainsborough possessed in a high degree. But, if we enlarge the concept of draughtsmanship into what the Italian theorists call *disegno*, we discern that Reynolds has a compensating feeling for mass and the solidity of bodies, in which Gainsborough is often strangely lacking. The outlines of Reynolds's masses may often strike us unfavourably, but their placing and value in a picture are rarely at fault. And in what Northcote, writing of Ramsay, has called 'the mental part' of a portrait, Reynolds is supreme, and this touches on his value as an historian. He had the unusual advantage, to a portrait painter, of being deaf during the years of his maturity. I cannot doubt that this sharpened and accelerated his power of reading character, and, as a painter of men and women who have played a part in history, there is hardly a single European painter who can touch him for variety. Gainsborough's well-known comment on Reynolds: 'Damn him, how various he is!' was a criticism wrung from the heart, and points surely to that aspect of his whole output which no longer abides our judgement.

It is worth while therefore to define the range of this variety, and to try and indicate the principles which controlled it, and which give a unity to Reynolds's work as a whole. A consideration of Reynolds in relation to Kneller and Van Dyck will help to make clear his range. Kneller had been a master of the 'historical portrait' in the sense that he had a fine eye for the lineaments of the face (in men) and for the outward and visible marks of char-acter: but he fitted his admirably observed faces into a set of stock patterns, which did nothing to bring out and a good deal to conceal the character of the sitter. His men are all dissimulators with different faces, and most of his women are puppets. Van Dyck on the other hand, as we have seen, was extremely sensitive to the shades of personal character and even modified his brushwork in accordance with his view of his sitter. But his sitters almost all belonged, in England, to the small circle of the Court and are invested with the same kind of elegance. If, however, we turn to Van Dyck's portraits of his brother artists, we shall see a range and variety much more akin to Reynolds. Reynolds had absorbed both traditions, and it is not for nothing that his earliest experiment in a large portrait group, 'The Eliot Family' 1746 (Port Eliot), is modelled on the Wilton Van Dyck, which he can then only have known from an engraving. The vitality of Kneller's heads, and a pattern and posture which would bring out the character in the style of Van Dyck, were two of the main elements in Reynolds's portrait style. But, in his best work, there is more than this.

The strata of society from which Reynolds drew his sitters were much more varied than had been the case with Van Dyck, and Reynolds, in his best portraits, shows as much concern with the character of the type to which his sitter belongs, as with the individual character of his sitter. In the earlier manuals, such as Lomazzo or de Lairesse, it was con-sidered enough to show, by some appropriately chosen symbol (as a globe for a navigator) what sort of profession your sitter had. Reynolds does not scorn such symbols, but he is concerned to reinforce their message by the pose and pattern of his figure. One of the most splendid examples is the 'Lord Heathfield' (National Gallery; Plate 135), as solid as the Rock of Gibraltar of which he was Governor, holding, by a chain round his wrist, the key of the fortress with a gesture which makes plain the security of his defence of the Rock. These are new resources in British portraiture, although they are not altogether new in European painting. Rembrandt had more poetically employed symbols in a double con-text, and Titian had invested his men, beyond their personal likeness, with what Reynolds himself called a certain 'senatorial dignity'. It was this enhancement of personality which Reynolds sought to emulate, and he did it by the assiduous study of the Old Masters and of classical statuary, whose formulas and poses, more familiar then than they are now to the subconscious of cultivated Europeans, could be translated from 'history' into por-traiture with the value of symbols. This translation, which has already been noted in Hogarth's 'Captain Coram' and Ramsay's 'Macleod of Macleod', is of the essence of Reynolds's style. It was described by Horace Walpole as 'wit', and it contributed more than anything else to raising the status of portraiture and of the painter in England, where the native practitioner had been despised for half a century as beneath comparison with what the travelling gentleman met with on his Grand Tour. This raising of the status of the British artist was the political objective of Reynolds's life and the mainspring of his conduct as first President of the Royal Academy. It was an objective in which he was wholly successful and his achievement in this field may be thought to have contributed more than anything to making possible the flowering of a British school of painting of which we can be legitimately proud.

There is a trait of character, revealed in a story from Reynolds's early youth, which marks him out from the generations before him and suggests the forerunner of the romantic period. Before serving his apprenticeship to Hudson in London, there was a discussion at home of an alternative career for him, and he broke out with the statement that 'he would rather be an apothecary than an *ordinary* painter'. Hogarth, one may surmise, would have sympathized with this, but the ambition of all earlier British eighteenth-century portraitists, even I suspect of Ramsay, was to be a successful ordinary painter. It was this spirit, in which he set out, which makes Reynolds's journey to Italy so memorable and so different from all earlier painters' years of Italian study. From the beginning of the century and the time of Jervas onwards the British portrait painter had been going to Italy and returning, at best, with nothing more than a reputation for connoisseurship. Reynolds, and Richard Wilson at the same time, went to Italy with a different kind of inquiring ambition. The light of the art of the Mediterranean world and its rich visual tradition broke over them, and they returned incomparably enriched. Something of the same kind had happened in the field of architecture thirty years earlier to Lord Burlington. We may fairly say that the plant of British painting, which had long been slowly maturing, suddenly ripened into flower about 1750 under the warmth of the Italian sun.

It may be that Reynolds swallowed this intoxicating nectar a little too rapidly. The sublimity of the figure style of the Italian High Renaissance, that quality about Michelangelo's statement of the human form which Reynolds, in his last *Discourse*, refers to so movingly as 'the language of the gods', was reached after many generations of endeavour. Yet it is this strong wine in which, in his writings, he recommends that the student with high aspirations should immerse himself. From his Italian notebooks, however, we can gather that Reynolds himself got more immediate profit from the more ornamental style of the Venetians, which, in his teachings, he affects to discourage as of inferior value. In his portraits he only rarely allows his devotion to 'the language of the gods' to get out of hand, and he can even adapt figures from the Sistine ceiling (as in the 'Duchess of Marlborough and Child' at Blenheim) with impeccable taste, but it is another story in the rather few historical subjects of his later years. Even in what is in many ways the finest of them, the 'Death of Dido' (Royal Academy 1781; Plate 137) at Buckingham Palace, we can discern the justness of Mrs Thrale's uncharitable lines,[1]

> A rage for sublimity ill-understood
> To seek still for the great by forsaking the good.

But there is no painter of such uneven gifts for whom familiarity breeds such respect as Reynolds. His vast output, as fully documented as that of any known painter, is widely scattered and there is no collection where he can be seen fully in the round. To give a fair account of his work there are hardly less than a hundred paintings which one would like to take into consideration, either for their success, their originality, or their influence. The fourteen *Discourses* which he delivered, as President, at the annual prize-givings at the Royal Academy Schools, remain the most practical, the most sensible and the best written discussions on the theory and practice of painting in the English language. They do not form a connected treatise and they deal often with problems of an occasional kind, but they lay down very clearly the terms in which the British school can be understood, as well as the attitude against which some of the romantic painters were to react at the end of the century.

A word should also be said about Reynolds's personal character, which has a bearing on his art and on his influence. It was so strongly in contrast to the character of Gainsborough that an understanding of the virtues of these two great rival portrait painters is made easier by a knowledge of their character. Reynolds was cool, businesslike, and eminently objective: to those who admired enthusiasm and a quick response to the impulses of the heart, his temper seemed too frigid. He was a man of letters and he chose his friends from the world of letters and never admitted a fellow painter to his intimacy, although his acts of kindness to young painters were numerous. His life passed without indiscretions, and one would be tempted, from some of his recorded observations, to think of him as cynical, if he were not so obviously in earnest about the noble qualities of art, and if a whole range of his portraits did not show such an unclouded response to beauty and strength and innocence of character.

Reynolds was apprenticed to Hudson for four years in October 1740, at the age of seventeen. He quickly acquired the routine knowledge of the work of an 'ordinary' portrait painter's studio, which was all that Hudson could give him, and this apprentice-ship was terminated amicably after two and a half years. From the middle of 1743 until May 1749, when he set out for Italy, he practised on his own, mainly in his native Devon-shire, but also for a year or two (1744/6), in London. Some twenty or so works of these years are known, some little better than pot-boilers, done hurriedly to earn a little money; some of his father and sisters, with a tender candour of approach which shows that he had looked at Hogarth rather than at his master, Hudson; some with passages of rich, creamy pigment which show already an interest in the texture of paint (which he is alleged to have derived from seeing the works of the elusive William Gandy at Exeter); others which show an eye to what Ramsay was doing in the 1740s. An accessible and perhaps char-acteristic example, signed and dated 1747, is the 'Lieutenant Roberts' (Plate 122B) at Greenwich. In style it is nearer to Ramsay than to any other painter, with a little more alertness than was common with Ramsay, and with an interest in bold light and shade, to give mood to the subject, which already shows one of the problems he was to give most detailed study to on his Italian travels.

He sailed for Italy with his friend Commodore (later Admiral and Viscount) Keppel; landed in January 1750, and remained in Rome until May 1752, when he came home over-land with short stays at Florence, Parma, Bologna, Venice, and Paris. Early in 1753 he settled in London. It was in Rome that his art and mind were formed, not, as with Ramsay, by the teaching of contemporary Italian painters and by study at the French Academy, but by daily communion with the great masters, with Raphael, Michelangelo, and the Antique. Here, in contrast to the narrow world of London, he bathed himself in the majesty of a long tradition of art. He approached this great tradition with humility and sought first for intellectual regeneration, and not, as his predecessors had done, merely for the tricks of the trade. He did not, of course, neglect the latter and made numerous studies of pose and arrangements of figures and patterns of light and shade, but all these were hints, memoranda, towards the understanding of the Grand Style. An over-simplified statement would be that Reynolds returned from Italy saturated with the idea of the Grand Style and determined, since the practical bent of his mind made him aware that there was no living to be made by a painter in London except through portraiture, to elevate the British portrait tradition by marrying it, as far as possible, to the Grand Style. In later life, in the 1780s, he came to see that the Grand Style should be used in portraiture only with considerable discretion and on a character which could bear it. But that was after it had won perhaps too overwhelming a victory in England, and the second phase of Reynolds's career, which may be said to culminate in the foundation of the Royal Academy in 1768, is centred on the naturalization into England of the Grand Style. By an understandable reaction almost the only original work Reynolds did during his Italian years was a series of caricature groups of British visitors to Rome. These throw considerable light on Reynolds's power of perceiving character, but he prudently decided to abandon this genre as one ill-calculated to advance the success of a professional portrait painter.[2]

Success followed immediately upon Reynolds settling in London, and by 1755 he had as many as a hundred sitters and was employing considerable studio help. In 1759 the number had risen to 150 and he had to raise his prices to reduce the volume of business. Many of the works of this period are naturally rather dull single heads, but it would be accurate to say that the wealth and variety of Reynolds's portraits in the 1750s revolutionized the taste of Britain and the older generation of artists were driven into retirement from fashionable practice and, if they could afford it, retired altogether.

The picture with which Reynolds secured his reputation was the 'Commodore Keppel' (Plate 125) of 1753/4 at Greenwich, and it is instructive to compare it with what seems to have been undoubtedly its model, Ramsay's 'Macleod of Macleod'.

The pose and the general pattern are nearly identical – the 'Apollo Belvedere' in reverse. There is a rock at the left, with a few scraggy trees, and the sea to right. But the difference is prodigious in the communication of life and energy. One is tempted to suppose that Reynolds knew exactly what he was doing: that he deliberately took a classical theme which had been arranged by Ramsay for chamber music and showed what he could make of it by scoring it for a full orchestra. Ramsay's figure is sharply and daintily silhouetted against a calm sky: it barely stands upon the shore and the right arm is thrust forward in a gesture rather of welcome than command. The landscape is little more than a photographer's backdrop for an elegant puppet and there is no motive to unite figure and background. The motive in Reynolds's 'Keppel' is that the Commodore had lately been shipwrecked and he is shown as a man of action, striding along the shore and braving the tempest. Walpole might have been thinking of these pictures when, in 1759, contrasting Reynolds and Ramsay, he says of the former that he is 'bold' and 'has a kind of tempestuous colouring' which Ramsay lacks. The difference in power and character made by Reynolds's alteration of the movement of the right arm, and the immense gain in the appearance of life by limiting the amount of the silhouette which is sharply outlined against the background are additional elements in Reynolds's new receipt for portraiture. In nothing is the new style so distinct from the old as in this marriage of the figure to an appropriate background by a use of light and shade which Reynolds had learned from his study of the Old Masters. In later years the setting of many of his full-length figures against parkland, evocative of the surroundings of the great country houses in which his sitters lived, is an extension of this method and the adaptation of a formula of Van Dyck to a modern theme. It is not surprising that this new style took the world by storm, or that Ramsay should soon have gone on a second journey to Italy to seek inspiration again at so invigorating a source. It is curious, however, that Reynolds should never have returned to Italy himself.

By no means all Reynolds's portraits make so complete a break with the old style. Heroic overtones were not always possible and the great bulk of his commissions were for more domestic portraits than for full-lengths. A much more typical example is the 'Mrs Francis Beckford' (Plate 123B) of 1756 at the Tate Gallery, a single three-quarter-length figure, in a far from easy or natural pose, and with as much emphasis on the dress as in any of Hudson's portraits. What is it which gives life to this and marks it of the new age? It is not, in the main, a question of lighting, although the shadows flicker in a more subtle fashion over Reynolds's surfaces, and more of the outline is lost in shadow. It is much more in the tender and sympathetic approach to a character, which cannot, in this instance, have been very strongly formed. There is an absence of Hudson's fixed expression, his stare, as it were, at the camera; a certain gracious shyness, a momentary quality, as of being caught unobserved. There is also an enchanting colour, the silvery blues which predominate in early Reynolds. It is a return of the Graces.

It is curious that Horace Walpole, as late as 1759, should have thought that Reynolds rarely succeeded with women, while Ramsay was formed to paint them. It is true, however, that Reynolds was keenly aware of what Ramsay, his only formidable rival in London at the time, was doing, and he may well have consciously set out, as he had done in his 'Keppel', to excel him in his own field. When Ramsay had painted Lord Bute in 1758, Reynolds is reputed to have said,[3] of a portrait he painted a little later, that he 'wished to show legs with Ramsay's "Lord Bute"'. I imagine that this picture was the 'James, 7th Earl of Lauderdale' (Thirlestane Castle; Plate 130) of 1759, one of the most lively of his full-lengths of Peers in robes, in which he has used the base of a twisted column beloved of Van Dyck, and invented a pose to justify the crossed legs, which was absent in Ramsay's figure. In selecting another Scottish Peer for this display of wit, there would be a conscious irony which was not alien to Reynolds's character. When the time came, in 1760, for the first public exhibition of artists' works at the Society of Arts Ramsay abstained from exhibiting and Reynolds emerged as the acknowledged leader of the English school. An article in the *Imperial Magazine*[4] at the time says that his 'merit is much beyond anything that can be said in his commendation'.

The ten years from 1759 to the first Academy Exhibition of 1769 are the culmination of Reynolds's earlier style. It is less classical than his style of the 1770s and less dramatic than his final phase. To many it seems the period when he was at the height of his gifts. A picture such as 'Georgiana, Countess Spencer and her Daughter' (Plate 132) of 1760/1 (Althorp) must count as one of the great masterpieces of English portraiture. It is not a masterpiece of formal design and it achieves its ends more by tenderness and human values than by the resources of art, although the colour and the texture of the paint are alike lovely. As Northcote said of Ramsay, it is the furthest possible removed from vulgarity, and that is a virtue more positive in portrait painting than one might at first suppose. It is in fact a *Madonna* design and the extremely tactful use of a formal pattern of this kind with the value of a symbol is a part of its haunting power. Something of the same quality lingers round the 'Nelly O'Brien' of about 1762 in the Wallace collection.

But Reynolds was hankering after a more powerful instrument of rhetoric than the style displayed in pictures of such quiet perfection. It may well be that he saw something of his own predicament in the picture he exhibited in 1762 of 'Garrick between Tragedy and Comedy' (on loan from Lord Rothschild to Birmingham; Plate 129). It was a modern parody on the old theme of 'Hercules between Virtue and Vice', and Reynolds has also given it a pictorial nuance by painting Comedy in the manner of Correggio and Tragedy in the manner of Guido Reni. It was also a symbol of a struggle he was going through himself between the more or less intimate portrait, of which he was a master, and the heroic portrait, with which he was beginning to experiment as early as 1760, in the 'Duchess of Hamilton and Argyll' at Port Sunlight. By 1765, in 'Lady Sarah Bunbury sacrificing to the Graces' (Chicago; Plate 131), Reynolds's second and classical manner is seen at the full, and it is hard to-day not to feel some suggestion of the 'sense of sublimity ill-understood'. Lady Sarah is, as it were, an illustration to much that he has to say in the *Discourses* about the Grand Style, antique drapery, and so on. She is conceived in the manner of Guido Reni, whose popularity was then at its height, and it was perhaps in an attempt to emulate the Old Masters that Reynolds conceived this somewhat unfortunate portrait style. It was a deliberate innovation of his own, for it does not correspond to any contemporary European fashion nor to a perceptible reaction towards classicism apparent in British society.

It was under the influence of this high-minded and doctrinaire style that Reynolds set about his duties as first President of the Royal Academy, and his contributions to the first exhibition are all in this vein – the Duchess of Manchester as 'Diana' removing a bow from her infant son as 'Cupid' (taken from Albano); Lady Blake as Juno receiving the cestus from Venus (from a Roman statue); two ladies moralizing at a tomb inscribed 'Et ego in Arcadia' (a fancy from Guercino); and an exercise in the manner of Correggio with the title of 'Hope nursing Love'. It is impossible to avoid the impression that the President was seeking to impart a lesson in style.

From the time of the exhibition of 1769 nearly all Sir Joshua's most important works appeared at the Academy. One can name hardly a dozen really major works from 1769 to 1790 which were not so exhibited, and Reynolds's importance as the arbiter of contemporary taste and as setting the example by his exhibits of one year for what the ambitious youth of the next would paint, becomes paramount. He was never so unremittingly classical again as in 1769, but the predominance of his high classical manner persists until the completion of his designs for the window of New College Chapel at Oxford in 1781. In each exhibition he sought to include a subject picture and, parallel with his sublime or heroic subjects, such as 'Ugolino' (Royal Academy 1773: at Knole), we begin to find in 1773 single figures or fancy pieces of a more temperate caste, such as the 'Strawberry Girl' (Wallace Collection). Reynolds does not seem himself to have set great store by these, as a number did not find their way into the exhibitions, but they gradually came, especially through engravings, to have a powerful influence on popular taste. These were often excursions into the style of the Old Masters. The 'Shepherd Boy' *c.* 1772 (Earl of Halifax) was an experiment in the vein of Murillo, and the 'Children with Cabbage Net' (Royal Academy, 1775: Buscot; Plate 128B) is an essay in Rembrandtesque lighting and simple genre. The former anticipates Gainsborough's fancy pieces, and the latter is a precursor of the early (and best) style of Opie. Then the fancy piece and the child's portrait become blent as in the 'Master Crewe as "Henry VIII" ' (Royal Academy, 1776: Lord O'Neil), which is a fancy picture in parody of Holbein engagingly combined with a portrait. In this, and in the 'Lady Caroline Scott as "Winter" ' (Royal Academy, 1777: Duke of Buccleuch; Plate 134) he showed that, even in the middle of his most didactically classical phase, when the subject could not justify such treatment he had lost nothing of the freshness and perception of his understanding. There is a blend in such pictures of detached sympathy and authentic visual or pictorial values uncomplicated by those sentimental overtones which make similar works by Sir John Millais so nauseous to those who respect the work of the creative artist. It is this fact that, in so much of his best work, pictorial and human values reinforce one another, which makes Reynolds such a difficult painter for the purist critic to appreciate.

The most ambitious of all Reynolds's portrait commissions, the great group of 'The Family of the Duke of Marlborough' (Blenheim; Plate 133) appeared at the Academy of 1778. It remains still the most monumental achievement of British portraiture, worthy of Blenheim, which was to house it. There is nothing on this scale which can count seriously between Van Dyck's group at Wilton and this, unless it be the Hudson group at Blenheim of the 2nd Duke and his family, which is stiffly composed, though not without some ingenuity. As a composition the Van Dyck is a failure, while the Reynolds errs perhaps a little in being in accordance with all the rules. But it is not what other such groups had been in England, conversation pieces enlarged to the scale of life; it is a history picture. It is the one occasion when Reynolds was able to demonstrate to the full the possibilities of applying the historical grand style to portraiture. It is thus the very centrepiece of his public style. From this time onwards Reynolds was to experiment with great success in a more informal mode.

One of the most brilliant of such experiments was the 'Lady Worsley' (Royal Academy, 1780: Harewood House; Plate 138). Towards the end of the 1770s his devotion to a more or less classical style of drapery abated and he came to realize that he could infuse more life, with no loss of monumentality, into his full-length portraits, by the scrupulous observance of contemporary costume. It may be that it was Gainsborough's arrival in London in 1774 which partly led to this change. In the 'Countess of Bute' 1777/9 (Mount Stuart), an old lady slowly walking across a park with a folded blue parasol, and in the 'Lady Worsley' in a red riding-habit and a black feathered hat, he suddenly makes his Goddesses come down to earth. In such pictures he inaugurates his third and final style, which reverts once more to the human values of his earlier manner, but retains overtones of the classical style which it supersedes.

Reynolds's interest in the informal was supported and enriched by a journey that he made to Flanders and Holland in the summer of 1781. On this occasion he particularly studied Rubens and was impressed by the combination of dramatic and informal elements in some of his portraits, and also by the rich texture of his picture surface. The result was apparent at once in his own work and at its height in the Academy of 1786, at which he showed 'The Duchess of Devonshire and her Daughter' (Duke of Devonshire; Plate 136) and Viscount Cowdray's 'Joshua Sharpe' (Plate 127). It is instructive to compare the picture of the Duchess with the Althorp group of her mother with herself as a child painted a quarter of a century before. Both are, in a sense, intimate pictures of a mother and child. But the serenity of the earlier picture, which owes allegiance to the Italian masters of the High Renaissance, has given way to a lively and dramatic style akin to Rubens's baroque. The timeless has given place to the momentary, and there is something more modish about the later work which announces the age when fashions in dress and gesture made up a large part of the character of men and women. It is from Reynolds's works of the middle 1780s that Hoppner and Lawrence derived their style. Reynolds himself kept a fine balance between his baroque curtains of sealing-wax red, the shimmering muslins and the glossy blacks of men's or women's dresses, and his closely characterized faces, but the next generation was not always so scrupulous in its observance of the balance between the two interests in a portrait.

The 'Joshua Sharpe' and the 'Lord Heathfield' (Royal Academy, 1788) may be taken as among the finest examples of his latest style in men's portraits, one a study of a man of thought, the other of a man of action. Both are pictures of types as well as of individuals, and much richer compositional resources have gone to their making than in his earlier portraits. The head of the grave lawyer is placed low on the canvas, the mass of the body slumped and concentrated, while the arrangements of the soldier's body are reversed. In both the figure is off centre, and there is a dramatic intention in this displacement and in the lighting. Not all Reynolds's later work is contrived with such thought, and he used the classical mode, which perhaps came most easily to him, on appropriate occasions even in his latest works. But until his eyesight began to fail in 1789 and he was forced to give up painting, he was constantly developing new resources in his art. We know so much more of the routine production of his studio than we do in the case of earlier painters, that it is not altogether easy to judge him fairly, but, judged by the standard of the very considerable number of his finer works, we can say without hesitation that he was the chief intellectual force in the first great age of British painting.

Reynolds's Pupils

Few of Reynolds's direct pupils deserve attention, for he does not seem to have had the qualities of a teacher and there was a tendency for his pupils to degenerate into 'assistants'. The best known was Northcote, who finds his place under the history painters, but one or two, who were portraitists, deserve a passing mention. The best was Thomas Beach (1738–1806) a man from the West Country, who was a pupil of Reynolds about 1760/2 and finally settled in Bath, from at least 1769 until a few years before his death. In the middle 1770s Beach would spend a few months in London, but his chief practice was in

Bath itself, or in the West Country, in which he would make a summer tour, visiting a succession of country houses at which he was commissioned to paint portraits. His work can be followed from about 1768, when it owed a good deal to Reynolds's formulas, up to about 1800. It is never without a certain individual character and includes a number of group portraits (which are never 'conversation pieces'). These have a certain agreeable *gaucherie* in their composition, but his single busts or half-lengths are at least as good as Beechey's, whose work they anticipate, and have no disagreeable modishness.

Reynolds's only other direct pupil who merits notice is William Doughty, who died in 1782 on his way to India. He was a native of York and studied with Reynolds (*c.* 1775–1778), but is best known as a mezzotint engraver. He did not often reach the level of the portrait of his chief patron, 'William Mason', now in the York Gallery, which is perhaps the closest to Reynolds in style of any work by his pupils.

NOTES TO CHAPTER 16

1. First published by C. H. Collins Baker in *Gainsborough and Reynolds* (Pasadena, 1936) – a small pamphlet in the 'Enjoy your Museum' series.

2. Thomas Patch (1725–82), who lived mainly in Italy, carried on this tradition of caricature groups of travelling Englishmen: see F. J. B. Watson in *Walpole Society*, xxvii (1939/40), 15 ff.

3. Quoted from Sir James Caw in *Walpole Society*, xxv, 59.

4. W. T. Whitley, *Artists and their Friends . . .*, i, 167.

CHAPTER 17

RICHARD WILSON (1713–82)

WILSON fills much the same place in the development of a tradition of landscape painting in Britain that Reynolds does in the development of portraiture. Both appear on the scene at the same kind of moment, when the ground had already been broken for the establishment of a new style; both were sons of the clergy and had some pretensions to scholarship; both were in Italy in the early 1750s and became saturated with the Mediterranean tradition. But there the likeness ends and, in their outward circumstances, there was great disparity. Reynolds imposed his style upon contemporary public taste, but Wilson – although his qualities were always esteemed in the professional circle of artists and he became a foundation Royal Academician – had to wait until a generation after his death for serious appreciation. Reynolds had accommodating manners, a cool temper, and an eye for fame: Wilson had a sharp and explosive tongue and was no respecter of formality, and he loved his art more than his reputation. Wilson has less variety and range than Reynolds, nor did he steadily develop from strength to strength over a period of forty years: once formed his style changed little, and his best work was produced in a period of little more than twenty years. But it might be held that Wilson shows a greater intensity and power of creative imagination in establishing the classical British landscape than Reynolds required to establish the classical British portrait. His precursors had advanced less far along the road.

It is still matter for surprise that Wilson's landscapes met with such little success amongst an aristocracy which was modelling the landscape of its parks on the Italian scene, and hailed Claude as the master of the picturesque and Gaspard and Salvator Rosa as masters of the sublime. Wootton and Lambert had already introduced the conventions of Claude and Gaspard to some extent into British landscape painting. But a landscape to them was either a mere piece of decorative furniture or a record of an actual scene. It was Wilson who first charged the 'landscape' in Britain with the values of an independent work of art, sometimes – and in these he was less successful – by attempting the Grand Style and combining 'history' with landscape, and sometimes, which was his great achievement, by infusing into his scene a feeling, either solemn or lyrical, for the divine element in nature which can best be apprehended by likening it to the feeling which is the constant theme of Wordsworth. One cannot sum this up more clearly than by quoting Ruskin's words that with 'Richard Wilson the history of sincere landscape art founded on a meditative love of nature begins in England'.

We know something of Wilson's own views on landscape from a story related by Beechey,[1] who once asked Wilson whom he considered the best landscape painter, and received the reply: 'Claude for air and Gaspard for composition and sentiment. ... But there are two painters whose merit the world does not yet know, who will not fail hereafter to be highly valued, Cuyp and Mompers.'[2] Even without this, we should have no difficulty in claiming Claude, Gaspard, and Cuyp as the three principal ancestors of Wilson's style. Indeed, in speaking of Claude and Gaspard, Wilson was doing no more than echo the prevailing views on those masters. The building up of a formal composition with a dark foreground, tree or rock masses at either side, and the eye carried in the centre to a far mountain distance, the gradations finely articulated by a sarcophagus, a temple, and other nostalgic memorials of an ancient or Arcadian civilization, and peopled with appropriate figures, are the elements of Claude's formula. Gaspard, more than any other painter, had loved the sites at Tivoli, Frascati, Albano, and Nemi, which form much of the material of Wilson's repertory. From Cuyp, who was to come into his own at the end of the century – with Wilson himself – he learned the devoted study of clouds and the play of light in northern climates, which is absent in Claude's airy vault of Mediterranean sky, and a feeling for transient gleams of splendid light which can sometimes start tears in the beholders' eyes. In his finest designs, when produced at moments of unclouded sensibility, these qualities are to be found. That he repeated these designs, sometimes with subtle variations, sometimes mechanically, sometimes with downright carelessness as mere pot-boiling (in his latter days he called such compositions 'good breeders'), is a matter for regret at times, but does not affect the value of the original inspiration. All Wilson's own work, even when slovenly in execution – and his own shortfalling has enabled much rubbish to pass to-day falsely under his name – retains something of this core of seriousness which lingers from its original inspiration and has a solid formal framework. We can perhaps appreciate this most easily by comparing it with the work of a popular rival, who had been friendly with Wilson in Italy, Francesco Zuccarelli.

Zuccarelli (1702–88) was a painter of Tuscan origin who had found success at Venice in the production of fancy landscapes in rather watered imitation of Marco Ricci. He was in London from about 1751 to 1762 and again in 1768, when he became a foundation member of the Royal Academy, but he was back in Venice by 1772. In London he met with great success and Windsor Castle is still full of his facile works. Some contemporary critics held it against George III that, just as he patronized Ramsay and neglected Reynolds, he patronized Zuccarelli and neglected Wilson – and the charge seems true enough. Wilson's first biographer relates a story that, soon after Wilson's return from Italy (probably about 1758) a group of artists who considered themselves the arbiters of taste came to a resolution 'that the manner of Mr Wilson was not suited to the English taste, and that, if he hoped for patronage, he must change it for the lighter style of Zuccarelli'.[3] Wilson's style seemed solemn and severe (which indeed are his virtues) and his contemptuous refusal to change to the *lighter* style lost him much success. Zuccarelli's style is indeed 'light'. Although a few of his pictures include compositions from classical story treated in the spirit of a snuff-box, the bulk of them are loosely composed picturesque views of a predominantly Italian caste, peopled with shepherds or *contadine*. This passion for the frivolous was by no means confined only to George III and an echo of the same sort of complaint can be heard in Reynolds's *Fourteenth Discourse*, when he objects, of Wilson, that he has been 'guilty... of introducing gods and goddesses, ideal beings, into scenes which were by no means prepared to receive such personages. His landscapes were in reality too near common nature to admit supernatural objects.' It looks as though Sir

Joshua were not willing that *two* people should introduce the Grand Style into England, and, when he goes on to say that to do what Wilson was trying to do 'requires a mind thrown back two thousand years, and, as it were, naturalized in antiquity, like that of Niccolo Poussin', he seems also to be passing unfavourable judgement on his own works. To-day Wilson's landscapes do not seem to be too near to common nature, and Wilson never laid claim to emulating the heroic landscapes of Nicolas Poussin. Rather he was creating a new genre out of Claude and Gaspard, which one might have thought specifically appropriate to the taste of Northern gentlemen who were steeped in classical culture. His figure-scale is larger than Claude's and his Italian landscapes with classical figures are meant rather as nostalgic evocations of the ideal landscape of the Mediterranean world visibly inhabited by the proper persons, either mythological or historical – Diana and her nymphs at Nemi, and Cicero and his friends at Arpinum. His views of Nemi in fact are as convincing with classical beings in the foreground as they are when peopled only by the monks from the Convent at Genzano, or mere nameless figures from the contemporary scene.

Wilson was a Welshman, born at Penegoes in Montgomeryshire. He was apprenticed to a portrait painter in London and became himself a portraitist at least as advanced as, and of equal distinction with, anyone working in London in the middle of the 1740s. His 'Admiral Thomas Smith' (Plate 128A) at Greenwich (engraved 1746: a rather less free full-length variant of 1744 is at Hagley) is very little below Hogarth in its genial interpretation of character and in the attractive quality of its paint surface. But he was not suited by temperament to be a fashionable portraitist, and that he had leanings towards landscape painting at this time is clear from the fact that the pictures he chose to contribute to the collection at the Foundling Hospital in 1746 were two small circular prospects of London hospitals which are executed in a style very close to that of George Lambert. He had certainly painted a view of Dover before 1747[4] and it is possible that he had begun also to specialize in 'views of gentlemen's seats' before he left for Venice late in 1750. In the general history of British painting, however, his work is of little moment before his Italian journey and his decision, made after 1750, to become a painter of landscape.

Wilson remained in Venice (where he painted a few portraits, such as those at Cardiff and in the Tate Gallery) from about November 1750 until at least the latter part of 1751. Then, still torn between landscape and portrait, according to William Lock who was his fellow traveller, he passed through Rimini and Florence and reached Rome by January 1752.[5] It was Rome – and perhaps, in some slight degree, the encouragement of Vernet – which settled his uncertainty, and from 1753 he can be considered only as a painter of landscapes.

Wilson remained based on Rome from 1752 until 1756 or 1757. He ranged as far up the Tiber Valley as Terni and Narni and he went south, probably with Lord Dartmouth, to the classical sites round Naples, but it was the Roman Campagna which won his heart, as it had won Gaspard Poussin's a century earlier. The landscape of the Campagna did for Wilson what Michelangelo's and Raphael's works did for Reynolds during the same years. It saturated him with an ideal beauty from which his imagination was never to escape. From Claude he no doubt learned the bare grammar of classical landscape, but he studied the scene on the spot, with its accidents of cloud and shadow as Claude himself had done in his drawings. Wilson's own drawings on the ground are little more than memoranda, sometimes only of rocks or tombs or antique fragments. They have nothing of Claude's splendours about them and may rather be compared with the drawings such Dutchmen as Berghem must have brought back with them, which were to serve them for painting Italian scenes for the rest of their lives. But Wilson also had some practice in making drawings of studio compositions of the Roman scene, such as the series he made for Lord Dartmouth in 1754.[6] He probably also made a set of such compositional models or patterns for himself, and at least half of his output after his return to England was of Italian scenes. Except for a few favourite compositions such as the 'Bridge at Rimini', these fall mainly into two groups, scenes from the country immediately round Rome, Tivoli, Albano, Castelgandolfo, and Nemi, and scenes from the classic landscape of the Phlegraean fields, Cape Misenum, the Lucrine Lake, the Lago di Agnano, and the Bay of Baiae.

A few large paintings can be identified with certainty, from their bearing dates, as having been painted during Wilson's years in Rome. Two companion pictures, one dated 1753, are in Lord Dartmouth's collection, and one, dated 1755, is at Wrotham Park (Plate 140B). In these the tone is muted, almost subdued, and has none of that clear, hard brilliance of high Italian summer which we find in some of his later repetitions. The figures are meditative and pastoral, never classical, and in the Wrotham picture Wilson re-uses an old *motif* which makes it almost an account of his own feelings for his Italian years. Two classically dressed shepherds are conversing near a tombstone, on which is written 'Ego fui in Arcadia'. Zuccarelli had been commissioned, about 1751, by a Scottish patron, to do a picture with a similar tomb, which was to symbolize that his Grand Tour days were over, but Wilson invests his picture with a melancholy poetry unknown to Zuccarelli, and the nostalgia, which is a prominent element in his style, is here unusually explicit. It may be that Wilson also did a few oil studies more or less on the spot while in Italy. Such a picture as the 'Lago di Agnano' (Plate 140A) at Oxford, with its unforced range of tone and its lack of the dramatic contrasts which are natural in the studio, can hardly have been produced in any other way. It is nearer to Corot's early Roman studies than to any other paintings, and it suggests what possibilities were latent in Wilson's art if the times had been ripe for their development. One or two of the late battered sketches in the National collections, which were among Wilson's possessions at his death, reveal that he went on painting such things for his own pleasure into later life.

Wilson was settled in London by 1758 and we are on less secure ground for his chronology in his later years. But his work falls readily into three categories, the later Italian views, the interpretations of the British landscape scene, and commissioned views of country houses. These can most easily be considered in turn, premising that he seems to have done little work beyond copying his own old compositions after about 1774, and he retired to Wales, a broken man, about a year before his death in 1782.

The Italian landscapes can be divided into two classes, the dramatic 'histories' in the Grand Style, and the more tranquil compositions, whether peopled by divinities or peasants. The dramatic histories, at which Sir Joshua tilts in his *Discourses*, are very few in number (not more than half a dozen) but are important as they are presumably the pictures with which Wilson hoped to obtain the highest class of patronage. Probably all were painted before the foundation of the Academy in 1768 and they were finely engraved between 1761 and 1768. The earliest (? *c.* 1760/1) seems to have been the 'Niobe' (Plate 142) of which the finest (though perhaps not the earliest) recension was the picture in the Tate Gallery destroyed during the war. It is hardly distinguishable in spirit from Gaspard Poussin and it is difficult not to consider Reynolds's strictures as provoked by jealousy. That they were felt as justified by others, however, seems indicated from the fact that Wilson himself later tried to introduce more Salvatorial figures into such a scene (as in 'The Unransomed' at Port Sunlight) and that the classical figures in his later 'histories', such as 'Apollo and the Seasons', are hardly to be distinguished from pastoral personages.

The remaining Italian views make up about half of Wilson's output after he had returned to London. They are sunnier and more glowing – as if enriched by memory – than the scenes painted in Italy, and later versions are richer and more buttery in pigment than the earlier. But, aside from mere pot-boiling copies, they are wonderfully true in tone and have very little air of having been confected in the studio. Of certain popular designs, such as 'The White Monk', there are at least a dozen originals, each varying a little in the number or disposition of the figures, or in the contour of the distant hills. This does not indicate, as similar duplicates perhaps do in El Greco, a constant search for perfection of composition, but simply that, like all true artists who are forced by circumstances to repeat themselves, he could not bear to be always merely copying. In some arrangements there are adaptations which almost amount to a new picture, and the way, for instance, in which Wilson has converted the small upright design engraved as 'Hadrian's Villa' (of which one of the best versions is in the National Gallery) into a new oblong picture in the example at Manchester (Plate 141B), shows the bent of his art.

It is, however, in his interpretations of the British scene that Wilson made his most original contributions to landscape painting. His range of country is not very wide, Kew and Syon House, the Thames and Windsor Park, certain districts in the South-West, and, above all, the streams and mountains of his native Wales. His Welsh views are the cream of his work and he saw the country with a mind rich in memories of the Roman Campagna. His eye sought those aspects of the country which fell into the classic mould, and he composed landscape true to the tones of Wales but invested with the authority of the classical tradition. Sometimes we may wonder whether the river is the Arno or the Dee and, in a picture like 'A Road by a River' (Plate 145) at Gosford House, the air of Italy is so strong and the effect of the design (which unexpectedly echoes Canaletto) so powerful, that we have to look hard to distinguish the British figures and hollyhocks and the British trees. Such pictures are not imitations of Claude or the Old Masters, but the application of one of the great traditions of landscape painting, in a quite personal way, to the native scene. In what is perhaps the finest of all his designs, the 'Snowdon' (of which there are admirable examples both at Liverpool (Plate 143) and Nottingham), he produced the most classical of all British landscapes under the stress of the same deep feeling for mountain scenery as inspired so much of the finer portion of Wordsworth's poetry. Its deep sincerity shines out most fully if it is compared with Turner's brilliant imitations of this kind of Wilson, which always keep something of a borrowed sentiment about them.

In another field Wilson continued the line which had been marked out by George Lambert and brought the 'country house portrait' to its finest perfection. It may be that the singular view of 'Old Chatsworth House' (Duke of Devonshire), as it was at the close of the seventeenth century and based on a drawing by Siberechts, was painted before his Italian journey: in all probability the 'View of Woburn' (Duke of Bedford; Plate 141A) may have been painted before the old house was reconstructed in 1759. Wilson employs in this the resources of the poet and takes the genre right out of the province of the topographer. A modest piece of water in the foreground has become a lake: the wooded slopes behind the house have become steeper and more enchanted, and a distant view of hills, which is a pure memory of Italy, has been invented. Other views of this kind followed. The 'Moor Park' 1765 series (Marquess of Zetland) is only a fine continuation of the tradition of Lambert; but the five 'Views of Wilton', of uncertain date but probably fairly early, are of the highest originality. Picturesque views are taken of the house and park from all points: one is painted in emulation of a 'blue' Claude, another of a 'pink' Claude; the compositions of Dutch painters such as de Koninck are used as models, and bold experiments in light, such as the 'South View of Wilton from Temple Copse' (Plate 144), combine a close study of local atmospheric effects with the attempt at rivalling Ruisdael in a *coup de soleil*. The whole series is a succession of poems in the picturesque style unrivalled in the painting or poetry of the age, and has never been surpassed. In his romantic prospect of 'Houghton House' (Royal Academy, 1771: Woburn), Wilson is obviously emulating Ruisdael's views of the 'Castle of Bentheim'; and in 'Muswell Hill with Minchenden House' (Royal Academy, 1775: Stoneleigh Abbey) Philips de Koninck is again the model. Occasionally Turner, in his 'Somer Hill' (Edinburgh), or Constable continued this tradition of portraits of country houses, but Wilson explored the whole range of this specially British field and established the models which his successors have been more or less bound to follow. The whole range of Wilson's art has not yet been fully illustrated, but there can be little doubt that, when this is done, he will emerge as one of the major masters in the history of the British school.[7]

Rivals and Followers of Wilson

Worldly success, which passed Wilson by, was for a time liberally accorded to his younger contemporary George Barret (1732?–84), an Irishman whose landscapes were uncharitably (but not altogether unperceptively) described by Wilson as 'spinach and eggs'. Barret formed his landscape style in Ireland, in the Park at Powerscourt and amid the mildly Salvatorial scenery of the Dargle, and settled in London in 1762. In England he soon specialized in the painting of landscapes faithfully representing a particular spot or picturesque view, usually within the private demesne of a noble patron. He was a foundation member of the Royal Academy; and at the first Academy exhibition, whereas Wilson's pictures, as works of imagination, are simply entitled 'a landskip', Barret's scenes are particularized to the nearest milestone. Barret had a sound sense of what was picturesque in a commonplace way, he was troubled neither with the knowledge nor the love of classic landscape, and he provided what his noble patrons wanted. The dukes of

Portland and Buccleuch were his most notable patrons, and his best work can be seen in their collections to-day. In later life he tried to imitate something of Wilson's classical manner, but his design lacks Wilson's authority, his tone Wilson's sureness, and his trees Wilson's sense of organic growth. His work is chiefly interesting to-day as serving, by comparison with its prose, to set off the poetic quality of Wilson's vision.

Next in age after Barret was William Marlow (1740–1813), who had been a pupil of Samuel Scott from about 1756 to 1761, but is also listed by Wright among Wilson's pupils. His use of paint, in his best works, comes very close to Wilson, and the pattern of his career also resembles that of Wilson, except that, at the end of his life, Marlow never lacked money. From 1762 to 1765 Marlow travelled England and Wales as a wandering landscape painter, but the patronage of the Duchess of Northumberland enabled him to travel in France and Italy from 1765 to 1768. From the studies made on these journeys he produced French and Italian views for the rest of his life, repeating, like Wilson, favourite patterns. His prevailing tone is silvery and he experimented also in coast scenes in the style of Vernet, in admirable views (more literal than Wilson's) of country houses, such as the four of 1772 at Castle Howard, and even in such freaks of fancy as what Canaletto had called *capricci*. At Benham Park was a picture of St Paul's in which a Venetian canal has taken the place of Ludgate Hill (Plate 146), and in which the styles of Scott and Wilson meet. The topographer and the painter of picturesque landscape meet on the same canvas, as if to explain the fusion of the two styles which was taking place in the middle of the eighteenth century. By 1785 Marlow had retired professionally and only continued to paint a few landscapes for his own amusement.

Of the painters whose style was wholly formed by Wilson, only Thomas Jones (1743–1803) and William Hodges (1744–97) deserve attention, for Joseph Farington (1747–1821), although later a personality of high importance in the art world, was of little account as a painter. Thomas Jones, like Wilson a Welshman of good family, was at first educated for the Church: but he became a pupil of Wilson in 1762, first exhibited independently in 1765, and spent the years 1776 to 1782/3 in Italy, mainly at Rome and Naples. He painted some ambitious 'histories' in the style Wilson was practising in the 1760s (the most famous is at Leningrad), and, while in Italy, painted a few Italian views saturated with memories of Wilson, but lacking his sureness of tone and betraying rather a botanist's interest in foreground plants. He had little of value to contribute of his own and was much less of a personality than Hodges.

William Hodges (1744–97) was probably the most accomplished painter of fake Wilsons. He studied with Wilson *c.* 1763/6, and his style in 1772[8] was so close to his master's that rather more than the evidence of the eye is needed to distinguish between the two. But he did not meet with much success in London and, in 1772, joined Captain Cook's second voyage to the South Pacific as official landscape painter. He was employed on this journey 1772 to 1775, and he later visited India from 1780 to 1784. Something 'strange' in nature or architecture was needed to bring out Hodges' best qualities and he succeeded to a considerable extent 'in combining the documentary with the picturesque without sacrificing the requirements of either'.[9] A number of his views in the South Pacific were done for the Admiralty (he repeated them also for commercial purposes) and are now at Greenwich and the 'Tahiti' (Plate 147A) is a characteristic example. Wilson's rules of picture making and technique are both apparent, but Hodges skilfully adapted them to exotic material, to which he gave an air of documentary fidelity. He became a Royal Academician in 1787 and travelled in Europe, but his original contribution to landscape is limited to his handling of his Pacific and Indian sketches with few exceptions. He abandoned painting for banking in 1795 and committed suicide two years later.

NOTES TO CHAPTER 17

1. Quoted in W. T. Whitley, *Artists and their Friends* …, 380.

2. Thomas Wright, in his *Life of Wilson*, 1824 (and others since), has talked a great deal of nonsense about de Momper and his influence on Wilson. It is likely that Wilson's idea of 'Momper' was formed by two pictures acquired under that name by his early patron, Lord Dartmouth, which seem to be Neapolitan works of the seventeenth century.

3. T. Wright, *op. cit.*, 72.

4. J. S. Müller published an engraving in 1747 of 'Dover' after Wilson. A small picture belonging to Sir Alec Martin (in the style of the Foundling Hospital roundels) may well be the original for this, and I am inclined to think that the pictures at Cardiff and in Mrs Butler's possession are post-Italian variants.

5. Brinsley Ford, 'R. Wilson in Rome' in *Burl. Mag.*, XCII (May 1951), 157 ff.

6. Published by Brinsley Ford in *Burl. Mag.*, XC (Dec. 1948), 337 ff. Mr Ford's book on Wilson's drawings has elucidated further Wilson's manner of approach to his compositions.

7. Mr W. G. Constable has in hand a book which will be the first to illustrate Wilson's whole range.

8. See his 'View of a Greek House at Weston' (Society of Artists, 1772) illustrated in *Country Life*, 26 Apr. 1946, p. 760. Both in the Morland sale in 1863 and in Lord Hillingdon's sale in 1939 this passed as a classical scene by Wilson.

9. Bernard Smith in *Journal of the Warburg and Courtauld Institutes*, XIII (1950), 73.

CHAPTER 18

THOMAS GAINSBOROUGH

GAINSBOROUGH is the most difficult to assess fairly of all the major painters who make up the first great age of the native British School. His genius was lyrical: it developed altogether independently of the Mediterranean tradition, which cast a dominating shadow over the work of his chief contemporaries; his mind was wholly without the strong intellectual bias of Reynolds's, and sought its recreation with music and musicians and not in literature and the society of *hommes de lettres*. Yet he seemed, even to Reynolds, an artist of sufficient stature to become, after his death, the central theme of one of the *Discourses* (the Fourteenth) which he delivered at the Royal Academy prize-giving – an honour he accorded to no one else. For Reynolds his rival, because he never attempted 'history', was a 'genius in a lower rank of art'; yet he observes that 'if ever this nation should produce genius sufficient to acquire to us the honourable distinction of an English School, the name of Gainsborough will be transmitted to posterity, in the history of the art, among the very first of that rising name'. What he is captivated with in Gainsborough's art is 'the powerful impression of nature, which he exhibited in his portraits and in his landscapes, and the interesting simplicity and elegance of his little ordinary beggar children'. Reynolds's detailed comments are still the most judicious account of Gainsborough's virtues, in spite of, and because of, the fact that they were to some extent wrung from his reluctant admiration by a style and an approach to painting which were the reverse of his own. To Reynolds Gainsborough seemed something of what we should to-day call an 'impressionist', allowing too much to be filled in by the spectator: yet he praises 'his manner of forming all the parts of a picture together', and the great protagonist of the study of the Antique and of the Italian masters praises Gainsborough because 'he very judiciously applied himself to the Flemish school' and because 'his grace was not academical or antique, but selected by himself from the great school of nature'.

Nor can we do better than begin an attempt at appraising Gainsborough's work by asserting with Reynolds that he possessed the 'quality of lightness of manner and effect... to an unexampled degree of excellence' and that 'whether he most excelled in portraits, landscapes, or fancy pictures, it is difficult to determine'. The great mass of his surviving work is in portraiture, yet he several times complains in letters that he painted portraits only for a living and that his heart was in landscapes – and to-day he is mainly thought of as the only serious rival to Reynolds in portraits. An intelligent contemporary, who had been admirably painted by both Reynolds and Gainsborough, writes in 1787 to her husband that she cannot bear anyone having a Sir Joshua of him but herself, but that she thinks 'a daub by Gainsborough' would do well enough for his College.[1] By a 'daub' she probably meant only a sketchy, 'impressionist' likeness, and not what we would mean to-day. She realized that the full man would emerge only from the more intellectual and psychological approach of Reynolds, and it is true that Gainsborough is at his best with sitters who have almost no positive character and can be treated as arabesques with that lightness of manner and effect which made Lady Spencer call them 'daubs', and which causes them to become to-day, if they have been badly cleaned, little but expensive smudges. His landscapes present the same relation to reality and are animated by the same pervasive rhythm. For them we have Gainsborough's own words in a letter to Lord Hardwicke[2] that 'if his Lordship wishes to have anything tolerable of the name of Gainsborough, the subject altogether, as well as figures &c., must be of his own brain'. Curiously enough, it is in his 'fancy pictures' that he came closest to the direct imitation of nature, for he selected his 'little ordinary beggar children' (as Reynolds incorrectly called them, for they were far from 'ordinary') from a model or models which came close to his own ideal of the beauty of innocence in children. In all three genres his prevailing interest as a painter was the same – in the beauty of fleeting effects of shadow and texture. This led him not only to do much of his painting by candlelight, but also to dislike increasingly for his finished pictures the glare of public exhibitions, so that he finally withdrew altogether from showing his pictures at the Royal Academy. Gainsborough is thus a painter apart from the main stream of British painting during the first hundred years of the Academy's life – perhaps up to the time of Rossetti – in that he never submitted to the tyranny of the 'exhibition picture'. In the same way he never submitted (or did submit so rarely as makes no matter) to the co-operation of the drapery painter. In all his works he was something of a lyrical individualist and it is this quality which makes him so hard to judge fairly in an age of reason.

Reynolds and Wilson made their great contributions to the British school on the side of 'sense', Gainsborough's was all on the side of 'sensibility'. Gainsborough's first direct heir in British painting was Constable. On looking at Gainsborough's landscapes, says Constable, 'we find tears in our eyes, and know not what brings them', so that it will be seen that a history of British painting which closes with the dawn of the romantic age must treat Gainsborough as something of an isolated phenomenon. It would be convenient if, following the remarks of Reynolds and of most contemporary commentators, we could see in Gainsborough an artist who really sought his inspiration direct from nature, and specifically from the English scene. But, unfortunately, the better we know Gainsborough, the further this view seems to be from the truth. We have his own word for it that he held no very high opinion of the beauties of English landscape in the raw, and that his pictures had to be the creations of his own brain; and we even know that, towards the close of his life, he painted landscapes from little models made up of moss and pebbles, which he had arranged in his studio. Yet, if we compare them with the landscapes of painters from any other country, there remains something incomparably English about them, a perception of light and a feeling of English woodland growth. There can be no doubt that he loved to draw the rural scene direct, but the result was always transmuted into lyrical terms.

In the Victoria and Albert Museum is a drawing wrongly ascribed to Fuseli of Gainsborough sketching in the country, which is not without satirical overtones. It shows a gay, almost raffish, person reclining at ease, rather than settled with the high-minded earnestness of purpose of a pure artist communing with nature. He is drawing the landscape but his eye is at least as busily directed at a promising female form which diversifies the scene. I cannot help feeling that we shall come much nearer to understanding Gainsborough's work if we approach it after this first revealing glimpse of the man, than if, as was proper for Reynolds, we come to him with a letter of introduction from Dr Johnson. Gainsborough's art is gay, nervous, and full of 'enthusiasm': he was endowed with a heaven-sent sensibility to linear rhythms, and he loved the use of line in drawing and that effect in painting which he called 'the touch of the pencil'. Where Reynolds's figures are all fee-fi-fo-fum, standing solidly planted in English parks, Gainsborough's are sometimes almost wraiths, exhalations of the autumn foliage. Reynolds concentrates on mass and solid textures: Gainsborough loves everything which is flickering and evanescent, the play of shadow on a silk dress in movement, and his most astounding prodigies of painting can only be enjoyed to-day when, as in the 'Queen Charlotte' at Windsor, the old concealing, discoloured varnish has been removed and the texture of the painting below has remained unharmed.

In character he was blithe, optimistic, *enjoué*: everything that Reynolds was not. His letters are delightfully incautious and one of his daughters admitted to Farington that he would sometimes give way to conviviality to such an extent that he was unable to paint for a day or two. He was very good company and had no fine manners, and Mr Whitley, whose biography, in the matter of documentation, is one of the best things ever written on an English painter, seems to me to have falsified Gainsborough's character (and our understanding of his art) by trying to make him out to be much more of a model of the domestic virtues than he was. But, with all his 'Bohemian' leanings, he too, like Reynolds, must have been a prodigious worker. We have at present record of more than seven hundred portraits[3] (about 125 of them full-lengths), pretty well all painted, as all Reynolds's were not, with his own hand; perhaps two or three hundred landscapes of various sizes, a few fancy pieces, and an enormous quantity of landscape drawings.

Thomas Gainsborough was the son of a once prosperous cloth-merchant of Sudbury. He was the youngest of five sons (and there were also four daughters) and was born in 1727. He showed a decided leaning towards painting at an early age (conflicting evidence says towards landscape or portraiture) and was sent to London, with a view to becoming an artist, about 1740. The evidence about his training is obscure and conflicting, but a hypothetical account of his life between 1740 and about 1753, when he was settled in Ipswich, might be something like the following: these years were spent mainly in London, with periodic visits to Suffolk; the last few years mainly in Sudbury. He had no academic training, but two influences predominated: the influence of Gravelot, with whom he worked in London as an assistant in his engravings (before 1745), and the influence of Dutch seventeenth-century painters (notably Ruisdael and Wynants), whom he copied whenever he could and whose works he restored for dealers in London. This combined French and Dutch influence orientated him away from the prevailing Mediterranean tradition, but the French and the Dutch styles pulled in opposing directions. Gravelot's influence made for daintiness in the figure and for an emphasis on the city-dweller's conception of the pastoral idea in the tradition of Boucher and the lesser Frenchmen of the time: the Dutchmen brought him back to nature, but with the presupposition that nature needed 'composing'. To these influences must be added the fact that Gainsborough himself was clearly most sensitive to the specific beauties of the Suffolk scene, to the play of light on the trees, to the movements of clouds, and to the details of leafy growth. At the very end of this period, perhaps on a short visit to London in the early 1750s, Gainsborough seems to have come into direct contact with Hayman and to have been influenced by his figure style.

The certainly datable pictorial and other evidence for these years is rather meagre, but it is enough for our purpose. In 1745, no doubt on a visit to Suffolk, he painted a portrait of a dog named Bumper (more or less a bull-terrier, but described on the back of the canvas as 'a most remarkable sagacious Cur') which now belongs to Sir Edmund Bacon. In this Gainsborough's neat and natural touch and sense of the tone of tree and cloud in Suffolk landscape is already perfectly developed. In July 1746 he married in London (at Dr Keith's Chapel, which secured only legality and not parental consent) a girl named Margaret Burr, who added to personal charm (which declined as she grew older) the substantial advantage of having an annual allowance of £200, which was paid to her as being a natural daughter of a Duke of Beaufort. In 1748, certainly in London, he painted the view of 'The Charterhouse' (Plate 148), which he presented that year to the Foundling Hospital, as one of the series of views of London Hospitals contributed by Richard Wilson, Wale, and Haytley. Among its companions, which have all a topographical intention, it was a revolutionary work. Its companions all show the general plan and aspect of the building, but this is purely a picturesque landscape, with the emphasis on the play of light and shade, with the clouds as important as the buildings, and with the main emphasis on two children playing on the flagstones in a patch of sunlight. It is the loveliest and the most natural English landscape that had been painted up to date, the work of a youth of twenty-one. If the taste of the time had encouraged Gainsborough to continue on these lines, which were clearly natural to his genius, we may fairly suppose that he would have anticipated Constable. But it was not to be.

At the close of 1748, at Sudbury, where he had gone to help wind up his father's estate, he seems to have finished (perhaps, in its present form, to have painted entirely) the picture known as 'Gainsborough's Forest' (Plate 151) in the National Gallery. We have his own authority for its date, and it is an epitome of his early, artificial, landscape style, what he calls, in a letter written at the end of his life,[4] his 'imitations of little Dutch landscapes'. All the component details are Suffolk, and the light and tone are the very breath of a native English landscape, yet the composition is intensely artificial, a blend of Ruisdael and Wynants, with the eye carried far into the distance, down a break in the trees, by a winding sandy lane, with a horseman or a pedestrian to articulate each bend, to a distant church spire on the horizon. The foreground weeds, the donkeys, the flying duck, all the resources of composition he had learned from the then still unfashionable Dutch naturalist painters, are combined in this almost classic work, and it is not surprising that, when Boydell bought it in 1788, at the end of Gainsborough's life, and had it engraved, it should have been regarded as something of a phenomenon – for its Dutch prototypes were then beginning to come again into fashion. Gainsborough never again in his Suffolk period, which lasted until 1759, put all his learning into one composition, for there is matter in this for half a dozen of his normal little Suffolk landscapes. But it serves perhaps better than any other picture to epitomize his first landscape style, and it shows very clearly the subordinate part which the direct representation of nature played even in his earliest landscapes.

Not long after this, probably not later than 1749, Gainsborough painted one of the first, and certainly the loveliest, of his portrait groups, 'Mr and Mrs Andrews' (Plate 150). In this, for the first time, the old tradition of the 'conversation piece' becomes transmuted in the hands of an artist for whom the portrait and the landscape are both of equal interest. There is a dewy freshness about this picture, a friendly naturalness of vision of an artist as yet untainted by any preoccupation with fashionable taste, which makes it one of the eccentric masterpieces of English painting. In a sense it is at once the promise and fulfilment of all that Gainsborough might have been. For another fifteen years Gainsborough tried fitfully, in a series of experiments in compromise, to paint the English country gentleman at ease in the native English landscape, but it found no favour with his clients and he had at last to fall back on the kind of landscape setting as artificial as the Victorian photographer's backdrop.

It may well be that we must credit (or blame) Gainsborough himself for first experimenting with the artificial backdrop. The 'Heneage Lloyd and his Sister' at Cambridge can be only very little later than 'Mr and Mrs Andrews', and yet much of the freshness and lack of sophistication of the earlier picture has evaporated. Even in the matter of the lighting there is no common bond between the figures and the landscape, and the suggestion that the whim was Gainsborough's own and not his patron's becomes probable when we find him exploiting the two modes in portraits of the same family. The 'Unknown Lady and Gentleman' at Dulwich, resting by a stile in a lovely and natural Suffolk landscape, are companions to the 'Unknown Girl' in the Cook collection at Richmond,[5] who sits against the pompous backdrop of an Italianate villa. By the middle 1750s he had probably given up altogether portraiture on this neat and exquisite scale and turned to the more lucrative practice of portraits on the scale of life.

It is generally believed that Gainsborough settled at Ipswich about 1752, and the date is probably correct to within a year: but it may well be that he was not so much a stranger to London at this time as is usually inferred. The next certainly dated landscapes are the two of 1755 at Woburn,[6] which enable us to place in the early 1750s the group of landscapes with Suffolk scenes with a prevailing hot red-brown tone in the foreground, pinky-grey skies, and an abundance of swinging curves, which are the nearest an English painter ever got to the rococo style. The Woburn pictures, which were painted as overmantels, and thus to be considered as 'furniture pieces' rather than as serious landscapes, show an altogether different intention from the earlier 'little Dutch landscapes'. It is probable that the inspiration behind their new style is French, and that one of the main channels of that style was Gainsborough's remembrance of his time working for Gravelot. One of them is a rustic idyll: a milkmaid is resting her pails under a tree and is coyly half-refusing to give a bowl of milk to a boy who has been chopping wood (Plate 147B). The figures are a lovely echo in paint of Gravelot's engravings, and the cow is richly and thickly executed in a manner (unparalleled elsewhere in Gainsborough) which almost suggests that he had seen a Fragonard. In the other Woburn picture there is a group of figures loading a hay-cart in the background as naturally observed and as musical in rhythm as a passage from Watteau, and already heralding the spirit of his best landscapes of the Bath period.

But commissions for such works were rare and his living was mainly made from portraiture on the scale of life during his Ipswich years. We can discern how relatively ill at ease he still was in this genre by comparing the commissioned portraits with a number of portraits of himself and of his own family which he painted for pleasure during these years. Secure dates are very scarce. The formal and gauche 'Admiral Vernon' (National Portrait Gallery) can be dated about 1754: in 1756 he dated a portrait of one of the officers of the First Dragoon Guards,[7] who seem to have been stationed near Ipswich, for there is a companion portrait of a fellow officer, 'Hon. Charles Hamilton', (Tyninghame). This is beautifully drawn in the face, but the costume is still relatively hard and awkward. Gainsborough has set his head and shoulders in a feigned oval, which is based in design on the heavy fruited stone ovals of Mary Beale, but he has treated it with such fluency of paint and lightness of feeling that it gives the effect of a rococo setting. Here again we can discern the spirit of Gravelot and are reminded of the report that Gainsborough helped in engraving the decorations for the series of Houbraken's *Heads*. As an example of the latest and maturest phase of Gainsborough's Ipswich portraiture we can take the 'William Wollaston' (Christchurch Mansion, Ipswich; Plate 153), who can probably be dated about 1759 since the sitter was M.P. for Ipswich. His fondness for music obviously made him a sympathetic sitter and the result, though it shows, almost for the first time, Gainsborough's mature style as a fashionable portrait artist, has an informality that few Members of Parliament would have appreciated.

But his potential capacity as a portraitist only comes out in these years when there is no question of pleasing a patron. The lovely unfinished bust of himself belonging to the Marchioness of Cholmondeley is dated by good tradition about 1754, and the likeness in handling to the Woburn milkmaid gives a date of about 1755/6 for the picture of 'Gainsborough's Daughters chasing a Butterfly' (National Gallery; Plate 149). This is one of the most enchanting, most original, most native, and most natural things in English painting. It is unfinished, as all Gainsborough's private masterpieces tended to be – like the picture of the same two girls with a cat, of about two years later, also in the National Gallery; and perhaps we must put it into the same class as Hogarth's 'Servants', of pictures outside the direct line of their artist's development, which show what they might have been had they not been for ever involved in the economic system of their times. It is only in lyrical outbursts like these that we see Gainsborough's full gifts, which makes him so difficult to judge against Reynolds whose full powers were displayed in the business of exploiting a splendid sitter.

Gainsborough disposed of his house and furniture at Ipswich in October 1759 and moved to Bath, where he was established until he finally settled in London in the summer of 1774. Even during these years he paid periodical visits to London, but his main clientele was drawn from the fashionable visitors to Bath. It is clear that he was an instant success – he had, on his going, no one better than William Hoare to compete with, and the number of his portraits which date from about 1760 to 1764 is perhaps greater than the number for any other period. It includes also more thoroughly dull portraits than any other period, and it is perhaps worth noting that Reynolds in London was also busiest during just these years and also produced more pedestrian work than at any other time.

In the large world of fashion Gainsborough was very little known when he settled in Bath. By 1768, when the Royal Academy was formed in London, he was without hesitation asked to become a foundation member and he was the only portraitist so honoured who was not established in the metropolis. His first nine years at Bath were thus the period during which he gained this eminent position and the really formative years for his mature style.

He set about to remodel himself on the example of Van Dyck, whose work he had had little chance to see before he moved to Bath. For he realized that the English aristocratic idea of elegance was modelled on notions imbibed from portraits by Van Dyck. That he visited Wilton we know, and he made a small copy from memory (aided by the engraving) from Van Dyck's great family piece. Others of his large direct copies, such as the 'Lords John and Bernard Stuart' (St Louis, Mo.), are imitations of rarely exampled sympathy. The newly formed Society of Artists in London opened its first exhibition in London in 1760, but Gainsborough, who perhaps had nothing ready as yet of sufficiently ambitious scope, sent no picture to it until the exhibition of 1761. We can follow his exhibits yearly from then on until the first show of the Royal Academy in 1769, when he transferred his allegiance to the new institution. The portraits that he sent were almost all his finest full-lengths and most can be identified to-day, and when we survey this series we cannot be surprised that through them and timely appearances in London, perhaps at least once a year, his reputation had spread by 1768 so that he was as well known there as in Bath.

Yet he did not adapt his natural leaning towards a certain easy informality into the more solemn style, which the patrons of the age demanded, altogether easily. His first Bath portraits of men are the direct continuation of the late Ipswich style of the 'William Wollaston'. The 'Earl Nugent' (Corporation of Bristol) can be dated securely to 1760 and it is so nearly identical with the 'Sir William St Quinton' (Plate 152) at Scampston Hall, that the latter also must date from 1760. In this Gainsborough had the advantage of a sitter with whom he was on terms of considerable friendship and his sympathetic power of presenting character is at its best. The picture is in the tradition of Hogarth rather than of Reynolds, and the lesson of Van Dyck appears only in the curtain in the background. The overwhelming impact of Van Dyck appears, however, in the first of his ambitious female full-lengths, which we know to have been begun the same year (its execution dragged on for some years), the 'Miss Ford' (soon to become 'Mrs Thicknesse') now at Cincinnati (Plate 139). This was seen at Gainsborough's house by Mrs Delany, on 23 October 1760, and her comment on it in her letter to Mrs D'Ewes reveals the kind of feeling which Gainsborough had to contend with in his patrons: 'a most extraordinary figure,' – she calls it – 'handsome and bold; but I should be very sorry to have anyone I loved set forth in such a manner.' It was from people whom his patrons loved that Gainsborough hoped to earn his living by painting. He had to tame his perceptiveness and not make his ladies look 'bold'. In the same way his gentlemen's portraits at first must have looked to his sitters altogether too easy and rural, too informal. The 'William Poyntz', with his dog and gun at Althorp, resting against a tree trunk, was sent to the Society of Artists in 1762, and in 1763 he sent 'Mr Medlycott' (Watlington collection, Bermuda), who is sitting at ease on a rustic stile. We are perhaps right in seeing in these a gallant attempt at popularizing a more or less informal type of full-length, in which Gainsborough would not have to contend with Reynolds on his own field. But commissions of this sort did not follow and Gainsborough settled down to a more solemn manner.

How well he succeeded can be seen from the 'Mrs William Henry Portman' (lent by Viscount Portman to the Tate Gallery; Plate 156), which can be dated about 1767/8 from its close similarity of style with the securely datable 'Duchess of Montagu' at Bowhill. If we compare it with Reynolds's 'Lady Sarah Bunbury' (Plate 131), its contemporary within a year or two, we can discern very clearly the difference between these two pre-eminent masters of their time – although one should add in fairness that the Reynolds is not one of his happiest creations. In Gainsborough's picture the uniform beauty of the painting in face, hands and arms, dress, and even in the fragment of a Gainsborough land-scape in the room behind, is what most strikes one. It is lovely painting throughout, in harmony with the tender interpretation of the character of the lady, who was a widow of sixty. It is essentially modest in spirit and makes no claims which it cannot substantiate. The Reynolds is essentially immodest: it goes all out for an impression of grandeur and skimps the details. At this moment of his career Gainsborough reached the finest balance of observed truth and imagination.

This golden period lasted for a few years only, from just before the founding of the Royal Academy in 1768 until a little after Gainsborough migrated from Bath to London. His most remarkable exhibit at the first Academy exhibition in 1769 was the 'Isabella, Lady Molyneux', later Countess of Sefton, still in Lord Sefton's possession. It partakes of the same character as the 'Mrs Portman', and the figure, for all its lightness of painting in reflected silk, is solidly planted in the space and stands firmly upon her feet. When Gains-borough settled in London in 1774 he was at the height of his powers and he seems to have experienced no difficulty in finding a sufficient stream of sitters to keep him busy and bring in a substantial income. In fact he did not even exhibit at the Academy for the years 1773 to 1775. By 1780 he had gained the patronage of the Court (who were tempera-mentally averse to Reynolds) and he sent to the Academy in 1781 the full-lengths, now at Windsor, of 'George III' and 'Queen Charlotte', of which the latter is one of his most splendid pieces of painting. It is also among the latest of his really solid portraits.

For the portraits of Gainsborough's later London years, although they include what are some of his most famous and most expensive masterpieces, are strange, airy stuff. After a quarrel with the Academy in 1784 he never exhibited there again but held private ex-hibitions in his own house, where he could control the hanging and the lighting so that he had no need to give his pictures that weight and body which a portrait that must stand up to the rigours of an Academy exhibition requires. His genius became more and more feminine and fanciful, and the really memorable portraits of men of his London years are surprisingly few. The solid British male, in whose portraiture Reynolds excelled, was outside Gainsborough's sympathy. His best male portraits of these years are of a few dandies in the Prince of Wales's world; of foreign musicians, such as his friend Abel and his son-in-law, Fischer; and of young men in the flower of their almost feminine youth, such as the two 'Swinburne' portraits at Detroit, of 1785; or the 'Samuel Whitbread' of 1788 at Southill. The portrait of 'Johann Christian Fischer' (Plate 158), the hautboy-player (Royal Academy, 1780) at Buckingham Palace, is perhaps the finest of these as a work of art. Yet its virtues, the very emphasis on the sitter's sensibility, would put it beyond the pale as a portrait of an English gentleman of middle age (for Fischer was forty-seven when it was painted). The truth is that Gainsborough, in his latest years, was only supremely fitted to paint the portraits of lovely creatures who were all heart and sensibility. The finest of them are 'Mrs John Douglas' 1784 at Waddesdon (Plate 159); 'The Morning Walk' 1785 (lent by Lord Rothschild to Birmingham; Plate 157) – an incomparable picture of young love; 'Mrs Sheridan' 1785/6 at Washington; and 'Lady Bate-Dudley' 1787 (Baroness Burton). These are celestial beings, devoid of the grosser qualities of human personality, almost the loveliest garden-statues come to life. They belong to a world as artificial and as tenderly melancholy as the creations of Watteau, but they are life-size. They hardly belong to the history of portraiture so much as to the world of the 'fancy pictures' which Gainsborough was painting in his last few years.

These fancy pictures (the name was given to them by Reynolds) may be said to have developed naturally out of the landscapes that Gainsborough was painting, at first more for his own pleasure than for profit, from the time he settled in Bath. Very few such landscapes seem to have found buyers before he moved to London, and there is no firmly established chronological series (as there is with his portraits) by which we can trace his development as a landscape painter. We may presume that a picture such as 'Carthorses drinking at a Ford' (Tate 310) dates from about 1762, since the trees and foliage recall the background to 'Mr Poyntz': and a 'Milkmaid and Farmer's Boy' at Scampston has an old date of 1766 on its label and was probably exhibited at the Society of Artists that year. Both of these pictures are concerned with the same pictorial matter as the Woburn landscapes of 1755. It is a countryside in which the details are drawn from nature, inhabited by ideal small figures of persons of the peasant class whose life is unclouded by the existence of the world of towns or fashions – a sort of *faubourg* of Arcadia. As Gainsborough's imagination matured, he got nearer to Arcadia itself. The landscape broadens, the horizons become vaster, beyond ranges of pearly hills, and the peasant inhabitants become more closely summarized and more ideally lovely. But they remain figures seen at a distance and do not take on the stature of life-size creatures. The great masterpieces of Gainsborough's early mature landscape style, from the last years of his Bath period, are 'The Harvest Wagon' (Barber Institute, Birmingham; Plate 154), which traditionally dates about 1771, and 'Going to Market: Early Morning' (Holloway College, Egham), which was seen by Mrs Lybbe Powys at Stourhead in 1776.

'The Harvest Wagon' can claim to be one of the supreme masterpieces of British painting. It has a musical rhythm, kept exquisitely under control, both in the line and in the play of light and shade, and the single figures, both of people and horses, combine a genial naturalness with a perfection of grace which makes the most studied arrangement seem natural. The girls, probably taken from the painter's own daughters, are lovely creatures, fit inhabitants of a pastoral Arcadia. They are almost portraits, yet the distance from which they are seen gives them a certain generalized air which suggests that we are not peering too closely at an ideal world. Later, in his fancy pictures, Gainsborough was to try and take its actual portraiture. In terms of style the picture is almost Watteau re-created in an English landscape with ideal rustic humanity substituted for the fine ladies and fine gentlemen. If we compare it with the picture of 'The Mall, St James's Park' (Frick Gallery, New York), which Gainsborough painted about 1783 as what one might call a 'society' equivalent, as a deliberate English Watteau, we can see how much was lost in the later transcription. Unpleasant as it still is for some of us to introduce the shade of Marx into the history of art, it may contribute to the understanding of Gainsborough to make plain that, unlike Reynolds, whose finest achievements owe a good deal to his sense of social values, Gainsborough's supreme quality lay in his awareness that the beauty of the English scene lay in the lyrical exploitation of the world which lay outside the canons of social distinctions.

After settling in London Gainsborough certainly found himself more remote from the kind of nature which he took pleasure in studying directly. He seems to have fallen back on the great number of landscape studies which he had made and, with these and the little compositional models he made of pebbles, weeds, etc., to have become more and more artificial in the construction of his landscapes. From the earlier London years, up to about 1780, he was perhaps preoccupied especially with the theme of 'The Cottage Door' (a townsman's nostalgic view of the country), of which the finest horizontal design is at Cincinnati and the finest upright design (possibly Royal Academy, 1780) in the Huntington Foundation in California. There is a more artificial quality about these than in 'The Harvest Wagon'. Trees 'crowd into a shade' more knowingly; and, in the Huntington picture, the young mother has such an air of Mrs Sheridan in disguise that one can under-stand the absurd title long given to an unfinished study in the National collection as 'Mrs Graham as a Housemaid'. The difference between Gainsborough and his slightly earlier French parallels is that, whereas the French pictures were quite clearly, say, 'Mlle Clairon en bergère', in Gainsborough's there remains a certain ambiguity, and the protagonist seems rather to be a peasant woman who recalls Mrs Sheridan. There is even early evidence that Arcadia was giving way to Bohemia (the native country of Gainsborough's musician friend, C. F. Abel), and Bohemia has more of a smack of the stage about it than Arcadia. In Mrs Piozzi's old age, in 1807,[8] she writes about a landscape in her possession: 'The subject cattle driven down to drink, & the first cow expresses something of surprize as if an otter lurked under the bank. It is a *naked* looking landscape – done to divert Abel the Musician by representing *his* Country Bohemia in no favourable light. ...' One should beware of trusting too much to Mrs Piozzi's fancies, but her description puts us on the look-out for the curious overtones which lie in Gainsborough's London landscapes.

In 1781 Gainsborough experimented with sea pieces (one is in the Duke of West-minster's collection) and he followed this in 1783 with 'The mouth of the Thames' at Melbourne, a picture which strangely anticipates Wilson Steer. But these pictures were not in the main current of Gainsborough's style and the next change of a decisive character occurred the year of a visit to the Lake District in 1783. This may well have been a deliberate visit to the most Gaspardesque scenery in England, since Gainsborough had already exhibited in the Academy of 1783 (just before his visit to the Lakes) a 'Romantic Mountain Landscape' (Duke of Sutherland; Plate 155), wholly typical of the new style which his Lakeland visit encouraged. It was clearly an attempt at playing to the taste of the collecting classes, who were still hypnotized by the wild sublimities of the landscape style of Salvator Rosa and Gaspard Poussin. The smiling glades and happy pastoral figures have gone: shepherds live a more uneasy life at the mercy of a more inhospitable nature, but the 'scenery' (for such it is) is the creation of Gainsborough's own fancy on the model of the sublimities of Salvator and Gaspard.

But Gainsborough's latest kind of picture, by which he set most store (for he charged the highest prices for it) was the 'fancy picture', to whose invention he seems to have been inspired by seeing a version of one of Murillo's paintings of the 'Child St John' in the later 1770s.[9] At the same time he discovered several models (notably children) who seemed to combine remarkable and unsophisticated beauty with the simplicity of common life. It was as if one of the figures in his Bath period landscapes had become real and could be treated on the scale of portraiture. His first experiment in this vein (which perished in a fire in 1810) was shown at the Academy of 1781. It was in the new spirit of the times, for a writer in the *Gentleman's Magazine* for 1780 (p. 76) writes, '... and you will find artists who know nothing of Greek or Latin, and can hardly talk English, paint a beggar-boy or gypsey-girl with all the propriety of Poussin or Rubens'. The 'aristocratic' critic did not like the new experiment, but the Academies of the 1780s were soon abounding in pictures of this genre, and Gainsborough's second attempt, 'A Girl with Pigs' (Royal Academy; Plate 160A) at Castle Howard, earned unstinted praise from Reynolds, who bought the picture himself. It was almost the first new kind of picture, which had appeared at an exhibition since the Academy had started, which Reynolds himself had not initiated, and we can estimate something of the stir it created from the fact that the provincial Beechey, meeting the London Fuseli at Houghton in August 1785, and asking what were the latest developments in art in London, was told that 'Gainsborough was painting pigs and black-guards'.[10] His popular fancy pictures were also used by Gainsborough to provide a new incentive to the sale of his landscapes, for the group of 'The Girl with Pigs' reappears, seen again at the distance from which these ideal creatures had emerged for a moment into the foreground, in a landscape of 1786 which belongs to Lord Tollemache. In his last years Gainsborough seems to have found a market for the kind of picture which he most liked to paint. Portrait and landscape and the pastoral idea were merging into a new synthesis which anticipates the spirit of *Lyrical Ballads*, and Gainsborough's latest fancy picture, 'The Woodman' (now preserved only in engraving), in which he had developed from unaffected childhood to a more mature theme from 'common life', is an almost perfect counterpart to Wordsworth's *Michael*. In this highly creative and original phase Gainsborough was struck down by illness and died in 1788.

Gainsborough Dupont (c. 1754–97)

Gainsborough was too individual a stylist to have founded a school even to the limited extent to which Reynolds did: but his nephew, Gainsborough Dupont, who perhaps played a larger part in his studio than has been generally admitted, carried on the tradition without his uncle's genius. He engraved his uncle's 'fancy pieces', and the small-scale 'engraver's copies' which exist of some of them (and usually pass as original Gainsboroughs) are probably by him. He completed the series of portraits of members of Whitbread's brewery (now at Southill), which Gainsborough had begun, and one would be hard put to it, without his signature, to say that some of them are not by Gainsborough. He did not exhibit independently at the Royal Academy until 1790, and a tinge of the age of Lawrence begins to creep into his theatrical portraits about 1794.

Traces of Gainsborough's style are also sometimes visible in Thomas Hickey (1741–1824), an Irish portraitist, who worked at Bath and London between 1771 and 1778, but the bulk of whose rather inferior work was done in India after 1784.

NOTES TO CHAPTER 18

1. Lavinia, Countess Spencer, to her husband, 24 May 1787 (Althorp MSS.).

2. Letter to Lord Hardwicke of 21 July 1763 (Whitley, 41).

3. A preliminary check list of Gainsborough's portraits will appear in *Walpole Society*, xxxiii.

4. See Whitley, 298–9.

5. Both pictures have identical Christie stencils on the back, but the sitters still elude identification.

6. Gladys Scott Thomson in *Burl. Mag.*, xcii (July 1950), 201 f.

7. Last in Anon. sale, 13 Mar. 1936, lot 52. It was at one time in Sir Cuthbert Quilter's collection and wrongly called a portrait of 'Philip Thicknesse'.

8. *Thraliana*, ed. K. C. Balderston (1942), ii, 1082 n. The picture *may* be the one now at Bowood, but the identification is far from certain.

9. See my article (with a full catalogue of the 'fancy pictures') in *Burl. Mag.*, lxxxviii (June 1946), 134 ff.

10. W. Roberts, *Sir William Beechey*, 22.

CHAPTER 19

OTHER FOUNDATION MEMBERS OF THE
ROYAL ACADEMY

WHATEVER may have happened at later times – and a spirit of secession from the Academy showed itself very early with Gainsborough and Wright of Derby – pretty well all the London painters of real distinction, who had made their name, were appointed foundation members of the new institution. The exceptions were Ramsay, who had more or less given up private practice and, as King's painter, may have thought himself outside and above the Academy; Romney (who, almost alone, never showed at the Academy) whose reputation hardly begins before 1769; and the specialists in certain picture genres, which ranked low in the hierarchy of the day, such as sporting painters. We can consider them in three groups: the portraitists, the decorators, and the history painters.

The Portraitists: Cotes, Hone, Dance, and Mason Chamberlin

Francis Cotes (1726–70) was the most important fashionable painter of portraits in the 1760s apart from Gainsborough and Reynolds. In the last six years of his life his business was perhaps as great as theirs and only his early death has caused his name to sink into relative oblivion. The place that he would have taken, both in the eyes of fashion and of the historian, was taken by Romney, and it is hardly an accident that Romney did in fact succeed to his handsome studio and residence in Cavendish Square.

Few painters are more easy to recognize than Cotes. He went all out for health and youth and fine clothes, a strong likeness and no nonsense. His complexions are usually of milk and roses, his men bear no burden of intellect and his ladies are neither bold nor pensive; his draperies (which were often executed by Peter Toms) look as if they had come out of a bandbox and are subjected to no delicate nuances of light and shade. He has a personal, sometimes almost gaudy, palette which owes a good deal to his early training as a painter in crayons.

He studied crayons under Knapton during the years the latter was painting his portraits for the Dilettanti Society, and he achieved considerable mastery at drawing the face in that medium pretty young. There is a pastel of a man in the Leicester Art Gallery, dated 1747, which is as good as anything he did for a number of years. His earliest oil that I have seen dates from 1753 and is only a much more timid transcription into oil of his crayon manner. Up to about 1753 he leans neither very strongly to the old conservative style of portraiture nor to the new, but he made up his mind in the middle 1750s, threw over the patterns of Knapton and, presumably under the influence of Reynolds's success, came out as a leading exponent in the new lively style. The pastel of 'Sir Richard Hoare' (162A) at Stourhead, of 1757, shows him completely at ease in the new manner. It is even a little more vivacious than most Reynolds's of this date and considerably in advance of Gainsborough's contemporary commissioned portraits. One may have to give Cotes some of the credit for being a leader in the new style, but his spirit in general was not that of the innovator.

Up to the end of the 1750s pastels predominate very strongly in his work and he never altogether gave up their practice, but, when he settled in Cavendish Square in 1763, his main output was in oils, and his prices, twenty, forty, and eighty guineas, were between those of Reynolds and Gainsborough. He was in full fashionable practice by 1764 and, in 1767, he did full-lengths of the Queen, of a pair of the Princesses, and, among others, of the Duchess of Hamilton and Argyll (Inveraray). This last, in which the sunflower is wilting before the bright radiance of the sitter's beauty, is Cotes's solitary flight into fancy. A wholly typical work is the 'Unknown lady' (Plate 162B) of 1768 (once called 'Kitty Fisher') in the National Gallery. The carefully instantaneous pose – as in the work of fashionable photographers of a later age – the suspicion of a large baroque pot, the luxuriance of accessory foliage and draperies, and the sharp accent of vivacity explain Cotes's popularity – and also why we need linger very little over his work. He is not known to have attempted anything beyond straightforward portraits.

Nathaniel Hone (1718–84)

Hone, an Irishman, was the oldest of the generation who survived in good practice as a portrait painter into the 1780s. He seems to have started as a miniature painter, especially on enamel, and the high polish of that medium never altogether deserted him, though he gave it up in the 1760s. He must have learned his art under a painter of the generation of Dahl or Richardson, for a portrait of 1741, in the days when he is said to have practised as an itinerant painter, looks like a Richardson with a polished surface.[1] But it already has Hone's main characteristics, a certain look of smugness and a bright gleam in the eye. In York in 1742 he married a lady with an allowance as the natural daughter of a Duke (as Gainsborough did later). This enabled him to settle in London, study in Italy from 1750 to 1752, and gradually give up miniature painting for the more lucrative trade of oils on the scale of life. Very few of these have been traced before about 1763, by which date his style was settled and remains unchanged up to his death. The 'Kitty Fisher' (Plate 163A) of 1765 in the National Portrait Gallery is a typical specimen, more attractive than the average. It has his invariable bright gleam in the eye and a self-conscious look of posing for the painter. Hone was a vain man and his numerous 'Selfportraits' (National Portrait Gallery; Royal Academy Diploma Gallery; Dublin; Manchester, etc.) show his limited range at its fullest. He painted a few fancy subjects, with his children as models, of which 'The Piping Boy' (Royal Academy, 1769) in the Dublin Gallery is a pretty example and an early attempt at the genre. But although he showed several such at the Academy, they were all in his possession in 1775, when he held a private exhibition as the result of a disagreement with that body over a picture called 'The Conjurer'.[2] This was a very interesting skit on the President's practice of cribbing from the Old Masters and shows considerable powers of satirical invention. It is also interesting as marking the moment of a change of taste, for it is one of the first criticisms of the habit of exploiting the traditional arrangements of the classical masters, and foreshadows the new ideology of the romantic age, and the revaluation of 'originality'. But Hone himself had little new in his genius.

Nathaniel Dance (1735–1811)

One of the youngest of the foundation Academicians, Dance never became more than a man of promise, for he retired from professional practice in 1776, on inheriting a fortune. In 1783 he married an enormously wealthy widow and he resigned altogether from the Academy in 1790, when he became a Member of Parliament. His career was crowned in 1800 when he was created a Baronet as Sir Nathaniel Dance-Holland. Even so, he cuts a moderately substantial figure as an artist.

He was a pupil of Hayman (1753–5) – just when Hayman was at his best in small-scale 'conversations' that recall Gainsborough – and Dance is said to have encountered Gainsborough during these years. But his style was mainly formed in Rome, where he spent the ten years 1755 to 1764, in company with his brother George, the architect, and where he nursed a hopeless infatuation for Angelica Kauffmann. The chief influence on him in Rome was Batoni who gave a certain 'tone' to the informal conversation style he had acquired from Hayman, and his most pleasing pictures are certain groups of young travelling Englishmen, which can quite simply be defined as Hayman made elegant in the spirit of Batoni. Perhaps the best is 'Hugh, Duke of Northumberland, and his Tutor Mr Lippyatt' (Syon House; Plate 164A), signed and dated 1763 and exhibited at the Society of Artists in 1764. It is obviously the work of a 'gentleman' (which some of Hayman's groups were not) and it includes the Coliseum and a handsome classical vase for full measure. With the connexions he had made in Rome, Dance had no difficulty in establishing himself as a successful portrait painter on his return to London – at prices the half of Reynolds's. His style is difficult to define, yet easy to recognize. Uncharitable contemporaries called his 'George III' 'a bit of wood', and there is an unfashionable, but not altogether disagreeable, stiffness about his life-size figures. The 'Pratt Children' 1767 (Bayham Abbey; Plate 163B) shows him at his best, and with a dark background. When he introduced landscape he could never keep figure and landscape in tone. During his short public career he tried his hand also at more heroic themes. The 'Garrick as Richard III' (Royal Academy, 1771), now belonging to the Corporation of Stratford-on-Avon, is the best, and owes something to the model. When he worked entirely out of his head, as in the 'Death of Mark Antony' (Royal Academy, 1776) at Knole, he is a less interesting exponent of the manner of Gavin Hamilton.

Mason Chamberlin (d. 1787), who perhaps drew his normal patronage from the merchant classes, is the most puzzling of all these portrait painters. Enough of his work survives to make it clear that he has no normal style, but echoes something of his more distinguished contemporaries without ever descending to imitation. His three works publicly accessible in London – 'George, Earl of Crawford and his two Sons' (Royal Academy, 1775) formerly at Hutchison House; 'A Naval Officer and his Son' (Royal Academy 1776) at Greenwich; and 'Dr Hunter', c. 1781, in the offices of the Royal

Academy – all rouse the interest as out of the ordinary, but Chamberlin awaits further study. Of other portraitists who were foundation Academicians, West and Penny are both more profitably considered as painters of history.

The Decorators: Cipriani and Angelica Kauffmann

The pretty stipple engravings of Bartolozzi and others after their designs have made the names of Cipriani and Angelica Kauffman well known beyond their deserts. Both of them assiduously exhibited pictures of historical subjects at the Academy, and one must bear in mind Edwards's remark about Hayman, that 'he was unquestionably the best historical painter in the kingdom, before the arrival of Cipriani'. Yet I cannot claim ever to have seen a single one of Cipriani's easel pictures.

Giovanni Battista Cipriani (1727–85), a Florentine, came to England in 1755, and Angelica Kauffmann (1741–1807), a Tyrolese with an Italian training and a gay and charming personality, arrived in 1766. Both were steeped in the tricks of classical composition and were rich in those accomplishments which our native artists lacked. They could arrange any subject you liked to name, but neither had any feeling whatever for the human drama which renders interesting the narratives of Homer, Shakespeare, or Klopstock. Every subject, no matter what its size, was reduced to the spirit of a decorative vignette, and they cannot be numbered among the painters of history.

Angelica only remained in England until 1781, when she married an Italian painter, Antonio Zucchi, who had been one of the chief decorative artists employed by the brothers Adam. They settled in Rome, and Angelica later became one of the Goethe circle, and succeeded to some extent to the practice of Batoni as the painter of portraits of travelling Englishmen. During her English years she painted a few rather vapid portraits but was at her best in single decorative figures such as the four ovals at Burlington House, of 'Painting', 'Design', 'Genius', and 'Composition' (Plate 161A), which were originally executed for the ceiling of the Lecture Room at Somerset House. The figure of 'Composition', with her dividers and a chess board, symbolizes neatly enough her contribution to the arts in England. If literature had been her *métier*, these attributes would fittingly have been replaced by scissors and paste.

Portraitists who were not Academicians: Pine and Kettle

Two portrait painters, each with rather pronounced mannerisms, who did not make the grade as Academicians, although the quality of their best work deserved that honour, may be best mentioned here. Robert Edge Pine (c. 1730–88)[3] won premiums at the Society of Arts for history painting in 1760 and 1763, but his main work was in portraiture and he was one of the first to paint actor portraits in character parts. His masterpiece is an extremely sinister full-length of 'George II' (1762: at Audley End), which was not painted from life. He was also a friend of Garrick, of whom he painted numerous portraits. His style is nearer to Hone than to other contemporaries and he can often be recognized by a fondness for a three-quarter view of the head in which the far top-corner of the cranium seems to have been sliced off. He worked at Bath about 1772 to 1779, and his most ambitious group, the 'Family of the 1st Lord Bradford' (Weston Park), dates from these years. In 1784 he emigrated to Philadelphia, taking with him a number of subject pictures from Shakespeare, and he died in 1788 after four years' considerable practice as a portraitist in America.

Tilly Kettle (1735–86) was a rather better painter than Pine. He studied in the St Martin's Lane Academy and improved himself by copying Reynolds's portrait of 'Marchi' with variations. Certainly his first work, in the early 1760s, is wholly dependent on Reynolds, and of rather good qualities. In the middle 1760s he was touring the Midlands and then settled in London, where he leaned somewhat to the style of Cotes. His masterpiece is 'An Admiral in his Cabin issuing Orders' 1768 at Highnam Court. This excellent and original composition should have won him a place in the Academy, but he was disappointed, and this may have led him to go to India in 1769, the first painter of any consequence to make that journey. In India he prospered exceedingly from 1769 to 1776, doing numerous portraits of the Native Princes and Nabobs. But success did not attend his return to London, although such portraits as 'Admiral Kempenfeldt' 1783 at Greenwich are fully up to the level of Dance and Hone. After a short visit to Dublin he died in the Syrian Desert on his way to India to recoup his fortunes. Kettle's portraits can be readily recognized by his tendency to render the human skull as of the shape of a football, but he has a pleasant and decorative key of colour and ranks fairly high among the lesser portraitists of the time.

NOTES TO CHAPTER 19

1. A portrait of 'George Gostling' in Lady Roundway sale, Sotheby's, 2 Oct. 1946, lot 122.

2. Now belonging to J. Maher in Ireland. First published, with a full commentary, by A. N. L. Munby in *The Connoisseur*, Dec. 1947, 82 ff.

3. I take the dates from the fullest published source, *The Dictionary of American Biography*. Another 'R. Pine', called by Vertue 'young Pine', was signing amateurish crayon portraits as early as 1742. Most sources confuse two painters or give Robert Edge Pine's dates as 1742–90.

CHAPTER 20

THE PAINTERS OF HISTORY

THE subject of 'history' painting in Britain has been sadly bedevilled. The idea and the practice were by no means the same, but the idea took an intolerable time to die. It was inherited from the French Academy in the later seventeenth century, was accepted as an article of faith by cultivated Europe in the first half of the eighteenth century, and was blandly enunciated by Reynolds in his *Fourth Discourse* as an unquestioned truth. Barry put it in the following form: 'History painting and sculpture should be the main views of any people desirous of gaining honours by the arts. These are the tests by which the national character will be tried in after-ages, and by which it has been, and is now, tried by the natives of other countries.' Barry believed this perverse nonsense, and so did Haydon after him, and the result was disaster for both. They tried to live by a theory and did not reckon with the state of patronage in the country where they worked. It was a general belief among the writers on art that, once art was linked to royal patronage – as it had been by the foundation of the Royal Academy – a time of prosperity would dawn for artists as it had in the time of Louis XIV. But they do these things much better in France – and much sooner. The first faint imitation of Colbert to have been produced in Britain was the Arts Council, and the difference between George III and Louis XIV was crisply but unkindly told by 'Peter Pindar', who wrote of George III:

> Of modern works he makes a jest –
> Except the works of Mr West.

The 'sublime' style which Reynolds inculcated, the kind of subject he favoured and its dependence on classical models, has already been seen in his 'Death of Dido' (Royal Academy, 1781; Plate 137). It may be that the President had more than an inkling of the direction from which the attack would come, for he sent to the Academy of 1774 'The Triumph of Truth, with the Portrait of a Gentleman' – which was in fact the portrait of 'Dr Beattie', now at Marischal College, Aberdeen – in which the public readily recognized, in the dim faces of Truth's opponents, the features of Voltaire, Hume, and Gibbon. These authors had been undermining the heroic conception of history, and the interesting trend in history painting during the first twenty years of the Academy's life is the gradual debunking of the Augustan tradition, in which everyone had to be dressed in classical draperies. The change was not all in one direction. One line, the most daring, introduced the representation of contemporary events, and culminates in the heroic *reportage* of Copley; another substituted for the classical trappings an equally artificial mode, based on popular misconceptions of 'contemporary' costume, and led to the Wardour Street medievalism of Northcote or Opie and of many of the lesser contributors to Boydell's Shakespeare Gallery; while yet a third treated subjects in themselves so gentle, or historical events in so mild a manner, that the 'grand style' was not involved at all – as was the case with Edward Penny. A romantic history style, more dependent on literature than on the tradition of classical painting, also arose in such painters as the Runcimans and Wright of Derby, which culminated, in the next generation, in the stormy style of Fuseli.

The latter years of the eighteenth century were certainly the golden age – if there ever was one – of the history picture in Britain. Benjamin West, by monopolizing royal patronage in this field, was paid over £34,000 by the Crown for his history pictures alone between 1769 and 1801: and Alderman Boydell, who almost alone seems to have learned Hogarth's lesson that history pictures could be made to pay by selling engravings after them, commissioned his Shakespeare Gallery in the years following 1786. More than one hundred and fifty pictures, both large and small, made up the final Shakespeare Gallery, commissioned from more than thirty artists, and Boydell's health as 'the commercial Maecenas of England' was drunk at the Academy banquet in 1789, on Burke's suggestion, by the President, the Prince of Wales and the assembled guests. Boydell's venture was followed by Macklin's 'Poets' Gallery', from 1788 onwards, but these groups of commissioned pictures were made to pay by the sale of engravings and of entrance money to the exhibitions, and they did not provoke any serious patronage of the history picture among British private collectors. When the Napoleonic wars put on the market Old Masters of a quality hitherto unobtainable by British collectors the patronage of our native produce very nearly evaporated altogether.

Of those artists who aspired to the grand style of history painting in the pure form in which Reynolds enunciated it, with heroic subjects and life-size figures, either nude or in classical draperies, only two painters need be considered – Gavin Hamilton and James Barry, the former a Scottish gentleman, the other an Irishman of very elevated enthusiasm. Gavin Hamilton (1723–98) must count as a considerable rarity in British painting, for his pictures were better known in Europe than at home, and even had a certain influence on French neo-classicism. He went young to Italy and was a pupil of Agostino Masucci in the 1740s: in London about 1752 he painted a few portraits – notably of the Gunning sisters – but he had an irresistible bent towards history and soon after settled in Rome for the rest of his life. In Rome he was a leading member of the classical school of which Mengs was the most reputed painter and Winckelmann the prophet, and he started his large-scale illustrations to the story of the *Iliad* in the 1760s. Being a man of some means he had these engraved by Cunego (from about 1764 onwards) and his reputation expanded throughout Europe. The Director of the French Academy at Rome mentions his work in 1763, and Grimm, writing to the Empress Catherine in 1779, mentions his painting with considerable approval. Only in Britain was he almost unknown, although he contrived to sell a number of his large works to British collectors by insisting on a commission as part payment for the works by Old Masters or classical statues in which he trafficked.[1] His pictures are rarely to be met with to-day, but the 'Hector's Farewell to Andromache' (Duke of Hamilton, Holyrood Palace; Plate 170B) is almost a Jacques Louis David *avant la lettre*. He deserves more attention than he has received and he boldly persisted in the old classical tradition after the innovations of West and Copley in the modern heroic manner had won the day, so that a writer in 1793[2] says of his works that they preserve 'a propriety with regard to *costume* which distinguishes them from most modern compositions, and a dignity of manner that is seldom attained by those who make living characters the principal object of their studies'. Perhaps no statement shows so clearly the revolution in history painting which had occurred between 1769 and 1793.

James Barry (1741–1806) was an altogether different character. His historical importance extends beyond the scope of this volume, for Barry and Fuseli between them made up a considerable part of the background which helps to account for Blake – and Fuseli can only be dealt with by the historian of the romantic period. Barry was an Irishman of humble origin, who had more than a spark, perhaps the real fire, of genius in his make-up. But he had a wild and arrogant enthusiasm, the tongue of an asp, and a voluble inconsiderateness for others which led to his undoing. As a self-trained stripling he brought a whole group of historical compositions to Dublin in 1763, impressed Edmund Burke with his genius, and was brought by Burke to London in 1764, where he was introduced to Reynolds and 'Athenian' Stuart, from both of whom he met with encouragement and kindness. No painter of his generation took the President's encouragement towards the 'grand style' so close to the letter and with so small a grain of the salt of common sense. Again financed by Burke, Barry went to Italy in 1766 and remained until 1771, saturating himself only too faithfully in the ancients and in Michelangelo. His genius, which was authentic, was recognized at once on his return, for he became an A.R.A. in 1772 and a R.A. in 1773. But he only became the more intransigent in his high classical principles and exhibited in 1776 a 'Death of Wolfe', which, no doubt as an attack on West's famous picture of 1771, appears to have been first painted in the classical nude and then draped with modern uniforms, as if to show the incompatibility of the heroic style with modern costume.[3] Whatever disagreements may have in fact arisen over this, he never exhibited at the Academy again. But the years 1777 to 1783 were wholly taken up with his major work and most serious claim to fame – the series of large canvases (two of them forty-two feet long) which he painted for the Great Room of the Society of Arts. The theme of the whole decoration is *The Progress of Human Culture* and these paintings must still be accounted the most considerable achievement in the true 'grand style' by any British painter of the century. They do not, as Barry believed, compare favourably with the work of Raphael, but they are works of genius and have a general grandeur of conception, in spite of peccancy in the taste of numerous details. Close in date to these, perhaps about 1784, must be Barry's portrait of 'Hugh, Duke of Northumberland' (Syon House; Plate 167), which has the gravity of their spirit and is more accessible to illustration. It has a kind of solemnity which was denied to Reynolds, and the resources of art which Barry here employs would perhaps have been more fitting for St George about to affront the dragon – and Barry did in fact paint a similar picture of the 'Prince of Wales as St George' now in the Municipal Gallery at Cork – than for a portrait of a peer in Garter Robes. But never was there a more vivid example of Reynolds's recommendation to elevate the style of portraiture by borrowing from the grand style. Barry's taste for sublimity was far better understood than Reynolds's, but lack of the right patronage turned him sour. Becoming Professor of Painting at the Academy about the time his work for the Society of Arts was completed, he used his lectures increasingly as a vehicle for the abuse of his colleagues, and was finally turned out of the Academy in 1799. To some extent his spirit was deranged, but it was a spirit of a noble fire.

Fire was what was lacking in Benjamin West, whose prodigious success provides the contrast to Barry's misery. Their pretensions had something in common, for Raphael's name was mentioned freely by West's admirers also and West gave his own son the Christian name of Raphael. Benjamin West (1738–1820) came of Pennsylvania Quaker stock, and it is significant that he and Copley (a New Englander) were the pioneers in modernizing British history painting. Forerunners of some of the characters in Henry James's novels, they came to Europe full of eagerness and appreciation but with minds free from the incubus of inherited tradition in the matter of high art. It may have seemed almost as strange to them as it does to us to-day to represent scenes from contemporary history in classical costume, and their minds were better attuned than were those of professional British artists to understand what was of interest to the common man. The native painters who worked for the upper classes had been saturated, from the beginning of their working life, with the prejudices of the 'connoisseurs'. West to some extent, and Copley more fully, realized the value for the artist of the new feeling of national pride in the achievements of one's own nation which had grown up with the generality of the public, and which had been fed hitherto, in the matter of art, only by the engravings in such volumes as Rapin's or Hume's histories. The stage too had begun to affect 'contemporary' costume when possible, and West and Copley, by the shortness of their roots in the European tradition, rather than by any profound originality in their own natures, were able to become the first articulate painters of a new range of subject-matter of general interest. It is the story of Hogarth over again with a different public. For the engraving of West's 'Death of Wolfe' (Plate 168B) is said to have earned as much as £15,000. West also was lucky in that the very mediocrity of his mind found a kindred spirit in the mind of George III.

A dispassionate study of West, whose importance at the time can be gauged from the fact that he succeeded Reynolds as President of the Royal Academy, is a desideratum. Writers who have been concerned with him incidentally have hitherto been forced to rely, however cautiously, on Galt's biography, published in part after West's death, but with his approval, which partakes of a somewhat legendary character. It is written in a spirit which we are more accustomed to find applied to South Italian Saints than to a Quaker Academician who lived into the last century, and it is probable that most of its famous anecdotes have been improved in the telling. The evidence of his pictures themselves, in so far as they can be identified to-day, is all that we can go upon securely at present.

Having learned 'the mechanical part' of painting in America, the young West spent the years 1760–3 in Italy, where he visited Rome, Florence, Bologna, and Venice. In Rome he was certainly in close contact with the circle of Mengs and Gavin Hamilton, and his notion of the subject-matter of history painting was certainly coloured by theirs. But he had had no experience of the academic practice of drawing from the Antique, and it may well have been this fact, rather than any more positive predilection, which turned West's ideas to the kind of history picture which Haydon later called scornfully 'Poussin size'.

In the meantime he improved his social contacts and became reasonably proficient as a portrait painter in a style nearer to Mengs than to Reynolds.

It was as a portrait painter that West set himself up in London, where he decided to settle soon after his arrival in 1763, but he sent two subject pieces to the exhibition of the Society of Arts in 1764. His success, both in Rome and in London, can be partly accounted for by his being an American, and thus a 'phenomenon' in which Society could allow itself to be interested. Cardinal Albani (who was blind) had naïvely supposed that he was a Red Indian, and it was an age when Wonders from the Western World were all the rage. At any rate his history pictures met with some response from the bench of Bishops, a body of men who have patronized the arts with effect on no other occasion, and one cannot help wondering whether the reason for this was not some obscure feeling of transferred missionary endeavour. It was Archbishop Drummond who introduced West to the King in 1768, with a picture of 'Agrippina landing at Brindisi', which had been commissioned by himself. The result was that the King suggested to West the subject of 'The final Departure of Regulus from Rome' (Plate 170A) as a commission for the royal collection. The 'Regulus' appeared at the first exhibition of the Academy in 1769 (of which West became a foundation member) and West's long association with the Crown began.

The 'Agrippina' and the 'Regulus' are remarkable works for their time. Their style is that of Gavin Hamilton, reduced to the more manageable size of Poussin. There is, above all, much of Raphael in them, but nothing of that extraordinary combination of harmony and purely formal qualities which gives Raphael's designs the air of being by an intellectually superior being. Their limitations made them the very pictures for George III and they were quickly popularized in engravings. A few British painters, such as Alexander Runciman, imitated West's choice of subjects, but this was reserved rather for the French, whose minor Academic painters followed West's choice of subjects with a fidelity which cannot be accidental.[4] But West himself soon graduated from classical subjects in the neo-classical manner to the baroque rendering of contemporary history, and showed at the Academy of 1771 his 'Death of Wolfe',[5] which is generally accepted, with reasonable accuracy, as marking the turning-point from the old style of history painting to the new.

The story, as related by West's hagiographer, is that Reynolds, hearing that West was painting a heroic history of the death of Wolfe in contemporary costume and not in classical draperies, came to persuade him against any such impropriety; that West used the various arguments that one would imagine to-day and asked Reynolds to suspend judgement until the work was finished; and that, on his final visit, Reynolds generously said: 'Mr West has conquered.... I foresee that this picture will not only become one of the most popular, but occasion a revolution in the art.' It is perhaps more parable than truth, but West's picture did in fact become extremely popular and helped to stimulate a movement away from classical subjects to the heroic rendering of national or contemporary history.

The picture itself has no claims to accuracy of historical presentation. Except for Wolfe himself, hardly any of the figures in the picture were present at his death, and the Red Indian is a purely symbolic figure. Without accepting all the sources put forward by Mr

Charles Mitchell[6] as contributing to West's design, we can agree that it is composed on a standard baroque formula and that the main group is based on the traditional pattern of a 'Mourning over the dead Christ'. What has not always been observed, in the heat of controversy, is that, within its limits, it is rather a good picture. West himself does not seem at the time to have thought he was doing anything revolutionary in the sense that it was 'modern', for he proposed to the King, for a series of companion pictures of 'historic deaths', those of 'Epaminondas' and 'Bayard', both of which were exhibited at the Academy of 1773. The former was treated in the classical manner, but the latter, as befitted a 'medieval' subject and in consonance with the new practices of the contemporary stage, is modelled on Salvator Rosa and in tune with the bandit pictures which were being popularized at exactly this time by John Hamilton Mortimer. It was this last style which West exploited most freely in his later works, and by which he belongs also to the romantic period.

Even by these pictures West's historical vein was not wholly exhausted, for a picture like 'The Apotheosis of Prince Alfred and Prince Octavius' (c. 1784: Kensington Palace; Plate 169) is altogether and literally in the style of Mengs. Unfortunately, like Gavin Hamilton, West had almost no feeling for colour or for the texture of paint. His contemporary fame and his legend have militated against a judicious appreciation of his work, which has an importance in the general history of European art, but left very little impression on the national school.

It was left to a second American painter, John Singleton Copley (1738–1815) to exploit to the full the popular subject from contemporary history, for which West had led the way. Unlike West, Copley was a Bostonian, and he had none of the curiosity value of West. What is more, he had waited fourteen years longer than West to come to Europe and had already formed a highly personal and distinguished style of his own in portraiture before he set out. Copley's New England style is unfortunately no part of the history of British painting: 'unfortunately' because, at its best, it is rivalled only by Hogarth for directness and sincerity of approach. Copley had had to work it out for himself to suit a clientele who accepted the general rule that Truth was to be preferred to Beauty, and who were prepared to give the painter long sittings. Neither of these conditions obtained in Europe and Copley felt that he must learn a new language during the period in 1774/5 that he spent in Italy and dashing through half Europe on his way from Italy to London. He learned it so effectively that no traces of his New England style survived, and he settled in London to paint portraits and groups in a style between Reynolds and West in 1775. As an American portraitist Copley rates very high indeed; as a European portraitist he can only be considered as an accomplished secondary painter except for his rare incursions into the rococo conversation piece, such as 'The Three Princesses' (Royal Academy, 1785) at Buckingham Palace, and 'The Sitwell Family' 1787 at Renishaw Hall. These are, in their way, masterpieces and owe a good deal of their charm to being so agreeably unEnglish, since the children conduct themselves in a manner which, though not uncommon with children, is more lively than most British parents liked to have perpetuated in a picture.

The prime virtue of these pictures rests in their composition, and 'composition' was what Copley found he had a genius for when he came to Europe. He had been so isolated from academic practice in Boston that he had no idea how a painter set about a group portrait, and it is astonishing to find the best painter in New England writing to his half-brother as follows on his first arrival in London at the age of thirty-six: 'The means by which composition is obtained is easier than I thought it had been. The sketches are made from life, not only from figures singly, but often by groups. This, you remember, we often talked of, and by this a great difficulty is removed that lay on my mind.' A new world of art had opened for him and he had discovered his personal gift. In Rome he painted an 'Ascension' (Boston) which is perhaps superior to any of West's compositions in his own style, and by 1778 he felt himself sufficiently established in London to send a composition to the Academy.

The picture of 'Brook Watson and the Shark' (examples are at Christ's Hospital (Plate 172), London, and at Boston), sent to the Academy in 1778, broke all the accepted rules of history painting. Much more than West's 'Death of Wolfe' does it deserve to be considered the pioneer work of a new age, for its like was not produced until the great days of the French romantics in the 1820s. The subject was contemporary and not classical: the hero was no national figure but rather the kind of person made familiar to-day by some of the Sunday newspapers: and the action has no grave historical import or moral lesson for mankind, but was frankly exciting and romantic. It is extremely unlikely that Copley had any idea how revolutionary his work was, and the reason why he turned from such pictures to more notable scenes from contemporary history was doubtless the fact that the engravings from them would sell to a much wider public. But the later works all partake of the same characteristics: they are dramatic, they have a contemporary subject, they are presented with a sufficient degree of accurate local colour to count as heroic *reportage*, and they gave Copley a chance to exploit his newly found passion for composition. The later ones were so vast that they had to be shown in special buildings by themselves, where they provided, to the exasperation of the Academicians, a new and popular rival to the exhibitions at the Royal Academy.

Copley's pictures of this class, which rank as the one series of great modern history paintings done in England in the eighteenth century, are as follows: the 'Death of Chatham', painted 1779/80 (Tate Gallery); the 'Death of Major Pierson' 1783 (Tate Gallery; Plate 173); 'The Repulse of the Floating Batteries at Gibraltar', finished 1791 (Guildhall, London: finished study in Tate Gallery); 'Admiral Duncan's Victory at Camperdown', finished 1799 (Camperdown House, Dundee). The unwieldy size of the last two has caused the first to be inaccessible and the last to be immovable, but the whole series of pictures was an artistic achievement of a new kind. The finest is the 'Death of Major Pierson', in which Copley was not faced with the difficulty of including a vast number of individual portraits. In the frightened mother and children at the right he has been able to include figures not essential to the story and so to concentrate less on documentary history and more on exciting and romantic elements in the scene. This splendid picture would hold its own and find its natural affinities in a room with *Les Pestiférés de Jaffa* and the great French romantic histories of the next century. One has only to compare Copley's works with the feeble historical subjects of George Carter, with whom Copley had travelled from London to Italy, to see how much that was new the American artist introduced into British painting. But for all the popular enthusiasm these pictures aroused, their lesson was lost on British artists and they founded no school of history painting.

The next type of history painter can be broadly classified as 'the Boydell group', from the stagy kind of history picture which made up Boydell's Shakespeare Gallery. The two most important members of this group are Opie and Northcote, who both started their London careers about the same time, and both became A.R.A. 1786 and R.A. 1787. Opie was much the younger, but much the more considerable talent, though he lacked the kind of training and knowledge of the Antique which Northcote had. They both came from humble West Country stock and became friends.

John Opie (1761–1807) had the makings of a serious painter in him and the fact that so many of his portraits are thoroughly dull, if not frankly bad, was due to the fact that he had no elegance in his make-up but was commissioned to do portraits of fashionable persons. His father was a Cornish carpenter, and the young Opie, who showed a precocious passion for drawing, was taken up, when he was fourteen, by John Wolcot, best known by his satirical verse under the name of 'Peter Pindar', who was then practising medicine in Cornwall. Wolcot had been a pupil of Richard Wilson and he constituted himself the young Opie's teacher and impresario. What training he gave him he kept remarkably dark, since his aim was to bring him upon the London stage as 'the Cornish Wonder', an untrained and self-taught prodigy, once he had rubbed off some of the young man's superficial asperities. Wolcot's scheme was largely successful and his advice both original and sound. He saw that the young man had a natural gift for local tone and for the strong rendering of rough natural types in a correspondingly strong chiaroscuro, and he fed him on Rembrandt and the Tenebrists, no doubt through the medium of prints. This was done with something of the secrecy which now attends the training of a race-horse, and Wolcot established himself with the young Opie in London in 1781 and pretended that the young prodigy had never seen an Old Master or had any serious training. At the Academy of 1782, and in the selection of pictures taken to show the King, only such morsels of common nature were selected as 'A Jew' or a 'Cornish Beggar' and Opie was successfully sprung on the world as a sort of modern Ribera. For a year or more Society flocked to him and demanded that he paint their portraits, and his old men and old women (such as 'Mrs Delany' 1782 in the National Portrait Gallery) were both novel and good. At this date Opie had a sense of paint texture and a broad touch which were refreshing, and his vaguely Rembrandtesque effects of lighting seemed original and pleased. Anything that was natural he could paint with sympathy, old people and children as well, for the four pictures of the four children of the Duke of Argyll of about 1784 at Inveraray are among his best portraits. At the Academy of 1784 he showed his first considerable subject piece, 'The School' (Loyd Collection, Lockinge; Plate 161B), which has a naturalness and rather pleasing awkwardness of composition which enabled Opie to excel in this kind of subject. It was a new voice in English painting, and the *Morning Post* presciently observed that: 'could people in vulgar life afford to pay for pictures, Opie would be their man'. This picture marks a return to Dutch and Flemish seventeenth-century painting as a source of inspiration, which was to reach its peak in Wilkie and to persist throughout the nineteenth century. As a history painter Opie was fully launched by 1786 when he began the first of seven pictures for Boydell's Shakespeare Gallery: in that year he also painted for Boydell 'The Assassination of James I of Scotland', and in 1787 'The Death of Rizzio', which Boydell gave to the Guildhall Gallery. These were destroyed by bombing in 1941, but they, and the Shakespeare subjects, and a number of others painted for Bowyer's 'Historic Gallery' in the 1790s, made Opie famous. To-day we have to judge them mainly from engravings, and find them turgid, with spurious 'period' costumes and stock stage expressions. But their influence was much greater than the much better history pictures of Copley and the tradition which culminated in Delaroche stems from these pictures of the 1780s and 1790s.

Opie's genius was of the kind which burns brightly at the outset and steadily goes dimmer with increasing contact with sophistication. The more positive the subject before him, the better he painted, and vague fancy pieces of his later years do little to enhance his reputation. His later subject-pieces belong thoroughly to the romantic period and are sometimes a novelette in themselves. Of these 'The angry Father' (or 'The Discovery of Clandestine Correspondence': Royal Academy, 1802) at Aston Hall, Birmingham, is a very complete example.

James Northcote (1746–1831) is at once the complement and antithesis to Opie. Their professional success was similar and their output of the same general character – great numbers of portraits, a number of histories in the Boydell vein, rather vapid fancy pieces: to which Northcote added some rather absurd series of moral stories in an unsuccessful attempt to emulate Hogarth. Intellectually and critically Northcote had the gifts to make an artist of a high order, and his training should have given him enormous advantages over Opie. From 1771 to 1775 he lived as a pupil and assistant in Sir Joshua Reynolds's house; from 1777 to 1780 he studied in Rome; and he settled in London about the same time as Opie in 1781. But, in spite of a strong sense of character, Northcote had no feeling for paint or for tone. Out of the combined virtues of Opie and Northcote one could have produced a painter of real eminence, but neither alone could achieve very high rank. Northcote embarked on scenes with a literary subject in 1784, and, in the next years, was one of the first to contribute to the Shakespeare Gallery. The only difference between his Shakespeare pictures and Opie's is that figures from the Antique and the Italian classics find their way more often into Northcote's compositions. Even in such a purely popular moral fable as 'The Wanton Servant in her Bedchamber', Northcote cannot resist modelling his frail female on the sleeping Ariadne. Opie had had too slight an acquaintance with the tradition of the classics, while Northcote's years with Reynolds and in Rome had numbed his powers of natural invention. Yet the later works of the two painters can sometimes quite readily be confused.

In strong contrast to this school is the work of Edward Penny, the earliest born and the least dramatic of narrative painters of the classic age. Penny (1714–91) would be important if his work had had any effect, for he was the first to paint the 'Death of Wolfe' (in 1764; Plate 168A). But he painted the subject, not as a dramatic modern history, but as a moral exemplar of a military virtue, and he painted as its companion 'Lord Granby relieving a Distressed Soldier and his Family'. Examples of both these designs are in the

Ashmolean Museum at Oxford and at Petworth, and, although 'in modern dress', they have a gently elegiac quality, which is characteristic of Penny's Muse. He had been a pupil of Marco Benefial in Rome, one of the forerunners of neo-classicism, and returned to England in 1743, where he at first practised in his native Cheshire and Lancashire as a portraitist in a style close to the contemporary work of Richard Wilson. From 1762 he exhibited at the Society of Artists and he became a foundation member of the Royal Academy and its first Professor of Painting, which shows the esteem in which he was held. He retired from that office in 1783 and made way for Barry.

Penny's narrative pictures (for such they are, rather than 'histories') are the continuation of Hayman's style. He had a nice sense of tone, gentle and silvery, which is apparent from 'The Generous Behaviour of the Chevalier Bayard'[7] of 1768, to the 'Lavinia and Acasto'[8] of 1781, but his defect was summed up by the contemporary critic who called the latter picture 'very tame indeed'. The picture was an illustration to Thomson's *Seasons*, one of the most popular sources for lesser painters of a literary caste, and the feeling for nature in Thomson, which finds its echo in Stubbs, crept into narrative painting in the work of Penny, who may yet turn out, when he has been more fully explored, to deserve more of our notice.

NOTES TO CHAPTER 20

1. Correspondence at Althorp over the purchase from Hamilton of the two large Guercinos and two Salvator Rosas for Spencer House.

2. Anonymous writer in *The Bee*, XVI, Edinburgh (10 July 1793), 3.

3. There are conflicting accounts of Barry's 'Death of Wolfe'. Edward Edwards says the figures were in the nude, but a contemporary newspaper account mentions a naval officer, a midshipman, and two Grenadiers – which seems to imply uniforms. I have not seen the original, but the account I have given may be inferred from the illustration of it in A. E. Wolfe-Aylward, *The Pictorial Life of Wolfe* (1924), 143. It then belonged to Sir Lees Knowles, Bt.

4. A suggestive list of subjects treated by Gavin Hamilton, West, and Barry, with their dates and the dates of their French imitations, is in J. Locquin, *La Peinture d'histoire en France de 1747 à 1785*, p. 157, note 9.

5. The first version, painted in 1770, is now at Ottawa. The later repetition at Kensington Palace shows no appreciable variation.

6. C. Mitchell in *Journal of the Warburg and Courtauld Institutes*, VII (1944), 20 ff.

7. Best known from Pether's mezzotint. The original was in the Heldmann sale at Worton Court, Isleworth, 13 Mar. 1939, lot 297.

8. Last in Anon. sale, Sotheby's, 15 May 1946, lot 59. For the criticism see *The Ear Wig* (1781), 10.

WRIGHT OF DERBY AND THE PAINTERS OF ROMANTIC LITERATURE

THE French pundits were very strict in their definition of a 'history picture', and the category of 'history painter' was the highest and most envied class in which to be received into the French Academy. In the year 1769, just about the time of the first exhibition of the Royal Academy in London, Greuze, in spite of having painted a 'Severus reproaching Caracalla', was only admitted as a 'painter of genre', a class to whom the highest academic honours were not open. Yet Greuze had developed a kind of picture, which had won the enthusiastic praise of Diderot and reflected the tastes of that highly intelligent body of men who were to affect most profoundly the direction of thought in Europe and America – the Encyclopaedists. In England, also in the 1760s, Wright of Derby reflects the same tendency, but since he found no literary champion, although a much more sincere artist than Greuze, we can best judge the place and importance of his early style in terms of what Diderot says of Greuze. This style answers to what Diderot calls *le genre sérieux* and its distinction from the current history style, which Diderot expressed in terms of the drama, was the difference between a *coup de théâtre* and a *tableau*, and the latter was defined as 'an arrangement of the characters so natural and so true that if faithfully rendered by a painter it would give me pleasure'. Had he known them, Diderot would probably have acclaimed Wright's first important pictures as models of this class. They have another character too, that of experiments in the scientific study of light, which reflects Wright's contact with the group of men – Erasmus Darwin, the Lunar Society, and the first founders of industry in the Midlands – who came nearest in England, in the direction of their thought, to the Encyclopaedists.

Joseph Wright (1734–97), generally known as 'Wright of Derby', is interesting for other reasons too. He was the first painter of real distinction to be settled for his whole life in the provinces (apart from Bath) and he was also 'the first professional painter to express the spirit of the industrial revolution'.[1] Trained as a portrait painter under Hudson (1751–1753), he returned again to Hudson's studio in 1756/7, to complete his technical knowledge after his first experience of practice in his native Derby. He was thus in London during the triumph of the 'new style' in portraiture but he remained faithful to the Hudson patterns until a year or two after 1760. Though based on Derby, we know that, apparently in the year 1760 alone, he was painting portraits at Newark, Lincoln, Boston, Retford, and Doncaster. But he soon established a permanent practice in Derby, where he remained, except for a substantial stay at Liverpool in 1769, until he went to Italy in the autumn of 1773, soon after his marriage.

His first style dates from these pre-Italian years, which can broadly be called his 'candle-light period'. In Derby, surrounded by a society devoted to scientific experiment, from which emerged two of his principal later patrons, Wedgwood, one of the pioneers of

207

pottery, and Arkwright, a pioneer of the cotton industry, it was natural that Wright should show in his art a bent towards science. The play of light, artificial at first, became his absorbing interest, and he was the first artist, above the level of the exponents of popular art, to give expression to the passionate interest of the Midlands in science. He must have seen some work by Honthorst or Schalken, and from these he evolved his own, wholly original, candlelight pictures. There are many single studies of figures in such lighting, but three finished masterpieces: 'Three Persons viewing "The Gladiator" by Candlelight', Society of Artists, 1765 (Bowood); 'The Orrery', Society of Artists, 1766 (Derby Gallery); and 'An Experiment on a Bird in the Air Pump', Society of Artists, 1768 (Tate Gallery; Plate 174B). This last is the masterpiece of the genre, and perhaps the most remarkable picture painted in what Diderot called *le genre sérieux*. The passionate interest in science of the Midlands is married to a complicated and successful design in which the whole group is both 'natural and true', and there is a great variety of tender human feeling. At the same time it was in no sense a 'history picture' and fell outside of any of the categories of contemporary appreciation. It is one of the wholly original masterpieces of British art, but it is amusing to observe that Wright was so wrapped up in observing nature under these artificial conditions of light, that some of his portraits of this period, such as 'Mrs Carver and her Daughter' (Derby Art Gallery), though feigned to be in the open air, show the drapery glossy and lit as by candlelight. With scenes of 'A Blacksmith's Shop' (British Association for the Advancement of Science) and 'The Forge' (Countess Mountbatten) he had nearly exhausted the possibilities of popular subjects in this style, and in 1772 he exhibited his first romantic history, 'Miravan opening the Tombs of his Ancestors' (Derby Gallery; Plate 176). The literary source of this has not been traced (although the story occurs, with other names, in Herodotus), but the picture is of an entirely new kind, with affinities to the novels of Mrs Radcliffe, and it includes a piece of furniture which suggests a Wedgwood nightmare. It is rare in England to find a painter so closely in line with contemporary trends in literature and fashionable artifacts.

From the same year dates Wright's first exhibited landscape, but it was not until his Italian journey (1773/5) that Wright began to appreciate how his interest in sources of light could be combined with landscape painting. The more monumental Italian art left little impression on him, but he was lucky to see Vesuvius in eruption and the annual fireworks at the Castel S. Angelo, and he exhibited landscapes of both of these phenomena on his return in 1776. He also appreciated in Italy the style and popularity of Vernet and saw the possibility of competing with his pictures of moonlight. 'Vesuvius' especially became one of Wright's favourite themes in later years and more than a dozen variants of the subject are known. But his most original contributions to English landscape painting were views of his native Derbyshire, especially the country round Matlock, seen under unusual conditions of sunlight or in moonlight arrangements. A typical example, signed and dated from an unreadable year in the 1780s is the 'Moonlight Scene' (Plate 171A) at Alfreton Hall. The architectonics of the scene are only a little different from those in the more topographical views of Thomas Smith (d. 1767 and known as 'Smith of Derby'), from which his own first taste for landscape may have derived. The moonlight gives a 'romantic air' to such pictures, but their aim was much more the faithful rendering of effects of moonlight than this air of romance. In fact, just as his earlier candlelight study had shown its effects in his daylight portraits, his study of the even, glassy, smoothness of moonlight is carried over into his daylight landscapes, giving them something of the disquieting effect of smooth linoleum.

Wright's study of the Antique in Rome had a curious and not altogether happy effect on his later portrait style. His draperies often cling to the form in a sheathlike fashion, which anticipates the extravagances of Fuseli, and his hands make more eloquent play than is normal among the more impassive peoples of the North. His best portraits date about 1781 and one of the most illuminating is the 'Sir Brooke Boothby' (Tate Gallery; Plate 165) of that year – a gentleman pensively reclining in a woodland glade and meditating on the volume which he clutches so carelessly and which is lettered 'Rousseau'. It well illustrates all the peculiarities of Wright's later style and points to one of their sources in the intellectual world of the Encyclopaedists. Soon afterwards he painted his masterpiece of group portraiture, 'The Coke Family', at Brookhill Hall.

In subject pictures Wright found that he had exhausted the vein of candlelight pieces by the time of his return from Italy in 1775. Hoping to become established as a fashionable portrait painter he moved to Bath (which Gainsborough had left in 1774) as soon as he was back, but clients did not come and he returned for good to Derby in 1777, where he found a steady stream of portrait clients and enough leisure to paint landscapes and the subject-pieces in which he was most interested. But literature, rather than history, was the source of his themes. To the Academy of 1778 he sent a study of 'Edwin' (no vulgar boy) from Beattie's *Minstrel*, of which at least three originals are known; and to that of 1781 a study of Sterne's 'Maria' (Derby Gallery), which, in style and arrangement, recalls the figures on Wedgwood's pottery; while for Wedgwood himself he painted in 1784 'The Maid of Corinth', a theme lately popularized by Hayley in a poem, and which had already been treated by Alexander Runciman and David Allan. For the first time contemporary poetry and painting went hand in hand, and Wright's masterpiece in this genre was 'The Dead Soldier'[2] (Plate 171B), a subject from Langhorne's poems, which was popularized by an engraving and, according to contemporary letters, brought tears to the eyes of beholders. The age of romantic sensibility has arrived and Wright's picture, shown at the Academy of 1787, is one of the finest of its early examples. About the same time he did two pictures for Boydell's Shakespeare Gallery, which had much more of the air of an illustration to the text than the stagy pictures of Opie and Northcote.

More nearly related to the work of Greuze and to *le genre sérieux* as it was practised in France is the rare work of Henry Walton (1746–1813), a gentleman painter who was a portraitist of only moderate ability, but who painted a few genre pictures between 1776 and 1780 of surprising perfection. He had been a pupil of Zoffany and first appears as a portraitist in 1771. There can be little doubt that he must later have visited France and seen the kind of subject Greuze (and others) were painting, and felt the perfection of Chardin's tone. Half a dozen pictures, beginning with the 'Girl plucking a Turkey' 1776 (National Gallery), are all that we have from him of this kind, but 'The Cherry Barrow' (Royal Academy, 1779: Sir Osbert Sitwell, Bt) is as near perfection in the genre as has been achieved in English painting, and the feeling for tone is worthy of Chardin. Why Walton gave up this kind of painting is obscure, for there was certainly in England at this time a small group of patrons with a taste for this kind of picture. William Lock of Norbury, receiving as a gift from his son two recent engravings after Greuze in 1789, writes 'I wish we had more painters of *Domestic Subjects*'.[3]

It is probable that the historian would be correct in considering John Hamilton Mortimer (1741?–79) more important than Wright or any other as the pioneer of romantic literary subjects, but at present we must take his work of this kind on trust, or guess at it from the considerable number of engravings which exist after his studies of Shakespearean heads and single figures. One of his works is known to have impressed and influenced Blake, and the kind of subject in which he latterly delighted paved the way for Fuseli. A pupil of Hudson at the same time as Wright (probably 1756/7), he later worked for a short time with Pine, but was practising on his own as a portrait painter in the early 1760s. In 1763 and 1764 he won premiums for straight history pictures from the Society for the Encouragement of the Arts, but he made his living in the later 1760s mainly by conversation pieces and small single figures in the style of Zoffany and in occasional theatre pieces (also in the style of Zoffany), such as the 'Scene from *King John*' 1768 at the Garrick Club. Only in 1770 did he first find his natural bent, which Edwards describes as 'representations of Banditti, or those transactions recorded in history, wherein the exertions of soldiers are principally employed, as also incantations, the frolics of monsters, and all those kind of scenes, that personify "Horrible Imaginings"'. Edwards's words are supported by the titles of Mortimer's pictures exhibited at the Society of Arts, and, in 1778 and 1779, at the Royal Academy – but hardly any of them can be traced to-day. They read like an anticipation of much of the subject-matter of Fuseli; and Mortimer too, in 1778, was one of the first to take a subject from Spenser, who became a favourite source for romantic history pictures. These themes read oddly as the work of a painter who was severely criticized by his biographers as preferring to excel at cricket rather than take his art seriously! But he was redeemed from the downward path by a virtuous marriage, about 1775, and exhibited the same year four companion pictures of 'The Progress of Virtue' (No. III; Plate 177), which have lately been acquired by the Tate Gallery. In the most lively of these his experience of vice stood him in good stead: the youthful hero is seen abandoning, at a rather late stage in the repast, a military dinner at which females are present, and removing a wreath of vine-leaves from his hair. No other British painting corresponds so precisely to the dubious sincerity of Greuze in his paintings of moral subjects. Wright and Walton represent in England the painting of 'moral subjects' (in Diderot's sense) of a neutral or domestic caste, while Mortimer represents the seamier side. His Banditti pictures no doubt owed something to Salvator Rosa, and it is characteristic of his temperament that he was latterly painting scenes from *Don Quixote*. As a portraitist, though he disliked the genre, he also deserves consideration, for his group of the 'Drake family'[4] (Royal Academy, 1778) at Shardeloes is the best conversation piece of its period in the Zoffany tradition, and distinctly superior to Zoffany's own work of this date. No doubt the pictures will gradually reappear which will enable a just estimate of Mortimer to be arrived at; even from the information available there can be little doubt of his historical importance, and the space devoted to him in Cunningham's biographies shows that the memory of him lingered.

Another notable exponent of what we have, perhaps rather unfairly, called 'the seamier side' of genre painting was Matthew William Peters (1742–1814). He has a link with Mortimer, since one of the most reputed of his half-length arrangements of young ladies 'in an undress' was a portrait of Mortimer's sister as 'Hebe', which was engraved in 1779. He has also a much stronger link with France than other British painters of genre, since he was in Paris in 1775 (when he was copying Rubens), and again in 1783/4, when he associated closely with Vestier and the young Boilly. Those who admired him (and they were less numerous than his detractors) called him 'the English Titian', not solely because he had spent the years 1773/4 in Venice, but because he had a lush juiciness of colour during his best years, and a rich creamy impasto, which remind one, at a long remove, of Venice. His high key and his feeling for texture of paint are certainly his most unusual and agreeable characteristics, but it must be admitted that his colour reminds us more often of the 'jammy' effects of Baroccio than of the sonorous harmonies of Titian. Peters too had been a pupil of Hudson in the later 1750s, perhaps at the same time as Wright and Mortimer. But we know nothing of his Hudsonesque phase and he quickly adapted himself to modern continental modes by study in Italy from 1762 to 1766. His first mature phase, from 1766 to 1772 is of little importance. Much of his work at this time was portraiture in crayons (though little has been identified) and he had developed in the later 1760s a tendency to imitate the cheesy impasto of Reynolds. In 1769 he became a Freemason and established a connexion with a body of patrons who stood him in good stead in his art, and later in the Church. But his really formative years were spent abroad from 1772 to 1776, at Venice, Parma, Paris, Rome, and probably elsewhere. It was during these years that he acquired a liking for a high key of colour, for the swimmy facial expressions of Correggio, for harmonies of pink and cream and smoke, and for genre subjects of a mildly *risqué* kind. On his return to London he exhibited at the Academy a series of lightly draped busts of smiling and inviting ladies, which caused a mild scandal and became instantly popular in engravings. These are the English equivalent of yet another aspect of Greuze's work, and they are, to modern taste, more agreeable than that phase of Greuze, since they are completely devoid of moral overtones and the yearning glances are given no cover by being made to appear to be motivated by a dead sparrow or an attitude of prayer. This phase only lasted until about 1778 (when Peters became an R.A.), but it is for the pictures of this period that he is famous. They were followed by genre scenes in the same key and with the same qualities of paint, such as his Diploma picture, 'Children with Fruit and Flowers' (deposited with the Academy in 1777; Plate 160B), and a few portraits, especially of women, which have an evanescent and very feminine charm – in single figures only, for his efforts at group portraits are all of them failures.

In 1779, perhaps for prudential rather than from higher motives, Peters was at Oxford, studying to be ordained. In 1781 he was ordained Deacon, in 1782 Priest, and he celebrated this change of life by exhibiting at the Academy of 1782 'An Angel carrying the Spirit of a Child to Paradise', which was followed by other works in the same vein. They became extremely popular in engraving, but they belong to the curiosities of the history of taste rather than to the history of art. Peters's last serious works as a painter (except for a few portraits, such as the lively 'Bishop Hinchliffe', engraved 1788, at Trinity College, Cambridge) were some history pictures for Boydell's Shakespeare Gallery and for Macklin's Poets' Gallery in the later 1780s. These did not altogether meet with ecclesiastical approval, for, although his scenes from *Henry VIII* are as dull and stagy as the worst of Northcote, his illustrations from *The Merry Wives of Windsor* and *Much Ado about Nothing* show something of the same spirit, under a cloak of Shakespearean respectability, as his studies of feminine genre of the 1770s. They are among the most light-hearted works of the Shakespeare Gallery, but Peters retired from professional painting and membership of the Academy in 1788 and settled down to the comfortable enjoyment of a plurality of livings. He was quite a good clergyman, but, before he took orders, he showed promise of being a painter of some individual talent.

These English pioneers of domestic genre and of the romantic literary subject can all be seen in some sense as a British counterpart to a popular continental mode, whose most famous exponent was Greuze, and some of them, such as Wright and Mortimer, can also be treated as among the forerunners of Fuseli. Their Scottish counterparts were of a more serious tone and their connexion with Fuseli was closer. Two brothers, sons of an Edinburgh builder, were the leaders: Alexander Runciman (1736–85), who was historically the more important, and his younger brother, John Runciman (1744–68), who had given promise, at the time of his early death, of becoming one of the most original and sensitive British painters of the century.

Alexander Runciman was apprenticed in 1750 to the decorative painting firm of 'Robert Norrie and Coy.', who were continuing to adorn the houses of Edinburgh in a tradition derived from a blend of Gaspard Poussin and Pannini. Unexpectedly he developed a passion for landscape for its own sake and it is said that, at the time of his starting independent practice in 1762, landscape was the object of his ambition. Certainly he was the first to paint watercolours, lightly tinted, of the Scottish scene in a more advanced romantic style than the pretty topographical views of Paul Sandby. The date of the half-dozen or so such watercolours in the Print Room of the Scottish National Gallery is uncertain, but they probably date from after his return from Italy, since they betray a knowledge of the landscape drawings of Claude as well as of those of Rembrandt. Alexander was presumably the teacher of his brother John, and Farington relates[5] in 1797 that he was shown by Stothard certain 'specimens in imitation of Rubens', who told him that 'much of the process he learnt from one of the Runcimans, whose father, a painter at Edinburgh, was taught it by a Fleming'. As Stothard can hardly have learned it from John, it must have been from Alexander, but it is John whose few pictures show a profoundly sympathetic use of something like a Rubens technique. They cannot be seen in public outside the Edinburgh Gallery, and the four best probably date from the end of his life, between 1766, when he accompanied Alexander to Rome, and 1768, when he possibly committed suicide in Naples after destroying much of his work in a fit of self-depreciation. Three of these are small scenes of religious genre, but the fourth is a larger picture, signed and dated 1767, of 'King Lear in the Storm' (Plate 174A). This is an altogether surprising masterpiece, mature in both technique and invention, remarkable as a subject at so early a date, and altogether unvitiated by any suggestion of an influence from the stage. The theatre was still forbidden in Edinburgh and this fact no doubt helped to keep John Runciman's style unsophisticated, but it does not account for a purely romantic painting which was about half a century in advance of its time. The Runcimans were probably the first British painters for whom the study of poetry was a direct source of inspiration, and their passion for Shakespeare is further documented by the 'Selfportrait' of Alexander with his friend John Brown, painted in 1784, where the two are discussing the interpretation of a passage in 'The Tempest' (Scottish National Portrait Gallery).[6] It is not unnatural that a mind attuned in this way would feel moved, among the splendours of Roman Antiquity, to turn to a subject from the greatest of British poets, but John Runciman seems to have been the first to do so. Fuseli, who reached Rome in 1770, after John's death, became friendly with Alexander Runciman and seems to have started in Rome his own series of paintings from Shakespearean themes, which first appeared at the Academy of 1774.

Of Alexander's own work in Rome, apart from some drawings and watercolours, we have no certain knowledge, but it is possible that 'The Origin of Painting' (the same subject that Wright later painted for Wedgwood), which is still at Penicuik House, dates from this period. He left Rome in 1771, and, after a brief stay in London, was appointed Director of the Edinburgh Academy in 1772. This body, which had hitherto had no loftier ambition than serving the needs of providing patterns for Scottish industry, was remodelled by Runciman to fall in line with the Academies of London and the rest of Europe. History painting was now esteemed in Scotland in the first place of honour and an 'academic' tradition was founded. Alexander Runciman himself painted a series of scenes (finished by 1773) from the story of Ossian in the great hall of Penicuik House, which were unfortunately destroyed by fire in 1899, but their intensely romantic and 'illustrative' character can be estimated from a number of studies which survive in the Print Room at Edinburgh. Perhaps they are too 'poetical', but they are in marked contrast to the stagy rhetoric of the Boydell group of painters, and their affinities are all with Fuseli, whom Runciman does not seem to have met again after his return to Scotland. In less ambitious works, such as the 'Landscape with a Hermit' at Edinburgh – one of the few British landscapes in a spirit akin to Richard Wilson – or 'David returning victorious after slaying Goliath' (Plate 166A) at Penicuik House, Alexander Runciman is seen operating within his range and shows a fresh imagination and a sense of design which promised well for the future of Scottish painting. That this promise was not fulfilled must be laid at the door of Scottish patronage.

As Master of the Edinburgh Academy Runciman was succeeded by David Allan (1744–1796), son of the shore-master at Alloa and a pupil of the Foulis Academy at Glasgow, who also had studied in Italy from 1764 until about 1775 or 1776. Allan had studied under Gavin Hamilton and had won a medal at the Academy of St Luke in Rome in 1773 with his *Origin of Painting* (Edinburgh), and he too had returned (at first to London) with aspirations to be a history painter. But he had abandoned this Utopian desire by the time he finally settled in Edinburgh in 1780, where he found there was little desire for anything but portraits on the scale of life, conversation pieces, and occasional scenes of genre.

Fortunately he had experimented with these lesser modes on a visit to Naples, where he had a letter to Sir William Hamilton. From 1775 date various versions of a conversation piece of 'Sir William and Lady Hamilton' (Earl Cathcart, etc.), and the first example of a genre scene from common life by a Scottish painter, the rather trivial 'The uncultivated Genius' in the Edinburgh Gallery. But this picture is interesting as the ancestor of one of the most characteristic types of Scottish genre, of which Wilkie was the best exponent. While at Naples peasant types from Procida attracted Allan and he painted a few studies in oil of such figures and many small watercolours, at Naples, Rome, and on his return through France, of characteristic local types of the sort which Wheatley had made popular with his *Cries of London*. Some of these, and typical scenes of common life in Rome and Naples, Allan exploited in a mixture of etching and aquatint, and he found a ready market for similar works of Scottish inspiration. These led on by natural stages to his illustrations to Allan Ramsay's pastoral, *The Gentle Shepherd*, by which Allan is best known to-day, and such works earned him the absurd title of the 'Scottish Hogarth'. His work is, in fact, pure rustic genre, without any overtones of satire, social, political, or moral preoccupations. But it is the ancestor of much of Wilkie, Carse, Lizars, Geikie, and one of the most natural and unaffected types of Scottish genre, which never altogether found its counterpart in England. As a portrait painter Allan is less important. He is well represented in every aspect of portraiture at Hopetoun House, but his most pleasing works are naïve conversation pieces, in which he followed the tradition of Zoffany without ever becoming falsely modish. One of the most lively is 'The Family of Sir James Hunter-Blair, Bart' (Plate 190A) 1785, at Blairquhan, which is almost an anthology of the various *motifs* which can be used for large groups of children of this kind, and also shows the attenuated form in which aspirations to historical composition had to find their outlet.

NOTES TO CHAPTER 21

1. F. D. Klingender, *Art and the Industrial Revolution* (1947), 46. Klingender's is the first book to give a serious appreciation of Wright's importance, and I have drawn several ideas from it.

2. What appeared to be the original, much darkened, appeared in Miss Heath Stubbs' sale, Sotheby's, 17 Dec. 1947, lot 105. There is a small copy in the Derby Gallery.

3. Duchess of Sermoneta, *The Locks of Norbury* (1940), 45.

4. Reproduced in Sacheverell Sitwell, *Conversation Pieces* (1936), figure 103.

5. *Diary*, I, 185, under date 16 Jan. 1797.

6. John Brown (1752–87) unfortunately can hardly be included in a history of painting, since he made only drawings and abandoned any idea of excelling in painting. He studied in Italy 1771 to about 1781, and perfected a style of portrait drawing which looks backward to Giles Hussey and forward to Ingres. He also was friendly with Fuseli's circle in Rome and did a few fantastic drawings in that style. His most remarkable works are the portrait drawings of the founder-members of the Scottish Society of Antiquaries, now in the Scottish National Portrait Gallery. A brief contemporary account of him is given in *The Bee*, xv, Edinburgh (8 May 1793), 27 ff.

CHAPTER 22

SPORTING PAINTERS FROM WOOTTON TO STUBBS

AFTER the portraits of himself, his wife, and his children the English patron of the eighteenth century liked best to have a portrait of his horse, and copies or engravings of portraits of famous horses or sporting scenes were in at least as great demand as portraits of the royal family or of popular heroes. But patrons were often less fastidious over the artistic quality of horse pictures than of human portraits, and the general run of sporting painting, although of absorbing interest to the social historian and to the student of the turf, is on a level with the work of those lesser portraitists whose achievements are passed over in silence in this book. To discuss the Sartorius tribe and such painters is no business of the historian of art, no matter how bitter the accusations of neglect are wont to be from those specialist writers who sometimes confuse the history of art with praising famous horses. The founder of sporting genre in England, Francis Barlow, was a distinguished painter in his own right; the Kneller of the field, John Wootton, made a valuable contribution to the British landscape tradition; George Stubbs was one of our great masters; and, after the period with which this book deals, Ben Marshall, who first emerges as a sporting painter in 1792, deserves a respectable niche in the history of British painting. The other figures who deserve mention are few.

The racecourse at Newmarket seems to have been the centre from which sporting pictures originated. The three founders of the school, Wootton, Tillemans, and Seymour, all worked there, and some of the most attractive early sporting pictures are panoramic views of Newmarket Heath with a string of horses. Such paintings are rather numerous, and, without the signatures, it is not always easy to tell a Wootton from a Tillemans. They show the first marriage of the topographical tradition of landscape with a sporting element.

John Wootton (d. 1756) was born early enough to have been a pupil of Wyck in the 1690s and to have assisted Siberechts in 1694. Wyck was a battle painter and Siberechts a specialist in a landscape style which was just beginning to break away from the topographical tradition. To this background Wootton himself added only a specialization in the painting of the horse, and, in the first reference to him among the Welbeck accounts, in 1714, he is described as 'ye horse painter'. He is very liberally represented at Welbeck and his horse portraits vary little in style from 1714 until the end of his career. The normal run is of pictures about 40 × 50 in., with the horse in profile, held by a groom, with a suspicion of a classic portico indicating a gentleman's stables at one side. Sometimes there are two grooms, sometimes a dog is added, sometimes a classical pot, but the formula is constant. Sometimes too the picture is life size. From this basic type Wootton's other kinds of picture evolve – the sporting conversation piece, hunt groups, and so on. He was nearly as prolific as Kneller and prospered proportionately. Hounds also did not come amiss to his brush and, in his earlier years, he was not above doing a portrait of a lap dog.

Sometimes he collaborated with Dahl (as in the 'Henry Hoare' 1726 at Stourhead) in doing the horse for a full-scale equestrian portrait. He was an adequate, but hardly a scrupulous, painter of the personality of individual horses and his best pictures are those in which his genuine bent for landscape could be given play. Two great series of sporting scenes, planned to be built into a hall as decoration, are at Longleat and Althorp, and the latter can be dated from a passage in Lord Egmont's Diary around 1734. In such a scene as 'Leaving the Kennel' (Plate 178A) at Althorp, Wootton appears as a good deal more than a sporting painter. He shows resource as a designer, a lively fund of human and animal observation, as well as a sympathy with his subject. If he had been given much chance to exploit this sort of vein he might even have become a sort of sporting Hogarth. Wootton is in fact at his best when he is doing something different from the pure horse portrait, and late works such as 'George II at Dettingen' 1754 (Hopetoun House) have an extremely lively battle scene in the background, which shows that he must have learned much from Wyck and refined that knowledge with something of the spirit of Vandermeulen. A great many nondescript pictures pass undeservedly under Wootton's name, but his original work has always a considerable level of competence. His importance in the history of British landscape painting has already been discussed.

Peter Tillemans, who died in 1734, was an Antwerp painter who must have been somewhat younger than Wootton. Brought over to England in 1708 he was employed at first in hack copying of Old Masters and then graduated into being an antiquarian draughtsman. In 1719 he did about 500 drawings for Bridges's *Northamptonshire*. From this to doing views of gentlemen's seats was a natural step, and from topographical panoramas to enlivening them with strings of horses was another. In his later years he did many such views of Newmarket and he also painted horse-portraits in Wootton's manner, but usually with more daintiness about his treatment of the sitter on horseback, a quality which can best be expressed by noting that he was the first teacher of Arthur Devis. To sporting genre he contributed nothing new.

The third of the 'Old Masters' of sporting painting was James Seymour (1702–52), a gentleman with some personal experience of the turf and a gift for drawing. He must count to some extent as an imitator of Wootton, but his drawings of horses suggest a quality of interest in the personality of the animal which Wootton did not have. He too settled at Newmarket and his interest, unlike Wootton's, was solely in horses and horse-painting. He is thus of more interest to the historian of the turf and it may well be that his horses give a much more accurate account of the originals than Wootton's do. But as pictures his works seem merely rather amateurish and amusing imitations of Wootton. Certain examples are not common, but there is an important group in Lord Hylton's collection at Ammerdown[1] which probably covers the full range of his achievement.

Between this first generation and the generation of Stubbs and Sawrey Gilpin there is no connecting link. Horse paintings continued to be produced but no progress was made in the genre, which, though lucrative, was considered very low in the artistic scale. With Stubbs it rises to a level with the most distinguished achievements of British painting, although the struggle which both Stubbs and Gilpin made to have their art recognized as on a level of seriousness with the portrait painter's and history painter's was not crowned with success.

To classify George Stubbs (1724–1806) as a 'sporting painter', as was done in his own lifetime, has been habitual since, and is repeated for convenience in this book, is assuredly wrong. He has no links with the sporting painters of the generation of Wootton, he never painted at Newmarket and horse pictures form only a part of his work, which embraces, in its affectionate study, man, the whole animal kingdom, and nature. His earliest passion was for anatomy and he seems at first to have practised portraiture as a means of livelihood while pursuing his anatomical studies. Wigan (1744), Leeds, York (about 1746 to 1752), Hull and Liverpool were the scenes of his early practice before he made a visit to Italy, allegedly in 1754, 'to convince himself that Nature is superior to all art'.[2] We know nothing of his paintings during these years, but he gave private lectures on human anatomy to the pupils in York Hospital in 1746, and he drew and etched the human embryo for a book on midwifery by Dr Burton of York, which was published in 1751. Instead of academies and the Antique he approached the study of painting through anatomy and this training isolated him from all his contemporaries in England. Another eccentric trait for an eighteenth-century character was that man was much less the centre of the universe for him than a mere element in the animal kingdom, and he was absorbingly interested in wild animals of all kinds and especially in the horse. Trees and plants also received the same loving attention. One can imagine the kind of superior criticism from some Italian-travelled face painter which must have exasperated this unspoiled student of the natural sciences into visiting Italy to see for himself that there was no need for him ever to have gone there! On this journey too he is said to have visited Morocco and to have seen a lion attack a frightened horse, an incident which laid the foundation for his interest in dramatic animal-history pictures. That he found horses to be preferable to human beings seems probable, and I cannot but suppose that he found encouragement for this view in some of the pictures of Albert Cuyp, which are the only artistic antecedent to which one can point. The dwarfing of his human figures by comparison with his horses, the emphasis on the noble characteristics of the beast, and the setting of it against an expanse of sunny sky and land-scape (often of a kind unsuited to the training of race-horses) all point to Cuyp as a formative influence. But Stubbs is not recorded ever to have mentioned the name of Cuyp. Soon after his return from abroad he went to Lincolnshire, where his earliest known por-traits are to be found at Scawby, and, from about 1756 to about 1760 he was engaged in making the drawings for a great work on *The Anatomy of the Horse*, in a remote Lincoln-shire farmhouse, where he lived in studious discomfort with the animals he was dissecting. These drawings were finally published in 1766, and it was this astonishing and monu-mental work, rather than any connexion with the turf, which – ironically enough – established Stubbs's reputation as a 'horse painter', and gradually forced him to take, in the hierarchy of fashionable art, a place below those who painted human beings with a complete disregard for their anatomy.

In his work and drawings for *The Anatomy of the Horse* Stubbs places himself among the great natural scientists England has produced, for it is not altogether beside the mark to liken his work on the horse to what Vesalius had done for human anatomy. At the end of his life, about 1802 onwards, Stubbs was engaged on *A comparative anatomical exposition of the structure of the human body with that of a Tiger and Common Fowls*, which was never completed, from which it is plain that the leading interests of his life remained unaltered. But the eye of the anatomist and the eye of the artist are not altogether at one, and it is sometimes a fair criticism of Stubbs's pictures that the artist yields to the anatomist. His animal figures will be beautifully and accurately drawn, his trees and foreground weeds will command admiration from the botanist, and there will be a charming landscape. Yet everything is not pulled together so as to produce the effect of a single act of vision. From uncompleted pictures such as the frieze of 'Brood Mares and Foals' (Plate 181) at Wentworth Woodhouse, we can see Stubbs's method. He concentrated first on the single figures of horses and arranged them in a lovely and flowing arabesque – and then the landscape would have been laboriously inserted, piece by piece, between the legs. For what he could see with a single look Stubbs had the artist's eye, but there were limits to his creative imagination – as is proper for an anatomist – and some of his arrangements of wild animals, such as the huge 'Lion slaying a Buck' and 'Lion seizing a Horse' formerly at Hutchinson House, have too much the air of habitat groups in a natural history museum.

After his labours on *The Anatomy of the Horse* were completed, about 1760, Stubbs settled in London and practised as a painter. He started exhibiting with the Society of Artists in 1761 and our knowledge of his painting begins about this time. Three large pictures at Goodwood – which date about 1761/2 – show the maturity and novelty of his work at this period. The finest is 'The 2nd Duke and Duchess of Richmond watching Horses exercising' (Plate 180), which is almost an anthology of his various abilities. Horses and dogs and human beings are portrayed with equal sympathy and affection, as well as trees and the broader aspects of English landscape. The lovely group of the horse being groomed at the right has a rival in English painting only in the freshest of Gainsborough's Suffolk landscapes, such as the pictures of 1755 at Woburn, and Stubbs reveals something of the same feeling for musical rhythm in the natural grouping of figures. Yet the composition as a whole tends to fall to pieces and is rather an assembly of fragmentary felicities. Much of Stubbs's finest work was painted between 1762 and the foundation of the Academy in 1769, conversation pieces (with or without horses), some studies of wild animals, and the most splendid of his large horse portraits, the life-size 'Whistlejacket' (probably about 1767) at Wentworth Woodhouse. Yet because he was considered to belong to that lowly genre of 'sporting painters', Stubbs did not become a founder-member of the Royal Academy. The three painters of real distinction whose work illustrated the exhibition of the Society of Arts, after the defection of the Academicians, in 1769, were Stubbs, Wright of Derby, and Zoffany. Stubbs's intellectual affinities are in fact closer with Wright of Derby than with any other painter. Both had a profound interest in the natural sciences and both, in later life, had professional relations with Wedgwood, one of the first scientific industrialists to seek the co-operation of serious artists in industrial production.

The effect of his exclusion from the Academy was to make Stubbs exhibit at the Society of Arts in 1770 only pictures which were not of a sporting kind. He showed a 'Hercules and Achelous' (a history subject in which it was proper to include a bull), a 'conversation', a 'repose after shooting', and the first of his pictures in enamel, a 'Lion devouring a Horse'. The 'conversation' seems to have been the 'Melbourne and Milbanke Families' (Plate 182) at Panshanger, in which it must be admitted that there are three horses and a dog, yet the picture counts as one of the most satisfactory English group portraits of the century. One of Stubbs's great qualities, which no doubt militated against his success, was that he had no eye for fashion at all. He saw human beings of all degrees at their best when they were affectionately associated with animals, and he shows us as a result the rural life of the English gentleman as no other painter succeeds in showing it, and the gentle rhythm of his designs, with their slow curves, makes the ideal formal language for this revelation.

From 1770 onwards he started to experiment in the use of enamel colours on copper, and, by 1778, Wedgwood had managed to produce china plaques, of considerable size which were suitable for the same pigments. This technique gives a smooth gloss and polish to some of his later works, even on canvas, which is rather distasteful by modern standards. It was at this time, and at first for these china plaques that he designed his rustic idylls, but he repeated them, with a greater breadth of feeling and a fuller range of tone in the shadows, on panel or canvas. This can be seen by comparing 'The Reapers' on china at Port Sunlight, with the version on panel of 1783 at Upton House (Plate 179B). The former is hardly more than gay and pretty, the latter has something of the mood, mystery, and poetic feeling of early Wordsworth. Stubbs's achievement in this kind of picture is very like that of Cuyp: the simple and veracious study of men and animals in a rural scene, as the faintly melancholy shadows of evening descend, conveys a hint of tears, and this feeling is echoed in a masterly way by Stubbs's use of the formal elements of picture-making.

Throughout his life Stubbs made pictures of any wild animal he had an opportunity of studying. Lions and tigers were his favourite subjects – after horses – but he painted sheep and cattle also and a zebra, a moose, a cheetah, and a monkey as the occasion offered. In the 1790s he enjoyed the patronage of the Prince of Wales, and, in certain pictures of the royal horses and servants – such as 'The Prince of Wales's Phaeton, with the State-Coachman, a Stable Boy, etc.' 1793 (Plate 179A) – Stubbs contrived to paint a picture which showed his opinion of the relative importance of men and animals. It is a picture more in the Chinese tradition than in that of eighteenth-century Europe, and has, more than most, that quality of strangeness which lifts many of Stubbs's pictures from the category of 'sporting art' into the realm of the poetry of creative observation. For imagination and a sense for the 'grand style' were equally lacking to Stubbs, and for this, in his own day, he was not forgiven.

Only one other horse-painter, Sawrey Gilpin, deserves to be considered as something more than a painter of 'sporting pictures', but two who were sporting painters and nothing more deserve mention as followers, to some extent, of Stubbs. Benjamin Killingbeck, probably a Leeds artist, who exhibited in London from 1769 to 1789 and had begun as a portrait painter, seems to have been considerably influenced by Stubbs when he was working at Wentworth Woodhouse, and, after Stubbs had quarrelled with Lord Rockingham, the latter turned to Killingbeck for portraits of his horses. One at Wentworth, dated 1776, is worthy of a follower of Stubbs, but such later examples as I have noted show a falling off which suggests that Killingbeck would not repay study. John Boultbee (1753–1812)[3] was a more serious painter from a respectable Leicestershire family and first exhibited in London in 1775. He does not seem to have been a direct pupil of Stubbs, but, during the 1780s, the influence of Stubbs is strong on him, the slow curves of his pattern and the rather hazy distances. Such horse pictures as 'Pagan and Monarch' 1784 at Althorp suffice to indicate the prevailing influence Stubbs's art had on the professional horse-painters before the emergence of Ben Marshall in the 1790s.

Sawrey Gilpin (1733–1807), like Stubbs, was not specifically trained to be a horse-painter. He came of a good family in Cumberland and was a brother of that eminent authority on the Picturesque, the Rev. William Gilpin. In 1749 he came to London and was apprenticed to Samuel Scott, the landscape and marine painter, with whom he remained until 1758. It is said that his market studies attracted the attention of the Duke of Cumberland, who took him under his patronage, and it was in the Duke's stud that he first devoted himself to horse-painting. Although lacking altogether Stubbs's detailed knowledge of the horse's anatomy, Gilpin had a good eye for nature and he liked lively movement in horses, whereas Stubbs preferred repose. With his training under Scott, Gilpin also was more experienced than Stubbs in marrying his animals with the landscape and giving the whole picture an air of unity. The Duke of Cumberland's horses provided him with the material for his first elaborate compositions and 'King Herod's Dam, with all her Brood, employed according to their Ages' (Society of Artists 1765), now at Scampston Hall, is a remarkable achievement. It contrives to make a lively picture, in an agreeable landscape, out of subject-matter which is primarily an equine genealogical tree. Composition, of the academic kind to which Stubbs was almost a stranger, came naturally to Gilpin and he, even more than Stubbs, must have been irked by the mean position accorded to the sporting painter and by not becoming a founder-member of the Academy. Even before the Academy was founded Gilpin had sought to elevate horse-painting by an admixture of history (as Reynolds was doing to portrait painting), and the outcrop of horse-history pictures during just these years was no doubt a bid for proper recognition. Between 1768 and 1772 Gilpin painted three histories of 'Gulliver and the Houyhnhnms' (Southill, York, and Beaumont collection) and in 1769 he showed a sketch for 'The Election of Darius' (Plate 178B), which was the result of the neighing of his horse. He later painted this picture on a large scale (York Gallery) in which something of Scott and Marlow's style is blent with a figure style which suggests Luca Giordano. But Gilpin had to wait until 1795 before he became A.R.A. (he became R.A. in 1797). By then he had painted dramatic pictures in the Snyders vein like 'The Death of the Fox' (1793), which have the advantage of a naturalistic liveliness over Stubbs's dramatic animal-histories although they look flimsy beside them. Gilpin's pictures are always the work of an artist (which cannot be said of some of the lesser sporting painters of the time) and they are more vivacious than many of the works of Stubbs, but Gilpin was much the lesser man. It is from Gilpin's style, however, that Ben Marshall and James Ward took the first elements of their art, which they were adapt to suit the landscape style of the next age.

NOTES TO CHAPTER 22

1. Most of the Seymours at Ammerdown are reproduced in *Country Life*, 26 Jan. 1929, 126 ff.

2. *Memoir of George Stubbs*, printed for Joseph Mayer, Liverpool (1879), 11. This is one of the few sources of information about Stubbs's beginnings. A full view of Stubbs will only be possible when the book on him in preparation by Mr Basil Taylor is published.

3. The few facts known about Boultbee are published by W. Shaw Sparrow in *The Connoisseur*, Mar. 1933, 148 ff.

CHAPTER 23

ROMNEY, AND FASHIONABLE PORTRAITURE

GEORGE ROMNEY (1734–1802) is accepted by common accord to-day as next after Reynolds and Gainsborough of the portrait painters before the age of Lawrence. This is a just estimate, and we may fairly place Romney on an isolated and lesser eminence midway between the greater heights of Reynolds and Gainsborough and the lower position of Hoppner and Beechey. Like Gainsborough, Romney was always complaining about the drudgery of face-painting, and we have the evidence of Flaxman (who became his friend only in later life) that 'his heart and soul were engaged in historical and ideal painting', yet there is little to show for this save a mass of drawings for high-flown compositions, mostly in the Fitzwilliam Museum at Cambridge, and one or two unsatisfactory pictures for Boydell's Shakespeare Gallery of 1787 onwards. These represent the aspirations of the shadowed side of Romney's life, and we know that he was nervous, introspective, unsociable, and took no part or apparent interest in the larger concerns of the world. Yet, by a curious irony, these very defects of character helped him to become the most successful of fashionable portrait painters. A 'fashionable' portrait painter is not one who, like Reynolds at his best, penetrates into the character of his sitter and forms a personal estimate of his position in the world of politics or society; nor one, like Gainsborough, who could impose his own artistic fantasy upon persons of a very slender personal character: it is one who brings forward all those neutral qualities which are valued by Society – health, youth, good looks, an air of breeding, or at least of the tone of the highest ranks of the social scale. No strong likeness is wanted by such sitters, and the artist who succeeds with them must have little curiosity into the secrets of personality. Romney, who seems to have shunned personal contact with most of his sitters as much as he shunned the risk of criticism by exhibiting his works, had the exact qualities of temperament which were required. Add to this that his prices always remained lower than those of either Reynolds or Gainsborough, that he was very sensitive to good looks in both sexes, and that he had a fine and easily recognizable sense of pattern, and you have the ingredients which made for his success. He was also, like his rivals, a prodigiously hard worker and had the ambition to succeed.

Romney was unlike Reynolds and Gainsborough in two things in particular. There are no overtones, either of character or sensibility, about his portraits, and he achieved his patterns predominantly by line. The flowing curves and easy poses of classical sculpture (of the Roman period) are at the back of all his best designs, and it was characteristic of him that, when passing through Genoa in 1773, he should write that the Genoese women's costumes 'produce the most elegant flowing lines imaginable'. He also had a very good eye for the placing of the figure in the canvas space so as to give it the greatest importance possible, and a number of his experiments in this way approach more closely to the patterns of the Society photographer of to-day than to the paintings of his contemporaries. A portrait such as the 'Samuel Whitbread' 1781 in the Provost's Lodge at Eton has this quality in a high degree, and the truth is that Romney, as a portrait painter, had the dispassionate eye of the camera in expert professional hands, who know that the instrument cannot lie but are not concerned in making it tell the truth.

Romney was the son of a Lancashire cabinet-maker and was apprenticed to a travelling portrait painter named Christopher Steele from 1755 to 1757, when he set up on his own in Kendal. Steele is said to have been a pupil of Vanloo and the two portraits by him that I have seen are far from contemptible. They are neat and hard and crisply drawn, neither gauche nor provincial, and stylistically related to Highmore. Romney's own earliest portraits, between 1757 and his moving to London in 1762, are not unlike harder and provincial variants on Highmore and they are less accomplished than the work of Christopher Steele.

On first coming to London the young painter, in 1763, won an award from the Society of Arts with a 'Death of Wolfe', which one assumes to have been in classical costume, but he soon settled down to portraiture. His first London period, which lasted until his visit to Italy in 1773, seems to have been devoted to acquiring the linear rhythms of classical drapery, and it is likely that the collection of casts at Richmond House was his principal source for this knowledge. In the ambitious works of this period (the only time when he exhibited his work in public) the figures are of unduly elongated proportions, and 'Sir George and Lady Warren and their Daughter' (Society of Artists 1769) and 'Mrs Yates as "The Tragic Muse"' (Society of Artists, 1771) are rather pretentious essays in the Antique with contemporary models. The same characteristics appear more agreeably in the small 'The Artist's Brothers' 1766 (Plate 183A). It is significant that, on a brief visit to Paris in 1764, he should have admired Le Sueur above all others. He had not yet seen Raphael, and it is understandable that Le Sueur's use of the Antique should have seemed to him to come nearer to his ideal than anything he had hitherto seen. One of the maturest works of this period is 'Mr & Mrs Lindow' 1772 (Tate Gallery), in which the papery quality of the folds suggests a blend of the classical with the style of Francis Cotes. It was the mantle of Cotes (who had died in 1770) that Romney was to inherit when he returned from Italy in 1775.

Romney's two years in Italy, 1773–5, were passed mainly at Rome, although he spent some months studying Titian at Venice. He copied many figures in the 'Stanze' of Raphael, and it was this direct experience of the Antique and of Raphael which matured him as an artist, gave that sense of poise to his figures, and smoothed out his draperies so that they no longer seem carefully arranged but fall in natural and graceful lines. This transformation from the groping to the mature is apparent in what was almost the first portrait he painted on his return, the lovely 'Mrs Carwardine & Son' 1775 (Plate 187), in Lord Hillingdon's collection. Romney never surpassed, perhaps later never equalled, the best of his works in the years 1775–80, while he was still fresh from his Roman experiences, and this portrait is the most direct expression of his indebtedness to Raphael, freely based as it is on the 'Madonna della Sedia'. In this case he was painting the family of a friend, with a more intimate feeling than was common for him, and we can discern perhaps what might have been Romney's stature had he not been content, or temperamentally compelled, to become a fashionable portrait painter.

In 1776 he took a lease of the fine house, with its painting-room, in Cavendish Square that had been Cotes's and he remained there until his final retirement to Kendal, when he sold the lease to Martin Archer Shee, who was to fulfil, in relation to Lawrence, the same sort of position that Romney filled in relation to Reynolds.

Romney's work, from 1776 onwards, is as well documented as that of Reynolds. We have most of his ledgers and his sitter books, and even his accounts with his frame-maker. He maintains an even level of accomplishment in his best work up to the middle of the 1780s, when his nerves and his powers began to flag. To some his powers seem to decline from 1781, when he first came into contact with Emma Hart (later to become Lady Hamilton), who exercised an almost hypnotic fascination upon his imagination, but a study of his dated work does not agree with this hypothesis. Seen in bulk his work is rather monotonous, since Romney's mind did not enlarge, nor did he seek further refinements and perfections in the art of portraiture as both Reynolds and Gainsborough did in their later years. But his colour is always strong and clear and sound, and the surface of his paint has stood up much better to the action of time than the experiments of Reynolds or Gainsborough's subtleties. He is at his best with people in the bloom of youth and health, with fine clothes and fine looks, young men about to leave Eton and young ladies first flowering upon the world and Society. Of the Eton leaving portraits 'Earl Grey' 1784 (Plate 183B) is as handsome as any, posed in a convention of which Romney was fond, as if seen both in the studio and against a summer sky. A young woman's portrait of the same date, and with the same arresting quality, is the 'Hon. Charlotte Clive' (Earl of Powis), whom one would take for an ancient divinity who has strayed into Society. The awareness of 'Society' is always there in Romney, in the look, in the conscious gracefulness of the pose, or in the movement of the arms. A comparison of what can be considered Romney's masterpiece, 'Sir Christopher and Lady Sykes' 1786 (Sledmere; Plate 184), a picture known as 'The Evening Walk', with Gainsborough's 'Morning Walk', is illuminating. The figures are Roman statues in modern dress, but with gestures more momentary and less eternal than ancient statues. They have an air of consequence and of the height of fashion, which Gainsborough's beings lack, and they could never be taken for anything but the portraits of individual persons, while Gainsborough's figures can stand for the image of young love.

In Lady Hamilton Romney found his own equivalent of what Gainsborough had found in his little beggar children, the visible realization of his dreams of an ideal world, and Romney's pictures of her of the 1780s are his equivalent to the fancy pieces Gainsborough was painting during the same years. There must be half a hundred pictures of his 'divine Emma', some made from direct sittings, some from drawings, and some from memory. She is Circe, she is Calypso, she is Alope, or a Bacchante, or a Magdalene, or Contemplation. The character parts which Romney selects for her show the nature of his infatuation. Oddly enough she is hardly ever what one would call 'a lady', and it may well be that the pictures of Lady Hamilton are something in the nature of an escape from the tyranny of for ever painting sitters who had to be made to look like ladies and gentlemen.

Whatever the truth, these fancy pictures are not, as Gainsborough's are, one of the glories of British art, and, for the student of Romney, in spite of their past expensiveness, they have rather a clinical than an aesthetic interest.

It is customary to dismiss Romney's last years with something like contempt, and it is true that his fashionable portraits of these years show a great falling off. Yet unhappiness seems to have given him for the first time something of a perception of mature character and the 'Warren Hastings' of 1795 (former India Office; Plate 185) is a noble and serious portrait. But it was a final flicker and Romney retired to Kendal in 1798 a broken man and an invalid, and died there four years later.

Nearest to Romney in the broad, flat, planes of his modelling and in the linear clarity of his English period was Gilbert Stuart (1755–1828). Born at Narragansett, Rhode Island, Stuart is the last of the American painters that need be considered, for, although many more came to England to become pupils of Benjamin West, the only one of them who settled and made any mark in London for a time was Washington Alston, who belongs wholly to the generation of the Romantics. Unlike West and Copley, Stuart returned to the United States (in 1793) to become the leading portrait painter of his own country.

Although Stuart's American style can hardly be said to belong to the history of British painting, we cannot understand Stuart without taking it into account, for it seems to have developed the moment he returned to America, and this instinctive adaptation to the requirements of patronage suggests a mind of considerable awareness. Stuart's New England style has something in common with Raeburn's Scottish idiom, but his lighting is less theatrical. He prefers a short bust, often cut with deliberate awkwardness, no hands, and a strong concentration on the character and likeness of the face. West had already said, in the early 1780s, that Stuart 'nails the face to the canvass', but his portraits of English and Irish sitters, who had no desire for such a strong likeness, hardly give that impression. During his English period, therefore, we must consider that Stuart showed his genius only in a muted form, calculated to the requirements of his patronage.

Stuart's first contact with European painting was a few months with Cosmo Alexander in Edinburgh, before the latter's death in 1772, but he returned almost immediately to New England and sailed for London in June 1775. He entered West's studio as an assistant in 1777, but was free to do portraits on his own, as he first exhibited at the Academy of that year. In 1782 he set up on his own and is reported by a contemporary as having 'had his full share of the bust business'. Extravagant living caused him to escape from his creditors to Ireland c. 1787/8, where he also did good business (and lived very extravagantly) until his return to America in 1792/3. But Stuart's style is not, even technically, dependent on West. His handling of paint is much more accomplished and his key of colour much gayer. It is difficult to suppose that he did not study Romney and he must certainly also have studied the portraits of Copley. His own portrait of 'Copley' (National Portrait Gallery; Plate 188A), of about 1785/6, is characteristic of the best work of his London period, a strongly lit, broadly modelled bust against a romantic sky. Ovals of this kind were the 'bust business' in which he specialized and the best surviving group of them is the half-dozen, ranging from 1781 to 1786, at Saltram. With a knowledge of Stuart's New England style we can read backwards into these the strong sense of character and likeness which Stuart has been at pains to under-emphasize. To show that he was not (as his detractors had alleged) incapable of drawing the human form below the waist, Stuart exhibited at the Academy of 1782 the full-length of 'Mr Grant, skating', now at Washington, which was a brilliant success. But most of his rare full-lengths are dull things, for Stuart could not impart the feeling of life, which it was natural for him to concentrate in the face, over the rest of the human form. The most ambitious of his English works is 'The Percy Children' of 1787 at Syon House, which is altogether in the style of Copley, but without Copley's liveliness.

The next portraitist in public repute after Romney is John Hoppner (1758–1810), who admittedly had a large name in his own day, but the recent fashion for him is due chiefly to assiduous puffing by the art trade some half a century ago and to the childlike desire of the very rich in that far-off age of collecting to fill their houses with portraits of beautiful women and lovely children. He had enough personal style usually not to leave any doubt as to whether a portrait is by him rather than by another, and yet he is for ever reminding us of the work of one or other of his greater contemporaries, at first of Reynolds and Romney, and later of Lawrence and Raeburn. He told Danloux that he kept a picture by Gainsborough in his studio as a model, and he bought some half-finished portraits at Romney's sale. He veered backwards and forwards between these rival influences, for – to take examples only from his best pictures – while Lord Dartmouth's 'Lady Charlotte Duncombe' of 1794 is entirely in the vein of Lawrence, the 'Lady Elizabeth Bligh' (Royal Academy, 1803; Governor Fuller, Boston) might be mistaken for a Reynolds. He is best in half-lengths, for his full-length ladies are little more than torrents of white muslin without form or shape.

A pupil at the Royal Academy schools in 1775, Hoppner first exhibited in 1780, and there can be little doubt that his earliest works, from the 1780s, in which he combined something of Reynolds's facture with Romney's feeling for large pattern, are the best. Unexpectedly he is well represented in the National Gallery. The 'Princess Mary' (Royal Academy, 1785; Plate 189B) at Windsor and 'Sir M. W. Ridley' c. 1786 at Blagdon represent about the peak of his achievement, and the former is a really very astute combination of elements taken from Reynolds and Romney. But every one of Hoppner's borrowings and combinations is contrived because it was calculated to please the flashy taste of those circles whose centre was the Prince of Wales. He had his reward, for in 1789 he was appointed Portrait Painter to the Prince of Wales, though he did not become A.R.A. until 1793 and R.A. until 1795. Happily death carried him off in time for the Prince, whose taste had matured, not to be too late to give his patronage to Lawrence. Lawrence's portraiture has given to the Regency and to the reign of George IV a *cachet* without which they would have cut a much poorer figure in history. Hoppner himself was attaining something nearer sobriety of style in his last years, as well as a more individual distinction, for his 'Earl Spencer' of 1808 at Althorp almost for the first time does not remind us of any other painter – or at least Hoppner has gone back to the Old Masters for strength rather than to his contemporaries. But the success of the portrait is a *tour de force* in spite of bad drawing.

Hoppner's chief rival – if we omit Lawrence – was Sir William Beechey (1753–1839), who was a better draughtsman and a more conscientious painter. But he is deadly dull. This praiseworthy dullness stood him in good stead, for, while Hoppner suited the flashy taste of the Prince of Wales, Beechey's stolid prose was more agreeable to Queen Charlotte and he was made Portrait Painter to the Queen in 1793. Beechey studied in the Academy schools in 1772 and first exhibited in 1776. He is said to have been a pupil of Zoffany and he began with small-scale full-lengths in Zoffany's manner, but painted as if by a pupil of Reynolds. The few of these which have been traced are pleasing and original. From 1782 to 1787 Beechey was settled at Norwich and painted the Norfolk gentry and his sound, provincial, unfashionable style is well represented by the 'George Maltby' of 1785 in the Hall of Durham Castle. It is much more solid and respectable than his attempts at pleasing London taste after he had settled there in 1787. Half a dozen portraits of the children of the Duke of Buccleuch (at Bowhill) show Beechey in 1789 and have something of the uneasy charm of the newcomer from the country after the first impact of the London fashions. But, by 1791, when he exhibited the 'Dashwood Children' (Toledo, Ohio), Beechey had arrived at his final style, which was modified only by the increasingly ugly fashions of the next fifty years. His roots always go back to the age before Lawrence and his respectable prose was always a counterweight to the more fancy style, first of Hoppner, and later of Lawrence. We may compare with Hoppner's 'Princess Mary' (Plate 189B) Beechey's portrait of the same sitter (Royal Academy, 1797; Plate 189A) at Windsor. It is modest and gentle and unassuming and has all those domestic virtues which the royal family (other than the Prince of Wales) appreciated.

Between them Hoppner and Beechey show the two opposite sides of the pre-romantic tradition in its last phase, and Beechey, who answers to Dahl a hundred years earlier, carried on the tradition for persons who preferred the old modes until after Lawrence's death. The other portrait painters of the early nineteenth century, Shee, Owen, Harlow, and Jackson, all belong to Lawrence's following. Often distinguished in half-lengths, their pursuit of an elegance of which Lawrence alone held the knack gives an unfortunate quality to their whole-length portraits, which Haydon neatly summed up by calling them the 'tip-toe school' of portraiture.

One of the lesser rivals of Beechey who just deserves not to be omitted – perhaps because his portrait of 'Lord Nelson' and one or two others have become well known from engravings – was Lemuel Francis Abbott (c. 1760–1802). From about 1780 he had a considerable vogue, especially in naval circles, and his bust portraits have distinct individuality. When he essayed the human form below the waist he was less a master. Good work by him can be seen at the National Portrait Gallery and at Greenwich.

CHAPTER 24

ZOFFANY: THEATRE GENRE AND LATER CONVERSATION PIECES

THE class of picture which can be called the 'theatrical conversation piece' was rare before the 1760s, when Garrick seems to have become alive to its advertising possibilities. A 'theatrical conversation' is by no means merely a scene from a play: it shows certain well-known actors in parts for which they were famous and its rise to popularity coincides with a change in the social position of actors, just as the conversation piece proper had appeared with the emergence of the prosperous middle classes. Although Richard van Bleeck had painted stage scenes, no actor was identifiable in them, and Hogarth's 'Beggar's Opera' picture, of 1728/9, which can be called the ancestor of the genre, was famous mainly because it combined the drama on the stage with drama in real life, and showed the young Duke in the box who ran away with the heroine. Hayman's Shakespearean scenes are also usually unconcerned with particular actors, and it is probable that it was Pieter van Bleeck (1697–1764), the son of Richard, who first introduced the genre. A large and gloomy picture in the Garrick Club of 'Griffin and Johnson in *The Alchymist*' was engraved by van Bleeck himself in 1748, with the statement that it was painted in 1738, but a far finer, and rather later, example is 'Mrs Cibber as "Cordelia" '[1] at present on loan to the theatre at Stratford. This and Hogarth's 'Garrick as "Richard III" ' are both large pictures and have little of the stage about them and nothing of the conversation piece. The marriage of the two genres was due either to Zoffany or to Benjamin Wilson.

Benjamin Wilson (1721–88) is an elusive and unsatisfactory figure. A native of Leeds, he is said to have been a pupil of Hudson, and he was at first equally addicted to painting and to scientific experiment. After two years in Dublin he settled in London in 1750 and was in a good way of business as a portrait painter for the next twenty years. To contemporaries his vaguely Rembrandtesque use of chiaroscuro seemed a sign of the new age, and as late as 1759 he seemed to some to be superior to Reynolds. His signed and dated portraits on the scale of life are not numerous but enough exist, ranging in date from about 1752 to 1769, for us to feel sure that he was a thoroughly bad painter. The curious can see examples in the Leeds and Dulwich Galleries. In spite of this the art trade and its satellites have in recent years attached his name to a number of conversation pieces and small-scale portraits of undoubted elegance which are obviously not by Zoffany. I have not found a shred of evidence that any of these are by Wilson and do not believe it. None the less he seems to have been a pioneer in the theatrical conversation piece in the 1750s. In 1754 there was published an engraving after his 'Garrick as "Hamlet" ' (a single figure), later came a 'Garrick and Mrs Bellamy in *Romeo and Juliet*' (which may be a small, battered, and feeble object now at Stourhead), and in 1761 a conversation of 'Garrick as "King Lear" ' was also engraved. It is possible that the execution of some of these may have been due to Zoffany, who was kept by Benjamin Wilson in his house as a sort of unseen painter's 'devil', but the evidence is conflicting and obscure. What is certain is that Zoffany freed himself, with Garrick's assistance, from some unsatisfactory arrangement of this sort with Wilson about 1762, and Wilson painted no more theatrical conversations. From about 1770 Wilson devoted himself more and more to experiments into the efficiency of lightning conductors, and strays out of the purview of the historian of art.

Whatever the truth about his early connexion with Benjamin Wilson, Johann Zoffany or Zauffelij (1734/5–1810) was the real creator and master of this genre. A native of Frankfurt, he seems to have spent a long period in his youth copying Old Masters in Rome, and he arrived in England within a year or two of 1760 with a neat, polished, highly finished German style and a tendency to the lively and minute imitation of natural objects in the vein of the Flemish little masters. It is probable that his introduction to the genre of theatrical conversation pieces came while he was working as drapery painter to Benjamin Wilson, but it is a reasonable hypothesis that the inventor of this genre was Garrick himself, who was a close friend of Wilson. Garrick was the first of the great actor-managers with a real flair for publicity and he saw how pictures of this character, popularized by engravings, would be the best publicity in the world. Certainly our continued awareness to-day of Garrick as a vital and living personality is largely due to his relations with artists, and not least to Zoffany. By a happy arrangement of Providence, Garrick discovered in the young man working in Benjamin Wilson's studio an artistic talent of limited capacity which was almost perfectly suited to his purpose. The details of the transaction are obscure, but it is certain that, in August 1762, Zoffany, who had lately exhibited his first theatrical conversation, had escaped from Wilson and was living in Garrick's house. Eight of Zoffany's works were in Garrick's possession at his death, mainly theatrical conversations, but some of them views of his villa and domestic conversation pieces.

The first of these theatre pictures was exhibited at the Society of Artists in 1762 and showed 'Garrick in "The Farmer's return from London"' (Plate 191A), of which at least three versions are known, but the first original, which was Garrick's, belongs to the Earl of Durham. Its novelty and its immediate success, and the reasons for that success, can be gauged by Horace Walpole's remark in his copy of the 1762 catalogue: 'Good, like the actors, and the whole better than Hogarth's'. We should not take Walpole's judgement to refer to the quality of the painting (although Zoffany never did better) but rather to the fact that the subject-matter is more properly pictorial and more fully under control than it is in Hogarth. There is no preaching and no attempt to compress into the small compass of a picture the whole matter of a novel. There is, in fact, no real ground for comparison at all.

This picture was followed in 1763 by an illustration of Garrick in a tragic role, 'Garrick and Mrs Cibber as Jaffier and Belvidera' (Earl of Durham), and Zoffany continued later with pictures of other actors in other plays. The theatrical series continued until 1770, when the vogue may have become exhausted, for Zoffany did not again exhibit portraits of actors until his decline in the 1790s. The eight or nine theatrical masterpieces of these years – of which the most accessible are two at Birmingham – constitute one of Zoffany's chief claims to fame. They are better composed and more lively than his other pictures, and although this may be in part due to their accurate rendering of skilful production on the stage, it seems unlikely that, for instance, 'Garrick in *The Provoked Wife*', Society of Arts, 1765 (Marquess of Normanby), is really an accurate rendering of the scene as it was performed. During the same decade one or two other painters produced occasional examples of this genre nearly as good – there are single examples by Mortimer and Benjamin Vandergucht at the Garrick Club – but this vogue, created by Garrick, did not persist as a lively tradition. Samuel de Wilde (1748–1832) was Zoffany's only close follower in this respect, but he mainly limited himself to single figures of actors, in character parts, of great neatness, and the real theatre conversation piece was not effectively revived until the work of George Clint in the second decade of the nineteenth century.

It was inevitable that Zoffany should turn his hand from the theatrical to the domestic conversation piece, which at last emerged in the 1760s from its middle-class smugness. Domesticity was in the air in the new reign of George III and it became fashionable to have groups of one's children painted on a small scale or family groups with all one's children round one. Zoffany may have been introduced to the King by Lord Bute, whose children he painted in two admirable groups, and the beginnings of royal favour date from about 1766. But Zoffany still exhibited at the Society of Arts in 1769, the year of the first Royal Academy, though in 1770 he was an R.A. and showed a group of the 'Royal Family', not altogether judiciously attired in Van Dyck costumes, at the Academy.

It is not surprising that George III should have shown an appetite for the work of a painter who was both a German and a limner of domesticity, and Zoffany's most accomplished conversation piece is 'Queen Charlotte and her two eldest Children' (Plate 191B) of about 1766/7, at Buckingham Palace. It is one of the prettiest and neatest of English eighteenth-century pictures. Though very far removed from anything which can be called 'great art', in British painting before the age of Turner and Constable we should be grateful for small mercies – and this is one of them. It is the best designed of all Zoffany's works and in the minute imitation of nature, a thing which usually pleases royalty, it is unexcelled. We can recognize the clock, which is still at Windsor, the picture over the door, and there is a perfectly recognizable image of a lady-in-waiting seen reflected in a mirror in the ante-room. Although George III's father, Frederick, Prince of Wales, had set the fashion for royal portraits of a certain informality, this is the first picture of the kind to be commissioned by a British king, and Zoffany later did admirable life-size half-lengths of the King and Queen in an informal manner, as if they had been private citizens. This tendency was directly opposed to the formality of Reynolds in doing portraits of important personages, and in Zoffany we have, almost by accident, the leader of a sort of popular reaction, sponsored by royalty, against the high-flown tendency of official art.

Support will never be lacking for the meticulous imitation in paint of the precise setting of daily life, and the attempt at arriving at a presentation of reality by simple enumeration has been at the bottom of such earnest painting as that of the Pre-Raphaelites. In the domestic conversation piece Zoffany carried it to its extreme in 'Sir Lawrence Dundas and his Grandson', of about 1769 (Marquess of Zetland), in an interior where not only the chairs, the carpet, and the standish are portraits, but all the eleven pictures on the walls and all the seven bronzes on the mantelpiece can be identified. Zoffany became hypnotized by his own skill and produced for the Academy of 1772 'The Life-Class at the Royal Academy' (Windsor; Plate 190B), which is almost a miracle of improvisation, for we have Walpole's evidence that he made no design or plan for the picture but 'clapt in' the figures of the Academicians, one by one, as he got the chance of taking their likeness. It is from this point that we can mark Zoffany's decline. His skill remained the same at first but he became lazy about the intellectual operation involved in composing a picture. From 1772 to 1776 he was at Florence, where he devoted untiring patience to a picture of 'The Tribuna of the Uffizi' (Windsor), with all its pictures and statues, most of the British colony in Florence, and a good deal of bric-à-brac for full measure. This has ceased to be a picture, and is simply a prodigy – and a historically fascinating one – of pictorial imitation. He was back in England (by way of Vienna) by 1779 and carried his bric-à-brac method of designing even into his conversation pieces, as in 'The Sharp Family' (Royal Academy, 1781) in Miss Lloyd-Baker's possession. A visit to India (1783–9) increased his prosperity but further undermined his artistic conscience, and the work of his last years adds nothing to his reputation, although the 'Charles Towneley among his Marbles' (Royal Academy, 1790) in the Burnley Art Gallery is a rather better organized experiment in the vein of 'The Tribuna' and showed that his powers of imitation had not flagged. Zoffany also occasionally painted fancy pieces and portraits on the scale of life. The full-length of 'Mrs Oswald' in the National Gallery, of about 1770, is altogether exceptional, but it deserves mention as one of the best pictures of its kind and period by one who does not figure among the great names in British life-scale portraiture.

Zoffany's pupil, Henry Walton (1746–1813), has already been mentioned as one of the best painters of fancy pictures in *le genre sérieux* and he also occasionally tried his hand at the conversation piece, adding to Zoffany's formula just what Zoffany lacked, a sense for tone and a sense of breeding. But his work in this genre is exceedingly rare, as also is that of Hugh Barron (*c.* 1747–91), a pupil of Reynolds who executed a few conversations in Zoffany's style at the end of the 1760s and early 1770s. It is Francis Wheatley whose work in portraiture is most often confused with that of Zoffany.

Francis Wheatley (1747–1801) was an artist of much greater variety than Zoffany and is best remembered to-day for his latest style, pictures from common life in the country or the rural side of city life, of which the *Cries of London*, engraved in 1795, are the most familiar. The originals of these were shown at the Academy in 1792/3 and some are now at Upton House. These are in a tradition which descends from Mercier and Hayman, through Henry Robert Morland[2] (1716–97), the father of George Morland, and may owe something of their added sweetness to a tincture of Greuze. But Wheatley has a richer personality than these late works would suggest.

He first exhibited at the Society of Arts in 1765 and these early works were almost wholly small-scale portraits or conversations. He may well even have been a pupil of Zoffany, but he looked elsewhere for the qualities which Zoffany lacked, a broadness of touch and a feeling for tone and the quality of English landscape. Indeed his 'Landscape with a Harvest Wagon' 1774 (Nottingham) is a shameless, but not insensitive, crib of Gainsborough's picture in the Barber Institute at Birmingham. From 1779 to 1783/4 Wheatley worked in Dublin and painted the pictures in which his indebtedness to

Zoffany is most manifest. 'The Irish House of Commons' 1780 (A. D. F. Gascoigne) is exactly in the spirit of Zoffany's 'Life-School at the Royal Academy' but is more sensitive in touch, and the 'Family of the Earl of Carlisle riding in Phoenix Park' 1781 (Castle Howard) has married Zoffany's minuteness to something of the broad feeling for landscape of Stubbs. On his return to London Wheatley continued small-scale portraiture until the end of the 1780s, and pictures such as 'Arthur Philip' 1786 (National Portrait Gallery; Plate 164B), with its broad touch, clean outline, and clear Romney-like colour, show how superior he had become to Zoffany in everything which goes to make a work of art. It may well be that Wheatley is the correct candidate for the best of the conversation pieces which have been masquerading under Benjamin Wilson's name.

But Wheatley abandoned this vein for the sentimental bourgeois genre which was beginning to be popular, and in his 'Mr Howard offering Relief to Prisoners' 1787 (Plate 192A) at Sandon (which was exhibited at the Academy of 1788) he made the nearest approach to a Greuze achieved by an English painter. The 'proper' relations between the upper and lower classes are here fully displayed, and, in all his later works of this kind, although the representative of the upper classes is not present, he is there by implication in the spectator. It is not surprising that pictures of this kind should have become popular in the more idealistic period of the industrial revolution, and they have kept their popularity among the collecting classes to-day. Periodically, in the history of taste, it is discovered that the lower orders are very picturesque. Wheatley also painted a number of pictures for Boydell's Shakespeare Gallery and he contrived to introduce exactly the same social sentiment into 'Polixenes and Camillo in the Shepherd's Cottage' as he had shown in the picture of Mr. Howard's benevolence.

In the later 1780s the conversation piece almost vanished from the fashionable scene and the small-scale full-length was limited either to the provinces, as in the work of the young Beechey at Norwich, or to very secondary painters, such as Mather Brown, an American pupil of Benjamin West, whose even leatheriness (enlivened only very occasionally by flashes of insight) barely deserves notice. Only in Scotland, in the work of David Allan and the young Nasmyth, did the tradition of conversation painting persist. The fashionable world of London preferred the watercolours of Downman and the miniatures of Cosway. In the pre-Regency and Regency world these two artists took the place of the conversation painters of the earlier years of the reign of George III.

John Downman (c. 1750–1824) came to London in 1767 and became a pupil of West, entering the Academy schools on their first formation. His early oil portraits on the scale of life are gauche, but he visited Rome 1774/5, and was settled for a time at Cambridge in 1777, where he painted a number of small-scale oil half-lengths on copper of both Town and Gown, which are like neat and elegant large miniatures in the style of West's best portraits. He travelled round the country for a year or so and soon settled in London, having perfected a method of taking charming likenesses. He would make his studies in coloured chalks and then produce one or more repetitions in lightly tinted watercolours. The earlier are usually ovals and have something French about them, the air of a *bibelot*. He excelled with children and with young and lovely people of fashion, and he achieves a faint fragrance of character exactly suited to his almost evanescent medium. This evaporates in his own oil portraits on the scale of life, and when he attempts small-scale histories in oil, such as 'The Return of Orestes' (Royal Academy, 1782), or 'Edward IV and the Duchess of Bedford' (Royal Academy, 1797), he only gives the impression of a number of desperately modish persons performing private theatricals. But, in his own medium, he captures the fleeting charm of Regency society as Hoppner, in his clumsier paint, never did. His quality hardly alters throughout his long life, but the dowdier clothes of the years after 1800 suit his medium less. His art is gracious, while that of Cosway is foppish.

Richard Cosway (1742–1821) was a youthful prodigy, who won many prizes for his drawings in the 1750s. Although he had exhibited throughout the 1760s, he studied in the Academy schools at their first opening and was rewarded by becoming A.R.A. in 1770 and R.A. the following year. He set up as a fashionable portraitist on the scale of life and his oil portraits are more numerous and less deplorable than is usually made out. He painted large oils right into the nineteenth century, but his forte was in miniatures, which are invariably exquisite in execution and of tip-top elegance. Cosway was a fop and a 'character' and was for some years intimate with the Prince of Wales, and he made a stir in Regency society such as no miniaturist had made before. No portraits give quite such a convincing image of that artificial world as the miniatures of Cosway and of his more pedestrian rival, George Engleheart (1750–1829), and the miniature again, after a long lapse since the days of the Restoration, deserves to be mentioned by the historian of British painting. It is presumably no accident that this medium should have flourished luxuriantly at two periods which show a certain similarity with one another in the corruption of their manners and the prodigality of their wealth.

NOTES TO CHAPTER 24

1. Reproduced in *Journal of the Warburg and Courtauld Institute*, x (1947), Plate 25A.

2. For what is known or surmised about Henry Morland see Martin Davies' National Gallery Catalogue, *The British School, sub voce.*

CHAPTER 25

LATER LANDSCAPE IN OILS:
EARLY WATERCOLOURS

I<small>T</small> would be natural to expect that something like a continuous development could be traced in landscape painting in oils to mark the gradation from the classical landscape of Wilson and the rococo landscape of Gainsborough to the consummate presentation of the English scene which flowered in Turner and Constable. But no such gradual transition is to be discerned and the fructifying influences on Turner and Constable were the early watercolour painters and the great masters of the Dutch school. This is not to say that landscape painting in oil was not practised abundantly, and that a few names are not deserving of mention. The chief painters are de Loutherbourg, George Morland, and Ibbetson.

It is probable that, of these, Philip James de Loutherbourg (1740–1812) was the most important and influential painter. He was an Alsatian, son and pupil of a miniature painter, and had studied under various practised hands, more particularly the battle painter Francesco Casanova. In 1767 he became a member of the French Academy and exhibited at the Salon of that year battle-pieces, marines, and landscapes, which earned a good deal of comment from Diderot, who admired their workmanlike qualities, but compared them unfavourably with Vernet's works. De Loutherbourg was in fact an extremely capable professional artisan. He could paint anything he liked out of his head, but was too lazy to refer back to nature. All this professional baggage he brought over to London in 1771, with an introduction to Garrick, who induced him in 1773 to become his stage and scenery designer. After Garrick's death he continued to practise this art with aplomb up to 1785. This gives a clue to the style of Loutherbourg's landscapes: they are generally arrangements of scenery. Loutherbourg knew his Wouvermans and his Berghem by heart and his contribution to British landscape painting was this European background. Curiously enough, it is in his earlier work that he took more trouble to adapt his style to the English scene and his 'A Midsummer Afternoon, with a Methodist Preacher' (Royal Academy, 1777, at Ottawa; Plate 192B), has a good deal of the savour of Rowlandson transferred to oil paint. In Mr R. S. de Quincey's 'Storm' (probably Royal Academy,1778) the same characteristics have been added to a dash of Gainsborough and the result is a more vigorous picture of the type which Morland was soon to make popular, only the trees and the landscape have a slightly 'foreign' air. But soon Loutherbourg gave up attempting to represent the English scene and simply painted out of his head landscapes with pastoral figures or soldiers foraging, or even views of the Danube. His religious scenes for Macklin's Bible can be passed over in silence, and after 1800 his preoccupation with stage scenery and a sort of panoramic moving peepshow, called the *Eidophusikon*, which he had opened in 1781, led him to devote his energies to an enormous 'Battle of

Valenciennes', which found its way to Easton Neston. These are works of ingenuity rather than art, and he was also associated with a polygraphic method for reproducing his and other people's pictures which still sometimes deceives the unwary to-day. But for all this, in his best pictures he anticipated all that was worth anticipating in George Morland.

George Morland (1763–1804) was the son of a painter apparently named Henry Robert Morland, who was an occasional portraitist but is best known for genre pieces in the style of Mercier, which he repeated with too great frequency. A 'Ballad Singer' by him is in the National Gallery and versions of his two most popular designs of 'Laundry Maids' are at the Tate. More important for his son's education was the fact that he was a restorer of Old Masters and presumably a dealer as well, and he employed young George, who was something of an infant prodigy in executive ability, to repair and to fake Old Masters of the Dutch school of landscape. George Morland, who was articled to his father from 1777 to 1784 and seems to have been kept in fairly strict durance, thus acquired by force something of the same cosmopolitan training that de Loutherbourg had received, and was a master of the international landscape style as soon as he set up on his own. Although more abundantly forged in his own lifetime than the works of any other painter, Morland's paintings have long continued to fetch high prices quite independently of changes in fashionable taste. The same unusual phenomenon is found in the works of Teniers and we may not unreasonably consider Morland a sort of English Teniers. The works of both painters are nicely, and even freshly, executed and they are quite brilliantly lacking in intellectual qualities. As long as there are private collectors of means there will always be some to whom Morland will readily appeal, and once such a person starts collecting Morland, he collects him in bulk. Morland's more recent apologists have sought to explain this by considering him one of the most 'essentially English' of painters, but Morland's only 'essentially English' qualities were his liking for gin and low company, and his style was nearly as international as that of de Loutherbourg. If the best of Morland's landscapes be compared with one of Turner's English views this distinction will become clear. But Morland does come very close to the heart of common things. The piggishness of his pigs and the dampness of his wet woodlands are very complete, but for all that, he did not love trees and shrubs as Constable did, hardly even enough to have been an inspiration to Constable. A good and typical specimen of his work is 'The Tavern Door' (Plate 175A).

Morland's youthful exhibited works were stained drawings, but when he first set up on his own, for a few months in 1785 at Margate and later in the same year at St Omer, it was as a portraitist. But he first came into public notice with works in Wheatley's latest style, fancy pseudo-rustic pictures, a sort of Greuze in muslin. A series of pictures of 'Lavinia' (not from Thomson's *Seasons*, but from *The Adventures of an Hackney Coach*), one of which was shown at the Academy of 1785, represents his first mature style. These were popularized by engravings, and one would be hard put to it, from the engravings and without Morland's name, to guess that they were not by Wheatley. In 1786 Morland married the sister of the engraver William Ward and his works were largely popularized by engravings of excellent quality from then onwards.

Morland's best work was done between 1788 and 1798 and is wholly consistent in style, though uneven in execution: peasants and animals in and about the farm, the interiors of stables, rustic figures in a landscape and occasionally such poignant figures of common life as soldiers, sailors, or deserters. It is a characteristic virtue that he is at best with children and animals, and the more dressed up his people are, the further they are from nature. The very large 'Inside of a Stable' of 1791 in the National Gallery is as fine an example as any, of his best period. It is sufficiently remarkable that a man who chiefly painted in the intervals of dissipation should have been able to bring to completion a picture so large and of such sure design. All Morland's natural talent and effortless ability is to be seen here, but he never improved upon these. Had he given his genius any encouragement he might have been worthy to rank with the masters of the succeeding age. But he spent much of his time evading his creditors and profited by hiding in the Isle of Wight in 1799 to paint some coastal landscapes. His pictures become more slipshod with advancing years and it is no longer possible to distinguish altogether between his own inferior work and that of his innumerable copyists. But at his best he has a freshness of touch and a command of tone which lift his works above those of most of his contemporaries.

The third painter who deserves mention is Julius Caesar Ibbetson (1759–1817). The background of his style is equally international, for he came to London in the later 1770s and was employed in copying or forging Dutch landscapes and also the works of English painters, such as Gainsborough or Wilson. Imitations or copies of Gainsborough's Suffolk landscapes of the 1750s are particularly deceptive and this sort of work formed the chief element in Ibbetson's style: the other element was de Loutherbourg, and the small Shakespearean scenes which Ibbetson painted for Boydell's Gallery would pass very well as the work of Loutherbourg. Most of Ibbetson's life after 1800 was spent in his native Yorkshire, where the sweeping landscapes and the old topographical tradition had a better effect on his art than all the learning of the studios. His later Yorkshire views are competent and neat and charming, but they are closer in style to the topographers of the 1750s than to the giants of landscape painting who were practising in London at the same time.

Far more important than these painters in oil were one or two watercolour artists, whose direct study of nature and observation of the particular tone of the British scene led up to the work of Girtin and Turner in the 1790s. It is with Turner and Girtin that the historian of our great age of landscape painting must begin.

The climate of the United Kingdom is decidedly moist, and the particular beauties of atmospheric effect with which those who put up with it are sometimes rewarded are the result of this moisture. Watercolour is undoubtedly the medium best adapted to render these transient effects, and we need look no further afield for the reason which has made watercolour painting one of the peculiar glories of British art. But this discovery was not made until men began to see beauty in these transient effects of nature, and it is no accident that the first mature period of watercolour painting should have coincided with the appearance of the early poems of Wordsworth and Coleridge. But for it to have developed so rapidly, once the desire for it was felt, demands a long tradition in the use of the medium, and the medium of watercolour had been in use in humble hands, whose names need not find mention in a general history of British painting, throughout the whole of the eighteenth century.

At the beginning of the century there were many skilled topographical draughtsmen who employed watercolour in the service of antiquarian persons. The professional used mainly a greyish or brownish wash, which he enlivened with occasional notes of colour: but amateurs sometimes used a livelier and more varied palette. The aim of these tinted drawings was to render faithfully the lineaments of buildings or ruins, and the picturesque effects of light and tone produced by the vagaries of our climate were a hindrance to this purpose and not taken into account. The great landscape artists of the classical period of British painting were not interested in accurately portraying existing natural beauties, and we can capture the exact tone of contemporary thought in a letter from Gainsborough (undated, but written probably about 1762) to the Earl of Hardwicke, who had asked him to paint a picture of some particular spot: 'Mr Gainsborough presents his humble respects to Lord Hardwicke, and shall always think it an honour to be employed in anything for his Lordship, but with respect to real views from Nature in this country he has never seen any place that affords a Subject equal to the poorest imitations of Gaspar or Claude. Paul Sandby is the only man of genius, he believes, who has employed his pencil that way.'[1] It is with Paul Sandby, the only watercolour painter of landscapes to be one of the foundation R.A.s, that we may reasonably begin.

Paul Sandby (1725/6–1809),[2] the younger brother of the architect (and topographical draughtsman) Thomas Sandby, lived right through the rise and blossoming of British watercolour painting. He himself would probably have said that he survived into the time of its decay into a 'wild rumble-tumble (or anything else you please) of penciling', if, as one may suppose, that expression, used by his son in his obituary notice of his father, echoes the old man's exasperated words. He himself was trained in a more austere tradition and he emerges quite literally from the tradition of the topographical draughtsmen. He and his brother came to London from Nottingham in 1741 to take up appointments in the Drawing Office of the Tower, the ancestor of the present Ordnance Survey Department, and Paul was sent as draughtsman with the Ordnance Survey party which went to survey the Highlands of Scotland after the rebellion of 1745. Up to 1751 he worked on the survey or in Edinburgh and this period in Scotland is the formative period for his art. Kept constantly to the faithful imitation of nature by the meticulous requirements of map-making, he was yet surrounded with some of the most picturesque scenery in the kingdom, and by a landscape which was exceptionally prone to atmospheric variations. He emerged a loving and faithful interpreter of the British scene and he did not neglect figure studies from the daily life of Edinburgh or from the soldiers on the survey party. About 1752 he came to London and he lived the rest of his life mainly in London or with his brother in Windsor Great Park, but made several excursions (after 1770) to Wales. He occasionally practised in oils but nearly all his work is either in transparent watercolour or in gouache, and many of his most important drawings he reproduced as aquatints, a process which he introduced into England. He was one of the first who drew in watercolour with the brush and did not limit himself to washing or tinting drawings made first with the pencil, and the most splendid series of his works is in the collection at Windsor Castle, where nearly every phase of his art can be studied, not least the series of views of the Castle itself. Sandby's works are the first 'real views from Nature' to form the bulk of the achievement of a considerable artist, and they are not, as Samuel Scott's had been, arranged into compositions according to the principles of Canaletto. His aim, in his son's words, was to 'give to his drawings a similar appearance to that seen in a *camera obscura*' and he 'never introduced, or depended at all upon violent contrasts for effect'. A later generation was to discover that violent contrasts could also be an important element in the truthful rendering of the English atmosphere. Sandby's studies of trees in Windsor Great Park also deserve attention as the beginnings of that loving portraiture of individual trees which was to become a passion with Constable. With the after-knowledge of Constable's work Sandby's trees seem still to be rather formal beings, but they are much closer to English nature than those in the classical English landscape painters, and a date which deserves to be recorded in the annals of British painting is 1793, when Sandby painted a room at Drakelowe entirely with forest foliage (Plate 175B). This room has now found its way into the Victoria and Albert Museum.

The figures are not the least among the charms of Sandby's watercolours, but they rarely predominate in his art. Exactly the opposite is the case with the other great watercolour master of this phase of painting, Thomas Rowlandson (1756–1827). Although a full generation younger than Sandby, he belongs to the same technical phase of the art as the older man and remained equally uninfluenced by the innovations of his younger contemporaries. His style became fixed about 1780 and he never altered it. He deserves attention for his great gifts as an artist, which appear with surprising frequency in the torrent of drawings which flowed from his pen. But he is an isolated figure, since his subject-matter never entered the traditional repertory of British watercolour painting, and that subject-matter was the rollicking life of the times. He is a Morland of greater gifts run to caricature.

Like Morland, Rowlandson benefited by some study in France, where he was trained in figure drawing from 1771 to 1773, and his sense of rhythm and the bounding life of line is in the French rococo tradition and unlike anything English. Like Morland too, he spent his life predominantly in low company, but with much greater profit to his art, for he depicts it with an amoral objectivity which gives it life, and the characters in Morland's pictures, for all that they were studied from his boon companions, appear refined into the creatures of a respectable female novelist when compared with Rowlandson's. But Rowlandson had an over-developed sense of the ridiculous, which, though a comfortable armour for a layman in his passage through life, is a disadvantage for an artist of such natural gifts who is not inspired as well – as Hogarth and Gillray were – by a social conscience and a divine indignation. It is where Rowlandson comes closest to Sandby, as in his 'Skaters on the Serpentine' of 1784,[3] where his rollicking feeling for life is added to great truth of atmospheric tone, that we can see his contribution to the landscape tradition. There are as yet no violent contrasts of effect, but Sandby's placid style has been shaken up and enriched and an advance has been made towards the full interpretation of wind and sky.

Parallel with this purely native tradition there grew up, during the same years, what has been called the 'Southern School' of watercolour painting, practised by artists who drew their subjects from the scenery of Italy or Switzerland. Starting in the same way as the topographical school had started, with gentlemen taking a watercolour painter with them on their tours to depict the splendours of the scenery, a new attitude towards the subject-matter was soon evolved. The grandeur of mountain prospects, solitude, and the moods which the poetic traveller associated with southern landscapes became the painter's object. The great initiators of this school are Alexander Cozens (c. 1715–86), who settled in England in 1746, and his son, John Robert Cozens (c. 1752–99). Both were associated with William Beckford, one of the prime figures of the Romantic period, and their work forms a necessary prelude to the consideration of Turner. It was from the marriage of these two traditions that the great British school of watercolour painting emerged.

NOTES TO CHAPTER 25

1. Quoted from W. T. Whitley, *Gainsborough*, 358.

2. The earlier literature on Sandby has been substantially corrected in A. P. Oppé, *Sandby Drawings at Windsor Castle* (1947); and by articles by A. P. Oppé in *Burl. Mag.*, LXXXVIII (June 1946), 143 ff.; and by E. H. Ramsden in *Burl. Mag.*, LXXXIX (Jan. 1947), 15 ff.

3. Reproduced in Laurence Binyon, *English Watercolours* (1933), 68. This book forms the best short general introduction to the whole subject. A full account of many minor craftsmen has been published by Iolo Williams (1952).

CHAPTER 26

PAINTING IN SCOTLAND IN THE EIGHTEENTH CENTURY

SCOTTISH painting of this period is still a very lightly explored field. Most of the painters of real stature, from the time when Aikman in 1723 had migrated to London, went south and the most distinguished of them all, Allan Ramsay, although he made periodical visits to Edinburgh (and probably stole the best commissions from the local painters), was based on London and has to be considered in the broader panorama of British painting. The same is true of the history painters, Gavin Hamilton and the Runcimans, whose works, in so far as they were exhibited at all, were shown in London. It was not until the beginning of the 'romantic' period, with Raeburn, that Scottish society reached a condition when it could fully employ a native painter of international quality – and Raeburn belongs with Lawrence to the nineteenth century. There was, however, a steady stream of patronage to artists who never strayed south of the Border between the 1720s and 1780s, and a consistent body of portraiture survives (and a few other paintings), which makes a slight sketch possible. Outside London there is nowhere else in the kingdom where a continuous tradition can be traced to anything like the same extent. A certain number of the painters had Jacobite leanings, which found them ready patrons at home and made them unwilling to stray into the sister kingdom.

The first in date is John Alexander, a great-grandson of George Jamesone, who was probably born in Edinburgh about 1690. He was in London in 1710, copying Scottish historical portraits, and in Rome at least from 1714 to 1719. Back in Scotland in 1720 he painted the unique example of Scottish baroque painting, an enormous canvas of 'The Rape of Proserpine' 1720/1 for the roof of the staircase at Gordon Castle. The big picture has vanished, but the little 'modello' (Plate 166B) is in the Edinburgh Gallery. Though hard and liny in outline, it is not altogether negligible in design and shows that the baroque spirit had found its way to north of Aberdeen. In Gordon Castle too – the collection was dispersed in 1938 – were thirteen portraits by John Alexander ranging in date from 1736 to 1743. A few of these now belong to the Duke of Hamilton and are as capable as the secondary line in London portraits at the time. Alexander was 'out' in 1745, and may have gone to Rome with his son. But he was back by the 1750s and working at Aberdeen till he disappears from view about 1757. His son, Cosmo Alexander (1724–72), also claimed to be a history painter but nothing but portraits have survived. These exist in relatively large numbers in houses throughout Scotland and are more sophisticated in style than his father's. He too was 'out' in 1745 and retired to Rome, where he is recorded in 1749. Back in Scotland by 1754 he improved his mind and style by travelling and was a member of the painters' guild at The Hague 1763/4. From his Dutch period dates a group of Hope portraits, one of which, 'Adrian Hope', is in the Edinburgh Gallery and shows marked affinities with the style of such Dutch painters as Troost or F. van der Mijn. After a visit to

London in 1765 he toured the eastern seaboard of the United States from 1768 to 1772 and returned to Edinburgh shortly before his death, bringing with him the young Gilbert Stuart, whose first teacher he seems to have been. The family dynasty was carried on by Cosmo Alexander's brother-in-law, Sir George Chalmers (c. 1720–91). His father had been a herald painter and his own portrait work (and engraving) begins 1738. He was in Minorca in 1755 but back in Scotland by 1760, where he married Isabella Alexander in 1768. He had looked at Reynolds but he had the Alexanders' wiry outline. In his best work, such as 'William Hay' 1770 at Duns Castle, he is on a level with such a painter as Tilly Kettle. Scottish patronage does not seem to have sufficed for him, as he settled in Hull about 1776/9 and later in London, where he died.

Aberdeen was also the main base and home of the most interesting of the earlier portraitists, William Mosman (c. 1700–71), whose work there can be traced from 1731. There is some evidence that Mosman may have studied in Rome under Imperiali, probably in the 1730s and a little before Ramsay entered Imperiali's studio. Ramsay in 1740 seems to have thought him the best painter working in Scotland and he was then working in the southern part of the country. His 'Mrs James Stuart' 1740 (Edinburgh) still has a faint Mediterranean flavour about it and Mosman's best work dates from the 1740s. Later it becomes more provincial and he was settled in Aberdeen by the middle 1750s, where he taught drawing at the two universities.

Mosman may have been driven north by abler practitioners of the London modes who came to Edinburgh. Peter De Nune (of a family from Ross), signed portraits from 1742 to 1751, and, at his best, was very close to Hudson in style; and from 1751 to 1763 a painter who signs 'R. Harvie' was active in the Border Country in a closely related style. But the ablest of the native Edinburgh painters in the middle of the century was William Millar. Millar is first found copying Ramsay portraits in 1751 and he modelled his style upon Ramsay, who, although not his teacher, expressed a high opinion of him. He was active until at least 1775 and his 'Thomas Trotter' 1767 at Edinburgh has a real grasp of Scottish character and an agreeable quality of paint.

In 1760 William Delacour, a Frenchman who is recorded in London in 1747 and who had Jacobite connexions, came to Edinburgh to be the first Master of the Trustees Academy. He painted occasional portraits, but his most interesting works are large wall paintings in a mixed Gaspard Poussin-cum-Pannini style which put the provincial work of the Norie firm in the shade. The ballroom at Yester was decorated in this way by Delacour with large panels dated 1761, and these seem to have served as models for the similar and competent work by Charles Steuart, a Gaelic-speaking Athollman, who painted the Saloon at Blair Atholl from 1766 to 1778.

Painters in Scotland would suddenly become fashionable for a year and then disappear. A certain F. Lindo, probably an Englishman, painted a number of portraits in 1761, and one J. Clark was acquiring a reputation in 1767, when he was enabled (in about 1768) to go and study in Naples by the generosity of Sir Ludovic Grant and Sir John Dalrymple. He seems to have flourished moderately as a painter in Naples until his death about 1801.

It was in the 1770s that painters who had been trained in London began to return to Scotland for a livelihood. John Thomas Seton, a pupil of Hayman, who had first exhibited in London in 1761, settled in Edinburgh in 1772 and painted life-size portraits as well as a few conversations, of which one in the Edinburgh Gallery was long understandably mistaken for a Zoffany. These works were certainly up to the level of works in the London exhibitions. From 1776 to 1785 Seton visited India, where he made a considerable fortune and painted a number of Nabobs, from Warren Hastings downwards. He returned once more to Edinburgh, where he was living as late as 1806. The ambitious full-lengths of his last period, such as the 'Lady Catherine Charteris' 1786 at Gosford, which is planned in the Reynolds tradition of twenty years earlier, were the first of this class of picture actually to be painted north of the Border. Another Edinburgh painter with a similar career was George Willison (1741–97), who first exhibited in London (1767), made a fortune in India (1772–81), and settled in Edinburgh (1784/5). The rather little of his work which has been traced is varied and reflects a pliable mind which was open to the influence of Gainsborough as well as to the prevailing style.

Finally there came David Martin (1737–97), who provides the rather tenuous link between Ramsay and Raeburn. Martin had been Ramsay's direct pupil and remained his studio assistant into the 1760s, but when we recognize his first independent work, about 1765, he had already veered over towards the more forceful patterns of Reynolds, and the rough texture of his paint in later years seems also to have been due to seeking for something of Reynolds's style. In 1775 he settled in Edinburgh and became the fashionable portrait painter for the next twenty years, his reputation not being eclipsed by the young Raeburn, to whom he is said to have lent one of his portraits to copy. He was always slovenly in execution and his hands are often astonishingly feeble, but his portraits have an individual tang and cannot readily be mistaken for the work of any other painter. He was well suited by sympathy to depict some of the more characteristic kinds of Scottish face, and his masterpiece is 'George Murdoch' (Plate 188B) 1793 in the Glasgow Gallery. It may be that he was not above taking a hint from Raeburn's sense of pattern and method of lighting the head in his later years, but what we know of Raeburn's chronology (and the knowledge is very imperfect) rather suggests that the influence was the other way about. Martin was appointed Painter to the Prince of Wales, and he seems to have been the first painter since the days of Sir John Medina to have made a good and steady income out of painting portraits in the capital of Scotland.

CHAPTER 27

PORTRAITISTS IN CRAYONS OR PASTEL

THE art of portraiture in crayons or pastel or kindred media was in sufficient vogue throughout much of the eighteenth century to demand separate treatment here. Most of the painters involved practised in oil also, but a number of them hardly made a name outside of their work in crayons to demand consideration as oil painters. Writing of the collection at Stourhead in the early years of the nineteenth century, Sir Richard Colt Hoare refers to 'painting in crayons, a style now quite unfashionable', so that we may properly conclude with a chapter on a form of painting which came to a temporary close with the period of which this volume treats.

It has been plausibly suggested that portraiture in crayons was introduced into England from France about the time of the Restoration. At any rate such work first appears in the 1660s among the circle of Lely's immediate associates. Two theatrical portraits by John Greenhill are the earliest which have been traced, 'Betterton as Tamerlane' 1663 at Kingston Lacy and 'Harris as Wolsey' in the President's Lodgings at Magdalen College, Oxford. It may be that something more highly coloured than the ordinary portrait drawing was felt as appropriate for the first portraits of actors in character parts, and the new medium gives them a strikingly modern air. But crayons were not confined to actors' portraits, as the two surviving crayon portraits (one in the Ashmolean Museum, Oxford) by an otherwise unknown associate of Lely, T. Thrumpton, are of more conventional sitters. They date from 1667.

The first artist whom we may reasonably consider to have been a professional specialist in crayon portraits was Edmund Ashfield, who can be certainly traced only from 1670 to 1675. He was copying Lely portraits in oil in 1670 but is stated by Walpole to have been the pupil of Michael Wright, which seems plausible on grounds of style. His crayons are about 11 × 9 in. in size, sometimes rich in colour and of high quality, when in good preservation. The best signed examples are at Ham House. We also learn from Walpole that Ashfield enriched the crayon-painter's palette and was the teacher of Edward Lutterell, who is a hardly more tangible figure.

Lutterell is reputed to have been an Irishman and trained to the Law. What is certain is that he also practised as a mezzotint engraver. He first emerges with any certainty about 1680 and he may have been living as late as 1723. His only crayons of note at present traced date from the 1690s and his work answers to some extent to Kneller's in painting. It is technically of considerable originality, since he devised a means of using crayons on copper by first preparing the ground as if for mezzotint. His clear key of colouring is very different from Ashfield's more sombre and sonorous colouring.

For the first quarter of the eighteenth century crayon portraits do not seem to have been in high fashion, although the work of a number of provincial masters is occasionally met with. But it was brought into repute again by three artists after their return from

Italy. Arthur Pond (*c.* 1705–58) came back from Italy in 1727; George Knapton (1698–1778) returned in 1732; and William Hoare (*c.* 1707–92) in 1737. As crayon painters, although Pond was the first to become fashionable, Knapton was the best and most important. The first report of the new fashion comes from Mrs Delany, writing to her sister, Anne Granville, 30 June 1734. 'Lady Dysart', she says, 'has got to crayons, and I design to fall into that way. I hope Mr Pond will help me too, for his colouring in crayons I think *the best* I have seen of any English painter.' Pond's quality in crayons, to judge from a signed example of 1737 at Melbury, is little higher than his quality in oils, but his work found favour and imitators as well. George Vertue disapproved of the vogue for crayon portraits and a singularly ungrammatical passage in his notes for 1741 gives his views (III, 109/10): 'crayon painting has met with so much encouragement of late years here, that several painters – those that had been in Italy to study, Knapton, Pond, Hoare, for the practice of painting in oil – found at their return that they could not make any extraordinary matter of it, and turned to painting in crayons, and several made great advantages of it. It looked pleasant, and, covered with glass (and in) large gold frames, was much commended for the novelty. And the painters, finding it much easier in execution than oil colours, readily came into it.' I have modified Vertue's punctuation, but retained his meaning. He closes his paragraph with the words: 'the want of ambition in art thus shows its declining state. Small pains and great gains is this darling modish study.' Knapton worked at London, Hoare in Bath. Knapton's tonality is rather brownish and greyish, while Hoare's is gayer, but it was Knapton who became the teacher of Francis Cotes, who brought the crayon portrait onto the same level as the portrait in oils, and who was the first of what Vertue calls the 'crayoneers' to adopt the portrait style of the new age. Independent of these was Catherine Read (1723–78), a Scottish lady who studied in Paris and Rome, worked in London from 1754, and went to India in 1775.

Francis Cotes (1726–70) first appears as an independent crayon artist in 1748. Even in his first years he is much brighter in colour than Knapton and he expresses admiration for the work of Mengs and Rosalba in a way which suggests that he had seen their works and profited by them. Indeed, a visit to Italy is not improbable, but is not documented. Rosalba herself never visited England but Cotes must have been put on his mettle by the appearance of Jean-Étienne Liotard (1702–89) the Swiss painter, who arrived in London in 1753 with an international reputation and a considerable English clientele. Liotard was in London from 1753 to 1755 and was at first a tremendous success, rousing the jealous criticism of the young Reynolds. Horace Walpole remarks that Liotard's likenesses were 'too like to please those who sat to him' and that he had great business the first year and very little the second. 'Freckles, marks of the small pox, everything found its place, not so much from fidelity, as because he could not conceive the absence of anything that appeared to him.' But for liveliness and vivacity of colour they were something quite new in portraiture in England. The series of portraits at Windsor of the Princess of Wales and her children (1755) is the most modern in appearance of any portraits of the age, and the fact that one can discern which of the children had adenoids is perhaps more interesting to posterity than it was to contemporaries. Certainly such work convinced Cotes that he must abandon altogether the old tonality of Knapton and he brought his crayons to a very high pitch of technical perfection and employed bright colours along the same lines. Although Cotes turned more and more to oils after 1763, he still took pupils in crayons, and Russell was in his studio as late as 1767. Liotard returned to London from 1772 to 1774, but the force of his first impact was spent.

A passing mention may be made of François Xavier Vispré, a native of Besançon, who worked in London (and a little in Dublin) from 1760 to 1789. His rather infrequent but charming crayon portraits brought to England something of the French manner of Perronneau, but seem to have been without influence. Nor did the work of Quentin de la Tour, although mentioned with praise by Allan Ramsay, find any echo in England. A neat painter of small-scale crayon heads, rather out of the main tradition, was Hugh Douglas Hamilton (c. 1739–1808), who is reputed to have acquired the technique at the Dublin school of art. He worked in London about 1764 to 1778, and the charming little ovals of this period are his best work, anticipating the small watercolour portraits of Downman, who succeeded to his vogue. Hamilton's work is generally subdued in colour and unrelated to the contemporary style of Cotes. From 1778 to 1791 Hamilton worked in Rome, specializing in small-scale full-length crayons which are like miniature portraits by Batoni. But he was persuaded by Flaxman to take to oils and retired to Dublin, where he prospered as an oil painter, but where his work lost its pristine elegance and neat charm.

The tradition of Cotes was maintained by John Russell (1745–1806), who was his pupil up to 1767. Russell bought certain works by Rosalba Carriera which he studied to advantage and cultivated a rather smudgier technique than had prevailed before, 'rubbing in' his crayons, as his contemporary, Bacon, reported. His personality is rather difficult to grasp, as he was a churchman of unusual devoutness, much given to favouring the Methodists in the days of their early enthusiasm. Yet he turned out a steady stream of portraits which seem to make his sitters more modish, or more mannered, than reality. He became A.R.A. as early as 1772, but was not elected R.A. until 1788. In 1785 he was appointed 'Crayon Painter to the Prince of Wales' and his prices in the 1790s were as high as those of Reynolds. From the end of the 1790s his London vogue lessened and most of his commissions came from Yorkshire, where he made extended tours, and where he died. There is an insipidity about his style which must have appealed to his contemporaries, who continued to sit to him, in spite of his preaching at his sitters.

Russell's rival towards the close of his career was Ozias Humphry (1742–1810), who had begun as a miniature painter of some distinction, settling in London in 1763. In 1773 he accompanied Romney to Italy, returning in 1777, and he visited India 1785 to 1788. An accident which affected his eyesight, in 1772, had diverted him from miniatures to oil painting, but he was never better at oil portraits than a third-rate echo of Romney's style. In 1791, however, he became R.A. and switched over to crayons, becoming soon afterwards 'Portrait Painter in crayons to His Majesty', no doubt as a sort of antidote to Russell's corresponding appointment to the Prince of Wales. In his crayons Humphry shows a rather greater probity than Russell and adopted a more linear and less smudgy style.

The youngest of the three chief masters of the crayon, Daniel Gardner (1750–1805), was the most distinguished and at the same time the most original. A native of Kendal, where Romney had first practised, he became a pupil of Romney and studied at the Royal Academy schools. But from Romney he learned nothing, except that it was not necessary to exhibit at the Academy, and the late style of Reynolds, in its least solid aspect, was Gardner's model. It has even been suggested that Gardner was Reynolds's assistant towards the close of his life. His first practice was in crayons, and in a letter of 12 November 1779 he describes the portrait of Philip Egerton as 'absolutely the first oil picture I ever finished'. Certain early oil portraits of the Pennington family (personal friends of Gardner) which have passed through the auction rooms in recent years, suggest that, although technically far from accomplished, he was capable of a vein of tender and romantic sentiment in this medium which is surprising. His masterpiece in oil, the 'Heathcote Hunting Group' belonging to the National Trust and exhibited at Montacute, is based on Reynolds's latest style, but retains, as always with Gardner, something of the effect of having been painted on a rough towel. This roughness of texture he evidently valued, for he carried it over into his pastels. These are technically highly original, for Gardner mixed brandy or spirits of wine with his crayons, which had been scraped to dust with a knife, and drew with this highly loaded preparation. The result is something half-way between crayons and oil painting and achieves a violent and almost harsh brilliance of effect unparalleled in any other medium. To this lush material Gardner added a very flashy style, torturing his white draperies more with the art of the *pâtissier* than of the painter, and organizing his family groups (or even his single figures) in a riot of voluptuous curves. Except for Cosway's miniatures, no paintings give quite such a complete synthesis of the artificial world of pre-Regency and Regency times, and it is understandable that Gardner's art died with him. But in fact the three chief painters in crayons all died in the early years of the nineteenth century and left no successor to carry on their art, which, almost overnight, ceased to be fashionable. Nor has it ever been, to any serious extent, revived.

BIBLIOGRAPHY

(Articles in periodicals are mentioned in the notes to the text)

BIBLIOGRAPHIES

There is no standard Bibliography of British Art. A beginning was made by the Courtauld Institute with an annual *Bibliography of the History of British Art* of which four volumes have appeared which cover the literature for the years 1934 to 1945 (Cambridge 1936 to 1951). The few books with useful special bibliographies have this fact recorded below.

DICTIONARIES

The articles on British painters in Thieme-Becker, *Allgemeines Lexikon der bildenden Künstler* are usually scrappy but are valuable for their (often excessive) bibliographical references. Certain articles on minor painters contain small items, derived from British scholars, which are unpublished elsewhere. The last edition of *Bryan's Dictionary of Painters and Engravers* revised by G. C. Williamson 1903/4 (and often republished up to 1925) contains some useful articles on the more flimsy painters of the eighteenth century in whom Dr Williamson specialized. The *Dictionary of National Biography* has some useful articles on the earlier painters by (Sir) Lionel Cust and is worth consulting for a few well-informed articles on minor painters. For the few painters of note of American origin, or who worked in the United States (e.g. Pine, West, and Copley) the *Dictionary of American Biography*, New York, 1928 to 1936, is much superior to any of the others.

GRANT, Colonel Maurice Harold. *A Chronological History of the Old English Landscape Painters (in oil).* I and II, London, 1926; III, Leigh-on-Sea, 1947.
>Much of this has reappeared in a *Dictionary*, 1952.

LONG, Basil S. *British Miniaturists.* London, 1929.
>This is a source book of the greatest value, with a full bibliography.

REDGRAVE, Samuel. *A Dictionary of Artists of the English School.* 2nd and revised edition, London, 1878.
>Still the most useful quick work of reference.

REES, Rev. T. Hardy. *Welsh Painters, Engravers, and Sculptors (1527–1911).* Carnarvon, 1912.
>An amateurish but diligent production.

STRICKLAND, Walter G. *A Dictionary of Irish Artists*, 2 vols. Dublin, 1913.
>A valuable book of reference, in which the term 'Irish' is most liberally interpreted.

GENERAL WORKS

There are many popular compilations on British or English painting. I include only works which can be regarded as source material or give evidence of a considerable degree of research.

Aspects of Art in England c. 1700–c. 1850. B.B.C., London, 1950.
>An illustrated brochure which includes certain illustrations not readily accessible elsewhere. The talks illustrated were published in *The Listener* for 1950.

BAKER, C. H. Collins. *Lely and the Stuart Portrait Painters*, 2 vols. London, 1912.
>The pioneer work on the seventeenth century.

BAKER, C. H. Collins, and CONSTABLE, W. G. *English Painting of the Sixteenth and Seventeenth Centuries.* Florence and Paris, 1930.
>With a valuable bibliography.

BAKER, C. H. Collins, and JAMES, M. R. *British Painting.* London, 1933.
>The best short history of the whole field.

BAKER, C. H. Collins, and BAKER, Muriel I. *The Life and Circumstances of James Brydges, first Duke of Chandos.* Oxford, 1949.

BINYON, Laurence. *English Watercolours.* London, 1933.

The Boydell Gallery. A reproduction on a reduced scale of 97 engravings from the original edition of 1805. London, 1874.

BUCKERIDGE, B., in R. DE PILES, *The Art of Painting.* 3rd edition of English translation, London (*c.* 1706).

CAREY, William. *Letter to I— A— Esq.* Manchester, 1809.

CUNNINGHAM, Allan. *The Lives of the Most Eminent British Painters.* Revised edition, with continuations, by Mrs Heaton, 3 vols. London, 1879/80.
>The most convenient edition to consult.

CUST, (Sir) Lionel, and COLVIN, (Sir) Sidney. *History of the Society of Dilettanti.* London, 1898 (reprinted 1914).
>See also: HARCOURT SMITH under heading 'Catalogues'.

CUST, (Sir) Lionel. *Notes on Pictures in the Royal Collections*. London, 1911.

DAYES, Edward. *The Works of the late Edward Dayes*. London, 1805.
> This contains biographical material on eighteenth-century painters.

EDWARDS, Edward. *Anecdotes of Painters . . .* 'intended as a continuation to the *Anecdotes of Painting* by the late Horace, Earl of Orford. London, 1808.

ENGLEFIELD, W. A. D. *The History of the Painter-Stainers Company of London*. London, 1923.

FARINGTON, Joseph. *The Farington Diary*. Ed. James Greig, 8 vols. London, 1922 ff.
> A very incomplete publication. The full MS. is in the Royal Library at Windsor and a complete typescript can be consulted in the Print Room of the British Museum.

FREY, Dagobert. *Englisches Wesen in der bildenden Kunst*. Stuttgart, 1942.

GREEN, David. *Blenheim*. London, 1952.

HERVEY, Mary F. S. *The Life, Correspondence, and Collections of Thomas Howard, Earl of Arundel*. Cambridge, 1921.

[HERVEY, S. H. A.]. *The Diary of John Hervey, First Earl of Bristol, with Extracts from his Book of Expenses*. Wells, 1894.

KLINGENDER, Francis D. *Art and the Industrial Revolution*. London, 1947.

LENYGON, Francis. *Decoration in England 1640 to 1760*. 2nd and revised edition. London, 1927.

MANWARING, Elizabeth Wheeler. *Italian Landscape in Eighteenth-Century England*. New York, 1925.

MILNER, Edith, and BENHAM, Edith. *Records of the Lumleys of Lumley Castle*. London, 1904.
> The first publication of the Lumley Inventory. It is more accurately transcribed in the *Walpole Society*, VI, 1918.

NICHOLS, John Gough. *Notices of the Contemporaries and Successors of Holbein*. London, 1863 (reprinted from *The Archaeologia*, XXXIX).

NICHOLS, R. H., and WRAY, F. A. *The History of the Foundling Hospital*. London, 1935.

NORTH, Roger. *The Lives of the Norths*. Augustus Jessopp edition, 3 vols. London, 1890.
> The matter relating to Lely is to be found only in Jessopp's edition.

PYCROFT, George. *Art in Devonshire, with the Biographies of Artists born in that County*. Exeter, 1883.

PYE, John. *Patronage of British Art*. London, 1845.

REDGRAVE, Richard and Samuel. *A Century of Painters of the English School*, 2 vols. London, 1866.
> Illustrated reprint, without the last chapter, 1949.

SAINSBURY, W. Noel. *Original unpublished Papers illustrative of the Life of Sir Peter Paul Rubens &c.* London, 1859.
> Contains documentary material on the patronage of artists by Charles I.

SAXL, Fritz, and WITTKOWER, Rudolph. *British Art and the Mediterranean*. Oxford (and Warburg Institute), 1948.

SHAW SPARROW, Walter. *British Sporting Painters*. London, 1922.

SHAW SPARROW, Walter. *A Book of Sporting Painters*. London, 1931.
> Has an index-dictionary at the end.

SITWELL, Sacheverell. *Conversation Pieces*. London, 1936.

SITWELL, Sacheverell. *Narrative Pictures*. London, 1937.
> Useful collections of plates with many sensitive observations but no pretensions to research.

SMITH, John Thomas. *Nollekens and his Times*. 2nd edition 1829. Annotated edition, ed. Wilfred Whitten. London, 1920.
> Whitten's edition is the most convenient for consultation.

SMITH, John Thomas. *A Book for a Rainy Day*. 1st edition 1845. Annotated edition, ed. Wilfred Whitten. London, 1905.

STEEGMAN, John. *The Artist and the Country House*. London, 1949.

THOMPSON, Francis. *A History of Chatsworth*. London, 1949.

TINKER, Chauncey Brewster. *Painter and Poet*. Harvard, 1938.

VERTUE, George. MS. notes. Published by the *Walpole Society*, XVIII (Vertue I), 1930. XX (Vertue II), 1932. XXII (Vertue III), 1934. XXIV (Vertue IV), 1936. XXVI (Vertue V), 1938. XXIX (Index to Vertue I to V), 1947.
> A further volume is in press.

WALPOLE, Hon. Horace (Earl of Orford). *Anecdotes of Painting in England*. 4 vols. 1765 to 1771. Another edition (including Dalloway's notes) ed. Ralph N. Wornum, 3 vols. London, 1876. Vol. v. ed. F. W. Hilles and P. D. Daghlian. Yale, 1937.
> The Wornum edition is most convenient for con-

sultation. Volume V consists of Walpole's own collection of contemporary extracts for the years 1760 to 1795.

WHITLEY, William T. *Artists and their Friends in England, 1700 to 1799.* 2 vols. London, 1928.
> The MS. collections on which these were based are now in the print room of the British Museum.

WILLIAMSON, G. C. *English Conversation Pieces.* London, 1931.
> A collection of plates, with very careless notes.

WOOD, Sir Henry Trueman. *A History of the Royal Society of Arts.* London, 1913.

WOODWARD, John. *Tudor and Stuart Drawings.* London, 1951.

CATALOGUES

Only such catalogues as have especial value as works of reference for the study of British painting are listed here: a few others will be found listed under the Bibliography of individual painters.

ADAMS, C. K. *A Catalogue of the Pictures in the Garrick Club.* London, 1936.

BAKER, C. H. Collins. *Catalogue of British Paintings in the Henry E. Huntington Library and Art Gallery.* San Marino, California, 1936.

Catalogue of an Exhibition of Late Elizabethan Art. Burlington Fine Arts Club. London, 1926.

Commemorative Catalogue of the Exhibition of British Art, R.A. 1934. Oxford, 1935.

CUST, (Sir) Lionel. *Exhibition illustrative of Early English Portraiture.* Burlington Fine Arts Club, 1909. Illustrated catalogue.

CUST, (Sir) Lionel. *Eton College Portraits.* London, 1910.

DAVIES, Martin. *National Gallery Catalogues: British School.* 1946.

DEVONSHIRE. *Report and Transactions of the Devonshire Association for the Advancement of Science, Literature and Art,* vol. XIV (1882) to XIX (1887).
> Catalogues of pictures in Devonshire collections are published in these reports.

DULEEP SINGH, Prince Frederick. *Portraits in Norfolk Houses,* 2 vols. Norwich, 1927.

FARRER, Rev. Edmund. *Portraits in Suffolk Houses (West).* London, 1908.
> The MS. for Suffolk (East) is in the Ipswich Public Library.

FRY, Frederick M. *A Historical Catalogue of the Pictures ... at Merchant Taylors' Hall.* London, 1907.

GOULDING, Richard W., and ADAMS, C. K. *Catalogue of Pictures belonging to His Grace the Duke of Portland.* Cambridge, 1936.
> There is new documentary material among the biographical index of artists.

GRAVES, Algernon. *The Royal Academy of Arts,* 8 vols. London, 1905/6.
> A complete dictionary of its contributors and their work from its foundation in 1769 to 1904.

GRAVES, Algernon. *The Society of Artists of Great Britain (1760–91): The Free Society of Artists (1761–1783).* London, 1907.
> A complete dictionary of contributors and their work.

GRAVES, Algernon. *A Century of Loan Exhibitions (1813–1912),* 5 vols. London, 1913/15.

HAILSTONE, Edward. *Portraits of Yorkshire Worthies,* 2 vols. London, 1869.
> Illustrated catalogue of selection from Leeds Exhibition 1868.

HARCOURT SMITH, Sir Cecil. *The Society of Dilettanti, its Regalia and Pictures.* London, 1932.

HAWKESBURY, LORD, and LAWRANCE, Rev. Henry. *East Riding Portraits in The Transactions of the East Riding Antiquarian Society,* X to XII. Hull, 1903/4.

National Portrait Exhibitions, South Kensington, 1866 to 1868.
> Illustrated Albums to these were published and many of the negatives survive in the Victoria and Albert Museum.

O'DONOGHUE, Freeman, and HAKE, (Sir) Henry M. *Catalogue of Engraved British Portraits ... in the British Museum,* 6 vols. London, 1908–25.

OXFORD. Illustrated catalogues of Loan Collections of Portraits, 1904–6, 3 vols. Oxford, 1904/6: (1) those who died prior to 1625; (2) those who died between 1625 and 1714; (3) those who died between 1714 and 1837.
> With introductions by (Sir) Lionel Cust: the portraits are nearly all from Oxford Collections.

POOLE, Mrs Reginald Lane. *Catalogue of Portraits in the possession of the University, Colleges, City and County of Oxford,* I, Oxford, 1912: II and III, 1925.
> Mr J. W. Goodison is engaged on a comparable work for Cambridge.

Royal Academy, The first hundred years of the. Catalogue of Exhibition, R.A. London, 1951/2.

RUBENS, Alfred. *Anglo-Jewish Portraits.* London, 1935.

SHAW, W. A. *Three Inventories of Pictures in the Collections of Henry VIII, Edward VI*. London, 1937.

SMITH, John Chaloner. *British Mezzotinto Portraits*, 5 vols. and portfolio of plates. London, 1878 to 1883.

VERTUE, George. *A Catalogue and description of King Charles the First's Capital Collection of Pictures &c*. London, 1757.

VERTUE, George. *A Catalogue of the Collection of Pictures &c. belonging to King James the Second &c*. London, 1758.

Later Royal Inventories remain unpublished.

WORKS ON INDIVIDUAL ARTISTS

ALLAN, David.
T. Crouther Gordon. *David Allan*. Alva, 1951.

BARRY, James.
Ed. Dr Fryer. *The Works of James Barry, Historical Painter*, 2 vols. London, 1809.

BEACH, Thomas.
Elise S. Beach. *Thomas Beach*. London, 1934 (Catalogue).

BEECHEY, Sir William.
W. Roberts. *Sir William Beechey*. London, 1907.
Material for catalogue.

COPLEY, John Singleton.
Letters and Papers of John Singleton Copley and Henry Pelham. Massachusetts Historical Society Collections. Vol. 71, 1914. J. T. Flexner. *John Singleton Copley*. Boston, 1948.
Has a full bibliography.

COSWAY, Richard.
G. C. Williamson. *Richard Cosway*. London, 1917.

DAHL, Michael.
Wilhelm Nisser. *Michael Dahl and the contemporary Swedish School of Painting in England*. Uppsala, 1927.
Catalogues and full bibliography for the period.

DEVIS, Arthur, &c.
Sydney H. Paviere. *The Devis Family of Painters*. Leigh-on-Sea, 1950.
Catalogues.

DOBSON, William.
Oliver Millar. *Catalogue of Dobson Exhibition at the Tate Gallery*. London, 1951.

DOWNMAN, John.
G. C. Williamson. *John Downman*. London, 1907.

DYCK, Sir Anthony van.
W. Hookham Carpenter. *Pictorial Notices of Sir Anthony van Dyck*. London, 1844.
This is still the only available work in which the chief documents relating to Van Dyck's work for the Crown are available.

(Sir) Lionel Cust. *Anthony van Dyck*. London, 1900.
This contains the fullest list of his English works (but no attempt is made at sorting originals from school works).

Gustav Glück. *Van Dyck* (Klassiker der Kunst). 2nd edition, 1931.
A good selection of his best English work is here illustrated.

GAINSBOROUGH, Thomas.
G. W. Fulcher. *Life of Thomas Gainsborough*. London, 1856.
This is the first attempt at a catalogue; a second edition allegedly of the same year has a slightly increased list.

Sir William Armstrong. *Gainsborough*. 2nd and revised edition, 1904.
A later catalogue, but uncritical.

William T. Whitley. *Thomas Gainsborough*. London, 1915.
This contains a very full biography.

Mary Woodall. *Thomas Gainsborough*. London, 1949.
The best general short account of the artist.

Mary Woodall. *Gainsborough's Landscape Drawings*. London, 1939 (with catalogue).

Album of the Gainsborough Loan Exhibition held at 45 Park Lane. London, 1936.
The fullest selection of plates is in this album.
Note: A preliminary check list of Gainsborough's portraits will appear in *Walpole Soc*. XXXIII.

GARDNER, Daniel.
G. C. Williamson, *Daniel Gardner*. London, 1921.

HILLIARD, Nicholas.
Graham Reynolds. *Catalogue of the Nicholas Hilliard Exhibition*, Victoria & Albert Museum. London, 1947.

John Pope-Hennessy. *A lecture on Nicholas Hilliard*. London, 1949.

HOGARTH, William.
Austin Dobson. *William Hogarth*. Last edition. London, 1907.
The fullest biography, with a bibliography of the earlier literature.

R. B. Beckett. *Hogarth*. London, 1949.
This contains the fullest collection of plates.

A. P. Oppé. *The Drawings of Hogarth*. London, 1948.
The best critical appreciation.

Hogarth. *Analysis of Beauty*. Ed. Joseph Burke.
Professor Burke is at the moment engaged on an edition of this book.

Robert Etheridge Moore. *Hogarth's Literary Relationships*. University of Minnesota, 1948.
This aspect of Hogarth's life will no doubt be more fully treated in Dr F. Antal's forthcoming book.

HOLBEIN, Hans.
Arthur B. Chamberlain. *Hans Holbein the Younger*. 2 vols. London, 1913.
Still the fullest account available.

Paul Ganz. *The Paintings of Hans Holbein*. London, 1950.
This contains the best collection of plates.

Alfred Schmid. *Hans Holbein der Jüngere*. Basel, 1945 (Plates), and 1950 (Text).
This is a more searching study of Holbein.

K. T. Parker. *The Drawings of Hans Holbein ... at Windsor Castle*. Oxford, 1945.
The other three are supplemented by this volume.

HOPPNER, John.
William McKay and William Roberts. *John Hoppner*. London, 1909, with a supplementary volume.

HUMPHRY, Ozias.
G. C. Williamson. *Ozias Humphry*. London, 1918.

IBBETSON, Julius Caesar.
Rotha Mary Clay. *Julius Caesar Ibbetson*. London, 1949.

JAMESONE, George.
John Bullock. *George Jamesone*. Edinburgh, 1885.
This has an attempt at a catalogue.

KAUFFMANN, Angelica.
Lady Victoria Manners and G. C. Williamson. *Angelica Kauffmann*. London, 1924.

KENT, William.
Margaret Jourdain. *William Kent*. London, 1948.

LELY, Sir Peter.
C. H. Collins Baker. *Lely and the Stuart Portrait Painters*, 2 vols. London, 1912.

R. B. Beckett. *Peter Lely*. London, 1951.

MORLAND, George.
W. Collins. *Memoirs of a Picture&c*. London, 1805.

F. W. Blagden. *Authentic Memoirs of George Morland*. London, 1806.

J. Hassel. *Memoirs of the Life of George Morland*. London, 1806.

George Dawe. *The Life of George Morland*. London, 1807.
These four are all early works on the painter.

Ralph Richardson. *George Morland's Pictures: their present possessors*. London, 1897.
A catalogue of the painter's work.

G. C. Williamson. *George Morland*. 1904.

NORTHCOTE, James.
Stephen Gwynne. *Memorials of an Eighteenth-Century Painter*. London, 1898.

Conversations of James Northcote with James Ward. Ed. Ernest Fletcher. London, 1901.

OPIE, John.
J. Jope Rogers, *Opie and His Works*. London, 1878.

Ada Earland, *John Opie and His Circle*. London, 1911.
This book has a catalogue.

PETERS, Matthew William. Lady Victoria Manners, *Matthew William Peters*. London, 1913.
This has a catalogue.

RAMSAY, Allan. Alastair Smart, *The Life and Art of Allan Ramsay*, London, 1952.

REYNOLDS, Sir Joshua.
A. Graves and W. V. Cronin, *A History of the Works of Sir Joshua Reynolds*, 4 vols. London, 1899–1901.
This contains the fullest documentation.

E. K. Waterhouse, *Reynolds*. London, 1941.
This has the largest collection of plates and an annotated bibliography and catalogue.

ROMNEY, George.
William Hayley, *Life of George Romney*. London, 1809.

Rev. John Romney, *Memoirs of the Life and Works of George Romney*. London, 1830.
Both are early works.

Humphry Ward and W. Roberts, *Romney*, 2 vols. London, 1904.
Has a very full catalogue.

RUSSELL, John.
G. C. Williamson, *John Russell*. London, 1894.
This has a catalogue.

ROWLANDSON, Thomas.
A. P. Oppé, *Thomas Rowlandson*. London, 1923.

SMIBERT, John.
Henry Wilder Foote, *John Smibert*. Harvard, 1950.

STUART, Gilbert.
Lawrence Park, *Gilbert Stuart*, 2 vols. text and 2 vols. plates. New York, 1926.
Contains a catalogue.

William T. Whitley, *Gilbert Stuart*. Harvard, 1932.

STUBBS, George.
Joseph Mayer, *Memoirs of Thomas Dodd, William Upcott, and George Stubbs*. Liverpool, 1879.

Sir Walter Gilbey, *Life of George Stubbs*. London, 1898.

W. Shaw Sparrow. *Stubbs and Ben Marshall*. London, 1929.
Mr Basil Taylor is engaged on a full study of Stubbs.

WEST, Benjamin.
John Galt, *The Life, Studies and Works of Benjamin West*. 2 parts. London, 1920.
See also Catalogue of West exhibition at Philadelphia, 1938.

WHEATLEY, Francis.
W. Roberts, *Francis Wheatley*. London, 1910.
This work is more concerned with engravings after Wheatley than with his paintings.

WILSON, Richard.
T. Wright. *Some Account of the Life of Richard Wilson*. London, 1824.

Thomas Hastings. *Etchings from the Works of Richard Wilson with some Memoirs of his Life, etc.* London, 1825.
This is better than the early and empty biography by Wright.

Adrian Bury. *Richard Wilson*. Leigh-on-Sea, 1947.
A little can be gleaned from this; it has a rudimentary catalogue.

Brinsley Ford. *Richard Wilson's Drawings*. London, 1951.
W. G. Constable is engaged on a full study of Wilson.

WRIGHT (of Derby), Joseph.
William Bemrose. *The Life and Works of Joseph Wright*. London, 1855.
Contains material for a catalogue. Charles Edward Buckley is engaged on a Doctoral Thesis on Wright for Harvard.

ZOFFANY, Johann.
Lady Victoria Manners and G. C. Williamson. *Johann Zoffany*. London, 1920.
Contains a catalogue.

SCOTTISH PAINTING

BROCKWELL, Maurice W. *George Jamesone and some primitive Scottish Painters*. London, 1939.
Extracts from Musgrave's eighteenth-century lists of portraits in Scottish houses.

BRYDALL, Robert. *Art in Scotland: its Origin and Progress*. Edinburgh, 1889.

CAW, (Sir) James L. *Scottish Portraits*. 4 portfolios. Edinburgh, 1902.

CAW, (Sir) James L. *Scottish Painting, Past and Present (1620–1908)*. Edinburgh, 1908.

CAW, (Sir) James L., with others. *Catalogue of the Exhibition of Scottish Art, R.A.* London, 1939.
This has an album of plates.

CURSITER, Stanley. *Scottish Art to the Close of the Nineteenth Century*. London, 1949.
This has a bibliography.

(B) English: Margaret, Countess of Salisbury. ±1535.
National Portrait Gallery, London

(A) English, early sixteenth century: Henry VI.
National Portrait Gallery, London

I

Holbein: Henry VIII and Henry VII
(Fragment of cartoon for lost fresco at Whitehall). 1537. *Chatsworth*

4

Follower of Holbein: Henry VIII. *Walker Art Gallery, Liverpool*

5

(B) Follower of Holbein: Unknown Lady. *T. W. Fitzwilliam,*
Milton Park, Northants

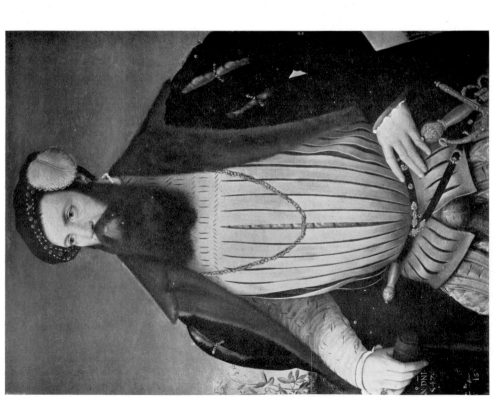

(A) G. Flicke: Unknown Man. 1547. *National Gallery of Scotland,*
Edinburgh

(B) Unknown: Queen Elizabeth I as Princess. ±1546.
Windsor Castle. By gracious permission of Her Majesty The Queen

(A) Unknown: Edward VI. ±1550. *Windsor Castle.*
By gracious permission of Her Majesty The Queen

Unknown: Young Man in Red. ±1550. *Hampton Court.*
By gracious permission of Her Majesty The Queen

8

Guillim Scrots: Henry Howard, Earl of Surrey. 1546.
Hon. Clive Pearson, Parham Park, Sussex

(B) Hans Eworth (?): Mary Tudor.
Captain Sir Bruce Ingram

(A) Antonio Moro: Queen Mary Tudor. 1554.
Marquess of Northampton, Castle Ashby, Northants

(B) Hans Eworth: A Turk on Horseback. 1549.
Earl of Yarborough, Brocklesby Park, Lincs

(A) Hans Eworth: Lady Dacre. *National Gallery of
Canada, Ottawa*

II

Hans Eworth: Sir John Luttrell. 1550. *G. F. Luttrell, Dunster Castle, Somerset*

THIS BETH SONES OF HE RIGHT HONERABLES TERLLE OF LENOXE AD
TE LADY MARGARETZ GRACE COVNTYES OF LENOXE AD ANGWYSI

1563

CHARLLES STEWARDE
HIS BROTHER, ÆTATIS, 6,

HENRY STEWARDE LORD DAR̄
LEY AND DOWGLAS, ÆTATIS, 17

Hans Eworth: Lord Darnley and his Brother. 1563. *Windsor Castle.*
By gracious permission of Her Majesty The Queen

13

Hans Eworth: Queen Elizabeth I and the Goddesses. 1569. *Hampton Court. By gracious permission of Her Majesty The Queen*

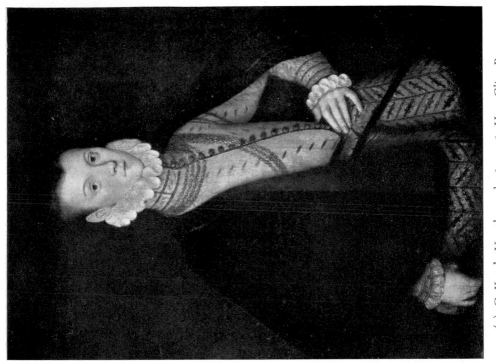

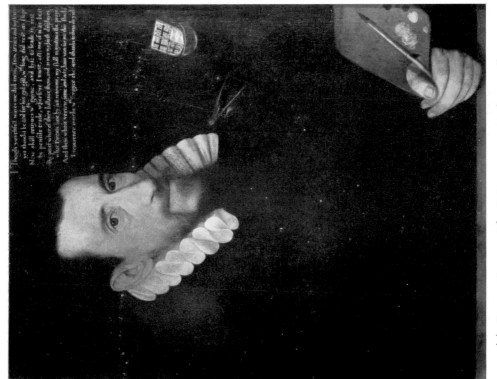

(B) C. Ketel: Youth aged 16. 1576. *Hon. Clive Pearson,*
Parham Park, Sussex

(A) George Gower: The Painter. 1579. *Earl Fitzwilliam,*
Milton Park, Northants

15

(B) J. Custodis: Lady Elizabeth Bruges. 1589. *Duke of Bedford,*
Woburn Abbey, Beds

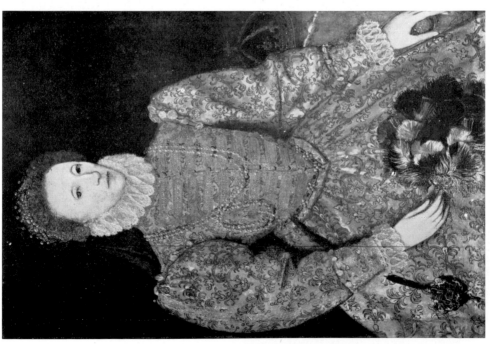

(A) Unknown: Queen Elizabeth I (The Cobham Portrait).
National Portrait Gallery, London

15

M. Gheeraerts: Lady Sidney and her Children. 1596. *Lord de L'Isle and Dudley, Penshurst Place, Kent*

Unknown: Queen Elizabeth I. ±1591. (The Ditchley Portrait.)
National Portrait Gallery, London

Nicholas Hilliard (miniature): George Clifford, Earl of Cumberland. ±1590.
National Maritime Museum, Greenwich

19

(B) F. Zuccaro: Queen Elizabeth I. 1575. *British Museum*

(A) M. Gheeraerts: Queen Elizabeth I. *Duke of Portland*

20

(B) R. Peake: Prince Charles. 1613. (Detail.)
Cambridge University Library

(A) J. de Critz (?): James I and VI. 1610.
National Maritime Museum, Greenwich

21

Unknown: Countess of Suffolk.
Margaret, Countess of Suffolk and Berkshire, Redlynch Park, Somerset

22

Unknown: Anne, Countess of Stamford.
Margaret, Countess of Suffolk and Berkshire, Redlynch Park, Somerset

I. Oliver (miniature): Richard, Earl of Dorset. 1616. *Victoria and Albert Museum, London (Crown Copyright)*

I. Oliver (?): Edward, Earl of Dorset. 1613.
Margaret, Countess of Suffolk and Berkshire, Redlynch Park, Somerset

(A) Style of Isaac Oliver: Frances, Countess of Essex.
Duke of Portland

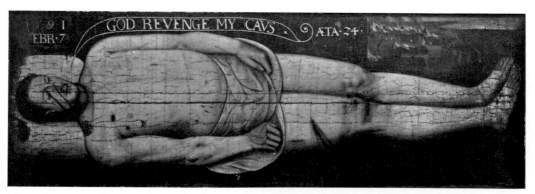

(B) Unknown: The Bonnie Earl of Moray. 1591. *Earl of Moray, Darnaway Castle, Morayshire*

Paul van Somer. Queen Anne of Denmark. 1617. *Windsor Castle.*
By gracious permission of Her Majesty The Queen

Sir Nathaniel Bacon: The Painter. *Earl of Verulam, Gorhambury, Herts*

Daniel Mytens: Thomas, Earl of Arundel. ±1618.
Duke of Norfolk, Arundel Castle, Sussex

D. Mytens: George Calvert, Lord Baltimore. 1627.
Earl Fitzwilliam, Wentworth Woodhouse, Yorks

D. Mytens: James, Duke of Hamilton. 1629. *Duke of Hamilton*
(*Loan to Edinburgh Gallery*)

D. Mytens: Charles I. 1633. *Earl Fitzwilliam, Wentworth Woodhouse, Yorks*

Van Dyck: Charles I. 1636.
Windsor Castle. By gracious permission of Her Majesty The Queen

33

(B) Cornelis Johnson: Susanna Temple. 1620.
Formerly with Messrs Vicars

(A) Cornelis Johnson: Lady of Kingsmill family. 1632.
Hon. Clive Pearson, Parham Park, Sussex

(B) George Jamesone: The Young Montrose. 1629. *Earl of Southesk, Kinnaird Castle, Kincardine*

(A) Cornelis Johnson: Sir Robert Dormer. 1642. *T. Cottrell-Dormer, Rousham, Oxon*

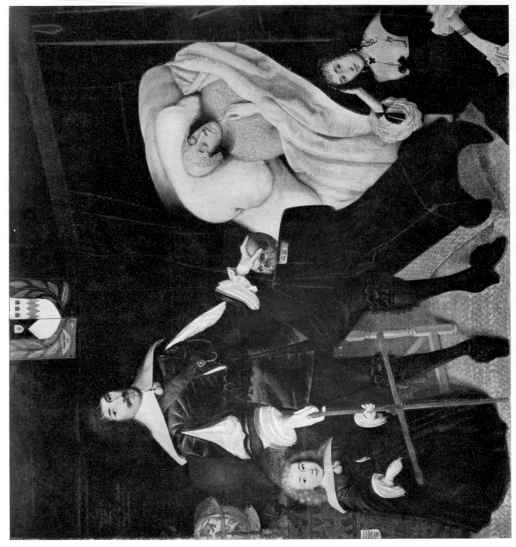

John Souch : Sir Thomas Aston at Death Bed of his First Wife. 1635. *City Art Gallery, Manchester*

David des Granges: The Saltonstall Family. ±1637. *Sir Kenneth Clark, London*

(A) Van Dyck: Charles I in Three Positions. ±1637. *Windsor Castle.*
By gracious permission of Her Majesty The Queen

(B) Van Dyck: Thomas Killigrew and Thomas Carew. 1638. *Windsor*
Castle. By gracious permission of Her Majesty The Queen

Van Dyck: King Charles on Horseback. *National Gallery, London*

(B) Sir Peter Lely : Blind Harper. *Earl Spencer, Althorp, Northants* (*Copyright Country Life*)

(A) T. Leigh : Robert Davies. 1643. *National Museum of Wales, Cardiff*

Emmanuel (?) de Critz: John Tradescant and Zythepsa. *Ashmolean Museum, Oxford*

(B) E. (?) de Critz: John Tradescant, Jr. *Ashmolean Museum, Oxford*

(A) H. Stone: Thomas, Lord Leigh. 1649. *Lord Leigh, Stoneleigh Abbey, Warwickshire*

W. Dobson: Prince Rupert, Colonel William Murray, and Colonel John Russell. *Lord Sandys, Ombersley, Worcs*

W. Dobson: Charles II as Prince of Wales. *Scottish National Portrait Gallery, Edinburgh*

W. Dobson: Endymion Porter. *National Gallery, London*

W. Dobson: Dobson, Sir C. Cotterell, and Sir B. Gerbier. *Duke of Northumberland, Albury (Copyright Country Life)*

(B) R. Walker: Mrs Hutchinson and her Daughter.
Earl Fitzwilliam, Milton Park, Northants

(A) R. Walker: Colonel John Hutchinson and his Son.
Earl Fitzwilliam, Milton Park, Northants

49

(A) Van Dyck: The Painter. *Duke of Westminster*

(B) R. Walker: The Painter. *Ashmolean Museum, Oxford*

Van Dyck (?): First Lord Denbigh. *National Gallery, London*

(B) Isaac Fuller: The Painter. *Bodleian Library, Oxford*

(A) Isaac Fuller: The Poet Cleveland. 1644. *Lt-Col H. G. Sotheby, Ecton, Northants*

(B) Lely: Lady Dering. 1651. *Hon. Clive Pearson,*
Parham Park, Somerset

(A) Lely: Sir William Compton. *Ham House, Surrey*
(Crown Copyright)

53

(A) Lely: Charles I and James, Duke of York. 1647. *Duke of Northumberland Syon House (Copyright Country Life)*

(B) Lely: The Younger Children of Charles I. 1647. *Hon. John Wyndham, Petworth, Sussex*

Lely: Henry Sidney, later Earl of Romney. *Lord de L'Isle and Dudley, Penshurst Place, Kent*

Lely: Family of Charles Dormer, Earl of Carnarvon. ±1658/9. *Sir John Coote, Bt*

56

(B) Lely: Francis Mercury van Helmont. 1671.
National Gallery, London

(A) Lely: Admiral Sir Jeremy Smith. ±1666/7.
National Maritime Museum, Greenwich

(B) Lely: Elizabeth, Countess of Northumberland. *Hampton Court.*
By gracious permission of Her Majesty The Queen

(A) Lely: Lady Barbara Fitzroy.
City Art Gallery, York

G. Soest: Lord and Lady Fairfax. *National Portrait Gallery, London*

G. Soest: Lord Baltimore. *State of Maryland*

Lely: The Duet. 1654. *Lord Dulverton, Batsford Park, Glos.*

(A) G. Soest: John, Second Marquess of Tweeddale.
Marquess of Tweeddale, Yester House, Midlothian

(B) G. Soest: Unknown Lady.
Formerly at Bradbourne

J. Huysmans: Children of John Coke of Melbourne. *Marquess of Lothian, Melbourne Hall, Derby*

J. Huysmans: Queen Catherine of Braganza. *Windsor Castle.*
By gracious permission of Her Majesty The Queen

H. Gascars: James, Duke of York, as Lord High Admiral.
National Maritime Museum, Greenwich

(B) Michael Wright: Third Lord Arundell of Wardour (?).
Wardour Castle

(A) Michael Wright: Mrs Claypole. 1658.
National Portrait Gallery, London

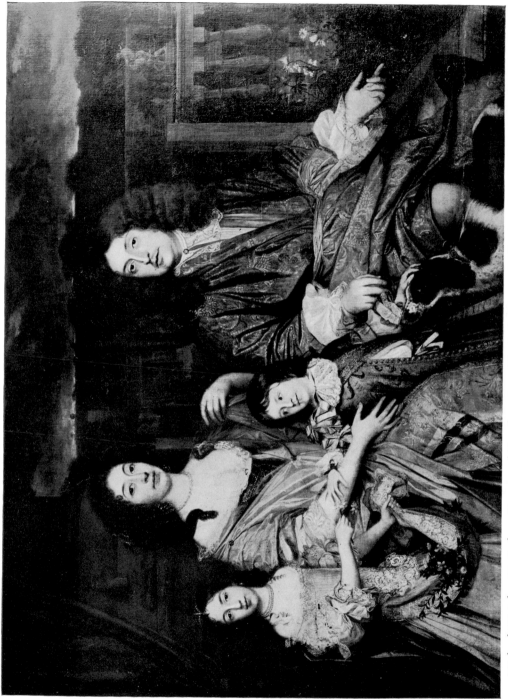

Michael Wright: Sir Robert Vyner and Family. 1673. Cdr C. G. Vyner, Studley Royal, Yorks (Copyright Country Life)

67

(B) J. Greenhill: The First Mrs Cartwright.
Dulwich College

(A) J. Greenhill: Unknown Naval Officer.
National Maritime Museum, Greenwich

70

(A) W. Wissing: The Lord Burleigh. (*Engraving*)

(B) W. Wissing: Miss Elizabeth Brownlow. (*Engraving*)

71

R. Streeter: Boscobel House. Hampton Court. By gracious permission of Her Majesty The Queen

J. Siberechts: Nottingham and the Trent. *Lord Middleton, Birdsall House, Yorks*

Sir J. Thornhill: Ceiling of Painted Hall, Greenwich

(A) Verrio: Ceiling of the King's Dining Room. *Hampton Court, Copyright H.M.M.O.W.*

(B) Pellegrini: Fresco on Staircase. *Kimbolton Castle, Hunts*

J. Rousseau: Decorative Landscape from Montagu House.
Duke of Buccleuch and Queensberry

J. Amigoni: Mercury and Argus, *Moor Park*, *Herts*

J. Riley: Bridget Holmes. 1686.
Windsor Castle. By gracious permission of Her Majesty The Queen

J. Riley: The Scullion. *Christ Church, Oxford*

Kneller: James, Duke of Monmouth. *Duke of Richmond and Gordon,*
Goodwood, Sussex

Kneller: Duchess of Portsmouth. 1684. *Duke of Richmond and Gordon,*
Goodwood, Sussex

(B) Kneller: Sir Charles Cotterell. 1683. *T. Cottrell-Dormer, Rousham, Oxon*

(A) Kneller: Philip, Earl of Leicester. 1685. *Lord de L'Isle and Dudley, Penshurst Place, Kent*

84

(B) Kneller: Sir Samuel Garth. (Kitcat series.)
National Portrait Gallery, London

(A) Kneller: Jacob Tonson. 1717. (Kitcat series.)
National Portrait Gallery, London

85

(B) Dahl: Admiral Sir Cloudesley Shovell.
National Maritime Museum, Greenwich

(A) Riley: Duke of Lauderdale. *Duke of Northumberland, Syon House*
(Copyright Country Life)

86

(B) Kneller: Duchess of Marlborough and Lady Fitzhardinge.
1691. *Duke of Marlborough, Blenheim Palace*

(A) T. Hill: Miss Susanna Strangways. *Earl of Ilchester,
Melbury, Somerset*

87

J. Closterman: Hon. Alexander Stanhope. 1698. *Earl Stanhope, Chevening, Kent*

J. Richardson: Lord Chancellor Cowper. *Heirs of Lady Desborough,*
Panshanger, Herts

R. Griffier: A Regatta on the Thames. 1748. *Duke of Buccleuch and Queensberry*

Samuel Scott: The Tower of London. 1753. *Viscount Hambleden, Hambleden, Bucks*

(A) Egbert van Heemskerk: An Oxford Election. 1687.
Town Hall, Oxford

(B) Canaletto: The Thames from Richmond House. *Duke of Richmond and Gordon, Goodwood, Sussex*

94

(A) Samuel Scott: Engagement between 'The Lion' and 'The Elizabeth'. 1745.
Earl of Sandwich, Hinchingbrooke, Hunts

(B) Samuel Scott: An Arch of Westminster Bridge. *Baroness Lucas and Dingwall,*
Woodyates Manor, Wilts

Hogarth: The Beggar's Opera. 1728/9. Colonel the Hon. J. J. Astor, Hever Castle, Kent

Hogarth: The Indian Emperor. 1731/2. *Earl of Ilchester, London*

J. Vanderbank: Queen Caroline. 1736. *Duke of Richmond and Gordon, Goodwood, Sussex*

Hogarth: Captain Coram. 1740. *Foundling Hospital, London*

Hogarth: Marriage à la Mode II, Early in the Morning. *National Gallery, London*

Hogarth: O the Roast Beef of Old England! 1748/9. *Tate Gallery, London*

Hogarth: Sigismunda. 1759. *Tate Gallery, London*

Hogarth: Hogarth's Servants. *National Gallery, London*

Highmore: Pamela telling Nursery Tales. *Fitzwilliam Museum, Cambridge*

Highmore: Mr Oldham and his Friends. *Tate Gallery, London*

Highmore: Samuel Richardson. 1750. *National Portrait Gallery, London*

Knapton: Hon. John Spencer and his Son. 1745. *Earl Spencer, Althorp, Northants*

B. Dandridge : The Price Family. *Metropolitan Museum, New York*

B. Du Pan: Children of Frederick, Prince of Wales. *Windsor Castle. By gracious permission of Her Majesty The Queen*

(A) Gawen Hamilton: An Artists' Club. 1735. *National Portrait Gallery, London*

(B) M. Laroon: A Party. *Duke of Buccleuch and Queensberry*

112

Hudson: Sir John and Lady Pole. 1755. *Sir John Carew Pole, Bt, Antony House, Devon*

(B) Mercier: Frederick, Prince of Wales.
National Portrait Gallery, London

(A) J. Smibert: Sir Francis Grant, Lord Cullen.
Scottish National Portrait Gallery, Edinburgh

Mercier: Viscount Tyrconnel and his Family. ± 1726. *Lord Brownlow, Belton House, Rutland*

Hudson: Admiral Byng. 1749. *National Maritime Museum, Greenwich*

Arthur Devis: Gentleman at Reading Desk. 1761. *City Art Gallery, Manchester*

(A) The Rev. James Wills: The Andrews Family. 1749. *Fitzwilliam Museum, Cambridge*

(B) Hayman: Sir Robert Walpole in the Artist's Studio. *National Portrait Gallery, London*

Ramsay: Dr Mead. *Foundling Hospital, London*

(B) Reynolds: Lt Roberts. 1747. *National Maritime Museum, Greenwich*

(A) Ramsay: Samuel Torriano. 1738. *Earl of Haddington, Mellerstain, Berwickshire*

(B) Reynolds: Mrs Francis Beckford. 1756. *Tate Gallery, London*

(A) Ramsay: The Painter's Wife. *National Gallery of Scotland, Edinburgh*

123

Ramsay: Norman MacLeod, Chief of MacLeod. 1748.
Mrs MacLeod of MacLeod, Dunvegan Castle, Skye

124

Reynolds: Commodore Keppel. 1753. *National Maritime Museum, Greenwich*

Ramsay: Hew Dalrymple, Lord Drummore. 1754.
Lady Broun Lindsay, Colstoun, East Lothian

Reynolds: Joshua Sharpe. 1786. *Viscount Cowdray, Cowdray, Sussex*

(B) Reynolds: Children with Cabbage Net. 1775.
Lord Faringdon, Buscot Park, Berks

(A) Richard Wilson: Admiral Smith. *National Maritime Museum,
Greenwich*

Reynolds: Garrick between Tragedy and Comedy. *Lord Rothschild (lent to Birmingham Gallery)*

Reynolds: James, Earl of Lauderdale. 1759. *Earl of Lauderdale,*
Thirlestane Castle, Berwickshire

Reynolds: Lady Sarah Bunbury. 1765. *Art Institute, Chicago*

Reynolds: Lady Caroline Scott as 'Winter'. 1777. *Duke of Buccleuch and Queensberry, Bowhill, Selkirk*

Reynolds: Lord Heathfield. 1788. *National Gallery, London*

Reynolds: Georgiana, Duchess of Devonshire and Daughter. 1786. *Trustees of the Chatsworth Settlement*

Reynolds: Death of Dido. 1781. *Buckingham Palace. By gracious permission of Her Majesty The Queen*

137

Reynolds: Lady Worsley. *Earl of Harewood, Harewood House, Yorks*

Gainsborough: Mrs Philip Thicknesse. 1760. *Cincinnati Art Museum*

(A) R. Wilson: Lago di Agnano. *Ashmolean Museum, Oxford*

(B) R. Wilson: Et in Arcadia Ego. *Lady Elizabeth Byng, Wrotham Park, Kent*

(A) R. Wilson: View of Woburn Abbey. *Duke of Bedford, Woburn Abbey, Beds*

(B) R. Wilson: Hadrian's Villa. *City Art Gallery, Manchester*

R. Wilson: Niobe. *Formerly National Gallery, London (destroyed)*

R. Wilson: Snowdon. *Walker Art Gallery, Liverpool*

W. Marlow: A Capriccio. St Paul's and a Venetian Canal.
Sutton Trustees, Benham Park (formerly)

(A) W. Hodges: Tahiti. *National Maritime Museum, Greenwich*

(B) Gainsborough: Milkmaid and Woodcutter. 1755. (Detail.)
Duke of Bedford, Woburn Abbey, Beds

147

Gainsborough: Mr and Mrs Andrews. G. W. Andrews, Redhill, Surrey

Gainsborough: Gainsborough's Forest. *National Gallery, London*

151

Gainsborough: Sir William St Quintin, 4th Bt. *Mrs L'Estrange Malone, Scampston Hall, Yorks*

Gainsborough: William Wollaston. *Christchurch Mansion Museum, Ipswich*

Gainsborough: The Harvest Waggon. *Barber Institute of Fine Arts, Birmingham*

Gainsborough: Mountain Landscape with Sheep. *Duke of Sutherland, Sutton Place, Surrey*

Gainsborough: Mrs William Henry Portman. *Lent to Tate Gallery by Viscount Portman*

Gainsborough: The Morning Walk. 1785. *Lord Rothschild (lent to Birmingham Gallery)*

157

Gainsborough: Johann Christian Fischer. 1780. *Buckingham Palace.*
By gracious permission of Her Majesty The Queen

Gainsborough: Mrs John Douglas. 1784. *James A. de Rothschild,*
Waddesdon Manor, Bucks.

(A) Gainsborough: Girl with Pigs. *George Howard, Castle Howard, Yorks*

(B) M. W. Peters: Children with Fruit. *Royal Academy, London (Diploma Gallery)*

(A) Angelica Kauffmann: Composition. *Royal Academy of Arts, London*

(B) Opie: The Schoolmistress. 1784. *C. Loyd, Wantage, Berks*

(B) F. Wheatley: Arthur Philip. 1786.
National Portrait Gallery, London

(A) N. Dance: Hugh, Duke of Northumberland and his Tutor.
1763. *Duke of Northumberland, Syon House (Copyright Country Life)*

164

Wright of Derby: Sir Brooke Boothby, Bart. 1781. *Tate Gallery, London*

(A) Edward Penny: Death of Wolfe. *Ashmolean Museum, Oxford*

(B) Benjamin West: Death of Wolfe. *Kensington Palace.*
By gracious permission of Her Majesty The Queen

Benjamin West: Apotheosis of Prince Alfred and Prince Octavius. *Buckingham Palace.*
By gracious permission of Her Majesty The Queen

J. S. Copley: Brook Watson and the Shark. *Christ's Hospital*

J. S. Copley: The Death of Major Pierson. *Tate Gallery, London*

Wright of Derby: Miravan breaking open the Tombs of his Ancestors. 1772.
Derby Art Gallery

J. H. Mortimer: The Progress of Virtue III. *Tate Gallery, London*

G. Stubbs: Duke and Duchess of Richmond watching Horse Exercises. *Duke of Richmond and Gordon, Goodwood (Copyright Country Life)*

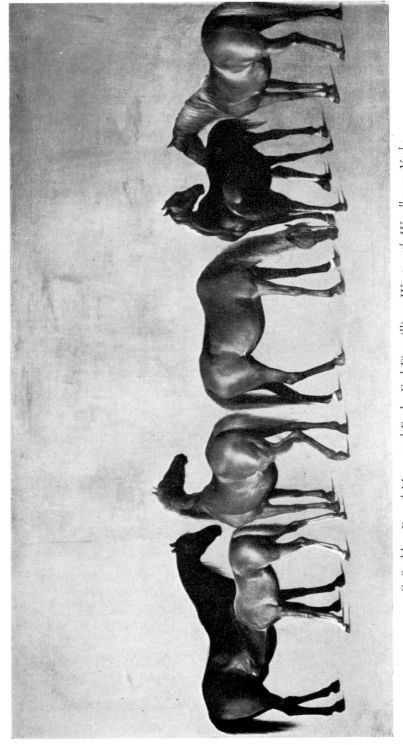

G. Stubbs: Brood Mares and Foals. *Earl Fitzwilliam, Wentworth Woodhouse, Yorks*

G. Stubbs: The Melbourne and Milbanke Families. 1770. *Heirs of Lady Desborough, Panshanger, Herts*

(B) Romney: Earl Grey. 1784. *The Provost's Lodgings, Eton College*

(A) Romney: Peter and James Romney. 1766. *(Owner untraced)*

183

Romney: Sir Christopher and Lady Sykes. 1786.
Sir Richard Sykes, Bt, Sledmere, Yorks

Romney: Warren Hastings. 1795. *Former India Office, London*
(By permission of H.M. Govt in U.K.)

H. Walton: The Cherry Barrow. 1779. *Sir Osbert Sitwell, Bt, Renishaw Hall, Derbyshire*

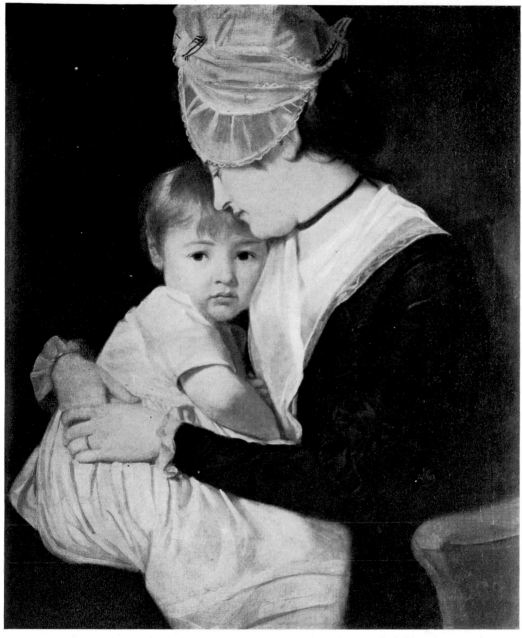

Romney: Mrs Carwardine and Child. 1775. *Lord Hillingdon, Wakefield Lodge, Northants*

(B) David Martin: George Murdoch. 1793. *City Art Gallery, Glasgow*

(A) Gilbert Stuart: J. S. Copley. *National Portrait Gallery, London*

(B) J. Hoppner: Princess Mary. 1785. *Windsor Castle.*
By gracious permission of Her Majesty The Queen

(A) Sir William Beechey: Princess Mary. 1797. *Windsor Castle.*
By gracious permission of Her Majesty The Queen

(A) F. Wheatley: Mr Howard offering Relief to Prisoners. 1787.
Earl of Harrowby, Sandon, Staffs

(B) De Loutherbourg: A Midsummer Afternoon with a Methodist Preacher,
National Gallery of Canada, Ottawa

INDEX

Titles of pictures and other works of art are printed in *italics*; names of owners, museums, galleries, and other indications of location in CAPITALS. Galleries are indexed under the town in which they are situate: thus, NATIONAL GALLERY will be found under LONDON. Where several references to an artist are given, that in **heavy type** is the principal. References in the notes are indexed only where some matter is dealt with in the note that is not evident from the text; in such cases the page on which the note appears, and the number of the note concerned, are given, thus: 63[18]. Numbers in *italics* refer to plates.